Eating Disorders

Eating Disorders

Understanding Causes, Controversies, and Treatment

Volume 1: A–M

JUSTINE J. REEL, EDITOR

An Imprint of ABC-CLIO, LLC

Santa Barbara, California • Denver, Colorado

Library of Congress Cataloging-in-Publication Data

Names: Reel, Justine J., editor.
Title: Eating disorders : understanding causes, controversies, and treatment
    / Justine J. Reel, editor.
Description: Santa Barbara, California : Greenwood, an imprint of ABC-CLIO,
    LLC, [2018] | Includes bibliographical references and index.
Identifiers: LCCN 2017046933 (print) | LCCN 2017048728 (ebook) | ISBN
    9781440853012 (eBook) | ISBN 9781440853005 (set : alk. paper) | ISBN
    9781440853029 (volume 1 : alk. paper) | ISBN 9781440853036 (volume 2 :
    alk. paper)
Subjects: LCSH: Eating disorders—Diagnosis. | Eating disorders—Treatment.
Classification: LCC RC552.E18 (ebook) | LCC RC552.E18 E293 2018 (print) | DDC
    616.85/26--dc23
LC record available at https://lccn.loc.gov/2017046933

ISBN: 978-1-4408-5300-5 (set)
        978-1-4408-5302-9 (vol. 1)
        978-1-4408-5303-6 (vol. 2)
        978-1-4408-5301-2 (ebook)

22 21 20 19 18   1 2 3 4 5

This book is also available as an eBook.

Greenwood
An Imprint of ABC-CLIO, LLC

ABC-CLIO, LLC
130 Cremona Drive, P.O. Box 1911
Santa Barbara, California 93116-1911
www.abc-clio.com

This book is printed on acid-free paper ∞

Manufactured in the United States of America

This book is dedicated to my mentor, friend and colleague, Dr. Carole Oglesby. Carole has been there for me personally and professionally every step of my journey. She has made a game changing impact on girls and women in sport as well as female faculty members and leaders. Carole, you helped me secure a faculty position at West Chester University and Temple University when no one was hiring recently graduated PhDs. Carole, we will always remember the symphony in Philadelphia and hiking in Yosemite with fondness. You are one in a million and we will always love you.

Contents

VOLUME 2

Acknowledgments

Thank you to the contributors and to Maxine Taylor who has served as my developmental editor for the past five years. Your patience in the process as well as your tireless effort to make the work stronger are admirable. I appreciate the unwavering commitment of ABC-CLIO to publish relevant books that offer accessible language for parents, teens, and the general public. Finally, I am grateful to my friends and family members who serve as my biggest cheerleaders.

Introduction

My fascination with eating disorders and body image began in the 1980s after Karen Carpenter died from an eating disorder in 1983. As a teenager, I did recognize any drawbacks to being too thin or being overly disciplined with regard to one's diet. In fact, the term "anorexia nervosa" was new to me, as eating disorders were not discussed in health classes or in blogs. Pro-ana websites and social media did not exist. I understood the emotions and the psyche linked to striving for a different body and wanting to be smaller, blonder, and more attractive to the opposite sex.

As a master's student, my goal was to study weight pressures associated with high school and college cheerleaders that can contribute to body dissatisfaction and disordered eating behaviors. At the time of this publication, I have studied weight pressures among female and male athletes across sports and dance for the past 22 years as a researcher. I have also investigated the influences of age, race/ethnicity, and gender on body image and eating behaviors in a variety of populations. My current research focus has expanded to include the role of exercise in treatment of eating disorders.

As a licensed professional counselor in the states of Utah and North Carolina, I have observed eating disorders from the other side of the office working in residential, inpatient, and outpatient settings. I had the opportunity to help develop the first eating disorder residential treatment program in Salt Lake City and created an exercise education component as part of the treatment and recovery process to address exercise dependence. As a primary therapist, I observed clients who lost their jobs, lost their families, dropped out of school, and/or were hospitalized due to dangerously low potassium levels. I realized that the treatment process resembled a rollercoaster, with some clients improving in the residential setting and showing symptom reduction only to slip when they transitioned to an outpatient level of care. Other clients would begin to develop self-harming behaviors once their eating disorder behaviors subsided.

Being an eating disorder treatment provider is extremely rewarding; however, more recently, I have been focusing on prevention by integrating eating disorder and obesity prevention efforts in programming for adolescents and their parents. I started a student organization at the University of Utah in 2002 called Students Promoting Eating Disorder Awareness and Knowledge to increase awareness about eating disorders and to promote positive body image. Although societal awareness has improved exponentially since Karen Carpenter's death, over 10 million individuals suffer from eating disorders in the United States. Many cases go undiagnosed for years and many individuals are overlooked because they do not meet the traditional stereotype of having an eating disorder—being young, white, thin, and female. It is estimated that 10–25 percent of eating disorder cases are males who have severely deteriorated when they finally present for treatment.

Fortunately, treatment options have improved and now include eating disorder treatment facilities in most states. Treatment continues to be expensive and can run upward of $1,000/day and may not be covered by one's insurance. Families struggle to make decisions on what is affordable versus what is necessary for their daughter's or son's health and survival. Exceptions to this expensive treatment include Eating Disorder Anonymous, a few nonprofit treatment centers, and Overeaters Anonymous, which provide free support groups in communities across the country.

Eating disorders are often oversimplified and misunderstood as being only about eating and food. However, the tendency to develop disordered eating can be attributed to a complex set of factors including biological, genetic, psychological, and social components. A person can be predisposed to develop mental health concerns based on family history. Psychological influences may include the intense emotions underlying a dysfunctional relationship with food, exercise, and the self. Individuals with eating disorders express poor self-esteem, perfectionism, and intense body dissatisfaction. Social factors may include relationships with other people who model dieting behavior or the media, which promotes a message emphasizing the importance of being thin. These media messages can help guide an inner dialogue that focuses on appearance flaws and weight. Having a desire to change the way one looks coupled with exhibiting a strong fear of gaining weight can lead to behaviors such as restricting, purging (e.g., self-induced vomiting, laxatives), or binge eating episodes. The diagnostic categories of eating disorders (anorexia nervosa, bulimia nervosa, and binge eating disorder) seek to classify disorders by symptoms largely for insurance purposes. However, disordered eating behaviors exist along a spectrum, and it is important to recognize that the underlying psychological characteristics and emotions can be interconnected for binge eating and restricting behaviors. Therefore, programs that target the country's obesity epidemic should be careful to address underlying emotional eating; adequate emphasis should be placed on developing a more positive relationship with food and with one's body. In this volume you will read about a few prevention programs, such as Healthy Buddies and Full of Ourselves, which seek to promote health and prevent eating disorders.

Finally, the volume includes information about how to refer someone who is suspected of having an eating disorder. Being a friend or family member can be extremely difficult, so to help them eating disorder resources are provided as well as specific entries on treatment modalities (e.g., nutritional treatment approaches). Case studies and interviews are presented to illuminate the intricacies associated with various presentations of eating disorders. It should be noted that although patterns exist across individuals with eating disorder symptoms, each person is and should be treated as an individual and unique case.

In sum, as a voice of recovery, an eating disorder researcher, an eating disorder therapist, and the author/editor of this two-volume encyclopedia about the causes, treatment, and prevention of eating disorders, I hope that you will use this book for your own personal and professional needs. If you are writing a research paper you will find the necessary background information here. You will also be able to locate valuable resources and information about how best to support someone with an eating disorder. If you are struggling with an eating disorder you may even see yourself on these pages.

Justine J. Reel, PhD, LPC, CMPC

Chronology

1300s	A female saint, Catherine of Siena (1347–1380), is said to eat "only a handful of herbs each day," representing food refusal and prolonged fasting common among female and male saints from 1200 to 1500.
1686	First medically diagnosed case of anorexia nervosa, a 20-year-old female, is termed by Richard Morton as "nervous atrophy" and described as "a skeleton only clad with skin."
1865	Dunglison's dictionary defines anorexia as "absence of appetite."
1874	British Physician Sir William Gull formally uses the term "anorexia nervosa" (lack of desire to eat due to a mental condition).
1903	Psychiatrist Pierre Janet describes "mixed" eating disorder case of Nadja and emphasizes the obsession with thinness, refusal of food, and secret binges leading to the medical term "bulimia" (derived from Latin meaning "hunger of an ox").
1950s	Binge eating is observed and reported in obesity studies by Dr. Albert Stunkard of the University of Pennsylvania; clients referred to as "compulsive overeaters."
1952	Anorexia nervosa is included in the original *Diagnostic and Statistical Manual of Mental Disorders* as a "psychophysiological reaction."
January 1960	Overeaters Anonymous (OA) is founded by Rozanne S. and two women to provide a twelve-step group that addresses issues related to food.
1968	Anorexia nervosa is listed under special symptoms/feeding disturbances in the *Diagnostic and Statistical Manual of Mental Disorders*, second edition (*DSM-II*).
1978	Hilde Bruch publishes *The Golden Cage* to depict anorexia nervosa for lay audiences.
1980	First classification of eating disorders as a separate section; bulimia nervosa receives first mention as a psychiatric disorder in *Diagnostic and Statistical Manual of Mental Disorders*, third edition (*DSM-III*).
1981	First scientific journal for eating disorders, *International Journal of Eating Disorders*, publishes first volume.

February 1983	Karen Carpenter dies of heart failure associated with anorexia nervosa at age 32.
1985	The Renfrew Center, the first freestanding eating disorder treatment facility, opens its doors in Philadelphia, Pennsylvania.
1985	International Association of Eating Disorder Professionals (IAEDP) is formed to provide training to eating disorder providers.
1987	De Coverley Veale introduces the term "exercise dependence" to describe a negative mood state experienced in the absence of exercise.
1992	The term "binge eating disorder" is formally introduced in the scientific literature by Robert Spitzer in the *International Journal of Eating Disorders*.
1992	Christy Henrich, an Olympic gymnast, dies from complications due to an eating disorder.
1993	Professional organization Academy for Eating Disorders (AED) hosts its first meeting of 33 clinicians and researchers in Tulsa, Oklahoma.
1994	Binge eating disorder (BED) is included in the research criteria for the *Diagnostic and Statistical Manual of Mental Disorders*, fourth edition (*DSM-IV*).
1997	Heidi Guenther, a professional ballet dancer from the Boston Ballet Company, dies from an eating disorder.
2000	Eating Disorders Anonymous (EDA) is formed by Alcoholics Anonymous members in Phoenix, Arizona, to offer a twelve-step group for eating disorders.
2001	National Eating Disorder Association (NEDA), a nonprofit eating disorder organization, is formed to help families.
2002	Students Promoting Eating Disorder Awareness and Knowledge is founded at the University of Utah to conduct eating disorder research and outreach.
2013	The *Diagnostic and Statistical Manual of Mental Disorders*, fifth edition (*DSM-5*) is published with substantial changes to eating disorder and feeding disorder diagnoses. The diagnosis of eating disorder not otherwise specified is eliminated.

ACADEMY FOR EATING DISORDERS

The Academy for Eating Disorders (AED) was founded in 1993 by Dr. Craig Johnson. Like other eating disorder professional associations (e.g., International Association of Eating Disorder Professionals and Binge Eating Disorder Association), AED provides a place for practitioners and researchers to convene to advance the field. The first AED conference, which included 33 eating disorder professionals who treated individuals with eating disorders or conducted research on the topic, met in Tulsa, Oklahoma, to discuss challenges associated with the treatment of eating disorders, including insurance practices and managed care. Currently, AED meets annually in various locations around the world and has an international membership of more than 1,000 physicians, psychologists, nurses, social workers, dietitians, and researchers from a variety of fields. The 2017 Annual Conference met in Prague, Czech Republic, to discuss diverse perspectives and shared goals between eating disorder researchers.

The AED is an international association of professionals devoted to leadership, research, education, treatment, and prevention of eating disorders. AED identified several strategic objectives for the organization to advance knowledge about eating disorder treatment and prevention, supporting research efforts, and developing guidelines for evidence-based practices. AED currently supports 23 special interest groups that focus on topics ranging from bariatric surgery and eating disorders to males and eating disorders. Members of this organization are given an opportunity to engage in advocacy to expand accessibility of treatment to individuals with eating disorders. In a position paper published in 2009, the AED emphasized eating disorders are serious mental illnesses that warrant the same level of health care coverage as other mental disorders. Another advocacy paper published in 2015 defied myths around anorexia nervosa being linked to traits of narcissism. In addition to advocacy work, AED supports the integration of research to practice through the publication of the *International Journal of Eating Disorders*. This journal's mission is to advance knowledge in the scientific community by publishing rigorous studies about eating disorders and obesity as well as healthy eating.

Justine J. Reel

See also: Advocacy Groups; Bariatric Surgery; Binge Eating Disorder Association; International Association of Eating Disorder Professionals

Bibliography

Academy for Eating Disorders. Accessed November 16, 2016. www.aedweb.org.

Klump, Kelly L., Cynthia M. Bulik, Walter H. Kaye, Janet Treasure, and Edward Tyson. Academy for Eating Disorders Position Paper: "Eating Disorders Are Serious Mental Illnesses." *International Journal of Eating Disorders* 42, no. 2 (2009): 97–103. https://doi.org/10.1002/eat.20589.

ACCEPTANCE AND COMMITMENT THERAPY

A common therapeutic approach used with clients who have eating disorders is called *acceptance and commitment therapy* (ACT). The underlying philosophy of this treatment approach is to help individuals experience a meaningful life while acknowledging the evitable pain and suffering that will reemerge over time. The focus of ACT lies with thinking and the response to negative thoughts. In many cases, individuals tend to respond in a self-destructive manner even when they are in a healthy and happy state. Therefore, ACT promotes the need for mindfulness, the ability to pay attention to one's thoughts with a degree of open-mindedness and flexibility without judgment. In other words, being mindful allows us to be aware of our thoughts and emotions, as well as how those effect our behaviors and our happiness. The goal of ACT is to be mindful and to experience a life we value. The central feature of ACT is psychological flexibility. That is, a person needs to be open, be flexible, and do what matters. In addition to the central component, there are six specific tenets of this therapeutic approach often described as the "ACT hexaflex."

Six Core Principles of ACT

An important focus of ACT directly related to mindfulness is to focus on the present. It is easy to spend long lengths of time dwelling on past events, like abuse or loss, rather than staying in the moment. Likewise, many individuals tend to obsess on what will happen in the future with thoughts like, "I will be happy when I am five pounds lighter." The first principle is to psychologically focus on the present, being mindful and engaged here and now rather than operating on automatic pilot.

The second characteristic of ACT relates to the ability to step back from thoughts. *Cognitive defusion* refers to a technique to create awareness of thoughts without being controlled by them. A person should detach and observe thoughts in a neutral fashion and see them for what they are—words or pictures in our head.

A third aspect of ACT relates to acceptance, which allows us to open and be vulnerable. Rather than avoid thoughts, acceptance helps us avoid resisting or fighting unwanted thoughts. In other words, acceptance provides the space for taking the time to understand these thoughts from a detached perspective. Being more neutral allows clients to avoid judgment and the tendency to tie their self-worth into their negative emotions and experiences.

Another key element of ACT is the ability to see self *as context*. For this principle, a client is encouraged to understand the *thinking* self and the *observing* self. The observing self is important to understand how we have changed over time instead of being stuck in our thoughts.

A unique characteristic of the ACT approach is the importance placed on a client's values. In other words, what does a person find important? By understanding one's values it is possible to see what gives someone direction in life.

Finally, a commitment to action is critical for the ACT approach. One's values are the driving force, but a commitment pushes us to do what it takes to achieve them. This may result in pain or discomfort, but these uncomfortable sensations are temporary and better than avoidance. Developing necessary coping skills is important to help individuals continue their committed action.

Why Is the ACT Approach Useful for Clients with Eating Disorders?

The strategies of ACT, such as being in the moment, align well with some other common struggles individuals with eating disorders face. Individuals with eating disorders may lack flexibility or the ability to be spontaneous in the moment. ACT reinforces the importance of maintaining a present-moment focus and avoiding the tendency to dwell on past negative events and painful memories. Likewise, the rigid focus of an eating disorder will benefit from increased flexibility and a willingness to adapt to one's present situation.

Individuals with eating disorders tend to struggle with rigid routines around eating and labeling certain foods as *good* or *bad*. ACT teaches clients to prepare for challenging situations and to change negative thoughts and harsh expectations. Instead of judging oneself, clients are encouraged to embrace their experiences without attempting to change them. Although individuals with eating disorders tend to avoid tough situations, ACT reinforces the need to accept responses to triggering experiences.

Another important piece of ACT is the concept of valued living. Individuals with eating disorders tend to place their lives on hold. They focus their energies and attention on engaging eating-disordered thoughts and behaviors. Individuals with eating disorders can benefit from exploring their values—what is important to them—and then making life choices that support those values. Finally, clients in ACT are encouraged to ensure their actions or behaviors align with their values. In other words, if painting is something a person values, how much time is spent engaging in this activity?

The key for growth is to be more aware of one's thoughts, emotions, and responses while developing a level of detachment. Staying in the moment and recognizing that experiences are temporary can prevent individuals from tying negative experiences to their sense of self-worth. In sum, the ACT approach uses a philosophy of promoting acceptance while using skill-based training to help clients view thoughts and emotions differently.

Justine J. Reel

See also: Cognitive Behavioral Therapy; Dialectical Behavior Therapy; Mindfulness; Psychodynamic Psychotherapy Approaches; Treatment

Bibliography

Harris, Russ. *ACT Made Simple: An Easy-to-Read Primer on Acceptance and Commitment Therapy.* Oakland, CA: New Harbinger Publications, 2009.

Haynos, Ann F., Evan M. Forman, Meghan L. Butryn, and Jason Lillis. *Mindfulness and Acceptance for Treating Eating Disorders and Weight Concerns: Evidence-Based Interventions.* Oakland, CA: Context Press, 2016.

Huoma, Jason B, Steven C. Hayes, and Robyn D. Walser. *Learning ACT: An Acceptance & Commitment Therapy Skills Training Manual for Therapists.* Oakland, CA: New Harbinger Publications, 2007.

Sandoz, Emily K., Kelly G. Wilson, and Troy Dufrene. *Acceptance and Commitment Therapy for Eating Disorders: A Process-Focused Guide to Treating Anorexia and Bulimia.* Oakland, CA: New Harbinger Publications, 2011.

ADOLESCENT DEVELOPMENT

Adolescence refers to the developmental transition from childhood (i.e., 10–13 years of age) to adulthood (i.e., 18–22 years of age). Adolescence is a challenging time for boys and girls, even when development occurs at a natural and healthy rate. Discussed in this entry are physical, cognitive, moral, social, and self-identity developmental processes.

Physical Development

The beginning of adolescence is marked by the onset of puberty (i.e., the process leading to physical, sexual, and psychosocial maturation). From a biological perspective, puberty is the maturation of the reproductive system, after which an individual can produce children. The physical changes associated with puberty are triggered by hormonal changes (e.g., increased release of androgens and estrogens that lead to increased physical changes in height, weight, body shape, and genital development).

This growth spurt for girls occurs at approximately age 9 with the peak of pubertal change occurring at age 11.5. During this time, girls increase in height by approximately 3.5 inches per year. By the time they reach their peak height at approximately age 12, girls have gained an average of 18 pounds. In addition to an increase in height and weight, girls' hips widen, and this is associated with an increase in estrogen. Unlike girls, boys typically begin puberty later, at age 11 or 12. A boy's peak growth spurt occurs midpuberty when testosterone levels rapidly increase. The peak growth spurt for boys is generally between ages 14 and 15 with an increase of 11 to 12 inches in height and an increase in strength. The change in body composition (i.e., redistribution of fat and increase in muscles) is related to males having more and larger muscle cells than females. In fact, boys have 1.5 times the lean body mass and bone mass of girls, and girls have twice as much body fat as boys.

Adrenarche refers to the earliest phase of puberty when the adrenal glands are activated. It usually begins between the ages of six and nine in girls, and approximately one year later in boys. This early part of puberty is usually characterized by external physical signs (e.g., adult body odor, axillary hair growth, breast buds). *Gonadarche* is the second phase of puberty, which is characterized by the maturation of the primary sexual characteristics (ovaries and testes) and full development of the secondary sexual characteristics (pubic hair, breast, and genital development). Gonadarche usually begins at age nine or ten in girls and appears a year later in boys. Certainly, the appearance of these bodily characteristics contributes to increased attention from the opposite sex and often leads to heightened self-consciousness about one's body.

For girls, sexual development includes breast development, enlargement of ovaries, and appearance of pubic hair. Usually the first sign of puberty for boys is testicular enlargement, followed by development of pubic hair and growth of the penis. With these reproductive changes, menarche occurs during the late-gonadarche phase. *Menarche*—or the onset of menses in girls—is the most common sign of sexual maturation in girls. It occurs at an average age of 12.8 years (range 11–13 years) in the general U.S. adolescent population. For boys, the clearest sign of puberty during gonadarche is *spermarche*, the onset of nocturnal emission, generally occurring at 13.5 or 14 years. In addition to sexual maturation and physical changes, other dimensions of pubertal maturation include changes in self-perception, social interactions, and perceptions by peers. This maturational process has a profound influence on the cognitive functioning of adolescents.

Cognitive Development

In recent years, researchers have tried to understand changes that occur in the brain during adolescence. Structural brain imaging studies over the past decade have challenged the belief that structural brain development ends in early childhood, revealing that changes occur through early adulthood. In addition, these studies provide insight into the biological basis for understanding adolescent thinking and behavior. For example, the ventromedial prefrontal cortex of the brain is responsible for evaluating risk and reward to guide a person making a decision. Imaging studies have shown this part of the brain is the last to mature in adolescents, which supports behavioral studies that find adolescents take greater risks than adults in activities such as substance abuse. Adolescents tend to engage in more reckless behaviors because the area of the brain that assesses risks and benefits has not yet completely developed. These findings, along with other studies examining the maturation of other regions of the prefrontal cortex during adolescence, suggest the spontaneity, shortsightedness, and risk-taking behaviors associated with adolescence could be partially biological in nature.

According to Piaget's theory of cognitive development, adolescents begin to shift from rule-bound and concrete styles of problem solving that occur in childhood to gain a greater capacity for abstract and flexible problem-solving skills during adolescence. Concrete operational thoughts occur approximately between the ages 7 and 11 when individuals can engage in mental actions that are reversible (e.g., mentally reverse liquid from one jar to another jar of different height or width) and divide things into sets and reason about their interrelations. Logical reasoning replaces intuitive thoughts if the principles can be applied to concrete examples. However, it is not until the formal operational stage starting at age 12 that individuals to think more abstractly than individuals in the concrete operational stage. They can think hypothetically and generalize from observations to aid them decision making.

Individuals in the operational stage can manage problems with many factors. For example, they can accurately display sticks by color and length. They can also think of many possibilities. In other words, adolescents at this stage can generate multiple possibilities for any given situation. Therefore, they can assess a problem, generate all the possible hypothetical outcomes, and then test hypotheses one at a time.

One mechanism that causes cognitive change during adolescence is biological maturation. As children grow physically, they encounter new possibilities for development. Just as biological development is salient to cognitive growth, experience with the physical world and the social environment also influence cognitive development. The quality of the experiences and the social context (home and school) affect the rate at which individuals move from one cognitive stage to the next. Providing new experiences and a comfortable environment to practice new skills facilitates cognitive development. According to Piagetian perspective, cognitive conflict is the main mechanism of cognitive change. For example, arguing about the rules of the game with peers stimulates cognitive conflict, helping individuals move from one cognitive stage to the next. In addition, Piaget believed cognitive conflict was important for moral development.

Moral Development

Although the debate on moral development continues, it is clear cognitive, social, and emotional growth in adolescence underpin the changes in moral reasoning that build a foundation to guide adolescents through adulthood. Lawrence Kohlberg interviewed many people across the life span regarding moral dilemmas and described six stages of moral development. At the preconventional level, children younger than age nine have an individualistic perspective where they follow rules to avoid punishment for personal reasons. During adolescence, girls and boys move from the preconventional to the conventional level of moral reasoning where they are guided by interpersonal relationships and place in society. Adolescents in this conventional level are concerned with helping and pleasing others, being a "good boy" or "good girl." The shift from preconventional to conventional level is also connected to cognitive and social development. Abstract thinking, ability to take another's perspective, and concern for others are prerequisites to be in the conventional level.

Social Development

Parent–Adolescent Relationship

The parent–adolescent relationship has been studied extensively in the adolescent development literature. Studies examining family dynamics during adolescence have focused on the parent–adolescent conflict (i.e., frequency and content of conflict). Parents and teenagers tend to experience arguments without knowing why there is a breakdown in communication. In addition, when there is more fighting between parents and teenagers, closeness (i.e., time spent with parents) declines. Subsequently, there could be mental health implications for parents and psychological maladjustment for teenagers. For example, parents have reported having difficulty adjusting to their adolescents' desire to be autonomous, and adolescents can develop aggression, depression, and hostility. As a result, teenagers can engage in unhealthy behaviors such as dieting or purging to cope or to attempt to be in control.

According to the separation-individuation theory, parent–child conflicts facilitate the increase in the adolescent's development of autonomy and independence. Distance in the relationship is needed to redefine the parent–adolescent relationship under conditions where the teenager still feels loved. Because of this process, adolescents gain more power and parents become more egalitarian. Furthermore, attachment theory emphasizes that parents who share activities and have emotional connections with their teenagers show support, and, in turn, provide space for adolescents to explore the world outside the family and form new relationships.

The amount of parental support (intimacy and warmth) declines from early to middle adolescence, and then stabilizes in late adolescence. There seems to be a consensus that conflict becomes more intense during early adolescence and less intense during middle to late adolescence. An explanation for an increase in conflict intensity during early adolescence is the biological and psychological changes that accompany puberty.

Boys and girls receive the same amount of support from parents during early adolescence; however, there is an increase in bonding between mothers and daughters from middle to late adolescence. Girls have more conflict with parents than boys, and girls have more conflicts (frequency and intensity) with mothers than fathers. Girls tend to be more autonomous than boys in early adolescence, but this difference disappears later in adolescence. A possible reason for these findings is that girls have an earlier pubertal development than boys. In addition, daughters and mothers argue over everyday concerns because mothers are typically more involved than fathers. Recent results from a longitudinal study show that the development of relationships with both parents is similar for girls and boys: (1) conflict is more intense during middle adolescence, (2) support from parents temporarily declines, and (3) conflict with parents temporarily increases. Thus, parent–adolescent relationships do become more equal over time, confirming that adolescents do develop more independence and autonomy over time.

Relationships with Peers

As adolescents develop more autonomy and independence, they spend more time alone and with their friends. Adolescents bring many qualities they have learned from spending time with their family to peer relationships. Adolescents from warm and supportive families are more socially competent and have more positive friendships.

There are several findings on how peers influence adolescent development. First, peers have positive and negative effects on adolescents. Peers influence academic performance and prosocial behaviors, but also unhealthy behaviors such as smoking and drinking alcohol. Second, adolescents follow their peers because they admire them and respect their opinions not because of peer pressure. Third, adolescents choose friends who are like them in cognition, attitudes, behaviors, and identities. Fourth, adolescents are most influenced by peers during middle adolescence compared to early and late adolescence.

Relationships with peers become more appealing during their teenage years because peers are less controlling, fairer, and less judgmental than adults. Thus, adolescents spend twice as much time with peers than parents, and they rely less on their parents to resolve problems. Adolescents want to be accepted by their peers. Being accepted by peers provides a sense of belonging in a peer group. It is also crucial for social and cognitive development. In contrast, being rejected by peers has detrimental effects on the social, psychological, and emotional development of adolescents. While popular adolescents report having closer friendships, and tend to be outgoing, humorous, and friendly, rejected adolescents tend to be aggressive, withdrawn, anxious, and socially awkward. Rejected adolescents may also be lonely, have low self-esteem, suffer from depression, and be vulnerable to teasing, bullying, and victimization by their peers. Some of the teasing surrounds weight, body size, and shape resulting in fat bias. Peer victimization can lead to the development of a poor self-image. However, adolescents rejected in middle school can become more popular and accepted in later adolescence, as adolescents become less strict in defining what is normal behavior and more tolerant of individual differences.

Friendships are more intimate during adolescence. More than half of U.S. adolescents reported having a romantic relationship in the past 18 months. By middle adolescence, most individuals have been involved in at least one romantic relationship. Research conducted prior to 1999 on romantic relationships during adolescence has been purely descriptive. More recent work has focused on the quality of relationships and the potential positive and negative implications.

Adolescents with positive romantic experiences have higher self-esteem, self-confidence, and social competence. In contrast, teenagers who worry about saving a relationship often suppress their thoughts and opinions (self-silencing) out of fear of losing their intimate partner and relationship. Self-silencing leads to poorer communication skills with partners, higher levels of depression, and greater sensitivity to rejection from a partner. This can cause adolescents to partake in alcohol and drug use, do poorly in school, and have poorer emotional health. Romantic experiences during adolescence have been found to have qualities similar to romantic relationships in later life.

Development of the Self

Adolescence has been characterized as a time of self-exploration for adolescents to determine who they are and how they fit in the world. For many years, studies have supported Erik Erikson's theory that adolescent identity is formed in early adolescence, but recent work has shown that identity formation occurs in late adolescence and even extends into young adulthood. Thus, the focus of research has been on the development of self-conceptions.

As mentioned earlier, in moving from childhood to adolescence, individuals begin to develop more abstract thinking and self-concepts become more differentiated and better organized. Harter expressed that adolescents begin to view themselves based on personal beliefs and standards instead of comparing themselves to others. During middle adolescence, individuals can view themselves differently depending on the situation (e.g., shy with classmates and outgoing with family members), but the discrepancies decline over time with adolescents forming a more constant view of themselves in late adolescence. They view themselves in a variety of domains, including academics, athletics, appearance, and morality. For example, if adolescents, especially girls, have high perceptions of their appearance, then they have high self-esteem. In addition, adolescents who do not act their true self because they devalue their true self develop depression. On the other hand, if they engage in false self-behaviors to please others, they will likely not have depression.

Sonya Soohoo

See also: Body Esteem; Children and Adolescents; Depression; Puberty; Substance Abuse; Teasing

Bibliography

Carver, Karen, Kara Joyner, and J. Richard Udry. "National Estimates of Adolescent Romantic Relationships." In *Adolescent Romantic Relationships and Sexual Behavior: Theory, Research, and Practical Implications,* edited by Peter Florsheim, 291–329. New York: Cambridge University Press, 2003.

Collins, W. Andrew, and Brett Laursen. "Parent–Adolescent Relationships and Influences." In *Handbook of Adolescent Psychology,* edited by Richard M. Lerner and Lawrence D. Steinberg, 331–361. Hoboken, NJ: John Wiley & Sons, 2004.

Collins, W. Andrew, Deborah P. Welsh, and Wyndol Furman. "Adolescent Romantic Relationships." *Annual Review of Psychology* 60 (2009): 631–652. https://doi .org/10https://doi.org/10.1146/annurev.psych.60.110707.163459.

De Goede, Irene H. A., Susan J. T. Branje, and Wim H. J. Meeus. "Developmental Changes in Adolescents' Perceptions of Relationships with Their Parents." *Journal of Youth Adolescence* 38, no. 1 (2009): 75–88. https://doi.org/10.1007/s10964-008-9286-7.

Dorn, Lorah D., Ronald E. Dahl, Hermi R. Woodward, and Frank Biro. "Defining the Boundaries of Early Adolescence: A User's Guide to Assessing Puberty Status and Pubertal Timing in Research with Adolescents." *Applied Developmental Science* 39 (2006): 625–626.

Erikson, Erik H. *Identity, Youth, and Crisis.* New York: W.W. Norton Company, 1968.

Furman, Wyndol, and W. Andrew Collins. "Adolescent Romantic Relationships and Experiences." In *Handbook of Peer Interactions, Relationships, and Groups,* edited by Kenneth H. Rubin, William M. Bukowski, and Brett Laursen. New York: Guilford Press, 2008.

Harter, Susan. "The Development of Self-Representations during Childhood and Adolescence." In *Handbook of Self and Identity,* edited by Mark R. Leary and June P. Tangney, 610–642. New York: Guilford Press, 2003.

Hazen, Eric, Steven Schlozman, and Eugene Beresin. "Adolescent Psychological Development: A Review." *Pediatric Review* 29 (2008): 161–167.

Kronenberg, Henry M., Shlomo Melmed, Kenneth S. Polonsky, and Larsen P. Reed. *Williams Textbook of Endocrinology,* 11th ed. New York: Elsevier, 2007.

McLeod, Saul. "Erik Erikson." *Simply Psychology*. 2013. Accessed November 21, 2017. https://www.simplypsychology.org/Erik-Erikson.html.

Meeus, Wim, Jurjen Iedema, Gerard Maassen, and Rutger Engels. "Separation-Individuation Revisited: On the Interplay of Parent–Adolescent Relations, Identity and Emotional Adjustment in Adolescence." *Journal of Adolescence* 28 (2005): 89–106. https://doi.org/10.1016/j.adolescence.2004.07.003.

Pinyerd, Belinda, and William B. Zipf. "Puberty—Timing Is Everything!" *Journal of Pediatric Nursing* 20 (2005): 75–82. http://dx.doi.org/10.1016/j.pedn.2004.12.011.

Santrock, John W. *Adolescence*. New York: McGraw-Hill, 2009.

Shanahan, Lilly, Susan M. McHale, Ann C. Crouter, and D. Wayne Osgood. "Warmth with Mothers and Fathers from Middle Childhood to Late Adolescence: Within- and Between-Families Comparisons." *Developmental Psychology* 43 (2007): 551–563. http://dx.doi.org/10.1037/0012-1649.43.3.551.

Steinberg, Lawrence, and Amanda S. Morris. "Adolescent Development." *Annual Review of Psychology* 52 (2001): 83–110. https://doi.org/10.1146/annurev.psych.52.1.83

ADVOCACY GROUPS

Advocacy groups play a critical role in eating disorder education. These groups serve different roles, including lobbying governments, establishing support communities for patients and families, offering professional advancement opportunities, creating innovative treatment programs, and funding projects related to eating disorders. Advocacy groups have played pivotal roles bringing eating disorders to the forefront of public awareness over the past several decades. Advocacy groups can take many forms and serve a variety of functions in the eating disorder community. Among the most well-known advocacy groups are the Eating Disorders Coalition, F.E.A.S.T., and the Academy of Eating Disorders, in addition to dozens of other organizations.

The Eating Disorders Coalition

One of the earliest advocacy groups established for eating disorders was the Eating Disorders Coalition (EDC), an American nonprofit established in April 2000. Originally, the EDC consisted of only five major groups, both from the scientific community and public sector. Currently, there are over 40 organizations that comprise the EDC, as well as numerous individual members. The EDC has six goals related to eating disorder prevention, intervention, and education:

1. Raise awareness among policy makers and the public about the health consequences of eating disorders
2. Promote federal support for improved access to quality care
3. Increase resources for education, prevention, and improved training for mental health practitioners
4. Increase fiscal support for scientific research on eating disorders
5. Promote initiatives that focus on healthy childhood development
6. Mobilize interested citizens to effectively advocate for the eating disorder community

Eating Disorder Advocacy: An Interview with the Cofounder of Rooted Recovery, Katie Fraser

Katie Fraser, along with her sister and fellow colleagues, founded Rooted Recovery. She is a therapist who specializes in the treatment of addictions, trauma, and eating disorders. Currently, she serves as a board member of the Columbia River Eating Disorder Network and an adjunct instructor for Lewis and Clark Graduate School. With broad experience as a therapist, she's worked in outpatient, intensive outpatient, partial hospitalization, and residential eating disorder treatment settings. As an avid consumer of research, she is committed to continual learning and conducts her own research as well. Katie is most interested in conducting and reading about research that investigates contextual factors that contribute to eating disorder treatment and recovery outcomes, positive and negative. Her work is driven by the belief that each person can learn to cultivate a healthy, value-driven, rich, and dynamic life.

What is the history of and mission for Rooted Recovery? Why was it important to you to start this organization?

Rooted Recovery's mission is to improve recovery outcomes by providing greater access to specialized community-based care. We believe that everyone should be able to access affordable, effective, and individualized treatment.

Rooted Recovery is an outgrowth of empirical research that involved the study of clinical recovery coaching as a supplement to traditional forms of treatment. The research also investigated the barriers and mitigating factors involved in both cultivating and sustaining eating disorder recovery. The results were so encouraging, with both participants and outside community members requesting that we continue our services, that we grew our research and pilot program into a company.

On both a personal and professional level, Rooted Recovery's founding members have been deeply impacted by eating disorders. On some level, we have experienced the potential complications involved in finding, securing, and receiving effective treatment, and the challenges involved in cultivating sustainable recovery. We do not believe treatment should cost $2,000+/day if a positive outcome cannot be guaranteed. We believe that everyone who needs treatment should be able to access and afford it. We believe that the treatment received should result in sustainable recovery. It is estimated that up to 90 percent of people with eating disorders do not receive the treatment they need. It is not uncommon for the 10 percent of those who do receive treatment to leave prematurely; in some research studies, dropout rates are as high as 51 percent. With treatment completion, relapse rates can be as high as 65 percent. These are not encouraging statistics. This is why Rooted Recovery exists; we want to reach out to those who haven't been able to access treatment. We want to help those who are receiving treatment by providing supplementary support. We want people to live the lives they deserve, free of the eating disorder.

Rooted Recovery believes that motivation, although helpful, is not necessary to recover from an eating disorder. Feelings of motivation can easily be obscured by the presence of an all-consuming and devastating disorder. Eating disorders are incredibly complex; constructs of recovery and relapse should not be built around esoteric and veiled factors like motivation. Rather than implicitly or explicitly blaming the patient, when a treatment isn't working we need to evaluate the treatment provided. Poor treatment outcome should never result in the conclusion that the patient wasn't yet ready for treatment and recovery, or didn't desire it strongly enough. As a community of providers, supporters, and sufferers, we need to agree that we don't know enough about eating disorders, what causes them, what maintains them, or how best to treat them. This does not mean that all treatment is ineffective. This does not mean that recovery is impossible. What this does mean is that we need to commit to living in community with one another. We need to commit to finding better solutions, more solutions. We must never give up hope; when suffering exists we must respond with compassion, curiosity, respect, and love. Rooted Recovery was developed to provide a supportive community for those in need, free of blame and judgment.

What is Rooted Recovery doing to help in the fight against eating disorders? What do you hope to accomplish in the next 3–5 years?
Rooted Recovery provides a range of specialized support services built to be highly customizable to the needs of each person throughout their recovery process. We provide grocery shopping assistance, meal support, 1:1 therapy, support groups, recovery coaching and accountability check-ins. In addition to traditional, in-person support, Rooted Recovery increases access to services through a mobile application and a HIPAA compliant teletherapy platform.

What do you believe are the keys to the prevention of eating disorders?
There are many challenges to the prevention of eating disorders. Our understanding of eating disorders, both the etiological and maintenance factors, and consequent treatment and recovery needs are embryonic; we have a lot of work yet to do, a lot more questions to ask, and even more answers to evaluate and reevaluate. Complacency and the belief that we understand eating disorders are our primary threats to prevention. We must remain curious. As providers, community members, and sufferers (past and present), we must remain humble and commit to continued dialogue with one another.

Is it possible to be "recovered" from an eating disorder? If so, how does someone know when he or she is fully recovered?
In other words, what does recovery look like? Some people believe it's possible to "recover" while others assert that only "recovery" is possible; there is debate as to whether this is just a matter of semantics or whether this difference in wording signifies a divide in our understanding of the overall recovery process, and what is possible. Rooted Recovery believes that this is something that individuals have the right to determine for themselves. Whether a person is "recovered" or lives in "recovery" we whole-heartedly believe that it is possible to live a life outside of the eating disorder.

The recovery process can be tricky, and it is certainly difficult. It can be hard to trust in the process, especially when someone is unable to know what life outside of the eating disorder looks or feels like. This is one reason why it's important to be surrounded with a healthy community of people who can help serve as guides, who can provide compassionate, informed, and consistent feedback during the process.

If someone wants to get involved in the fight against eating disorders, what can he or she do to make a difference? What is the most important thing for parents to know related to preventing eating disorders and creating a positive body image culture in the home?

There are many ways to get involved. Advocacy starts at home; make sure to maintain your own health and well-being. There are advocacy groups you can join. You can start your own group. Rooted Recovery welcomes you to contact us as well.

There are several things parents can do to create a positive body image culture in the home: (1) don't comment, positive or negative, on your kid's appearance; (2) Reinforce their positive qualities and traits; (3) Encourage them to openly dialogue about their experiences with themselves and the world around them; (4) Help them learn how to recognize, experience, and communicate emotions; (5) Encourage socialization with healthy communities; (6) Encourage participation in hobbies, sports, or other interests; (7) Praise children for the process, not the result (example: A process comment is "I see that you worked really hard on your paper." Conversely, a result comment is "Congratulations on getting an A." By being praised for results, just as with appearance, a child is learning that acceptance is associated with a static condition; (8) Treat your body with compassion, acceptance, and respect. Lead by example.

The EDC has been instrumental in several pivotal policy changes over the past 15 years. Chief among these was the Eating Disorders Awareness, Prevention, and Education Act of 2003 (H.R. 873), which increased funding for programs to identify students with eating disorders and for education programs to promote eating disorder awareness among parents and students. The EDC was also instrumental in the IMPACT Act (S. 1172), which, expanded a grant-funding program for the education of health professions students in eating disorders.

Central to the mission of the EDC is advocating for mental health parity. This movement seeks to protect mental health disorders and substance abuse disorders from being discriminated against in health care and insurance practices. For example, prior to the Paul Wellstone and Pete Domenici Mental Health Parity and Addiction Equity Act (passed by Congress in 2008), it was common for an insurance company to offer unlimited coverage for doctor visits for a chronic biological condition, such as diabetes, but restrict number of visits eligible for a mental health disorder, like schizophrenia. Since the first piece of legislation on mental health parity was passed in 1996, the EDC has been influential educating policy makers on the importance of health coverage for mental illness (including eating disorders) and advocating for Congress to pass laws to ensure that mental health parity becomes a reality.

International Organizations

Eating disorder advocacy is also present at the international level. As opposed to nationally based groups, which are principally concerned with lobbying governments for laws that promote the well-being of individuals suffering or recovered from an eating disorder, international groups focus on education and community building. Many international groups use social media and the Internet to connect with families, afflicted individuals, and professionals from all parts of the world and establish online communities. One such group is the Families Empowered and Supporting Treatment for Eating Disorders (F.E.A.S.T.), established in 2008. F.E.A.S.T. focuses on promoting support for caregivers and therapy models that integrate families into the treatment of eating disorders. F.E.A.S.T. has spoken out against *Parentectomy*, which it refers to as the removal of caregivers from the treatment process. F.E.A.S.T. has also advocated for more caregiver representation at academic conferences on eating disorders and created support groups for family members of individuals with eating disorders.

Treatment Groups

Other organizations under the umbrella of advocacy groups focus specifically on providing quality treatment options to individuals with eating disorders. Instead of lobbying for governmental reform, establishing support groups, or providing professional advancement opportunities, these groups prioritize the creation of innovative and comprehensive treatment programs. Rooted Recovery is one such example. Rooted Recovery offers treatment options for patients who suffer from eating disorders, support for caregivers and family members, and consultation services for clinicians who treat eating disorders. Although the organization is tangentially involved in advocacy efforts and promoting high standards in the mental health profession, its self-reported focus is on providing accessible, high quality, and personalized care to patients.

List of Advocacy Groups

Below is a list of advocacy groups, with a brief description. This does not represent an exhaustive list, but the authors believe these represent a breadth of topics. For a comprehensive list of advocacy groups organized by location, please visit the F.E.A.S.T. registry at www.feast-ed.org/?page=WorldAdvocacyOrgs.

- National Association for Anorexia Nervosa and Associated Disorders (ANAD)
  ANAD is one of five original advocacy groups instrumental in establishing the Eating Disorders Coalition in 2000. ANAD is the oldest nonprofit advocacy group in the United States and is headquartered in Naperville, Illinois. ANAD offers a 9–5 helpline, works primarily in the areas of support, awareness, and treatment referrals, and has a free quarterly publication, *Working Together,* available to the public on its website.
- Eating for Life Alliance
  The Eating for Life Alliance promote mental health awareness and eating disorder prevention among college students. The Eating for Life Alliance has a number of resources for college students on its website, including resources for specific populations (e.g., athletes, males, Freshman).

- Project HEAL
  Project HEAL was organized by two women who met in recovery for anorexia nervosa while they were teenagers. Project HEAL raises money for individuals seeking treatment for an eating disorder who cannot afford quality care.
- The National Association for Males with Eating Disorders (NAMED)
  Although males are not affected by eating disorders such as anorexia nervosa at equal rates with women, there is still a great need for understanding the male experience of body image and disordered eating. NAMED promotes research, education, and awareness of men's eating disorders. The NAMED website features a blog written by male survivors, resources on relevant research articles and books, as well as a place for professionals who treat males to network and share their experiences.
- MentorCONNECT
  MentorCONNECT is a global mentoring community for individuals suffering and recovered from an eating disorder. It is a nonprofit organization that offers live 24/7 support community access for members. Only individuals who have recovered from an eating disorder can be involved in the mentorship process.

Hannah J. Hopkins

See also: Binge Eating Disorder Association; Legislation on Eating Disorders; National Eating Disorders Association; Prevention; Students Promoting Eating Disorder Awareness and Knowledge (SPEAK)

Bibliography

"Academy for Eating Disorders." *AED.* Accessed February 3, 2017. http://www.aedweb.org/.

Alexander, Lamar. "Text—S.2680—114th Congress (2015–2016): Mental Health Reform Act of 2016." *Congress.gov.* Last modified April 26, 2016. Accessed November 22, 2017. https://www.congress.gov/bill/114th-congress/senate-bill/2680/text/is.

Cogan, Jeanine C. "Question & Answer: Why Is Advocacy on Eating Disorders Needed?" Edited by Russell D. Marx. *Eating Disorders* 8, no. 4 (2000): 353–354. https://doi.org/101080/10640260008251242.

Cogan, Jeanine C., Debra L. Franko, and David B. Herzog. "Federal Advocacy for Anorexia Nervosa: An American Model." *International Journal of Eating Disorders* 37, no. S1 (2005): S101–S102. https://doi.org/10.1002/eat.20127.

Cogan, Jeanine C., and David B. Herzog. "Questions & Answer: Why Is It Important to Address Eating Disorders through Federal Advocacy?" Edited by Russell D. Marx. *Eating Disorders* 13, no. 3 (2005): 307–312. https://doi.org/10.1080/10640260590932904.

"Eating Disorders Coalition: Mission & Goals." *Eating Disorders Coalition.* Accessed February 3, 2017. http://www.eatingdisorderscoalition.org/inner_template/about_us/mission-and-goals.html.

"F.E.A.S.T. (Families Empowered and Supporting Treatment of Eating Disorders)." *Feast.* Accessed February 3, 2017. http://www.feast-ed.org/.

"NAMI: National Alliance on Mental Illness: Understanding Health Insurance." *NAMI.* Accessed February 3, 2017. http://www.nami.org/Find-Support/Living-with-a-Mental-Health-Condition/Understanding-Health-Insurance/What-is-Mental-Health-Parity.

"Our Community—Rooted Recovery Wellness." *Rooted Recovery.* Accessed February 3, 2017. http://rootedrecovery.com/our-community/.

"Summary of the New Parity Law." *APA Practice Organization.* Accessed February 3, 2017. http://www.apapracticecentral.org/news/2008/parity-summary.aspx.

AEROBICS

The term *aerobics* was first coined by Dr. Kenneth Cooper in 1968 to represent a system of exercise for preventing coronary artery disease. Jackie Sorenson developed aerobic dance (i.e., a series of dance routines to improve cardiovascular fitness) a year later. The aerobic dance movement spread across the United States and into other countries in the 1970s and 1980s. In 1983, *sportaerobics* was developed by the Sport Fitness International (SFI) organization, which hosted the first national U.S. aerobics championship. Since then, world aerobics competitions have continued and aerobics are a global phenomenon. Although the competition aspect of aerobics is important, aerobic dance classes are available in almost every fitness center across the United States. Female and male aerobics class participants with a variety of motives exercise in group classes.

Body Image and Aerobics

Aerobics classes are not just a means to get fit in a 60-minute session; they can also become a culture. Group exercise classes present some body image concerns and opportunities for scrutiny. Like dancers, aerobics class participants generally face a mirror while they participate in aerobics routines. Participants may experience dissatisfaction with the image in the mirror, or they may sense pressure to wear a particular outfit to fit in with the other participants or to dress up for the mirror. Exercise attire may be form fitting or revealing and this can contribute to body consciousness. Aerobics class participants may also compare their bodies to those of other participants or the group leader.

Although aerobics participants are most likely to compare their bodies to their peers' bodies, it is interesting to note that aerobics instructors' bodies are on display and serve as models of correct form and sources of motivation. Therefore, there are certain expectations for aerobics class instructors regarding size, shape, and appearance. In fact, it was reported in 2002 that the Jazzercise company did not hire a five foot eight, 240-pound female to teach aerobics class because her size, stature, and physique did not represent the body ideal of a fitness leader.

In one study, 171 aerobics participants were surveyed about the ideal characteristics of aerobics instructors. Interestingly, appearance, age, or body type were less frequently cited characteristics than physical fitness, enthusiasm, motivation, the ability to lead a group exercise class, strong cue skills, and demonstration of proper technique. Only 6 percent of participants stated that "being thin" was an important quality for instructors and "under age 40" was less important (5 percent of participants).

Aerobics Instructors and Eating Disorders

Well-known aerobics instructors who have struggled with eating disorders include Jane Fonda and Richard Simmons. Research studies about eating disorder rates among aerobics and fitness instructors have yielded mixed results. For one Swedish study, 27 percent of female fitness instructors admitted to having a history of anorexia nervosa and/or bulimia nervosa. In a follow-up study with a similar population of Swedish fitness instructors, 30 percent of instructors reported binge eating episodes and uncontrollable eating, 15 percent reported restricted eating, and 72 percent were dissatisfied with their body weight. Additionally, 35 percent of these instructors reported a history of eating disorders with 11 percent admitting to having a current eating disorder. Exercise dependence characteristics were present in fitness instructors with 71 percent continuing to exercise despite suffering from a cold or illness. For a study looking at 30 U.S. aerobics instructors, 40 percent of instructors reported having an eating disorder history with 23 percent identifying bulimia nervosa and 17 percent indicating a history of anorexia nervosa. The instructors appeared to have greater preoccupation with body weight, higher body dissatisfaction, more perfectionism, and greater drive for thinness, predictive of greater risk for developing and maintaining disordered eating behaviors or clinical eating disorders.

In contrast to the Swedish and American studies, a study of 286 Canadian female aerobics instructors determined instructors did not score higher on commitment to exercise, drive for thinness, body dissatisfaction, bulimia or other eating disorder predictors compared to high-exercising populations or the general population. Therefore, more research is needed to better understand which aerobics instructors may be at increased risk for body image disturbances and eating disorders.

Justine J. Reel

See also: Dancers; Exercise; Personality Characteristics

Bibliography

Evans, Retta R., Ellen M. Cotter, and Jane L. Roy. "Preferred Body Type of Fitness Instructors among University Students in Exercise Classes." *Perceptual and Motor Skills* 101 (2005): 257–266. https://doi.org/10https://doi.org/10.2466/pms.101.1.257-266.

Fonda, Jane. *My Life So Far.* New York: Random House, 2005.

Hoglund, K. and L. Normen. "A High Exercise Load Is Linked to Pathological Weight Control Behavior and Eating Disorders in Female Fitness Instructors." *Scandinavian Journal of Medicine & Science in Sports* 12 (2002): 261–275. https://doi.org/10https://doi.org/10.1034/j.1600-0838.2002.10323.x.

Manley, Ronald S., Karina M. O'Brien, and Sumerlee Samuels. "Fitness Instructors' Recognition of Eating Disorders and Attendant Ethical/Liability Issues." *Eating Disorders* 16 (2008): 103–116. https://doi.org/10https://doi.org/10.1080/10640260801887162.

Martin, Kathleen A., and Heather A. Hausenblas. "Psychological Commitment to Exercise and Eating Disorder Symptomatology among Female Aerobic Instructors." *The Sport Psychologist* 12, no. 2 (1998): 180–190. https://doi.org/10.1123/tsp.12.2.180

Olson, Michele S., Henry N. Williford, Leigh Anne Richards, Jennifer A. Brown, and Steven Pugh. "Self-Reports on the Eating Disorder Inventory by Female Aerobic Instructors." *Perceptual and Motor Skills* 82 (1996): 1051–1058. https://doi.org/10https://doi.org/10.2466/pms.1996.82.3.1051.

Thogersen-Ntoumani, Cecilie, and Nikos Ntoumanis. "A Self-Determination Theory Approach to the Study of Body Image Concerns, Self-Presentation and Self-Perceptions in a Sample of Aerobics Instructors." *Journal of Health Psychology* 12, no. 2 (2007): 301–315. https://doi.org/10https://doi.org/10.1177/1359105307074267.

AESTHETIC SPORTS

The term *aesthetic* generally refers to beauty or art that judge is pleasing to the eye. Sports have often been classified into categories such as aesthetic, endurance, ball, or team sports to distinguish various demands. Aesthetic sports represent those sports in which successful athletic performance is often related to a certain look or specific standard of physical appearance. Often, aesthetic sports consider leanness, low body weight, and/or a petite body size to be beautiful, artful, and an indicator of optimal athletic performance. Sports in the aesthetic category are gymnastics, figure skating, dance, diving, bodybuilding, and cheerleading.

Examples of Aesthetic Sports

The success of rhythmic gymnastics routines is highly dependent on both technical and artistic components. More specifically, flexibility (e.g., 180-degree splits), detailed choreography, disciplined execution of movements (e.g., pointed toes), careful control of an apparatus (i.e., hoop, ball, rope, clubs, or ribbon), and the purposeful incorporation of music are emphasized. Figure skaters are also judged based on technical and artistic elements of a program. A skater's choreography, expression, and style of skating are just as important as successful completion of jumps, spins, and footwork sequences. For competitive dancers, performances are often evaluated on the appropriateness of the music and dance costume in addition to advanced technical skills. Each of these aesthetic sports tends to favor a graceful exterior and long and lean body lines. In contrast, bodybuilders are judged on muscularity, skeletal structure, body proportion, balance, and symmetry, while cheerleading has been associated with sex appeal and audience entertainment.

Some aesthetic sports (e.g., diving, gymnastics, pairs skating) demand prepubescent body shapes with long lines and minimal curvature to meet specific standards of physical appearance and allow for maximum flexibility, movement, or flight. This is especially true for aesthetic sports that involve difficult lifts, such as pairs skating and cheerleading. Lighter and leaner athletes are far easier to lift and maneuver in the air, thereby allowing for successful and potentially more competitive athletic performances.

Aesthetic Sports, Body Image Concerns, and Disordered Eating

Research shows that because of an emphasis on weight, shape, and physical appearance, athletes in aesthetic sports are at greater risk for disordered eating as compared to nonaesthetic sport athletes (e.g., ball sport participants like softball or soccer players) and nonathletes. This trend has been demonstrated in meta-analyses of the literature, which are summaries of findings across many studies. Unfortunately, aesthetic sport participants (i.e., dancers, gymnasts, cheerleaders, baton twirlers, swimmers, aerobics participants, and figure skaters) as young as ages 5-7 have been shown to experience significantly greater weight concerns than nonaesthetic sport participants (i.e., volleyball, soccer, basketball, softball, hockey, tennis players, martial arts participants, and track athletes) and nonathletes.

Other studies examining body image concerns and disordered eating in aesthetic sports alone have produced astounding statistics. The prevalence of eating disorders in female aesthetic sport athletes at the elite level have been reported at 42 percent. In a study of 35 ballet dancers, 41 percent met criteria for a clinical or subclinical eating disorder. The lifetime prevalence rate of developing an eating disorder as a professional dancer has been found to be as high as 50 percent. Another study of 215 collegiate female gymnasts found over 60 percent met criteria for a moderate form of disordered eating, and only 22 percent were categorized as having normal eating habits. In an examination of 42 collegiate female gymnasts, 100 percent reported dieting and over 60 percent reported they used at least one pathogenic weight control behavior (e.g., self-induced vomiting; use of diet pills, laxatives, or diuretics). Similar trends have been demonstrated in figure skaters. For example, in a study of 40 male and female national-level figure skaters, 48 percent reported symptoms indicative of an eating disorder.

Females involved in aesthetic sports may also be more vulnerable to negative self-perceptions and low perceived competence, especially during puberty. The physical changes associated with puberty can include breast development and fat gain in girls, greater muscle mass in boys, rapid growth spurts, and weight increases. Each of these changes may not only influence athletic performance by altering balance, stability, speed, and coordination but also negatively affect body image. In short, aesthetic sport athletes may begin to perceive themselves poorly relative to both the technical and appearance-based aspects of their sport as they experience natural pubertal changes.

Role of Coaches

Scholars believe pressures from an athletic environment influence athletes' thoughts, beliefs, and attitudes toward weight, shape, appearance, eating, and exercise. The role of coaches in the onset of body image disturbances and disordered eating in aesthetic sport athletes has been a primary area of concern. Among 603 elite female athletes, 67 percent of those who met criteria for a clinical eating disorder were told by a coach to diet. Another study revealed that nearly 70 percent of 42 collegiate female gymnasts reported their coaches told them they were too heavy. Seventy-five percent of those who received a disparaging comment from their coach resorted to a pathogenic weight control behavior. Similar findings have been shown in figure skaters, where the greatest reported pressure to lose or maintain weight is from skaters themselves, followed by coaches.

Coaches are believed to be powerful, key figures in the lives of athletes. Athletes may therefore take extreme measures to meet the expectations of their coaches when it comes to appearance, weight, shape, and body size. Unfortunately, coaches tend to make comments about weight based on subjective evaluations of appearance rather than objective measurements and evidence-based practice to improve performance. Therefore, athletes' efforts to lose and maintain weight are often both unstructured and unhealthy.

Due to the strong influence of coaches, the National Collegiate Athletic Association (NCAA) has taken strides to protect aesthetic sport athletes by providing educational materials to coaches regarding the topic. However, much more can and should be done to increase coaches' awareness of their influence on the weight management practices of athletes. In a study examining collegiate coaches' knowledge of eating disorders, nearly 25 percent of coaches scored between 60 and 69.5 percent, and only 4.3 percent of coaches scored a 90 percent or greater. Nearly 40 percent reported that they were unaware of any eating disorder resources offered by their athletics department.

Role of Judges

Given the subjective scoring system in aesthetic sports, the role of judges is especially important. Judges' scoring in aesthetic sports can be affected by an athlete's shape; leaner athletes with longer lines tend to receive higher scores. Research demonstrates the primary reason many aesthetic sport athletes engage in dieting and weight management behaviors is because they believe such practices will help achieve athletic success by improving their performance and their appearance. For example, in a study of 28 elite and nonelite gymnasts, 32 percent expressed the need to look good in a leotard, 25 percent believed being thin would improve performance, and a substantial number reported concern about weight because of the emphasis on appearance (18 percent) and being continuously judged (18 percent). Unfortunately, the dieting and weight management practices associated with the demands of aesthetic sports may evolve into severe disordered eating attitudes and behaviors or a clinical eating disorder, such as anorexia nervosa or bulimia nervosa. A tragic example of this tendency of an athlete to engage in harmful eating practices is Christy Henrich, an Olympic gymnast who was told by a judge to lose weight. Her long-standing battle with an eating disorder resulted in a rapid performance decline and eventual death.

Role of Teammates and Parents

Although weight pressures from coaches and judges appear to be a primary concern, teammates and parents are also a source of pressure for aesthetic sport athletes. For example, of 28 female collegiate gymnasts, 17 percent reported experiencing pressure from other gymnasts to lose weight. In a study of 32 female figure skaters, parents were the third-most significant source of pressure to lose or maintain weight, followed by the skaters themselves and coaches. Male skating partners have also been shown to be a source of pressure to lose or maintain weight in ice dancers and pairs skaters because of the difficult lifts and flight patterns necessary to succeed in these particular disciplines.

Males in Aesthetic Sports

Popular belief suggests the relationship between aesthetic sport participation and the risk for disordered eating and body image distortions is only evident in females.

Although more research is needed, preliminary evidence indicates males in aesthetic sports may also be vulnerable to pressures associated with the demands to maintain a certain weight, shape, and appearance. This has most recently been shown in male dancers who were equally at risk for an eating disorder as females, and where self-evaluative perfectionism (e.g., perceived pressure from others) and conscientious perfectionism (e.g., striving for excellence) were predictive of disordered eating patterns. College male cheerleaders reported similar weight pressures—including coaches, weight requirements to tryout, and uniforms—as their female counterparts. However, in contrast to many females, male cheerleaders and other male athletes are expected to gain weight throughout the competitive season while maintaining low body composition and a lean physique.

Benefits of Aesthetic Sport Participation

Although participation in aesthetic sports is associated with negative struggles for some athletes relative to eating behaviors and body image, it is important to remember these sports are not all bad. In fact, aesthetic sports offer a unique combination of artistic expression and technical skills that define athleticism in new and interesting ways unlike any other sport type. Many scholars have noted the aesthetic appeal of sports in general is one reason we both appreciate and continue to participate in sports as athletes, coaches, spectators, and sponsors.

Moreover, many aesthetic sport athletes at the youth, high school, collegiate, and elite levels demonstrate positive outcomes. For example, the development of important life skills across sport types has been well documented and includes learning important values, behaviors, and interpersonal skills. To maximize these benefits and minimize the risks associated with aesthetic sport participation, much should be done to prevent disordered eating and body image disturbances in this unique population of athletes. To achieve this goal, many governing bodies of aesthetic sports offer educational resources on proper nutrition for optimal performance, healthy body image, and eating disorder prevention available to athletes, coaches, and parents.

Dana K. Voelker

See also: Bodybuilding; Cheerleading; Coaches; Dancers; Figure Skating; Gymnastics; Weight Class Sports

Bibliography

Galli, N., and Justine J. Reel. "Adonis or Hephaestus? Exploring Body Image in Male Athletes." *Psychology of Men and Masculinity* 10 (2009): 95–108. https://doi.org/10https://doi.org/10.1037/a0014005.

Hausenblas, Heather A., and Albert V. Carron. "Eating Disorder Indices and Athletes: An Integration." *Journal of Sport & Exercise Psychology* 21 (1999): 230–258. https://doi.org/10.1123/jsep.21.3.230

Neumark-Sztainer, Dianne. "Preventing the Broad Spectrum of Weight-Related Problems: Working with Parents to Help Teens Achieve a Healthy Weight and a Positive Body Image." *Journal of Nutrition Education & Behavior* 37 (2005): S133–S139. https://doi.org/10.1016/S1499-4046(06)60214-5.

Sundgot-Borgen, Jorunn. "Risk and Trigger Factors for the Development of Eating Disorders in Female Elite Athletes." *Medicine and Science in Sports and Exercise* 26 (1994): 414–419.

Sundgot-Borgen, Jorunn, and Monica Klungland Torstveit. "Prevalence of Eating Disorders in Elite Athletes Is Higher Than in the General Population." *Clinical Journal of Sports Medicine* 14 (2004): 25–32.

Thompson, Ron A., and Roberta Trattner Sherman. *Helping Athletes with Eating Disorders.* Champaign, IL: Human Kinetics, 1993.

Turk, Joanne C., William E. Prentice, Susan Chappell, and Edgar W. Shields. "Collegiate Coaches' Knowledge of Eating Disorders." *Journal of Athletic Training* 34 (1999): 19–24.

AGING AND BODY IMAGE

Although most publicity surrounding eating disorders and body image disturbances targets adolescent and college females, it is important to consider what happens to body-related and appearance concerns as people age. A youthful appearance has been equated with beauty and social status that has generated a billion-dollar industry for antiaging products that claim to reduce cellulite, eliminate wrinkles, and wash away gray hairs. In addition to these antiaging products many males and females have resorted to drastic measures such as cosmetic surgery to stall time and to change appearance. According to the American Society of Plastic Surgeons, 9.9 million females undergo cosmetic procedures annually and a majority of women are older than age 40. Specifically, 45 percent of women ages 40–50, 26 percent of women age 50 years and over, 19 percent of women in ages 30–39 years, and 7 percent of women ages 20–29 years underwent cosmetic surgical (e.g., liposuction, breast augmentation, eyelid surgery) and/or minimally invasive procedures (e.g., Botox injections, chemical peels). Men also seek cosmetic surgery to enhance body parts, including pectoral implants for a more defined chest and calf implants. Beyond monetary issues, combating natural changes that occur with age (e.g., wrinkles, thinning or graying hair, decreased skin elasticity and sagging skin) can contribute to body dissatisfaction and disordered eating among individuals in their 30s, 40s, 50s, and beyond.

Body Image and the Media

Youthfulness symbolizes beauty and desirability, while aging has become something to be avoided by exercising, restricting certain foods, undergoing cosmetic surgery, or using products marketed by the media. Studies that analyzed media trends found models in magazines did not represent the age or size of the readership. Researchers have discovered models ages 25–34 years were overrepresented in the over-35 magazines (e.g., *Country Living, Martha Stewart*), models were even younger (18–24 years) in the under-35 magazines (e.g., *Cosmopolitan),* and younger models were thinner. This underrepresentation of older female images and celebration of youthful appearance qualities can reinforce body dissatisfaction.

Originally, it was assumed adolescent females would be most at risk for body image disturbances and eating disorders due to developmental concerns (e.g., puberty and peer pressures). However, several studies have found no age-related differences in body image and some have found the midlife group (usually 39–59 years) to show higher body dissatisfaction than younger and older females. These results suggest women of all ages may be dissatisfied with their bodies and serve as a caution that individuals do not simply grow out of eating disorders at a certain age. Although aging in males has often been associated with looking more distinguished or wise, 70-year-old former bodybuilder and ex-governor, Arnold Schwarzenegger, admitted during a 2011 interview he has developed poor body image because of age-related bodily changes.

Eating Disorders

Eating disorders are recognized as psychological disorders that primarily afflict adolescent girls and young women. Although traditionally, researchers argued the onset of eating disorders is less common later in adulthood, recent research has revealed an increase in the prevalence of eating disorders in older women and case studies involving midlife and late onset. It is difficult to know how many women in midlife and beyond suffer from eating disorders because the disorder may be underdiagnosed or females with disordered eating thoughts or behaviors may refuse to seek treatment. Across studies, middle-aged women report wanting to be thinner, engaging in unhealthy weight loss methods (e.g., self-induced vomiting), and being more aware of the sensations of hunger and satiety than elderly women. Middle-aged women were also at a higher risk for an eating disorder and endorsed a stronger fear of aging than their older counterparts. Elderly women displayed similar levels of body dissatisfaction as the younger groups, and recently, the phenomenon of late-life and late-onset eating disorders has received attention in treatment settings.

Forman and Davis (2005) investigated eating attitudes and body image in young and midlife adults and found that women over age 35 years with eating disorders had similar desires and thoughts such as wanting to be thin, body image dissatisfaction, experiencing perfectionism, having a sense of general inadequacy, as younger women with eating disorders. In addition, another study suggested young women (18–31 years old) and elderly women (60–78 years old) have similar dieting restraints and eating attitudes. Although older women are concerned with their physical appearance like younger women, the factors (e.g., pregnancy) that lead older women to develop bodily concerns and disordered eating may be different.

Toward a Thin Ideal

The literature on risk factors of body image concerns and eating disorders in girls and young women has generally overlooked older populations. This research suggests that a thin ideal is conveyed and reinforced by many sociocultural factors including family, peers, schools, sports, and, most significantly, the media. Flashy images of an extremely slim body promoted ubiquitously in magazines, television advertisements, reality shows, and movies may cause people to internalize that a female's body is her most salient attribute. Women are socialized to view their bodies as objects to be scrutinized for flaws and work to sculpt their bodies closer to the advertised body ideal. Women who view themselves as objects and conform to societal pressure by comparing themselves to other people and societal ideals may internalize observers' perspectives, experience shame and anxiety, and experience emotional and behavioral body image disturbances closely tied to the natural processes of aging.

Developmental Adulthood Milestones

Several developmental milestones that occur as women age may contribute to changes in body image and eating behaviors. Pregnancy represents body changes outside of a female's control. Although viewed as the healthy growth of a fetus, weight is often highly monitored and difficult to control. Menopause is associated with biological changes (e.g., weight gain, slowed metabolism) and may contribute to negative body image. Other life transitions may occur as women age, such as experiencing loss, divorce, or empty nest syndrome, all of can play a role in the development of eating disorders in older women. Women may engage in appearance-sculpting strategies (e.g., overexercise, cosmetic surgery) to cope or may engage in emotional eating (i.e., overeating or restricting).

Justine J. Reel

See also: Cosmetic Surgery and Eating Disorders; Late Life and Late-Onset Eating Disorders; Media; Menopause; Movies and Eating Disorders; Pregnancy; Puberty; Television Shows and Eating Disorders

Bibliography

American Society of Plastic Surgeons. "2006 Gender Quick Facts: Cosmetic Plastic Surgery." (2007). Accessed November 16, 2016. https://d2wirczt3b6wjm.cloudfront .net/News/Statistics/2006/plastic-surgery-gender-quick-facts-2006.pdf.

Bailey, Holly. "Arnold Schwarzenegger Is Sad He's Not Young Anymore." *The Ticket.* (2011). Accessed November 16, 2016. https://www.yahoo.com/news/blogs/ticket /arnold-schwarzenegger-sad-not-young-anymore-20110418-081648-118.html.

Bedford, Jennifer L., and Shanthi C. Johnson. "Societal Influences on Body Image Dissatisfaction in Younger and Older Women." *Journal of Women and Aging* 18 (2006): 41–55. http://dx.doi.org/10.1300/J074v18n01_04.

Bessenoff, Gayle R., and Regan Del Priore. "Women, Weight, Age: Social Comparison to Magazine Images across the Lifespan." *Sex Roles* 56 (2007): 215–222. https://doi .org/10.1007/s11199-006-9164-2.

Bordo, Susan. *Unbearable Weight: Feminism, Western Culture, and the Body.* Berkeley, CA: University of California Press, 1993.

Brandsma, Lynn. "Eating Disorders across the Life Span." *Journal of Women & Aging* 19 (2007): 155–172. https://doi.org/10.1300/J074v19n01_10.

Cumella, Edward J., and Zina Kally. "Profile of 50 Women with Midlife-Onset Eating Disorders." *Eating Disorders* 16 (2008): 193–203. https://doi.org/10.1080/10640260802016670.

Deeks, Amanda A., and Marita P. McCabe. "Menopausal Stage and Age and Perceptions of Body Image." *Psychology and Health* 16 (2001): 367–379. http://dx.doi.org/10.1080/08870440108405513.

Ferraro, F. Richard, Jennifer J. Muehlenkamp, Ashley Paintner, Kayla Wasson, Tracy Hager, and Fallon Hoverson. "Aging, Body Image, and Body Shape." *The Journal of General Psychology,* 135, no. 4 (2008): 379–392. http://dx.doi.org/10.3200/GENP.135.4.379-392.

Forman, Maryelizabeth, and William N. Davis. "Characteristics of Middle-Aged Women in Inpatient Treatment for Eating Disorders." *Eating Disorders: Journal of Treatment and Prevention* 13 (2005): 41–48. https://doi.org/10.1080/10640260590932841

Kearney-Cooke, Ann, and Florence Isaacs. *Change Your Mind, Change Your Body: Feeling Good about Your Body and Self after 40.* New York: Atria, 2004.

Lapid, Maria I., Maria C. Prom, M. Caroline Burton, Donald E. McAlpine, Bruce Sutor, and Teresa A. Rummans. "Eating Disorders in the Elderly." *International Psychogeriatrics* 22, no. 4 (2010): 523–536. https://doi.org/10.1017/S1041610210000104.

Lewis, Diane M., and Fary M. Cachelin. "Body Image, Body Dissatisfaction, and Eating Attitudes in Mid-life and Elderly Women." *Eating Disorders* 9 (2001): 29–39.

Mangweth-Matzek, Barbara, Claudia I. Rupp, Armand Hausmann, Karin Assmayr, Edith Mariacher, Georg Kemmler, Alexandra B. Whitworth, and Wilfried Biebl. "Never Too Late for Eating Disorders or Body Dissatisfaction: A Community Study of Elderly Women." *International Journal of Eating Disorders* 39 (2006): 583–586.

Midlarsky, Elizabeth, and George Nitzburg. "Eating Disorders in Middle-Aged Women." *The Journal of General Psychology* 135, no. 4 (2008): 393–407. http://dx.doi.org/10.3200/GENP.135.4.393-408.

Patrick, Julie H., and Sarah T. Stahl. "Understanding Disordered Eating at Midlife and Late Life." *The Journal of General Psychology* 136, no. 1 (2008): 5–20. http://dx.doi.org/10.3200/GENP.136.1.5-20.

Peat, Christine M., Naomi L. Peyerl, and Jennifer J. Muehlenkamp. "Body Image and Eating Disorders in Older Adults: A Review." *The Journal of General Psychology* 135, no. 4 (2008): 343–358. http://dx.doi.org/10.3200/GENP.135.4.343-358.

Reel, Justine J. "Body Image and Physical Self-Perceptions among African-American and Caucasian Women across the Adult Life Span." *Dissertation Abstracts International* 61, no. 5-B (2000).

Reel, Justine J., Sonya SooHoo, Franklin Summerhays, and Diane L. Gill. "Age before Beauty: An Exploration of Body Image Concerns among African-American and Caucasian Women." *Journal of Gender Studies* 17, no. 4 (2008): 321–330.

Scholtz, Samantha, Laura S. Hill, and Hubert Lacy. "Eating Disorders in Older Women: Does Late Onset Anorexia Nervosa Exist?" *International Journal of Eating Disorders* 43, no. 5 (2010): 393–397. https://doi.org/10.1002/eat.20704.

SooHoo, Sonya, Justine J. Reel, and Judy Van Raalte. "Chasing the 'Fountain of Youth': Body Image and Eating Disorders among 'Older' Women." In *The Hidden Faces of Eating Disorders and Body Image,* edited by Justine J. Reel and Katherine A. Beals. Reston, VA: NAGWS/AAHPERD, 2009.

Today Show. "Midlife Women with Eating Disorders." 2011. Accessed November 16, 2016. https://www.youtube.com/watch?v=azYhLOyzduU.

Zerbe, Kathryn J. "Eating Disorders in Middle and Late Life: A Neglected Problem." *Primary Psychiatry* 10 (2003): 80–82.

AIRBRUSHING

Airbrushing refers to a process of retouching or altering photographs used in advertising numerous products. The media's frequent use of airbrushing has recently come under scrutiny due to the evidence that digitally altered images contribute to negative body esteem in female adolescents and can trigger disordered eating.

History of Airbrushing

An airbrush is a small, air-operated tool that sprays ink, dye, or paint. Airbrushing has been used to alter photographs in the predigital era. The photograph could be extensively retouched or doctored to result in removing an entire person or surrounding objects, or to change the characteristics of the model. The first airbrush was developed and patented in 1876 by the makers of the Stanley Steemer. The first airbrush instruments were used for painting watercolors and for artistic purposes. Since the inception of airbrush technology, commercial artists and illustrators have used airbrushes to create and alter images for advertising, book covers, comic books, and graphic novels. One of the earliest manipulated photos is a famous image of President Lincoln that is a composite of Lincoln's head on another politician's body.

Body Image and Airbrushing

Currently the term *airbrushed* often refers to glamour photos (e.g., magazines) where models' imperfections (e.g., moles, scars) have been removed or body parts have been enhanced or altered (e.g., increased breasts, decreased waist). The resulting image represents a socially constructed standard of beauty and the perfection appears as a better version of the model. Some actresses (e.g., Jamie Lee Curtis in *More* magazine) have openly posed for photos showing before and after effects of intensive hair and make-up sessions. In 2010, Britney Spears released unairbrushed images of herself next to the digitally altered versions from a Candie's advertisement. It was determined that the resulting photos depicted an image of a female with a smaller waist, slimmer thighs, smaller bottom, and bruises, cellulite, and tattoo removed.

Airbrushing Regulations

The increased airbrushing has led to controversy and both magazines and models have been criticized for digitally enhanced photos (e.g., Kate Winslet in *GQ* magazine). L'Oréal makeup advertisements featuring airbrushed models Julia Roberts and Christy Turlington were banned in the UK because of their controversial use of airbrushing. Similar to the UK strictly regulated use of airbrushing, an Arizona lawmaker introduced a bill in February 2012 to require advertisers to provide a disclaimer for a photograph that has been altered or enhanced.

Justine J. Reel

See also: Celebrities and Eating Disorders; Cosmetic Surgery and Eating Disorders; Media; Models and Eating Disorders

Bibliography

"Airbrush Campaign by Former Anorexic." Last modified May 1, 2012. Accessed November 21, 2017. http://www.bbc.com/news/health-17904837.

"Crisis of Body Image." Wordpress.com. Last modified July 17, 2007. Accessed November 21, 2017. https://redsquirrel.wordpress.com/2007/07/17/the-crisis-of-body-image/.

Daily Mail Reporter. "Arizona Lawmakers Mull Bill to Outlaw Airbrushing and PhotoShopping in Ads." Dailymail.co.uk. Last Modified February 16, 2012. Accessed November 21, 2017. http://www.dailymail.co.uk/news/article-2101915/Arizona-law makers-mull-outlaw-airbrushing-Photo-Shopping-ads.html.

Daily Mail Reporter. "Britney Spears Bravely Agrees to Release Un-Airbrushed Images of Herself Next to the Digitally-Altered Versions." Dailymail.co.uk. Last modified April 13, 2010. Accessed November 21, 2017. http://www.dailymail.co.uk/tvshowbiz /article-1265676/Britney-Spears-releases-airbrushed-images-digitally-altered -versions.html#ixzz1VQHB9SqO.

Hayter, Alexandra. "The Effects of Airbrushing." *Alexandrahayterextendedproject.blogspot .com*. Last modified December 5, 2011. Accessed November 21, 2017. http:// alexandrahayterextendedproject.blogspot.com/2012/01/over-past-few-months-i-have -looked-at.html.

Jones, Bryony. "Britain Bans Airbrushed Julia Roberts Make-up Ad." *CNN.com*. Last modified July 28, 2011. Accessed November 21, 2017. http://www.cnn.com/2011 /WORLD/europe/07/28/airbrushed.advertisements.ban/.

Martin, Charlotte. "Airbrushed Pictures of Celebs Put Pressure on My 14-Year-Old Daughter to Look Perfect." *The Sun*. Last modified November 10, 2009. Accessed November 21, 2017. http://www.thesun.ie/irishsol/homepage/woman/2723569/Mums-and-teen-girls -on-body-image-and-airbrushing.html.

Tartakovsky, Margartia. "The Art of Airbrushing." *Psychcentral.com*. Accessed November 16, 2016. http://psychcentral.com/blog/archives/2008/12/09/the-art-of-airbrushing/.

Womack, Sarah. "Magazines Criticised for Airbrushing Models." *The Telegraph*. Last modified December 21, 2007. Accessed November 21, 2017. http://www.telegraph .co.uk/news/uknews/1573295/Magazines-criticised-for-airbrushing-models.html.

ALEXITHYMIA

Alexithymia is an inability to identify and describe one's feelings. Alexithymia is a common feature across both depression and eating disorders. Having alexithymic characteristics undermines an individual's ability to form healthy connections and to develop empathy and sensitivity toward others. Children who are physically and emotionally insecure and discouraged from expressing emotions have difficulties identifying and expressing varied emotions as adults. Alexithymia is related to low self-esteem and the inability to be assertive for individuals with anorexia nervosa or bulimia nervosa and can disrupt successful eating disorder treatment. Therefore, treatment of eating disorders needs to incorporate multidimensional approaches that include assertiveness training and self-esteem enhancement as part of a broader cognitive-behavioral therapy model to address alexithymic characteristics if present. The Toronto Alexithymia Scale (TAS-20), a 20-item questionnaire, was validated in 1994 by Bagby and colleagues to assess the degree of alexithymia.

Justine J. Reel

See also: Assertiveness Training; Cognitive Behavioral Therapy; Depression

Bibliography

Bagby, R. Michael, Graeme J. Taylor, and James D. A. Parker. "The Twenty-Item Toronto Alexithymia Scale-II. Convergent, Discriminant, and Concurrent Validity." *Journal of Psychosomatic Research* 38, no. 1 (1994): 33–40.

Bekker, Marrie H., Marcel A. Croon, Esther G. van Balkom, and Jennifer B. Vermee. "Predicting Individual Differences in Autonomy-Connectedness: The Role of Body Awareness, Alexithymia and Assertiveness." *Journal of Clinical Psychology* 64, no. 6 (2008): 747–765. https://doi.org/10.1002/jclp.20486.

Shina, Akihiro, Michiko Nakazato, Makoto Mitsumori, Hiroki Koizumi, Eui Shimizu, Mihisa Fujisaki, and Masaomi Iyo. "An Open Trial of Outpatient Group Therapy for Bulimic Disorders: Combination Program of Cognitive Behavioral Therapy with Assertive Training and Self-Esteem Enhancement." *Psychiatry and Clinical Neurosciences* 59 (2005): 690–696.

AMENORRHEA

Amenorrhea refers to a condition in which a female experiences a delayed start to her menstrual cycle or the absence of a period. When a female with secondary sex characteristics has failed to start her period by age 15 it is known as *primary amenorrhea*. Secondary amenorrhea is defined by the absence of three consecutive menstrual periods after menses has begun. Amenorrhea has been used as one of the ways to diagnose a female with anorexia nervosa in previous versions of the *Diagnostic and Statistical Manual of Mental Disorders,* used by clinicians to diagnose individuals with eating disorders. However, the realization that male clients or older women would not qualify for anorexia nervosa led to changes in the *DSM-5* (5th edition of the manual). Therefore, the current definition of anorexia nervosa has removed absence of menstrual cycle as a criterion to be more inclusive of males and postmenopausal females.

It is also important to note the loss of a female's menstrual cycle may occur for eating disturbances other than anorexia nervosa, such as bulimia nervosa. Further, non–eating-disordered women may also experience changes in their menstrual cycle that can be tied to factors such as restrictive eating behavior or excessive exercise that leads to an energy deficit.

Causes of Amenorrhea

Scientists initially believed having a low percentage of body fat led to disruptions in the menstrual cycle. However, recent studies suggest having low energy availability (i.e., the amount of dietary energy remaining for other physiological functions after exercise) may be the real culprit causing menstrual disturbances.

Specifically, when energy availability decreases to a certain threshold, the body compensates by slowing one's metabolism and reducing of energy used for reproductive functioning.

Health Consequences

Low energy availability and estrogen deficiency can slow the rate of increasing bone mass that occurs in adolescence and lead to bone loss that impedes peak bone mass. This can result in lower bone mineral density compared to women of the same age and result in fragile bone that increases risk of skeletal fractures. Loss in bone mineral density has been observed to occur at an average rate of 2.5 percent per year in women with anorexia nervosa who do not resume menses. Decreased dilation of blood vessels, an indicator of premature cardiovascular disease, and infertility, are additional consequences of amenorrhea.

Amenorrhea in Athletes

The athletic population is a high-risk group for amenorrhea. Sport-specific risk factors for disordered eating coupled with high exercise training increase an athlete's susceptibility to energy deficits. The interrelationship between energy availability, menstrual function, and bone mineral density is termed "the female athlete triad." Each component of the triad exists along a spectrum with amenorrhea as the most severe menstrual cycle disturbance.

Management of Amenorrhea

Hormonal treatments in women with anorexia nervosa, such as estrogen therapies, have not effectively restored bone mass or addressed the nutritional aspects of bone health. Increasing caloric intake and/or reducing exercise can restore lost weight and combat an energy deficit and are recommended to reduce the risk for poor bone health. The most significant improvements in bone mineral density have been noted in individuals who adequately restore energy balance and return to regular menstrual cycles. Anorexia nervosa clients who have resumed menstruation have higher metabolic rates and increased levels of reproductive hormones compared with weight-recovered nonmenstruating clients. Thus, it may be beneficial to monitor estrogen status and assess energy availability as indicators of sufficient caloric intake for reproductive function.

Holly E. Doetsch

See also: Female Athlete Triad, *Diagnostic and Statistical Manual of Mental Disorders*

Bibliography

Fenichel, Rebecca M., and Michelle P. Warren. "Anorexia, Bulimia, and the Athletic Triad: Evaluation and Management." *Current Osteoporosis Reports* 5, no. 4 (2007): 160–164. https://doi.org/10.1007/s11914-007-0011-3.

Hoch, Anne Z, Sophia Lal, Jason W. Jurva, and David D. Gutterman. "The Female Athlete Triad and Cardiovascular Dysfunction." *Physical Medicine and Rehabilitation Clinics of North America* 18, no. 3 (2007): 385–400. http://dx.doi.org/10.1016/j.pmr.2007.05.001.

Loucks, Anne B. "Energy Availability and Infertility." *Current Opinion in Endocrinology, Diabetes, and Obesity* 14, no. 6 (2007): 470–474. https://doi.org/10.1097/MED.0b013e3282f1cb6a.

Loucks, Anne B., and Jean R. Thuma. "Luteinizing Hormone Pulsatility Is Disrupted at a Threshold of Energy Availability in Regularly Menstruating Women." *Journal of Clinical Endocrinology and Metabolism* 88, no. 1 (2003): 297–311. https://doi.org/10.1210/jc.2002-020369.

Miller, Karen K., Ellen E. Lee, Elizabeth A. Lawson, Madhusmita Misra, Jennifer Minihan, Steven K. Grinspoon, Suzanne Gleysteen, Diane Mickley, David Herzog, and Anne Klibanski. "Determinants of Skeletal Loss and Recovery in Anorexia Nervosa." *Journal of Clinical Endocrinology and Metabolism* 91, no. 8 (2006): 2931–2937. https://doi.org/10.1210/jc.2005-2818.

Nattiv, Aurelia, Anne B. Loucks, Melinda M. Manore, Charlotte F. Sanborn, Jorunn Sundgot-Borgen, and Michelle P. Warren. "American College of Sports Medicine Position Stand. The Female Athlete Triad." *Medicine and Science in Sports and Exercise* 39, no. 10 (2007): 1867–1882.

Practice Committee of the American Society for Reproductive Medicine. "Current Evaluation of Amenorrhea." *Fertility and Sterility* 82 (2004): 266–272.

Sanborn, Charlotte F., Bruce H. Albrecht, and Wiltz W. Wagner. "Athletic Amenorrhea: Lack of Association with Body Fat." *Medicine and Science in Sports and Exercise* 19, no. 3 (1987): 207–212.

Sim, Leslie A., Lauren McGovern, Mohamed B. Elamin, Brian A. Swiglo, Patricia J. Erwin, and Victor M. Montori. "Effect on Bone Health of Estrogen Preparations in Premenopausal Women with Anorexia Nervosa: A Systematic Review and Meta-analyses." *International Journal of Eating Disorders* 43, no. 3 (2010): 218–225. https://doi.org/10.1002/eat.20687.

Sterling, Wendy M., Neville H. Golden, Marc S. Jacobson, Rollyn M. Ornstein, and Stanley M. Hertz. "Metabolic Assessment of Menstruating and Nonmenstruating Normal Weight Adolescents." *International Journal of Eating Disorders* 42, no. 7 (2009): 658–663. https://doi.org/10.1002/eat.20604.

ANOREXIA ATHLETICA

Anorexia athletica refers to athletes with eating disorder symptoms. Although not listed as an official eating disorder diagnoses in the *Diagnostic and Statistical Manual of Mental Disorders (DSM-5)*, anorexia athletica is also known as athletic nervosa or compulsive exercise and is particularly common in athletes who play a sport that emphasizes a lean physique, such as ski jumping, cycling, climbing, gymnastics, or long-distance running. Athletes with anorexia athletica show slightly different disordered eating symptoms and characteristics compared to nonathletes who have eating disorders. Primarily, anorexia athletica represents reduced energy intake and body mass despite high physical performance in athletes. Athletes who suffer from anorexia athletica do not enjoy exercise or training but rather are compelled to engage in workouts beyond what is required for one's sport. Typically, an athlete is driven more by sport performance than by body shape. By engaging in excessive exercise or training, an athlete attempts to gain confidence and reduce anxiety related to sport performance. These athletes usually prioritize practice schedules over family occasions, social events, or jobs. They will also exercise while injured and despite weather or other external barriers.

History of Anorexia Athletica

In the 1990s, the term *anorexia athletica* was coined to label athletes who exhibited partial anorexic behaviors, but who did not have full-blown eating disorders. Sundgot-Borgen and Torstveit, who introduced anorexia athletica, described disordered eating as occurring on a spectrum from abnormal eating behavior to a full-blown eating disorder that qualified for a clinical diagnosis. Thus, there are overlapping signs that appear across anorexia athletica, disordered eating, and eating disorders. First, an excessive concern about body shape can be seen in athletes who suffer from anorexia athletica when they compare their degree of fatness to that of other, remarkably more successful, athletes. Second, frequent weight cycling such as repeated weight loss and regain is used to control weight in some sports such as ski jumping and wrestling. Third, many athletes have lower body weight and percentages of body fat. Last, some athletes may engage in risky dietary restriction and/or definitive overexercising to burn calories.

Differences between Anorexia Athletica and Eating Disorders

In contrast, Sudi et al. explained clear distinctions between anorexia athletica and eating disorders. First, the reduction in body mass and/or the loss in body fat mass (considered as an unwarranted burden) associated with anorexia athletica is initiated for performance reasons, rather than for appearance or excessive concern about body shape, and it is often coaches and trainers who initiate dieting or overexercising. Second, the loss in body mass leads to a lean physique. Third, anorexia athletica should no longer be detectable after cessation of an athlete's career.

Maya Miyairi

See also: Aesthetic Sports; Dancers; Female Athlete Triad; Gymnastics; Ski Jumping; Weight Class Sports; Wrestling

Bibliography

Beals, Katherine A. *Helping Athletes with Eating Disorders.* Champaign, IL: Human Kinetics, 2004.

Reel, Justine J., and Katherine A. Beals, eds. *The Hidden Faces of Eating Disorders and Body Image.* Reston, VA: AAHPERD, 2009.

Sudi, Karl, Karl Ottl, Doris Payerl, Peter Baumgartl, Tauschmann Klemens, and Wolfram Muller. "Anorexia Athletica." *Nutrition* 20 (2004): 657–661. http://dx.doi .org/10.1016/j.nut.2004.04.019.

Sundgot-Borgen, Jorunn, and Monica K. Torstveit. "Prevalence of Eating Disorders in Elite Athletes Is Higher Than in the General Population." *Clinical Journal of Sport Medicine* (2004): 14–25.

ANOREXIA NERVOSA

The *Diagnostic and Statistical Manual of Mental Disorders*, fifth edition, identified three distinct clinical eating disorders: (1) anorexia nervosa (AN); (2) bulimia nervosa (BN); and (3) binge eating disorder (BED). Anorexia nervosa, dubbed the "self-starvation syndrome" is characterized by extreme weight loss or a demonstrably lower weight than what is expected for one's height. Other characteristics are fasting or restriction of food intake and body image disturbances with an intense fear of weight gain. In previous editions of the *DSM*, the loss of a female's menstrual cycle was a key diagnostic feature; however, with the most recent edition, it was removed.

Anorexia nervosa is the third most common chronic disease among adolescent females with a prevalence of 1 percent. However, onset of this disorder rarely occurs in women over age 40. Anorexia nervosa is most prevalent in industrialized nations with citizens who focus on being thin to be considered attractive in a culture. This eating disorder is most commonly pictured in psychology textbooks and is often visually represented by a female with pale skin and protruding collarbones.

History of Anorexia Nervosa

The first documented case of anorexia nervosa was a 20-year-old female client who was reported in the medical literature in 1686, although the diagnosis was formalized only much later. The term *anorexia* is of Greek origin and translates as "lack of appetite." This translation is inadequate for understanding the pervasive control and self-discipline features related to an anorexic person's eating behavior. In fact, individuals with anorexia nervosa report thinking about food 70–85 percent of the time despite feeling hunger pangs and other physical symptoms (e.g., stomach distress) associated with their food restricting and fasting behavior.

The full clinical term anorexia nervosa was adopted in 1874 by physician Sir William Gull to describe individuals who refused to eat and exhibited excessive weight loss, amenorrhea (loss of menstrual cycle), and other medical symptoms (e.g., low pulse rate, constipation) that could not be explained by other medical conditions. Gull described the condition as occurring typically in girls ages 16 to 25 who exhibited irritability, high energy despite poor nutritional intake and low weight, and excessive activity. Although Gull reported one fatality associated with anorexia nervosa, he viewed the condition as treatable. A case study of a 14-year-old girl in 1945 illustrated a common pattern of self-starvation, excessive exercise and a dysfunctional mother–daughter relationship.

Clinical cases of anorexia nervosa disappeared from medical documentation during the Great Depression and World War II when food insecurity (not having adequate available food to subsist) dominated concerns in society. However, post–World War II, with affluence in the 1960s, more cases were documented where female adolescents developed dysfunctional relationships with food and engaged in emotional eating. The American public was not exposed to anorexia nervosa until the 1970s when articles appeared in the popular press (e.g., *Reader's Guide to Periodic Literature, Science Digest*) about a "starving disease" found in certain young women who had an aversion to eating.

From a clinical perspective, anorexia nervosa was identified as a separate disorder from bulimia nervosa in 1980, in the *Diagnostic and Statistical Manual of Mental Disorders.* The disorder came into focus in the mainstream public in 1983 following the death of pop musician Karen Carpenter. By 1984, anorexia nervosa was in comedic skits such as on *Saturday Night Live,* which featured jokes about an anorexic cookbook" and in movies like *Down and Out in Beverly Hills,* filmed in 1986 with a character who had anorexia nervosa. Although the stereotype that anorexia nervosa primarily affects young affluent women has remained, it is important to recognize diverse individuals may meet clinical criteria for this disorder. Many celebrities have been suspected of having or admitted to having anorexia nervosa, including Victoria Beckham, Spice Girls' singer and fashion designer, who described her body image obsession and restriction of food intake to only vegetables in the 1990s.

Symptoms of Anorexia Nervosa

Clinical criteria for anorexia nervosa, according to the *Diagnostic and Statistical Manual of Mental Disorders,* require body weight to be lower than what is expected minimally to be healthy for one's height and a fear of fatness or gaining weight despite being severely underweight. Although not part of the *DSM-5* criteria for anorexia nervosa, body composition (percentage of body fat) or body mass index (BMI, a formula determined by height and weight) may be used to determine how much weight loss has occurred and what level of treatment is required. Using weight in kilograms divided by height in meters squared (W/H^2, or kg/m^2), a BMI value between 15.1 and 19.9 is considered underweight. To achieve weight loss or maintain an unhealthy low weight, individuals with anorexia nervosa engage in severe restricting behavior that resembles an extreme diet. It is common for individuals with anorexia to participate in periods of fasting or to limit their diet to a narrow selection of foods that are considered safe. Some anorexic individuals will become vegetarians or vegans as a way of justifying avoidance of meat or dairy products.

In addition to weight loss and severe underweight, anorexic individuals report being obsessed with body shape, size, and appearance and express exhibit body dissatisfaction about specific body parts. Body image distortion, in which one's perceived size does not fit with actual measurements, is common among anorexics. Individuals with anorexia nervosa are easy to recognize due to appearing severely underweight from severe caloric restriction. Previously, individuals were required to have secondary amenorrhea, the absence of a menstrual period for at least three cycles, to be diagnosed with anorexia nervosa; however, this criterion changed in the *DSM-5.* Using amenorrhea had restricted the anorexia nervosa diagnosis from being used for children or early adolescents who had not yet reached menarche and for postmenopausal women who no longer menstruate. Additionally, males may fit all anorexia nervosa criteria except for amenorrhea.

Outcome studies with hospitalized anorexia nervosa populations indicated that 44 percent of clients restored weight and resumed menstruation, which was classified as a "good" outcome. However, 24 percent were rated "poor" (unable to restore weight and menstruation), 28 percent were rated between "poor" and "good," and 5 percent had died (premature mortality). Mortality rates reached 20 percent for patients with anorexia nervosa followed for more than 20 years. It has been suggested a poorer prognosis is expected when there is a lower initial body weight, presence of vomiting, or poor familial support.

Personality Characteristics

Psychological characteristics associated with anorexia nervosa include perfectionism, being ego-oriented (i.e., showing strong focus on outcome rather than process), and demonstrating strong academic accomplishments or performing well in athletics or other areas. However, clients with anorexia nervosa tend to exhibit low self-esteem. Individuals with anorexia nervosa may appear socially isolated or withdrawn. Anorexic individuals overemphasize weight and size. Body and weight changes are directly connected to one's self-worth. The anorexia nervosa individual may be rewarded or reinforced for unhealthy restricting behaviors when receiving comments like "you look so thin." Other features of anorexia nervosa include alexithymia (inability to identify and express feelings), a strong need for control, and a lack of assertiveness. Individuals with anorexia may also be diagnosed with personality disorders such as borderline narcissistic obsessive-compulsive disorder (OCD) or dependent personality disorder. They may suffer from other comorbidities such as anxiety disorders or mood disorders or have a history of trauma.

Health Consequences of Anorexia Nervosa

Sudden cardiac arrest is the leading cause of death in anorexia nervosa. Mortality rates for anorexia nervosa are slightly higher (4 percent) than for bulimia nervosa (3.9 percent). However, there are numerous other health risks and medical complications. Inadequate nutrition due to anorexia nervosa results in amenorrhea (loss of period), which places a female at risk for loss of bone mineral density. Bone density loss has been associated with premature development of osteopenia and osteoporosis. Dehydration resulting from lack of fluid intake can cause dry skin, brittle nails, and hair loss. Additionally, lanugo (soft hair) may form on face, back, and arms to protect against the cold due to periods of starvation. Low body temperature leads to eating-disordered individuals being cold all the time. Sleep disturbances are common in both anorexia nervosa and bulimia nervosa individuals. Anorexia nervosa individuals are more likely to experience infertility compared to the general female population. Because individuals with anorexia nervosa may require refeeding to restore body weight and avoid being medically compromised, they may also experience the risks of refeeding syndrome, which includes edema (swelling of body tissue). Refeeding syndrome is discussed in more depth in a separate entry.

Anorexia Nervosa in Males

Identification of anorexia nervosa in males has been controversial because one of the requisite criteria for anorexia is amenorrhea. However, Gull observed this condition in males as well as young girls in the late 1800s, and clinicians documented case studies involving male clients who engaged in restricting food intake, experienced extreme weight loss, and otherwise fit the criteria for anorexia nervosa. A case (Jim) was presented in 1955 that details a 12-year-old male—an only child—who rapidly lost weight, going from 100 pounds to 67 pounds in a matter of months. He refused to eat and exhibited irritability and a dysfunctional relationship with his parents. A description of his medical treatment stated that he was forcibly tube-fed to save his life.

Males reported to be at risk for developing anorexia nervosa include wrestlers, jockeys, weight class athletes (e.g., lightweight boxers), and ski jumpers who face sport-specific pressures to lose weight or maintain an unhealthy low weight. Bahne Rabe (1963–2011), an Olympic rower who won eight gold medals for West Germany at the 1988 Seoul Olympics, suffered from anorexia nervosa during his competitive career. As a result, he experienced severe weight loss and weakness and eventually died of pneumonia. Similar to athletes, gay males are overrepresented in cases of males with anorexia nervosa. Although it is estimated that only 10–25 percent of eating disorder cases are male, it is suspected males are less likely to seek treatment or be diagnosed with an eating disorder that has been traditionally considered a "women's" disease.

Justine J. Reel

See also: Alexithymia; Amenorrhea; Body Mass Index; Bulimia Nervosa; Carpenter, Karen; *Diagnostic and Statistical Manual of Mental Disorders*; Medical and Health Consequences; Refeeding Syndrome

Bibliography

Abraham, Suzanne, and Derek Llewellyn-Jones. *Eating Disorders: The Facts.* New York: Oxford University Press, 1995.

American Psychiatric Association. *Diagnostic and Statistical Manual of Mental Disorders*, 4th ed., rev. Washington, DC: American Psychiatric Association Publishing, 2000.

American Psychiatric Association. *Diagnostic and Statistical Manual of Mental Disorders*, 5th ed. (*DSM-5*). Washington, DC: American Psychiatric Association Publishing, 2013.

Brumberg, Joan Jacobs. *Fasting Girls: The History of Anorexia Nervosa.* New York: Plume, 1989.

Chen, Eunice Yu, Michael S. McCloskey, Sara Michelson, Kathryn H. Gordon, and Emil Coccaro. "Characterizing Eating Disorders in a Personality Disorders Sample." *Psychiatry Research* 185 (2011): 427–432. https://doi.org/10.1016/j.psychres.2010.07.002.

Chui, Harold T., Bruce K. Christensen, Robert B. Zipursky, Blake A. Richards, M. Katherine Hanratty, Noor J. Kabani, David J. Mikulis, and Debra K. Katzman. "Cognitive Function and Brain Structure in Females with a History of Adolescent-Onset Anorexia Nervosa." *Pediatrics* 126 (2008): 426–437. https://doi.org/10.1542/peds.2008.0170.

Costin, Carolyn. *The Eating Disorder Sourcebook: A Comprehensive Guide to the Causes, Treatments and Prevention of Eating Disorders*, 3rd ed. New York: McGraw-Hill, 2007.

Costin, Carolyn. *100 Questions & Answers about Eating Disorders.* Sudbury, MA: Jones and Bartlett, 2007.

Courbasson, Christine, and Jacqueline M. Brunshaw. "The Relationship between Concurrent Substance Use Disorders and Eating Disorders with Personality Disorders." *International Journal of Environmental Research and Public Health* 6 (2009): 2076–2089. https://doi.org/10.3390/ijerph6072076.

"DSM-5 Diagnostic Criteria." *The Alliance for Eating Disorders Awareness*. Accessed November 16, 2016. http://www.allianceforeatingdisorders.com/portal/dsm-bed.

Falstein, Eugene I., Sherman C. Feinstein, and Ilse Judas. "Anorexia Nervosa in the Male Child." *American Journal of Orthopsychiatry* 26, no. 4 (1956): 751–772. https://doi.org/10.1111.j.1939-0025.1956.tb06220.x.

Krantz, Mori J., William T. Donahoo, Edward L. Melanson, and Philip S. Mehler. "QT Interval Dispersion and Resting Metabolic Rate in Chronic Anorexia Nervosa." *International Eating Disorders* 37, no. 2 (2005): 166–170. https://doi.org/10.1002/eat.20082.

Lock, James, Daniel Le Grange, W. Stewart Agras, and Christopher Dare. *Treatment Manual for Anorexia Nervosa: A Family-Based Approach*. New York: Guilford Press, 2001.

Mehler, Philip S. "Diagnosis and Care of Patients with Anorexia Nervosa in Primary Care Settings." *Annals of Internal Medicine* 134 (2001): 1048–1059. https://doi.org/10.7326/0003-4819-134-11-200106050-00011.

Mehler, Philip S., and Mori J. Krantz. "Anorexia Nervosa Medical Issues." *Journal of Women's Health* 12, no. 4 (2003): 331–340. https://doi.org/10.1089/154099903765448844.

Mehler, Philip S., and Kenneth L. Weiner. "Use of Total Parenteral Nutrition in the Refeeding of Selected Patients with Severe Anorexia Nervosa." *International Journal of Eating Disorders* 40, no. 3 (2007): 285–287. https://doi.org/10.1002/eat.20371.

Melanson, Edward Louis, William Troy Donahoo, Mori J. Krantz, Paul Poirier, and Philip S. Mehler. "Resting and Ambulatory Heart Rate Variability in Chronic Anorexia Nervosa." *The American Journal of Cardiology* 94 (2004): 1217–1220. https://doi.org/10.1016/j.amj card.2004.07.103.

Reel, Justine J., and Katherine A. Beals, eds. *The Hidden Faces of Eating Disorders and Body Image*. Reston, VA: AAHPERD/NAGWS, 2009.

Sernec, Karin, Martina Tomori, and Bojan Zalar. "Effect of Management of Patients with Anorexia and Bulimia Nervosa on Symptoms and Impulsive Behavior." *Collegium Antropologicum* 34, no. 4 (2010): 1281–1287. Accessed November 21, 2017. http://hrcak.srce.hr/62825.

"Victoria Beckham Tells of Her Obsession with Her Body." Sick Celebrities. Accessed November 21, 2017. http://www.sick-celebrities.com/celebrities/victoria-beckham-tells-of-eating-disorder-hell/.

ANXIETY DISORDERS

Anxiety disorders are mental disorders characterized by a persistent worry or fear that does not subside over time and may interfere with daily life functioning (e.g., school, work). Anxiety disorders can occur in individuals of any age per the *DSM-5*, the latest edition of the *Diagnostic Statistical Manual of Mental Disorders*. Anxiety is considered out of proportion of what would normally be expected for the situation. Panic attacks refer to a condition in which a person feels like he or she is experiencing a heart attack. Physiological responses such as intense sweating, palpitations, trembling, shaking, lightheadness, stomach pains, fear of losing control or dying, and smothering accompany this condition. According to *DSM-5*, panic attacks, both expected and unexpected, are not limited to anxiety disorders but may be applicable to any mental health disorder.

Anxiety disorders were first recognized as psychiatric disorders in the late 19th century. They are generally thought to be caused by a combination of genetic and biological factors— including family history—as well as environmental triggers or stress. The types of anxiety disorders included in the previous *DSM-IV-TR* were generalized anxiety disorder, social phobia and other specific phobias, panic disorder, and obsessive-compulsive disorder (OCD). In the *DSM-5*, OCD is included in the obsessive/compulsive and related disorders section or under post-traumatic stress disorder and acute disorder.

Generalized anxiety disorder is characterized by a persistent worry that is not tied to any particular event or object and is accompanied by nervousness and stress beyond what would normally be expected during any given day. On the other hand, an individual could have a specific phobia that results in an excessive fear of encountering a particular object. Social phobia, or social anxiety disorder, involves worry or fear associated with social interactions. Having a social phobia may result in avoidance of social situations (e.g., parties) and cause an individual to stay at home for risk of perceived embarrassment or scrutiny from others. Individuals with social phobia and specific phobias may also suffer from panic attacks. Panic disorder may accompany a social phobia but is marked by unanticipated panic attacks that may seem like heart attacks and includes several symptoms such as racing heartbeat, dizziness, upset stomach, or sweating. Obsessive-compulsive disorder is characterized by persistent and recurring thoughts and compulsive behaviors. Individuals who suffer from OCD often are compelled to engage in daily rituals (e.g., hand washing) to satisfy obsessive thoughts and to be in control.

Overlap between Anxiety and Eating Disorders

Anxiety disorders are often comorbid with other mental disorders. Approximately 60 percent of individuals with an anxiety disorder also suffer from clinical depression. Comorbidity (the co-occurrence of two mental disorders) between anxiety and eating disorders is incredibly common. Approximately 55–60 percent of anorexic individuals and 57–68 percent of bulimic individuals also experience an anxiety disorder. Although it is suspected that eating disorders and anxiety disorders share a genetic link, anxiety disorders also serve as a risk factor for eating disorders. Having a dual diagnosis creates challenges for treatment as the anxiety disorder may prevent the eating-disordered client from attempting certain social challenges (e.g., trying on clothing, eating out in public) or create the fear that panic attacks may be debilitating. However, the treatment team can address an anxiety disorder along with an eating disorder by using treatment approaches helpful for both disorders (e.g., psychotropic medications, stress reduction strategies). Psychotherapy that includes a cognitive-behavioral therapy approach has produced favorable treatment outcomes and is considered effective to address both anxiety and eating disorders. Social physique anxiety, which is anxiety specific to one's body or shape, is discussed in a separate entry.

Justine J. Reel

See also: Cognitive Behavioral Therapy; Comorbidity; Depression; Diagnostic and Statistical Manual of Mental Disorders; Medications and Eating Disorders; Obsessive-Compulsive Disorder; Social Physique Anxiety; Treatment

Bibliography

American Psychiatric Association. Diagnostic and Statistical Manual of Mental Disorders, 5th ed. (DSM-5). Washington, DC: American Psychiatric Association Publishing, 2013.

Andrews, Linda Wasmer. Encyclopedia of Depression, Vol. 1. Santa Barbara, CA: ABC-CLIO, 2010.

Anestic, Michael D., Jill M. Holm-Denoma, Kathryn H. Gordon, Norman B. Schmidt, and Thomas E. Joiner. "The Role of Anxiety Sensitivity in Eating Pathology." Cognitive Therapy Research 32 (2008): 370–385. https://doi.org/10.1007/x10608-006-9085-y.

Buckner, Julia D., Jose Sigado, and Peter M. Lewinsohn. "Delineation of Differential Temporal Relations between Specific Eating and Anxiety Disorders." Journal of Psychiatric Research 44 (2010): 781–787. https://doi.org/10.1016/j.jpsychires.2010.01.014.

Pallister, Emma, and Glenn Waller. "Anxiety in the Eating Disorders: Understanding the Overlap." Clinical Psychology Review 28 (2008): 366–386. https://doi.org/10.1016/j.cpr.2007.07.001.

Touchette, Evelyn, Adina Henegar, Nathalie T. Godart, Laura Pryor, Bruno Falissard, Richard E. Tremblay, and Sylvana M. Cote. "Subclinical Eating Disorders and Their Comorbidity with Mood and Anxiety Disorders in Adolescent Girls." Psychiatry Research 185 (2011): 185–192.

ART THERAPY

Art therapy is a type of therapy that allows for expression without the need to articulate emotions and thoughts into words. Traditional counseling approaches for eating disorders typically include individual talk therapy, group therapy to address body image, and family therapy to confront negative dynamics, communication, and relationships. Alternative forms of therapy, such as art therapy, have become increasingly popular as part of a multidisciplinary treatment approach. In fact, many eating disorder residential facilities employ an art therapist or offer a creative arts therapy group as part of a treatment schedule.

Art therapy can be especially effective for clients who have difficulty identifying or expressing their emotions, which is common for eating-disordered individuals or people with a history of trauma. By using clay, pastels, or paint, clients allow repressed feelings to flow without fear of judgment or the need for resistance. This is particularly important for eating-disordered individuals who are often people-pleasers and want to be good clients. Art therapy provides a medium for expressing and staying with a previously repressed emotion in that an object (e.g., mask) can be touched, changed, and manipulated with the swipe of a brush. For example, one client with exercise dependence drew herself shackled to a treadmill to represent her emotions of being imprisoned by her obligation to exercise.

While artwork can provide a safe mechanism for emotional expression, the act of engaging in art therapy activities can also serve a cathartic purpose. Clients who have been limited in their physical exercise may be stressed and anxious; however, art can provide a new coping skill for distracting and regulating one's arousal.

Art therapy goals can include nurturance, control, self-esteem, and an ability to cope with emotions and identity concerns. Initially, art therapy activities are less directed to encourage spontaneity and creativity in the moment and to avoid having a client attempt to create a perfect picture or art piece. As a client becomes more comfortable with the art therapy process, a trained art therapist gently processes the artwork and the feelings invoked by creating the piece with the client. It is common for sensitive and difficult topics (e.g., childhood abuse, cutting, suicidal thoughts) to arise in an individual or group art therapy session. Therefore, it is important for an art therapist to remain in close communication with the eating-disordered client's primary therapist.

Justine J. Reel

See also: Equine Therapy; Therapeutic Recreation; Treatment

Bibliography

Beck, Elizabeth H. *Art Therapy with an Eating Disordered Male Population: A Case Study.* Published thesis. Drexel University, Philadelphia, Pennsylvania, 2007.

Frish, Maria J., Debra L. Franko, and David B. Herzog. "Arts-Based Therapies in the Treatment of Eating Disorders." *Eating Disorders* 14 (2006): 131–142. http://dx.doi.org/10.1080/10640260500403857.

Levens, Mary. "Borderline Aspects of Eating Disorders: Art Therapy's Contribution." *Group Analysis* 23 (1990): 277–284. https://doi.org/10.1177/0533316490233008.

Rehavia-Hannauer, Dafna. "Identifying Conflicts of Anorexia Nervosa as Manifested in the Art Therapy Process." *The Arts in Psychotherapy* 30 (2003): 137–149. https://doi.org/10.1016/S0197-4556(03)00049-2.

ASSERTIVENESS TRAINING

Assertiveness refers to the ability to assert oneself and say no to requests one does not desire to fulfill. Assertiveness also includes skills that maintain healthy boundaries and an ability to express emotions in interpersonal relationships. Individuals with anorexia nervosa and bulimia nervosa feel significantly more controlled by external factors and are less likely to display self-assertion than non–eating-disordered comparison groups. Many individuals with eating disorders lack social skills, have difficulty with assertiveness, or display social inhibition. Therefore, assertiveness training to teach social skills should be part of a broader eating disorder treatment.

Assertiveness training helps individuals express thoughts and emotions effectively, change self-perceptions, and build self-confidence across situations. Common strategies include demonstrations of healthy assertive behaviors, role-playing to practice with feedback, relaxation exercises, and homework. Although assertiveness training can be introduced in individual psychotherapy sessions, researchers suggest a group approach to assertiveness training is superior because it allows for additional practice with peers and opportunities for more feedback. Assertiveness training as part of a cognitive-behavioral treatment group can be used for coping with interpersonal problems, social skills training, and self-esteem enhancement. Additionally, alexithymia can be addressed in assertiveness training using role-play.

Role-play allows for an individual to spontaneously respond to a situation that is simulated to create a challenge. A client has to respond using one's thoughts, perceptions, feelings, and individual tendencies. Group members can provide feedback and offer suggestions on how to change behaviors. Therefore, such role-play forces individuals with alexithymic characteristics and lack of assertiveness to recognize their emotions and express these to group members through their attitude and speech patterns (which should be congruent with how they feel).

Justine J. Reel

See also: Alexithymia; Cognitive Behavioral Therapy; Coping Skills; Treatment

Bibliography

Bekker, Marrie H., Marcel A. Croon, Esther G. van Balkom, and Jennifer B. Vermee. "Predicting Individual Differences in Autonomy-Connectedness: The Role of Body Awareness, Alexithymia and Assertiveness." *Journal of Clinical Psychology* 64, no. 6 (2008): 747–765. https://doi.org/10.1002/jclp.20486.

Hayakawa, Masaya. "How Repeated 15-Minute Assertiveness Training Sessions Reduce Wrist Cutting in Patients with Borderline Personality Disorder." *American Journal of Psychotherapy* 63, no. 1 (2009): 41–51.

Lin, Yen-Ru, Mei-Hsuen Wu, Cheng-I Yang, Tsai-Hwei Chen, Chen-Chuan Hus, Yue-Cune Chang, Wen-Chii Tzeng, Yuan-Hwa Chou, and Kuei-Ru Chou. "Evaluation of Assertiveness Training for Psychiatric Patients." *Journal of Clinical Nursing* 17 (2008): 2875–2883. https://doi.org/10.1111/j.1365-2702.2008.02343.x

Shina, Akihiro, Michiko Nakazato, Makoto Mitsumori, Hiroki Koizumi, Eui Shimizu, Mihisa Fujisaki, and Masaomi Iyo. "An Open Trial of Outpatient Group Therapy for Bulimic Disorders: Combination Program of Cognitive Behavioral Therapy with Assertive Training and Self-Esteem Enhancement." *Psychiatry and Clinical Neurosciences* 59 (2005): 690–696. https://doi.org/10.1111/j.1440-1819.2005.01438.x

Vagos, Paula, and Anabela Pereira. "A Proposal for Evaluating Cognition in Assertiveness." *Psychological Assessment* 22, no. 3 (2010): 657–665. http://dx.doi.org/10.1037/a0019782

ASSESSMENT

Assessment identifies whether symptoms are present for making a clinical diagnosis and prescribing appropriate treatment. An assessment may be conducted for research or clinical purposes, but a research-based assessment will probably look quite different when compared to an assessment conducted for the purpose of informing treatment decisions. The context in which an assessment is conducted also bears on the nature of the assessment itself. For research assessments, individuals may respond to an anonymous questionnaire without having further interaction with a researcher. Clinical assessments are more common, and may take place in inpatient hospitals, residential treatment facilities, or outpatient settings (e.g., college counseling center).

Who Assesses for Eating Disorders?

Because eating disorder assessments occur in numerous settings, a multidisciplinary approach is recommended. Therefore, an individual should be examined by a medical professional for vital signs and health status, by a mental health professional, and by a registered dietitian to assess psychological states and nutritional behaviors. Data should be gathered from the adolescent or adult suspected of having an eating disorder and, with client consent, from close family members who can provide an invaluable perspective regarding the duration and severity of an eating disorder.

What Are the Eating Disorder Criteria?

Eating disorders, as of this writing, are classified based on the fifth edition of the *Diagnostic and Statistical Manual of Mental Disorders* (*DSM-5*). This newest version of what many refer to as the "clinician's bible," was published in 2013 and contained significant changes to diagnostic criteria for eating disorders, including the name of the category itself, which will be changed to *Feeding and Eating Disorders*. Under the *DSM-5* classification system there are three eating disorders: anorexia nervosa, bulimia nervosa, and binge eating disorder. Each disorder is briefly discussed here.

Anorexia nervosa is currently characterized by being underweight for one's age and height, an intense fear of gaining weight or becoming fat, and a distorted body image. Although the *DSM-IV-TR* specified being underweight refers to weighing less than 85 percent of what would be expected for one's age and height, the *DSM-5* removed the actual percentage as it is possible for an individual to be significantly below expected weight at a percentage greater than 85 percent. A criterion that will be removed altogether is the criterion related to menses because it cannot be applied to premenarcheal females, postmenopausal females, or males.

According to the *DSM-5* bulimia nervosa is characterized by binge episodes and behaviors designed to get rid of food consumed or to offset a binge. A binge is characterized by consumption of a large quantity of food in a brief period by an individual. The food consumed during a binge is more than a typical person would eat given the circumstances. For example, it is not that unusual for individuals in the United States to consume large quantities of food on Thanksgiving Day. To meet the criteria, however, binge episodes would have to occur on a more regular basis for at least several months and the binge episode should be accompanied by a sense of loss of control over one's eating. In bulimia nervosa, an individual will repeatedly engage in negative behavior to prevent weight gain. These behaviors include self-induced vomiting, abuse of laxatives, diuretics, or syrup of ipecac, fasting, or excessive exercise. Finally, when considering self, an individual will place great emphasis on the shape and weight of the body.

Binge eating disorder (BED), widely recognized as a separate eating disorder, has previously been diagnosed as eating disorder not otherwise specified (EDNOS), but finally received a separate classification in the *DSM-5*. BED has used the same definition for a binge episode as bulimia nervosa and is characterized by eating rapidly, being uncomfortably full, eating a lot even when not hungry, being disgusted/depressed/guilty, or eating alone due to embarrassment. The EDNOS category was eliminated by name in the *DSM-5* and replaced with "Feeding and Eating Conditions Not Elsewhere Classified" (FECNEC).

Assessment Methods

There are a variety of methods to determine whether a particular client has an eating disorder. These include self-report measures, structured instruments, and diagnostic interviewing. Self-report measures allow a client to indicate what behaviors she may be experiencing. Although many of these instruments have good psychometric properties and are often inexpensive, they are limited in part by the degree to which the information provided by a client is accurate. Self-report measures include the Eating Disorder Examination-Questionnaire (EDE-Q) and the Eating Disorder Diagnostic Scale (EDDS).

Structured measures provide a professional with a set of specific items to address with a client. Each of these measurement tools gather specific information (e.g., eating disorder–related behavior) and generally do not allow an assessor to ad lib questions. Some tools in this category are referred to as *semistructured*. These tools require specific items be addressed by an assessor while allowing follow-up questions as needed. Structured measures have included the Eating Disorder Examination (EDE) and the Structured Interview for Anorexic and Bulimic Syndromes for *DSM-IV* and *ICD-10*. These will likely need to be revised to be in concordance with the *DSM-5*.

A clinical interview is helpful to elicit information from a client and to establish rapport. Establishing a rapport is critical for an ongoing therapeutic relationship and ensures the information provided by a client is as accurate as possible. Clinical interviews can be unstructured, semistructured, or structured in nature. The use of one type over another will depend on things such as time needed, type of information needed, and the assessment clinician's familiarity with the tool. Examples of diagnostic interviews include the Eating Disorder Examination and Structured Clinical Interview.

All the types of assessment tools mentioned are only as accurate as the information provided by a patient as well as the assessor's ability to communicate to a client the purpose and importance of an assessment. Therefore, all results should be interpreted in light of the limitations of a tool and the data gathered. Professionals, patients, and family members are encouraged to read more about eating disorder assessment tools to learn about their purpose and reported effectiveness.

Regardless of the method used, thorough and accurate assessment of eating disorders is important for an appropriate diagnosis so an individual can receive the proper treatment for his or her level of care. To help providers determine the appropriate level of care for a patient the American Psychiatric Association (APA) has published a set of practice guidelines that include recommendations for this type of assessment. The APA notes there are five levels of care from outpatient treatment to inpatient hospitalization. The degree of treatment required is determined by assessing severity of symptoms, including but not limited to medical stability, suicidal thoughts, weight, motivation, co-occurring disorders, environmental stressors, and geographic availability of treatment. The appropriateness of using a client's weight to determine level of wellness or illness has received considerable attention. The APA notes the weight percentages listed in its table are to be considered guidelines and that an appropriate weight for any patient should be considered on case-by-case.

Although typically the purpose of an assessment for an eating disorder is not to determine how much insurance coverage a patient will receive, payment for treatment is certainly a consideration. Insurance companies often require a diagnosis from a treating physician or mental health professional; however, the label is less important than understanding the way a disorder affects an individual. Conducting an assessment to determine whether a particular eating disorder is present may mean that equally serious, but not textbook, cases may be overlooked. Assessments should be conducted for the purpose of identifying and evaluating particular symptoms. This will inform the decision regarding the method of treatment needed on an individualized basis. Moreover, a focus on symptoms, rather than diagnostic categories or labels, will foster a more supportive climate for both the eating-disordered individual and his family so treatment options can be addressed.

It is important to note that although eating disorders are still heavily associated with adolescent or young adult white females and a majority of cases still fit in this demographic, the reality is that males, children, adults, and all ethnic minorities are also be at risk for an eating disorder. Therefore, the decision to encourage someone to be assessed for an eating disorder should not be influenced by the age, sex, gender, or race/ethnicity of an individual. Relying on demographics alone is likely to result in a delay identifying an eating disorder or in unidentified cases.

Assessment of Eating Behaviors

Identifying and understanding a client's eating behaviors will assists to determine an accurate diagnosis and inform treatment decisions. Eating disorder–related behaviors include limiting how much food is consumed, overeating, limiting the types of foods eaten, and eating only under certain circumstances or in certain environments. The more behaviors a client demonstrates, the greater the likelihood he or she is struggling with an eating disorder.

Depending on the purpose of the assessment, it may be important to differentiate between actual eating behaviors and a client's perception of his or her eating behaviors. For example, the terms *objective binge* and *subjective binge* have been used to differentiate between a binge as defined by the *Diagnostic and Statistical Manual of Mental Disorders* and a binge as defined by a client who may not meet the diagnostic criteria for a binge. Verifying the objective or subjective nature of what a client reports is important for treatment purposes. A client who engages in objective binges will need assistance to eliminate the behavior; a client who engages in a subjective binge (i.e., it *feels* like a binge but technically is not a binge) may benefit from cognitive restructuring and psychoeducation about what constitutes too much or too little food.

Assessing the quantity of food consumed in a typical day is an important facet of assessment. Having this information helps providers estimate weight loss or weight gain and extent of dietary restriction. This element of assessment can be elusive. Although individuals with eating disorders will seemingly know a great deal about calories, fat, and carbohydrate content for a wide variety of foods, they are not usually very accurate in estimating how much they consume in a typical day. This does not mean the amount consumed should not be assessed, but it does suggest the assessor should not assume the information receives is accurate. Independent verification of a patient's self-report by someone who witnesses a patient's eating behaviors may be necessary.

Assessment of Physical/Medical Symptoms

Determining the type and level of care needed for a patient is aided by knowing a client's current medical status. This can be ascertained by a medical provider able to perform assessments to target specific systems in the body (e.g., vital signs, gastrointestinal, cardiovascular, and neurological functioning, bone health). An indicator that one or more of a client's bodily systems may be compromised is a client's current weight and weight history. This may be especially true for individuals diagnosed with or suspected of having anorexia nervosa. Specific and serious medical conditions (e.g., heart arrhythmias) are associated with a severely low weight for one's age, sex, and height in comparison to weight history. Therefore, when a client is identified as having a seriously low weight (as assessed by an eating disorder expert applying current *DSM* criteria), it is paramount weight restoration be the first order of treatment. It is important to note, however, that weight alone is not an effective indicator of a client's health (or lack thereof). Clients classified as in a normal weight range may also be seriously medically compromised.

Related to a female client's weight is the whether she is menstruating regularly or at all. Although primary amenorrhea (missing three consecutive menstrual cycles in a postmenarcheal female) and secondary amenorrhea (delayed onset of menses) are currently a part of the symptom constellation of anorexia nervosa as defined by the *DSM-IV-TR*, these symptoms were removed in the *DSM-5*. Regardless of the diagnostic status of these symptoms, any significant change in a female's menstrual cycle, or a significant delay in the onset of menses for a preadolescent or adolescent female, may indicate she has not maintained or achieved a sufficient weight to support this physiological function. In addition to compromised reproductive functioning, an absent or irregular menstrual cycle can result in poor bone health. Osteopenia, mild loss of bone density, is the precursor to osteoporosis or severe loss of bone density, which can result in bone fractures or breaks. Therefore, assessing an individual's bone density (assessed by a medical professional ideally using a DXA scan) can confirm evidence of bone deterioration. It is important to note clients with menstrual irregularity who regularly engage in high-impact/weight-bearing activities should have an assessment to measure bone density on a non-weight-bearing location (e.g., lumbar spine). Weight-bearing joints in athletes and regular exercisers are likely to be particularly strong and may not be accurate indicators of what is occurring throughout the rest of the skeleton.

Although it is common to associate serious medical problems with anorexia nervosa due in large part to the low weight many patients reach, patients with bulimia nervosa are also at risk for serious medical problems involving the gastrointestinal system (e.g., esophageal rupture). They are also at risk for cardiac problems (e.g., arrhythmias), oral and dental problems (e.g., gum recession), and reproductive problems (e.g., infertility). Therefore, it is important to assess the frequency of binge episodes as well as accompanying episodes of pathogenic compensatory behaviors (e.g., vomiting, use of laxatives or diuretics, use of syrup of ipecac, excessive exercise). Although the binge–purge cycle is typically associated with bulimia nervosa, patients with anorexia nervosa can also engage in these behaviors and should be assessed accordingly.

Assessment of Cognitions

The beliefs and attitudes held by clients with eating disorders are typically rigid, affect nearly all aspects of a client's life, and often linger far beyond the stabilization and elimination of eating disorder–related behaviors and the accompanying medical consequences. Therefore, an essential element of assessment is to identify the nature of a client's thought processes. It is also important to look into a client's awareness of and thoughts about these cognitions and identify the forces that reinforce these cognitions.

It is common for clients to spend a great deal of mental energy on attitudes and beliefs surrounding weight, body shape and size, and self-worth. Often, clients' self-worth is directly tied to beliefs about what a current weight means and the degree of body satisfaction. Many clients' belief systems are heavily influenced by media images and messages (i.e., the *thin ideal* for females and *muscular ideal* for males), friends and family who hold specific ideas about how one ought to look, and the beliefs of important others including dating partners or athletic coaches. Knowing the influences on a client's belief system has a direct effect on treatment. Interventions can be designed to target specific cognitions or to manage the messages a patient hears from those around her.

A related but separate element of a client's belief system that needs to be assessed is the degree to which a client identifies with or values a belief system. That is, are the client's beliefs ego-syntonic or ego-dystonic? Ego-syntonic belief systems suggest an investment in these cognitions that will be resistant to intervention. Clients will often indicate there is something they like about their thought patterns or that their thought patterns are helpful in some way. Clients who report they do not like their thought patterns or that patterns are detrimental in some particular way are more likely to respond favorably to interventions designed to alter or eliminate these beliefs.

Assessment of Interpersonal Functioning

It is also important to assess the quality of and any changes in interpersonal relationships. Frequently, eating-disordered individuals are secretive about their behaviors due to the shame and guilt they experience, and they may isolate themselves from others. This interpersonal change may be presented by consistently turning down social invitations they previously would have accepted.

Christine L. B. Selby

See also: Amenorrhea; Anorexia Nervosa; Binge Eating Disorder; Bulimia Nervosa; Diagnostic Interview; *Diagnostic and Statistical Manual of Mental Disorders*; Medical and Health Consequences; Referring Someone for Eating Disorder Treatment

Bibliography

American Psychiatric Association. *Diagnostic and Statistical Manual of Mental Disorders*, 5th ed. (*DSM-5*). Washington, DC: American Psychiatric Association Publishing, 2013.

American Psychiatric Association. *Diagnostic and Statistical Manual of Mental Disorders,* 4th ed., text rev. Washington, DC: American Psychiatric Association Publishing, 2000.

American Psychiatric Association. "Feeding and Eating Disorders." *American Psychiatric Association: DSM-5 Development.* Accessed November 21, 2017. http://dsm5.org /ProposedRevision/Pages/FeedingandEatingDisorders.aspx.

American Psychiatric Association. *Practice Guideline for the Treatment of Patients with Eating Disorders,* 3rd ed. June 2006. Accessed November 21, 2017. https:// psychiatryonline.org/pb/assets/raw/sitewide/practice_guidelines/guidelines/eating disorders.pdf.

Anderson, Drew A., Jason M. Lavender, and Kyle P. De Young. "The Assessment Process: Refining the Clinical Evaluation of Patients with Eating Disorders." In *Treatment of Eating Disorders: Bridging the Research-Practice Gap,* edited by Margo Maine, Beth Hartman, and Douglas W. Bunnell, 71–87. San Diego, CA: Elsevier Academic Press, 2010.

Anderson, Drew A., and Andrea D. Murray. "Psychological Assessment of the Eating Disorders." In *The Oxford Handbook of Eating Disorders,* edited by Stewart W. Agras, 249–258. New York: Oxford University Press, 2010.

"DSM-5 Diagnostic Criteria." *The Alliance for Eating Disorders Awareness.* Accessed November 16, 2016. http://www.allianceforeatingdisorders.com/portal/dsm-bed.

Mitchell, James E., and Carol B. Peterson, eds. *Assessment of Eating Disorders.* New York: Guilford Press, 2005.

Tyson, Edward P. "Medical Assessment of Eating Disorders." In *Treatment of Eating Disorders: Bridging the Research-Practice Gap,* edited by Margo Maine, Beth Hartman, and Douglas W. Bunnell, 89–110. San Diego, CA: Elsevier Academic Press, 2010.

Yager, Joel. "Assessment and Determination of Initial Treatment Approaches for Patients with Eating Disorders." In *Clinical Manual of Eating Disorders,* edited by Joel Yager and Pauline S. Powers, 31–77. Washington, DC: American Psychiatric Association Publishing, 2007.

ATHENA

Athletes Targeting Healthy Exercise and Nutrition Alternatives (ATHENA), refers to a prevention program for sports teams to reduce disordered eating and substance abuse in female athletes. ATHENA parallels a program called ATLAS (Adolescents Training and Learning to Avoid Steroids), developed for male athletes to improve nutrition and exercise while decreasing alcohol and illicit and performance enhancement substances. ATHENA, a peer-led program, has been implemented in a team setting and 70 percent of sessions are led by a trained team member. This trained group leader attends a 90-minute orientation in advance of sessions and is provided with a script to be used to facilitate lessons. The prevention program consists of eight 45-minute sessions that take place when athletes are not training or competing and can meet as a group.

Lessons of ATHENA cover topics like depression, self-esteem, healthy norms, and societal pressures to be thin. Interactive sessions include efforts to deconstruct negative media messages that reinforce ultrathin body ideals and glamorize alcohol, cigarettes, or nutritional supplements. Athletes receive information about healthy strength training and exercise habits. Sports nutrition education is provided covering necessary carbohydrate, protein, fat, and calcium intake. Because ATHENA is geared to female athletes at risk for developing disordered eating, caloric information of foods is not presented and instead the consequences of eating disorders are discussed. In concordance with evidence-based prevention research, the ATHENA program is interactive (rather than strictly didactic), focuses on females-only (rather than mixed-sex grouping), and provides participants with the opportunity to practice skills throughout the program.

Evaluation of the ATHENA program

ATHENA was shown to be feasible to implement by coaches and athletes in high school and college team sports. In one study with female high school athletes, athletes reported decreased disordered eating and body-shaping drug use (e.g., diet pills, steroids, amphetamines) and increased knowledge regarding sports nutrition and eating disorder consequences. Additionally, ATHENA athletes demonstrated healthy nutritional and exercise habits following the program. Interestingly, participants were less likely to ride in a car with a driver who had consumed alcohol and were more likely to wear seatbelts. Athletes reported less intention for vomiting or use of diet pills, tobacco, or creatine to try to lose weight in the future. At the college level, auxiliary dancers (i.e., majorettes, color guard dance teams) from Southeastern universities participated in the ATHENA program and reported increased knowledge of eating disorders and nutrition.

Justine J. Reel

See also: Anorexia Athletica; Prevention; Sports

Bibliography

Elliot, Diane L., Linn Goldberg, Esther L. Moe, Carol A. DeFrancesco, Melissa B. Durham, and Hollie Hix-Small. "Definition and Outcome of a Curriculum to Prevent Disordered Eating and Body-Shaping Drug Use." *Journal of School Health* 76 (2006): 67–73. https://doi.org/10.1111/j.1746-1561.2006.00070.x.

Elliot, Diane L., Linn Goldberg, Esther L. Moe, Carol A. DeFrancesco, Melissa B. Durham, and Hollie Hix-Small. "Preventing Substance Use and Disordered Eating: Initial Outcomes of the ATHENA (Athletes Targeting Healthy Exercise and Nutrition Alternatives) Program." *Archives of Pediatric and Adolescent Medicine* 158 (2004), 1043–1049. https://doi.org/10.1001/archpedi.158.11.1043.

Elliot, Diane L., Linn Goldberg, Esther L. Moe, Carol A. DeFrancesco, Melissa B. Durham, Wendy McGinnis, and Chondra Lockwood. "Long-Term Outcomes of the ATHENA (Athletes Targeting Healthy Exercise and Nutrition Alternatives) Program for Female High School Athletes." *Journal of Alcohol and Drug Education* 52, no. 2 (2008): 73–92.

Stice, Eric, Heather Shaw, and Nathan C. Marti. "A Meta-Analytic Review of Eating Disorder Prevention Programs: Encouraging Findings." *Annual Review of Clinical Psychology* 3 (2007): 207–231. https://doi.org/10.1146/annurev.clinpsy.3.022806.091447.

Torres-McGehee, Toni. M., James M. Green, Deidre Leaver-Dunn, James D. Leeper, Phillip A. Bishop, and Mark T. Richardson. "Attitude and Knowledge Changes in Collegiate Dancers Following a Short-Term, Team-Centered Prevention Program on Eating Disorders." *Perceptual and Motor Skills* 112, no. 3 (2011): 711–725. https://doi.org/10.2466/06.PMS.112.3.711-725.

ATHLETIC TRAINERS

Athletic trainers are in a unique position to help athletes who display disordered eating behaviors, because they are both health care providers and part of an extended coaching staff. As health care professionals, athletic trainers focus on an athlete's overall health and well-being in addition to sport performance. Therefore, athletic trainers can identify eating-disordered behaviors and can access the coaching staff and other important sports personnel (e.g., team physician) to support an athlete. Athletic trainers serve as the first line of defense and can detect eating, exercise, and body weight changes in athletes when they occur.

Identification of At-Risk Athletes

Early identification of, and intervention with, athletes who exhibit disordered eating behaviors (e.g., restricting foods) increases the probability of treatment success. Interestingly, 2,800 NCAA coaches who were surveyed reported athletic trainers were often first responders when it came to identifying athletes at risk for eating disorders. Given the potential for athletic trainers to play such a key role in eating disorder identification and treatment referrals, it is necessary for athletic trainers to receive appropriate training. To this end, the National Athletic Trainers' Association (NATA) published a position statement in 2008 discussing the role of athletic trainers in the prevention, detection, and management of athletes with eating disorder–related behaviors.

The NATA position statement provides recommendations including action items that should take place immediately (e.g., establishing a well-qualified team of professionals), items for how to detect eating disorder–related behavior, items on how to manage athletes with eating-disordered behaviors, and ways to prevent eating disorder–related behaviors. Given these recommendations, NATA concluded certified athletic trainers should play an active role on the healthcare team. NATA also noted the knowledge base required for athletic trainers to be certified, in conjunction with experience working with athletes with eating disorder–related behaviors, suggests athletic trainers' overall effectiveness working with this unique population will hopefully increase in the coming years.

Recent studies have evaluated certified athletic trainers' perceptions of how prepared they are to work with athletes who develop eating-disordered behavior. The certified athletic trainers indicated they do not think they receive adequate preparation (educationally or professionally) to work with athletes who demonstrate eating disorder–related behaviors. This study also revealed despite this perceived lack of preparation, athletic trainers still acknowledged they are responsible for identifying and working with this population. The college athletic trainers surveyed in a different study reported that although nearly all participants had worked with a female athlete with eating disorder–related behaviors, just over one-quarter were confident they could identify an eating disorder, and nearly all respondents indicated more attention needs to be given to this subpopulation of athletes. Both studies concluded that there seems to be a need and a desire for continuing education about eating disorders in athletes. Moreover, the study on college athletic trainers recommended collegiate athletic programs develop institutional policies on how to manage athletes with eating disorders. By having policies, athletic trainers can be better equipped to identify at-risk athletes and to refer them for treatment.

Treatment of Eating Disorders

The importance of a multidisciplinary treatment team for individuals with eating disorders has been well documented. When an athlete is the client, members of that athlete's sport-related community may be a part of that team; however, it is more likely that sports personnel (e.g., coaches, athletic trainers) will be part of what Thompson and Sherman have called a *sport management team*. Although it may be appropriate for some sports personnel to be formal members of the treatment team—that is, the group of professionals providing treatment interventions—most sports personnel will be more appropriately a part of the sport management team. This team will ideally have contact with the treatment team to ensure an expedient recovery for an athlete. Athletic trainers will usually be a part of an athlete's sport management team.

Christine L. B. Selby

See also: Coaches; Sports

Bibliography

Bonci, Christine M., Leslie J. Bonci, Lorita Granger, Craig L. Johnson, Robert M. Malina, Leslie W. Milne, Randa R. Ryan, and Erin M. Vanderbunt. "National Athletic Trainers' Association Position Statement: Preventing, Detecting, and Managing Disordered Eating in Athletes." *Journal of Athletic Training* 43, no. 1 (2008): 80–108. https://doi.org/10.4085/1062-6050-43.1.80.

Sherman, Roberta T., Ron A. Thompson, Denise Dehass, and Mary Wilfert. "NCAA Coaches Survey: The Role of the Coach in Identifying and Managing Athletes with Disordered Eating." *Eating Disorders* 13 (2005): 447–466. http://dx.doi.org/10.1080/10640260500296707.

Thompson, Ron A., and Robert T. Sherman. *Eating Disorders in Sport.* New York: Routledge, 2010.

Vaughan, Jennifer L., Keith A. King, and Randall R. Cottrell. "Collegiate Athletic Trainers' Confidence in Helping Female Athletes with Eating Disorders." *Journal of Athletic Training* 39, no. 1 (2004): 71–76.

Whitson, Emily J., Mitchell L. Corova, Timothy J. Demchak, Catherine L. Stemmans, and Keith A. King. "Certified Athletic Trainers' Knowledge and Perception of Professional Preparation Involving Eating Disorders among Athletes." *Journal of Allied Health* 35, no. 1 (2006): 18–29.

AVOIDANT/RESTRICTIVE FOOD INTAKE DISORDER

Avoidant/restrictive food intake disorder is usually referred to by its acronym ARFID. This new eating disorder classification was added to the most recent publication of the *Diagnostic and Statistical Manual for Mental Disorders* (*DSM-5*). ARFID is a pattern of eating behaviors that result in significant nutritional deficiencies or an inability to meet daily energy requirements. Unlike in the case of anorexia nervosa and bulimia nervosa, ARFID is not associated with a body image disturbance or a fixation on shape/weight. Research has shown ARFID is more common in children, but it has been shown to persist into adulthood. ARFID has been associated with trauma and other disorders, such as autism spectrum disorders and attention deficit disorder.

ARFID is a significant impairment in diet quality due to a highly restricted diet. Restriction can be a result of sensory aversions (e.g., taste, smell, and/or texture), emotional eating difficulties, fear of physical sensations associated with eating, or phobias related to consequences of eating, usually traumatic in nature (like choking). ARFID affects both children and adults. In children, ARFID looks very different from both anorexia and bulimia. However, in adults, ARFID shares several important characteristics with anorexia. Importantly, a common set of warning flags exist independent of age that may indicate a problem.

Symptoms of ARFID

To meet criteria for avoidant/restrictive food intake disorder, one must have significant weight loss, demonstrate nutritional deficiency, have significant impairment in psychosocial functioning, and/or be dependent on medically administered feeding (e.g., enteral feeding) or oral supplements. In children, a failure to meet expected growth markers or weight gain can also qualify for an ARFID diagnosis. Additionally, the nutritional deficiency must be considered clinically significant. For example, a calcium deficiency, a problem for the American population in general, would not qualify as a clinical concern.

It is also important to note ARFID can be seen as a failure to meet nutritional requirements, a failure to meet daily caloric/energy requirements, or both. This is particularly important when considering how ARFID relates to preexisting terms for similarly restrictive eating behaviors, such as picky eating. Picky eating (alternatively referred to as "selective eating") is a similar pattern of food refusal and restrictive dieting. Individuals who identify as picky eaters typically refuse foods on the basis of undesirable sensory characteristics, usually taste, smell, and/or texture. However, picky eaters do not experience the nutritional or growth deficiencies associated with ARFID. This distinction is particularly important for children, where the line between picky eating (a normative childhood behavior) and ARFID is easily blurred.

The *DSM-5* also adds the hallmark restrictive diet in the ARFID diagnosis falls into one of three distinct categories. First, individuals may demonstrate an emotional barrier to eating. Apathy toward eating and sadness or anxiety that interfere with eating are the two most frequent examples of emotions that interfere with eating. Second, restrictive eating may be a result of an aversion to specific characteristics of food, such as the taste, texture, or smell. This is particularly common in children. And last, individuals may eat a very restrictive diet due to an eating-related fear. Choking and vomiting are common phobias that may affect someone's willingness to eat, and result in a diagnosis of ARFID.

To qualify for a diagnosis of ARFID, the eating disturbance must be separate from another medical condition, such as irritable bowel syndrome. In some cases, individuals may have concurrent conditions (e.g., autism); in these cases, the impairment caused by eating-related behaviors must be severe enough to warrant attention aside from typical treatments for any other co-occurring conditions. Additionally, the restrictive eating patterns must be unrelated to body disturbances. Last, restrictive diets must not be explained by a lack of food availability and/or culturally sanctioned practices.

ARFID in Children

A recent study that approximately 13 percent of children who sought treatment at an adolescent and childhood eating disorder program met criteria for avoidant/restrictive food intake disorder. Compared to anorexia and bulimia nervosa, individuals with ARFID were younger and had a longer duration of illness. Males accounted for a larger percentage of ARFID cases (29 percent) than in the case of anorexia (15 percent male) or bulimia (6 percent male). Additionally, patients with ARFID had an average BMI between the average BMI for anorexia (lowest) and for bulimia (highest). Last, ARFID was associated with co-occurring psychiatric disorders significantly more often than anorexia or bulimia. Approximately 30 percent of ARFID patients had demonstrated picky eating since early childhood, 22 percent suffered from anxiety, 19 percent had a fear of choking/vomiting, and 5 percent had specific food allergies.

Researchers agree ARFID is a more meaningful diagnosis than the disorder it replaced. In the *DSM-IV-TR, feeding disorder of infancy and early childhood* was used to capture what is now referred to as ARFID. However, the vague criteria and problematic inclusion of infants (for whom it is very difficult to determine normal versus abnormal eating behaviors) made this diagnosis unpopular in the medical and scientific communities. It was rarely given out, and only a handful of research studies attempted to investigate the disorder. Comparatively, ARFID captures a significant number of children and young adolescents who previously did not meet criteria for any disorder (other than the catchall diagnosis of eating disorder not otherwise specified, which has been criticized for its lack of associated intervention techniques). Additionally, patients diagnosed with ARFID differ in important ways from patient with anorexia or bulimia. This differentiation allows physicians, dietitians, and mental health professionals a greater degree of sensitivity when determining appropriate treatment options. Previously, children who met criteria for ARFID fell into one of three categories regarding treatment: they were either treated on the anorexia model, on the picky eating model, or they were not treated at all. Now that ARFID has been introduced, researchers will be able to develop intervention techniques specifically tailored to the needs of these individuals.

ARFID in Adults

Very few studies have investigated ARFID among adults. However, adults do suffer from ARFID even if the symptoms might be attributed to reasons different than younger patients. Whereas children were likely to refuse food because of smell, taste, or texture, the majority of adults with ARFID report emotional eating difficulties, gastrointestinal complications (e.g., stomach aches), and choking/vomiting phobias as the primary reasons behind food refusal. Additionally, one study found that in a sample of 95 adults with ARFID, all were women.

This same study found the adult presentation of avoidant/restrictive food intake disorder shared two defining traits of anorexia nervosa. First, adult ARFID patients did not differ in BMI from patients with anorexia, highlighting adults with ARFID tend to be significantly underweight. Second, all the ARFID patients exhibited amenorrhea (abnormal absence of menstruation), which is a primary diagnostic criterion for anorexia nervosa. Amenorrhea is the result of an interruption in the body's production of a specific hormone that triggers menstruation; in anorexia, it is the state of starvation that interrupts this process. Although research has yet to investigate amenorrhea in ARFID, it is likely being underweight is the cause, given that ARFID patients shared similar BMIs with anorexia. Despite these similarities, ARFID patients were hospitalized significantly less than patients with anorexia, suggesting health professionals are not as readily able to identify ARFID patients.

Future Directions in the Study of ARFID

Now that ARFID represents a formal diagnosis in the *DSM-5*, researchers can begin to design studies to investigate this population. Future research should focus on further characterizing the disorder. Identifying genetic, behavioral, environmental, and personality risk factors will make early identification and intervention easier, for example. Understanding ARFID in adults is particularly crucial given the paucity of epidemiological studies on ARFID and related symptomology (i.e., picky eating) in adult populations. Current treatment options for anorexia nervosa, bulimia nervosa, and picky eating will need to be reevaluated in the context of ARFID populations; more likely than not, significant revisions and additions will need to be made to these interventions. Further differentiating ARFID from picky/selective eating is also needed in the literature on children.

Hannah J. Hopkins

See also: Dietary Restraint; Food Phobia; Picky Eating

Bibliography

Bryant-Waugh, Rachel, and Richard E. Kreipe. "Avoidant/Restrictive Food Intake Disorder in DSM-5." *Psychiatric Annals* 42, no. 11 (2012): 402–405. http://dx.doi.org/10.3928/00485713-20121105-04.

Cardona Cano, Sebastian, Henning Tiemeier, Daphne Van Hoeken, Anne Tharner, Vincent W. V. Jaddoe, Albert Hofman, Frank C. Verhulst, and Hans W. Hoek. "Trajectories of Picky Eating during Childhood: A General Population Study." *International Journal of Eating Disorders* 48, no. 6 (2015): 570–579. https://doi.org/10.1002/eat.22384.

Fisher, Martin M., David S. Rosen, Rollyn M. Ornstein, Kathleen A. Mammel, Debra K. Katzman, Ellen S. Rome, S. Todd Callahan, Joan Malizio, Sarah Kearney, and B. Timothy Walsh. "Characteristics of Avoidant/Restrictive Food Intake Disorder in Children and Adolescents: A 'New Disorder' in DSM-5." *The Journal of Adolescent Health: Official Publication of the Society for Adolescent Medicine* 55, no. 1 (2014): 49–52. https://doi.org/10.1016/j.jadohealth.2013.11.013.

Kenney, Lindsay, and B. Timothy Walsh. "Avoidant/Restrictive Food Intake Disorder (ARFID): Defining ARFID." *Eating Disorders Review* 24, no. 3 (2013): 1–13. Accessed February 3, 2017. http://eatingdisordersreview.com/nl/nl_edr_24_3_1.html.

Kurz, Susanne, Zoé van Dyck, Daniela Dremmel, Simone Munsch, and Anja Hilbert. "Variants of Early-Onset Restrictive Eating Disturbances in Middle Childhood." *International Journal of Eating Disorders* 49, no. 1 (2016): 102–106. https://doi.org/10.1002/eat.22461.

Murphy, Jillian, and Kimberly R. Zlomke. "A Behavioral Parent-Training Intervention for a Child with Avoidant/Restrictive Food Intake Disorder." *Clinical Practice in Pediatric Psychology* 4, no. 1 (2016): 23–34. https://doi.org/10.1037/cpp0000128.

Nakai, Yoshikatsu, Kazuko Nin, Shun'ichi Noma, Satoshi Teramukai, and Stephen A. Wonderlich. "Characteristics of Avoidant/Restrictive Food Intake Disorder in a Cohort of Adult Patients: Avoidant/Restrictive Food Intake Disorder." *European Eating Disorders Review* 24, no. 6 (2016): 528–530. https://doi.org/10.1002/erv.2476.

Norris, Mark, Wendy Spettigue, and Debra Katzman. "Update on Eating Disorders: Current Perspectives on Avoidant/Restrictive Food Intake Disorder in Children and Youth." *Neuropsychiatric Disease and Treatment* 19, no. 12 (2016): 213–218. https://doi.org/10.2147/NDT.S82538.

Schreck, K., and K. Williams. "Food Preferences and Factors Influencing Food Selectivity for Children with Autism Spectrum Disorders." *Research in Developmental Disabilities* 27, no. 4 (2006): 353–363. https://doi.org/10.1016/j.ridd.2005.03.005.

Wildes, Jennifer E., Nancy L. Zucker, and Marsha D. Marcus. "Picky Eating in Adults: Results of a Web-Based Survey." *International Journal of Eating Disorders* 45, no. 4 (2012): 575–582. https://doi.org/10.1002/eat.20975.

Williams, Keith E., Helen M. Hendy, Douglas G. Field, Yekaterina Belousov, Katherine Riegel, and Whitney Harclerode. "Implications of Avoidant/Restrictive Food Intake Disorder (ARFID) on Children with Feeding Problems." *Children's Health Care* 44, no. 4 (2015): 307–321. https://doi.org/10.1080/02739615.2014.921789.

Zucker, Nancy, William Copeland, Lauren Franz, Kimberly Carpenter, Lori Keeling, Adrian Angold, and Helen Egger. "Psychological and Psychosocial Impairment in Preschoolers with Selective Eating." *Pediatrics* 136, no. 3 (2015): e582–e590. https://doi.org/10.1542/peds.2014-2386.

BALLET

Ballet, a style of performance dance, dates to 15th-century Italy where it emerged as a dance interpretation of fencing. Ballet has since spread across Europe and the United States, and numerous professional ballet companies have evolved. In the United States, choreographer George Balanchine choreographed routines in the 1920s and formed his first professional ballet company in 1935. His choreography and techniques had a significant influence on a recognizable ballet body represented by tall dancers who had long limbs to create aesthetically pleasing performance lines. Ballet has been considered an at-risk activity for eating disorders associated with this ultrathin ideal. Recently, a movie, featuring actor Natalie Portman, entitled *Black Swan* showed the darker side of eating disorders and the pressure for ballerinas to remain slim.

Body Image and Ballerinas

Across studies, ballet dancers (anywhere from 37 to 84 percent) have reported body dissatisfaction and over half (58 percent) are preoccupied with body weight and food compared to 38 percent of nondancers. Ballet schools and professional ballet companies place a strong emphasis on body shape, weight, and the appearance of the body during movement. However, unlike cheerleading, ballet schools do not rely on weight requirements, but on the aesthetic of the body shape, length, and slenderness of body parts. Therefore, young dancers who develop less ideal body shapes as a result of puberty or genetics are often asked to leave or change to another style of dance (e.g., modern dance, which allows a more forgiving body ideal). In the most elite ballet schools in the United States, only 5 percent of eight-year-old ballet dancers complete the program. Similar to figure skating, ballet dancers have a small window in which to excel and perform in a professional dance company. Ballet dancers who compete for limited spots may experience pressure to meet a particular *ballet body* from many sources, including dance teachers, choreographers, themselves, and other dancers. Because of the separation of sex roles in ballet, female ballerinas are expected to be feminine and dainty. Strong and muscular male ballet dancers must lift female dancers to display lines and beauty. Dancers' bodies are constantly monitored by teachers and choreographers. However, the mirror serves as a constant reminder of one's body size, shape, and appearance during long training. Once a ballet dancer lands a professional role, the body-related evaluation is not over. In one case, a critic made disparaging remarks about a ballet dancer who had an eating disorder history.

Eating Disorders and Ballet

With the numerous pressures associated with ballet to maintain a low weight and thin appearance, it is no surprise the prevalence of anorexia nervosa is three to six times higher in ballet dancers than the general population. Forty percent of ballet dancers weighed below 85 percent of their ideal body weight and 27–47 percent of dancers experienced menstrual dysfunction (i.e., irregular menstrual cycle or amenorrhea). Bulimia nervosa rates among ballet dancers range from 2 to 12 percent depending on the study, but the use of purging methods including self-induced vomiting and laxatives have been well documented in the ballet population. Other weight loss strategies reported by dancers have included wearing rubber suits, smoking, and excessive exercising beyond dance training. A recent study reported 6 percent of adolescent ballet dancers met the criteria for anorexia athletica, demonstrating that excessive exercise was a concern for this population. The tragedy of eating disorders among ballerinas is shown by the 1997 death of Heidi Guenther, who at age 22 died from an eating disorder after being told she should lose weight or risk losing her role as a principal dancer in the Boston Ballet Company.

Justine J. Reel

See also: Aesthetic Sports; Anorexia Athletica; Anorexia Nervosa; Bulimia Nervosa; Dancers; Exercise Dependence; Figure Skating

Bibliography

Druss, Richard G., and Joseph A. Silverman. "Body Image and Perfectionism of Ballerinas: Comparison and Contrast with Anorexia Nervosa." *General Hospital Psychiatry* 1, no. 2 (1979): 115–121. http://dx.doi.org/10.1016/0163-8343(79)90056-2.

Herbrich, Laura, Ernst Pfeiffer, Ulrike Lehmkuhl, and Nora Schneider. "Anorexia Athletica in Pre-Professional Ballet Dancers." *Journal of Sports Sciences* 29 (2011): 1–9. https://doi.org/10.1080/02640414.2011.578147.

Hewitt, Bill. "Last Dance: A Desperate Desire to Be Slender May Have Cost 22-Year-Old Ballerina Heidi Guenther Her Life." *People* 48, no. 4 (1997). Accessed November 21, 2017. http://people.com/archive/last-dance-vol-48-no-4/.

Ravaldi, Claudia, Alfredo Vannacci, Enrica Bolognesi, Stefania Mancini, Carlo Faravelli, and Valdo Ricca. "Gender Role, Eating Disorder Symptoms, and Body Image Concern in Ballet Dancers." *Journal of Psychosomatic Research* 61 (2006): 529–535. https://doi.org/10/1016/j. jpsychores.2006.04.016.

Ringham, Rebecca, Kelly Klump, Walter Kaye, David Stone, Steven Libman, Susan Stowe, and Marsha Marcus. "Eating Disorder Symptomatology among Ballet Dancers." *International Journal of Eating Disorders* 39, no. 6 (2006): 503–508. https://doi.org/10.1002/eat.

Swaine, Jon. "'Sugar Plump Fairy' Ballet Dancer Says She Suffered from Eating Disorders." *The Telegraph.* Accessed November 21, 2017. http://www.telegraph.co.uk/news/worldnews/northamerica/usa/8202087/Sugar-Plump-Fairy-ballet-dancer-says-she-suffered-from-eating-disorders.html.

Thomas, Jennifer J., Pamela K. Keel, and Todd F. Heatherton. "Disordered Eating Attitudes and Behaviors in Ballet Students: Examination of Environmental and Individual Risk Factors." *International Journal of Eating Disorders* 38, no. 3 (2005): 263–268. https://doi.org/10.1002/eat.20185.

Toro, Josep, Marta Guerrero, Joan Sentis, Josefina Castro, and Carles Puertolas. "Eating Disorders in Ballet Dancing Students: Problems and Risk Factors." *European Eating Disorders Review* 17 (2009): 40–49. https://doi.org/10.1002/erv.888.

BARIATRIC SURGERY

Bariatric surgery, a medical weight loss procedure, has been used since the late 1990s to treat morbid obesity (body mass index, or BMI, greater than 40). The most common bariatric procedure in the United States is the Roux-en-Y gastric bypass, which accounts for 88 percent of bariatric surgeries and involves placing three staple lines in a vertical direction resulting in a pouch. The small size of the pouch leads to decreased dietary intake and results in a loss of up to 65 percent of excess body weight in morbidly obese patients.

Although most weight loss occurs in the short term (within two years) following bariatric surgery, over 50 percent of individuals reported regaining some weight, usually between two and five years later. Factors that may influence an individual's ability to maintain weight or vulnerability to weight gain include the type of surgery performed, age, presence of binge eating disorders, eating behaviors, depression, sleep patterns, patient adherence to support groups, and BMI before surgery. Gaining weight led clients to report shame and guilt to their treatment providers. Some clients, following bariatric surgery, reported feeling alone with their new body and their fears and admitted to a history of dysfunctional eating patterns, such as binge eating disorder, night eating syndrome, and emotional eating.

Emotional eating is defined as an automatic reaction to unrecognized negative emotions. In eating-disordered individuals, emotions are often suppressed (i.e., alexithymia) rather than expressed, and emotional eating becomes a vehicle for coping with stress. Similarly, research has suggested emotional eating was prevalent in gastric bypass patients before and after gastric surgeries and was accompanied by a belief that food acts as a sedative. This relationship with food predicted a continuation of disordered eating regardless of initial weight loss. Therefore, it is important to note that individuals are especially vulnerable for developing disordered eating or clinical eating disorders if the thoughts and emotions related to food and body image are not addressed before, during, and after surgery. It has been argued that individuals suffering from binge eating disorder be treated and stabilized before bariatric surgery.

Justine J. Reel

See also: Binge Eating Disorder; Body Mass Index; Diet Pills; Night Eating Syndrome; Obesity

Bibliography

Chen, Eunice, Megan Roehrig, Sylvia Herbozo, Michael S. McCloskey, James Roehrig, Hakeemah Cummings, John Alverdy, and Daniel Le Grange. "Compensatory Eating Disorder Behaviors and Gastric Bypass Surgery Outcome." *International Journal of Eating Disorders* 42, no. 4 (2009): 363–366. https://doi.org/10.1002/eat.20617.

Chesler, Betty E., Bernadette G. Harris, and Pamela H. Oestreicher. "Implications of Emotional Eating Beliefs and Reactance to Dietary Advice for the Treatment of Emotional Eating and Outcome Following Roux-en-Y Gastric Bypass: A Case Report." *Clinical Case Studies* 8 (2009): 277–295. https://doi.org/10.1177/1534650109341075.

Kruseman, Maaike, Anik Leimgruber, Flavia Zumbach, and Alain Golay. "Dietary, Weight and Psychological Changes among Patients with Obesity, 8 Years after Gastric Bypass." *Journal of American Dietetic Association* 110 (2010): 527–534. https://doi.org/10.1016/j. jada.2009.12.028.

Magro, Daniéla O., Bruno Geloneze, Regis Delfini, Bruna C. Pareja, Francisco Callejas, and José C. Pereja. "Long-Term Weight Regain after Gastric Bypass: A 5-Year Prospective Study." *Obesity Surgery* 18 (2008): 648–651. https://doi.org/10.1007/s11695-007-9265-1.

Sarwer, David B., Thomas A. Wadden, Reneé H. Moore, Alexander W. Baker, Lauren M. Gibbons, Steven E. Raper, and Noel N. Williams. "Preoperative Eating Behavior, Postoperative Dietary Adherence and Weight Loss Following Gastric Bypass Surgery." *Surgery Obesity Related Diseases* 4, no. 5 (2008): 640–646. https://doi.org/10.1016/j.soard. 2008.04.013.

White, Marney A., Melissa A. Kalarchian, Robin M. Masheb, Marsha D. Marcus, and Carlos M. Grilo. "Loss of Control Over Eating Predicts Outcomes in Bariatric Surgery: A Prospective 24-Month Follow-Up Study." *Journal of Clinical Psychiatry* 71, no. 2 (2010): 175–184. https://doi.org/10.4088/JCP.08m04328blue.

BIGOREXIA

Bigorexia is a condition related to people's perceptions regarding the size and shape of their body. Although the term *bigorexia* is not typically used as a formal diagnosis, it is believed to be a subtype of body dysmorphic disorder (BDD). BDD is a clinically diagnosable condition in which individuals are preoccupied with a physical defect (e.g., the size of one's nose) that is either minor or imagined. In the case of bigorexia, the defect is a perceived lack of muscularity. Also known as reverse anorexia, and more recently as muscle dysmorphia, bigorexia occurs almost exclusively in male bodybuilders. Bigorexia is characterized by a variety of cognitive and behavioral symptoms. The predominant cognitive symptom of bigorexia is an obsessive preoccupation with the idea that one's body is too small or weak. Preoccupation with the body can lead to inaccurate perceptions of body size and shape, high anxiety, and an inability to focus on other important aspects of life. Behavioral symptoms include excessive time spent lifting weights, monitoring diet, and mirror checking. Although research on bigorexia remains in its infancy, studies have shown that up to 10 percent of male bodybuilders exhibit symptoms of bigorexia and the average age of onset is 19.4 years.

Body Image Disturbances and Bigorexia

Although some level of body dissatisfaction is to be expected as individuals enter adolescence, there are several important differences between normal signs of development and pathological body image concerns associated with bigorexia. First, a person's body perception may be severely distorted, leading an individual to underestimate the total amount of muscle mass he possesses and the size and shape of individual muscles. Second, an individual's sense of self-worth may be highly dependent on the size and shape of his body. Third, efforts to achieve the ideal body are likely to interfere with school, work, and social interactions. Finally, individuals with bigorexia may engage in unhealthy practices such as dietary restrictions, taking diet pills, binge eating, or steroid use.

Nick Galli

See also: Body Image in Males; Body Dysmorphic Disorder; Masculinity Ideals; Muscle Dysmorphia; Substance Abuse

Bibliography

Mosley, Philip E. "Bigorexia. Bodybuilding and Muscle Dysmorphia." *European Eating Disorders Review* 17 (2009): 191–198. https://doi.org/10.1002/erv.897.

Olivardia, Roberto. "Mirror, Mirror on the Wall, Who's the Largest of Them All? The Features and Phenomenology of Muscle Dysmorphia." *Harvard Review of Psychiatry* 9 (2001): 254–259.

BINGE EATING DISORDER

Binge eating disorder (BED) has been described as having recurrent overeating episodes without engaging in a compensatory method of purging (e.g., self-induced vomiting). Although overeating has existed for centuries and was observed among the Romans, the first documented medical case of BED was of Laura in 1949. Binge eating behavior was reported across obesity studies in the 1950s by Dr. Albert Stunkard, and by the 1980s it was determined bulimia nervosa and binge eating disorder (which was then called *pathological overeating syndrome*) should be categorized as separate eating disorders. Likewise, it was important for medical professionals to distinguish between obese clients who engaged in binge eating and individuals who did not engage in overeating behaviors. In 1992, the term *binge eating disorder* was coined and discussed in the *International Journal of Eating Disorders*. The previous version of the *Diagnostic and Statistical Manual of Mental Disorders, fourth edition* (1994) only identified binge eating episodes associated with bulimia nervosa and included proposed BED research criteria in the appendix. Individuals who previously met the BED criteria were diagnosed with eating disorder not otherwise specified However, BED finally received a separate clinical diagnosis in the 2013 *DSM-5* publication. Although a highly secretive disorder, some celebrities have admitted to struggling with binge eating disorder, including Kara DioGuardi, an *American Idol* judge, Victoria Beckham (Posh Spice from the Spice Girls rock band), and Monica Seles, a tennis star. In 2009, Monica Seles revealed how a violent attack led to a dysfunctional pattern of emotional eating to deal with her overwhelming stress.

Symptoms of Binge Eating Disorder

The *DSM-5* criteria for binge eating disorder includes recurrent episodes of binge eating as the overarching behavioral component. The overeating occurs in a discrete period of time (usually within a two-hour time span) and the binge represents more consumption than would be typical for most people in a similar situation. The binges may last longer for an individual with BED than for someone with bulimia nervosa. Additionally, the binges are marked by a sense of being out of control over one's eating or how much food is consumed. Binge eating episodes need to include three or more of the following features to meet the criteria for a BED diagnosis: (1) eating more rapidly than normal, (2) eating until uncomfortable—past the point of fullness, (3) eating large amounts of food despite not being hungry, (4) eating alone due to embarrassment about how much food one is eating, and (5) being disgusted with oneself, experiencing depressed mood or guilt after the binge eating episode. Individuals with BED report significant distress regarding their binge eating. According to the *DSM-5*, the binge eating episodes occur at least once per week for at least three months (reduced from six months stated in the *DSM-IV-TR*). It is important to note that this duration for binge behavior is now consistent with bulimia nervosa (i.e., three months). The final criterion for BED requires that binge eating episodes not be accompanied by inappropriate compensatory methods such as vomiting, laxative abuse, and excessive exercise. As a result of the frequent overeating, many individuals with BED struggle with overweight and obesity.

Prevalence of Binge Eating Disorder

Approximately one-fifth to one-third of individuals who seek obesity treatment fit the criteria for BED. Seventy percent of individuals with BED in a community sample were obese and 20 percent of BED individuals had a body mass index over 40. BED is more common than either anorexia nervosa or bulimia nervosa. Approximately 3.5 percent of women and 2 percent of men reported having a binge eating disorder at some point in their lives compared with only 0.9 percent of women with anorexia nervosa, 1.5 percent of women with bulimia nervosa, or 0.5 percent of men with bulimia nervosa. There is some initial evidence that certain groups (e.g., football players) and minority populations (e.g., African American, Latino/Hispanic, Polynesian groups) may be considered at risk for developing binge eating disorder due to sport demands and cultural traditions (e.g., overeating for family meals).

Personality Characteristics and Coexisting Conditions

BED frequently occurs concurrently with mood and anxiety disorders and substance use. Studies have shown that up to 74 percent of BED individuals reported additional psychiatric disorders. In fact, individuals with BED were significantly more likely to have co-occurring psychiatric disorders than obese clients without BED. One study demonstrated that 60 percent of obese binge eaters met the criteria for one or more psychiatric disorders compared to only 28 percent of non–binge eaters of similar age and weight. Furthermore, binge eaters were more likely to struggle from an affective disorder (e.g., depression) than non–binge eaters with rates of 32 percent and 8 percent, respectively. For binge eating individuals, major depressive episodes were often accompanied by weight gain.

Although binge eating individuals were more likely to have psychiatric problems compared to the general population, when examining individuals with anorexia nervosa or bulimia nervosa, individuals with BED were no more likely to have comorbid psychiatric conditions. Although studies vary in terms of reported prevalence rates, approximately 36–44 percent of individuals who abused alcohol reported engaging in binge eating episodes.

Health Consequences of BED

Individuals who suffer from BED often experience the same health consequences associated with being overweight or obese. Being overweight or obese carries a higher risk for a number of damaging health conditions such as high blood pressure, high cholesterol, cardiovascular disease, and type 2 diabetes. With increased rates of obesity come additional risks of bone and joint problems, respiratory problems, and stroke. Additionally, gall bladder disease is more common among obese individuals, and obese women have twice the rate of bowel or rectal cancer as individuals at a normal weight. Due to binge episodes triggered by psychological states, binge eating individuals experience difficulty realizing fullness. They may also have difficulty in losing weight and in maintaining a normal or healthy weight for their height and age.

Justine J. Reel

See also: Binge Eating Disorder Association; *Diagnostic and Statistical Manual of Mental Disorders*; Food Addiction; Obesity; Overeaters Anonymous; Personality Characteristics

Bibliography

Abraham, Suzanne, and Derek Llewellyn-Jones. *Eating Disorders: The Facts*. New York: Oxford University Press, 1995.

American Psychiatric Association. *Diagnostic and Statistical Manual of Mental Disorders*, 5th ed. (*DSM-5*). Washington, DC: American Psychiatric Association Publishing, 2013.

American Psychiatric Association. *Diagnostic and Statistical Manual of Mental Disorders*, 4th ed., rev. Washington, DC: American Psychiatric Association Publishing, 2000.

Amianto, Federico, Luca Lavagnino, Paolo Leombruni, Filippo Gastaldi, Giovanni Abbate Daga, and Secondo Fassino. "Hypomania across the Binge Eating Spectrum: A Study on Hypomanic Symptoms in Full Criteria and Sub-Threshold Binge Eating Subjects." *Journal of Affective Disorders* (2011): 1–4. https://doi.org/10.1016/j.jad.2011.04.049.

Bulik, Cynthia M. *Carve: Why You Binge Eat and How to Stop*. New York: Walker Publishing Company, 2009.

Carrard, I., C. Crépin, P. Rouget, T. Lam, A. Golay, and M. Van der Linden. "Randomised Controlled Trial of a Guided Self-Help Treatment on the Internet for Binge Eating Disorder." *Behavior Research and Therapy* 49 (2011): 482–491. https://doi.org/10.1016/j.brat. 2011.05.004.

Castelnuovo, Gianluca, Gian Mauro Manzoni, Valentina Villa, Gian Luca Cesa, and Enrico Molinari. "Brief Strategic Therapy vs. Cognitive Behavior Therapy for Inpatient and Telephone-Based Outpatient Treatment of Binge Eating Disorder: The STRATOB Randomized Controlled Clinical Trial." *Clinical Practice & Epidemiology in Mental Health* 7 (2011): 29–37. https://doi.org/10.2174/1745017901107010029.

Chen, Eunice Yu, Michael S. McCloskey, Sara Michelson, Kathryn H. Gordon, and Emil Coccaro. "Characterizing Eating Disorders in a Personality Disorders Sample." *Psychiatry Research* 185 (2011): 427–432. https://doi.org/10.1016/j.psychres.2010.07.002.

Connolly, Anne M., Elizabeth Rieger, and Ian Caterson. "Binge Eating Tendencies and Anger Coping: Investigating the Confound of Trait Neuroticism in a Non-Clinical Sample." *European Eating Disorders Review* 15 (2007): 479–486. https://doi.org/10.1002/erv.765.

Costin, Carolyn. *A Comprehensive Guide to the Causes, Treatments and Prevention of Eating Disorders,* 3rd ed. New York: McGraw-Hill, 2007.

Costin, Carolyn. *100 Questions & Answers about Eating Disorders.* Sudbury, MA: Jones and Bartlett, 2007.

Courbasson, Christine, and Jacqueline M. Brunshaw. "The Relationship between Concurrent Substance Use Disorders and Eating Disorders with Personality Disorders." *International Journal of Environmental Research and Public Health* 6 (2009): 2076–2089. https://doi.org/10.3390/ijerph6072076.

De Bolle, Marleen, Barbara De Clercq, Alexandra Pham-Scottez, Saskia Meis, Jean-Pierre Rolland, Julien D. Guelfi, Caroline Braet, and Filip De Fruyt. "Personality Pathology Comorbidity in Adult Females with Eating Disorders." *Journal of Health Psychology* 16 (2011): 303–313. https://doi.org/10.1177/1359105310374780.

"DSM-5 Diagnostic Criteria." *The Alliance for Eating Disorders Awareness.* Accessed November 16, 2016. http://www.allianceforeatingdisorders.com/portal/dsm-bed.

Fairburn, Chris G. *Overcoming Binge Eating.* New York: Guilford Press, 1995.

Grilo, Carlos M., Marney A. White, and Robin M. Masheb. "DSM-IV Psychiatric Disorder Comorbidity and Its Correlates in Binge Eating Disorder." *International Journal of Eating Disorders* 42 (2009): 228–234.

Hall, Lindsey, and Leigh Cohn. *Bulimia: A Guide to Recovery.* Carlsbad, CA: Gurze, 2011.

Harvey, Kate, Francine Rosselli, G. Terence Wilson, Lynn L. DeBar, and Ruth H. Striegel-Moore. "Eating Patterns in Patients with Spectrum Binge-Eating Disorder." *International Journal of Eating Disorders* 44 (2011): 447–451. https://doi.org/10.1002/eat.20839.

Hudson, James I., Eva Hiripi, Harrison G. Pope, and Ronald C. Kessler. "The Prevalence and Correlates of Eating Disorders in the National Comorbidity Survey Replication." *Biological Psychiatry* 61, no. 3 (2007): 348–358.

Mehler, Philip S. "Bulimia Nervosa." *The New England Journal of Medicine* 349, no. 9 (2003): 875–882.

Parker-Pope, Tara. "Monica Seles Talks about Binge Eating." *New York Times.* Accessed November 21, 2017. https://well.blogs.nytimes.com/2009/04/24/monica-seles-talks-about-binge-eating/.

Robinson, Athen Hagler, and Debra L. Safer. "Moderators of Dialectical Behavior Therapy for Binge Eating Disorder: Results from a Randomized Controlled Trial." *International Journal of Eating Disorders* (2011): 1–6. https://doi.org/10.1002/eat.20932.

White, Marney A., and Carlos M. Grilo. "Diagnostic Efficiency of DSM-IV Indicators for Binge Eating Episodes." *Journal of Consulting and Clinical Psychology* 79, no. 1 (2011): 75–83. http://dx.doi.org/10.1037/a0022210.

BINGE EATING DISORDER ASSOCIATION

There are many national and international associations devoted to increasing awareness of eating disorders, such as the Academy of Eating Disorders, International Association of Eating Disorder Professionals, and National Eating Disorder Association. The Binge Eating Disorder Association (BEDA), a newer national association, was founded with the purpose of focusing on advocacy for persons who suffer from binge eating disorder (BED). Specifically, Chevese Turner, who organized BEDA in 2008, was dedicated to bringing attention to individuals with BED who were overshadowed by the more visibly shocking eating disorder diagnosis of anorexia nervosa. Although individuals with anorexia nervosa could be readily identified by low body weight and ribs protruding, people with BED often struggle with disordered eating thoughts and behaviors in silence. Importantly, BED represents the most prevalent eating disorder in the United States with 3.5 percent of women and 2 percent of men having the disorder. BED affects all people regardless of age, sex, gender, race or ethnicity, level of education, or income status.

Further, because binge eating episodes may lead to weight gain and being overweight, individuals with BED are often the recipients of weight stigma including teasing about one's body weight or appearance and judgment or bias. Weight stigma is defined as shaming or discriminating against someone based on body size and appearance. For example, a common stereotype is for overweight and obese people to be labeled as lazy or unmotivated due to their body size.

Mission and Values of BEDA

BEDA, a 501(c)3 nonprofit organization, works to support both individuals with BED and treatment providers. Specifically, the goal of BEDA is to advance prevention and treatment efforts of BED by providing leadership in the field. The organization, which also strives to improve diagnosis and assessment, was created before BED was formally listed in the clinical criteria for eating disorders in the *Diagnostic and Statistical Manual of Mental Disorders (DSM)*. This changed in 2013 when binge eating disorder became a separate and formal category in eating disorders for the fifth edition of the *DSM*.

BEDA is also strongly committed to fighting for excellent care for clients with BED. A Health at Every Size approach is promoted by BEDA to celebrate diversity of sizes and foster cultural acceptance. Although living a healthy lifestyle is supported with this philosophy, health promotion activities are not necessarily tied to subsequent weight loss changes.

As an organization, BEDA works to build a community of treatment profes sionals and advocates. Values include, but are not limited to, providing hope, supporting research, educating treatment professionals, identifying discrimination related to size and weight, and advocating for awareness about BED and weight stigma. Specifically, BEDA has the broad vision of developing a community to provide resources to help individuals recover from BED and to fight weight stigma. BEDA hosts an annual conference for treatment professionals from across disciplines as well as family members and individuals with BED. Advocacy efforts also include the opportunity to contact state legislators about topics related to BED and weight stigma.

Finally, BEDA has designed a toolkit for providers to educate a myriad of treatment professionals about the harms of weight stigma in health care practices. A separate toolkit is also available for families, friends, and individuals with BED who likely suffer from weight stigma. This practical resource helps people understand the best way to advocate for themselves and others to reduce weight stigma.

Justine J. Reel

See also: Advocacy Groups; Binge Eating Disorder; Health at Every Size Approach; International Association of Eating Disorder Professionals; National Eating Disorders Association; Weight Stigma

Bibliography

American Psychiatric Association. *Diagnostic and Statistical Manual of Mental Disorders*, 5th ed. (*DSM-5*). Washington, DC: American Psychiatric Association Publishing, 2013.

Cogan, Jeanine C. "Question & Answer: Why Is Advocacy on Eating Disorders Needed?" Edited by Russell D. Marx. *Eating Disorders* 8, no. 4 (2000): 353–354. https://doi .org/10.1080/10640260008251242.

"DSM-5 Diagnostic Criteria." The Alliance for Eating Disorders Awareness. Accessed October 25, 2016. http://www.allianceforeatingdisorders.com/portal/dsm-bed.

"What Is BEDA?" Binge Eating Disorder Association. Accessed October 25, 2016. http:// bedaonline.com/.

BODY ALIENATION

Body alienation refers to a condition in which an individual views his or her body as something separate, or alien. The term was first coined by French philosopher and social theorist Simone de Beauvoir in her 1949 book, *The Second Sex*. According to de Beauvoir, both girls and boys become alienated from their bodies at a young age. According to her, the alienation process is particularly problematic for girls, as they tend to use their dolls as models for how they should appear. Although dolls represent the body, they also represent the body as something passive and subject to the approval of society. The process of alienation can be further promoted by early sexual abuse or parents who place excessive emphasis on physical appearance. The sense of alienation is heightened during adolescence when girls' bodies begin to mature. Changes in body shape and size are often confusing to girls, and as a result their body image may become fragmented and described in terms of specific body parts (e.g., breasts, hips) rather than a whole. A study with teenage boys and girls revealed that while boys described their bodies in terms of physical function (e.g., strong), girls described their bodies in terms of physical attractiveness (e.g., pretty).

Relationship between Body Alienation and Eating Disorders

Body alienation has recently been linked to low self-esteem and self-harm behaviors, such as eating disorders and self-mutilation. With regard to eating disorders and other self-injurious behaviors, the body is viewed as an enemy that must be dealt with. Eating disorders are an attempt to maintain control over the body and perceive it as a part of the person's entire being. Research has shown body alienation is related to increased pressure to be thin in adolescent girls. Interviews with women who engaged in self-harming behaviors support the notion that these individuals tend to view their bodies as an entity separate from themselves. The interviewees often referred to themselves or their bodies, rather than integrating the two parts. For example, one woman discussed wanting to "kill her body." Other women noted using their body as a tool to manage others and maintain control. Because body alienation has been connected with a variety of negative psychological and behavioral outcomes, it has also been examined in several different at-risk populations, including athletes, nurses, and rheumatoid arthritis patients.

Body Alienation among Athletes

Body alienation may be observed in competitive athletes, as their success is dependent on the speed, strength, and agility of their bodies. Athletes who are alienated from their bodies may spend excessive hours training, attempt to perform despite illness or injury, or engage in disordered eating. Pressure to perform prompts many athletes to become isolated from their body and seek to improve performance by any means necessary. Elite athletes may be encouraged to treat their bodies as high-performance cars or strive to turn their bodies into well-oiled machines. Such a view of the body as a machine normalizes and encourages the use of nutritional supplements and performance-enhancing drugs to help the body achieve optimal performance. Body alienation in sports is closely tied to the ideal that truly dedicated athletes must constantly strive for success, accept risks, and play through pain if they are to be considered real athletes. There are three components to body alienation in sports: injury tolerance, training through pain, and the use of the body as a tool. Thus, athletes who are alienated from their body will play through injury despite the risk of causing permanent damage, push themselves beyond the boundaries of pain tolerance, and treat their body as if it is a mechanical device to help them achieve performance success. A 13-item survey was developed to assess the three components of body alienation in athletes. For example, one statement on the survey is, "I see myself as a machine designed to perform a specific sport." Answers to the survey represent the degree to which a respondent views this statement to be true. Although limited research has been conducted on body alienation in athletes, the results of a study on ultramarathoners suggested runners who identified strongly as exercisers showed more body alienation as indicated by higher injury tolerance than runners who identified less strongly as exercisers.

Body Alienation in Health Care Settings

For individuals who have a chronic illness such as arthritis, lupus, or bursitis, having a positive view of the body is a challenge. Indeed, it would be easy for individuals with a chronic illness to have the sense that one's body has betrayed them and is hindering the ability to live a healthy and happy life. A study of 168 individuals suffering from rheumatoid arthritis showed that feelings of body alienation were related to less self-esteem, and that feelings of harmony with the body were associated with higher self-esteem. Health care professionals who care for sick or injured individuals are also at risk for body alienation. Researchers interviewed seven Brazilian female nurses in critical care units to find how these women perceive their bodies. Nurses in Brazil work in a rigid hierarchical structure where they are treated as tools for production. A major finding from the interviews was that the nurses felt exploited and alienated from their bodies. A nurse discussed her body being used as a tool for production, "And there's that thing, nurses don't get sick, it's just whining, it's not illness . . . you see nurse colleagues who are having a breakdown, who need help, who are anxious . . . they have a lot of issues and aren't worried about it, because apparently it's still working, isn't it? They're working."

Contributing Factors to Body Alienation

A variety of social forces contribute to body alienation. Some have accused the Western medical profession of being largely responsible for alienating people from their bodies. Some sociologists argue a more egalitarian relationship between doctor and patient, in which a patient takes an active role in the treatment process, would lead to a more holistic view of the body, which would then lead to more effective treatment.

Nick Galli

See also: Body Distortion; Body Dysmorphic Disorder; Body Esteem; Body Image

Bibliography

Albini, Leomar, and Liliana M. Labronici. "Exploitation and Alienation of the Body of the Nurse: A Phenomenological Study." *Acta Paulista de Enfermagem* 20 (2007): 299–304. http://dx.doi.org/10.1590/S0103-21002007000300009.

Arp, Kristana. "Beauvoir's Concept of Bodily Alienation." In *Feminist Interpretations of Simone de Beauvoir,* edited by Margaret Simons, 161–172. College Park: The Pennsylvania State University Press, 1995.

Bologh, Roslyn W. "Grounding the Alienation of Self and Body." *Sociology of Health and Illness* 3 (1981): 188–206. https://doi.org/10.1111/1467-9566.ep11343883.

Cross, Lisa W. "Body and Self in Feminine Development: Implications for Eating Disorders and Delicate Self-Mutilation." *Bulletin of the Menninger Clinic* 57 (1993): 41–68.

de Beauvoir, Simone. *The Second Sex.* New York: Vintage Books, 2011.

Frederickson, Barbara L., and Tomi-Ann Roberts. "Objectification Theory: Toward Understanding Women's Lived Experiences and Mental Health Risks." *Psychology of Women Quarterly* 21 (1997): 173–206.

Lantz, Christopher D., Deborah J. Rhea, and Karin Mesnier. "Eating Attitudes, Exercise Identity, and Body Alienation in Competitive Ultramarathoners." *International Journal of Sport Nutrition and Exercise Metabolism* 14 (2004): 406–418.

Parent, Mike C., and Bonnie Moradi. "His Biceps Become Him: A Test of Objectification Theory's Application to Drive for Muscularity and Propensity for Steroid Use in College Men." *Journal of Counseling Psychology* 58 (2010): 246–256. http://dx.doi .org/10.1037/a0021398.

Reinhold, Sandra. "Alienation and Isolation from the Body: A Common Etiology for the Deliberate Self-Harm of Eating Disorders and Self-Mutilation?" PhD dissertation, The Chicago School of Professional Psychology, 2002.

BODY AVOIDANCE

Body avoidance, a behavioral component of body image, refers to the behavior of actively going out of one's way to avoid looking at one's body or in a mirror. To avoid negative emotions associated with their body, eating-disordered individuals may exhibit avoidance behavior, such as not looking in the mirror or wearing baggy clothing to hide bodily appearance. The opposite of body avoidance, body checking, represents another behavior associated with negative body image. It is unclear whether these behaviors represent opposite manifestations of body image disturbances or whether they are related to one another. However, checking and avoidance prevent individuals from disconfirming their worst fears about body shape and weight and serve to maintain dysfunctional attitudes about the body. Avoidance behaviors may also be associated with increased importance placed on shape and weight.

Treatment of Body Avoidance

Treatment for avoidance behaviors would follow a similar intervention as that aimed to improve body image. Cognitive-behavioral approaches that include a body exposure piece show promise and include systematically increasing one's exposure to observing one's body. Specifically, body image therapy with mirror confrontation has been shown to reduce body dissatisfaction, whereas body image therapy without exposure does not address body avoidance behaviors. By using a full-length mirror or other body exposure techniques (e.g., prescribing the client to gradually wear more form-fitting clothing), the body distortion component of body image can be addressed in treatment. Interestingly, many prevention strategies may encourage individuals to reduce body checking behaviors (e.g., weighing themselves, using the mirror as a form of evaluation) to promote decreased attention to appearance or evaluation of one's body and appearance. Therefore, body exposure therapy to reduce body avoidance behaviors should be used with caution so individuals do not develop excessive body checking behaviors (e.g., looking at oneself in the mirror, weighing or measuring one's body).

Assessment of Body Avoidance

The Body Image Avoidance Questionnaire (BIAQ) was developed by Rosen and colleagues in 1991 to assess behavioral manifestations of body image disturbances.

A general score is calculated from 13 items that represent body-related avoidance behaviors (i.e., the tendency to disguise or cover up one's appearance by wearing baggy, nonrevealing clothing and avoiding social situations in which weight or appearance could be the focus of attention). For example, one item reads, "I wear baggy clothes." This questionnaire includes additional subscales (e.g., grooming, weighing) that do not measure body avoidance behavior but are associated with body image. When using the BIAQ, eating-disordered individuals have scored significantly higher than healthy controls on body-related avoidance behaviors. Therefore, it is important to address this behavioral component of negative body image in eating disorder treatment.

Justine J. Reel

See also: Body Checking; Body Distortion; Body Esteem; Body Image; Exposure Therapy

Bibliography

Latner, Janet D. "Body Checking and Avoidance among Behavioral Weight-Loss Partici-pants." *Body Image* 5 (2008): 91–98. https://doi.org/10.1016/j.bodyim.2007.08.001.

Rosen, James C., Debra Srebnik, Elayne Saltzberg, and Sally Wendt. "Development of a Body Image Avoidance Questionnaire." *Psychological Assessment: A Journal of Consulting and Clinical Psychology* 3, no. 1 (1991): 32–37. http://dx.doi.org/10.1037/1040-3590.3.1.32.

Vocks, Silja, Joachim Kosfelder, Maike Wucherer, and Alexandra Wachter. "Does Habitual Body Avoidance and Checking Behavior Influence the Decrease of Negative Emotions during Body Exposure in Eating Disorders?" *Psychotherapy Research* 18, no. 4 (2008): 412–419. http://dx.doi.org/10.1080/10503300701797008.

BODY CHECKING

Body checking, a behavioral component of body image, refers to repeated attempts to evaluate or scrutinize one's body shape, size, or appearance. In addition to spending excessive time compulsively checking one's body in a mirror, body checking behaviors also include using the fit of clothing to judge whether one's size has changed. Another common behavior is obsessively feeling one's body parts for bones or fat. Although this body checking behavior has been observed among individuals with anorexia nervosa, bulimia nervosa, and binge eating disorder, as well as obese individuals and nonclinical populations, females with eating disorders engage in body checking strategies significantly more often than healthy females. Recent attempts have been made to measure body check-ing among males, which is believed to be tied to body dysmorphic disorder and muscle dysmorphia.

It is not clear what the relationship between body checking and body dissat-isfaction is, but it is predicted the overestimation of one's body size will naturally contribute to body dissatisfaction and this occurs more frequently among eat-ing-disordered individuals. In fact, researchers speculate body checking behavior is likely to be associated with body image distortion and needs to be addressed in eating disorder treatment to avoid a relapse triggered by body checking behaviors.

Individuals who engage in body checking behavior report using it as a way to reduce anxiety or to avoid the discomfort associated with not checking. Individuals who engage in body checking may also claim that watching one's size and appearance provides a way to take control of one's weight and eating patterns. Unfortunately, in practice, this body checking behavior brings attention to problem areas and serves to trigger body image disturbances or feed anxiety related to one's physique. Therefore, body checking should be discouraged and needs to be addressed as part of eating disorder treatment.

Treatment of Body Checking

Cognitive-behavioral therapy that includes a body exposure component shows promise for improving body image disturbances. During a session, a client is instructed to look into a full-length mirror to provide exposure in a systematic way. Because the session provides a safe place for the client to engage in taboo behaviors, the client has an opportunity to experience and express emotions to his or her therapist in the moment. A therapist may encourage exposure coupled with coping skills (e.g., relaxation techniques like deep breathing) to reduce stress. After continuing body exposure to the mirror over a number of sessions, a client becomes less anxious and the behavior becomes more normalized. There is hope using expose techniques in conjunction with newer virtual reality techniques will allow clinicians to help eating-disordered individuals manage intense body image feelings.

Assessment of Body Checking

The Body Checking Questionnaire (BCQ) was developed in 2002 to assess habitual body-related checking strategies. The BCQ consists of 23 items such as "I check my reflection in glass doors or car windows to see how I look." Studies have found that individuals with eating disorders scored significantly higher on the BCQ than nonclinical counterparts. More recently, a body checking questionnaire was constructed for use among males. The Male Body Checking Questionnaire (MBCQ) contains 19 items, uses the same format as the BCQ, and adapts questions to meet body image concerns of males. For example, the BCQ focuses on female problem areas (e.g., thighs) and fatness; however, males are more likely to be obsessed with muscularity and leanness.

Justine J. Reel

See also: Body Avoidance; Body Distortion; Body Dysmorphic Disorder; Body Image; Exposure Therapy; Muscle Dysmorphia; Virtual Reality

Bibliography

Haase, Anne M., Victoria Mountford, and Glenn Waller. "Understanding the Link between Body Checking Cognitions and Behaviors: The Role of Social Physique Anxiety." *International Journal of Eating Disorders* 40 (2007): 241–246. https://doi.org/10.1002/eat.20356.

Hadjustavropoulos, Heather, and Brandy Lawrence. "Does Anxiety about Health Influence Eating Patterns and Shape-Related Body Checking among Females?" *Personality and Individual Differences* 43 (2007): 319–328. https://doi.org/10.1016/j.paid.2006.11.021

Hildebrandt, Tom, D. Catherine Walker, Lauren Alfano, Sherrie Delinsky, and Katie Bannon. "Development and Validation of a Male Specific Body Checking Questionnaire." *International Journal of Eating Disorders* 43 (2010): 77–87. https://doi.org/10.1002/eat.20669.

Latner, Janet D. "Body Checking and Avoidance among Behavioral Weight-Loss Participants." *Body Image* 5 (2008): 91–98. https://doi.org/10.1016/j.bodyim.2007.08.001.

Shafran, Roz, Michelle Lee, Elizabeth Payne, and Christopher G. Fairburn. "An Experimental Analysis of Body Checking." *Behavior Research and Therapy* 45 (2007): 113–121. http://dx.doi.org/10.1016/j.brat.2006.01.015.

Smeets, Elke, Marika Tiggemann, Eva Kemps, Jennifer S. Mills, Sarah Hollitt, Anne Roefs, and Anita Jansen. "Body Checking Induces an Attentional Bias for Body-Related Cues." *International Journal of Eating Disorders* 44 (2011): 50–57. https://doi.org/10.1002/eat.20776.

Vocks, Silja, Joachim Kosfelder, Maike Wucherer, and Alexandra Wachter. "Does Habitual Body Avoidance and Checking Behavior Influence the Decrease of Negative Emotions during Body Exposure in Eating Disorders?" *Psychotherapy Research* 18, no. 4 (2008): 412–419. https://doi.org/10.1080/10503300701797008.

BODY DISTORTION

Body image broadly represents affective, cognitive, behavioral, or perceptual aspects of one's size, shape, or appearance. Body image distortion (or perceptual disturbance) refers to the perceptual component of body image and relates to an individual's ability to accurately perceive one's body size and shape. Eating-disordered individuals may perceive themselves as vastly larger than they are in reality, despite looking in the mirror or being told by other people that they are smaller than they believe. In fact, using objective measures (e.g., scales) to confront cognitive distortions may be met with skepticism that the scale is not functioning properly or has been tampered with by the medical professional.

Body perceptions should be distinguished from the more widely recognized component of body image, body dissatisfaction, which is defined by the subjective negative evaluation of one's body or body parts. However, both body dissatisfaction and body distortion are predictive of disordered eating and clinical eating disorders and should be considered for assessment and treatment. A concept related to body distortion, muscle dysmorphia, also called reverse anorexia, involves individuals who largely underestimate their bodies.

Measurement of Body Distortion

Clinicians and researchers recognize a strong correlation between eating disorders and perceived body size distortions. Unfortunately, previous body image distortion studies have been limited to using figural drawing scales (e.g., Figure Ratings Scale) to assess perceived body size. These silhouette-based instruments include a series of sex-specific drawings of bodies that range from extremely thin to overweight. An individual is asked to identify the silhouette that most resembles his or her current body, preferred body size, and the figure most attractive for dating others. To assess for perceptual disturbances, a subjective rater (the researcher or clinician) may also rate an individual's current body on the silhouette scale. Because the figure ratings scales are largely visual, researchers can survey participants across reading levels. However, figural drawing scales do not allow for a comprehensive measurement of size perceptions and may contain the potential for a memory bias for participants because mirrors are not provided during assessment.

Previous work using nonclinical populations demonstrates changes to one's body size can influence how participants perceive distance and size. For example, Stefanucci and Geuss manipulated participants' widths by having them hold their hands out wide, and found larger participants estimated the width of gaps to be significantly smaller. In addition, an earlier study had large and small participants judge their ability to pass through a horizontal gap without rotating their shoulders. Both large and small participants required the gap to be 16 percent larger than their shoulder width to indicate an ability to pass through. This measure directly tests participants' perceptions of environmental extents because they must compare these extents to their body size to decide whether they can pass through. A recent study showed that participants with anorexia nervosa indicated they needed wider gap widths to pass through. These results suggest individuals with anorexia nervosa perceive themselves as larger and this distortion of body size influences what they believe they are capable of performing. The emergence of virtual reality (VR) technology may allow for body distortion measurement to improve along with a means for addressing body distortions in treatment. Currently, cognitive-behavioral approaches with exposure therapy to mirrors or body tracings using art therapy have been the main ways to help a client overcome this debilitating aspect of an eating disorder.

Justine J. Reel

See also: Art Therapy; Body Dysmorphic Disorder; Body Image; Figural Rating Scales; Muscle Dysmorphia; Virtual Reality

Bibliography

Allen, Karina L., Susan M. Byrne, Neil J. McLean, and Elizabeth A. Davis. "Overconcern with Weight and Shape Is Not the Same as Body Dissatisfaction: Evidence from a Prospective Study of Pre-Adolescent Boys and Girls." *Body Image* 5 (2008): 261–270. https://doi.org/10.1016/j.bodyim.2008.03.005.

Gardner, Rick M., and Dana L. Brown. "Body Image Assessment: A Review of Figural Drawing Scales." *Personality and Individual Differences* 48 (2010): 107–111. https://doi.org/10.1016/j.paid.2009.08.017.

Grieve, Frederick G. "A Conceptual Model of Factors Contributing to the Development of Muscle Dysmorphia." *Eating Disorders* 15 (2007): 63–80. http://dx.doi.org/10.1080/10640260601044535.

McCabe, Marita P., Kelly Butler, and Christina Watt. "Media Influences on Attitudes and Perceptions toward the Body among Adult Men and Women." *Journal of Applied Biobehavioral Research* 12, no. 2 (2007): 101–118. https://doi.org/10.1111/j.1751-9861.2007.00016.x.

O'Riordan, Siobhan S., and Byron L. Zamboanga. "Aspects of the Media and Their Relevance to Bulimic Attitudes and Tendencies among Female College Students." *Eating Behaviors* 9 (2008): 247–250. https://doi.org/10.1016/j.eatbeh.2007.03.004.

Stefanucci, Jeanine K., and Michael Geuss. "Big People, Little World: The Body Influences Size Perception." *Perception* 38 (2009): 1782–1795. https://doi.org/10.1068/p6437.

BODY DYSMORPHIC DISORDER

Body dysmorphic disorder (BDD) refers to a mental disorder that is characterized by an excessive, often irrational, preoccupation with an imagined or very slight defect in physical appearance. Although concerns may be related to body weight or shape, BDD should be distinguished from anorexia nervosa, bulimia nervosa, and binge eating disorder. Although any body part can become the focus of preoccupation, the most common body parts are skin, hair, nose, and stomach. Less than 3 percent of individuals meet the diagnostic criteria for BDD with males and females. The *Diagnostic and Statistical Manual of Mental Disorders* identified the BDD criteria as (1) has preoccupation with an imagined defect; (2) preoccupation causes significant distress or impairment; and (3) preoccupation is not better accounted for by another mental disorder.

For individuals with BDD, concerns about appearance are accompanied by repetitive and time-consuming behaviors associated with camouflaging or enhancing appearance. Like eating-disordered individuals, persons suffering from BDD commonly resort to body checking and body avoidance behaviors. In one study, 80 percent of individuals with BDD excessively checked their appearance in a mirror, while the other 20 percent avoided mirrors altogether. Furthermore, individuals with BDD were found to engage in excessive grooming (e.g., excessive hair removal), compulsive skin-picking, and concealing of perceived flaws with a beard, baggy clothing, or makeup. Typically, BDD begins during adolescence and may not be diagnosed for many years. It can be related to a higher incidence of rhinoplasty surgery to change the shape of one's nose, other cosmetic surgery, or increased dermatologist visits. BDD is associated with poor functioning in areas of social interaction, school, and work. In one study of 200 individuals diagnosed with BDD, 36 percent reported missing a week or more of work in the past month and 11 percent dropped out of school because of a struggle with BDD. In the same study, 25 percent of BDD participants reported at least one suicide attempt. Other studies have found the rates of suicidal ideation (thinking about suicide) to be even higher (58–78 percent).

Treatment Considerations for Body Dysmorphic Disorder

Individuals with BDD have been found to have poor insight into their problem. Instead of recognizing BDD as a mental health concern, clients often seek cosmetic procedures to alter the perceived defect. Unfortunately, many clients with BDD report numerous surgeries on the same body part only to continue to struggle with the same negative and obsessive thoughts. Clinicians recognize individuals who meet the BDD criteria share many similarities with individuals with obsessive-compulsive disorder. Therefore, treatment approaches must address the need to replace compulsive behaviors and rituals as part of the recovery process. Furthermore, because of the high level of suicidal ideations and distress, individuals with BDD may struggle to maintain stability. Like clients with borderline personality disorder, BDD clients could benefit from receiving dialectical behavior therapy and skill-based training to regulate difficult emotions.

Barriers to treatment should be considered for this unique population of individuals with BDD. One study with over 400 BDD clients found the majority reported shame (56 percent) or wanting to handle the problem alone (57 percent) as the biggest deterrents for seeking help. In addition, 51 percent of participants thought treatment would not alleviate BDD symptoms and 50 percent thought it would be too expensive.

Muscle Dysmorphia

Muscle dysmorphia refers to an obsession with one's muscularity and the feeling of being too small. Often dubbed reverse anorexia, muscle dysmorphia is considered a subtype of BDD with the perceived defect being musculature. Most frequently males suffer from this condition and bodybuilders are overrepresented. This type of BDD is discussed in more detail in another entry.

Justine J. Reel

See also: Body Avoidance; Body Checking; Body Distortion; Body Image; Dialectical Behavior Therapy; Muscle Dysmorphia

Bibliography

American Psychiatric Association. *Diagnostic and Statistical Manual of Mental Disorders*, 5th ed. (*DSM-5*). Washington, DC: American Psychiatric Association Publishing, 2013.

Fang, Angela, and Stefan G. Hofmann. "Relationship between Social Anxiety Disorder and Body Dysmorphic Disorder." *Clinical Psychology Review* 30 (2010): 1040–1048. https://doi.org/10.1016/j.cpr.2010.08.001.

Marques, Luana, Hillary M. Weingarden, Nicole J. LeBlanc, and Sabine Wilhelm. "Treatment Utilization and Barriers to Treatment Engagement among People with Body Dysmorphic Symptoms." *Journal of Psychosomatic Research* 70 (2011): 286–293. https://doi.org/10.1016/j.psychores.2010.10.002.

Picavet, Valerie A., Emmanuel P. Prokopakis, Lutgardis Gabriels, Mark Jorissen, and Peter W. Hellings. "High Prevalence of Body Dysmorphia Disorder Symptoms in Patients Seeking Rhinoplasty." *Plastic Reconstructive Surgery* 128, no. 2 (2011): 509–517. https://doi.org/10.1097/PRS.0b013e31821b631f.

Reese, Hannah E., Richard J. McNally, and Sabine Wilhem. "Reality Monitoring in Patients with Body Dysmorphic Disorder." *Behavior Therapy* 42 (2011): 387–398.

Taillon, Annie, Kieron O'Connor, Gilles Dupuis, and Marc Lavoie. "Inference-Based Therapy for Body Dysmorphic Disorder." *Clinical Psychology and Psychotherapy* (July 25, 2011). https://doi.org/10.1002/cpp.767.

Wilhelm, Sabine. *Feeling Good about the Way You Look: A Program for Overcoming Body Image Problems*. New York: Guilford Press, 2006.

BODY ESTEEM

Body esteem refers to perceptions of self-esteem related to the body's abilities, worth, and appearance. Self-esteem is generally a more global concept that represents confidence in one's overall propensity for achievement in academic, social, and physical domains. Strong self-esteem can reduce anxiety across situations and often results from being positively reinforced by parents, teachers, and other social beings. The U.S. culture values the physical body and athletic prowess. The media acts as a vehicle for portraying body ideals and giving feedback on what types of bodies are most valued and considered attractive. Products and strategies for changing one's body to make it closer to the ideal are advertised so individuals can take action. There are numerous societal rewards (e.g., increased likelihood of being pursued romantically) for working toward appearance ideals and engaging in self-monitoring behaviors (e.g., checking one's body in the mirror). However, the development of body esteem is a largely internal process and may continue to be low despite eating, exercise, and body-related changes.

Sex Differences in Body Esteem

Body standards for males and females are different. In the media, females are portrayed as tall and thin. Because society is bombarded with these images, females are judged according to this standard of physical appearance; therefore, they tend to be self-conscious about their bodies. Particular areas of focus are legs, buttocks, face, chest, and lips. Self-esteem or confidence for males is based on their degree of muscularity or strength. Females tend to judge males based on those standards as the media have placed a high value on that type of male body.

Throughout the life span from infancy to childhood, adolescence, and adulthood, our bodies are constantly changing, and body esteem can be influenced. For example, during childhood, girls are highly influenced by their mothers' preoccupation with beauty and weight. Mothers might criticize their own bodies and express the need to lose weight. As a result, their daughters will observe this body scrutiny, learn to develop similar feelings of body shame, and report lower body esteem.

Puberty and Body Esteem

Likewise, adolescence and pubertal weight gain may influence body esteem. This natural weight gain can be difficult for adolescents to accept and can lead to a sense of being out of control in relation to one's body. Meanwhile, adolescents experience intense comparison with their peers and may be subject to teasing from peers or family members. Unfortunately, adolescents may face lower self-esteem and body esteem and may engage in eating disorder behaviors (e.g., skipping meals, overexercising, restricted eating, overeating followed by vomiting). Body esteem in adolescents has been addressed by programs such as Full of Ourselves. This program strives to accomplish the following objectives: (1) facilitate candid talk regarding the changes the body undergoes during puberty; (2) identify weightism as a prejudice; (3) discuss myths about body fat; and (4) practice body tolerance and self-acceptance.

Pregnancy and Body Esteem

Adults are not immune to experiencing poor body esteem as they continue to feel body dissatisfaction beyond adolescence. One trigger for low body esteem among female adults is pregnancy. The necessary weight gain during pregnancy that fosters a healthy baby can lead to negative body image that persists after birth due to slow or no weight loss. For women with an eating disorder history, the weight gain may reactivate past coping strategies such as food restriction, binge eating, and vomiting to return to prepregnancy weight. Breastfeeding allows for the mother and baby to bond by encouraging nurturing qualities. Although breastfeeding assists a mother to return to a healthy weight by burning calories, some women may abuse this opportunity by increasing the number of calories burned by breastfeeding more often or by pumping and disposing of milk.

Measurement of Body Esteem

The Body Esteem Scale (BES) was originally developed in 1982 for children to measure feelings about the body using a yes/no response format. The original BES has been modified into the current 23-item scale that uses a 5-point Likert scale with responses ranging from *never* to *always* for individuals 12 years and older. Sample questions include "I like what I look like in pictures" and "I'm proud of my body." The BES includes three areas of body esteem: BE-Appearance (general feelings about one's appearance), BE-Weight (satisfaction about one's weight) and BE-Attribution (others' evaluation of one's body and appearance). The BES is a valid and reliable measure for use with adolescents and adults.

Hailey E. Nielson

See also: Body Checking; Body Image; Full of Ourselves; Puberty

Bibliography

Cobelo, Alicia Wisz, Estima de Chermont Prochnik, E. Yoshio Nakano, Aparecida M. Conti, and Taki Athanassios Cordas. "Body Image Dissatisfaction and Eating Symptoms in Mothers of Adolescents with Eating Disorders." *Eating and Weight Disorders* 15, no. 4 (2010): 219–225.

Cousineau, Tara M., Debra L. Franko, Meredith Trant, Diana Rancourt, Jessica Ainscough, Anamika Chaudhuri, and Julie Brevard. "Teaching Adolescents about Changing Bodies: Randomized Controlled Trial of an Internet Puberty Education and Body Dissatisfaction Prevention Program." *Body Image* 7 (2010): 296–300. https://doi.org/10.1016/j.bodyim.2010.06.003.

Franzoi, Stephen L., and Jeffrey R. Klaiber. "Body Use and Reference Group Impact: With Whom Do We Compare Our Bodies?" *Sex Roles* 56 (2007): 205–214. https://doi.org/1007/s11199-006-9162-4.

Goldenberg, Jamie L., Shannon K. McCoy, Tom Pyszczynski, Jeff Greenberg, and Sheldon Solomon. "The Body as a Source of Self-Esteem: The Effect of Mortality Salience on Identification with One's Body, Interest in Sex, and Appearance Monitoring." *Journal of Personality and Social Psychology* 79, no. 1 (2000): 118–130. https://doi.org/10.1037//0022-3514.79.1.118.

Mendelson, Beverley K., Morton Mendelson, and Donna R. White. "Body-Esteem Scale for Adolescents and Adults." *Journal of Personality Assessment* 76 (2001): 90–106. http://dx.doi.org/10.1207/S15327752JPA7601_6.

Spangler, Diane, and Eric Stice. "Validation of the Beliefs about Appearance Scale." *Cognitive Therapy and Research* 25, no. 6 (2001): 813–827. https://doi.org/10.1023/A:1012931709434.

Steiner-Adair, Catherine, and Lisa Sjostrom. *Full of Ourselves: A Wellness Program to Advance Girl Power, Health, and Leadership.* New York: Columbia University, 2006.

BODY IMAGE

Body image refers to an individual's positive or negative perception of his or her body shape, measurements, weight, or appearance. Although the importance an individual places on this perception can vary greatly, research studies estimate that 80–90 percent of females report body dissatisfaction and about 33–45 percent of males are dissatisfied with their bodies. When compared with males, females are also more likely to engage in self-loathing about body size and weight and have a greater drive for thinness. Women are also more likely to be uncomfortable about their weight and have higher anxiety about how others perceive their body.

Body Dissatisfaction

The most common component of body image is referred to as *body dissatisfaction*, which literally means being dissatisfied with the physical appearance of one's body. Body dissatisfaction has been positively correlated with lower self-esteem, decreased self-confidence, dieting, eating disorders, and obesity. Body dissatisfaction is often a motivating factor behind weight loss efforts. When an individual gains weight, his or her body dissatisfaction typically increases as well. Individuals with a higher percentage of body fat are more likely to be dissatisfied with their shape.

Body image (body dissatisfaction) is influenced by environment, experiences, and behaviors, which interact to shape a person's attitude toward and perception of his or her body. The development of negative body image comes from both historical and proximal events. Historical events are experiences that influence the way an individual thinks about his or her body. These experiences can be molded by cultural socialization, teasing, peer or parental expectations, and the media. These historical events combine with proximal events, which are more immediate body image experiences, such as not fitting into a pair of old jeans or seeing a friend who is perceived to have a better body. These events are more influenced by social learning and a person's immediate environment.

One's body image vacillates constantly, changing daily or throughout the day for many people. A woman may feel positively toward her body in the morning, negatively toward it by afternoon, and positively toward it again by evening. There are many influences that affect body image and reinforce these positive or negative feelings toward the self, including exposure to media images, emotions related to eating and meals, and other events throughout the day.

Body Image Influences

Culturally Defined Beauty

Beauty and ideals in body shape and size are culturally defined, as individuals value the physical ideals of their society. Cultures have valued different physical attributes as an aesthetically pleasing physical form. For example, historically in China a woman who had small feet was more likely to achieve prestigious marriage. In that culture, bound feet were a physical ideal and some individuals would attribute value strictly based on that ideal. In the modern United States, many women believe the ideal body shape is tall and very thin. The prominence of cheekbones, application of makeup, fashion styles, teeth and skin color, and fat distribution are all examples of socially desirable ideals. A woman in this culture may assess herself according to that ideal, and her body image could be affected by this assessment. The same holds true for men as they may value similar ideals, such as tanned skin and white teeth, but they have ideals of a muscular, athletic body with broad shoulders. These ideals for beauty affect body image when an individual places great importance on obtaining the ideal and is unable to do so. For many people, trying to fit into the ideal formed by society is a frustrating and futile experience. Not measuring up to the ideal may then make a person feel worse about his or her body in comparison, thus contributing to a negative body image.

Media

The ideals of beauty are often perpetuated through the media. Traditionally, in television shows and movies, the central character fits the cultural ideal while the supporting role does not. The thin, beautiful women are happy, successful, and able to find love. With more than half of Americans currently overweight or obese, it is interesting that even reality shows feature beautiful, handsome, thin, and muscular people. Various research studies have found a woman's perception of her own to become more negative after watching television shows featuring women who meet the cultural ideal. The same result occurs with movies and magazines. A woman's response to these external images likely fluctuates depending upon several factors. It is suspected that the same is true for men who experience media with images for the male ideal. The influence of the media on body image appears to start relatively young, as children often model what they observe on television. It is believed most children gain an understanding of the cultural ideal through television watching.

Peers and Family

The influence of peers and family play a role in body image. A person's family is likely to represent his or her first encounter with perceptions of body shape and size. Young girls are more likely to want to lose weight if their mother is trying to lose weight. Similarly, if a child perceives thinness to be important to her parents, she will likely carry a similar ideal. Multiple studies have shown that weight-related concerns of parents are commonly passed on to their children. Similarly, siblings can have an influence by modeling behavior that reinforces cultural ideals and through teasing others about nonadherence to these ideals.

Even though body image is an extremely personal experience, it is influenced by one's peers, as people compare themselves to people of their social group. For example, an overweight woman may feel worse about her body if her social circle includes only underweight and normal weight women, whereas an overweight woman who has many overweight friends and associates may not feel as badly about herself. If a person's social comparisons are unfavorable, body dissatisfaction and unhealthy eating behaviors may increase.

Romantic relationships can also influence body image. Overweight women are less likely to be dating than their healthy weight peers and one study found having a boyfriend was associated with better body satisfaction. However, being in a relationship can positively or negatively affect body image, as negative comments made by a partner concerning body size or shape can dramatically increase body dissatisfaction, whereas positive comments can increase body satisfaction.

Self-Esteem

Although the cultural and family/peer influence is strong, an individual's life experience, which may dictate more accurately the way that a person feels, should not be overlooked. Individuals with higher self-esteem are more likely to have a more positive body image, regardless of actual body shape, size, or attractiveness. Many people experience body image shifts associated with aging that lead to a more accepting view of self and others. Other individuals make a concerted effort to improve their self-esteem and body image through classes, counseling, or other mind–body programs. In addition, nonphysical attributes or experiences can positively or negatively affect one's body image. For example, when a woman finds success in her employment, she may feel more positively toward her body, even while her physical attributes have remained unchanged.

Self-Awareness

Body image contains elements of self-assessment and self-awareness as an individual works to process the ideals of society and then apply them to his or her physical body. An incorrect self-assessment may be a sign of body distortion. An example of this would be a normal weight woman who thinks badly about her body because she thinks she is obese. Thus, body image is expected to be individual to each person but largely determined by the person's response to an examination of his or her body in comparison to societal images. The term *body image investment* has been used to refer to the importance placed on body image and achieving society-defined ideals.

News and Advertisements

Negative body image affects so many people and is a frequent headline on entertainment news shows and magazine covers. Numerous celebrities have admitted to struggling from body image disturbance or eating disorders, while other celebrities are accused or suspected of such behavior. Articles on loving your body are next to weight loss ads and liposuction promotions. Many dieting and plastic surgery companies prey on negative body image to attract clients. A classic example would be a woman on a television commercial explaining how miserable and unhappy her life was and how badly she hated herself until she lost weight through a certain product. The advertisement then promises the viewer equivalent results in both weight and body image by buying the product (e.g., Hydroxycut).

There are multiple reality shows on television where the sole purpose is to change the physical appearance of participants. Many of these shows claim high viewership levels and encourage audience members to undergo similar transformations. Shows also promote products available to help people make changes. Multiple shows and specials have been made highlighting children in beauty pageants where they are made up to look like adults with spray-on tans and perfect teeth and makeup (e.g., *Toddlers and Tiaras*, *Little Miss Perfect*). Articles about mothers giving their daughters Botox to help them be successful in beauty pageants have recently been in the news.

Multiple industries use the stereotypical ideals to sell products. The beach body ideal for men, with tanned skin, large muscles, broad shoulders, and rugged good looks, is used to sell everything from lotion to alcohol. These advertisements are to sell products and make viewers feel insufficient or inadequate and in need of the product. Such commercials reinforce the cultural ideal of beauty and can affect a person's body image. For example, Kim Kardashian and Paris Hilton have starred in provocative commercials promoting juicy burgers from Carl's Jr. Several celebrities including Jessica Simpson and Alicia Keys have endorsed Proactive acne solution which can underscore perceive beauty flaws.

In recent years, stories of underweight models near death from eating disorders have filled newspapers and Internet sites. In response, several European countries have made laws requiring models have a certain height-to-weight ratio to work.

Body Image Programs

Many programs have been conducted to help people improve their body image. One of the most widespread public campaigns has been the Dove Campaign for Real Beauty, a worldwide marketing campaign including advertisements, videos, workshops, sleepover events, and a book. Commercials celebrating the natural variation in women's bodies began in 2004. The goal is to inspire people and help them have confidence in themselves. Dove has also worked with young girls to change the concept of beauty from the ultrathin models with perfect features to making every girl feel positively about herself.

Body Image and Health

Body image perceptions are often associated with psychological consequences; however, recently positive body image has also been associated with improved physical health and healthy eating behaviors. Individuals with higher body dissatisfaction are more likely to engage in counterproductive weight loss behaviors, such as short-term starvation diets followed by binge episodes. Negative body image commonly affects the eating habits of individuals. Either they diet, often gaining back any weight lost, or they eat less or more than they should, putting them at risk for eating disorders and obesity.

Individuals with body image concerns are less likely to eat fruits and vegetables and more likely to consume meat and fast food. Body image can affect whether someone will engage in or avoid healthy amounts of physical activity. If an individual feels negatively about himself, he may engage in exercise to improve his appearance and even engage in obligatory exercise. However, if an individual experiences negative body image, he or she may express intense social physique anxiety that could result in avoiding public settings (e.g., pools, fitness centers) for exercise.

Body image can also affect the decision to quit smoking, especially if an individual fears he will gain weight because of cessation. Similarly, body dissatisfaction is associated with higher frequency of cigarette and alcohol use. Given the effects that negative body image can have on health behaviors, more health professionals are identifying negative body image as a serious threat to physical health and well-being.

TeriSue Smith-Jackson

See also: Body Dysmorphic Disorder; Body Esteem; Body Image Globally; Body Image in Males; Cosmetic Surgery and Eating Disorders; Dove Campaign for Real Beauty; Full of Ourselves; Intellectual Disabilities and Body Image; Media; Prevention; Self-Presentation Theory; Social Physique Anxiety; Tanning Behaviors and Body Image

Bibliography

Aruguete, Mara S., Kurt A. DeBord, Alayne Yates, and Jeanne Edman. "Ethnic and Gender Differences in Eating Attitudes among Black and White College Students." *Eating Behaviors* 6, no. 4 (2005): 328–336. http://dx.doi.org/10.1016/j.eatbeh.2004.01.014.

Cash, Thomas F. "Cognitive-Behavioral Perspectives on Body Image." In *Body Image: A Handbook of Theory, Research and Clinical Practice,* edited by Thomas F. Cash and T. Pruzinsky, 38–46. New York: Guilford Press, 2002.

Chu, Hui-Wen, Barbara Bushman, and Rebecca Woodard. "Social Physique Anxiety, Obligation to Exercise, and Exercise Choices among College Students." *Journal of American College Health* 57, no. 1 (2008): 7–14. http://dx.doi.org/10.3200/JACH.57.1.7-14.

"Dove Self-Esteem Project: Our Mission in Action." Selfesteem.dove.us. Accessed November 16, 2016. http://selfesteem.dove.us/Articles/Written/Our_Mission_in_Practice.aspx.

Forbes, Gordon B., Rebecca L. Jobe, and Raynette M. Richardson. "Associations between Having a Boyfriend and the Body Satisfaction and Self-Esteem of College Women: An Extension of the Lin and Kulik Hypothesis." *Journal of Social Psychology* 146, no. 3 (2006): 381–384. http://dx.doi.org/10.3200/SOCP.146.3.381-384.

Franzoi, Stephen L., and Jeffrey R. Klaiber. "Body Use and Reference Group Impact: With Whom Do We Compare Our Bodies?" *Sex Roles* 56 (2007): 205–214. https://doi.org/10.1007/s11199-006-9162-4.

Gleeson, Kate, and Hannah Frith. "(De)constructing Body Image." *Journal of Health Psychology* 11, no. 1 (2006): 79–90. https://doi.org/10.1177/1359105306058851.

King, Teresa K., Mala Matacin, Kamila S. White, and Bess H. Marcus. "A Prospective Examination of Body Image and Smoking in Women." *Body Image* 2 (2005): 19–28. http://dx.doi.org/10.1016/j.bodyim.2005.01.003.

Roy, Jane L. P., Gary R. Hunter, and Tamilane E. Blaudeau. "Percent Body Fat Is Related to Body-Shape Perception and Dissatisfaction in Students Attending an All Women's College." *Perceptual Motor Skills* 103, no. 3 (2006): 677–684. https://doi.org/10.2466/pms.103.3.677-684.

Shankar, Padmini, Jennie E. Dilworth, and Diana Cone. "Dietary Intake and Health Behavior among Black and White College Females." *Family and Consumer Science Research Journal* 33, no. 2 (2004): 159–171. https://doi.org/10.1177/1077727X04269613.

Sheets, Virgil, and Kavita Ajmere. "Are Romantic Partners a Source of College Students' Weight Concern?" *Eating Behaviors* 6, no. 1 (2005): 1–9. http://dx.doi.org/10.1016/j.eatbeh.2004.08.008.

Striegel-Moore, Ruth H., and Debra L. Franko. "Body Image Issues among Girls and Women." In *Body Image: A Handbook of Theory, Research, and Clinical Practice,* edited by T. F. Cash and T. Pruzinsky, 183–191. New York: Guilford Press, 2002.

Trampe, Debra, Diederik A. Stapel, and Frans W. Siero. "On Models and Vases: Body Dissatisfaction and Proneness to Social Comparison Effects." *Journal of Personality and Social Psychology* 92, no. 1 (2007): 106–118. http://dx.doi.org/10.1037/0022-3514.92.1.106.

BODY IMAGE GLOBALLY

Around the world, body ideals, appearance norms, and eating patterns are highly specific to the cultural norms of groups and countries. When considering body weight expectations and eating behaviors, it is important to consider access to mainstream media, the role of availability of food sources (food security), and the prosperity of nations. The effect of the media on body image is especially apparent in regions such as Fiji that were not previously exposed to media images of beauty. The Fiji study, discussed in a later entry, demonstrates how media influence resulted in more negative body image and the initiation of pathological dieting practices that did not exist prior to media presence in the country.

Food Availability

In developing countries, food availability is not always predictable. Therefore, the tendency to overeat when food is available is a survival strategy for individuals who face food insecurity. By gaining weight an individual who faces periods of involuntary starvation can conserve fat stores and calories for energy for times when food is not available. Generally, a heavy body figure or large size has been desirable in developing countries because having a rotund shape has been associated with wealth. Historically, thinness has been associated with both malnourishment and diseases (e.g., HIV, AIDS, malaria) that might be stigmatized in developing countries (e.g., Sub-Saharan Africa, South Africa, India, Brazil, Philippines). It is important to delineate the difference between eating disorders and malnutrition. Although malnutrition is a health consequence of restrictive behavior associated with eating disorders, malnutrition can also be a result of political instability, droughts, and disease; eating disorders, on the other hand, are largely psychological in nature. Although it is not possible to cover every country in this entry, certain countries will be highlighted to illustrate unique customs and expectations related to appearance and food intake.

The Influence of Westernization on Identity and Body Image

The term "*Westernization*" refers to other cultures looking to take on the identity of the body image and fashion trends seen in both the United States and Europe.

Americans and Body Image

Americans spend over $40 billion on dieting and diet-related products each year. What is even more surprising is that 35 percent of normal dieters progress to pathological dieting, and, of that 35 percent, 20–25 percent progress to partial or full syndrome eating disorders. The diet mentality has infiltrated the American way of life and not only impacts adults but also affects children and adolescents. The cultural pressure to be thin or at least prove one is trying to lose weight is not only promoted among adults but has also been inadvertently or directly taught to children and adolescents. Researchers discovered that 42 percent of first through third grade girls wanted to be thinner, while 81 percent of 10-year-old girls report being fat. There are many psychological factors that contribute to the development of eating disorders. However, the social and cultural environment plays an important role during critical developmental stages in the life cycle.

Prevalence of Eating Disorders

In the United States, as many as 10 million people have been diagnosed with an eating disorder. According to the American Psychiatric Association, women and girls account for 90–95 percent of individuals suffering from anorexia nervosa. In addition, 0.5–1.0 percent of women in America have the disorder. Forty percent of all new cases of anorexia nervosa are girls ages 15–19. In the same report, it was stated the incidence of bulimia in women ages 10–39 years tripled between 1988 and 1993. Girls and women make up 80 percent of bulimia nervosa clients. Overall, bulimia nervosa affects 1–2 percent of adolescents and young women. Estimates of the prevalence of binge eating disorder range from 1 percent to 5 percent of the population with 60 percent female and 40 percent male. Research conducted with diverse populations demonstrates eating disorders and body image concerns do not occur only among white female adolescents.

Etiology

Objectification theory suggests girls and women are naturally acculturated to internalize a person's observation about their physical features as the foremost view of themselves. This perspective regarding the self can lead to frequent and obsessive body monitoring, which can cause an increase in women's susceptibility to shame and anxiety, reduce motivation, and diminish awareness of internal bodily states. The media serve as a vehicle for reinforcing body image concerns and shame. Accumulations of such experiences may result in dieting behavior and ultimately disordered eating in young females. Eating disorders pose a public health risk and are associated with numerous health consequences. This theory is also pertinent to men, as certain kinds of communication in the media can influence both college-aged men and women to be at risk for weight control, disordered eating, and excessive exercise.

Exposure to images of highly attractive same-sex models rather than unattractive models heightens self-consciousness. This suggests attractive models in the media are likely to evoke a social comparison process, which is also referred to as the internalization of the thin ideal. To change this internalization of the thin ideal, researchers suggest a short educational message to counter negative body messages should be given to women. Although public service announcements (PSAs) have been the most effective thus far, researchers are now discovering adverse effects due to PSAs addressing the thin ideal incorrectly by showing too many thin models. This suggests an intervention without pictures might be more effective.

Both men and women experience body dissatisfaction to different extents. Both sexes being objectified in the media results in body dysmorphic disorder. For women it manifests as the thin ideal, while for men muscularity is perceived to be associated with positive attention. Researchers suggest an unrealistic comparison of bodies for both sexes can be successfully addressed with health messages using cognitive behavioral therapy (CBT). The use of narrative therapy in health messaging has been effective, as a philosophy of language proposes that meaning is socially constructed. This therapeutic approach assists persons to externalize negative body image messages by deconstructing the message into positive language.

Europe and Body Image

In the early 19th century, the Industrial Revolution took place in Europe. To illustrate the poverty that came because of this, artists would paint pictures of the thin, ill, tanned, and impoverished persons seen on the streets. Thinness and dark skin tone were associated with outside labor and were perceived as undesirable qualities in Europe. Instead, a heavier body ideal was desired and became synonymous with wealth and a limitless food supply. This more curvaceous ideal was enhanced and sexualized in the late 19th century with the invention of the corset that accentuated female body parts (i.e., hips and breasts). Today, body image dissatisfaction and disordered eating behavior in adolescent and female adults in the United Kingdom has reached the same rate as that in the United States through a similar vehicle, ultrathin models in the media. Similar to the United States, girls and women monitor their bodies and experience body shame and disordered eating. Milan has been noted as requiring ultrathin models for its catwalks. In 2006, as a result of the increase in body image disturbances and eating disorders, underweight models were banned on the Milan and Madrid catwalks. Males, on the other hand, experienced negative body image and have reported engaging in excessive exercise in attempts to strive for a more fit-looking physique. While Germany and the Netherlands had the lowest rates of eating disorders, France, Belgium, and Italy report the highest rates in Europe.

Japan and Body Image

Japanese females have been historically stereotyped by Western countries as pale-skinned, dark-haired, and subservient women in extravagant kimonos and referred to as *geishas*. This stereotype is outdated and far from reality. Japan is the fashion capital of Asia and is heavily influenced by Western models. This celebration of Western models and Caucasians as symbols of beauty has led some Asian women to reject Asiatic facial features. Although many Asian women possess epicanthic (slanted) eyes naturally, they report wanting larger eyes and resort to cosmetic surgery to create a pronounced crease on their eyelids to appear more Western. Likewise, Japanese women have elected for nose reconstructive surgery to flatten and widen their noses.

Hair color has also been a symbol of beauty for Japanese women. To strive for the more Western blond ideal, Japanese women in the 1990s would lighten their hair color by using juices from flowers and herbs. Currently, chemicals and dyes are used to lighten the naturally black hair of 80 percent of Asian females in their 20s.

Interestingly, Japanese participants have reported lower body esteem and are likely to desire the Western body ideals of Caucasians. Japanese women's reported body mass index (BMI) ideal is 19.0, while the country average is 20.7. This was significantly lower than the reported BMI ideal of Caucasian females (20.4). Data from Nakamura and colleagues indicated rates of anorexia nervosa and bulimia nervosa in Japanese females and males (ages 15–29) were 17 out of every 100,000 and 6 out of every 100,000, respectively. Over the past 25 years in Japan, eating disorders have increased six-fold and research regarding potential risk factors for the maintenance and onset of eating disorders is vital.

Nearly 20 percent of 10-year-old boys and girls have dieted in Japan; 30 percent of girls age 6 showed distorted body image, low body esteem and body consciousness, and greater social anxiety compared to other countries. In Japan approximately 30–50 percent of individuals are diagnosed and treated for social anxiety (i.e., avoidance of interpersonal relationships) called *Taijin Kyofusho*. Having overprotective or overcontrolling parents can lead to negative body image and eating disorders. Prevalence of eating disorders is high due to the inflexible nature of the modern Japanese family. Adolescents are sharing weight concerns and dieting behaviors with their mothers who encourage them to lose weight and stay thin. Comparatively, the influences that yield body dissatisfaction and restrictive dieting in American women are identical to those idealized by Japanese women. The reason is that although women in Japan today are liberated and have more freedoms, they are relegated to take a backseat and conform to traditional culture that supports male dominance. Assertiveness, a protective factor against eating disorders, is viewed in Japan as selfish, immature, and showing bad manners. Men in Japan have a tendency to want to gain weight, which leads to obsessive exercise to gain muscle. As they gain muscle they feel more positive about their bodies.

China

Although advertisements (e.g., Levi's) featuring Western models have bombarded Chinese media, Chinese people have not appeared to be as strongly influenced by them as Japanese individuals. Rather, they are influenced by the advertisements in the Chinese media that focus on the face more than the body and on selling cosmetics and hair products rather than clothing. Being thin and fragile has been connected to female beauty for centuries and it did not originate from Western ideals portrayed in the media. However, with recent cultural, political, and economic reforms in China, Western media has had the opportunity to be introduced to the people of China, since as early as 1980. Today, children in China are influenced by Western media more than their parents were. Since 970 CE, foot binding was a customary practice, as having small feet was a sign of beauty, attractiveness, identity, virtue, and womanhood. Foot binding is a two-year process that begins by wrapping binding (silk or cotton bandage) around a three- to five-year-old girl's feet to bend the toes back (minus the big toe). This forces the bones in the foot to break. Sharp objects are inserted in the bandages to be tightened daily to shrinks the foot and cuts off excess skin. The result was that a girl's feet had toes tucked under permanently meeting the heel. Mothers-in-law would choose their sons' wives based on the appearance of the feet. Foot binding was first banned in 1645, but the ban was later lifted. As a result of lifting the ban in 1895, anti–foot binding societies arose.

Centuries ago, women would mix dyes from various plants in their kitchens to create a rose color to be applied to their cheeks. Mixing oils to moisturize their skin was also common; however, there was not a concern for antiaging retinols and SPFs. The cosmetic company Estée Lauder caught wind of the Chinese women's drive for beauty through cosmetics. The company strategically placed cosmetic advertisements in the first ever Chinese magazine in 1988. Estée Lauder then opened a store in Shanghai in 1993 that led to great success and demand among Chinese women. The primary consumers of the cosmetics industry in China are women under age 50. Those older and living in the communist era have mostly rejected the modern beauty ideals of the cosmetics industry. Although there is no evidence regarding the degree of influence the Japanese *Hattou Shin* ideal has on Chinese magazine readers, there is a strong desire to have long legs. Shockingly, women will endure a painful surgical procedure where the bones in the legs are broken and then fitted with a metal brace that can be adjusted to stretch the tendons while the bone heals, adding one more inch to their height. Similar to Japanese women, Chinese women also desire a crease in their eyelid to resemble the shape of a Caucasian's eye. To fulfill this desire, women can buy beauty products such as glue to assist in the creation of a crease; however, plastic surgery is preferred.

As adolescent girls in the United States and Japan are influenced by their mothers' personal body image concerns, so are the Chinese girls. Mothers in China have been known to encourage their daughters to engage in dieting (i.e., food restriction) and exercise; mothers and daughters criticize their bodies together. This is further complicated by the controlling and strict nature of Chinese mothers and the pressure to fulfill their expectations. Young girls define diet, exercise, and body criticism by a healthy mother–daughter relationship that is disturbing and unhealthy. This activity is highly influenced by the 1979 one child only law set by the government. This law weakened family bonds and threatened the traditional understanding of self that is discovered in sibling relationships. It has also limited the opportunities for social comparison of the body and isolated a child from extended family networks, leading children to rely heavily on the media and peers to inform them about ideal body types. This has led to peers teasing and criticizing both male and female bodies. The diet behavior that both males and females glean as a result is food restriction. Interestingly, consuming Western foods is related to one's social standing and wealth, as McDonald's entered the Chinese market in the 1980s. Thus far it has resulted in sedentary work, high-calorie foods, and high-fat diets, leading to a 200 percent increase in obesity.

In Chinese culture, masculinity has been related to a man's character rather than physique and muscularity. About 30 percent of adolescent boys in China viewed themselves as underweight, felt pressure to be underweight, and had a clinical diagnosis of underweight, suggesting they were at risk for an eating disorder. Comparatively, overweight males were more likely to participate in exercise to build muscles due to body ideals seen in magazines.

India and Body Image

India has been exposed to Western media for more than a decade. Asian Indian girls and women face increasing pressures in meeting international standards in the economic sphere and in terms of body image. Girls start comparing their bodies to the thin models in magazines, leading to food restriction and bulimic behavior during adolescence. In comparison, adult women experience less body teasing than girls and adolescents, but still restrict food intake due to body dissatisfaction.

It is suggested by researchers that the Hindu religion plays a role in the disordered eating attitudes and the desire of women and girls to be thin. A vegetarian diet is frequently promoted in India, associated with health beliefs, and has roots in Ayurveda (ancient system of medicine in India) but is not specifically meant to avoid fat or energy intake. A vegetarian lifestyle supports nonviolence toward animals, a more easily digestible diet, and religious beliefs.

Africa

Ghana

In Ghana, 1.5 percent of female adolescents in two secondary schools were found to be underweight due to self-starvation to achieve perfectionist moral and academic standards. At the same time, they had a low sense of self-efficacy over academic pressures and family conflicts. The girls perceived their weight loss as positive and got the idea from religious fasting. Although religious fasting does not cause anorexia nervosa, it can be a risk factor for girls with low self-esteem and girls experimenting with diets; a short fast might give them the opportunity to enjoy feeling hungry and to discover food restriction as a coping mechanism. To compare, women in Ghana preferred an overweight body size because that meant they were more likely to marry, be successful, and prosper; however, women who were obese were dissatisfied with their bodies. This illustrates the current generational shift in body image.

Men in Ghana thought women were attracted to muscular men, and 50 percent reported a desire to become more muscular because Western media shows that muscularity brings prestige; they also believed muscularity helps intimidate other males to defend themselves and to be better at sports. It should be noted that despite a desire to increase muscle mass, Ghanaian men are generally more muscular than American men.

Senegal

Senegal is in the early stages of exposure to the Western media. Although men desire women who are overweight because a large body size is positively associated with having a good job, enough money, , a great personality, and eating healthy, 97.3 percent of women want to be thinner. Of this 97.3 percent, 12.3 percent are clinically underweight (BMI < 18.5). Women know that overweight and obesity are associated with heart disease, diabetes, and cancer. This knowledge stems from the influence of Western culture and an awareness of health. The largest effect Western culture has had in Senegal is the desire for lighter skin, which has led to chemical skin bleaching resulting in skin cancer.

South Africa

African women are thought to be protected from eating disorders because there has historically been less cultural pressure to be thin. Recently, changes in body image beliefs have been observed as South African women are pressured to be thin from an increasingly Westernized media. In South Africa, black female fashion models have a significantly lower BMI than Caucasians. In comparison, magazines in the United States show Caucasian models with a lower BMI than black models. Although attractiveness in South Africa is defined as the traditional rural heavy-set person , young black affluent people conform to the ideals in the media—that equate a thin body with a low BMI—at a higher rate than Caucasians. Male African fashion models in both South Africa and the United States have a significantly lower BMI than Caucasian models with the addition of a high muscle mass. Likewise, African men tend to engage in more disordered eating associated with gaining muscle than Caucasian males in the United States.

Meal patterns and food habits change during primary school to include food restriction, while beliefs about increased exercise change from primary school to secondary school to conform to body ideals in the media as discussed with friends. However, individuals exposed to persons diagnosed with HIV/AIDS or tuberculosis

(TB) do not want to be thin, as there is a severe societal taboo surrounding HIV/AIDS and TB-positive persons that leads to isolation. It is believed by a subset of people in South Africa that if someone is thin the person must have HIV/AIDS or TB. These people are ignored and isolated by society—thinness is not considered beautiful.

South America

Brazil is the so-called cosmetic surgery capital of the world, with more than 2.3 million reported surgical procedures in 2015. Eighty-five percent of these cosmetic surgeries were performed on women. While 15 percent of the surgeries were performed on adolescents under age 18, 38 percent were on individuals between ages 19–35, and 34 percent were on individuals ages 36–50.

Because cosmetic surgery prices are lower in Brazil than in Europe and the United States, many people travel to Brazil for breast enhancement and reduction, liposuction, tummy tucks, eyelid surgery, nose modification, and face-lifts. Two-thirds of individuals who traveled to Brazil for cosmetic surgery self-identified as Caucasian and one-third self-identified as black. In Brazil, the body has always played an important role in culture.

Brazilians have a saying that physical appearance is vital for the construction of *uma identidade nacional brasileira* (a national Brazilian identity). It is believed a beautiful body will give hope for a higher social class and eternal youth. Their body plays a role in economics and is a symbol of wealth. Women do not have cosmetic surgery for their husbands or partners who are opposed to the surgery. Rather, they are have surgery for themselves to address body dissatisfaction that occurs following a pregnancy. Reportedly women report their breasts and abdominal area are no longer tight, and cosmetic surgery can improve psychological well-being while avoiding exercise and dieting. In summary, women and female adolescents report they opt for cosmetic surgery to increase self-esteem, as plastic surgeons in Brazil perform surgery and provide psychological counseling to patients.

Mexico

Family relationships play a larger role in body image in Mexico, unlike in most other countries where the media play a big role. Although Hispanics are exposed to thin bodies in the media, families widely reject that ideal, which leads to persons less likely to use extreme measures, if any, to obtain a thin body as seen in magazines.

Hispanic girls tend to overestimate their weight, and this has resulted in body dissatisfaction and higher levels of eating disorder symptoms (i.e., fasting [4.2 percent], diuretics [7.9 percent], or laxatives [3.5 percent]) than in non-Hispanic white girls. This illustrates a social shift from the traditional ideal of a heavy body type to a thin body type as in the Western media. Although there is evidence of exposure to and influence of the Western media in Mexico, there are no data on whether Hispanic girls in Mexico have internalized the thin Western ideal.

However, in one study, low-income Hispanic girls living in Mexico showed a high rate of internalizing the thin ideal portrayed in the media, in addition to wanting to achieve a smaller body size than girls in the United States and Europe. It was unclear if girls in this study who internalized the thin ideal had strong family relationships—a protective factor in Mexico.

Hailey E. Nielson

See also: Body Image; Body Image in Males; Fiji Study; Food Security; Media; Skin Tone; Tanning Behaviors and Body Image

Bibliography

American Psychiatric Association. *Diagnostic and Statistical Manual of Mental Disorders*, 5th ed. (*DSM-5*). Washington, DC: American Psychiatric Association Publishing, 2013.

American Psychiatric Association. *Diagnostic and Statistical Manual of Mental Disorders*, 4th ed. (*DSM-4*). Washington, DC: American Psychiatric Association Publishing, 1994.

Amuna, Paul, and Francis B. Zotor. "Epidemiological and Nutrition Transition in Developing Countries: Impact on Human Health and Development." *Proceedings of the Nutrition Society* 67 (2008): 82–90. https://doi.org/10.1017/S0029665108006058.

Austin, Julia L., and Jane E. Smith. "Thin Ideal Internalization of Mexican Girls: A Test of the Sociocultural Model of Eating Disorders." *International Journal of Eating Disorders* 41 (2008): 448–457. https://doi.org/10.1002/eat.20529.

Bennett, Dinah, Michael Sharpe, Chris Freeman, and Alan Carson. "Anorexia Nervosa among Female Secondary School Students in Ghana." *British Journal of Psychiatry* 185 (2004): 312–317. https://doi.org/10.1192/bjp.185.4.312.

Calogero, Rachel M. "Objectification Processes and Disordered Eating in British Women and Men." *Journal of Health Psychology* 14 (2009). https://doi.org/10.1177/1359105309102192.

China Economic Review. "China Rises to World's Eighth Largest Beauty Market." *China Economic Review,* 2003.

Chisuwa, Naomi, and Jennifer A. O'Dea. "Body Image and Eating Disorders amongst Japanese Adolescents: A Review of the Literature." *Appetite* 54 (2010): 5–15. https://doi.org/10.1016/j.appet.2009.11.008.

Coetzeek, Vinet, and David I. Perrett. "African and Caucasian Body Ideals in South Africa and the United States." *Eating Behaviors* 12 (2010): 72–74. https://doi.org/10.1016/j.eatbeh.2010.09.006.

Dorneles de Andrade, Daniela. "On Norms and Bodies: Findings from Field Research on Cosmetic Surgery in Rio de Janeiro, Brazil." *Reproductive Health Matters* 18, no. 35 (2010): 74–83. http://dx.doi.org/10.1016/S0968-8080(10)35519-4.

Duda, Rosemary B., Naana A. Jumah, Joseph Seffah, and Richard Biritwum. "Assessment of the Ideal Body Image of Women in Accra, Ghana." *Tropical Doctor* 37, no. 4 (2007): 241–244. https://doi.org/10.1258/004947507782332883.

Duncan, Margaret Carlisle. "The Politics of Women's Body Images and Practices: Foucault, the Panopticon, and Shape Magazine." *Journal of Sport and Social Issues* 18 (1994): 48–65. https://doi.org/10.1177/019372394018001004.

Frederick, David A., Gregory M. Buchanan, Leila Sadehgi-Azar, Letitia A. Peplau, Martie G. Haselton, Anna Berezovskaya, and Ryan E. Lipinski. "Desiring the Muscular Ideal: Men's Body Satisfaction in the United States, Ukraine, and Ghana." *Psychology of Men and Muscularity* 8, no. 2 (2007): 103–117. http://dx.doi.org/10.1037/1524-9220.8.2.103.

Fredrickson, Barbara L., and Tomi-Ann Roberts. "Objectification Theory: Toward Understanding Women's Lived Experiences and Mental Health Risks." *Psychology of Women* 21 (1997): 173–206.

Hall, Howard K., Andrew P. Hill, Paul R. Appleton, and Stephe A. Kozub. "The Mediating Influence of Unconditional Self-Acceptance and Labile Self-Esteem on the Relationship between Multidimensional Perfectionism and Exercise Dependence." *Psychology of Sport and Exercise* 10 (2009): 35–44. https://doi.org/10.1018/j.psychsport.2008.05.003.

Hall-Iijima, Christine. "Asian Eyes: Body Image and Eating Disorders of Asian and Asian American Women." *Eating Disorders* 3 (1995): 5–19.

Hoek, Hans Wijbrand, and Daphne van Hoeken. "Review of the Prevalence and Incidence of Eating Disorders." *International Journal of Eating Disorders 34, no. 4* (2003): 383–396. https://doi.org/101992/eat.10222.

Holdsworth, M., A. Gartner, E. Landais, B. Maire, and F. Delpeuch. "Perceptions of Healthy and Desirable Body Size in Urban Senegalese Women." *International Journal of Obesity* 28, no. 12 (2004): 1561–1568. https://doi.org/10.1038/sj.ijo.0802739.

Howden-Chapman, Philippa, and Johan Mackenback. "Poverty and Painting: Representations in 19th Century Europe." *British Medical Journal* 325 (2002): 1502–1505. https://doi.org/10.1136.1502.

"ISAPS International Survey on Aesthetic/Cosmetic: Procedures Performed in 2015." *ISAPS.org.* Accessed November 21, 2017. https://www.isaps.org/Media/Default/global-statistics/2016%20ISAPS%20Results.pdf.

Jackson, Todd, and Hong Chen. "Factor Structure of the Sociocultural Attitudes towards Appearance Questionnaire-3 (SATAQ-3) among Adolescent Boys in China." *Body Image* 7, no. 4 (2010): 349–355. https://doi.org/10.1016/j.bodyim.2010.07.003.

Kayano, Mami, Kazuhiro Yoshiuchi, Samir Al-Adawi, Nonna Viernes, Atsu S. Dorvlo, Hiroaki Kumano, Tomifusa Kuboki, and Akira Akabayashi. "Eating Attitudes and Body Dissatisfaction in Adolescents: Cross-Cultural Study." *Psychiatry and Clinical Neurosciences* 62, no. 1 (2008): 17–25. https://doi.org/10.1111/j.1440-1819.2007.01772.x.

Kowner, Rotem. "Japanese Body Image: Structure and Esteem Scores in a Cross-Cultural Perspective." *International Journal of Psychology* 37, no. 3 (2002): 149–159. https://doi.org/10.1080/0020759014300298.

Leahy, Trisha, and R. Harrigan. "Using Narrative Therapy in Sport Psychology Practice: Application to a Psychoeducational Body Image Program." *The Sport Psychologist* 20 (2006): 480–494.

Long, Clive G., Jenny Smith, Marie Midgley, and Tony Cassidy. "Overexercising in Anorexic and Normal Samples: Behavior and Attitudes." *Journal of Mental Health* 4 (1993): 321. https://doi.org/10.3109/09638239309016967.

Macia, Enguerran, Priscilla Buboz, and Lamine Gueye. "Prevalence of Obesity in Dakar." *Obesity Reviews* 11, no. 10 (2010): 691–694. https://doi.org/10.1111/j.1467-789X.2010.00749.x.

Mao, John. "Foot Binding: Beauty and Torture." *The Internet Journal of Biological Anthropology* 1, no. 2 (2008).

Martinelli, Valentina, Ottavia Colombo, Cristiano Nichini, Ilaria Repossi, Piergiuseppe Vinai, and Anna Tagliabue. "High Frequency of Psychopathology in Subjects Wishing to Lose Weight: An Observational Study in Italian Subjects." *Public Health Nutrition* 14, no. 2 (2010): 373–376. https://doi.org/10.1017/S1368980010001576.

McNutt, Suzanne W., Yuanreng Hu, George B. Schreiber, Patricia B. Crawford, Eva Obarzanek, and Laural Mellin. "A Longitudinal Study of the Dietary Practices of

Black and White Girls 9 and 10 Years Old at Enrollment: The NHLBI Growth and Health Study." *Journal of Adolescent Health* (1997): 27–37. https://doi.org/10.1016 /S1054-139X(96)00176-0.

Mond, Jonathan J., Phillipa J. Hay, Bryan Rodgers, Cathy Owen, and James Mitchell. "Correlates of the Use of Purging and Non-Purging Methods of Weight Control in a Community Sample of Women." *Australian & New Zealand Journal of Psychiatry* 40 (2006): 136–142. https://doi.org/10.1080/j.1440-2006.01760.x.

Mukai, Takayo, Akiko Kambara, and Yuji Sasaki. "Body Dissatisfaction, Need for Social Approval and Eating Disturbances among Japanese and American College Women." *Sex Roles* 39 (1998): 751–763. doi: 0021-9630/94.

Nagaoka, Tomoaki, Solchi Watanabe, Kiyoko Sakurai, Etsuo Kunieda, Satoshi Watanabe, Masao Taki, and Yukio Yamanaka. "Development of Realistic High-Resolution Whole-Body Voxel Models of Japanese Adult Males and Females of Average Height and Weight, and Application of Models to Radio-Frequency Electromagnetic-Field Dosimetry." *Physics in Medicine and Biology* 49 (2004): 1–15. doi: 0031-9155/04/010001+15.

Nakamura, Kei, Kenji Kitanishi, Yuko Miyake, Kazuyuki Hahsimoto, and Mikiko Kubota. "The Neurotic Versus Delusional Subtype of Taijin-Kyofu-sho: Their DSM Diagnoses." *Psychiatry and Clinical Neurosciences* 56, no. 6 (2008): 595–601. https://doi .org/10.1046/j.1440-819.2002.01061.x.

Park, Sung-Yeon, Jacqueline Hitchon McSweeney, and Gi Woong Yun. "Intervention of Eating Disorder Symptomatology Using Educational Communication Messages." *Communication Research* 36 (5) (2009) 677–697. https://doi.org/10.1177/0093650209338910.

Preti, Antonio, Giovanni de Girolamo, Gemma Vilagut, Jordi Alonso, Ron de Graaf, Ronny Bruffaerts, Koen Demyttenaere, Alejandra Pinto-Meza, Josep Maria Haro, and Piero Morosini. "The Epidemiology of Eating Disorders in Six European Countries: Results of the ESEMeD WMH Project." *Journal of Psychiatric Research* 43 (2008): 1125–1132. https://doi.org/10.1016/j.jpsychires.2009.04.003.

Puoane, Thandi, Lungiswa Tsolekile, and Nelia Steyn. "Perceptions about Body Image and Sizes among Black African Girls Living in Cape Town." *Ethnicity and Disease* 20, no. 1 (2010): 29–34.

Shisslak, Catherine M., M. Marjorie Crago, and Linda S. Estes. "The Spectrum of Eating Disturbances." *International Journal of Eating Disorders* 18, no. 3 (1995): 209–219. https:// doi.org/10.1002/1098-108X(199511)18:<209::AID EAT2260180303>3.0CO;2-E.

Shroff, Hemal, and Kevin J. Thompson. "Body Image and Eating Disturbance in India: Media and Interpersonal Influences." *International Journal of Eating Disorders* 35, no. 2 (2004): 198–203. https://doi.org/10.1002/eat.10229.

Sira, Natalia, and Carmel Parker White. "Individual and Familial Correlates of Body Satisfaction in Male and Female College Students." *Journal of American College Health,* 58, no. 6 (2010): 507–513. https://doi.org/10.1080/07448481003621742.

Smith, Delia E., Marsha D. Marcus, Cora E. Lewis, Marian Fitgibbon, and Pamela Schreiner. "Prevalence of Binge Eating Disorder, Obesity and Depression in a Biracial Cohort of Young Adults." *Annals of Behavioral Medicine* 20 (1998): 227–232. https:// doi.org/10.1007/BF02884965.

Swami, Viren, Katia Poulogianni, and Adrian Furnham. "The Influence of Resource Availability on Preferences for Human Body Weight and Non-Human Objects." *Journal of Articles in Support of the Null Hypothesis* 4, no. 1 (2006): 17–28.

Thornton, Bill, and Maurice, Jason. "Physique Contrast Effect: Adverse Impact of Idealized Body Images for Women." *Sex Roles* 37 (1997): 433–439. https://doi .org/10.1023/A:1025609624848.

Victoria, Cesar G., Linda Adair, Caroline Fall, Pedro C. Hallal, Reynaldo Martorell, Linda Richter, and Harshpal Singh Sachdev. "Maternal and Child Undernutrition: Consequences for Adult Health and Human Capital." *Lancet* 371, no. 26 (2008). https://doi.org/10.1016/501406736(07)61692-4.

Xu, Xiaoyan, David Mellor, Melanie Kiehne, Lina A. Ricciardelli, Marita P. McCabe, and Yangana Xu. "Body Dissatisfaction, Engagement in Body Change Behaviors and Socio-cultural Influences on Body Image among Chinese Adolescents." *Body Image* 7, no. 2 (2010): 156–164. https://doi.org/10.1016/j.bodyim.2009.11.003.

Yamamiya, Yuko, Hemal Shroff, and Kevin J. Thompson. "The Tripartite Influence Model of Body Image and Eating Disturbance: A Replication with a Japanese Sample." *International Journal of Eating Disorders* 41, no.1 (2008): 88–91. https://doi.org/10.1002/eat.

BODY IMAGE IN MALES

Although it was once believed only women had body image concerns, researchers and practitioners have recently become aware of growing body dissatisfaction in men. Most experts before the 1990s dismissed body image concerns among males. In the past 25 years, it has become clear that many boys and men are dissatisfied with their bodies, although this dissatisfaction often stems from sources different from females. Advances in research have been accompanied by changes in the sociocultural climate have made body weight, size, and shape increasingly more important to boys and men.

Early Research on Body Image in Males

Increased awareness of the prevalence of anorexia nervosa and bulimia nervosa in females in the 1970s and 1980s encouraged a focus on the desire to lose weight in girls and women. Thus, most studies were designed to detect body image concerns related to perceptions of being overweight. In one study, men and women were presented with same-sex drawings that ranged from very thin to obese. The women rated their current body as heavier than their ideal drawing, but the men rated their current body as similar to their ideal drawing. Although most researchers ignored negative body image as a male concern, a nationwide survey of body image in 1986 revealed 44 percent of men were afraid of becoming fat. Furthermore, eating disorders have been acknowledged in males as far back as the 1600s, indicating that some men do express concerns about their body. Certain subpopulations of males may be more at risk for body image concerns related to weight loss. For example, boys and men who compete in sports where being lean is believed to give them a performance advantage (e.g., cross-country running, diving) or where there are distinct weight classes (e.g., wrestling) are more likely to engage in unhealthy eating behaviors than males who do not compete in these sports.

Sex Differences in Body Image

Researchers have discovered that body dissatisfaction may be experienced differently for males than for females. In one study, young adult males were nearly equally

Boys and Men with Eating Disorders: An Interview with Dr. Nick Galli

Dr. Nick Galli is an assistant professor in the Department of Health, Kinesiology, and Recreation at the University of Utah. In this role he teaches a variety of health-related courses, including those focused on body image and eating disorders for both undergraduate and graduate students. Dr. Galli's research related to body image, weight pressures, and disordered eating in competitive athletes has been published in scholarly journals such as *Body Image, Eating Behaviors,* and *The Journal of Clinical Sport Psychology.* He is a certified consultant of the Association for Applied Sport Psychology, and in this capacity works with athletes and sport teams on mental skills such as intensity regulation, concentration, communication, and self-confidence for performance improvement. Prior to his current position at Utah, he spent two years as faculty member in the Department of Kinesiology at California State University at Northridge. Dr. Galli holds a PhD in the Psychosocial Aspects of Sport from the University of Utah, an MS in Sport Studies from Miami (OH) University, and a BA in Psychology from Sacramento State University.

People tend to associate eating disorders with girls and women. Do boys and men also suffer from eating disorders? Why are boys and men often overlooked when it comes to eating disorder diagnosis and treatment?

Because anorexia nervosa (AN) and bulimia nervosa (BN) are characterized by a desire to lose weight, which aligns with the thin ideal for women in Western cultures, boys and men have not historically been considered at risk for eating disorders. However, as the research suggests approximately 10 million men in the United States will experience a clinical eating disorder at some point in their lives. Furthermore, men represent 25 percent of the cases of AN and BN, and 36 percent of binge eating disorder (BED) cases according to Dr. Hudson and his colleagues. Eating disorders have been stereotyped as a female disease, which contributes to a gender bias. We also know that boys and men are less likely to seek treatment than girls and women. The bias can even occur in the treatment setting as health care providers are much more likely to diagnose girls and women with eating disorders than their male counterparts. Previously the clinical criteria for anorexia nervosa excluded boys and men due to the lack of menstrual cycle requirement, but this has changed with the latest edition of the *Diagnostic and Statistical Manual of Mental Disorders.*

What does negative body image look like for boys and men? What are contributing factors for disordered eating and body image disturbances among males? Can media play a role too?

In some ways negative body image for boys and men appears similar to negative body image in girls and women. Low body satisfaction, distorted perception of body shape and size, and behavioral efforts to alter the body are characteristic of poor body image for both men and women. The difference lies in the desired outcome. Whereas many women seek a body that is toned yet petite, many men prefer a body that is bigger, leaner, and more muscular than they perceive their body to be. The male body ideal is just as unrealistic as the female body ideal.

Contributing factors to eating disorders for both men and women include biological (e.g., brain structure), personality (e.g., traits such as perfectionism), familial (e.g., parental role modeling), and environmental (e.g., media) factors. As compared to women, one difference for men who experience anorexia nervosa and bulimia nervosa is that they are more likely to have been overweight in youth in a recent research study. And just as in girls and women, mass media does play a role in shaping the body image of boys and men. In a recent study, the consumption of men's magazines such as *Men's Health* predicted a higher drive for muscularity in teenage boys.

Are certain male athletes at risk for developing eating disorders? Why or why not?

It does appear that boys and men who participate in certain sports are more at risk for disordered eating and eating disorders. One study found that wrestlers were significantly more likely than male nonathletes to engage in disordered eating. Because wrestlers must compete within a specified weight class, the pressure to maintain or lose weight is heightened. Furthermore, long-standing norms create a culture wherein "cutting weight" by any means necessary (e.g., exercising in a sauna, food restriction) is often considered a normal, accepted, and even expected part of the sport by coaches and teammates. Beyond wrestling, male athletes in sports such as distance running and diving may also be at higher risk for disordered eating due to perceived performance and aesthetic gains associated with losing weight.

What should coaches, family members, and other sport professionals do to prevent eating disorders among male athletes?

The number one thing that coaches, family members, and sport professionals can do to prevent eating disorders in male athletes is to create a culture where health is valued over appearance and performance. Although an emphasis on health over performance may be easier to maintain at the lower levels of sport, even at the elite level it can be argued that athletes cannot perform at their best when their health is compromised through behaviors such as dietary restriction, purging, and excessive exercise. Unless an athlete's weight is becoming an obvious health issue, coaches should leave such discussions to a registered dietician with training and experience in sport nutrition. In other words, having formal weight requirements for team tryouts or public weigh ins should be avoided. Furthermore, teammates, coaches, and family members should refrain from teasing or weight-related comments.

How can we do a better job recognizing problems in boys and men?

The first step is an awareness that boys and men can and do experience body image disturbances and eating disorders. Although these issues can manifest in a desire to lose weight and be thin, and obsessive desire to gain muscle mass is an added concern for boys and men. Second, we should pay attention to their language and body-related comments. How do they talk about their body? Do they seem to make frequent comparisons with the bodies of men portrayed on TV and online? Third, pay attention to their behaviors. Drastic dietary changes, new or increased use of dietary supplements, and/or spending an excessive amount of time exercising are all warning signs of a possible eating disorder.

divided between a desire to lose weight (45 percent) and a desire to gain weight (40 percent). Only 5 percent of the men expressed satisfaction with their current weight, which refuted the notion that most men have a positive body image. The findings from studies in the 1980s suggested body image concerns were not just a problem for women. However, the nature of the concerns (i.e., weight gain vs. weight loss) appeared to differ between males and females. Research on body type preference identified another dimension of body image dissatisfaction in males. One study revealed that although 60 percent of males identified themselves as endomorphs (i.e., a body type characterized by high body fat and a tendency to gain weight easily), 95 percent reported a preference for the mesomorph type (i.e., a body type characterized by an athletic physique and the ability to easily gain or lose weight).

Beyond Weight: Contemporary Body Image Research in Males

Research conducted in the 1990s and 2000s highlighted the role of muscularity in constructing males' body image. Specifically, researchers and practitioners developed a dual-pathway model to depict body image dissatisfaction in boys and men that includes both weight and muscularity for male body image. Western males' drive for muscularity may predict a higher tendency toward the use of body/performance enhancing substances, and enhanced risk for weight-related health conditions such as type 2 diabetes and coronary heart disease.

Muscle Dysmorphia

In extreme cases, the drive for muscularity by males may lead to a body image disturbance known as muscle dysmorphia. Also known as reverse anorexia, or bigorexia, muscle dysmorphia is characterized by a variety of cognitive and behavioral symptoms related to weight and muscle gain. The predominant cognitive symptom of muscle dysmorphia is an obsessive preoccupation with one's body being too small or weak. Preoccupation with the body can lead to inaccurate perceptions of body size and shape, high anxiety, and an inability to focus on other important aspects of life. Behavioral symptoms include excessive spent lifting weights, monitoring diet, and mirror checking. The condition was first noted by psychiatrist Harrison Pope in a series of studies with male bodybuilders conducted in the late 1980s and early 1990s. In one study published in *Comprehensive Psychiatry* in 1993, Pope and his colleagues conducted clinical interviews with 108 bodybuilders. Although three of the bodybuilders reported formerly suffering from anorexia nervosa, nine bodybuilders reported symptoms of muscle dysmorphia. Of these nine, four used steroids because they believed they looked too small and another four developed muscle dysmorphia symptoms after taking steroids. Pope and colleagues' initial findings sparked a plethora of studies focused on muscle dysmorphia. Researchers have been particularly interested in the factors that lead to body image dissatisfaction and muscle dysmorphia in males.

Causes of Body Image Dissatisfaction in Males

Just as with females, a variety of body biological, psychological, and sociocultural factors contribute to body image dissatisfaction in males. In a study of 434 adolescent boys, two of these factors were related with body modification strategies aimed at weight loss, weight gain, and the use of food supplements. Specifically, more pubertal growth (a biological factor) was related to increased use of food supplements, and pressure from parents and peers to increase muscle mass, increase weight, and decrease weight (sociocultural factors) was related to greater use of weight and muscle change strategies. In another study, higher self-esteem (a psychological factor) was related to less body image dissatisfaction in men and women across a two-year time period. Thus, it is clear that body image dissatisfaction in males results from numerous sources.

Male Body Image Dissatisfaction and Hegemonic Masculinity

Perhaps the most intriguing influences on male body image dissatisfaction are sociocultural or environmental. For many males, muscularity is a powerful symbol of masculinity. Muscularity is just one aspect of hegemonic masculinity. Hegemonic masculinity refers to the dominant conceptions of what it means to be a man. In Western culture, the hegemonically masculine male is physically and mentally strong, competitive, and willing to take risks. Research findings have supported the link between masculinity and muscularity. In one study, men with traditional attitudes about masculinity (i.e., men who subscribed to hegemonic masculinity) wanted to be more muscular than men with less traditional attitudes. Thus, body image dissatisfaction associated with muscularity signals simultaneous low self-worth and insecurity regarding one's masculinity. According to many experts, the most important reason for body image concerns on the rise for males is that they are exposed to increasingly objectified images of the male body. These images serve as a constant reminder to males of the muscular ideal inherent to hegemonic masculinity (i.e., lean and muscular). Three specific sources appear to be most influential (1) parents and peers, (2) media images, and (3) action figures.

Parents and Peers

Weight- and body-related messages from friends and family are a powerful source of influence for adolescent boys. In one study of boys ages 12–15, body feedback from fathers and male friends was influential in the boys' adoption of body change strategies, such as the use of food supplements and exercise to add muscle mass. Another study revealed that males rated peers of the opposite sex as most important in evaluating their body. However, peer teasing was not related to a drive for muscularity. Although females generally report more weight- and body-related parental pressure than males, parents may be less aware of signs of body image dissatisfaction in boys. For example, a vigorous commitment to lifting weights and consuming food supplements by their sons may appear to be quite healthy behaviors to many parents. However, due to the relatively recent awareness of male-specific body image disturbances such as muscle dysmorphia, parents may fail to evaluate their son's body image attitudes and behaviors as carefully as they would a daughter who decided to go on a diet. Thus, potentially dangerous body change strategies may go unnoticed by the parents of boys. Although parental knowledge and awareness of body image concerns in boys is yet to be examined, such research would add to professionals' understanding of parents' role in preventing and/or exacerbating male body image dissatisfaction.

Media Images

Just as females can be negatively influenced by media images of ultrathin women, so too can portrayals of hyperlean and muscular men increase body image dissatisfaction in males. Supporting the idea that body shape changes are more relevant for males than body weight changes, one study showed that popular men's magazines contain a significantly higher ratio of shape advertisements (17) to weight-change advertisements (5). Male models in men's magazines help shape perceptions of the ideal male body. A recent examination of the depiction of male bodies in men's magazines revealed that sexualized and objectified images of men were commonplace. Further, the magazines included content to help men either gain muscle mass or lose weight. Photographs and stories in men's magazines do not go unnoticed by males. There is clear evidence that exposure to male models in men's magazines results in depression, anxiety, drive for muscularity, and body image dissatisfaction in males. Men are not alone in their exposure to idealized body images. White preadolescent boys exposed to video game magazines displayed an increased drive for muscularity over a one-year period. Some researchers have suggested boys have not been taught to be critical of magazine content as girls have and this is a necessary step to protect them from the influence of objectified media images.

Action Figures

Perhaps the most intriguing source of body image influence are the toy action figures played with by many children. Much information about conceptions of the ideal male body can be learned by simply observing how these toys have changed over time. In one study comparing the scaled body measurements of G.I. Joe figures from the 1970s to the 1990s, the figures exhibited notable growth in their waist (31.7 to 36.5 inches), chest (44.4 to 54.8 inches), and biceps (12.2 to 26.8 inches). Hypermuscular action figures have a negative influence on males' body image. In one study, young adult men who emulated unrealistically muscular action figures had more body image dissatisfaction than men who emulated more lifelike action figures.

Programs to Promote Positive Body Image in Males

Given the multifaceted nature of body image dissatisfaction, programs to promote healthy body image in males should focus on both psychological and sociocultural factors. The few systematic programs implemented have focused on self-esteem, peer relationships, and acceptance of individual differences. However, the programs have yielded mixed results. Professionals interested in developing a program should consider the following guidelines: (1) as previously stated, include a focus on both psychological and sociocultural factors, (2) target older adolescents (15–18 years), as issues of body weight, shape, and size are likely to be more salient for this group than for younger adolescents, and (3) develop programs for specific at-risk populations (e.g., low self-esteem, poor peer relations) rather than all-in-one programs.

Nick Galli

See also: Bigorexia; Body Image; Bodybuilding; Drive for Muscularity; Masculinity Ideals; Media; Military; Muscle Dysmorphia; Sports

Bibliography

Cash, Thomas F. "Body-Image Attitudes: Evaluation, Investment, and Affect." *Perceptual & Motor Skills* 78 (1994): 1168. https://doi.org/10.2466/pms.1994.78.3c.1168.

Cash, Thomas F., Barbara A. Winstead, and Louis H. Janda. "The Great American Shape-Up: Body Image Survey Report." *Psychology Today* 20 (1986): 30–37.

Drewnowski, Adam, and Doris K. Yee. "Men and Body Image: Are Males Satisfied with Their Body Weight?" *Psychosomatic Medicine,* 49 (1987): 626–634. https://doi.org/10.1.1.504.7078.

Hobza, Cody L., and Aaron B. Rochlen. "Gender Role Conflict, Drive for Muscularity, and the Impact of Ideal Media Portrayals on Men." *Psychology of Men & Masculinity* 10 (2009): 120–130. http://dx.doi.org/10.1037/a0015040.

Jones, Diane C., and Joy K. Crawford. "Adolescent Boys and Body Image: Weight and Muscularity Concerns as Dual Pathways to Body Dissatisfaction." *Journal of Youth & Adolescence* 34 (2005): 629–636. https://doi.org/10.1007/s10964-005-8951-3.

Lerner, Richard M., and Sam J. Korn. "The Development of Body-Build Stereotypes in Males." *Child Development* 43 (1972): 908–920. https://doi.org/10.2307/1127641.

McCabe, Marita P., and Lina A. Ricciardelli. "Parent, Peer, and Media Influences on Body Image and Strategies to Both Increase and Decrease Body Size among Adolescent Boys and Girls." *Adolescence* 36 (2001): 225–240. http://dx.doi.org/10.1016/j.brat.2004.05.004.

Neumark-Sztainer, Dianne, Melanie M. Wall, Mary Story, and Cheryl L. Perry. "Correlates of Unhealthy Weight-Control Behaviors among Adolescents: Implications for Prevention Programs." *Health Psychology* 22 (2003): 88–98. http://dx.doi.org/10.1037/0278-6133.22.1.88.

Pope, Harrison G., David L. Katz, and James I. Hudson. "Anorexia Nervosa and 'Reverse Anorexia' among 108 Male Bodybuilders." *Comprehensive Psychiatry* 34 (1993): 406–409. http://doi.org/10.1016/0010-440X(93)90066-D.

Pope, Harrison G., and Roberto Olivardia. "Evolving Ideals of Male Body Image as Seen through Action Toys." *International Journal of Eating Disorders* 26 (1999): 65–72.

BODY MASS INDEX

Body mass index (BMI) is a way to measure whether one is underweight, healthy weight, overweight, or obese. In 2017, two-thirds of U.S. adults and one-fifth of U.S. children were considered overweight or obese based on BMI scores. BMI is calculated by taking body weight in kilograms and dividing by height in meters squared (i.e., kg/m²). BMI does not measure one's body fat or consider the size of one's frame.

History of Body Mass Index

The body mass index, originally the Quetelet index, was invented in Belgium between 1830 and 1850 by Adolphe Quetelet. The term *body mass index* was popularized by Ancel Keys in his 1972 paper discussing obesity. The current U.S. BMI charts indicate a BMI greater than or equal to 30 is considered obese and that 25–29.9 is considered overweight for adults. Children are measured for BMI using sex-specific, age-growth charts; children at or above the 95th percentile for sex and age are defined as obese; children with BMIs between 85th and 95th percentiles were considered overweight. Studies using competitive athletes have illustrated the controversy about the measure of obesity, such as a well-known study that found 60 percent of National Football League players were overweight or obese. A separate study with varsity high school football players found 28 percent of players were at risk of being overweight, 45 percent were overweight, and 9 percent met the criteria for being morbidly obese. Although obesity has become a major societal concern, many researchers use body composition (percentage of body fat) and waist circumference (distance around the smallest point of the waist) in addition to BMI to determine overweight and obesity.

BMI and Eating Disorders

Although the BMI formula has received more attention to assess levels of obesity, BMI can also be used to determine whether an individual is underweight. Generally, optimal weight has been represented by a BMI score between 20 and 25; however, this varies by country. For example, Hong Kong and Japan have stringent cutoffs for overweight (BMI = 23) and obesity (BMI = 25 and higher). The World Health Organization reported a BMI lower than 18.5 may indicate malnutrition or an eating disorder, with severely underweight indicated by a score lower than 16.0. For eating disorders, consideration of being underweight (BMI < 17.5) is often used by medical professionals as an informal criterion for the diagnosis of anorexia nervosa and/or to determine an individual's appropriate level of care. However, BMI is not formally included in the *Diagnostic and Statistical Manual of Mental Disorders, fifth edition*. Furthermore, BMI is typically monitored in a hospital or residential eating disorder treatment setting to ensure adequate weight restoration occurs. If BMI drops below a certain level (as determined by the medical provider on an individual basis), an anorexic client may require tube feeding and is likely to be restricted from physical activity (i.e., advised bed rest).

BMI Report Cards

Using BMI for identifying children at risk for weight-related problems has been a controversial practice due to the limitations of BMI and the ability to offer adequate education. Some states (e.g., Texas) have introduced BMI report cards in schools notifying parents if their children are overweight or obese. There have been concerns about how the weighing takes place and the possibility that focusing on weight could contribute to dieting and disordered eating. Another concern is whether parents will become the food police once they receive the BMI report card without having the tools to provide healthy meals at home.

Justine J. Reel

See also: Assessment; Obesity; Teasing; Treatment; Weight Stigma

Bibliography

Cole, Tim J., Katherine M. Flegal, Dasha Nicholls, and Alan A. Jackson. "Body Mass Index Cut Offs to Define Thinness in Children and Adolescents: International Survey." *British Medical Journal* 335 (2007): 194–202. https://doi.org/10.1136/bmj.39238.399444.55.

Dietz, William H., Mary T. Story, and Laura Leviton. "Introduction to Issues and Implications of Screening, Surveillance, and Reporting of Children's BMI." *Pediatrics* 124 (2009): S1–S2. https://doi.org/10.1542/peds.2008-3586C.

Harp, Joyce B., and Lindsay Hecht. "Obesity in the National Football League." *Journal of the American Medical Association* 292, no. 24 (2005): 2999. https://doi.org/10.1001/jama.293.9.1061-b.

Khan, Laura K., Kathleen Sobush, Dana Keener, Kenneth Goodman, Amy Lowry, Jakub Kakietek, and Susan Zaro. "Recommended Community Strategies and Measurements to Prevent Obesity in the United States." *Morbidity and Mortality Weekly Report: Recommendations and Reports* 58 (2009): 1–29.

Laurson, Kelly R., and Joey C. Eisenmann. "Prevalence of Overweight among High School Football Linemen." *Journal of the American Medical Association* 297, no. 4 (2007): 363–364. https://doi.org/10.1001/jama.297.4.363.

Schocker, Laura. "More Schools Including Weight, BMI on Report Cards." *The Huffington Post.* Last modified June 19, 2011. Accessed November 21, 2017. http://www.huffingtonpost.com/2011/04/19/bmi-schools_n_850776.html.

BODYBUILDING

Bodybuilding has been around for more than 100 years, but the sport did not become a part of mainstream culture until the 1960s when personalities such as Arnold Schwarzenegger and Lou Ferrigno became household names. However, bodybuilding has slowly increased its visibility supported by magazines, such as *Men's Health* and *Flex*.

Although stone lifting, for example, occurred in ancient Greek and Egyptian societies, it was not primarily for physical display, as is the case in bodybuilding. The term *bodybuilder* refers to someone who trains regularly with free weights or machines to increase muscularity and reduce body fat for the purpose of competing. A person who is into bodybuilding engages in weight training to enhance his physique and appearance. However, he or she does not necessarily compete in the sport of bodybuilding. Competitive bodybuilding is generally divided into natural (with drug testing) and non-natural (no drug testing) competitions.

There are several reasons why someone might want to be a bodybuilder. For both males and females, self-esteem and empowerment, emulation of a hero figure, health reasons, or even previous participation in sports are all frequently cited reasons. A recent study of male bodybuilders found previous sport participation and emulation were more important than self-esteem in making the decision to be a bodybuilder.

Bodybuilding and Body Image

Competitive bodybuilding and body image are intertwined; how one's image is perceived on stage determines victory or defeat. Therefore, it is not surprising that many bodybuilders exhibit poor body image. It is a vicious cycle where a bodybuilder continues to train, but is unable to see the improvements made, or thinks the improvements are inadequate. In sum, a bodybuilder is unable to accept his or her physique and there is the perception that a body part can be improved in some way.

Although competitive bodybuilders wear revealing attire while they compete, many do not like to expose their bodies for public inspection outside of their sport. This physique protection demonstrated by many bodybuilders may lead to them wearing bulky clothing to cover their physique or to appear larger. Conversely, other competitive bodybuilders prefer to expose their muscularity and engage in body checking to monitor progress (e.g., mirror checking). These bodybuilders may also seek attention from the opposite sex and other competitors. They may make social comparisons with other bodybuilders during training and competitions.

Competitive bodybuilders are not the only athletes who experience poor body image perceptions. Athletes who weight train for physique motives but do not compete as bodybuilders also exhibit similar behaviors as competitive bodybuilders. What is clear is that a continual focus on one's physique can contribute to a negative body image and other harmful practices.

Bodybuilding and Eating Disorders

It is hardly surprising a bodybuilder focused on his physique relies heavily on a strict nutritional regimen. In fact, most bodybuilders are very knowledgeable regarding nutrition and supplements and take great care monitoring what they put in their bodies. Due to the restrictive practices that are normative in bodybuilding, many competitive bodybuilders exhibit eating practices that resemble clinical eating disorders. Although many competitive bodybuilders are significantly more conscientious about nutritional habits than the average person, the more accurate label is usually disordered eating, unless the practices continue during the off-season.

Because a bodybuilder goes through a period of competition followed by an off-season, nutritional behaviors usually vary radically. During the off-season, the main aim of a competitor is to build as much muscle as possible through anabolism.

This dietary practice requires consuming large quantities of both carbohydrates and protein and a bodybuilder is likely to gain substantial weight. Then, during the preseason, which lasts for approximately 6–12 weeks prior to competition, a bodybuilder begins to restrict diet with the intention of burning fat while retaining muscle mass. During the competitive season, a bodybuilder continues to burn as much fat as possible while retaining muscle mass.

Although this yo-yo dieting follows strict caloric guidelines, there is little doubt the method by which this occurs is of serious concern. These radical shifts in diet result in extreme changes in weight, and the preseason can be extremely painful and dangerous. For example, when preparing for a competition, one bodybuilder experienced extreme pain in the soles of his feet caused by lack of fat in the tissue. He also reportedly suffered from dizziness, shortness of breath, increased heart rate and palpitations, and several psychological disturbances. Immediately following a major competition close, many bodybuilders will gorge themselves on food, as their body has been craving it for days or even weeks. Weight gain is often rapid and the cycle of weight gain followed by reduction begins for another season.

Timothy M. Baghurst

See also: Body Image in Males; Drive for Muscularity; Muscle Dysmorphia; Sports

Bibliography

Baghurst, Timothy M., and Cathy Lirgg. "Characteristics of Muscle Dysmorphia in Male Football, Weight Training, and Competitive Natural and Non-natural Bodybuilding Samples." *Body Image* 6 (2009): 221–227. http://dx.doi.org/10.1016/j.bodyim.2009.03.002.

Chapman, David L. *Sandow the Magnificent: Eugen Sandow and the Beginnings of Bodybuilding.* Urbana: University of Illinois Press, 1994.

Fussell, Samuel W. *Muscle.* New York: Avon Books, 1992.

Klein, Alan M. "Special Issue." *Sport in Society* (2007): 1073–1119.

Lambert, Charles P., Laura L. Frank, and William J. Evans. "Macronutrient Considerations for the Sport of Bodybuilding." *Sports Medicine* 34 (2004): 317–327. https://doi.org/10.2165/00007256-200434050-00004.

Parish, Anthony, Timothy M. Baghurst, and Ronna Turner. "Becoming Competitive Amateur Bodybuilders: Identification of Contributors." *Psychology of Men & Masculinity* 12 (2010): 152–159. http://dx.doi.org/10.1037/a0018091.

BODYWORKS

The BodyWorks educational program was developed in 2006 by the Office on Women's Health in the U.S. Department of Health and Human Services to teach parents and caregivers of adolescents about healthy nutrition and exercise habits. Using a social cognitive theoretical framework that focuses on both an individual and his or her environment, the BodyWorks curriculum uses parents as role models for healthy behaviors in a family system. Parents are taught experiential lessons with opportunities for hands-on practice of healthy skills. The parent training is conducted through ten 90-minute sessions each week. Adolescents join parents for two of the sessions to reinforce the lessons and give teenagers an exposure to healthy nutrition and activity concepts.

The BodyWorks program follows a train-the-trainer model in which leaders receive training so they can teach parents in their community. BodyWorks trainers represent almost all of the 50 states. Although receiving the training to conduct the BodyWorks program may vary in cost, a free toolkit is provided to all trainers and parent participants. Each toolkit includes guides for parents, teen females and teen males, quizzes, games, and interviews. Additionally, food and fitness journals allow for tracking of eating and exercise behaviors and a recipe book is provided with quick healthy food selections. A meal planner magnet and shopping list (i.e., a form to help families plan weekly menus before they go to the grocery store) are also included in the BodyWorks toolkits.

The BodyWorks program includes lessons regarding portion sizes of fruits, vegetables, and cheese as well as the benefits of various vitamins in the diet. The significance of eating breakfast and some healthy options (e.g., smoothies) are suggested. Fast food alternatives are provided to parents with quick meal ideals and accompanying recipes. Many programs will allow participants to practice preparing a healthy snack (e.g., fruit kabobs) during the lesson to increase confidence and the likelihood that nutritional choices will be replicated in the home environment. Strategies for increasing the physical activity of teens (e.g., limits on screen time) are also covered to educate parents about obesity prevention.

Implementation of BodyWorks

The BodyWorks program has been implemented in English and Spanish through community-based organizations, state health agencies, nonprofit organizations, health clinics, hospitals, health care systems, and insurance wellness programs. The actual BodyWorks curriculum about nutrition and physical activity is evidence-based; however, more evaluation of individual programs is needed. To date, very little data has been published about the efficacy of the program for changing parent and teen health behaviors.

Justine J. Reel

See also: Parents; Prevention

Bibliography

"BodyWorks." Womenshealth.gov. Last Modified June 26, 2014. Accessed January 20, 2017. https://www.womenshealth.gov/bodyworks/.

"A Project of the U.S. Department of Health and Human Services Office on Women's Health." Womenshealth.gov. Accessed November 16, 2016. http://www.womenshealth.gov.

Reel, Justine J., Carlie Ashcraft, Rachel Lacy, Robert A. Bucciere, Sonya SooHoo, Donna-Richards, and Nicole Mihalopoulos. "Full of Ourselves PLUS: Lessons Learned from an Obesity and Eating Disorder Intervention." *Journal of Sport Psychology in Action* 3, no. 1 (2011): 109–117. http://dx.doi.org/10.1080/21520704.2010.534545.

Utz, Rebecca, Darrin Cottle, Kori Fitschen, Julie Metos, Justine Reel, and Nicole Mihalopoulos. "Eat & Live Well: Lessons Learned from an After School Weight Management Program." *Utah's Health: An Annual Review* 13 (2008): 81–88.

BOOKS ABOUT EATING DISORDERS

Many people affected by eating disorders, such as parents/family, friends, health care professionals, school personnel, and others, turn to books about eating disorders as a source of information. Generally, the available literature on eating disorders can be divided into two categories: (1) fictional books and memoirs; and (2) educational and medical works. Both types of books provide valuable information and lend insight into how eating disorders are experienced, what contributes to them, and best practices for helping someone with an eating disorder. However, just like other forms of media that depict eating disorders, books also pose a risk for harm or serve as a potential trigger to the reader.

Fictional Books and Memoirs

Many fictional accounts of eating disorders have been published over the years. In addition to works of fiction, a considerable number of memoirs written by people who have struggled with eating disorders have also been published. Oftentimes, these books are written to be accessible even to those without any formal training in the field. However, research and anecdotal evidence has that some of these works can be potentially dangerous and triggering for people with a predisposition to disordered eating.

The Dangers of the Written Word

People first became aware of the potential dangers the written word could have on vulnerable individuals following publication of Marya Hornbacher's 1998 memoir, *Wasted*. The book describes Hornbacher's struggle with anorexia in her adolescent and young adult life. Once this book became popular, personnel at treatment centers and hospitals began seeing patients trying to smuggle *Wasted* into their facilities with them. Many people with anorexia have described Hornbacher's book as the anorexia bible and have intentionally used it to exacerbate their anorectic behaviors and thoughts. Interestingly, in Hornbacher's *Wasted*, she describes a similar process whereby her eating disorder was triggered by reading *The Best Little Girl in the World* by Steven Levenkron.

Many have criticized the assertion that reading a text can effectively cause an eating disorder, arguing that reading is not a powerful enough medium to create a psychological state capable of triggering disordered behaviors. However, a seminal study in the mid-1940s established a link between how people read and process information and their eating behaviors. The Minnesota Starvation Experiment, conducted in 1944–1945, was originally to test the most effective weight restoration strategies for people who had been starved on a long-term or chronic basis. Motivation for the experiment arose out of the famine conditions many civilians and concentration camp prisoners endured in Europe during World War II; medical professionals needed evidence-based strategies to best nourish these individuals back to a healthy weight in a safe and controlled manner. Surprisingly, one of the most critical results from the Minnesota Starvation Experiment centered on the participants' behaviors related to books: the participants exhibited obsessive-compulsive behaviors and began hoarding cookbooks and recipes and reading them repetitively. This was the first study that showed how starvation and the physiological state associated with it directly affects reading behaviors.

More recent research investigating the effect of eating disorders on reading behaviors has focused specifically on viewing online pro–eating disorder content. Multiple studies have shown that exposure to such content (i.e., pro-anorexia websites) increases negative mood and body image disturbance. Additionally, given the notoriety *Wasted* specifically received for its effects on disordered eating, a study conducted in 2006 investigated the effects that the book had on healthy college-aged women. In direct contrast with the widespread reports of the book worsening eating disorder symptoms among individuals with anorexia, the healthy college-aged women in this study reported no direct effects on their self-esteem, body satisfaction, or eating/exercising behaviors. The researchers concluded individuals who have a predisposition to disordered eating would be more likely to consider *Wasted* and other memoirs as personally relevant and this sense of relevancy could make recalling the information in these types of books easier.

Educational and Medical Books

These books are typically written for a specialized audience, including counselors, dietitians, doctors, physical therapists, and others who see eating disorders in settings that are focused on treatment or diagnosis. Unlike the available fictional literature on eating disorders, these types of books typically do not receive as much critical evaluation given that the content of these books is (often) backed by scientific evidence. An important consideration to keep in mind when selecting a book written from an educational and/or medical perspective on eating disorders is the specificity of the topic and the accessibility of the writing relative to the reader's knowledge-base. Some books—like this one—are written in the hopes of providing an overview to eating disorders; others focus on specific disorders, such as anorexia nervosa or binge eating disorder, or on specific populations, such as men or athletes. Other books have a narrower focus that can be more in-depth than the average reader may find useful. Last, as is the case with all scientific writing, currency of the writing is important to consider. Eating disorders is a widely studied field, and therefore significant new research and findings are generated every year. Choosing a book that has been recently published is important to ensure it contains the most up-to-date information.

Suggested Books about Eating Disorders

These suggestions have been compiled from lists provided by recovery centers and advocacy groups and are identified as some of the most helpful, comprehensive, and important books written about eating disorders to date.

The Eating Disorder Sourcebook: A Comprehensive Guide to the Causes, Treatments, and Prevention of Eating Disorders. Written in 2006 by Carolyn Costin, this book focuses on information on the causes of eating disorders, the types of treatments available, and various prevention strategies. It is appropriate for loved ones/family members, patients, and medical professionals.

Surviving an Eating Disorder: Strategies for Family and Friends. Dr. Michele Siegel, Dr. Judith Brisman, and Margot Weinshel published this work in 1988 and it has since been considered a classic in the field. It was written specifically to provide information, insight, and support to person who are affected by a loved one's eating disorder.

Talking to Eating Disorders: Simple Ways to Support Someone with Anorexia, Bulimia, Binge Eating, or Body Image Issues. Dr. Jeanne Albronda Heaton and Claudia Strauss's 2005 manual provides information on how to talk with someone struggling with an eating disorder. In the book's description, the authors caution that many people's natural inclination is to intervene and fix a problem, which can end up causing more harm than good. This is a great book for the layperson hoping to provide support to a friend or family member.

Hope, Help, and Healing for Eating Disorders. Published in 2010 by Dr. Gregory Jantz, this book describes Jantz's holistic approach to treating anorexia, bulimia, and other forms of disordered eating. Designed primarily for individuals in the medical and/or helping professions, it is a great introduction to treatment and counseling of eating disorders.

The Invisible Man: A Self-Help Guide for Men with Eating Disorders, Compulsive Exercise, and Bigorexia. John Morgan's 2008 book seeks to provide men and boys with the tools to initiate their journey to recovery. The book covers cultural factors that impact male body image, eating disorder features unique to males, facts and fictions related to eating disorders, as well as a seven-step treatment approach that individuals can explore at their own pace and comfort level.

The Stepdaughter. Caroline Blackwood's 1976 novella is an easy, one-sitting read about comfort eating. *The Stepdaughter* is the story of 13-year-old Renata, who subsists on a steady diet of television and box-mix cakes, as told through the perspective of her anorectic and unsympathetic stepmother. Blackwood's novella focuses on how food—or a lack thereof—often becomes about the relationships that take place in and around food.

The Brief Wondrous Life of Oscar Wao. Oscar Wao, the main character in Junot Diaz's 2007 novel, is defined by his weight and binge eating. Told from a third-person perspective that highlights how harshly obesity is often judged in Western cultures, readers follow Oscar—a Dominican immigrant to the United States—on a journey of growing up overweight and ostracized in a strange country.

An Experiment in Love. Written by Hilary Mantel in 1995, *An Experiment in Love* takes place in Britain and follows the story of working-class girl, Carmel McBain, and her experience living in an all-women's residence hall during university in London. What initially begins as an attempt to save money by skipping meals becomes problematic and Carmel slowly begins to obsess over her starvation. Mantel's novel has been praised as an exploration of how anorexia, similar to other addictions, is a form of poverty.

Hannah J. Hopkins

See also: Internet and Eating Disorders; Movies and Eating Disorders; Pro-Ana; Television Shows and Eating Disorders

Bibliography

"Book Recommendations from the Emily Program." *The Emily Program.* Accessed April 10, 2017. https://www.emilyprogram.com/resources/books.

Costin, Carolyn. *The Eating Disorder Sourcebook: A Comprehensive Guide to the Causes, Treatments, and Prevention of Eating Disorders.* New York: McGraw-Hill Education, 2007.

"Reading List for Recovery." *Eating Disorders Victoria.* April 10, 2017. https://www.eatingdisorders.org.au/resources/reading-list-for-recovery.

Seaber, Emma. "Reading Disorders: Pro-Eating Disorder Rhetoric and Anorexia Life-Writing." *Literature and Medicine* 34, no. 2 (2017): 484–508. https://doi.org/10.1353/lm.2016.0023.

Thomas, Jennifer J., Abigail M. Judge, Kelly D. Brownell, and Lenny R. Vartanian. "Evaluating the Effects of Eating Disorder Memoirs on Readers' Eating Attitudes and Behaviors." *International Journal of Eating Disorders* 39, no. 5 (2006): 418–425. https://doi.org/10.1002/eat.20239.

Wilson, Bee. "The Author of 'First Bite: How We Learn to Eat' on Eating Disorders." *Wall Street Journal.* Last modified February 12, 2016. Accessed November 22, 2017. https://www.wsj.com/articles/bee-wilson-1455308366?tesla=y.

BULIMIA NERVOSA

Bulimia nervosa is a clinical eating disorder that is characterized by cycles of overeating binges followed by purging behavior such as vomiting, laxative abuse, or obligatory exercise. *Bulimia* is a Latin word meaning *hunger of an ox.* The practice of overeating and then vomiting was a Roman practice. However, this binge–purge behavior was first documented as a medical case in 1903 by psychiatrist Pierre Janet. Initially, bulimia was considered part of anorexia nervosa and was therefore dubbed *bulimarexia.* However, bulimia nervosa was included as a separate diagnosis in the *Diagnostic and Statistical Manual of Mental Disorders* beginning in the 1980 edition. Many famous celebrities have admitted to suffering from bulimia nervosa including singer Paula Abdul, actress Justine Bateman, and *American Idol* winner Kelly Clarkson. Lady Gaga and Elton John have both discussed their histories with bulimia nervosa. Sharon Osbourne, a television cohost and wife of Ozzy Osbourne, admitted to a 35-year struggle with bulimia nervosa despite having had gastric bypass surgery. Well-known actress and fitness expert, Jane Fonda, discussed being a secret bulimic beginning at age 12 and having an eating disorder for 30 years.

Symptoms of Bulimia Nervosa

To be diagnosed as having bulimia nervosa using the *Diagnostic and Statistical Manual of Mental Disorders, fifth edition* (DSM-5) criteria, individuals must engage in both binge eating episodes and inappropriate compensatory methods. Recurrent binge episodes are described as secretively eating large amounts of food often in a short period of time (usually two hours). However, binges may last anywhere from 15 minutes to several weeks in duration. Although a binge may start at any time of the day and occur on weekdays or weekends, individuals with bulimia nervosa tend to report having certain days and times of increased vulnerability to binge behavior. A binge is represented by 3 to 30 times the amount of food usually consumed on a typical day. A person experiences a lack of control during the binge episodes, continuing to eat despite feeling full and having a desire to stop eating. Typically, binge foods consist of trigger foods that may be high in calories, sugar, or fat content such as potato chips, cookies, or ice cream. In fact, individuals may consume thousands of calories (30,000+) in one binge. Individuals may purchase binge foods from multiple drive-through fast-food restaurants, contributing to financial strain. Interestingly, the initial motivation behind binge behavior is a desire to calm emotions, reduce anxiety, or numb uncomfortable feelings. However, following a binge episode, an individual with bulimia nervosa experiences intense shame and guilt. In between binge episodes, an individual with bulimia nervosa typically engages in dieting behavior and may restrict forbidden binge foods.

To prevent weight gain and to dampen guilt, the food is purged using a compensatory method of choice. Self-induced vomiting may be used or an individual may misuse laxatives, diuretics, or enemas, or engage in excessive exercise to burn calories. Usually an individual with bulimia nervosa has a preferred method of purging. However, he or she may use different methods depending on the setting (e.g., dorm room, home). The binge–purge cycle occurs at least twice a week for at least three months to receive a bulimia nervosa diagnosis.

It is important to consider that bulimia nervosa is not solely about eating too much food and feeling compelled to eliminate it afterward. Like anorexia nervosa, individuals with bulimia nervosa express deep concern about body shape, size, and appearance. Body checking (e.g., weighing) and avoidance behaviors (e.g., wearing baggy clothing) are common for individuals with bulimia nervosa. Individuals with bulimia nervosa may appear to be at a normal or slightly-above-normal weight that results in less detection based on weight changes. Individuals with bulimia nervosa struggle with intense body dissatisfaction internally and may think they do not deserve to be in eating disorder treatment because they are not thin or sick enough.

Prevalence of Bulimia Nervosa

Because individuals who suffer from bulimia nervosa are secretive about their disorder, the problem may go undetected for many years and it is suspected that the overall prevalence is underreported. It is estimated that at least 1.0–1.8 percent of college women meet the bulimia nervosa criteria with another 2.6–3.3 percent having characteristics of bulimia nervosa at subclinical levels (disordered eating). Studies vary widely, but generally more adult females (1.5 percent) than males (0.5 percent) have bulimia nervosa. In some high school samples, bulimia nervosa rates are reported as much higher (15 percent) than the adult population. Onset is most commonly during the adolescent and early adulthood years. Recently, however, treatment centers are reporting an insurgence of women in their midlife years with eating disorders triggered by life events (e.g., divorce, menopause).

Personality Characteristics and Coexisting Conditions

Most individuals with bulimia nervosa also suffer from an anxiety disorder or mood disorder (e.g., depression). A relationship has been found between bulimia nervosa and substance abuse as well as sexual promiscuity. As with other eating disorders, individuals with bulimia nervosa may have a history of sexual trauma and in some cases, a traumatic event (e.g., an accident, abuse, divorce) may trigger the onset of binge–purge episodes. Figures for bulimic individuals who report sexual abuse range from 7–70 percent depending on the study. Some individuals with bulimia nervosa also have personality disorders such as borderline, narcissistic, and obsessive-compulsive disorders. Characteristics of being impulsive and compulsive may put individuals with bulimia nervosa at risk for other addictive behaviors (e.g., shopping, gambling, excessive exercise). Therefore, it remains important to teach adaptive coping strategies as part of the treatment process so that individuals with bulimia nervosa do not develop a new addiction. Likewise, body image concerns should be addressed in therapy so that the binge–purge behavior does not evolve into a different type of eating disorder (anorexia nervosa or binge eating disorder).

Health Consequences

Although medical complications will be addressed in more depth in a separate entry, it is important to note that there are numerous medical complications resulting from bulimia nervosa. In addition to mortality, individuals with bulimia nervosa may experience electrolyte imbalances, gastrointestinal difficulties (e.g., constipation, diarrhea), and other symptoms like severe acid reflux, bloating, and dehydration. Oral problems including erosion of tooth enamel, cavities, loss of teeth, gum inflammation, sore throat, and dry mouth frequently occur. Individuals with bulimia nervosa report having cold hands and feet as well as calluses on the back of their hand from vomiting. Additional complications associated with bulimia nervosa include, but are not limited to, internal bleeding, pancreatitis, impaired fertility, compromised bone health leading to osteoporosis, and brain changes. Although less common, some individuals with bulimia nervosa use syrup of ipecac, detergents, or foreign objects to induce vomiting (as a purging method). Abuse of ipecac, a dreadful tasting liquid, can lead to muscle weakness and cardiac arrest.

Justine J. Reel

See also: Assessment; Celebrities and Eating Disorders; Dehydration; *Diagnostic and Statistical Manual of Mental Disorders*; Medical and Health Consequences; Mortality Rates; Purging

Bibliography

Abraham, Suzanne, and Derek Llewellyn-Jones. *Eating Disorders: The Facts.* New York: Oxford University Press, 1995.

American Psychiatric Association. *Diagnostic and Statistical Manual of Mental Disorders*, 5th ed. (*DSM-5*). Washington, DC: American Psychiatric Association Publishing, 2013.

Chen, Eunice Yu, Michael S. McCloskey, Sara Michelson, Kathryn H. Gordon, and Emil Coccaro. "Characterizing Eating Disorders in a Personality Disorders Sample." *Psychiatry Research* 185 (2011): 427–432. https://doi.org/10.1016/j.psychres.2010.07.002.

Connolly, Anne M., Elizabeth Rieger, and Ian Caterson. "Binge Eating Tendencies and Anger Coping: Investigating the Confound of Trait Neuroticism in a Non-Clinical Sample." *European Eating Disorders Review* 15 (2007): 479–486. https://doi.org/10.1002/erv.765.

Costin, Carolyn. *A Comprehensive Guide to the Causes, Treatments and Prevention of Eating Disorders*, 3rd ed. New York: McGraw-Hill, 2007.

Costin, Carolyn. *100 Questions & Answers about Eating Disorders.* Sudbury, MA: Jones and Bartlett, 2007.

Courbasson, Christine, and Jacqueline M. Brunshaw. "The Relationship between Concurrent Substance Use Disorders and Eating Disorders with Personality Disorders." *International Journal of Environmental Research and Public Health* 6 (2009): 2076–2089. https://doi.org/10.3390/ijerph6072076.

De Bolle, Marleen, Barbara De Clercq, Alexandra Pham-Scottez, Saskia Meis, Jean-Pierre Rolland, Julien D. Guelfi, Caroline Braet, and Filip De Fruyt. "Personality Pathology Comorbidity in Adult Females with Eating Disorders." *Journal of Health Psychology* 16 (2011): 303–313. https://doi.org/10.1177/1359105310374780.

Hall, Lindsey, and Leigh Cohn. *Bulimia: A Guide to Recovery.* Carlsbad, CA: Gurze, 2011.

Mehler, Philip S. "Bulimia Nervosa." *The New England Journal of Medicine* 349, no. 9 (2003): 875–882.

Mehler, Philip S., Allison L. Sabel, Tureka Watson, and Arnold E. Andersen. "High Risk of Osteoporosis in Male Patients with Eating Disorders." *International Journal of Eating Disorders* 41, no. 7 (2008): 666–672. https://doi.org/10.1002/eat.20554.

Rowe, Sarah L., Jenny Jordan, Virginia V. W. Mcintosh, Frances A. Carter, Chris Frampton, Cynthia M. Bulik, and Peter R. Joyce. "Complex Personality Disorder in Bulimia Nervosa." *Comprehensive Psychiatry* 51 (2010): 592–598. http://dx.doi.org/10.1016/j.comppsych.2010.02.012.

Sernec, Karin, Martina Tomori, and Bojan Zalar. "Effect of Management of Patients with Anorexia and Bulimia Nervosa on Symptoms and Impulsive Behavior." *Collegium Antropologicum* 34, no. 4 (2010): 1281–1287.

Williams, Kim D., Tracey Dobney, and Josie Geller. "Setting the Eating Disorder Aside: An Alternative Model of Care." *European Eating Disorders Review* 18 (2010): 90–96. https://doi.org/10.1002/erv.989.

C

CARPENTER, KAREN

Karen Carpenter was a lead singer for The Carpenters, a vocal and instrumental duo in the 1970s. She shocked the world when she died at age 32 from cardiac arrest due to complications associated with anorexia nervosa. During the 1970s, hard rock was in great demand, but Carpenter and her brother Richard produced an alternative soft rock musical style and recorded 11 albums during their 14-year career. Carpenter, who was born in 1950, was identified for her musical talent while still a teenager. In 1966, she sang at a demo session where a trumpet player was auditioning for a part. Los Angeles bassist Joe Osborn stated, "Never mind the trumpet player, this chubby little girl can sing."

Karen Carpenter and Eating Disorders

Carpenter's dieting was first observed in 1967 when her doctor placed her on a water diet resulting in marked weight loss over a short period. By Fall 1975, Carpenter weight had dipped to below 80 pounds and she was abusing thyroid pills, vomiting, and abusing laxatives. In 1975, she collapsed on stage in Las Vegas while performing. When she was hospitalized it was determined that she was 35 pounds underweight and had an eating disorder. Although she sought treatment for her disorder, she died February 4, 1983, of a cardiac arrest

Her death was significant for raising public awareness regarding anorexia nervosa and advancing eating disorder treatment approaches. Prior to her death, dieting and disordered eating had been seen as normative behavior for teenage girls without cause for alarm or health consequences. The secretive nature of the disorder had kept many individuals believing they struggled alone from the disorder.

Justine J. Reel

See also: Anorexia Nervosa; Celebrities and Eating Disorders; Media; Mortality Rates

Bibliography

Coffey, Edel. "The Real Reason Karen Carpenter Was Driven to Anorexia." Independent. ie. Last modified November 29, 2010. Accessed November 21, 2017. http://www.independent.ie/life/the-real-reason-karen-carpenter-was-driven-to-anorexia-26703889.html.

"Eating Disorders." Foodsuperbook.wordpress.com. Last modified November 7, 2014. Accessed November 21, 2017. https://foodsuperbook.wordpress.com/2014/05/07/eating-disorders/.

Latson, Jennifer. "How Karen Carpenter's Death Changed the Way We Talk about Anorexia." Time.com. Last modified May 23, 2016. Accessed November 21, 2017. http://time .com/3685894/karen-carpenter-anorexia-death/.

Schmidt, Randy L. *Little Girl Blue: The Life of Karen Carpenter*. Chicago, IL: Chicago Reviewer Press, 2010.

CAUSES

The causes of eating disorders are multifaceted and usually include a combination of psychological, familial, sociocultural, and biological or genetic factors rather than a sole determinant of the disorder. Furthermore, not all individuals who possess a genetic predisposition or certain biological factors will develop clinical eating disorders. On the other hand, other individuals who have no family history of anorexia nervosa, bulimia nervosa, or substance abuse can still suffer from disordered eating or clinical eating disorders.

Given the difficulties of identifying causal factors at the epidemiological or individual level, some researchers have suggested identifying the cause may not be as important as identifying the maintaining factors of an eating disorder. One researcher noted that there may be a difference between the factor that initiates an eating disorder and the factor that maintains the eating disorder. If the maintaining factors replace causal factors, the treatment of an eating disorder must focus on what keeps eating disorder behaviors going. What follows is a summary of factors thought to contribute to the development of eating disorders.

Psychological Factors

Individual factors thought to contribute to the development of an eating disorder can be categorized as cognitive factors, interpersonal experiences, emotions, or degree of body dissatisfaction. With respect to cognitive factors, research findings consistently point to cognitive patterns that are often associated with eating disorders. These patterns include obsessive thoughts (a comorbid diagnosis of obsessive-compulsive disorder with anorexia nervosa is common with lifetime prevalence rates ranging from 9.5 percent to 62 percent) about which most clients report being frustrated; they also report having attempted to decrease the obsessive thinking. Some clients, however, report a strong identification with these thought patterns and are not, therefore, invested in making them diminish or disappear. Cognitive patterns associated with eating disorders can also involve perfectionistic thinking that drives perfectionistic behaviors (e.g., behaviors related to the eating disorder itself or other pursuits such as academics or sport). Some studies have demonstrated that despite being weight-restored, individuals with anorexia nervosa will continue to score high on measures of perfectionism. This finding has led some to conclude that perfectionism should be considered as an antecedent of anorexia nervosa and therefore is a causative factor.

Interpersonal experiences consistently linked to eating disorders include trauma, abuse, and teasing. Typically, in the context of eating disorders, the teasing some individuals experience is focused on weight, body shape, and size. Thus, to end the teasing, an individual may engage in behaviors intended to change one's weight, body shape, or size, which for some may mean engaging in eating disorder–related behaviors. Some professionals have suggested the presence of sexual abuse or other forms of abuse and trauma is overestimated in the eating disorder population. However, there is evidence to suggest the presence of trauma and abuse is associated with eating disorders.

The connection between emotions and eating disorders typically involves the regulation of emotions. Eating disorder–related behaviors are often linked to an individual being aware of an unpleasant emotional experience, becoming overwhelmed by his or her emotions, and using eating disorder behaviors as a way to cope. Eating disorders can serve as a way to cope with overwhelming emotional experiences (e.g., restricting) and to numb feelings.

Finally, body dissatisfaction has been strongly linked to eating disorder behaviors and is included in the diagnostic classification of eating disorders. Some have suggested body dissatisfaction can be linked to nearly all other potential causative factors. For example, if an individual is teased about her body weight/shape/size and she is dissatisfied with her body an eating disorder may develop. Additionally, an individual who is dissatisfied with his or her body may be more detrimentally affected by media images illustrating the perfect body for his or her sex. Some researchers have also suggested that body dissatisfaction is directly tied to one's sense of self or identity. If an individual is dissatisfied with who she is as a person and remains unclear about how to become more satisfied with herself, she may focus efforts (cognitive, behavioral, interpersonal) on manipulating how she looks, if she also has a high degree of body dissatisfaction. Engaging in eating disorder–related behaviors, therefore, is seen as an unhealthy solution to a problem concerning one's identity. If a dissatisfied person can become the one with self-control, or the skinny one, or the muscular one, then he or she is likely to experience a sense of purpose and a sense of self. This identity, of course, is tenuous at best.

Sociocultural Factors

There are a multitude of sociocultural factors that have been linked to eating disorders. One such factor involves living in a culture where food resources are abundant. In such cultures there is a corresponding valuation of thinness as the preferred physique for females, whereas in cultures where food is scarce, a larger female body type tends to be idealized. This idealization of a specific physique is often discussed in terms of the *thin ideal* for females; however, recently there has been recognition that the *muscular ideal* is the standard to which males in abundant cultures are typically held. Regardless of the particular standard, many studies have pointed to Western cultures as contributing factors to the development of eating disorders.

Another sociocultural factor involves media influence. Numerous studies have been conducted to examine the effect of various media on self-esteem and self-worth, cognitions around the desire to achieve the ideal standard. Typically, media images often portray unrealistic images of both males and females. Those individuals portrayed often represent a statistical minority or are engaged in extraordinary (and potentially harmful) behaviors to achieve this ideal body type.

The above findings are tempered by a recent meta-analysis examining the influence of cultural factors on the development of eating disorders. The findings suggested that eating disorders *may* be culture-bound syndromes. This depends in part on the eating disorder considered and how an eating disorder is defined (not all researchers faithfully follow *DSM* diagnostic criteria or apply the criteria in the same way). Therefore, while culture may have the types of influences noted above, it is best and probably more accurate to take into account the myriad other potential factors that are briefly discussed below in this section and the sections that follow.

The effect of one's peers on maladaptive behaviors has been studied widely and has included eating disorders. Researchers indicate individuals with eating disorders can learn or perfect their pathogenic eating-related behaviors from peers. Additionally, they may share similar attitudes and beliefs with respect to a desire to achieve a specific body type that will probably entrench these attitudes and beliefs. While changing peer groups will not necessarily prevent an eating disorder from developing, the evidence suggests that the peers with whom one associates can be potentially harmful.

Although the sociocultural factors discussed above demonstrate converging evidence for their effects on the development and maintenance of eating disorders, Polivy and Herman remind us these influences are so ubiquitous that many more people should demonstrate eating-disordered behaviors. The fact remains that eating disorders only exist in a small minority of individuals exposed to these factors. Therefore, if these factors were causative in the way that many believe they are, we would see a much higher incidence of eating disorders.

Familial Factors

Historically, familial factors were blamed for eating disorders. To date, there are numerous studies documenting familial influences on eating disorders, including the encouragement of eating disorder–related behavior by family members. For example, family members may reinforce efforts to lose weight or express envy about an individual's slimness or self-control. Additionally, other studies have pointed to certain family dynamics (e.g., being highly critical, intrusive, hostile, emotionally dismissive) as breeding grounds for eating disorders. Evidence has also been reported that daughters of mothers with eating disorders can be particularly negatively influenced by their mothers' struggles with these disorders and as a result develop an eating disorder.

Few research studies examining the effect of family on development of eating disorders are experimental in nature, which means the findings reported above are correlational. Thus, dysfunctional family dynamics often reported when a family member has an eating disorder may mean the presence of the eating disorder itself may be a causal factor in the dysfunction and not the other way around. Moreover, individuals with eating disorders can also be found in families where dysfunctional family dynamics do not exist. Thus, many have declared that it is no longer appropriate to consider families as causal agents of eating disorders. The Academy for Eating Disorders condemns the suggestion that families are the cause of a child's illness. Therefore, as is the case with sociocultural factors, to the extent that families have any effect on the development of eating disorders it is clear the emergence of an eating disorder is dependent on factors apart from familial factors.

Genetic Factors

Genetic studies (i.e., studies on factors inherited from biological relatives) usually involve investigating families and twins of individuals with eating disorders. Historically, reports of eating disorders in families have relied on imprecise data collection methods and definitions of the disorders, anecdotal reports, and other nonrigorous methods. Contemporary studies of family transmission processes are well designed and have the benefit of a diagnostic classification system that can make identifying individuals with various forms of eating disorders more accurate. Thus, these studies have revealed that eating disorders are much more common in families that have biological relatives with eating disorders in comparison to the population at large. This in part supports the notion that genetics plays a role in the presence of an eating disorder.

Twin studies parcel out the question of whether the findings revealed in family studies reflect the intergenerational transmission of genetic material or environmental influences. Studies examining monozygotic and dizygotic twins indicate monozygotic twins are more likely to show both individuals of the twin dyad with an eating disorder than dizygotic twins. This provides additional evidence for the genetic transmission of eating disorders. Genetic researchers caution, however, that it is important to consider all plausible causes for the development of eating disorders.

Christine L. B. Selby

See also: Family Influences; Media; Personality Characteristics; Risk Factors; Teasing

Bibliography

Collier, David A., and Janet L. Treasure. "The Aetiology of Eating Disorders." *British Journal of Psychiatry* 185, no. 5 (2004): 363–365. https://doi.org/10.1192/bjp.185.5.363.

Godart, Nathalie T., M. F. Flament, F. Perdereau, and P. Jeammet. "Comorbidity between Eating Disorders and Anxiety Disorders: A Review." *International Journal of Eating Disorders* 32, no. 3 (2002): 253–270. https://doi.org/10.1002/eat.10096.

Keel, Pamela K., and Kelly L. Klump. "Are Eating Disorders Culture-Bound Syndromes? Implications for Conceptualizing Their Etiology." *Psychological Bulletin* 129, no. 5 (2003): 747–769. http://dx.doi.org/10.1037/0033-2909.129.5.747.

le Grange, Daniel, James Lock, Katharine Loeb, and Dasha Nicholls. "Academy for Eating Disorders Position Paper: The Role of the Family in Eating Disorders." *International Journal of Eating Disorders* 43, no. 1 (2010): 1–5. https://doi.org/10.1002/eat.20751.

Palmer, Bob. "Causes of Eating Disorders." In *ABC of Eating Disorders,* edited by Jane Morris, 5–8. Williston, VT: Wiley-Blackwell Publishing, 2008.

Polivy, Janet, and C. Peter Herman. "Causes of Eating Disorders." *Annual Review of Psychology* 53 (2002): 187–213. https://doi.org/10.1146/annurev.psych.53.100901.135103.

Schmidt, Ulrike. "Aetiology of Eating Disorders in the 21st Century: New Answers to Old Questions." *European Child & Adolescent Psychiatry, suppl. 1,* 12 (2003): 30–37. https://doi.org/10.1007/s00787-003-1105-9.

Strober, Michael, and Cynthia M. Bulik. "Genetic Epidemiology of Eating Disorders." In *Eating Disorders and Obesity: A Comprehensive Handbook,* edited by Christopher G. Fairburn and Kelly D. Brownell, 238–242. New York: Guilford Press, 2002.

CELEBRITIES AND EATING DISORDERS

Some of the best-known and, unfortunately, tragic cases of eating disorders have been in celebrities. Understanding how celebrity culture contributes to eating disorders, and, in turn, how a celebrity's struggles with body image inform a layperson's experiences may shed light on the eating disorder epidemic. Many celebrities have publicly disclosed struggles with anorexia and bulimia, such as Princess Diana, Elton John, and Karen Carpenter. In some cases, these public figures brought much-needed attention and awareness to eating disorders. The willingness of celebrities to disclose problems with substance use disorders and eating disorders reduces the stigma associated with admitting one has a problem. Celebrity culture and media in general have been implicated broadly in the development of body dissatisfaction, and many researchers have highlighted how celebrities are embodiments of societal values and stereotypes surrounding weight and eating disorders.

Karen Carpenter

Karen Carpenter has been widely cited as one of the first celebrities to suffer from an eating disorder. Carpenter died at the age of 32 from heart failure in 1983 attributed to her anorexia. Carpenter achieved fame for her role as half of the soft rock band The Carpenters that she formed with her brother Richard. Although Carpenter maintained an extremely gaunt frame throughout the duration of her stardom, it was not until after her death that her struggle with anorexia became public. Her brother and bandmate confessed that he believed that his sister's fame contributed to her eating disorder. Beginning with an intense workout regimen she put herself on following comments from critics that she looked "paunchy" on stage, Richard said that his sister Karen the muscularity she put on while working out. This triggered a dieting binge, and, for the remaining decade of her life, she struggled with restrictive dieting that grew progressively worse. She has often been cited as the first celebrity who brought eating disorders into public awareness as well as a catalyst for women struggling with anorexia in the 1980s and 1990s to come forward with their disorder.

Princess Diana

Princess Diana was one of the most beloved female celebrities of the 1980s and 1990s, particularly in the United Kingdom. She rose to international fame after her marriage to Prince Charles. Princess Diana's struggle with bulimia went

Recovery from Eating Disorders: An Interview with Movie Stuntwoman Luci Romberg

Luci Romberg is a professional stuntwoman in Hollywood, California. Luci is a member of the Stunt Women's Association of Motion Pictures and Tempest Freerunning. Luci has appeared in numerous films such as *Ghostbusters* (2016), *Spy*, *Zombieland*, *Transformers 4*, *The Conjuring*, and *Indiana Jones and the Kingdom of the Crystal Skull*. She also performs stunts for TV shows, commercials, and freerunning competitions. She is the 11-time female world champion in Red Bull Art of Motion. As a national champion gymnast and all-league soccer player in college, Luci's transition into stunts was seamless. In 2014 she won a Taurus World Stunt Award for Best Overall Stunt by a Stuntwoman for her car hit doubling Melissa McCarthy on *Identity Thief*.

What factors do you believe contributed to the development of your eating disorder?

The peer pressures of the media and being perfect and thin definitely contributed but I think the biggest factor was being a young gymnast and having to wear a leotard in front of all my friends and peers put added pressure on being thin. Watching all my friends obsess over their bodies from the time I was about 13 got the ball rolling for disaster.

Was negative body image a part of this and if so, how did that relate to your eating behaviors?

When I was younger I could eat anything and everything I wanted. Once I went through puberty that was no longer the case and I still had the same eating habits but the weight began adding on. I was by no means overweight but I was no longer the stick thin athlete that I was used to being and I hated the changes in my body and the way I looked.

What type of treatment did you seek for your eating disorder? What was helpful and what was less than helpful?

In high school I attempted to be anorexic but it literally lasted for like a day. I couldn't get past feeling sick but I always hated the way I looked. Once I got to college and discovered bulimia I was all in. I kept it a secret from everyone for about a year. Once I gained the courage to tell my friends and family I went to a counselor but I only went a few times. I wasn't good at talking about my struggles and feelings and I guess I wasn't ready for recovery. Throughout college my eating disorder would come and go. Meaning, I was able to manage it sometimes and not others and I don't know why. What was helpful to me was maturity and finding a sport (freerunning) that I felt I was born to do and gave me the confidence I needed to accept myself for who I truly am.

What role did sport/movement play in helping you overcome an eating disorder?

Once I got into stunts the pressures of being thin never left so again my eating disorder was still present on and off. Once I discovered freerunning I was a bit older and was able to gain more confidence to be happy with who I was as a person and the way that I looked. Basically, sports and movement as I got older gave me the confidence to know that I didn't need to binge and purge. But unfortunately the thought and urge never leaves. As I got older I realized that bingeing and purging didn't work. I never lost weight and the guilt of the eating disorder weighs so heavy. With age and freerunning, I learned how to eat healthier and how to have a stronger and healthier mind. I will never be 100 percent happy with my body but the ability to have control and overcome my disorder is the most freeing feeling I've ever felt.

What did recovery look like for you? How do you feel about your relationship with food, exercise and your body now?
I still struggle with body image but I now have a clean and healthy mind and am free. It took me a long time to get there. I now know how to eat healthy, not overexercise, and appreciate my body!

How does the movie industry feed a thin-ideal culture or show value of certain body types?
In my experience it's tough because as a stunt person you have to be strong enough to save and protect yourself but at the same time be thin enough to double the actresses that are a lot of the time obviously stick thin. The movie industry portrays a body image type that is ideal that all women should strive for. I think women need to be realistic and strive for being healthy rather than being thin.

What should we do to prevent eating disorders?
I wish I knew the answer to this. It has been thrown in women's faces from an early age that thin equals beautiful and beautiful equal success. I hope that someday as a society we can change that tune. Beauty needs to be viewed as who we are and what we're capable of rather than what we look like on the outside. I think as role models and parents we can do more to tell our girls how beautiful they are and what healthy looks like! I think the eating portions in this country give us a false sense of how much our body needs. We need way less food than what restaurants and food sellers tell us we need.

Anything else you'd like to add?
Being free of the unhealthy mind-set of bulimia is seriously the best feeling in the world. To not carry the internal guilt of not being able to control my actions (bingeing and purging) is the most freeing feeling and I am so much happier as a person not carrying around that guilt!

public in a biography published about her early life in 1992 titled *Diana: Her True Story*. Throughout the 1990s, Diana continued to advocate for awareness about eating disorders and encouraged women to seek treatment. Diana herself admitted to struggling with bulimia for almost a decade, beginning in 1981 shortly before her wedding and continuing until late in the 1980s, when she finally sought treatment. Many people in the media and in research referred to the spike in the number of bulimia cases reported following Diana's public admission of the disease as the *Diana Effect*. In 1996, Princess Diana and Prince Charles divorced, but she remained a beloved public figure. She died in a car crash in Paris in 1997.

Elton John

Although men are underrepresented in the literature on eating disorders and report higher levels of stigma associated with an eating disorder, Elton John went public with his bulimia nervosa. Sir Elton John is a British singer-songwriter, musician, and composer with a five-decade long career and over 30 albums to his name. John has been an advocate for HIV/AIDS awareness as well as for the LGBTQ community throughout his career.

In a 2002 interview with Larry King, Elton John was asked if he knew about his friend Princess Diana's bulimia, to which he replied, "Yes I did. We were both bulimic." Following this public announcement, Sir Elton John admitted to struggling with a cocaine addiction and bulimia nervosa for the early part of his career. He entered treatment in 1990 for both his substance addiction as well as his eating disorder.

Lady Gaga

Lady Gaga (born Stefani Joanne Angelina Germanotta) first opened up about her past eating disorder in 2012 at a conference in Los Angeles. When asked about her high school experience, Lady Gaga confided that she wanted to be small like a ballerina, but struggled with her voluptuous figure. Lady Gaga said, ultimately, her bulimia interfered with her ability to sing because of the detrimental effects of stomach acid from frequent vomiting on her vocal cords. Throughout her pop career, Lady Gaga has continued to advocate for body positivity and share her experiences with bulimia and anorexia. Following a barrage of speculation over her weight gain in various news outlets, Lady Gaga posted several pictures of herself in undergarments with the caption "Bulimia and anorexia since I was 15" on her social media website. In an interview with *Harper's Bazaar* in 2014, Lady Gaga discussed overcoming her struggles with body image and depression, saying "I'm a human being and not a doll . . . I learned that sadness never destroyed what was great about me."

Oprah Winfrey

One of America's most recognizable and loved TV icons, Oprah Winfrey, has publicly admitted to struggling with binge eating. During an interview with Piers Morgan in 2011, Oprah was asked about a particularly difficult time in her career. Shortly after the release of her movie *Beloved* in 1998, Oprah's show suffered a downward trend in ratings following criticism that some of its new segments were "too New Age-y." When asked how she coped with this time, Oprah confided she ate about 30 pounds of macaroni and cheese and bread pudding her chef made for her. "I really, literally, went into a tailspin," said Winfrey. Oprah has been particularly vocal in advocating for greater awareness of binge eating disorder and the important emotional factors involved. "I thought I just wanted some macaroni . . . I didn't connect the powerlessness [with the bingeing] until [much later]." Winfrey told Morgan in the same interview.

Dennis Quaid

Actor Dennis Quaid is best known for his roles in a number of Hollywood classics, including *The Parent Trap* (1998). In the mid-1990s, Quaid starred in the film *Wyatt Earp* (1994) as Doc Holliday. In the storyline, Quaid's character was dying of tuberculosis, and Quaid was instructed to lose a significant amount of weight to capture the gauntness of a man on the verge of death. Quaid later revealed that this tremendous weight loss—about 40 pounds, he estimates—catalyzed his struggle with what he described as *manorexia*. He said his arms were so frail and skinny that he could not pull himself out of a swimming pool following his weight loss. "I'd look in the mirror and still see a 180-pound guy, even though I was 138 pounds," Quaid said of his disorder. Despite struggling with restrictive eating and obsessive calorie counting for many years, Quaid says that he eventually overcame it and is now an advocate for awareness of men's body image and eating disorders.

Other Celebrities with Eating Disorders

Other celebrities have come forward in the past several decades to discuss their eating disorders, including:

- Lucy Hale—b. June 14, 1989, American actress best known for her role as Aria Montgomery on the TV show *Pretty Little Liars*, revealed in 2012 that she had previously suffered from an eating disorder
- Sally Field—b. November 6, 1946, American actress best known for starring roles in movies such as *Mrs. Doubtfire* (1993) and *Forrest Gump* (1994), admitted to struggling with bulimia and anorexia in her early 20s
- Katie Couric—b. January 7, 1957, American journalist and media personality best known for cohosting the *Today* show and anchoring *CBS Evening News,* discussed her battle with body dissatisfaction and bulimia in college
- Jane Fonda—b. December 21, 1937, American actress, political activist, and fitness guru, opened up about her struggle with bulimia and extreme perfectionism in her childhood in a public newsletter
- Billy Bob Thornton—b. August 4, 1955, American actor who starred in *Friday Night Lights* (2004) and *Armageddon* (1998) along with many other films, discussed his weight loss throughout his career and has come forward to discuss his anorexia
- Mary Kate Olsen—b. June 13, 1986, former child actress, fashion designer, entered treatment in 2004 for anorexia nervosa

Impact of Celebrity Culture on Public Health

In addition to acknowledging that many celebrities experience eating disorders, understanding how the culture surrounding celebrity bodies affects the general public is also important. Research has time and again demonstrated the important role media exposure plays in the development of body dissatisfaction and weight/shape concern. Although it is generally accepted that media exposure alone is not enough to trigger an eating disorder, it has been shown individuals who are exposed to more TV, movies, and/or magazines are more likely to develop disordered eating. Several studies have shown that introducing Western media into a previously media-naive culture increases the rate of eating disorders, body dissatisfaction, and dieting two- and threefold.

Many studies in fields such as cultural anthropology and sociology have illuminated the role that celebrities and celebrity culture play in embodying societal values. The thin ideal perpetuated in pop culture today reflects a social value we ascribe to thin bodies. The thin ideal has roots in historical movements and reflects a Western (and particularly American) emphasis on self-reliance. In many cultures around the world, and in pre-20th-century Europe and United States, being overweight is a symbol of financial stability and wealth. For example, much of the art that comes to us from the Renaissance period depicts women who are fleshier than today's standard of beauty. Carrying weight was an outward symbol that you/your family could afford ample food and did not need to participate in manual labor. Around the turn of the 20th century, the ideal began to change along with agricultural and industrial revolutions that made access to food much easier and more affordable for the lower classes. During the early 20th century, overweight became associated with greed, gluttony, and sloth, whereas being thin became a symbol of self-restraint and discipline. These values persist today and are reflected in the celebrity culture of Western society. Celebrities are often regarded as symbols of wealth, social status, and power in society, and many of them maintain slim figures (and struggle with eating disorders).

The values and stereotypes surrounding overweight and thin bodies persists in the language used to describe eating disorders. Bulimia and anorexia are typically considered *thin-oriented* disorders and share an emphasis on body weight/shape control, whereas binge eating disorder is often seen as a disorder that affects overweight individuals more so than normal or underweight persons. One study that investigated media coverage of eating disorders over a 10-year period found anorexia and bulimia were often attributed to a variety of external pressures, thereby eliminating individual blame for the disorders. In contrast, news pieces describing binge eating disorder construed it as rooted in a lack of control over normal eating behaviors, and a majority of interventions described for binge eating emphasized individual-level interventions. This pattern highlights society's different understandings of the thin-oriented disorders versus disorders such as binge eating. This idea is also perpetuated in celebrity culture, where celebrities (who act as symbols of power and wealth) often maintain thin figures and frequently go public with their struggles with bulimia and anorexia.

Hannah J. Hopkins

See also: Carpenter, Karen; Media; Models and Eating Disorders

Bibliography

Boodman, Sandra G. "Eating Disorders: Not Just for Women." *Washington Post*. Last modified March 13, 2007. Accessed November 21, 2017. http://www.washingtonpost.com/wp-dyn/content/article/2007/03/09/AR2007030901870.html

"Bulimia: The Princess Diana Eating Disorder." *Mirror Mirror Eating Disorders*. Accessed February 3, 2017. http://www.mirror-mirror.org/princess-diana-eating-disorder.htm.

"Carpenters Biography 2005, Richard and Karen Carpenter." *Richard and Karen Carpenter.* Last modified June 4, 2008. Accessed February 2, 2017. http://www.richardandkaren carpenter.com/biography.htm.

"Celebrity Culture Is Not to Blame for Eating Disorders." *Nursing Children and Young People* 23, no. 7 (2011): 5. http://dx.doi.org/10.7748/ncyp2011.09.23.7.5.p6249.

Cohen, Elizabeth. "Don't Overeat like Oprah." CNN.com. Last modified January 20, 2011. Accessed November 21, 2017. http://www.cnn.com/2011/HEALTH/01/20/binge.eating/.

Corkery, Claire. "Jane Fonda Reveals How Her Father Encouraged Her Body Issues." Mail Online. Last modified April 11, 2016. Accessed November 21, 2017. http://www.dailymail .co.uk/femail/article-3532382/Jane-Fonda-reveals-told-diet-father-stepmothers -led-developing-eating-disorders.html.

Derenne, Jennifer L., and Eugene V. Beresin. "Body Image, Media, and Eating Disorders." *Academic Psychiatry* 30, no. 3 (2006): 257–261. https://doi.org/10.1176/appi .ap.30.3.257.

King, Natalie, Stephen Touyz, and Margaret Charles. "The Effect of Body Dissatisfaction on Women's Perceptions of Female Celebrities." *International Journal of Eating Disorders* 27, no. 3 (2000): 341–347. https://doi.org/10.1002 /(SICI)1098-108X(200004)27:3<341::AID-EAT12>3.0.CO;2-P.

Lopez, John, and Mia De Graaf. "Mary-Kate Olsen Sparks Surgery Rumours after Recent Red Carpet Turn." Mail Online. Last modified November 11, 2014. Accessed November 21, 2017. http://www.dailymail.co.uk/tvshowbiz/article-2828062/Mary-Kate-Olsen -sparks-surgery-rumours-looking-noticeably-different-recent-red-carpet-event-twin -sister-Ashley.html.

Peterson, Todd. "Dennis Quaid: I Battled Anorexia." People.com. Last modified March 10, 2006. Accessed November 21, 2017. http://people.com/celebrity/dennis-quaid-i -battled-anorexia/.

Rothman, Michael. "Lady Gaga Reveals Past Eating Disorder, Depression." *ABC News.* Last modified February 6, 2014. Accessed November 21, 2017. http://abcnews.go.com /Entertainment/lady-gaga-reveals-past-eating-disorder-depression/story?id=22394704.

Saguy, Abigail C., and Kjerstin Gruys. "Morality and Health: News Media Constructions of Overweight and Eating Disorders." *Social Problems* 57, no. 2 (2010): 231–250. https:// doi.org/10.1525/sp.2010.57.2.231.

Saukko, Paula. "Rereading Media and Eating Disorders: Karen Carpenter, Princess Diana, and the Healthy Female Self." *Critical Studies in Media Communication* 23, no. 2 (2006): 152–169. https://doi.org/10.1080/07393180600714539.

Stewart, Dodai. "'Bulimia and Anorexia Since I Was 15': Lady Gaga Responds to 'Fat' Headlines with Half-Naked Pics and a Confession." Jezebel. Last modified September 25, 2012. Accessed November 21, 2017. http://jezebel.com/5946233/bulimia-and-anorexia-since -i-was-15-lady-gaga-responds-to-fat-headlines-with-half-naked-pics-and-a-confession.

Vandever, Leslie. "Bulimia Isn't Beautiful: Celebrities with Eating Disorders." *Eating Disorder Hope.* Accessed February 3, 2017. https://www.eatingdisorderhope.com/information /eating-disorder/bulimia-isnt-beautiful-celebrities-with-eating-disorders.

CHEERLEADING

More than three million individuals compete in cheerleading across the United States. Although cheerleaders are often stereotyped as blonde, bubbly, and beautiful women, the first cheerleaders were male yell leaders in the 1890s. Beginning in the 1920s, all-male squads of highly masculine members performed stunts and gymnastics to the delight of the crowds at college football games. Females were restricted from cheerleading participation due to fear of masculinization associated with raising and deepening one's voice and participating in a highly athletic endeavor. However, despite numerous female bans from cheerleading that were documented in both high schools and colleges into the 1950s, females entered the sport during World War II and were there to stay. Cheerleading grew more competitive and formalized in the 1980s, and ESPN televised the first national high school competition in 1981. A majority of today's cheerleaders are affiliated with junior highs, high schools, and colleges, but the squads may compete in national competitions. In the 1990s, all-star cheerleading competition squads emerged with the sole purpose of training and competing in local, regional, and national competitions without cheering for any particular team. Interestingly, when females entered the sport, cheerleading became regarded as a highly feminine endeavor despite the fact that males continued to participate. With increased opportunity to participate in competitions, difficulty levels have increased and led the way for stringent weight requirements.

Body Image and Cheerleading

In addition to gymnastics and figure skating, cheerleading is considered an aesthetic sport that values appearance as a successful component of performance. In cheerleading, being lighter is associated with more opportunity to become a flyer (the most desirable cheerleading position due to higher visibility than the base position) and more difficult partner stunts. The gymnastic elements of cheerleading also promote a lean physique with the perception that it improves the ability to perform flips and handsprings.

Few studies examining female athletes and body image have included cheerleaders. However, one study found that 70 percent of high school female cheerleaders were dissatisfied with their bodies. In another study, 34 percent of cheerleaders admitted to fasting to lose weight and another 30 percent reported vomiting to control weight. A researcher at University of South Carolina estimated eating disorder risk for college cheerleaders at 33 percent and found flyers (i.e., cheerleaders who are thrown in the air during stunts) were more at risk for disordered eating and body image dissatisfaction than other cheerleading positions (e.g., base). In a separate 1996 study of both college and high school cheerleaders, Reel and Gill found that of 157 high school and college cheerleaders, 84 percent reported pressure to lose weight or maintain an unhealthy weight. In this study, weight pressures specific to the sport of cheerleading were identified.

Weight Pressures

Cheerleaders at the college level reported significantly more sport-specific weight pressures than high school cheerleaders. Conversely, high school cheerleaders were more likely to report stronger body dissatisfaction, social physique anxiety, and eating disorder tendencies. Overall the most frequently reported weight pressure (58 percent) for competitive cheerleaders was a revealing team uniform. However, other sport-specific pressures included peers, stunt partner, coaches, a perceived performance advantage, and weight requirements for a sport including weigh-ins.

Uniform

A majority of high school (61 percent) and college (54 percent) female cheerleaders believed a team uniform contributed to pressure to lose weight or control eating to maintain an unhealthy size as compared with 41 percent of male cheerleaders. Over the decades, cheerleading uniforms have become more revealing and tighter fitting. Cheerleaders experienced the greatest body image dissatisfaction when wearing their most revealing uniforms that display midriffs. Interviews with adolescent competitive cheerleaders ages 10–17 demonstrated that uniforms often contributed to self-consciousness due to lack of coverage. One 16-year-old cheerleader explained, "It [the uniform] makes it hard sometimes because of the things we wear with the short skirts and tight shirts . . . everyone is looking at you . . . things bother me when I wear my uniform." The increasingly more revealing uniforms have sparked controversy in the news. The conservative fans and alumni at University of Idaho protested the short skirts and skimpy tops when the new cheerleading coach released an updated uniform, and this resulted in the team ordering more modest replacement uniforms.

Coach and Other Pressures

Another noteworthy pressure among competitive cheerleaders and other athletes is the coach. In cheerleading, 70 percent of female college cheerleaders, 88 percent of male college cheerleaders, and 25 percent of high school cheerleaders thought weight was important to their coaches. Furthermore, 49 percent of female and 65 percent of male college cheerleaders were subjected to a weight limit to try out and 40 percent of college cheerleaders had weigh-ins throughout the season to monitor body weight for their current cheerleading squad.

Being a flyer on a squad was associated with more pressure to stay light and more risk for disordered eating. Having different weight expectations by position (flyer versus base) meant comparison with other teammates to determine who would have the prestigious flyer role.

Stunt partners who lifted and threw other cheerleaders noticed when flyers gained weight. Therefore, 42 percent of high school and 30 percent of college cheerleaders reported a stunt partner as a weight pressure. It is likely that the ability to execute difficult stunts resulted in a perceived performance advantage with lower weight, which was expressed by 43 percent of college and 38 percent of high school cheerleaders.

Celebrities Paula Abdul and Nicole "Snooki" Polizzi, who were both former cheerleaders, have disclosed their histories with eating disorders. Snooki from the television show *Jersey Shore* admitted her eating disorder started in high school because she was worried about being replaced on the cheerleading squad by thinner and younger freshmen females. Cheerleading is a unique sport that combines appearance expectations with gymnastic and stunting skills designed to entertain a crowd. Body image concerns among college cheerleaders have included pressures to lose weight and maintain low weights for females and pressures to gain weight, strength, and muscles for males. Competitive cheerleaders report revealing team uniforms, coaches, position type, and weight requirements most frequently as sport-specific pressures.

Justine J. Reel

See also: Aesthetic Sports; Coaches; Figure Skating; Gymnastics; Social Physique Anxiety; Weight Pressures in Sport

Bibliography

Associated Press. "Cheerleaders Ditch Skimpy Uniforms after Complaints from Fans." Fox-News.com. Last modified September 23, 2008. Accessed November 21, 2017. http://www.foxnews.com/story/0,2933,426270,00.html

Lundholm, Jean K., and John M. Litrell. "Desire for Thinness among High School Cheer-leaders: Relationship to Disordered Eating and Weight Control Behaviors." *Adolescence* 83 (1986): 573–579.

Reel, Justine J., and Diane L. Gill. "Psychosocial Factors Related to Eating Disorders among High School and College Female Cheerleaders." *The Sport Psychologist* 10 (1996): 195–206.

Reel, Justine J., and Diane L. Gill. "Weight Concerns and Disordered Eating Attitudes among Male and Female College Cheerleaders." *Women in Sport and Physical Activity* 7, no. 2 (1998): 79–94.

SooHoo, Sonya. "Social Construction of Body Image among Female Adolescent Cheerlead-ers." PhD Dissertation, University of Utah, 2008.

Taub, Diane E., and Elaine M. Blinde. "Disordered Eating and Weight Control among Adolescent Female Athletes and Performance Squad Members." *Journal of Adolescent Research* 9 (1994): 483–497. https://doi.org/10.1177/074355489494006.

Torres-McGehee, Toni. "Eating Disorder Risk and the Role of Clothing on Body Image in College Cheerleaders." *Journal of Athletic Training* 47, no. 5 (2012): 541–548. https://doi.org/10.4085/1062-6050-47.5.03.

CHILDREN AND ADOLESCENTS

Historically, eating disorders have been most commonly associated with females in their late teens and early 20s. Individuals beyond the college years were assumed to outgrow eating disorders and body issues. Children and early adolescent boys and girls were thought to be too young to think about dieting or engage in disordered eating. However, one news story discussed young children aged five to seven years who were showing signs of eating disorders.

Alarmingly, the American Academy of Pediatrics issued a 2010 report that brought attention to the increased prevalence of eating disorders in children and adolescents. Specifically, hospitalizations for eating disorders rose 119 percent between 1999 and 2006 for children younger than age 12. Eating disorders represent the most common psychiatric problem in adolescents, and mortality rates for anorexia nervosa are among the highest for any psychiatric

Parent of High School Daughter with an Eating Disorder: An Interview with "Rosalyn"

"Rosalyn" (pseudonym used to preserve anonymity) is a recently remarried mother of two children. She grew up in the Southwestern United States and currently works in the health care field. She actively works to support others to become more healthy in their daily lives. As a mother, she continues to support her daughters as they grow into adult women.

What age was your daughter when you realized she had a problem? What were the telltale signs that indicated she had an eating disorder?

My daughter was 17 and a senior in high school when I realized she had a problem. She was an intensely involved high school athlete, exclusively running cross-country and track her senior year with previous participation in basketball, soccer, and softball. I first noticed an obsession with food, but quickly attributed the focus to being an athlete eating for performance and strength. The depth and severity of her obsession soon became apparent with her restrictive and unusual rules around food. She avoided treats, going out to dinner, and isolated herself from social activities with her family and friends. Life was entirely centered around food, or lack of. She had excessive mood swings and became withdrawn, spending a great deal of time alone in her room. *Everything, every day* was stressful to her. She was irritable, sad, and angry most of the time.

What do you believe were some of the contributing factors that played a role in the development of her eating disorder?

Years after her diagnosis, secrets came out in therapy revealing her need to have control over something in her life. Her father secretly controlled her every thought and action; to be perfect at everything. A perfect athlete, perfect demeanor and physical looks. She was rewarded treats hidden in his drawer because she worked out and wasn't overweight as he perceived her siblings to be. She was told to show no emotion because people could judge her if she did. He was perceived to be the perfect husband, father, teacher, and church leader to everyone that knew him. Away from the public eye he was quietly and calmly controlling and demanding. When she was 16 her father left home and lost his teaching license. The school district revealed multiple relationships with teenage female students. He took no accountability or acknowledgment for his behavior or actions, blaming the community and his family.

She was told and believed she was a bad girl if she didn't act or perform to her father's expectations. She was blamed for making people unhappy if she didn't act or do things a certain way. She was loved *conditionally* and then abandoned. Her perfectionism caused her extreme anxiety, which also led to depression. She could never be good enough in her own eyes. She did not have the ability to express emotions. My daughter experienced sexual and emotional abuse and suffers from severe complex post-traumatic stress disorder.

What was your daughter like before she had an eating disorder? How did she change as a result of her eating disorder identity?

She was fun, crazy, and spontaneous. She was very thoughtful toward her family and friends, always paying attention to details in their lives. Her creativity led to very silly times with lots of laughter. She was passionate and *present*.

She changed with the identity of her eating disorder. She became withdrawn from her family and friends. She was moody and angry at everyone and everything.

What were your biggest fears associated with your daughter's eating disorder?
My biggest fear . . . she would die. And if she survived, that her life would be imprisoned by the eating disorder causing great mental and physical suffering. Her care team prepared me for her demise. To this day they are amazed at her fight and resilience . . . that she is alive.

What factors or supports do you believed helped your daughter overcome her eating disorder?
First and foremost her amazing care team of therapists and medical doctors. Their honesty, sincere understanding and care to her as a person and our family helped us survive. Right alongside this care team was her family who offered unconditional and consistent love, support, and encouragement. Her family never gave up on her and allowed her to express emotions and exhibit her imperfections. She was also given opportunities to speak about her personal experience to eating disorder awareness groups with her colleagues and university professor.

What should parents do if they think their daughter or son has a problem?
The best advice I can give is to seek help from professionals, for her, yourself, and your family. I believe the most difficult thing is avoidance and denial of the signs you see, overlooking and justifying. Educating yourself to learn about eating disorders and available treatments gives you power in decision making. Confronting your loved one is scary and challenging. They make excuses and promises.

Do you believe it is possible for a person to be recovered from an eating disorder? Why or why not?
To some degree recovery is possible. However, the underlying reasons for the disorder are often replaced by other behaviors in order to cope. "An abscess cannot be healed with a band aid."

What else would you like to add from the perspective of a parent who had a daughter with an eating disorder?
It is a lifelong process. You feel completely helpless. You experience every possible emotion. I learned that it's okay to feel emotion, to walk through it and keep moving. The effects of the eating disorder are felt far beyond the person suffering from it. It is emotionally exhausting and painful. There is fear, sadness, guilt, and anger. You fight daily. You feel tired and discouraged. You feel like your insides have been ripped out. LOVE her, unconditionally! SUPPORT her SINCERELY every day so she doesn't feel alone. LISTEN openly and be PATIENT and NON-JUDGMENTAL. Ask what she is feeling with deep sincerity. Don't tell her what to do, how to think or feel, just listen, validate the emotions, feelings, and pain. Focus on her positive traits, those unconnected to her physical appearance. And . . . one of the biggest frustrations is if they are 18 years of age or older they have the ability to make their own choices and discontinue treatment if they so desire. NEVER give up!

disorder. It is estimated less than 1 percent of adolescent girls in the United States meet the criteria for anorexia nervosa, 1.0–3.0 percent for bulimia nervosa, and 0.8–14.0 percent fall into the "eating disorder not otherwise specified" category from the previous edition of the *Diagnostic and Statistical Manual of Mental Disorders (DSM-IV-TR)*. In a Canadian study, the incidence of restrictive eating disorders among children was two times greater than the incidence of type 2 diabetes in all children younger 18. Similar to other health problems, pediatricians are often the first line of defense for eating disorder detection. Unfortunately, although the eating disorders have the potential to cause health problems and medical complications in children and adolescents, treatment for this population has often been ineffective to address restrictive behaviors and eating disorders.

Barriers to Treatment of Children and Adolescents

There are many barriers associated with children and adolescents receiving treatment for eating disorders. First, many individuals under age 18 seek treatment on an involuntary basis, rather than making a choice to enter therapy. Clients who think they have been pushed into treatment may not be ready or motivated to change their behaviors or discard their eating disorder identity. Furthermore, children and adolescents may discover treatment is usually centered around individual therapy and participating in group therapy with other adults. Younger individuals may lack the cognitive development to process their thoughts and emotions related to their disorder. Additionally, children and adolescents often learn the disordered eating behaviors from their peers and such behavior is often part of their normative culture. If children and adolescents receive treatment in a residential or inpatient setting, they will return to a system (e.g., family and peers) with the same pressures and dynamics that contributed to the eating disorder in the first place. Family members may lack the insight to manage or support the child or adolescent when he or she returns to the home.

Treatment Recommendations for Children and Adolescents

Adolescents and children who can be treated in outpatient and inpatient settings should receive care from a physician, dietitian, and mental health therapist. A family pediatrician may refer the client to a physician or psychiatrist who specializes in monitoring and managing eating disorders. It is important for these treatment professionals to collaborate with one another to form an outpatient treatment team. Medical stabilization and developing healthy eating will be important goals for the initial phase of treatment. However, addressing mental health concerns and psychological factors that contributed to the eating disorder will require ongoing care. Mental health professionals may find that everything from alternative forms of therapy such as art therapy, equine therapy, and yoga therapy to the traditional talk therapy are needed to reach the younger client. It is generally recommended that family members receive education and be part of the treatment plan. A popular approach for family therapy, the Maudsley approach, is discussed in detail in another entry.

Justine J. Reel

See also: Adolescent Development; Puberty

Bibliography

Eddy, Kamryn T., Daniel le Grange, Ross D. Crosby, Renee Rienecke Hoste, Angela Celio Doyle, Angela Smyth, and David B. Herzog. "Diagnostic Classification of Eating Disorders in Children and Adolescents: How Does DSM-IV-TR Compare to Empirically-Derived Categories?" *Journal of American Academy of Child and Adolescent Psychiatry* 49, no. 3 (2010): 277–293. http://dx.doi.org/10.1016/j.jaac.2009.10.012.

Hill, Amelia. "More Children Have Anorexia Than Previously Thought, Study Finds." TheGuardian.com. Accessed November 21, 2017. https://www.theguardian.com/society/2011/apr/04/children-anorexia-study.

Lock, James. "Treatment of Adolescent Eating Disorders: Progress and Challenges." *Minerva Psichiatrica* 51, no. 3 (2010): 207–216.

Lock, James, and Kathleen Kara Fitzpatrick. "Advances in Psychotherapy for Children and Adolescents with Eating Disorders." *American Journal of Psychotherapy* 63, no. 4 (2009): 287–303.

Loeb, Katharine L., Diel Le Grange, Tom Hildebrandt, Rebecca Greif, James Lock, and Lauren Alfano. "Eating Disorders in Youth: Diagnostic Variability and Predictive Validity." *International Journal of Eating Disorders* 44 (2010): 1–11. https://doi.org/10.1002/eat.20872.

Parentables. "If You Want Your Children to Be Healthy, Don't Talk to Them about Weight." Yahoo.com. Last modified March 8, 2013. Accessed November 21, 2017. https://www.yahoo.com/news/blogs/parenting/want-children-healthy-don-8217-t-talk-them-140400513.html.

Pinhas, Leora, Anne Morris, Ross D. Crosby, and Debra K. Katzman. "Incidence and Age-Specific Presentation of Restrictive Eating Disorders in Children." *Archives of Pediatric Adolescent Medicine* 165, no. 10 (2011): 895–899. https://doi.org/10.1001/archpediatrics.2011.145.

Rosen, David S. "Identification and Management of Eating Disorders in Children and Adolescents." *Pediatrics* 126 (2010): 1240–1253. https://doi.org/10.1542/peds.2010-2821.

Sinton, Meghan M., Andrea B. Goldschmidt, Vandana Aspen, Kelly R. Theim, Richard L. Stein, Brian E. Saelens, Leonard H. Epstein, and Denise E. Wilfley. "Psychosocial Correlates of Shape and Weight Concerns in Overweight Pre-Adolescents." *Journal of Youth Adolescence* 41, no. 1 (2011): 67–75. https://doi.org/10.1007/s10964-011-9686-y.

COACHES

Coaches of sports teams are employed to teach sports skills, devise strategies, and improve the performance of athletes of all ages and competitive levels. Coaches are viewed as experts regarding the sport-specific demands, nutrition, strength and conditioning, and injury concerns. As a result, many athletes unconditionally accept coaching recommendations with hopes of achieving a competitive edge despite the potential for short- and long-term consequences (e.g., injuries). Some coaching recommendations are related to size, weight, and appearance and have been linked to pathogenic weight control methods and severe health concerns (e.g., eating disorders).

Weight-Related Coach Pressure

Athletes may experience pressure from their coaches to lose weight or maintain a low body weight in the pursuit of improved sport performance. Moreover, weight-related coach pressure may be reinforced by the use of weekly weigh-ins or weight-related tryout requirements. Coaches may also directly state weight-related goals for an athlete or team or may engage in teasing athletes about their weight, shape, or size. In one study, 50–70 percent of cheerleaders believed weight was important to their coach and almost 20 percent reported having coaches who openly encouraged weight loss.

Consequently, athletes who hear of weight concerns from coaches and others are almost three times more likely to develop unhealthy eating patterns (e.g., eating disorders and disordered eating). In one study, nearly half of the athletes who reported experiencing coach comments to lose weight or maintain a low body weight were upset and more self-conscious as a result of those comments. Unfortunately, the negative impact of coach comments regarding weight increases as the frequency and severity of those comments increases, leaving an athlete more upset and more self-conscious.

As a coach's job is to make athletes better—to win—coaches may notice what they perceive to be excessive weight on an athlete and recommend weight loss with the intention to help an athlete improve performance. It should be noted that many coaches probably give this advice based on the misguided belief that reduced weight improves performance, rather than on scientific evidence. Although some coaches may encourage athletes to lose weight inadvertently through public weigh-ins, uniform choice, or weight requirements, other coaches may bench athletes or cut athletes from the team if they do not "make weight." If the athlete thinks coaching recommendations are credible and he or she wants to avoid consequences (e.g., public humiliation, being benched), disordered eating behaviors (e.g., restricting calories or certain foods) may seem like the logical choice. Likewise, if an athlete experiences initial performance improvement after losing some initial weight, he or she may be more motivated to continue disordered eating behaviors to lose additional weight.

Sources of Weight-Related Coach Pressure

Whether athletes perceive pressure from coaches to lose weight or maintain a low body weight through direct instructions to lose weight, athletes who perceive weight-related pressure tend to believe that they *need* to lose weight, exhibit more disordered eating behaviors, and be diagnosed with eating disorders more often than athletes who have not experienced similar weight-related coach pressures. Research has indicated that perceived weight-related coach pressure can have a stronger effect on elite athletes' dietary patterns than their previous perceptions about their bodies.

Coach–Athlete Relationship

Experienced coaches understand that the coach–athlete relationship has a significant effect on the athlete's entire life. Athletes who report a strong relationship with coaches sense more support and less conflict than athletes who report having a weak coach–athlete relationship. Although research on coach–athlete relationships and eating disorders is sparse, one study indicated a coach–athlete relationship predicted 25 percent of disordered eating behaviors in youth athletes. That is, weak coach–athlete relationships were associated with disordered eating behaviors such that they accounted for 25 percent of the difference in disordered eating scores; they did not explain the other 75 percent of the difference in disordered eating behavior scores.

Ashley M. Coker-Cranney

See also: Athletic Trainers; Sports; Weight Pressures in Sport

Bibliography

Berry, Tanya R., and Bruce L. Howe. "Risk Factors for Disordered Eating in Female University Athletes." *Journal of Sport Behavior* 23 (2000): 207–218.

de Bruin, A. P. (Karin), Raoul R. D. Oudejans, and Frank C. Bakker. "Dieting and Body Image in Aesthetic Sports: A Comparison of Dutch Female Gymnasts and Non-Aesthetic Sport Participants." *Psychology of Sport and Exercise* 8 (2007): 507–520. http://dx.doi.org/10.1016/j.psychsport.2006.10.002.

Harris, Mary B, and Debbie Greco. "Weight Control and Weight Concern in Competitive Female Gymnasts." *Journal of Sport & Exercise Psychology* 12 (1990): 427–433.

Jowett, Sophia, and Duncan Cramer. "The Prediction of Young Athletes' Physical Self from Perceptions of Relationships with Parents and Coaches." *Psychology of Sport and Exercise* 11 (2010): 140–147. http://dx.doi.org/10.1016/j.psychsport.2009.10.001.

Kerr, Gretchen, Erica Berman, and Mary Jane De Souza. "Disordered Eating in Women's Gymnastics: Perspectives of Athletes, Coaches, Parents, and Judges." *Journal of Applied Sport Psychology* 18 (2006): 28–43. http://dx.doi.org/10.1080/10413200500471301.

Muscat, Anne C., and Bonita C. Long. "Critical Comments about Body Shape and Weight: Disordered Eating of Female Athletes and Sport Participants." *Journal of Applied Sport Psychology* 20 (2005): 1–24. http://dx.doi.org/10.1080/10413200701784833.

Reel, Justine J., and Diane L. Gill. "Psychosocial Factors Related to Eating Disorders among High School and College Female Cheerleaders." *The Sport Psychologist* 10 (1996): 195–206.

Reel, Justine J., Sonya SooHoo, Trent A. Petrie, Christie Greenleaf, and Jennifer E. Carter. "Slimming Down for Sport: Developing a Weight Pressures in Sport Measure for Female Athletes." *Journal of Clinical Psychology* 4 (2010): 99–111.

Thompson, Ron A., and Roberta Trattner Sherman. *Eating Disorders in Sport.* New York: Routledge, 2010.

Waldron, Jennifer J., and Vikki Krane. "Whatever It Takes: Health Compromising Behaviors in Female Athletes." *QUEST* 57 (2000): 315–329. http://dx.doi.org/10.1080/003 36297.2005.10491860.

Williams, Patti L., Roger G. Sargent, and Larry J. Durstine. "Prevalence of Subclinical Eating Disorders in Collegiate Female Athletes." *Women in Sport & Physical Activity Journal* 12 (2003): 127–145.

COGNITIVE BEHAVIORAL THERAPY

Cognitive behavioral therapy (CBT) is a psychotherapeutic approach to treat dysfunctional emotions, behaviors, and cognitions through a goal-oriented procedure. CBT has been used as an umbrella term to refer to therapies that share a foundation in behavior learning theory and cognitive psychology. The goals of CBT are to challenge the thoughts about troubling personal situations by identifying the cognitive traps and help a client identify less disturbing thoughts and behaviors that can then be tested in real-life situations.

CBT is an evidence-based treatment for mental disorders including mood disorders, anxiety disorders, personality disorders, eating disorders, substance abuse disorders, and psychotic disorders. CBT is often brief and time limited and is used in both individual therapy and group settings. CBT techniques can also be adapted for self-help applications, such as replacing destructive thoughts with verbal personal compliments while looking in the mirror. CBT therapists identify and monitor thoughts, assumptions, beliefs, and behaviors related to, and accompanied by, debilitating negative emotions. A therapist guides a client to replace or transcend inaccurate or unhelpful emotions with realistic and useful cognitive and behavioral tools.

History

CBT can be traced back to the development of behavior therapy in the early 20th century, the development of cognitive therapy in the 1960s, and the subsequent merging of the two. Behavioral approaches appeared as early as 1924, with Mary Cover Jones's work on the unlearning of fears in children. However, between 1950 and 1970, the field emerged with researchers who were inspired by the behaviorist learning theories of Ivan Pavlov, John Watson, and Clark Hull. Psychologists also began applying the radical behaviorism of B. F. Skinner to clinical use.

CBT was primarily developed through a merging of behavior therapy with cognitive therapy during the late 1980s and early 1990s. Although rooted in different theories, cognitive and behavioral therapies found common ground in focusing on the here and now and symptom removal. Many CBT treatment programs have since been developed to address symptoms of specific disorders, such as depression, anxiety, and eating disorders. The health care trend of evidence-based treatment has favored CBT over other approaches such as psychodynamic treatments. For example, in the United Kingdom, the National Institute of Health and Clinical Excellence recommends CBT as the treatment of choice for bulimia nervosa.

In the 1960s, cognitive therapy rapidly became a frequently used intervention based on the work of Albert Ellis who developed Rational Emotive Behavior Therapy in the early 1950s. Aaron Beck, inspired by Ellis, became known as the father of cognitive therapy and the inventor of the widely used Beck Scales. Beck also distinguished three levels of cognition that cause and maintain psychopathology: (1) schemas/core beliefs, which are internal models of the self and the world that develop over the course of experiences beginning early in life. Schemas may lie dormant until they are activated by conditions similar to those under which they originally developed; (2) maladaptive assumptions, which include must/should and if-then statements; and (3) automatic thoughts, which include negative view of self, negative view of the future, and negative view of the world. During the 1980s and 1990s, cognitive and behavioral techniques were merged into cognitive behavioral therapy. Core beliefs often fuel development of eating disorders. Maladaptive assumptions and automatic thoughts contribute to the maintenance of eating disorder symptoms, including a negative view of the inner self and a negative image of the physical body. As such, addressing the three levels of cognition assists an eating disorder client in achieving relief from symptoms and beginning to heal.

Techniques

CBT techniques commonly include (1) keeping a diary of significant events and associated emotions, thoughts, and behaviors; (2) questioning and testing unhelpful and unrealistic cognitions, assumptions, evaluations, and beliefs ; (3) gradually facing activities that have been avoided; and (4) trying new ways of behaving and reacting. Relaxation, mindfulness, and distraction techniques are also commonly used. More specific to keeping a diary is maintaining a dysfunctional thought record to identify, evaluate, and change automatic thoughts. A thought record has columns for objectively describing triggering situations and associated automatic thoughts and emotions, and alternative, self-enhancing responses.

Eating Disorders

CBT as a therapeutic approach can treat all eating disorders regardless of actual diagnosis. Diaries of events, for example, can be useful for binge eaters to track the time, the amount of food consumed, and emotional triggers of a binge over a certain period. Patterns can then be identified, and unhelpful thoughts are recorded in thought records along with healthy thought substitutes. Additionally, individuals who suffer from anorexia nervosa can try eating a forbidden food at a restaurant with a support person. Someone with bulimia nervosa may be challenged to take a walk or write in a journal for 45 minutes following a meal or until the urge to purge abates.

Furthermore, CBT for anorexia nervosa employs behavioral strategies like establishing a regular pattern of eating and systematic exposure to several forbidden foods, while simultaneously addressing cognitive aspects of a disorder, such as motivation for change and a disturbance in an experience of shape and weight.

Specifically, what are a client's reasons for seeking treatment? Is motivation internal? How does an individual view the physical body and what are the automatic thoughts associated with examining the body in a mirror or other reflection? CBT challenges schema-level core beliefs and the inextricable tie between personal identity, body image, and an eating disorder. Healing is facilitated, for example, by a change in core beliefs about the value of self from the inside out, thus reducing the desire to control the physical weight or appearance. CBT is also a leading treatment for bulimia nervosa. For instance, a thought record can track automatic thoughts prior to, during, and after a binge. Helpful thoughts are suggested to replace automatic thoughts and a client is encouraged to keep a written record of results. Additionally, replacement behaviors (walks, journaling, visiting with supportive friends) are recommended following meals to help a client avoid purging until the feeling passes. A similar thought record can be used for binge eating disorder. Food diaries can be coupled with thought records to identify a pattern of binge behaviors and the food consumed during binges. Behaviors to replace binge episodes are suggested. Automatic thoughts associated with new behaviors are monitored and replacement thoughts are suggested. Ideally, the replacement thoughts become automatic as a client ventures into emotional health and well-being.

Obstacles

Obstacles to using CBT in early intervention are excessive avoidance, dissociation, anger, grief, extreme anxiety, catastrophic beliefs, prior trauma, comorbidity (specifically borderline personality disorder and psychotic disorders), substance abuse, depression and suicide risk, poor motivation, ongoing stressors, and certain cultural characteristics. Dissociation, for example, occurs when an individual detaches from the present or escapes to a safe emotional place because present thoughts remind him or her of a traumatic past event and are too painful to endure. The detachment can interfere with a person's ability to focus on the here-and-now, a premise of CBT. Dissociation is often seen in other disorders such as borderline personality disorder and schizophrenia. Therefore, having more than one diagnosis can impair a client's ability to positively respond to CBT. Substance abuse, for instance, chemically removes the client from here-and-now reality and reduces the effectiveness of CBT.

Juliann Cook Jeppsen

See also: Cognitive Behavioral Therapy Guided Self-Help Treatment; Cognitive Dissonance Interventions; Dialectical Behavior Therapy; Substance Abuse; Treatment

Bibliography

Alford, Brad, and Aaron Beck. *The Integrative Power of Cognitive Therapy.* New York: Guilford Press, 1998.

Beck, Aaron T. *Cognitive Therapy and Emotional Disorders.* Madison, CT: International Universities Press, 1975.

Beck, Aaron T., John A. Rush, Brian F. Shaw, and Gary Emery. *Cognitive Therapy of Depression.* New York: Guilford Press, 1979.

Fairburn, Christopher G., Zafra Cooper, and Roz Shafran. "Enhanced Cognitive Behavior Therapy for Eating Disorders (CBT-E): An Overview." In *Cognitive Behavior Therapy and Eating Disorders,* edited by Christopher G. Fairburn, 23–34. New York: Guilford Press, 2008.

Halmi, Katherine A., W. Stewart Agras, Scott Crow, James Mitchell, G. Terrance Wilson, Susan W. Bryson, and Helena C. Kraemer. "Predictors of Treatment Acceptance and Completion in Anorexia Nervosa: Implications for Future Study Designs." *Archives of General Psychiatry* 62, no. 7 (2005): 776–781. https://doi.org/10.1001/archpsyc.62.7.776.

COGNITIVE BEHAVIORAL THERAPY GUIDED SELF-HELP TREATMENT

One of the biggest challenges in the field of eating disorders is ensuring individuals who require care have access to treatment. Unfortunately, treatment for eating disorders can be prohibitively expensive (e.g., $1,000 or more per day for residential facilities). Further, insurance coverage for eating disorder treatment varies widely with one's plan and may not cover the necessary length of stay or adequate number of sessions. Availability of trained therapists and properly equipped facilities are other significant challenges. Mental health professionals are often required to seek specialized training before being certified to work with individuals who have an eating disorder. Although these specially certified clinicians may be relatively common in large cities, smaller towns and rural areas often do not attract these types of professionals. Moreover, efficacious treatments for eating disorders, such as cognitive behavioral therapy (CBT), require multiple visits per week, lasting at least an hour each, over the course of several months. For individuals who live in rural areas, who do not have reliable transportation, or whose schedules do not allow for such flexibility, this type of intensive, long-term commitment is often not possible.

For this reason, many mental health professionals and health care providers have advocated for treatments that find creative ways to bypass these barriers. Cognitive behavioral therapy guided self-help (or CBTgsh) is one such treatment. Often administered electronically, CBTgsh was first developed in the late 1990s to address obesity and binge eating disorder (BED). In the original study that tested CBTgsh, the intervention was found to successfully alleviate BED symptoms. During the first investigations of this particular treatment, BED was a relatively new concept and many clinicians had little or no exposure to it. Therefore, discovering an effective intervention tool was critical, given that many people suffering from BED were limited by a therapist's lack of experience with the disorder. Subsequent research on CBTgsh has verified this alternative to traditional psychotherapy reduces binge eating behaviors.

Treatment Protocol and Content

CBTgsh is based on the treatment manual *Overcoming Binge Eating*, written by international eating disorder expert Dr. Christopher Fairburn in the mid-1990s. This book was based on a popular treatment manual designed for mental health professionals that detailed CBT practices specifically for patients with eating disorders. *Overcoming*

Binge Eating was found to be an effective self-help manual soon after its first publication, and since then it has become the centerpiece for CBTgsh interventions.

The book is divided into two sections that correspond to different treatment focuses. In the first section, readers are educated on the nature of binge eating, associated problems, and potential causes of this behavior. The first section also provides a background on the theory of a guided self-help intervention and explains the rationale for treatment design. The second section details six specific steps that participants take to relieve binge eating symptoms. The six steps build upon each other and a person must complete the steps in order.

One particular aspect of CBTgsh that has been thought to contribute to its efficacy is the establishment of a regular eating pattern. One of the main predictors of binge episodes is previous dietary restriction. Individuals who restrict caloric intake for a brief period—from several hours to a week—are at a higher risk for a subsequent binge episode. This pattern of restriction followed by binge eating is extremely common in many eating disorders that involve binge episodes, such as BED and bulimia nervosa. In CBTgsh, the formation and adherence to a regular eating schedule combats the yo-yo effect of restriction and binge eating. Research has shown the more successful a person is in adhering to an eating schedule, the more positive outcomes at the conclusion of the CBTgsh protocol.

If conducted in a research environment, CBTgsh takes 12 weeks to complete. Most self-help treatment protocols require face-to-face therapy; whereas the standard for CBTgsh is six 15–20-minute appointments held biweekly for the duration of the treatment. However, one of the strengths of this treatment approach is that it is entirely self-paced. For the purposes of research integrity and standardization, researchers require participants in studies to complete the CBTgsh protocol at a particular pace. Laypersons, however, who purchase the treatment manual independently are free to complete the protocol at their own pace.

Research on CBTgsh

In the first study testing the effectiveness of CBTgsh in treating binge eating disorder, guided self-help (that included contact with a facilitator and use of the *Overcoming Binge Eating* manual) was compared to pure self-help (no contact with facilitator, provided with manual) and a wait-list condition. Seventy-two women with binge eating disorder were randomly assigned to one of the three treatment options for 12 weeks; the severity of their eating disorder as well as other measures of mental health were given to participants both before and after completing the 12-week treatment. Both the guided self-help and pure self-help had positive effects on participants' binge eating disorder severity, and improvements in overall psychiatric health. The guided self-help treatment option—that was the first iteration of CBTgsh—was particularly potent for its participants, which was even more optimistic given the relatively low therapist burden associated with CBTgsh.

Subsequent research has replicated these findings multiple times, lending support for the effectiveness of CBTgsh to treat BED. Other research has focused on the efficacy of CBTgsh to treat bulimia nervosa (BN). In one study, 81 women with

BN were assigned to receive either an 18-week CBTgsh protocol or 18 weeks of group CBT (hour-and-a-half-long weekly office visits with a trained therapist in a group). Patients were contacted a year after treatment protocol and asked to report on their eating disorder behaviors and general mental and emotional well-being. The majority (75 percent) of individuals who completed the CBTgsh were free of bulimic symptoms after one year, compared to only 44 percent of individuals in the traditional CBT group. This study, among others, has supported the utility of CBTgsh in treating BN and BED. The program emphasis on establishing and maintaining a routine eating schedule has been credited with explaining its utility to treat eating disorders.

CBTgsh in the Modern Age

All of the mental health field, including the area of eating disorders, is faced with new challenges unique to modern society. Treatments are now tested in populations of different cultural and ethnic backgrounds to determine whether the therapeutic content transfers across culture and language barriers. Technology, including social media, is being probed as a potential new frontier for prevention, education, and intervention efforts. Several researchers have studied the effects of cross-cultural efficacy and technology-based administration could have on CBTgsh.

In one study, researchers evaluated whether CBTgsh was equally as effective in a native Mexican, Spanish-speaking population as it has been in U.S./Canadian, English-speaking samples. Thirty-one Mexican American women were recruited to participate in a culturally adapted CBTgsh protocol; the treatment gains reported by this sample were equally as potent and long-lasting as gains found in non-Mexican samples. This finding suggests CBTgsh is an effective treatment for binge eating across cultural contexts, which strengthens the argument for its widespread availability and implementation, even in culturally diverse settings.

Another study looked at whether CBTgsh would be equally as helpful if administered solely over the Internet. One hundred fifty-five women with BN were randomly assigned to complete traditional CBTgsh (use of the *Overcoming Binge Eating* treatment manual in hard copy) or Internet-based CBTgsh (no hard copy provided, material available in full via Internet platform). Although the researchers hypothesized the Internet-based protocol would be more effective at treating the bulimic symptoms than the traditional CBTgsh protocol, no significant differences between the groups were found. Additionally, a significant number of participants who were assigned to the Internet-based CBTgsh protocol never completed the program. Although the convenience and ease-of-access typically associated with electronic-based interventions are often touted as major advantages over traditional psychotherapies, this study (among others that have shown a similar dropout rate) suggests future research is required to identify why some participants never complete an Internet-based treatment protocol.

Hannah J. Hopkins

See also: Cognitive Behavioral Therapy; Self-Help Interventions; Treatment

Bibliography

Bailer, Ursula, Martina de Zwaan, Friedrich Leisch, Alexandra Strnad, Claudia Lennkh-Wolfsberg, Nadia El-Giamal, Kurt Hornik, and Siegfried Kasper. "Guided Self-Help versus Cognitive-Behavioral Group Therapy in the Treatment of Bulimia Nervosa." *International Journal of Eating Disorders* 35, no. 4 (2004): 522–537. https://doi.org/10.1002/eat.20003.

Cachelin, Fary M., Munyi Shea, Phoutdavone Phimphasone, G. Terence Wilson, Douglas R. Thompson, and Ruth H. Striegel. "Culturally Adapted Cognitive Behavioral Guided Self-Help for Binge Eating: A Feasibility Study with Mexican Americans." *Cultural Diversity and Ethnic Minority Psychology* 20, no. 3 (2014): 449–457. https://doi.org/10.1037/a0035345.

Carter, Jacqueline C., and Christopher Fairburn. "Cognitive-Behavioral Self-Help for Binge Eating Disorder: A Controlled Effectiveness Study." *Journal of Consulting and Clinical Psychology* 66, no. 4 (1998): 616–623.

Fairburn, Christopher G. *Overcoming Binge Eating.* New York: Guilford Press, 1995.

Grilo, Carlos M., and Robin M. Masheb. "A Randomized Controlled Comparison of Guided Self-Help Cognitive Behavioral Therapy and Behavioral Weight Loss for Binge Eating Disorder." *Behaviour Research and Therapy* 43, no. 11 (2005): 1509–1525. https://doi.org/10.1016/j.brat.2004.11.010.

Striegel-Moore, Ruth H., G. Terence Wilson, Lynn DeBar, Nancy Perrin, Frances Lynch, Francine Rosselli, and Helena C. Kraemer. "Cognitive Behavioral Guided Self-Help for the Treatment of Recurrent Binge Eating." *Journal of Consulting and Clinical Psychology* 78, no. 3 (2010): 312–321. https://doi.org/10.1037/a0018915.

Wagner, Gudrun, Eva Penelo, Christian Wanner, Paulina Gwinner, Marie-Louise Trofaier, Hartmut Imgart, Karin Waldherr, Çiçek Wöber-Bingöl, and Andreas F. K. Karwautz. "Internet-Delivered Cognitive–Behavioural Therapy v. Conventional Guided Self-Help for Bulimia Nervosa: Long-Term Evaluation of a Randomised Controlled Trial." *The British Journal of Psychiatry* 202, no. 2 (2013): 135–141. https://doi.org/10.1192/bjp.bp.111.098582.

Wilson, G. Terence, and Laurie J. Zandberg. "Cognitive–Behavioral Guided Self-Help for Eating Disorders: Effectiveness and Scalability." *Clinical Psychology Review* 32, no. 4 (2012): 343–357. https://doi.org/10.1016/j.cpr.2012.03.001.

Zendegui, Elaina A., Julia A. West, and Laurie J. Zandberg. "Binge Eating Frequency and Regular Eating Adherence: The Role of Eating Pattern in Cognitive Behavioral Guided Self-Help." *Eating Behaviors* 15, no. 2 (2014): 241–243. https://doi.org/10.1016/j.eatbeh.2014.03.002.

COGNITIVE DISSONANCE INTERVENTIONS

Eating disorders have always presented challenges in treatment, including resistance, concealment of symptoms, and high rates of comorbidity and mortality. Because of these challenges, there has been an increased focus on prevention programs to reduce risk factors for subsequent eating disorders. Researchers and practitioners have investigated a variety of prevention programs, encompassing psychoeducation to exercise programs and everything in between. One particularly promising prevention program for eating disorders is cognitive dissonance training. Cognitive dissonance uses an exploration of an individual's viewpoint around a certain topic to create dissonance, or tension, between arguments both for and against that viewpoint. The goal is to heighten awareness of potential benefits and drawbacks of a particular action or belief to help in decision making. In eating disorder prevention, cognitive dissonance programs typically ask clients to explore their attitudes and beliefs about the thin ideal prevalent in Western cultures. Cognitive dissonance is also used in interventions for eating disorders, although a majority of research on applying this theory to eating disorders is on prevention.

Overview of Cognitive Dissonance Theory

Cognitive dissonance theory was originally developed in social psychology (a branch of psychology that focuses solely on social interactions and their effects on emotions, thoughts, and behaviors) in the late 1950s. The theory is based on the idea that people seek to minimize conflict between their actions and their beliefs by altering their beliefs. For example, if an individual believes it is important for everyone to do their part to protect the environment, but simultaneously drives a non–environmentally friendly car, she may readjust her beliefs about taking care of the environment. Another example may be someone who believes that junk food is unhealthy and should not be consumed but goes to the movie theater and has a large bag of popcorn. That individual may readjust his or her previous belief (I should not eat junk food) to something that permits eating popcorn (e.g., junk food is OK as long as I don't eat it regularly).

The conflict between someone's beliefs and their actions is referred to as *dissonance* and is thought to be an uncomfortable sensation; hence, individuals act to reduce or eliminate the tension. In addition to changing beliefs, individuals can also change their behavior to make it more in line with their beliefs. Returning to the example of the person who believes in protecting the environment but has a non–environmentally friendly car, rather than changing their thoughts about the importance of protecting the environment, they may choose to sell their car in favor of one that is environmentally friendly.

In therapy, cognitive dissonance is used to motivate behavior change or attitude shifts. Dissonance-based interventions (or DBIs) are considered particularly potent because they motivate change based on an individual's self-concept, which produces longer lasting change than using an external motivator. Typically, clients are asked to describe their beliefs on a certain topic (e.g., importance of dieting) and then defend the opposing belief. Through the process of arguing for a belief contradictory to the original belief, individuals are more likely to endorse a modified belief at the conclusion of an exercise.

History of Prevention Programs for Eating Disorders

A majority of prevention programs been designed for and tested in at-risk populations for eating disorders have shown little or no significant improvement. Some researchers claim that as few as 5 percent of all prevention programs for eating disorders result in reductions of disordered eating behaviors and/or reduce the likelihood of developing an eating disorder. Prevention programs take many forms. Initially, many of these preventive efforts were primarily psychoeducation-based, taking the form of traditional classroom learning where individuals listened to a presentation regarding the causes of eating disorders, healthy eating, and weight management behaviors. Evidence has shown these didactic, teacher–student type programs typically do not produce significant results compared to interactive programs.

Once researchers and clinicians realized psychoeducation programs did not produce results, the focus switched to risk reduction. These prevention programs focus on reducing demonstrated attitudes, beliefs, and behaviors that correlate to disordered eating, including body dissatisfaction, internalization of the thin ideal, dieting, and negative affect. Risk reduction programs also simultaneously promote protective strategies, including critical consumption of mass media and stress management techniques. Although noticeably more effective than psychoeducational prevention programs, these programs also produced limited results.

Following these two waves of largely unsuccessful prevention programs, researchers began to turn to cognitive dissonance and dissonance-based interventions. DBIs were widely known and revered for the ability to challenge and change maladaptive beliefs and attitudes, and anecdotal evidence from clinicians supported the efficacy of DBIs for treating eating disorders. Beginning in the mid-1980s, DBIs became a larger focus for clinicians exploring preventive measures against eating disorders.

Results from Dissonance-Based Preventions and Interventions

Prior to their application to eating disorders, DBIs had been used in a variety of problem areas, including specific phobias, obesity, environment protection behaviors, smoking cessation, interpersonal and dating violence, substance abuse, and others. When DBIs appeared in the field of eating disorders, they focused particularly on challenging internalization of the thin ideal, or the degree to which someone buys into the Western cultural standard of thinness for female beauty. Other topics explored and emphasized in dissonance-based prevention programs were body dissatisfaction, extreme dieting, and negative affect. Individuals were generally given an option to participate in these types of programs as previous research indicated results were more potent when participants chose whether to participate. These programs often required participants to write a speech, deliver a presentation, or participate in a debate on the issue(s) at hand. Following completion of the program, participants largely reported greater intentions to change their behaviors or a modified belief regarding the issue. The structure of DBIs is largely identical between prevention programs targeted at populations with higher risk for eating disorders and intervention programs targeted at persons already diagnosed with an eating disorder or experiencing disordered eating behaviors.

DBIs have been used in a variety of populations and have produced widely positive results. One study investigated the efficacy of a dissonance-based prevention program in a sample of female athletes, a population at high risk for disordered eating behaviors. Women who participated were asked to participate in what was called *body activism* behaviors that directly challenged beliefs about their bodies through actions. Examples of body activism tasks included wearing shorts even though you believe your thighs are big or standing in front of a mirror in the least amount of clothing you feel comfortable in and repeating positive statements regarding physical and intellectual qualities. Results showed that individuals experienced a reduction in depression and sadness, an internalization of an in-shape body ideal (as opposed to the thin ideal), and increases in body satisfaction as a result of a DBI program.

Similar results were seen when sorority members were exposed to a dissonance-based prevention program targeting internalization of the thin ideal of female beauty. Following program participation, women reported lower dietary restraint, fewer disordered eating behaviors, and enhanced body satisfaction. Other studies have replicated these findings in different populations, and the positive results produced by DBIs persist to for two to three years, which is extremely rare. Additionally, DBIs have been shown to work among the spectrum of disordered eating behaviors, with anorexia, bulimia, obesity, and extreme dieting all showing responsiveness to dissonance-based programs.

Hannah J. Hopkins

See also: Prevention; Treatment

Bibliography

Becker, Carolyn Black, Lisa M. Smith, and Anna C. Ciao. "Reducing Eating Disorders Risk Factors in Sorority Members: A Randomized Trial." *Behavior Therapy* 36, no. 3 (2005): 245–253. http://dx.doi.org/10.1016/S0005-7894(05)80073-5.

Festinger, Leon. *A Theory of Cognitive Dissonance*. Redwood City, CA: Stanford University Press, 1962.

Smith, Ariane, and Trent Petrie. "Reducing the Risk of Disordered Eating among Female Athletes: A Test of Alternative Interventions." *Journal of Applied Sport Psychology* 20, no. 4 (2008): 392–407. https://doi.org/10.1080/10413200802241832.

Stice, Eric, Heather Shaw, Carolyn Black Becker, and Paul Rohde. "Dissonance-Based Interventions for the Prevention of Eating Disorders: Using Persuasion Principles to Promote Health." *Prevention Science* 9, no. 2 (2008): 114–128. https://doi.org/10.1007/s11121-008-0093-x.

Witcomb, Gemma L., Jon Arcelus, and Jue Chen. "Can Cognitive Dissonance Methods Developed in the West for Combatting the 'Thin Ideal' Help Slow the Rapidly Increasing Prevalence of Eating Disorders in Non-Western Cultures?" *Shanghai Archives of Psychiatry* 25, no. 6 (2013): 332–340. https://doi.org/10.3969/j.issn.1002-0829.2013.06.002.

COMORBIDITY

Comorbidity is the co-occurrence of more than one mental disorder and is sometimes referred to as a dual diagnosis. Eating disorders have high rates of coexisting with other mental illnesses. In fact, mood disorders, the most common comorbid condition, are estimated to coexist with eating disorders in 50 percent of clients

However, one study that separated participants by type of eating disorder diagnosis found mood disorders are present in 64.1–96.0 percent of clients with anorexia nervosa and in 50–90 percent of clients with bulimia nervosa.

It is important to consider any comorbid conditions with eating disorders for treatment planning to maximize successful treatment outcomes and increase chances of recovery. In addition to depression, it is common for individuals with eating disorders to concurrently be diagnosed with an anxiety disorder or obsessive-compulsive disorder (OCD). Additionally, eating-disordered clients may also present with bipolar disorder (i.e., a mood disorder with periods of mania and depression), substance abuse, personality disorders, a history of trauma, or self-harming behaviors. These conditions are discussed in separate entries of this volume.

Clients should be assessed for the potential for overlap in psychiatric conditions and treated accordingly. For example, clients who are diagnosed with depression and eating disorders may receive psychotropic medications, which may lessen the intensity of emotional triggers to engage in eating-disorder behaviors and improve overall mood. A client with comorbid conditions may appear more resistant to treatment recommendations. However, it is important to establish which diagnosis should receive primary diagnosis status and match treatment accordingly. For example, individuals who present with substance abuse and an eating disorder should be assessed carefully for placement in an eating disorder specialty or substance abuse treatment center for appropriate care. On a positive note, many eating disorder facilities have recognized the high prevalence of comorbidity and offer dual diagnosis treatment.

Justine J. Reel

See also: Anxiety Disorders; Depression; Obsessive-Compulsive Disorder; Personality Disorders; Substance Abuse

Bibliography

Bardone-Cone, Anna M., Megan B. Harney, Christine R. Maldonado, Melissa A. Lawson, D. Paul Robinson, Roma Smith, and Aneesh Tosh. "Defining Recovery from an Eating Disorder: Conceptualization, Validation, and Examination of Psychosocial Functioning and Psychiatric Comorbidity." *Behaviour Research and Therapy* 48, no. 3 (2010): 194–202. https://doi.org/10.1016/j.brat.2009.11.001.

Jordan, Jennifer, Peter R. Joyce, Frances A. Carter, Jacqueline Horn, Virginia V. W. Mcintosh, Suzanne E. Luty, Janice M. McKenzie, Christopher M. A. Frampton, Roger T. Mulder, and Cynthia M. Bulik. "Specific and Nonspecific Comorbidity in Anorexia Nervosa." *International Journal of Eating Disorders* 41, no. 1 (2008): 47–56. https://doi.org/10.1002/eat.

McElroy, Susan L., Renu Kotwal, and Paul E. Keck. "Comorbidity of Eating Disorders and Bipolar Disorder and Treatment Implications." *Bipolar Disorders* 8 (2006): 686–695. https://doi.org/10.1111/j.1399-5618.2006.00401.x.

Mischoulon, David, Kamry T. Eddy, Aparna Keshaviah, Diana Dinescu, Stephanie L. Ross, Andrea E. Kass, Debra L. Franko, and David B. Herzog. "Depression and Eating Disorders: Treatment and Course." *Journal of Affective Disorders* 130 (2011): 470–477. https://doi.org/10.1016/j.jad.2010.10.043.

COPING SKILLS

Coping skills is a broad term for behaviors a person can use in response to a situation, emotion, thought, or experience. Coping skills represent a variety of common behaviors and thought patterns that serve a specific purpose, such as reducing stress or distracting someone from negative emotions. Coping skills are intricately related to disordered eating and eating disorders. For many people, eating-related behaviors represent a way of coping, albeit negative, for emotional relief during times of stress or sadness. Another example is individuals who cope by exerting control over their food intake by counting calories or restricting certain types of foods. For people who struggle with eating disorders, their disordered eating behaviors might reflect a dysfunctional form of coping with personal difficulties. Therefore, treatment approaches for eating disorders, including cognitive behavioral therapy (CBT), interpersonal therapy (IPT), and dialectal behavior therapy (DBT), have incorporated coping skills training to educate clients to better respond in stressful situations.

Types of Coping Skills

Coping skills can be separated into three distinct categories: task-oriented, emotion-oriented, and avoidance-oriented. Task-oriented coping skills involve actively working toward resolution of a problem. Examples of task-oriented coping skills may include seeking social support from friends and family for stress or being assertive in relationships. One of the challenges with task-oriented coping skills is that they typically work best for specific problems and are not as effective in reducing generalized anxiety or stress. For example, for students who reported stress related to academics, the use of task-oriented coping skills was not found to significantly reduce stress levels. In students who reported specific academic stressors (e.g., too many classes, an anxiety-provoking project), task-oriented coping skills did reduce stress.

The second category, emotion-oriented coping skills, is often considered to be negative coping, such as crying or engaging in self-blame. Rumination, or constantly thinking about something distressing and its potential causes, is another example of emotion-oriented coping. Emotion-oriented coping skills are almost always considered unhealthy because they provide little lasting benefit to an individual and can in some cases worsen affect or stress. Typically, this set of skills is targeted in therapy because it is unproductive in moving someone closer to a solution.

Finally, the third category is avoidance-oriented coping skills. Predictably, these behaviors often involve distracting one's self from the distressing situation. Although avoidance-oriented coping mechanisms are generally seen as unhealthy, when used in concert with task-oriented coping, they can be adaptive. For example, someone may choose to go for a run (avoidance-oriented) to clear his or her head and then go home and confront his or her spouse in a healthy manner (task-oriented) over a disagreement. Other examples of avoidance-oriented coping skills include abusing drugs or alcohol, physically withdrawing from unpleasant situations (e.g., skipping classes), and watching a movie or television show for distraction purposes.

Coping Skills and Eating Disorders

Generally, research has shown people with eating disorders exhibit maladaptive coping skills. Conversely, individuals with lower eating disorder symptomology report more adaptive coping skills. Studies have found individuals with more disordered eating behaviors report using more emotion- and avoidance-oriented and fewer task-oriented coping skills than healthy controls. Similarly, when individuals are fully recovered from an eating disorder—physically, behaviorally, cognitively, and emotionally—the coping skills they report using are almost identical to the coping skills reported by healthy controls. However, when people are in early recovery from eating disorders (i.e., their weight has been restored and they no longer engage in the disordered behaviors but are not fully cognitively or emotionally recovered), their coping skill set more closely resembles that of someone in the throes of an eating disorder. This suggests development of healthy coping mechanisms is integral to recovery and may even provide the demarcation line between someone who is still recovering versus someone who is recovered.

Another interesting finding that connects coping skills to disordered eating behaviors is how well people believe they cope with stress. Although research on this topic is not as robust as research on the connection between types of coping mechanisms and eating disorders, one study conducted with college students found students who had less confidence in their ability to effectively manage day-to-day stress were more likely to engage in dysfunctional eating behaviors. The confidence individuals believe they can cope with stress is known as *coping self-efficacy* and is closely related to a person's belief in problem solving abilities. This latter idea—confidence in one's ability to problem-solve—has also been connected to disordered eating behaviors in both clinical samples (i.e., among people with a diagnosed eating disorder) and nonclinical samples (people without a diagnosed eating disorder). These findings suggest that it is not only the nature of the coping mechanisms used by individuals that puts them at higher risk for an eating disorder but also the confidence these individuals have in their ability to handle stress and solve daily problems impacts their eating behaviors.

Much attention has been given to binge eating episodes as a form of maladaptive coping. Research has shown binge episodes are almost always preceded by a state of negative affect, whether anger, sadness, anxiety, or loneliness. Subjective reports of binge eating episodes reveal individuals often experience a temporary lift in the negative mood while engaging in the binge eating episode, supporting the argument that people associate the binge episode with a way to cope. However, binge eating as a coping mechanism becomes maladaptive when it is uncontrollable to an individual and is followed by intensified negative emotions (often mixed with guilt and shame over the binge). In fact, this second episode of negative mood following a binge episode often causes individuals to resort to purging methods, like self-induced vomiting, laxative abuse, or overexercising, as another maladaptive coping skill. In this sense, the entire cycle of binge eating disorder and bulimia nervosa can be viewed as a series of maladaptive coping mechanisms.

Similarly, some researchers have hypothesized caloric restriction in anorexia nervosa functions as a maladaptive coping mechanism in the same way that binge eating does in binge eating disorder and bulimia nervosa. Although binge eating is usually a coping mechanism used in response to negative mood, studies have found caloric restriction in anorexia is more often caused by a sense of loss of control. This sense of control has also been reported in individuals who are dieting but not diagnosed with anorexia nervosa, indicating dietary restriction is also used by healthy individuals as a form of coping. Therefore, all the major eating disorders and their related behaviors are at least in part the result of maladaptive coping mechanisms taken to the extreme.

In the treatment of eating disorders, the focus is to identify precursors or precipitating stressors and respond to stressors with different, healthier coping mechanisms rather than binge eating, overexercising, or self-starvation. The differences between the treatment approaches relate to specific types of coping skills emphasized and how skills are taught. For example, in CBT the primary emphasis of the treatment is on challenging and correcting incorrect behaviors and thoughts that maintain an eating disorder and/or contribute to negative moods. Therefore, the coping skills emphasized in CBT are cognitive in nature and focus on changing someone's interior monologue. Interpersonal therapy focuses solely on relationships someone has with other people in their life, so the coping skills emphasized in IPT often involve having social support, confronting others over disagreements, and assertiveness skill training. Coping skills emphasized in DBT include mindfulness training, distress tolerance skills (e.g., self-soothing, emotional validation), and emotion regulation skills.

Hannah J. Hopkins

See also: Cognitive Behavioral Therapy; Dialectical Behavior Therapy; Resiliency; Self-Care; Treatment

Bibliography

Bryan, J., and M. Tiggemann. "The Effect of Weight-Loss Dieting on Cognitive Performance and Psychological Well-Being in Overweight Women." *Appetite* 36, no. 2 (2001): 147–156. https://doi.org/10.1006/appe.2000.0389.

Christiano, Beth, and J. Scott Mizes. "Appraisal and Coping Deficits Associated with Eating Disorders: Implications for Treatment." *Cognitive and Behavioral Practice* 4, no. 2 (1997): 263–290. https://doi.org/10.1016/S1077-7229(97)80004-1.

Ekern, Jacquelyn. "Effective Coping Skills: Eating Disorder Self-Soothing." Eating Disorder Hope. Last modified June 6, 2016. Accessed November 22, 2017. https://www.eatingdisorderhope.com/recovery/self-help-tools-skills-tips/self-soothing-advice.

Fitzsimmons, Ellen E., and Anna M. Bardone-Cone. "Coping and Social Support as Potential Moderators of the Relation between Anxiety and Eating Disorder Symptomatology." *Eating Behaviors* 12, no. 1 (2011): 21–28. https://doi.org/10.1016/j.eatbeh.2010.09.002.

Fitzsimmons, Ellen E., and Anna M. Bardone-Cone. "Differences in Coping across Stages of Recovery from an Eating Disorder." *International Journal of Eating Disorders* 43, no. 8 (2010): 689–693. https://doi.org/10.1002/eat.20781.

Kelly, Nichole R., Janet A. Lydecker, and Suzanne E. Mazzeo. "Positive Cognitive Coping Strategies and Binge Eating in College Women." *Eating Behaviors* 13, no. 3 (2012): 289–292. https://doi.org/10.1016/j.eatbeh.2012.03.012.

MacNeil, Laura, Christianne Esposito-Smythers, Robyn Mehlenbeck, and Julie Weismoore. "The Effects of Avoidance Coping and Coping Self-Efficacy on Eating Disorder Attitudes and Behaviors: A Stress-Diathesis Model." *Eating Behaviors* 13, no. 4 (2012): 293–296. https://doi.org/10.1016/j.eatbeh.2012.06.005.

Shea, Maureen E., and Mary E. Pritchard. "Is Self-Esteem the Primary Predictor of Disordered Eating?" *Personality and Individual Differences* 42, no. 8 (2007): 1527–1537. https://doi.org/10.1016/j.paid.2006.10.026.

COSMETIC SURGERY AND EATING DISORDERS

Cosmetic surgeries are extremely popular in many Western countries. Between 1992 and 2002, the number of U.S. adults who underwent a cosmetic surgery rose 1,600 percent from 400,000 to 6.6 million. Many procedures are classified as noninvasive, such as microdermabrasion, Botox injections, or chemical peels. Of the invasive cosmetic surgeries, the most common in the United States are breast augmentation, rhinoplasty (nose reshaping), and liposuction. Body dissatisfaction and low self-esteem have been repeatedly connected with a desire for cosmetic surgery in research studies. Although the potential link between cosmetic surgery and eating disorders has long been noted in the scientific community, it remains a vastly understudied topic. Most existing literature on the topic is in the form of case studies thatlimit the extent to which results can be interpreted as widespread phenomena. However, results from the handful of larger studies that have investigated eating disorders and cosmetic surgery have provided support for a close connection between the two.

A History of Research on Cosmetic Surgery

Many studies have found individuals who report a higher interest in cosmetic procedures or who have undergone these procedures are often plagued by lower self-esteem, dysfunctional body image, and a history of teasing or bullying. Most of these studies have focused on body contouring procedures, such as liposuctions, tummy tucks, and breast augmentations, but similar results have been noted for surgeries on the face (rhinoplasty, eye lifts, etc.). The earliest studies on this topic were conducted in the 1950s and 1960s by doctors at Johns Hopkins hospital in Baltimore, Maryland. These studies were largely patient self-report and interpreted from a psychodynamic orientation, the dominant theory in psychology at the time. Patients seeking cosmetic surgeries were overwhelmingly diagnosed with different psychopathologies, including neurotic depression and passive-dependent personality disorder.

Following this first wave of investigations, more standardized measures were incorporated into psychological studies in the 1970s and 1980s that allowed results to be generalized and compared. As it related to the study of cosmetic surgery and body image, the consensus seemed to shift considerably with the inclusion of more rigorous and standardized tests. Patients receiving cosmetic surgeries were tested before and after procedures and compared to control groups that did not receive surgery; the results did not show any measurable difference between the groups. Unlike the studies from the 1950s and 1960s, which found individuals who received cosmetic surgery had higher rates of psychopathology than the general population, the second generation of studies on this topic found little evidence for this pattern.

The third generation of studies, beginning in the 1990s and continuing to present day, has adjusted for the limitations of previous studies. Self-report interviews with patients have been used in conjunction with standardized psychological tests to provide researchers with a rich, nuanced picture of the experiences of individuals who have cosmetic surgery. Additionally, the prevalence of these procedures has skyrocketed, offering researchers access to larger samples that produce more statistically trustworthy results. Current research on cosmetic surgery and its relationship with mental health suggests people who seek body-altering procedures have higher rates of anxiety and depression prior to surgery but experience improvements in mood and self-esteem following surgery.

Cosmetic Surgery and Mental Health

Although results vary considerably depending on the type of surgery studied, results generally support the conclusion that individuals who have cosmetic procedures are more likely to experience a mental disorder. One study compared rates of mental illness between a group of people who had undergone a consultation for a cosmetic procedure and a group of controls (individuals who had recently undergone a noncosmetic procedure). A significantly higher percentage of people who expressed interest in a cosmetic procedure had a history of diagnosed mental illness compared to the control group: 19 percent versus 4 percent, respectively. Additionally, 18 percent of people interested in a cosmetic procedure reported being on a psychiatric medication at the time of consultation, compared to 5 percent of the noncosmetic procedure sample.

Further research on this topic has focused more pointedly on the role body image and body dissatisfaction play in the desire for cosmetic procedures. Numerous studies have repeatedly shown greater body dissatisfaction, lower self-esteem, and a history of body-related teasing correlate with an increased desire for cosmetic procedures. Other variables associated with a higher self-reported interest in cosmetic surgeries include lower educational attainment, being divorced or separated, and a greater internalization of sociocultural messages about beauty standards. Some procedures (primarily liposuction and abdominoplasty, or "tummy tuck") have also been associated with disordered eating behaviors.

Poorer mental health appears to be a reliable predictor of increased interest in cosmetic procedures *prior* to surgery, but research suggests individuals generally experience positive results in their mental well-being *after* surgery. One study conducted in northern Europe compared scores on self-report measures of mental health and body satisfaction between pre- and postsurgery, as well as against scores from the general population. Results showed body image evaluation and self-esteem improved pre- to postsurgery. The cosmetic procedure group was significantly different from the general population group on all measures prior to their procedures but did not differ from the general population group after their procedures. These results and similar trends from other studies, suggest cosmetic procedures can cause improvements in mental well-being.

Cosmetic Surgery and Eating Disorders

As mentioned, certain cosmetic procedures have been shown to correlate with higher rates of disordered eating, particularly surgeries of the stomach. Although the connection between cosmetic surgeries and body image is well studied, the relationship between these procedures and eating disorders is far less studied. The research that has been conducted on this topic is most often in the form of case studies. These case studies have given rise to several theories explaining the connection between cosmetic procedures and eating disorders. One theory suggests liposuction (subcutaneous fat removal) is a variant of purging behavior found in bulimia nervosa (BN); this is supported by the temporary reduction in depression noted in one individual diagnosed with BN following liposuction surgery, a pattern almost identical to the reduction in depression seen following other forms of purging (e.g., vomiting, overexercising). Additionally, one of the only large-scale studies on this topic found a distinct connection between cosmetic surgery and purging behaviors. Another theory suggests the desire for cosmetic surgery is prompted by an unhealthy hypercompetitive personality type, which contributes to higher levels of disordered eating. Although each of these theories have been moderately supported, most researchers hypothesize disordered eating behaviors and cosmetic surgery are connected by body dissatisfaction and other body image variables.

Hannah J. Hopkins

See also: Airbrushing; Body Image; Celebrities and Eating Disorders; Media; Tanning Behaviors and Body Image

Bibliography

Calogero, Rachel M., Afroditi Pina, Lora E. Park, and Zara Rahemtulla. "Objectification Theory Predicts College Women's Attitudes toward Cosmetic Surgery." *Sex Roles* 63, no. 1–2 (2010): 32–41. http://dx.doi.org/10.1007/s11199-010-9759-5.

Coughlin, Janelle W., Colleen C. Schreyer, David B. Sarwer, Leslie J. Heinberg, Graham W. Redgrave, and Angela S. Guarda. "Cosmetic Surgery in Inpatients with Eating Disorders: Attitudes and Experience." *Body Image* 9, no. 1 (2012): 180–183. https://doi.org/10.1016/j.bodyim.2011.10.007.

Jávo, Iiná Márjá, Gunn Pettersen, Jan H. Rosenvinge, and Tore Sørlie. "Predicting Interest in Liposuction among Women with Eating Problems: A Population-Based Study." *Body Image* 9, no. 1 (2012): 131–136. https://doi.org/10.1016/j.bodyim.2011.08.002.

Markey, Charlotte N., and Patrick M. Markey. "Correlates of Young Women's Interest in Obtaining Cosmetic Surgery." *Sex Roles* 61, no. 3–4 (2009): 158–166. http://dx.doi.org/10.1007/s11199-009-9625-5.

Sarwer, D. B., H. A. Zanville, D. LaRossa, and S. P. Bartlett. "Mental Health Histories and Psychiatric Medication Usage among Persons Who Sought Cosmetic Surgery." *Plastic and Reconstructive Surgery* 114, no. 7 (2004): 1927–1933. https://doi.org/10.1097/01.PRS.0000142999.86432.1F.

Sarwer, David B., and Canice E. Crerand. "Body Image and Cosmetic Medical Treatments." *Body Image* 1, no. 1 (2004): 99–111. https://doi.org/10.1016/S1740-1445(03)00003-2.

Soest, T. von, Ingela Lundin Kvalem, H. E. Roald, and K. C. Skolleborg. "The Effects of Cosmetic Surgery on Body Image, Self-Esteem, and Psychological Problems." *Journal of Plastic, Reconstructive & Aesthetic Surgery* 62, no. 10 (2009): 1238–1244. https://doi.org/10.1016/j.bjps.2007.12.093.

Thornton, Bill, Richard M. Ryckman, and Joel A. Gold. "Competitive Orientations and Men's Acceptance of Cosmetic Surgery." *Psychology* 4, no. 12 (2013): 950–955. https://doi.org/10.4236/psych.2013.412137.

Thornton, Bill, Richard M. Ryckman, and Joel A. Gold. "Competitive Orientations and Women's Acceptance of Cosmetic Surgery." *Psychology* 4, no. 1 (2013): 67–72. https://doi.org/10.4236/psych.2013.41009.

D

DANCERS

Dance has been used for ceremony, rituals, and entertainment since the earliest days of human civilization. Although ballet was formalized in 18th-century Italy and France (e.g., at the Paris Opera), other forms of dance (e.g., modern dance) emerged a few centuries later. Relative to body image and eating disorder concerns, ballet (typically represented by thin and feminine dancers) has received the most notoriety in the media and in research. However, other forms of dance (e.g., modern and belly dance) have important implications for body identity and health and will be discussed in this entry. Modern dance is particularly salient because some dancers trained in classical ballet are encouraged to change to modern dance if their bodies do not fit the ballet ideal.

Modern Dance

Modern dance, later dubbed "contemporary dance," emerged in the early 20th century. Modern dance is typically perceived as a more forgiving form of dance than ballet. For example, unlike ballerinas who traditionally wear black leotards and pink tights to train, modern dancers are given flexibility to choose training attire and sometimes costumes. However, in body image studies, modern dancers tend to report body dissatisfaction equivalent to ballet dancers and high levels of social physique anxiety (i.e., anxiety surrounding physique or body shape).

Body Image

Modern dancers in university dance programs revealed they experienced significant weight pressures associated with preparing to be professional dancers. Despite the stereotypes of modern dance as more forgiving of body type, dancers felt constrained by the desires of various choreographers who would be hiring dancers for their company. Modern dancers reported choreographers had distinct preferences in height, size, and appearance of dancers based upon the aesthetic desired in the performance. In some cases, a decision of which dancer was hired came down to who could fit into the last dancer's costume. Most frequently reported weight pressures for college modern dancers included mirrors (100 percent), costumes (99 percent), performance advantages (97 percent), other dancers (83 percent), and the audience (70 percent). Like their ballet counterparts, modern dancers thought weight was not the sole feature of the ideal dancer's body. However, the majority (65 percent) of dancers stated they would perform better if they lost five pounds.

Eating Disorders

Modern dancers in university settings have reported strong body dissatisfaction and pressure to lose weight; however, they have lower rates of disordered eating and clinical eating disorders than ballet samples. In one study, college modern dancers reported controlling their weight by excessively exercising (39 percent), fasting (38 percent), restricting fat or calories (29 percent), and vomiting (26 percent). Another 29 percent of dancers reported using fad diets and 14 percent wore plastic clothing to maintain low body weight or lose weight. Interestingly, 23 percent of dancers admitted to smoking cigarettes to control their weight, underscoring the health risk associated with the weight-focused nature of the dance culture.

Belly Dance

History and Costumes of Belly Dance

Belly dance, the Western label for traditional Middle Eastern dance or Arabic dance, has roots in the Middle East and North Africa. Belly dancing originated as a dance dedicated to the goddess of fertility and for entertainment purposes. In the United States, belly dancing first received attention in the late 19th century at the Chicago World Fair. During the 1960s and 1970s, belly dancing in the United States grew as a performance and participatory activity and has recently been valued as a form of exercise.

Belly dance, traditionally popular in Egypt, Lebanon, Turkey, the United States, and Canada, has different costume variations depending on the country. In Egypt, women have been prohibited from baring their midriffs or showing excessive skin since the 1950s. The Egyptian belly dance costume typically consists of a long, form-fitting, one-piece Lycra gown with sheer body stocking to cover the midsection. By contrast, in Lebanon and Turkey belly dancers wear bedleh-style costumes, with shorter skirts, sheer material, an exposed midriff. American belly dancers' costumes resemble those from Egypt or Turkey but also include a headband with fringe instead of a veil. Women may choose to wear harem pants or a skirt rather than the Egyptian Lycra gown.

Body Image of Belly Dance

The costume for belly dance is widely recognized for its revealing characteristics and decorative flourishes that may leave a bare midriff and plunging neckline. However, compared to other forms of dance, belly dance tends to use costuming as a way to accentuate the female form. Belly dancers also report less body dissatisfaction or desire to change their bodies than modern dancers and ballet dancers. Only 18 percent of female belly dance participants were dissatisfied with their bodies in one study. This percentage is considerably lower than other dancers or nondance populations of females. Likewise, belly dancers did not experience the same types of weight pressures (e.g., choreographer, other dancers, performance advantage) reported by modern dancers. Audience scrutiny (40 percent) was the sole pressure reported by belly dancers who as a group reported a supportive, body-accepting community of dancers. Curves were celebrated, and belly dance seemed to play a positive role in promoting positive body image and health.

Other Types of Dance

Similar to belly dance, street dancers have reported being more satisfied with their bodies than other dancers or nondancers. Street dance became popularized in the 1970s with the Jackson 5 and the television show *Soul Train*. Meanwhile, hip-hop dance from Jamaica emerged in the United States in 1967, with b-boys and b-girls performing breakdancing movements on the streets. These dance styles (e.g., breakdancing, locking, krumping, popping) evolved outside of formal settings and are typically improvisational and social in nature. More recently, these dance trends have expanded to exercise settings (e.g., cardio funk or hip-hop aerobics classes) and televised reality show competitions (e.g., *So You Think You Can Dance?*). In a rare study of 83 female street dancers, it was discovered street dancers reported higher body appreciation than nondancers, reflecting higher body acceptance. More body image research is needed to investigate specific body image concerns and disordered eating rates in street dance as well as other types of dance, such as folk dance, ballroom dance, and jazz dance.

Justine J. Reel

See also: Aesthetic Sports; Ballet; Drill Team/Dance Team; Social Physique Anxiety; Weight Pressures in Sport

Bibliography

Clabaugh, Alison, and Beth Morling. "Stereotype Accuracy of Ballet and Modern Dancers." *The Journal of Social Psychology* 144, no. 1 (2004): 31–48. http://dx.doi.org/10.3200 /SOCP.144.1.31-48.

Downey, Dennis J., Justine J. Reel, Sonya SooHoo, and Sandrine Zerbib. "Body Image in Belly Dance: Integrating Norms into Collective Identity." *Journal of Gender Studies* 19, no. 4 (2010): 377–393. https://doi.org/10.1080/09589236.2010.514209.

Langdon, Susan W., and Gina Petracca. "Tiny Dancer: Body Image and Dancer Identity in Female Modern Dancers." *Body Image* 7 (2010): 360–363. https://doi.org/10.1016/j .bodyim.2010.06.005.

Reel, Justine J., Sonya SooHoo, Katherine M. Jamieson, and Diane L. Gill. "Femininity to the Extreme: Body Image Concerns among College Female Dancers." *Women in Sport and Physical Activity Journal* 14, no. 1 (2005): 39–51.

Swami, Viren, and Martin J. Tovee. "A Comparison of Actual-Ideal Weight Discrepancy, Body Appreciation, and Media Influence between Street-Dancers and Non-Dancers." *Body Image* 6 (2009): 304–307. http://dx.doi.org/10.1016/j.bodyim.2009.07.006.

Tiggemann, Marika, and Amy Slater. "A Test of Objectification Theory in Former Dancers and Non-Dancers." *Psychology of Women Quarterly* 25 (2001): 57–64. https://doi .org/10.111j/1471-6402.00007.

Wright, Jan, and Shoshana Dreyfus. "Belly Dancing: A Feminist Project?" *Women in Sport and Physical Activity Journal* 7, no. 2 (1998): 95–114.

DEHYDRATION

Dehydration occurs when there is inadequate fluid intake to maintain bodily systems. Six to 10 cups of noncaffeinated, nonalcoholic beverages daily are required to maintain fluid balance in the body. Fluid requirements increase with exercise, and consuming six to eight ounces of fluid every 15 minutes during exercise is necessary to maintain proper hydration status.

Eating Disorders and Dehydration

Individuals with eating disorders may experience dehydration resulting from self-induced vomiting, diuretic abuse, and laxative use behaviors. An eating-disordered individual may also avoid fluids fearing weight gain that leads to liquid restriction, including water. Individuals who abuse laxatives and diuretics are often motivated to lose a large amount of weight in a short period. However, most of the weight loss from these purging methods is water loss and dehydration. Therefore, these pounds will be regained once an individual's hydration status is returned to normal. Severe dehydration can lead to alterations in electrolytes and cause kidney failure and cardiac problems.

Laboratory tests confirm dehydration in eating-disordered individuals. Blood tests may show high blood urea nitrogen and fluctuations in serum sodium. A urinalysis may show an elevation in an individual's urine specific gravity. In individuals who purge, lab results may reveal metabolic alkalosis (increased serum bicarbonate). In addition to dehydration, eating-disordered individuals who purge can also experience electrolyte abnormalities, including hypokalemia (low serum potassium), hyponatremia (low serum sodium), hypomagnesemia (low serum magnesium), and hypocalcemia (low calcium). Dehydration triggers the body's renin–angiotensin system that results in secretion of high levels of the hormone aldosterone from the adrenal cortex. This prevents low blood pressure and fainting in the presence of ongoing purging behaviors or fluid restriction.

Clinical Manifestations

An individual who is dehydrated may experience constipation, dizziness, light-headedness, and weakness. An individual may also complain of headache, dry mouth, dry skin, and muscle cramps. Decreased urine output, low blood pressure, and tachycardia (high heart rate) may also occur. In severe cases of dehydration, confusion, breathing difficulty, seizures, kidney damage, and death are possible.

Orthostatic Hypotension

It is not unusual for a dehydrated individual to experience orthostatic hypotension. This is a form of hypotension in which an individual's blood pressure falls suddenly when he or she shifts from sitting to standing. The most common symptom of orthostatic hypotension is dizziness on standing. However, this marked drop in blood pressure can cause fainting, blurred vision, confusion, or nausea.

Treatment

Dehydrated individuals are treated with aggressive oral hydration, or in severe cases, intravenous infusions of sodium chloride saline to shut off the renin–angiotensin system and stop aldosterone production. Individuals who are being rehydrated need to be carefully monitored for electrolyte imbalances. In hypokalemic individuals, high levels of aldosterone will continue to cause potassium loss if dehydration is not treated first. In eating-disordered individuals who have significant hyponatremia (low sodium), saline solutions should be run slowly to prevent development of a neurological complication called central pontine myelinolysis. Rapid infusions may cause edema in some individuals. Doctors need to reassure these individuals that edema will resolve with continuing treatment and avoiding eating disorder behaviors.

Shelly Guillory

See also: Diuretics; Electrolyte Imbalance; Medical and Health Consequences; Purging; Weight Manipulation

Bibliography

Brunzell, Carol, and Mary Hendrickson-Nelson. "An Overview of Nutrition." In *The Outpatient Treatment of Eating Disorder: A Guide for Therapists, Dietitians, and Physicians,* edited by James E. Mitchell, 222–223. Minneapolis: University of Minnesota Press, 2001.

"Dehydration." MayoClinic.com. Last modified October 29, 2016. Accessed November 21, 2017. http://www.mayoclinic.org/diseases-conditions/dehydration/home/ovc-20261061.

Mehler, Philip S., and Arnold E. Anderson. "Evaluation and Treatment of Electrolyte Abnormalities." *Eating Disorders: A Guide to Medical Care and Complications,* 2nd ed., 97–107. Baltimore, MD: Johns Hopkins University Press, 2010.

Miller, Karen K., Steven K. Grinspoon, Julia Ciampa, Joan Hier, David Herzog, and Ajnne Klibanski. "Medical Findings of Outpatients with Eating Disorders." *Archives of Internal Medicine* 135, no. 5. (2005): 561–566. https://doi.org/10.1001/archinte.165.5.561.

"Orthostatic Hypotension." MayoClinic.com. Last modified May 13, 2014. Accessed November 21, 2017. https://www.mayoclinic.org/diseases-conditions/orthostatic-hypotension/symptoms-causes/syc-20352548.

DENTAL COMPLICATIONS

People with eating disorders may experience numerous medical consequences that affect all of the body. In fact, an eating disorder may be initially detected at the dentist's office due to oral complications. Oral complications are a common result of self-induced vomiting behavior associated with a purge episode for bulimia nervosa. These oral complications result from the constant regurgitation of acidic gastric contents and include a variety of problems. Dental complications include angular cheilosis (sores on the lip), perimolysis (loss of enamel on the surface of teeth), dental caries, gingivitis, enlargement of salivary glands, and hyperamylasemia.

Angular Cheilosis

One complication associated with self-induced vomiting is angular cheilosis. Although this condition is uncommon and occurs in fewer than 10 percent of patients, cheilosis refers to lesions or sores on the angles of the lips. These sores may leave scar tissue and are directly caused by acid in the vomit as well as from vitamin deficiencies associated with eating disorders. It is important to differentiate between cheilosis and herpes, which typically presents with sores in the middle of the mouth. In addition, cheilosis lesions are also usually more painful than herpes. Treatment involves keeping the area clean and dry. Patients are usually advised to apply a topical petroleum jelly to the sores to expedite healing.

Perimolysis

Another complication associated with eating disorders is perimolysis or the erosion of enamel on the teeth's surface. The loss of enamel is the most obvious sign of bulimia nervosa. Perimolysis is reported to occur in 38 percent of dental patients with bulimia nervosa. This condition results from the chronic contact with acid from the stomach from self-induced vomiting. The appearance of teeth becomes dull with an irregular edge. The teeth may also appear shorter as a result of this condition. When loss of enamel is readily visible to a dental provider, an assumption is made that purging has been happening for at least two years. Other factors, such as the types of foods consumed, one's quality of tooth structure, and oral hygiene habits also affect the rate and severity of enamel loss. In addition to impacting the appearance of the teeth, perimolysis can also cause sensitivity to hot and cold foods. Chipping around the edges of the teeth can also take place. The treatment for perimolysis typically involves cessation of vomiting behavior along the use of mouthwashes to reduce acid content. Crowns or other restorative dental work may be required to address the resulting damage.

Dental Caries

Although the exact association is unclear, it is suspected some people with eating disorders suffer from dental caries. Binge episodes that include foods rich in sugar and high carbohydrates put a person at risk for dental caries. Other factors that may increase the likelihood of the development of dental caries include the type of water (whether it is fluorinated), one's diet, genetics, and oral hygiene. The best way to address this is to stop vomiting behavior. Another recommendation has been to rinse the mouth with a baking soda solution to neutralize the acidic content.

Gingivitis (Gum Disease)

Gingivitis or gum disease is relatively uncommon and afflicts fewer than 10 percent of patients. Gum disease can be caused by irritation resulting from exposure to stomach acid while vomiting. The condition is painful. There is an increased incidence in patients with bulimia nervosa.

Enlargement of Salivary Glands

Sialadenosis refers to an enlargement or hypertrophy of the salivary glands. This condition is a common occurrence and is present in almost half of patients with bulimia nervosa. The swelling is typically painless, but is noticeable two or three days following a self-induced vomiting episode. The frequency and severity of purging behavior correlates with the severity of sialadenosis. This swelling, caused by chronic regurgitation of stomach acid, may also be associated with higher risk for the development of enamel erosion. As with other dental complications, the best course of treatment is to stop the purging behavior. Hot compresses or medications are also used to decrease swelling.

Hyperamylasemia

Hyperamylasemia is the elevation of the serum amylase blood level and is associated with sailadenosis. This condition has a prevalence rate of 10–66 percent in all patients. Hyperamylasemia occurs most commonly in individuals who struggle with binge eating episodes and vomit as a purging method. Similar to other dental complications, it is important to treat bulimia nervosa and stop the purging behavior to resolve the condition.

Justine J. Reel

See also: Medical and Health Consequences; Purging

Bibliography

Mehler, Philip S. "Medical Complications of Bulimia Nervosa and Their Treatments." *International Journal of Eating Disorders*, 44, no. 2 (2011): 95–104. https://doi.org/10.1002/eat.20825.

Mehler, Philip S., and Arnold E. Andersen. *Eating Disorders: A Guide to Medicare Care and Complications*, 2nd ed. Baltimore, MD: Johns Hopkins University Press, 2010.

Mitchell, James E., and Scott Crow. "Medical Complications of Anorexia Nervosa and Bulimia Nervosa." *Current Opinion in Psychiatry*, 19, no. 4 (2006): 438–443. https://doi.org/10.1097/01.yci.0000228768.79097.3e.

DEPRESSION

Depression is an affective or mood disorder characterized by depressed mood, sadness, low energy, fatigue, and feelings of hopelessness. Depression in the form of major depressive disorder or another type of mood disorder commonly exists in individuals with an eating disorder. Over half the clients with eating disorders are thought to have a mood disorder, but some studies have found higher rates when considering age, type of eating disorder, and level of care. For example, one study found the prevalence of mood disorders varied between 64.1 and 96 percent for individuals, whereas a more recent study found the comorbidity rate to be between 12.7 and 68 percent for anorexia nervosa. By contrast, 50–90 percent of individuals with bulimia nervosa were reported to suffer from a mood disorder compared to a current comorbidity rate of 40 percent.

Explanations for Overlap between Depression and Eating Disorders

Although it is difficult to come to a clear conclusion regarding whether depression causes the eating disorder or the other way around, there have been several theories forwarded to explain the coexistence of depression and eating disorders. One theory is that depression might pave the way for an eating disorder because a depressed mood may contribute to reduced sleep and increased vulnerability to stress and dysfunctional coping strategies. A second explanation is that both disorders may be the outgrowth of a common foundation. Genetic factors are related for depression and eating disorders, and it is common for individuals with eating disorders to have a family history of depression. Another possible explanation for the co-occurrence of depression and eating disorders is that an eating disorder may lead to increased vulnerability for depression. A further complication is that starvation can produce physiological and psychological symptoms resembling depression diagnostic criteria.

Justine J. Reel

See also: Anxiety Disorders; Comorbidity; Family Influences; Substance Abuse

Bibliography

Casper, Regina C. "Depression and Eating Disorders." *Depression and Anxiety* 8, no. 1 (1998): 96–104.

Ferreiro, Tatima, Gloria Seoane, and Carmen Senra. "A Prospective Study of Risk Factors for the Development of Depression and Disordered Eating in Adolescents." *Journal of Clinical Child & Adolescent Psychology* 40, no. 3 (2011): 500–505. http://dx.doi.org/10.1080/15374416.2011.563465.

Giovanni, Abbate-Daga, Carla Gramaglia Carla, Enrica Marzola, Federico Amianto, Maria Zuccolin, and Secondo Fassino. "Eating Disorders and Major Depression: Role of Anger and Personality." *Depression Research and Treatment* (2011): 1–7. https://doi.org/10.1155/2011/194732.

Mischoulon, David, Kamry T. Eddy, Aparna Keshaviah, Diana Dinescu, Stephanie L. Ross, Andrea E. Kass, Debra L. Franko, and David B. Herzog. "Depression and Eating Disorders: Treatment and Course." *Journal of Affective Disorders* 130 (2011): 470–477. https://doi.org/10.1016/j.jad.2010.10.043.

Touchett, Evelyne, Adina Henegar, Nathalie T. Godart, Laura Pryor, Bruno Falissard, Richard E. Tremblay, and Sylvana M. Cote. "Subclinical Eating Disorders and Their Comorbidity with Mood and Anxiety Disorders in Adolescent Girls." *Psychiatry Research* 185 (2011): 185–192. https://doi.org/10.1016/j.psychres.2010.04.005.

DETOX DIETS AND CLEANSES

It is common to hear celebrities discuss their latest *detox* or *cleansing* programs. The detox they are referring to is a type of fasting or dietary restriction that should be distinguished between a detoxification used in substance abuse treatment. Whereas substance abuse treatment employs a gradual detox that supports a client to achieve abstinence, a detox diet is only temporarily used to rid toxins found in foods. For substance abuse detox, it is anticipated support will need to be provided for withdrawal symptoms.

Detox diets, like other fad diets, have become a popular way for people to attempt to lose weight. They may involve fasting entirely, eating an entirely raw diet or narrow diet of selected foods, ingesting certain prescribed substances or juices, or using other herbal remedies believed to cleanse the body. The Master Cleanse, one example, involves consuming warm salt water, laxative teas, and a mixture of lemon juice, maple syrup, and cayenne pepper exclusively (no other foods) for 10 days straight. The theory is that detoxification, which refers to eliminating the body of toxic or harmful substances, can be used to drop pounds and promote a healthy lifestyle. Detox diets are promoted by advocates who claim detoxification can decrease disease risk by ridding the body of toxins that cause cancer and other diseases. The idea of cleansing oneself of toxins is purported to bring health benefits such as weight loss, increased energy, decreased sugar cravings, and better skin.

Detox diets are not without controversy. Researchers argue there is no scientific evidence detox diets actually work or produce the stated benefits. Further, the body is designed to cleanse itself through organs like the kidneys and liver. Medical experts indicate indulging in a healthy and balanced diet that includes increasing a person's fruit and vegetable intake would be more beneficial than a detox diet.

Side Effects of Detox Diets and Cleanses

Meal plans that incorporate detox diets are deemed unnecessary despite their popularity. Participating in detox diets and cleanses can actually be harmful to the body. Some of the common side effects that result from detox therapies include stomach pain, vomiting, and diarrhea. As with other dietary restrictive practices, the body's electrolytes will be affected. Depending on the particular cleanse, a person may experience a large loss of electrolytes, such as sodium and potassium. Dehydration is another potential side effect associated with fasting or detox diets. More severe consequences include more serious medical conditions including liver failure, blood infections, kidney failure, and death. Moreover, certain groups face additional risk associated with detox diets and cleansing such as pregnant women, people with reduced immune systems, and people with chronic conditions. It is also important that children and teenagers avoid fad diets including detox diets and cleansing. Detox diets could impede growth and development.

Justine J. Reel

See also: Dietary Restraint; Diet Pills; Fad Diets

Bibliography
Altshul, Sara. "Your Simple 3-Day Diet Detox." Prevention.com. Last modified March 27, 2014. Accessed November 21, 2017. http://www.prevention.com/weight-loss/weight-loss-tips/your-simple-3-day-diet-detox.
"Are Detox Diets Safe?" Kidshealth.org. Last modified March 2015. Accessed November 21, 2016. http://kidshealth.org/en/teens/detox-diets.html.
Cosgrove, Ben. "The Truth about Detox Diets." Berkeley Wellness. Last modified March 9, 2015. Accessed November 21, 2017. http://www.berkeleywellness.com/healthy-eating/diet-weight-loss/nutrition/article/truth-about-detox-diets.

Palermo, Elizabeth. "Detox Diets & Cleansing: Facts & Fallacies." Live Science. Last modified February 9, 2015. Accessed November 21, 2017. http://www.livescience.com/34845-detox-cleansing-facts-fallacies.html.

DIABETES

Individuals with type 1 diabetes, an autoimmune disease in which the pancreas ceases to produce insulin, represent a high-risk group for eating disorders and subclinical eating disorders. This is often referred to as *diabulimia*. Insulin is a hormone that regulates blood glucose levels. Type 1 diabetes is managed by routinely self-administering insulin, checking blood glucose levels, and monitoring dietary intake of carbohydrates that increase blood sugar levels. Although overexercising, binge eating, purging, dietary restriction, and laxative abuse are disordered eating behaviors present in the general population, insulin omission is a weight control behavior unique to eating-disordered individuals with type 1 diabetes. Neglecting to take one's prescribed insulin has been identified as an alternative method of purging. Missing insulin doses or taking less insulin than required can cause blood sugar levels to rise and the kidneys then work to rid the body of excess blood sugar resulting in rapid weight loss.

Rates of diagnosable eating disorders and subclinical eating disturbances in a diabetic population have varied across studies, depending on how eating disorders were defined. According to the results of many research studies, the prevalence of bulimia nervosa, but not anorexia nervosa, is higher in female adolescents and adults with type 1 diabetes compared to age-matched peers. A higher prevalence of subclinical eating disorders among females with type 1 diabetes is also a common finding, especially when insulin omission is included as a weight loss method. The prevalence of eating disorders among males who have type 1 diabetes and individuals with type 2 diabetes is unknown.

Risk Factors

Similar to eating disorders in the general population, psychological, physical, and family factors have been associated with eating disorders in individuals with type 1 diabetes. These factors include low self-esteem, depression, perfectionism and borderline personality characteristics, negative and avoidant coping styles, body dissatisfaction, a higher BMI and being overweight, parental dieting behaviors and negative eating attitudes, infrequent family meals, and impaired family functioning. There may also be specific aspects of diabetes management that increase risk for eating disorders.

Diabetes Care and Weight Gain

Weight loss is a common symptom of new onset type 1 diabetes; consequently, once an insulin regimen begins to manage blood sugar levels, weight gain occurs. The fear of excessive weight gain with improved blood glucose may lead some individuals to omit insulin as a weight loss method. Weight-related concerns may also stem from experiencing hypoglycemia (i.e., low blood sugar levels) in that additional calories must be consumed to normalize levels or an individual will be triggered to overeat. Interestingly, some individuals with both type 1 diabetes and eating disorders initially restricted insulin to avoid hypoglycemia or other factors that affect adherence to diabetes management. When people notice the weight loss from not taking medication, they are motivated to continue the disordered behavior.

Preoccupation with Food

Dietary management of type 1 diabetes involves monitoring carbohydrate intake. Although current dietary regimens allow considerable flexibility over traditional meal planning for diabetes in that strict limits on the types and amounts of food are no longer promoted, it has been suggested that constant awareness of food portions and carbohydrate content reinforce perfectionism, rigid thinking about food, and dietary restraint in individuals already at risk for eating disorders. Dietary restraint may lead to hypoglycemia and binge eating episodes, leading to insulin omission to avoid weight gain.

Stressors Related to Diabetes Management

The strict regimen required for diabetes management may trigger a low sense of control over one's life. The pubertal years, in particular, are a time when individuals strive for more autonomy and control over their lives. However, due to rapid growth and development, insulin requirements are greater and glycemic control may be difficult to achieve during adolescence. The increased responsibilities and changes associated with diabetes management during adolescence may adversely impact one's sense of control and disordered eating behaviors may be a resultant coping strategy. Promoting an environment of autonomy in conjunction with addressing the challenges of diabetes management can be difficult for families to balance. Individuals with diabetes may experience a loss of independence if family members are overprotective or anxious about their health and diabetes regimen. On the other hand, an absence of familial support and validation may contribute to helplessness and ineffectiveness in individuals with diabetes. Similarly, the perceived lack of support from health professionals has been described by people with both type 1 diabetes and eating disorders. People who adhere to a diabetes care regimen and yet are unable to achieve the standards put in place for them by health professionals may experience hopelessness and depression, especially if receive consistent disapproval from a provider as well as family.

Health Consequences

The combination of type 1 diabetes and eating disorder behaviors is associated with poor blood sugar control. Thus, individuals face an increased risk for diabetes-related medical complications, including diabetic ketoacidosis, an acute life-threatening complication in which a shortage of insulin promotes high blood sugar levels. Because the body cannot use blood glucose for energy without insulin, there is an increased breakdown of fat for energy, and the production of acidic ketone bodies. This condition leads to dehydration and electrolyte imbalances, nausea, vomiting, abdominal pain, confusion, and, if not treated quickly, loss of consciousness, fluid swelling in the brain, and death. Treatment requires hospitalization. Health consequences of having both type 1 diabetes and eating disorders also include an increased risk for diseases of the smallest arteries of the body, particularly damage to the eye (diabetic retinopathy) that can lead to blindness, as well as kidney disease (nephropathy), and nerve damage (neuropathy), and can affect organ systems. Furthermore, higher mortality rates have been reported among clients with both eating disorders and diabetes than either diagnosis alone.

Management of Diabetes

Routine use of an effective and efficient screening tool that considers diabetes-related risk factors for disordered eating is important for early detection and intervention. A multidisciplinary team approach is the standard of care for addressing various aspects of treatment for concurrent eating disorders and type 1 diabetes; this team includes, but is not limited to an endocrinologist (a physician who specializes in treating hormonal diseases) to assist clients with developing an appropriate insulin regimen; a diabetes nurse educator (nurses who maintain a special certification in diabetes) to provide education on various aspects of diabetes management as needed, such as how to correctly monitor blood sugar levels and provide insulin injections; a registered dietitian to provide dietary education and counseling; and a psychotherapist to provide mental health counseling and address the underlying thoughts and feelings that contribute to disordered eating. Established treatments for eating disorders may be implemented but should be modified to address insulin omission, glycemic control, and diabetes-related risk factors.

It is suggested small, gradual goals be negotiated with a client to improve diabetes care and eating disorder recovery and to reduce the risk of relapse. For example, instead of the fully prescribed amount of multiple insulin injections per day, clients may start with twice per day insulin injections as a manageable first step. It is important to discuss fears related to diabetes management (e.g., weight gain with insulin restart, hypoglycemia). The treatment provider should also offer education and coping skills to reduce stress and discomfort with the treatment plan. Family therapy may also be beneficial in terms of fostering communication and support between family members. Enforcing the need to take medication as part of one's self-care will be an important piece of a therapeutic process for a client with diabetes who omits insulin as a purging method.

Holly E. Doetsch

See also: Dietary Restraint; Disordered Eating; Medical and Health Consequences; Self-Care

Bibliography

Daneman, Denis, Gary Rodin, Jennifer Jones, Patricia Colton, Anne Rydall, Sherry Maharaj, and Marion Olmsted. "Eating Disorders in Adolescent Girls and Young Adult Women with Type 1 Diabetes." *Diabetes Spectrum* 15, no. 2 (2002): 83–105. http://dx.doi.org/10.2337/diaspect.15.2.83.

Goebel-Fabbri, Ann E. "Disturbed Eating Behaviors and Eating Disorders in Type 1 Diabetes: Clinical Significance and Treatment Recommendations." *Current Diabetes Reports* 9 (2009): 133–139. https://doi.org/10.1007/s11892-009-0023-8.

Hillege, Sharon, Barbara Beale, and Rose McMaster. "The Impact of Type 1 Diabetes and Eating Disorders: The Perspective of Individuals." *Journal of Clinical Nursing* 17, no. 7B (2008): 169–176. https://doi.org/10.1111/j.1365-2702.2008.02283.x.

Jones, Jennifer M., Margaret L. Lawson, Denis Daneman, Marion P. Olmsted, and Gary Rodin. "Eating Disorders in Adolescent Females with and without Type 1 Diabetes: Cross Sectional Study." *British Medical Journal* 320, no. 7249 (2000): 1563–1566. http://dx.doi.org/10.1136/bmj.320.7249.1563.

Maharaj, Sherry I., Gary M. Rodin, Marion P. Olmsted, Jennifer A. Connolly, and Denis Daneman. "Eating Disturbances in Girls with Diabetes: The Contribution of Adolescent Self-Concept, Maternal Weight and Shape Concerns and Mother–Daughter Relationships." *Psychological Medicine* 33, no. 3 (2003): 525–539. https://doi.org/10.1017/S0033291702007213.

Maharaj, Sherry I., Gary M. Rodin, Marion P. Olmsted, and Denis Daneman. "Eating Disturbances, Diabetes, and the Family: An Empirical Study." *Journal of Psychosomatic Research* 44, no. 3–4 (1998): 479–490. http://dx.doi.org/10.1016/S0022-3999(97)00273-0.

Mannucci, Edoardo, Francesco Rotella, Valdo Ricca, Sandra Moretti, Gian F. Placidi, and Carlo M. Rotella. "Eating Disorders in Patients with Type 1 Diabetes: A Meta-analysis." *Journal of Endocrinological Investigation* 28 (2005): 417–419. https://doi.org/10.1007/BF03347221.

Markowitz, Jessica T., Michael R. Lowe, Lisa K. Volkening, and Lori M. B. Laffel. "Self-Reported History of Overweight and Its Relationship to Disordered Eating in Adolescent Girls with Type 1 Diabetes." *Diabetic Medicine* 26, no. 11 (2009): 1165–1171. https://doi.org/10.1111/j.1464-5491.2009.02844.x.

Mellin, Allison E., Dianne Neumark-Sztainer, Joan Patterson, and Joseph Sockalosky. "Unhealthy Weight Management Behavior among Adolescent Girls with Type 1 Diabetes Mellitus: The Role of Familial Eating Patterns and Weight-Related Concerns." *Journal of Adolescent Health* 35, no. 4 (2004): 278–289. http://dx.doi.org/10.1016/j.jadohealth.2003.10.006.

Nielsen, Soren. "Eating Disorders in Females with Type 1 Diabetes: An Update of a Meta-analysis." *European Eating Disorders Review* 10, no. 4 (2002): 241–254. https://doi.org/10.1002/erv.474.

Nielsen, Soren, Charlotte Emborg, and Anne-Grethe Molbak. "Mortality in Concurrent Type 1 Diabetes and Anorexia Nervosa." *Diabetes Care* 25 (2002): 309–312. http://dx.doi.org/10.2337/diacare.25.2.309.

Olmsted, Marion P., Patricia A. Colton, Denis Daneman, Anne C. Rydall, and Gary M. Rodin. "Prediction of the Onset of Disturbed Eating Behavior in Adolescent Girls with Type 1 Diabetes." *Diabetes Care* 31, no. 10 (2008): 1978–1982. http://dx.doi.org/10.2337/dc08-0333.

Peveler, Robert C., Kathryn S. Bryden, H. Andrew W. Neil, Christopher G. Fairburn, Richard A. Mayou, David B. Dunger, and Hannah M. Turner. "The Relationship of

Disordered Eating Habits and Attitudes to Clinical Outcomes in Young Adult Females with Type 1 Diabetes." *Diabetes Care* 28 (2005): 84–88. http://dx.doi.org/10.2337/diacare.28.1.84.

Pollock-BarZiv, Stacey M., and Caroline Davis. "Personality Factors and Disordered Eating in Young Women with Type 1 Diabetes Mellitus." *Psychosomatics* 46 (2005): 11–18. http://dx.doi.org/10.1176/appi.psy.46.1.11.

Rydall, Anne C., Gary M. Rodin, Marion P. Olmsted, Robert G. Devenyi, and Denis Daneman. "Disordered Eating Behavior and Microvascular Complications in Young Women with Insulin-Dependent Diabetes Mellitus." *New England Journal of Medicine* 336 (1997): 1849–1854. https://doi.org/10.1056/NEJM199706263362601.

Steel, Judith M., Robert J. Young, Geoffrey G. Lloyd, and Basil F. Clarke. "Clinically Apparent Eating Disorders in Young Diabetic Women: Associations with Painful Neuropathy and Other Complications." *British Medical Journal* 294, no. 6576 (1987): 859–862. http://dx.doi.org/10.1136/bmj.294.6576.859.

Walker, James D., Robert J. Young, Jill Little, and Judith M. Steel. "Mortality in Concurrent Type 1 Diabetes and Anorexia Nervosa." *Diabetes Care* 25 (2002): 1664–1665. http://dx.doi.org/10.2337/diacare.25.9.1664-a.

Young-Hyman, Deborah L., and Catherine L. Davis. "Disordered Eating Behavior in Individuals with Diabetes." *Diabetes Care* 33, no. 3 (2010): 683–689. http://dx.doi.org/10.2337/dc08-1077.

DIAGNOSTIC AND STATISTICAL MANUAL OF MENTAL DISORDERS

Prior to the middle of the 20th century, psychiatrists viewed the use of diagnoses for mental health conditions in a negative way. They argued using labels could be dangerous for patients and could likely cause more harm than good. The downside of this philosophy was the delay in developing standardized ways to identify and treat eating disorder cases.

In 1972, a groundbreaking piece was published in the *Archives of General Psychiatry* that argued for the need for and use of standardized diagnostic criteria for various mental health disorders including anorexia nervosa. This paper served as a catalyst to provide specific definitions of the mental health disorders in one place. The resulting *Diagnostic and Statistical Manual of Mental Disorders* (DSM) has been considered a "clinician's bible" since the American Psychiatric Association published its first version, the *DSM-III*, in 1980. The *DSM-III* finally provided a much-needed systematic method for diagnosing eating disorders.

The introduction of this important manual allowed for standardizing the identification of mental health diagnoses. This was an important step for detection and treatment of eating disorders. There have been substantial changes with each revision to reflect a need for greater specification of diagnosis categories. The most recent version, *DSM-5* represents significant changes that will influence assessment and diagnosis for eating disorders.

DSM-III *and* DSM-III-R

The first version of the *Diagnostic and Statistical Manual of Mental Disorders*, the *DSM-III*, included two eating disorders (anorexia and bulimia) as well as a feeding disorder (pica). Anorexia nervosa (AN) had been discussed in the literature since the 1870s with numerous documented medical cases. However, bulimia nervosa (BN) was not formally named until 1979, in a paper by a British psychiatrist named Gerald Russell. AN and *bulimia* (rather than bulimia nervosa) represented the sole eating disorder classifications in the *DSM-III*; however, an additional residual category called *atypical eating disorder* was provided for eating disorders that did not fit either AN or BN. For example, if someone did not meet the strict AN criteria of losing at least 25 percent of original body weight, then the atypical eating disorder diagnosis was assigned.

In 1987, with the publication of *DSM-III-R*, the name of the residual category changed from atypical eating disorder to eating disorder not otherwise specified (EDNOS). Additionally, the diagnostic criteria were revised for both AN and BN. For example, to meet the criteria for AN, a person was at only 85 percent of expected weight as opposed to 75 percent of expected weight in the original *DSM-III*. For bulimia, which became bulimia nervosa, the requirement of binge episodes twice a week was added. Further, reporting compensatory behaviors such as vomiting and laxative abuse were added to BN criteria. Being overly concerned with body shape was not included in the original diagnostic criteria for bulimia in *DSM-III*, but it was later added for the *DSM-III-R*. EDNOS tended to include individuals who only met the partial criteria for either AN or BN.

DSM-IV and DSM-IV-TR

The *DSM-IV* and *DSM-IV-TR* (text revision) were published by the American Psychiatric Association in 1994 and 2000, respectively. The EDNOS diagnostic category was expanded to include a variety of disordered eating behaviors and binge eating disorder (BED) was mentioned. BED did not represent a separate diagnostic category in this edition, but was identified as a disorder warranting further investigation. In both the *DSM-IV* and *DSM-IV-TR*, BED was characterized by recurring binge eating episodes at least twice weekly for six months without any accompanying compensatory behaviors.

DSM-5

From the time that the *DSM-IV* was introduced to prior to the development and refinement of the *DSM-5*, it was clear that a large chunk of eating disorder cases was falling in the catchall EDNOS diagnostic category. This was a concern of clinicians and patients who worried EDNOS was seen as not really meeting the full criteria for an eating disorder. Given that individuals engaging in disordered eating behaviors face health consequences regardless of diagnostic category, it seemed important to give more validity to the 40–60 percent of individuals who fit the EDNOS label. Therefore, a major thrust for the *DSM-5*, published by the American Psychiatric Association in 2013, was to clearly identify disorders that had previously fallen into the EDNOS diagnostic category for eating disorders. Binge eating disorder finally became a separate diagnosis with criteria coming from the *DSM-IV* research criteria section. The only exception was that the binge episode frequency was reduced from twice to once per week and the duration was reduced from five to three months, identical to the frequency changes for BN.

The residential category name was changed from EDNOS to *other specified feeding or eating disorder* (OSFED). Additionally, emergency department personnel tend to use unspecified feeding or eating disorder (UFED). This diagnosis applies to individuals who do not have symptoms that meet typical eating disorder criteria but who have significant struggles with eating and food that warrant clinical attention. Another diagnostic category new to the *DSM-5* was avoidant/restrictive food intake disorder (ARFID). This diagnosis expands the previous diagnosis of feeding disorder of infancy or early childhood. The key feature of ARFID is avoidance or restriction of food intake by significantly failing to meet requirements for nutrition or oral energy intake of food. For example, a person who meets the criteria for ARFID may have problems obtaining enough calories or meeting nutritional needs through diet. Some of the issues may include, but are not limited to, having problems digesting certain foods, avoiding specific textures or colors of foods, reporting no appetite, or exhibiting a fear of choking or vomiting.

Other changes to the *DSM-5* included the removal of amenorrhea as a requirement to fit the AN criteria. This allowed for male and postmenopausal clients to meet the AN diagnosis. Additionally, the wording clarified how to judge if an individual is at, or below, a significantly low weight and has a fear of weight gain that interferes with weight gain. The atypical anorexia category was provided for individuals who met all criteria for AN without meeting the weight cutoff.

Justine J. Reel and Robert A. Bucciere

See also: Assessment; Diagnostic Interview; History of Eating Disorders

Bibliography

American Psychiatric Association. *Diagnostic and Statistical Manual of Mental Disorders Disorders*, 5th ed. (*DSM-5*). Washington, DC: American Psychiatric Association Publishing, 2013.

"DSM-5 Diagnostic Criteria." *The Alliance for Eating Disorders Awareness.* Accessed September 1, 2016. http://www.allianceforeatingdisorders.com/portal/dsm-bed.

Feighner, John P., Eli Robins, Samuel B. Guze. "Diagnostic Criteria for Use in Psychiatric Research." *Archives of General Psychiatry* 26, no. 1 (1972): 57–63. https://doi.org/10.1001/archpsyc.1972.01750190059011.

Flett, Mary L. *Mastering the DSM-5: Integrating New & Essential Measures into Your Practice.* Eau Claire, WI: PESI Publishing & Media, 2014.

Zayas, Lazaro, and Jennifer J. Thomas. "The History of BED and ED-NOS." In *The Wiley Handbook of Eating Disorders: Volume 1, Basic Concepts and Foundational Research*, edited by Linda Smolak and Michael P. Levine, 39–49. West Sussex, UK: John Wiley & Sons, 2015.

DIAGNOSTIC INTERVIEW

A diagnostic interview, commonly referred to as a clinical interview, is a well-established way to identify eating disorder characteristics in clinical and research settings and is considered the gold standard for assessment of mental health conditions.

Used in a clinical setting, a diagnostic interview can provide valuable information to guide treatment planning and can h establish rapport and buy in for treatment. It is necessary to identify symptoms and formulate an accurate diagnosis (anorexia nervosa, bulimia nervosa, binge eating disorder) to develop a treatment approach and facilitate health insurance support for payment if relevant.

A diagnostic interview approach can also be used to collect research data and allows an individual to tell his or her story. More rich and in-depth information can be gathered than using a standard survey. Another advantage of using a diagnostic interview rather than a standardized questionnaire is that clients respond in their words to key questions. Clinicians who can build trust with clients can also read nonverbal cues allowing for follow-up questions and probing to gather more in-depth information. Like other forms of assessment (e.g., eating disorder questionnaires), the information provided in a diagnostic interview is self-report. Therefore, the challenge is whether a client is comfortable enough to share the level and intensity of the problem and whether memory creates a bias in what information is reported. It is not uncommon for eating-disordered individuals to minimize symptoms or normalize eating behaviors during a diagnostic interview.

Topics Covered during a Diagnostic Interview

To understand the complexity of an eating disorder case and provide an individualized treatment approach, questions should be asked about all types of disordered eating symptoms ranging from binge eating episodes to restricting and purging behaviors. If a client admits to engaging in a particular behavior, it is critical to gauge the intensity and frequency of its occurrence. For example, an interviewer should ask, "How often did you binge in the last week?" and "Can you tell me more specifically what you ate during your last binge?" In addition to eating patterns, an interviewer should ask about body weight, body image and dissatisfaction, and overall self-worth. To understand a client's level of body preoccupation, an interviewer will ask about body checking and body avoidance behaviors. Finally, clinicians will attempt to ascertain whether comorbid conditions are present, such as substance abuse, depression, anxiety, or personality disorders.

Justine J. Reel

See also: Assessment; Comorbidity; *Diagnostic and Statistical Manual of Mental Disorders*

Bibliography

Cooper, Zafra, and Christopher Fairburn. "The Eating Disorder Examination: A Semi-structured Interview for the Assessment of the Specific Psychopathology of Eating Disorders." *International Journal of Eating Disorders* 6, no. 1 (1987): 1–8. https://doi.org/10.1002/1098-108X(198701)6:1<1::AID-EAT2260060102>3.0.CO;2-9.

Goldfein, Juli A., Michael J. Devlin, and Claudia Kamenetz. "Eating Disorder Examination-Questionnaire with and without Instruction to Assess Binge Eating in Patients with Binge Eating Disorder." *International Journal of Eating Disorders* 37, no. 2 (2005): 107–111. https://doi.org/10.1002/eat.20075.

Mitchell, James E., and Carol B. Peterson. *Assessment of Eating Disorders.* New York: Guilford Press, 2005.

Mond, Jonathan M., Phillipa J. Hay, Bryan Rodgers, Cathy Owen, and Pierre J. V. Beumont. "Temporal Stability of the Eating Disorder Examination Questionnaire." *International Journal of Eating Disorders* 36 (2004): 195–203. https://doi.org/10.1002/eat.2007.

Sysko, Robyn, B. Timothy Walsh, and Christopher Fairburn. "Eating Disorder Examination-Questionnaire as a Measure of Change in Patients with Bulimia Nervosa." *International Journal of Eating Disorders* 37 (2005): 100–106. https://doi.org/10.1002/eat.20078.

Wolk, Sara L., Katharine L. Loeb, and B. Timothy Walsh. "Assessment of Patients with Anorexia Nervosa: Interview versus Self-Report." *International Journal of Eating Disorders* 47 (2005): 92–99. https://doi.org/10.1002/eat.20076.

DIALECTICAL BEHAVIOR THERAPY

Dialectical behavior therapy (DBT) was developed as a targeted treatment for chronically parasuicidal women and was introduced to the scientific community in 1987. The treatment was designed by Marsha Linehan to treat individuals with borderline personality disorder (a personality disorder listed in the *Diagnostic and Statistical Manual of Mental Disorders*) who had usually remained resistant to traditional forms of therapy and exhibited a poor prognosis for improvement. DBT, a skills-based form of cognitive behavioral therapy (CBT), addresses key tenets of acceptance and change. Used in both inpatient and outpatient settings with clients diagnosed with borderline personality disorder, DBT targets suicidal behaviors, self-injury, treatment interfering behaviors, and behaviors that prolong hospitalization. Ever since its development, this treatment approach has been helpful for individuals suffering from other mental disorders including substance abuse, eating disorders, and depression.

Description of DBT

DBT is often implemented in a group setting with multiple sessions varying from 50 minutes to 2.5 hours in length. Most eating disorder clients also participate in individual therapy, and if substance abuse is present, they may also attend twelve-step groups. In one treatment program that reported success with bulimia nervosa and binge-eating-disordered clients, treatment involved 20 sessions of weekly 50-minute meetings to teach emotional regulation skills to specifically address an eating disorder.

In the first two sessions, the client is usually introduced to the idea that there is a relationship between disordered eating behaviors and emotions. Clients are asked to pick a recent episode of purging or binge eating and to report the circumstances and emotions that came before the event. Clients receive a diary card to record frequency of targeted behaviors (e.g., vomiting), to rate the intensity of emotions, and to note the skills practiced each day. Clients begin to brainstorm about healthier behaviors (e.g., singing, knitting) that can replace the problematic behaviors. In DBT, mindfulness is taught as a way to increase awareness of emotions before reacting to them. Clients are taught to observe emotions in a nonjudgmental way so they can describe and analyze emotions and behaviors. Clients are encouraged to engage in mindful eating so they consume food with a higher degree of awareness of bodily cues of hunger and fullness as well as taste.

Clients who participate in DBT also learn how to manage emotions more effectively by identifying triggers, reducing vulnerability to intense emotions, and changing emotional experiences. Clients practice distress tolerance skills to gain strength to cope with painful emotions that accompany stressful situations. Some of these survival strategies include distracting (e.g., going for a walk), self-soothing (e.g., taking a bubble bath), and visualization (e.g., imagining a relaxing setting like the beach). Throughout, the sessions apply and practice the skills to eating-disordered behaviors.

DBT as Eating Disorder Treatment

DBT has been used with eating-disordered clients for over a decade. It is important to consider that many eating-disordered clients are diagnosed with comorbid mental health conditions (e.g., substance abuse, borderline personality disorder) that add to the complexity of treatment needs and serve as an additional barrier for recovery. It has been estimated that at least one-third of eating-disordered clients who did not respond to traditional cognitive behavioral therapies could be concurrently diagnosed with borderline personality disorder. DBT, demonstrated as the most established treatment for borderline personality disorder, shows much promise for individuals with anorexia nervosa, bulimia nervosa, and binge eating disorder who engage in impulsive behaviors (e.g., cutting) or struggle to manage emotions in a healthy way. DBT focuses on helping clients develop self-awareness of problems, impulsivity, and emotional dysfunction. Clients receive training and practice for emotional regulation strategies and coping skills (e.g., mindfulness meditation).

Comorbidities with Eating Disorders

When DBT was applied to individuals diagnosed with both eating disorder and borderline personality disorder, reductions in both self-harm behaviors and eating disorder behaviors were observed. In a separate study of 25 clients with an eating disorder and substance abuse, DBT was helpful to reduce binge eating episodes, bulimic or restricting tendencies, and weight concerns as well as reduce substance abuse. A greater retention rate for treatment was observed for the DBT group versus traditional therapy and clients reported positive feedback about receiving mindfulness training. Furthermore, several clients expressed being validated and more motivated for change after participating in a treatment they thought addressed both of their problems simultaneously; they reported they were empowered to recover.

Binge Eating Disorder and Bulimia Nervosa

Even in eating-disordered individuals without personality disorders or other comorbid conditions, DBT has been an effective form of treatment. Eighty nine percent of clients with binge eating disorder in a DBT skills group were able to eliminate binge eating episodes compared to only 13 percent in a control group. In a separate study with bulimia nervosa, 29 percent of clients abstained from purging or binge eating behaviors after completing DBT compared to none of the participants in a control group. A case study report of a 36-year-old bulimia female who participated in 20 DBT sessions yielded positive feedback regarding the skills provided to address eating disorders. The client thought she was better equipped to handle inevitable stressful situations in a healthy way rather than sliding back into disordered eating behaviors. This client was able to maintain a healthy weight and experience higher levels of body satisfaction following treatment.

Justine J. Reel and Robert A. Bucciere

See also: Cognitive Behavioral Therapy; Depression; Mindfulness; Treatment

Bibliography

Ben-Porath, Denise D., Lucene Wisniewski, and Mark Warren. "Differential Treatment Response for Eating Disordered Patients with and without a Comorbid Borderline Personality Diagnosis Using a Dialectical Behavior Therapy (DBT)-Informed Approach." *Eating Disorders* 17 (2009): 225–241. https://doi.org/10.1080/10640260902848576.

Chen, Eunice Y., Lauren Matthews, Charese Allen, Janice R. Kuo, and Marsha M. Linehan. "Dialectical Behavior Therapy for Clients with Binge Eating Disorder or Bulimia Nervosa and Borderline Personality Disorder." *International Journal of Eating Disorders* 41 (2008): 505–512. https://doi.org/10.1002/eat.20522.

Courbasson, Christine, Yasunori Nishikawa, and Lauren Dixon. "Outcome of Dialectical Behavior Therapy for Concurrent Eating and Substance Use Disorders." *Clinical Psychology and Psychotherapy* (2011): 1–16. https://doi.org/10.1002/cpp.748.

Kroger, Christoph, Ulrich Schweiger, Valerija Sipos, Soren Kliem, Ruediger Arnold, Tanja Schunert, and Hans Reinecker. "Dialectical Behaviour Therapy and An Added Cognitive Behavioral Treatment Module for Eating Disorders in Women with Borderline Personality Disorder and Anorexia Nervosa or Bulimia Nervosa Who Failed to Respond to Previous Treatments. An Open Trial with a 15-Month Follow-Up." *Journal of Behavioral Therapy and Experimental Psychiatry* 41 (2010): 381–388. https://doi.org/10.1016/j.jbtep.2010.04.001.

Palmer, Robert L., Helen Birchall, Sadhana Damani, Nicholas Gatward, Lesley McGrain, and Lorraine Parker. "A Dialectical Behavior Therapy Program for People with an Eating Disorder and Borderline Personality Disorder—Description and Outcome." *International Journal of Eating Disorders* 33 (2003): 281–286. https://doi.org/10.1002/eat.10141.

Safer, Debra L., Christy F. Telch, and W. Stewart Agras. "Dialectical Behavior Therapy Adapted for Bulimia: A Case Report." *International Journal of Eating Disorders* 30 (2001): 101–106. https://doi.org/10.1002/eat.1059.

Telch, Christy F., W. Stewart Agras, and Marsha M. Linehan. "Group Dialectical Behavior Therapy for Binge Eating Disorder: A Preliminary, Uncontrolled Trial." *Behavior Therapy* 31 (2000): 569–582. http://dx.doi.org/10.1016/S0005-7894(00)80031-3.

DIET PILLS

The allure of losing weight sets the stage for fast fixes like a fad diet or diet pills. Diet pills are medications or herbal supplements claiming to have properties that lead to weight loss without dietary or physical activity changes. In general, diet pills purport to suppress a person's appetite or speed up a body's metabolism, but there may be harmful side effects. Diet pills have also been identified as a purging method used as part of an eating disorder. There is a wide array of prescription and over-the-counter drugs on the market touting weight loss, but most of them can be separated into two broad categories: diet pills people should avoid due to negative effects and medications that should be taken only under direct supervision of a physician. Ultimately, there are a variety of drugs and supplements claiming weight loss effects. There seems to be no magic bullet to address obesity and diet pills can be extremely harmful. Side effects range from stomach problems and sleep disturbances, severe heart and nervous system complications, and even death.

Types of Diet Pills

A type of diet pills been popular for people seeking weight loss is prescription obesity drugs. One such drug, Xenical, works to block up to 30 percent of fat absorbed by the body. Then undigested fat can be eliminated via bowel movements rather than absorbed by the body, resulting in reduced caloric intake. Although this drug is thought to be a promising option for morbidly obese individuals unable to achieve necessary weight loss through exercise and diet alone, Xenical may have serious side effects including intestinal discomfort, diarrhea, flatulence (i.e., gas), severe cramping, and leaky stools.

Another example of a prescription diet pill was Meridia (sibutramine) designed to suppress appetite by increasing brain chemicals. This drug was approved by the Food and Drug Administration (FDA) in 1997. It included a warning that the drug should not be used by individuals with high blood pressure or a history of cardiac disease as it could increase heart rate and blood pressure. Additional side effects of Meridia are constipation, insomnia, headache, and dry mouth.

Other drugs, such as Bontril, Desoxyn (methamphetamine), Ionamin, and Adipex-P (phentermine), have been prescribed for short-term use to lose weight. Despite approval by the FDA, the drugs were like speed pills. In this case people with high blood pressure and heart disease as well as an overactive thyroid gland or glaucoma were warned against using the drugs. In addition to being highly addictive, side effects are irritability, dizziness, dry mouth, sleep disturbances, upset stomach, blurred vision, and constipation.

Over-the-counter drugs include labels that have drug facts that identify side effects of a particular drug the way a food label lists ingredients. The FDA has actively banned most over-the-counter diet drugs as they have been shown to have risks and dangerous side effects. Another problem with these drugs has been the inability of companies to support marketing claims. However, one exception, Alli was approved by the FDA for adults over 18 years of age. This weight loss drug was supposed to be part of a larger health promotion plan inclusive of physical activity and a healthy nutrition plan. Actually, Alli is a reduced-strength version of Xenical, discussed earlier. Concerns with the drug included a study published in 2010 that reported liver problems. Side effects for Alli have included itching, loss of appetite, brown urine, yellow eyes and skin, and light-colored stool.

Some diet drugs have been recalled because they are found to contain hazardous substances or are believed to be a health risk. For example, Cal-Ban 3000, Cal-Lite 1000, Cal-Trim 5000, and Medi Thin have been banned because they contained the ingredient guar gum. Guar gum swells the stomach so a person experiences a sensation of being full, that is helpful for weight loss. However, this ingredient also can result in blockages in the stomach and throat that are dangerous to a person. Another example, phenylpropanolamine, found in Dexatrim and Acutrim, was associated with a public health advisory urging people to stop taking drugs that contain this ingredient due to an increased risk for stroke.

Dietary supplements have typically not received the same level of scrutiny from the FDA. Although some supplements include warning labels and list side effects, the presence of this information is inconsistent across products. There may be small print or nothing at all listed relative to a supplement. Instead consumers must contact the manufacturer directly if they have an concern. Ephedra was the first dietary supplement banned by the FDA. This diet supplement was touted to promote weight loss and enhance sport performance. However, use of the popular supplement led to a number of adverse effects including irregular heartbeats, strokes, heart attacks, and death. Ephedra was thought to be responsible for 92 deaths. The substance was banned in 2003 due to the serious health hazards mentioned as well as other side effects (e.g., insomnia, light-headedness, and high blood pressure).

Justine J. Reel

See also: Detox Diets and Cleanses; Fad Diets; Medical and Health Consequences

Bibliography

Fleig, Lena, Rudolf Kerschreiter, Ralf Schwarzer, Sarah Pomp, and Sonia Lippke. "'Sticking to a Healthy Diet Is Easier for Me When I Exercise Regularly': Cognitive Transfer between Physical Exercise and Healthy Nutrition." *Psychology and Health* 29, no. 12 (2013): 1361–1372. https://doi.org/10.1080/08870446.2014.930146.

Gattellari, Melina, and Gail Huon. "Restrained and Unrestrained Females' Positive and Negative Associations with Specific Foods and Body Parts." *International Journal of Eating Disorders* 21, no. 4 (1997): 377–383. https://doi.org/10.1002/(SICI)1098-108X(1997)21:4<377::AID-EAT11>3.0.CO;2-W.

Golden, Robert N., Fred L. Peterson, Gerri F. Kramer, William Kane, and Mark J. Kittleson. *The Truth about Eating Disorders*, 2nd ed. New York: Facts on File, 2009.

Goldfield, Gary S., and Andrew Lumb. "Effects of Dietary Restraint and Body Mass Index on the Relative Reinforcing Value of Snack Food." *Eating Disorders* 17 (2009): 46–62. https://doi.org/10.1080/10640260802570106.

Gonzalez, Vivian M. M., and Kelly M. Vitousek. "Feared Food in Dieting and Non-Dieting Young Women: A Preliminary Validation of the Food Phobia Survey." *Appetite* 43 (2004): 155–173. https://doi.org/10.1016/j.appet.2004.03.006.

Radtke, Theda, Daphne Kaklamanou, Urte Scholz, Rainer Hornung, and Christopher J. Armitage. "Are Diet Specific Compensatory Health Beliefs Predictive of Dieting Intentions and Behaviour?" *Appetite* 76 (2014): 36–43. https://doi.org/10.1016/j.appet.2014.01.014.

DIETARY RESTRAINT

Dietary restraint is a psychological construct that refers to one's intention to restrict food intake due to concern with weight. Restrained eating was introduced by researchers in the 1970s to describe chronic dieting. Restrained eating ranges from restricting certain foods or meals to intense caloric restriction that resembles anorexic behavior. Restrained eaters report successful dieting when they believe they self-discipline and control over eating by ignoring physiological cues of hunger. These periods of dietary restraint predictably become undermined by disinhibiting events. Disinhibiting eating occurs when a restrained eater engages in excessive eating or overeating in response to a triggering event. Most commonly reported disinhibiting events are alcohol consumption that decreases sensitivity to eating cues, negative emotional states (e.g., stress), and consumption of forbidden foods.

Characteristics of Restrained Eaters

Restrained eating has been associated with clinical eating disorders, disordered eating, and obesity. With regard to personality characteristics, restrained eaters have been described as narcissistic, perfectionistic, and highly impulsive. Research studies have shown while restrained eaters tend to report negative body image, they also tend to have high self-esteem compared to eating-disordered clients. In a study of 1,470 middle-aged women, eating behavior beyond hunger (disinhibition) was related to higher weight and larger size for restrained eaters. Individuals who reported high dietary restraint were not significantly thinner or lighter than nonrestrained eaters, indicating that restrained eating is often counterproductive. A well-known ice cream study conducted in the 1980s with 48 female undergraduates observed eating behavior in a blinded taste test scenario. College students arrived to sample bowls of vanilla, strawberry, and chocolate ice cream. However, the researcher left the subjects alone for 15 minutes and instructed them to eat whatever amount they desired before throwing out the containers. The amount consumed was correlated with tendency toward dietary restraint. The most noteworthy finding from the study was that measurement of dietary restraint (how it was labeled) was most important. Several surveys have been developed to measure dietary restraint.

Measurement of Dietary Restraint

The most commonly used instrument for measuring dietary restraint is the Revised Restraint Scale (RS), a 10-item self-report questionnaire created in 1975 to assess cognitive components of self-control inherent in people's attempts to restrict food intake and lose weight. A sample item of the RS is "Do you eat sensibly in front of others and splurge alone?" In attempts to address the disinhibition quality of restrained eaters, the Three Factor Eating Questionnaire (TFEQ) was developed in 1985 by Stunkard and Messick. The TFEQ, a 51-item self-report scale, measures dietary restraint, disinhibition, and hunger. Dietary restraint refers to control over food intake to influence body weight and shape. Disinhibition represents episodes experienced by restrained eaters that involve a loss of control over eating. Finally, the hunger items assess subjective sensations of hunger and food cravings.

Another popular instrument for measuring dietary restraint is the Dutch Eating Behavior Questionnaire (DEBQ). The 33-item DEBQ measures several aspects of eating behaviors using several subscales: restrained eating, emotional eating, and external eating. Restrained eating is demonstrated by items like, "Do you try to eat less at mealtimes than you would like to eat?" Emotional eating asks participants questions like, "Do you have a desire to eat when you are irritated?" External eating measures responses to environmental cues and a sample item is "If you walk past the bakery do you have the desire to buy something delicious?"

Justine J. Reel

See also: Disordered Eating; Fad Diets; Intuitive Eating; Nutrition Treatment Approaches

Bibliography

Atlas, Jana G., Gregory T. Smith, Leigh Anne Hohlstein, Denis M. McCarthy, and Larry S. Kroll. "Similarities and Differences between Caucasian and African American College Women on Eating and Dieting Expectancies, Bulimic Symptoms, Dietary Restraint, and Disinhibition." *International Journal of Eating Disorders* 32 (2002): 326–334. https://doi.org/10.1002/eat.10081.

Dykes, J., E. J. Brunner, P. T. Martikainen, and J. Wardle. "Socioeconomic Gradient in Body Size and Obesity among Women: The Role of Dietary Restraint, Disinhibition and Hunger in the Whitehall II Study." *International Journal of Obesity* 28 (2004): 262–268. https://doi.org/10.1038/sj.ijo.0802523.

Goldfield, Gary S., and Andrew Lumb. "Effects of Dietary Restraint and Body Mass Index on the Relative Reinforcing Value of Snack Food." *Eating Disorders* 17 (2009): 46–62. http://dx.doi.org/10.1080/10640260802570106.

Lejeune, M. P. G. M., D. P. C. van Aggel-Leijssen, M. A. van Baak, and M. S. Westerterp-Plantenga. "Effects of Dietary Restraint vs. Exercise during Weight Maintenance in Obese Men." *European Journal of Clinical Nutrition* 57 (2003): 1338–1344. https://doi.org/10.1038/sj.ejcn.1601697.

Safer, Debra L., Stewart Agras, Michael R. Lowe, and Susan Bryson. "Comparing Two Measures of Eating Restraint in Bulimic Women Treated with Cognitive-Behavioral Therapy." *International Journal of Eating Disorders* 36 (2004): 83–88. https://doi.org/10.1002/eat.20008.

Stein, David M. "The Scaling of Restraint and the Prediction of Eating." *International Journal of Eating Disorders* 7, no. 5 (1988): 713–717.

Yeomans, M. R., H. M. Tovey, E. M. Tinley, and C. J. Haynes. "Effects of Manipulated Palatability on Appetite Depend on Restraint and Disinhibition Scores from the Three-Factor Eating Questionnaire." *International Journal of Obesity* 28 (2004): 144–151. https://doi.org/10.1038/sj.ijo.0802483.

DISORDERED EATING

Disordered eating refers to destructive, unhealthy weight control patterns that may lead to a diagnosable clinical eating disorder (e.g., anorexia nervosa or bulimia nervosa) if left untreated. Individuals who engage in disordered eating may present with a variety of symptoms including, but not limited to, restricting overall food intake or certain types of foods (e.g., food with high fat or caloric content), occasional purging (e.g., vomiting, laxatives), frequent weighing, secretive eating, or excessive exercise to lose weight or to compensate for a meal.

The term *disordered eating* was used by the American College of Sports Medicine (ACSM) to refer to dysfunctional eating patterns associated with the female athlete triad. In ACSM's original position stand, disordered eating was a spectrum of negative eating behaviors used for weight loss. The spectrum ranges in severity from restricting food intake, to binge episodes and purging, to the *DSM-IV* defined disorders of anorexia nervosa and bulimia nervosa (American College of Sports Medicine 1997). In a recent update to ACSM's position stand the "disordered eating" was replaced with the term *energy availability*.

Disordered Eating versus Clinical Eating Disorders

Disordered eating has been commonly used to identify dysfunctional eating behaviors that may result in health consequences (e.g., menstrual and bone complications), but may not be severe enough to meet the clinical threshold for either anorexia nervosa or bulimia nervosa. By recognizing a problem before an individual has a full-blown eating disorder, early intervention can take place. Furthermore, disordered eating is more common in athletes and the general population, and can be addressed as part of prevention programs. Studies found that 18.2 percent of high school athletes, 26.1 percent of college athletes, and 46.2 percent of elite athletes engaged in disordered eating behaviors.

Justine J. Reel

See also: Anorexia Nervosa; Bulimia Nervosa; Dietary Restraint; Energy Availability; Female Athlete Triad

Bibliography

American College of Sports Medicine (ACSM). "The Female Athlete Triad." ACSM.org. Accessed November 16, 2016. https://www.acsm.org/docs/brochures/the-female-athlete-triad.pdf.

American College of Sports Medicine (ACSM). "Position Stand: The Female Athlete Triad." *Medicine & Science in Sport & Exercise* 29 (1997): i–ix. https://doi.org/10.1097/00005768-199705000-00037.

American College of Sports Medicine (ACSM). "Team Physician Concensus Conference." ACSM.org. Accessed November 16, 2016. http://forms.acsm.org/2014ATPC/TPCC/Master%20TPCC%20-%201999-2007.pdf.

Beals, Katherine A. *Disordered Eating among Athletes: A Comprehensive Guide for Health Professionals.* Champaign, IL: Human Kinetics, 2004.

Nichols, Jeanne F., Mitchell J. Rauh, Mandra J. Lawson, Ming Ji, and Hava-Shoshana Barkai. "Prevalence of Female Athlete Triad Symptoms among High School Athletes." *Archives of Pediatric and Adolescent Medicine* 160 (2006): 137–142. https://doi.org/10.1001/archpedi.160.2.137.

Reel, Justine J., Sonya SooHoo, Holly Doetsch, Jennifer Carter, and Trent Petrie. "The Female Athlete Triad: Is the Triad a Problem for Division I College Female Athletes?" *Journal of Clinical Sport Psychology* 1 (2007): 358–370.

Thompson, Ron A., and Roberta Trattner Sherman. *Eating Disorders in Sport.* New York: Routledge, 2010.

Torstveit, Monica K., Jan H. Rosenvinge, and Jorunn Sundgot-Borgen. "Prevalence of Eating Disorders and Predictive Power of Risk Models in Female Elite Athletes: A Controlled Study." *Scandinavian Journal of Medicine & Science in Sports* 18 (2008): 108–118. https://doi.org/10.1111/j.1600-0838.2007.00657.x.

DISTANCE RUNNING

The ability to run was developed about four and a half million years ago as a means to hunt animals in an upright position. Competitive running emerged from religious festivals in Greece, Egypt, Asia, and Africa. The Tailteann Games, an Irish sports festival to honor the goddess Tailtiu, is one of the earliest records (1829 BCE) of competitive running. The rules and traditions of cross-country running were formalized in Britain with the first English National Competition in 1876 and the International Cross-Country Championships in 1903.

Distance Running and Eating Disorders

Distance running (e.g. marathons cross-country), has been identified as an endurance sport that put athletes at risk for disordered eating and eating disorders. As early as the late 1980s, researchers found that almost half (48 percent) of female runners and 24 percent of male runners were preoccupied with being thinner. In the same study, 48 percent of female runners and 20 percent of male runners feared gaining weight and 57 percent of females and 37 percent of males were dissatisfied with their body weight, size, or appearance. Another study in the 1980s found that half of runners were engaging in at least one pathogenic weight control method.

A more recent study with elite women runners in the United Kingdom revealed that 16 percent of athletes had an eating disorder at the time of the study and additional participants reported a past eating disorder. Runners with eating disorders were found to be significantly less satisfied with their physical appearance, increased dieting, and reported poorer psychological health than nondisordered runners. This eating disorder prevalence was higher than the general population, but consistent with other studies of distance runners. For example, in a separate study, 24 percent of female runners and 8 percent of male runners admitted to eating disorder symptoms. As a group, distance runners experience overuse injuries, body image distortion, and excessive weight concerns.

Weight Pressures in Distance Running

Distance runners face unique performance demands associated with their sport. The perception that losing weight will improve performance is rampant. Although performance may initially increase, once an athlete faces an energy deficit, performance drops sharply. Cross-country runners have reported revealing team attire (e.g., short shorts) as contributing to body dissatisfaction. Likewise, coaches often promoted weight loss and dieting behaviors. Stereotypes were associated with a larger runner being labeled as slow or lazy and thinner runners receiving positive comments and extra attention from a coaching staff. Pressure to be the thinnest runner was present with intense comparisons of body sizes occurring at high school and college ranks for distance runners.

Justine J. Reel

See also: Anorexia Athletica; Endurance Sports; Female Athlete Triad; Sports; Weight Pressures in Sport

Bibliography

Barrack, Michelle T., Mitchell J. Rauh, Hava-Shoshana Barkai, and Jeanne F. Nichols. "Dietary Restraint and Low Bone Mass in Female Adolescent Endurance Runners." *American Journal of Clinical Nutrition* 87 (2008): 36–43.

Baum, Antonia. "Eating Disorders in the Male Athlete." *Sports Medicine* 36, no. 1 (2006): 1–6. https://doi.org/10.2165/00007256-200636010-00001.

Hulley, Angela J., and Andrew J. Hill. "Eating Disorders and Health in Elite Women Distance Runners." *International Journal of Eating Disorders* 30 (2001): 312–317.

Karlson, Kristine A., Carolyn Black Becker, and Amanda Merkur. "Prevalence of Eating Disordered Behavior in Collegiate Lightweight Rowers and Distance Runners." *Clinical Journal of Sport Medicine* 11 (2001): 32–37.

Tenforde, Adam S., Lauren C. Sayres, Mary L. McCurdy, Herve Collado, Kristin L. Sainani, and Michael Fredericson. "Overuse Injuries in High School Runners: Lifetime Prevalence and Prevention Strategies." *America Academy of Physical Medicine and Rehabilitation* 3 (2011): 123–131. http://dx.doi.org/10.1016/j.pmrj.2010.09.009.

Wilmore, Jack H., C. Harmon Brown, and James A. Davis. "Body Physique and Composition of the Female Distance Runner." *Annals of the New York Academy of Sciences* 301 (1977): 764–776. https://doi.org/10.1111/j.1749-6632.1977.tb38245.x.

DIURETICS

Diuretics are medications that cause the kidneys to get rid of water and salt from the tissues and the bloodstream through urination. Diuretics are sometimes prescribed to help control blood pressure, heart problems, and other medical conditions. However, abusing diuretics may represent a purging method by an eating-disordered individual to lose weight in a short time. The weight lost from diuretic use is regained quickly once an individual rehydrates by consuming water in foods and fluids.

Types of Diuretics

A study in the April 2011 edition of *International Journal of Eating Disorders* reported that thiazide, loop, and potassium-sparing diuretics are the most commonly abused diuretics. Thiazide diuretics inhibit sodium chloride reabsorption in the distal renal tubule of the kidney, causing excretion of sodium in the urine via the kidneys. The excretion of sodium and water decreases plasma volume and reduces edema in individuals with complications from fluid retention. Sodium and water loss can also stimulate the renin–angiotensin system that can lead to hypokalemia (low serum potassium) and metabolic alkalosis (high serum bicarbonate).

Loop diuretics inhibit reabsorption of sodium by blocking the sodium chloride–potassium chloride cotransporter. Loop diuretics also activate the renin–angiotensin system. Using loop diuretics can also result in hypokalemia and metabolic alkalosis. Hypomagnesemia (low serum magnesium), hypocalcemia (low serum calcium), and hyperuricemia (high uric acid) can also occur.

Potassium-sparing diuretics act on epithelial sodium channels. This class of medication causes sodium and water loss but does not cause a loss of potassium. In contrast to thiazide and loop diuretics, potassium-sparing diuretics put individuals at risk for hyperkalemia (high serum potassium) and metabolic acidosis (low serum bicarbonate).

Diuretic Abuse

To prevent dehydration from ongoing diuretic abuse, the body's renin–angiotensin system is activated. A high level of the hormone aldosterone is secreted, which increases sodium and bicarbonate reabsorption in the kidney in exchange for potassium and hydrogen. This system is further potentiated by dehydration. According to *Eating Disorders: A Guide to Medical Care and Complications*, the metabolic alkalosis in individuals who abuse diuretics is milder than that found in individuals who induce vomiting. But because electrolyte imbalances and metabolic acidosis are rarely seen in anorexia nervosa, high or low bicarbonate levels and other electrolyte abnormalities present in laboratory results of individuals with anorexia nervosa who deny purging can be useful to physicians who suspect purging behaviors.

Clinical Manifestations

Eating-disordered individuals with electrolyte abnormalities may complain about vague symptoms, including weakness, fatigue, constipation, dizziness, and depression. Hypokalemia can cause serious, life-threatening cardiac arrhythmias leading to sudden death. Cardiac complications can be diagnosed by an electrocardiogram. Although hypomagnesemia and hypocalcemia are not common in individuals with bulimia, hypomagnesemia should always be assessed in eating-disordered individuals who purge using diuretics. Hypomagnesemia and hypocalcemia can contribute to cardiac arrhythmias and can cause tetany, an involuntary contraction of the muscles.

Pseudo-Bartter Syndrome

According to an article published in the *International Journal of Eating Disorders*, pseudo-Bartter syndrome is widely recognized in eating-disordered individuals who abuse diuretics. Bartter syndrome is characterized by hypokalemia, metabolic alkalosis, hyperaldosteronism (high aldosterone), and normal blood pressure. There is also hyperplasia of the juxtaglomerular apparatus in the kidney. The juxtaglomerular cells stimulate the secretion of the adrenal hormone aldosterone causing sodium and bicarbonate reabsorption. The author further reports that unlike Bartter syndrome, in pseudo-Bartter syndrome there is a lack of intrinsic pathology in the renal tubules and a normal urinary chloride level. Once the purging is eliminated, pseudo-Bartter syndrome resolves.

Treatment

When treating individuals with electrolyte imbalances and dehydration from diuretic use, hydration status must be restored before treating the electrolyte abnormalities. Because dehydration stimulates aldosterone production, hydration status must be corrected first to shut off the renin–angiotensin system and stop the loss of potassium in the urine. Normalizing aldosterone levels may take from one to two weeks after an individual ceases purging behaviors. Rapid, intravenous infusions of normal saline can cause further sodium and water retention, and the resulting edema may cause individuals with bulimia to be reluctant to give up diuretics or other purging methods. Eating-disordered individuals should be reassured the edema will cease with continued treatment. *Eating Disorders: A Guide to Medical Care and Complications* recommends dietary salt restriction, elevation of legs for 10 to 15 minutes a few times each day, and a slow infusion of saline to prevent edema. In some cases, a low dose of spironolactone, a potassium-sparing diuretic that inhibits the action of aldosterone and aids in hypokalemia correction, is given daily to prevent or treat edema.

Shelly Guillory

See also: Dehydration; Detox Diets and Cleanses; Fad Diets; Medical and Health Consequences

Bibliography

Mascolo, Margherita, Eugene S. Chu, and Philip S. Mehler. "Abuse and Clinical Value of Diuretics in Eating Disorders Therapeutic Applications." *International Journal of Eating Disorders* 44, no. 3 (2011): 200–202. https://doi.org/10.1002/eat.20814.

Mehler, Philip S., and Arnold E. Anderson. "Evaluation and Treatment of Electrolyte Abnormalities." *Eating Disorders: A Guide to Medical Care and Complications,* 2nd ed., 96–107. Baltimore, MD: Johns Hopkins University Press, 2010.

Mitchell, James E., Claire Pomroy, Marvin Seppala, and Marguerite Huber. "Pseudo-Bartter's Syndrome, Diuretic Abuse, Idiopathic Edema, and Eating Disorders." *International Journal of Eating Disorders* 7, no. 2 (1988): 225–237. https://doi.org/10.1002/1098 -108X(198803)7:2<225:AID-EAT2260070209>3.0.CO;2-2.

DOLLS

Dolls and action figures have been around for centuries and they represent a multi-billion-dollar industry. However, only in the past several decades have we begun to consider the way that dolls influence or shape a child's perceptions of body image. This is in part due to the emergence of plastic figures in the late 1950s with Barbie and early 1960s with G.I. Joe. The transition to plastic allowed manufacturers to better manipulate the figures to resemble a particular person or physique, modeling societal trends of the time.

Barbie and Body Image

There has been extensive research focusing on the unrealistic physical proportions of toys and action figures. Most of this research has focused on dolls such as Barbie. Barbie is often viewed as an icon of female beauty. For example, it has been reported that preadolescent girls viewed Barbie as perfect, and adult social scripts can be enacted by playing with Barbie. In one study, a Barbie doll was scaled to the same height as another female doll—Army Norma—modeled on female army recruits. The researcher found if Barbie was five feet four inches, her physical measurements would be 32 x 17 x 28 inches, representing an anorexic physique. There has been some media and parental concern about the extreme figure of dolls such as Barbie. In response to these body image concerns, Mattel, the makers of Barbie, has altered some Barbie dolls by increasing waist and hip circumferences and decreasing breast size. However, these dolls still reinforce unrealistic expectations of a woman's body shape. In another study, girls who played with Barbie dolls showed greater desire for thinness and lowest self-esteem compared to preadolescents who played with an Emme doll or no doll at all. The researchers concluded dolls such as Barbie could lead to future body image concerns including weight cycling and disordered eating.

Action Figures and Body Image

Although a majority of research focuses on sex-based female dolls and toys, action figures are an important part of a boy's socialization. Boys tend to prefer action figures to other male figures as they represent masculinity, strength, and invincibility. An action figure differs from a doll such as Barbie in several ways. Typically, the figure is a superhero made of plastic that is capable of bending at the limbs and standing on its own. It is distinguished from other figures primarily because it is designed for boys. G.I. Joe is considered the first action figure, appearing in the U.S. market in the mid-1960s.

Although action figures are socially acceptable for boys, some researchers question the violent symbolism behind action figures. In addition, action figures represent unrealistic and unattainable physiques for the average male. Baghurst and colleagues compared the physical dimensions of original action figures to today's version. They found that the current action figures have much larger measurements for the neck, chest, arms, forearms, thighs, and calves. In one study, these action figures were presented to a group of adolescent boys to determine their opinions about the figures. The boys overwhelmingly preferred the current action figure due to its larger size and increased muscularity.

Body Image

Every toy is educational and sends an intended or unintended message. Thus, it is important to understand dolls and action figures may influence the body image of males and females. Viewing dolls (e.g., Barbie or G.I. Joe) as having a desirable appearance may lead to internalizing larger societal expectations. Seeking a physique disproportionate to real life could lead to unattainable and unhealthy body image ideals. Simply playing with a toy can influence one's body esteem. Interestingly, even adults who emulate a figure may be affected and body esteem may be lowered a result.

Timothy M. Baghurst

See also: Body Esteem; Body Image; Masculinity Ideals; Media; Parents

Bibliography

Baghurst, Timothy M., David Carlston, Julie Wood, and Frank Wyatt. "Preadolescent Male Perceptions of Action Figure Physiques." *Journal of Adolescent Health* 41 (2007): 613–615. http://dx.doi.org/10.1016/j.jadohealth.2007.07.013.

Baghurst, Timothy M., Dan B. Hollander, Beth Nardella, and G. Gregory Haff. "Change in Sociocultural Ideal Male Physique: An Examination of Past and Present Action Figures." *Body Image* 3 (2006): 87–91. http://dx.doi.org/10.1016/j.bodyim.2005.11.001.

Barlett, Chris, Richard Harris, Scott Smith, and J. Bonds-Raake. "Action Figures and Men." *Sex Roles* 53 (2005): 877–885. https://doi.org/10.1007/s11199-005-8304-4.

Kline, Steven. "Toys as Media: The Role of Toy Design, Promotional TV and Mother's Reinforcement in Young Males (3–6) Acquisition of Pro-Social Play Scripts for Rescue Hero Action Toys." Presentation at the International Toy Research Association Conference, Halmstadt, Sweden, June 18, 1999.

Kuther, Tara L., and Erin McDonald. "Early Adolescents' Experiences with and Views of Barbie." *Adolescence* 39 (2004): 39–51.

McCreary, Donald R., and Doris K. Sasse. "An Exploration of the Drive for Muscularity in Adolescent Boys and Girls." *Journal of American College Health* 48 (2000): 297–304. http://dx.doi.org/10.1080/07448480009596271.

Thomas, Jeannie B. *Naked Barbies, Warrior Joes, & Other Forms of Visible Gender.* Urbana: University of Illinois Press, 2003.

Urla, Jacqueline, and Alan C. Swedlund. "The Anthropometry of Barbie: Unsettling Ideals of the Feminine Body in Popular Culture." In *Deviant Bodies: Critical Perspectives in Science and Popular Culture,* edited by Jennifer Terry and Jacqueline Urla, 277–313. Bloomington: Indiana University Press, 2004.

DOVE CAMPAIGN FOR REAL BEAUTY

The Dove Campaign for Real Beauty was a global effort launched in 2004 as a starting point to widen the definition and discussion of beauty and celebrate diverse and healthy body shapes. The campaign included videos, advertisements, workshops, sleepover events, a book, and a play production to improve self-esteem in girls and women of all ages. It is currently available in 30 different countries. Dove has released marketing campaigns in video formats that reveal the truth behind the media images with a mission statement on its website that commits to inspiring women and girls to reach their potential.

Evolution of Beauty Video

The *Evolution of Beauty* takes a viewer through a visual journey of the harsh world of modeling. At the beginning of the video a female model is seen plainly dressed with hair that has not been styled and no makeup. Professional hair and makeup artists go to work to mold her into a more desirable media-ready photograph by styling her hair and layering on makeup. The photographer manipulates the lighting on set to make her look thinner than she is in person. After the photographs have been meticulously shot from various eye-pleasing angles, they are transferred to a computer for digital enhancement. Enhancements or changes that are made to the model's body might include changing her eye color, eyebrow shape, eye size, and face shape (to make it thinner and longer). They may also involve enlarging her lips, moving her cheekbones, elongating her neck, and removing fat from her body. All the changes made to the models' bodies are unrealistic. The emerging image of the model does not resemble her original real appearance and the video depicts this transformation.

Dove Advertisements

Dove has thoughtfully placed advertisements of its products through magazines using models of all sizes. Their appearances, unlike most other advertisements, have not been digitally enhanced or changed. A model's body seen in the Dove advertisements in magazines will look the same when placed next to the model in person. This real depiction teaches girls and women of all ages that they are beautiful regardless of body shape, size, height, or color. Emphasizing a positive body image message is refreshing, as it is easy to criticize one's body after viewing ultrathin models in advertisements.

Dove Workshops

The Dove Campaign for Real Beauty offers free workshops around the world. These workshops can be conducted by any person willing to learn and teach the curriculum. To obtain the curriculum go to the Dove website. Curriculum lesson plans include assertiveness training, media literacy, and self-esteem training. Media literacy involves being able to critically analyze manipulated and negative media images and advertisements. Dove also offers online workshops for parents and daughters. One workshop activity involves building a "self-esteem bubble" by dragging names and images that evoke happiness into a bubble shape and printing it out. The *Playing with Beauty* activity shows what the proportions of a Barbie doll would look like if the doll's measurements were extrapolated into a human being's size and height. The *True You for Mothers and Daughters* workbook, which aims to strengthen mother–daughter relationships, is available online as a resource to build body image and self-esteem.

Hailey E. Nielson

See also: Body Image; Media; Prevention

Bibliography

"Dove Self-Esteem Project." Selfesteem.dove.us. Accessed November 16, 2016. http://selfesteem.dove.us/.

"Dove Self-Esteem Project: Our Mission in Action." *Selfesteem.dove.us.* Accessed November 16, 2016. http://selfesteem.dove.us/Articles/Written/Our_Mission_in_Practice.aspx.

Falcione, Olivia, and Laura Henderson. "The Dove Campaign for Real Beauty Case Study." *The Dove Campaign* (2009).

DRILL TEAM/DANCE TEAM

Historically, drill teams have been squads of individuals (typically females) who performed line dances and high kick and jazz routines often in association with a school's marching band. The Universal Dance Association (UDA) was founded in 1980 as Universal Dance Camps to educate dancers about proper techniques and fitness. UDA changed the name from drill teams to dance teams to better represent the fitness associated with the activity. To date, there are numerous dance championships across the United States.

Athletes and dancers are identified as at risk for body image disturbances, disordered eating, and clinical disorders due to the weight-focused nature of training and competition. Dance squads and drill teams perform separately from cheerleaders and other athletes and have been largely ignored in large-scale eating disorder studies with athletes. However, the training and performance schedules are stringent, practice of difficult choreography and skills is rigorous, and like in cheerleading and ballet, a certain body type may be selected or valued by choreographers and dance team coaches.

Body Image and Eating Disorders in Auxiliary Team Members

Although auxiliary units (e.g., dance team squad members, majorettes) have been overlooked in most athlete studies, they may experience physical and psychological pressures associated with their participation. Expectations to be feminine and pretty to fit into the stereotype of dance performers—apart from types of uniforms and choreographers—contribute to pressure to maintain a low body weight or size. Dance teams may wear tight stretch pants, boy shorts, short skirts, and tops that display midriffs. Similar to cheerleaders, there may be weight requirements associated with trying out for a dance team and dancers may be told to lose weight to fit the appearance desired for a squad. Naturally, majorettes are the central focus of a marching band and are scrutinized for their appearance and beauty. A rare study of 101 female auxiliary unit members representing three National Collegiate Athletic Association Division I universities found approximately 30 percent of women were at risk for eating disorders with 31 percent of color guard members, 26 percent of dance line members, and 37 percent of majorettes displaying disordered eating risk factors. Color guard members reported the highest frequency for binge eating (20 percent) compared to 15 percent for the whole sample. Vomiting to lose weight (14 percent) was also higher in color guards than the entire sample (10 percent). However, majorettes were more likely to admit laxative, diet pills, or diuretic abuse (26 percent) than the rate for all participants (19 percent).

Auxiliary team members may be overlooked in studies that examine disordered eating behaviors and risk for eating disorders in athletic populations. However, some initial research indicates dance team members and majorettes also face pressures associated with body weight, size, and appearance. When considering the revealing team uniforms and the focus on appearance associated with performing, it is important to examine this potentially at-risk group.

Justine J. Reel

See also: Ballet; Cheerleading; Dancers; Gymnastics; Sports; Weight Pressures in Sport

Bibliography

Black, David R., Laurie J. S. Larkin, Daniel C. Coster, Larry J. Leverenz, and Doris A. Abood. "Physiologic Screening Test for Eating Disorders/Disordered Eating among Female Collegiate Athletes." *Journal of Athletic Training* 38, no. 4 (2003): 286–297.

Kurtzman, Felice D., John Landsverk, Diane C. Bodurka. "Eating Disorders among Selected Female Student Populations at UCLA." *Journal of the American Dietetic Association* 89, no. 1 (1989): 45–53.

Torres-McGehee, Toni M., James M. Green, Deidre Leaver-Dunn, James D. Leeper, Phillip A. Bishop, and Mark T. Richardson. "Attitude and Knowledge Changes in Collegiate Dancers Following a Short-Term, Team-Centered Prevention Program on Eating Disorders." *Perceptual and Motor Skills* 112, no. 3 (2011): 711–725. https://doi.org/10.2466/06. PMS.112.3.711-725.

Torres-McGehee, Toni M., James M. Green, James D. Leeper, Deidre Leaver-Dunn, Mark T. Richardson, and Phillip A. Bishop. "Body Image, Anthropometric Measures, and Eating-Disorder Prevalence in Auxiliary Unit Members." *Journal of Athletic Training* 44, no. 4 (2009): 418–426.

"Universal Dance Association." UDA.varsity.com. Accessed November 16, 2016. https://uda.varsity.com/About/About.

DRIVE FOR MUSCULARITY

Drive for muscularity (DM) is the tendency of certain individuals in Western society to strive for lean and muscular bodies. Drive for muscularity was first introduced in a 2000 issue of the *Journal of American College Health* by researcher Donald McCreary. McCreary noted that although males have a low drive for thinness, they do display a desire for increased body size and muscularity. For example, 40 percent of college men in one study desired to gain weight. In another study, 95 percent of adult males preferred to be a mesomorph, a body type characterized by an athletic physique and the ability to easily gain or lose weight. According to McCreary, DM has two components: (1) muscularity-oriented body image (e.g., wanting to be more muscular), and (2) muscularity behavior (e.g., lifting weight to build more muscle). DM parallels the drive for thinness pervasive in females of all ages. Just as many women report being larger and heavier than their actual size, many men view themselves negatively as smaller than their actual size. As a result, a substantial number of normal weight adolescent boys seek to gain weight, primarily through increasing muscle mass.

Although the prevalence of DM is unknown, a 2010 study of 235 college men and women revealed 41 percent of participants scored above the median on a paper-and-pencil measure of DM. Calculating an exact prevalence of DM may be problematic, as the concept is currently viewed as existing on a continuum rather than as a discrete condition. Thus, individuals may be classified as "high" or "low" on DM, but specific criteria to identify someone as really experiencing DM do not yet exist.

Assessment of Drive for Muscularity

The systematic assessment of male body image to measure DM has only recently been addressed by researchers. Perceptual tests (e.g., photos and videos) to measure individual ability to correctly estimate body measurement and subjective tests, (e.g., paper-and-pencil surveys and drawings) to measure individual thoughts about the body, are used to assess DM. Most perceptual tests focus on body size and weight without consideration for muscularity and are thus ill equipped to assess DM. However, several subjective tests show promise to assess DM. Most subjective assessments are paper-and-pencil surveys scored using Likert rating scales (e.g., 0 = "strongly disagree" to 5 = "strongly agree") to assess individuals' attitudes about muscularity (e.g., "I think I have too little muscle on my body"). An abundance of paper-and-pencil tests specifically focused on DM have been developed in the past 10 years. These tests include the Drive for Muscularity Scale (DMS), the Male Body Attitudes Scale (MBAS), the Muscle Appearance Satisfaction Scale (MASS), and the Drive for Muscularity Attitudes Questionnaire (DMAQ). The DMS was the first test created, and is by far the most widely used of the paper-and-pencil subjective assessments. Example items from the 15-item DMS include "I wish that I were more muscular," and "I drink weight-gain or protein shakes."

Used less to subjectively assess DM are contour-drawn silhouette scales. Assessment using silhouette scales involves presenting individuals with a series of same-sex body figures ranging from very large to very small. Individuals are asked to select the figure that most accurately portrays their body, as well as the figure that represents the body they would most like to have. Early silhouette scales were characterized by figures that ranged from low to high adiposity and did a poor job of assessing DM. However, the somatomorphic matrix (SM) consists of a 10 x 10 matrix of 100 figures that vary in terms of both muscularity and body fat. Because it portrays figures based on both muscularity and body fat, the SM is the most valid silhouette scale assessment of DM.

Sex Differences in Drive for Muscularity

Although girls and women do exhibit DM, the drive for muscularity is higher in males. Further, DM seems to be more relevant to the mental and physical health of males than the health of females. Regardless of sex, excessive DM can lead to a variety of negative consequences, including binge eating, the use of body/performance enhancing substances, the development of body image disturbances such as muscle dysmorphia, and enhanced risk for weight-related health conditions such as type 2 diabetes and coronary heart disease.

Although males report higher DM than females, DM should not be ignored in girls and women. DM in females centers more on a lean and toned physique, than a big and muscular physique. One study did reveal differences between men and women on DM disappeared when the focus was on muscle tone instead of muscle mass. The same study also found DM was related to similar behaviors (e.g., physical activity, diet) in men and women. Thus, efforts to build muscle in persons who score high on DM are similar regardless of sex.

Gay Men and Drive for Muscularity

Researchers have determined gay males as a population may be at increased risk for body dissatisfaction and DM, as a desire for a muscular body may represent a vehicle for overcoming years of teasing and questions related to their masculinity. In one study, gay males perceived themselves as less muscular and reported more body dissatisfaction specific to their muscles than heterosexual men. Another study compared DM between 70 gay and 71 heterosexual men. The gay males reported more awareness and internalization of a lean and muscular ideal than the heterosexual men. Thus, due at least partially to the stigma associated with being gay, gay males are a subpopulation that may be particularly at risk for high DM.

Race and Ethnicity

Unfortunately, very few researchers have examined racial and ethnic differences for DM. A study comparing muscularity satisfaction between college men in the United States and those in Hong Kong revealed the Hong Kong men were significantly more satisfied with their muscularity than their U.S. counterparts. Western conceptions of masculinity and the muscular ideal remain largely rejected by males in Hong Kong, as they conflict with the traditional Chinese notion of a more well-rounded masculinity that includes either physical *or* scholarly traits. The lone study focused on DM in African American men showed that muscularity was an important component of their racial/ethnic identity.

Athletes and Drive for Muscularity

Competitive athletes are a subpopulation of interest when considering DM. Athletes face the same pressures as nonathletes to conform to societal body ideals of muscularity, but they also encounter pressures from coaches and teammates to achieve sufficient muscularity for their sport. Male and female athletes in team and individual sports report a strong DM. In support of a dual pathway of body image dissatisfaction, one study of college-aged male athletes showed participants reported a desire to gain an average of 3.2 pounds while at the same time *lose* an average of 5.1 percent body fat. In another study, 100 percent of college male athletes reported a desire to be muscular. Female athletes also express DM, although at lower levels than male athletes. In a recent study, college female athletes expressed a significantly stronger DM than female nonathletes. In the same study, the 84 percent of female athletes who wanted to be muscular reported that muscularity was important for several reasons, including functionality (i.e., sport performance), health, external gratification (i.e., sex appeal), and internal gratification (i.e., self-esteem).

Other Characteristics Associated with Drive for Muscularity

A variety of factors have been suggested as leading to DM, including biology, personality, physical attributes, sex role perceptions, and social environment. The results of one study found that prenatal testosterone exposure was related to higher DM in adult males. In terms of personality, men with high DM may also be anxious, perfectionistic, and strongly focused on fitness and appearance. Surprisingly, the only physical measure related to DM is bicep circumference. Thus, body mass index (BMI), body fat percentage, and other anthropometric measures have not shown a relationship with DM.

In comparison to biology, personality, and physical attributes, much more research has focused on the influence of gender and sex roles and social environment on DM. In Western society, muscularity is often equated with masculinity and individuals who identify as more masculine tend to show higher DM. Men who endorse more traditional views of masculinity such as the taking of risks, being physically strong and tough, and controlling one's emotions are also more likely to have a stronger DM.

The social environment is believed to have a strong influence on men's conceptions of masculinity, and what it means to have a masculine body. Images of the ideal male body have evolved from the strong and burly John Wayne in the 1950s and 1960s to the tanned, ripped, and muscular action heroes of the 2000s and 2010s. Arnold Schwarzenegger is largely credited for bringing bodybuilding to the mainstream with his 1977 documentary, *Pumping Iron* that made lifting weights socially acceptable for boys and men and signaled a shift in the male body ideal.

Movies are not the only media source to normalize hypermuscularity in males. Male models in health and fitness magazines tend to have less fat and more muscle mass today than they did in the 1970s and 1980s. Changes to the design of action figures have ensured young boys are exposed to the muscular ideal. Whereas action figures from the 1970s and early 1980s depicted men's bodies as relatively skinny, the same characters portrayed in the 1990s showed marked upper body development. Video games and gaming magazines are another source of information for boys about the type of body they should strive to attain. Many researchers believe changes to the portrayal of the male body have had the strongest influence on DM in boys and men today. Research supports this link, as numerous studies have shown exposure to muscular male models in magazines leads to worsened mood and increased body dissatisfaction, depression, and DM in males.

Nick Galli

See also: Bigorexia; Body Image in Males; Bodybuilding; Dolls; Masculinity Ideals; Media; Movies and Eating Disorders

Bibliography

Cafri, Guy, and Kevin J. Thompson. "Measuring Male Body Image: A Review of the Current Methodology." *Psychology of Men and Masculinity* 1 (2004): 18–29.

Davis, Caroline, Kristina Karvinen, and Donald R. McCreary. "Personality Correlates of a Drive for Muscularity in Young Men." *Personality & Individual Differences* 39 (2005): 349–359.

Drewnowski, Adam, and Doris K. Yee. "Men and Body Image: Are Males Satisfied with Their Body Weight?" *Psychosomatic Medicine* 49 (1987): 626–634.

Galli, Nick, and Justine J. Reel. "Adonis or Hephaestus? Exploring Body Image in Male Athletes." *Psychology of Men and Masculinity* 10 (2009): 95–108. https://doi.org/10.1037/a0014005

Giles, David C., and Jessica Close. "Exposure to 'Lad Magazines' and Drive for Muscularity in Dating and Non-dating Young Men." *Personality & Individual Differences* 44 (2008): 1610–1616. http://dx.doi.org/10.1016/j.paid.2008.01.023.

"Han Solo 1970s Action Figure Vintage." Pinterest.com. Accessed November 16, 2016. https://s-media-cache-ak0.pinimg.com/236x/16/ce/72/16ce72a9ef7bcf7b380e3543167febbe.jpg.

"Han Solo 1990s Action Figure." Google.com. Accessed November 16, 2016. http://designbyelena.com/ebay/AuctionImages6/sw-beastpack-3.jpg.

Harrison, Kristen, and Bradley J. Bond. "Gaming Magazines and the Drive for Muscularity in Preadolescent Boys: A Longitudinal Examination." *Body Image* 4 (2007): 269–277. http://dx.doi.org/10.1016/j.bodyim.2007.03.003.

"John Wayne." Allposters.com. Accessed November 16, 2016. http://cache2.allpostersimages.com/p/LRG/21/2115/UG4ED00Z/posters/john-wayne.jpg.

Jung, Jaehee, Gordon B. Forbes, and Priscilla Chan. "Global Body and Muscle Satisfaction among College Men in the United States and Hong Kong-China." *Sex Roles* 63 (2010): 104–117. https://doi.org/10.1007/s11199-010-9760-z.

Kelley, Courtney C., Jennie M. Neufeld, and Dara R. Musher-Eizenman. "Drive for Thinness and Drive for Muscularity: Opposite Ends of the Continuum or Separate Constructs?" *Body Image* 7, no. 1 (2010): 74–77. http://dx.doi.org/10.1016/j.bodyim.2009.09.008.

Kyretjo, Jacob W., Amber D. Mosewich, Kent C. Kowalski, Diane E. Mack, and Peter R. E. Crocker. "Men's and Women's Drive for Muscularity: Gender Differences and Cognitive and Behavioral Correlates." *International Journal of Sport and Exercise Psychology* 6 (2008): 69–84. http://dx.doi.org/10.1080/1612197X.2008.9671855.

Lerner, Richard M., and Sam J. Korn. "The Development of Body-Build Stereotypes in Males." *Child Development* 43 (1972): 908–920. https://doi.org/10.2307/1127641.

McCreary, Donald R., and Doris K. Sasse. "An Exploration of the Drive for Muscularity in Adolescent Boys and Girls." *Journal of American College Health* 48 (2000): 297–304. http://dx.doi.org/10.1080/07448480009596271.

McCreary, Donald R., Deborah M. Saucier, and Will H. Courtenay. "The Drive for Muscularity and Masculinity: Testing the Associations among Gender-Role Traits, Behaviors, Attitudes, and Conflict." *Psychology of Men and Masculinity* 5 (2005): 83–94. http://dx.doi.org/10.1037/1524-9220.6.2.83.

Pope Jr., Harrison G., Katharine A. Phillips, and Robert Olivardia. *The Adonis Complex: The Secret Crisis of Male Body Obsession.* New York: Free Press, 2000.

"Pumping Iron." YouTube.com. Accessed November 16, 2016. http://www.youtube.com/watch?v=IjH9lJVofh0.

Smith, April R., Sean E. Hawkeswood, and Thomas E. Joiner. "The Measure of a Man: Associations between Digit Ratio and Disordered Eating in Males." *International Journal of Eating Disorders* 43 (2010): 543–548. https://doi.org/10.1002/eat.20736.

Steinfeldt, Jesse A., Hailee Carter, Emily Benton, and Matthew C. Steinfeldt. "Muscularity Beliefs of Female College Athletes." *Sex Roles* 64 (2011): 543–554. https://doi.org/10.1007/s11199-011-9935-2.

Tiggemann, Marika, Yolanda Martins, and Alana Kirkbride. "Oh to Be Lean and Muscular: Body Image Ideals in Gay and Heterosexual Men." *Psychology of Men and Masculinity* 8 (2007): 15–24. http://dx.doi.org/10.1037/1524-9220.8.1.15.

"Vin Diesel." Hitfix.com. Accessed November 16, 2016. http://images.hitfix.com/photos/689885/Vin-Diesel-in-Fast-Five_gallery_primary.JPG.

EATING DISORDER NOT OTHERWISE SPECIFIED

Eating disorder not otherwise specified (EDNOS) was an eating disorder diagnosis in previous editions of the *Diagnostic and Statistical Manual of Mental Disorders*; however, in the fifth edition (i.e., *DSM-5*), EDNOS was removed. The purpose of addressing EDNOS in the *DSM-5* was to give more information about the 40–60 percent of eating disorder cases that fit into this catchall category. Therefore, the decision was made to replace EDNOS with more specific categories including binge eating disorder.

Specifically, the previous edition of the *Diagnostic and Statistical Manual of Mental Disorders (DSM-IV-TR)* identified three categories of eating disorders: anorexia nervosa, bulimia nervosa, and EDNOS. EDNOS was diagnosed when an individual with an eating disorder did not meet the full criteria for anorexia nervosa or bulimia nervosa. EDNOS has been labeled the *garbage can* for eating disorder diagnoses because it was only used when an individual presented with eating-related syndromes not yet covered by the *DSM-IV-TR* such as binge eating disorder, night-eating syndrome, selective eating disorder, and orthorexia.

Examples of EDNOS Diagnoses

Individuals who are considered subclinical cases—that is, they present with disordered eating that is not as severe as full-blown eating disorder—and show potential to develop into clinical eating disorders previously received the EDNOS diagnosis.

EDNOS was also given as a diagnosis when an individual with a severe eating disorder did not fit the category for anorexia nervosa (e.g., everything except for amenorrhea) or bulimia nervosa (e.g., frequency less than twice a week or duration less than three months). Additionally, individuals who exhibited what has been dubbed as *bulimiarexia*, a disorder where they alternate between restricting and binge–purge behaviors usually received an EDNOS diagnosis.

The EDNOS category has represented a catchall eating disorder category in previous editions of the *DSM*. Discontinued in *DSM-5* to allow for more specificity in diagnosing eating disorders, EDNOS is still widely referred to in the literature.

Justine J. Reel

See also: Assessment; *Diagnostic and Statistical Manual of Mental Disorders*; Disordered Eating

Bibliography

American Psychiatric Association. *Diagnostic and Statistical Manual of Mental Disorders*, 5th ed. (*DSM-5*). Washington, DC: American Psychiatric Association Publishing, 2013.

American Psychiatric Association. *Diagnostic and Statistical Manual of Mental Disorders*, 4th ed., text rev. Washington, DC: American Psychiatric Association Publishing, 2000.

"DSM-5 Overview: The Future Manual." Dsm5.org. Accessed November 16, 2016. http://www.dsm5.org/about/Pages/DSMVOverview.aspx.

"Eating Disorders." Nami.org. Accessed November 16, 2016. http://www.nami.org/Learn-More/Mental-Health-Conditions/Eating-Disorders/Overview.

EATING DISORDERS ANONYMOUS

Eating Disorders Anonymous (EDA) was formed in 2000 by Alcoholics Anonymous members in Phoenix to bring together individuals struggling with eating disorders who could share their common experience in a support group. Until that time, individuals with eating disorders would either attend Overeater's Anonymous (OA) or other twelve-step groups as part of treatment and recovery. However, individuals with anorexia nervosa and bulimia nervosa did not always think their experience fit with these groups.

Unlike other eating disorder associations (e.g., National Eating Disorder Association) that engage in activist work to change societal beliefs and combat harmful media messages, EDA self-identifies as not wanting to participate in controversies or affiliate with any particular sect, denomination, political party, organization, or institution. EDA's primary purpose is help people recover from eating disorders and help other to recover as well. EDA defines recovery as living a life free of obsessions with on food, weight, or body image and making healthy choices in life, regaining trust in self, and practicing self-care. The only requirement for being an EDA member is to have the desire for recovery from an eating disorder.

EDA Meetings

EDA meetings function as support groups for males and females of all ages who suffer from an eating disorder. Groups average eight attendees but often range from 2 to 20 participants. The EDA's proposed solution parallels the twelve steps and twelve traditions of EDA published in a workbook format. Each meeting begins with a serenity prayer followed by a reading of the twelve steps or traditions. Participants have an opportunity to share their stories and members can seek support by relating to individuals in the group who have a shared experience. Currently, meetings take place as face-to-face, online, or over the phone in almost all of the states in America, as well as Canada, Ireland, South Africa, and Ukraine. There is no cost to attend meetings or to join EDA, but donations are accepted to support the foundation.

EDA been provided support groups and meetings using a traditional twelve-step format since 2000. Individuals with eating disorders are welcome to attend free meetings to find solace hearing from others who struggle from eating disorders.

Like other anonymous groups, EDA mentions a "higher power"; however, the group is not affiliated with any particular religion or group. Because eating disorder treatment has traditionally been extremely expensive (sometimes ranging from $1,000 to $2,000 for a night's stay in a residential facility), EDA offers a free option for receiving support to recover.

Justine J. Reel

See also: Advocacy Groups; National Eating Disorders Association; Overeaters Anonymous; Twelve-Step Programs

Bibliography

The Alliance for Eating Disorders. Accessed November 16, 2016. http://www.alliancefor eatingdisorders.com.

Eating Disorders Anonymous. Accessed November 16, 2016. http://www.eatingdisorders anonymous.org/.

Overeaters Anonymous. Accessed November 16, 2016. https://oa.org/.

EDEMA

Edema is swelling caused by fluid accumulation between cells. In eating-disorder clients, edema most frequently affects tissue in the lower legs, usually around the feet and ankles. Some cases of edema are described as *pitting*, an indentation in the skin when pressure is applied to the area. Many cases of edema are mild, but severe prolonged lower limb edema may result in increasingly painful swelling, leg stiffness, and difficulty walking. For eating disorder clients, the acute, rapid weight gain that edema causes may intensify body image disturbances and reinforce the fear of gaining too much weight or becoming fat that could trigger a return to eating-disordered behaviors.

Causes of Edema

There can be multiple causes of edema and those that affect eating-disordered clients are not entirely understood. However, the most commonly proposed causes of edema in eating-disordered clients involve (1) the retention of sodium and fluid by the kidneys and (2) the movement of fluid from blood vessels into tissues between cells. However, other causes of edema should not be ruled out, including heart, liver, or kidney failure.

Sodium and Fluid Reabsorption
Purging and Edema
Self-induced vomiting and laxative and diuretic abuse are common purging methods for eating-disorder clients and may lead to chronic dehydration. To adapt, the body increases production of aldosterone, a hormone that signals the kidneys to reabsorb fluid and sodium. When purging behaviors are discontinued abruptly, or if an individual undergoes rapid rehydration (e.g., via intravenous administration), aldosterone levels may remain elevated and lead to edema.

Refeeding Edema

Refeeding syndrome is characterized by a myriad of metabolic complications that develop when nutrition is reintroduced, including fluid and electrolyte disturbances (see "Refeeding Syndrome" in Volume 2 of this work for the full description). Edema may be one of the first signs of refeeding syndrome. Under-nourished clients may have an increased sensitivity to insulin, a hormone that regulates carbohydrate and fat metabolism. The elevation in insulin levels that occurs when carbohydrates are provided in higher amounts and used again by the body after a period of starvation may stimulate sodium reabsorption and, thus, fluid retention.

Blood Vessel Permeability

Reproductive Hormones

Menstrual cycle disturbances are a common symptom of malnutrition when the body's production of reproductive hormones decreases. During nutrition and weight repletion, these hormone levels increase leading to the return of menses. It is possible estrogens cause blood vessels to widen, causing fluid to leak from vessels and build up in surrounding tissues.

Management of Edema

Edema usually resolves on its own over time without any form of treatment. The length of time that it takes for edema to go away varies depending on the situation but may take a few weeks for some. However, mental health providers should discuss the possibility of edema with the client to help prepare them psychologically for any acute physiological changes when nutrition is reintroduced, or refeeding occurs. For severe edema, leg elevation is helpful in reducing the swelling in some clients. Sometimes, diuretics are prescribed in low doses; however, use of diuretics is closely monitored by a physician to prevent abuse. Edema may also occur less often in clients who consume a low sodium diet during the initial weeks of refeeding to reduce sodium retention. To prevent or reduce the severity of edema, nutritional rehabilitation should occur gradually in undernourished clients, with a slow increase in caloric intake, close monitoring of electrolyte levels, avoidance of excessive fluid intake, and regular physical examinations.

Holly E. Doetsch

See also: Diuretics; Laxative Abuse; Medical and Health Consequences; Refeeding Syndrome; Relapse

Bibliography

Ehrlich, Stefan, Uwe Querfeld, and Ernst Pfeiffer. "Refeeding Oedema: An Important Complication in the Treatment of Anorexia Nervosa." *European Child and Adolescent Psychiatry* 15 (2006): 241–243. https://doi.org/10.1007/s00787-006-0528-5.

Kalambokis, Georgios N., Agathocles A. Tsatsoulis, and Epameinondas V. Tsianos. "The Edematogenic Properties of Insulin." *American Journal of Kidney Diseases* 44, no. 4 (2004): 575–590. http://dx.doi.org/10.1053/j.ajkd.2004.06.025.

Mascolo, Marguerita, Eugene S. Chu, and Philip S. Mehler. "Abuse and Clinical Value of Diuretics in Eating Disorders Therapeutic Applications." *International Journal of Eating Disorders* 44 (2011): 200–202. https://doi.org/10.1002/eat.20814.

Rigaud, Daniel, Alain Boulier, Isabelle Tallonneau, Marie Claude Brindisi, and Raymond Rozen. "Body Fluid Retention and Body Weight Change in Anorexia Nervosa Patients during Refeeding." *Clinical Nutrition* 29 (2010): 749–755. http://dx.doi.org/10.1016/j.clnu.2010.05.007.

Roerig, James L., Kristine J. Steffen, James E. Mitchell, and Christie Zunker. "Laxative Abuse: Epidemiology, Diagnosis and Management." *Drugs* 70, no. 12 (2010): 1487–1503. https://doi.org/10.2165/11898640-000000000-00000.

Tey, Hong Liang, Su Chi Lim, and Alison M. Snodgrass. "Refeeding Oedema in Anorexia Nervosa." *Singapore Medical Journal* 46 (2005): 308–310.

Yücel, Başak, Nese Özbey, Aslihan Polat, and Joel Yager. "Weight Fluctuations during Early Refeeding Period in Anorexia Nervosa: Case Reports." *International Journal of Eating Disorders* 37 (2005): 175–177. https://doi.org/10.1002/eat.20050.

ELECTROCARDIOGRAM

An electrocardiogram, also known as EKG or ECG, is a noninvasive, painless test to measure the heart's electrical activity. During the 10- to 15-minute test, a person is asked to lie flat. Twelve electrodes, called leads, are placed on the arms, legs, and chest. The leads are connected to a machine to record the electrical signals of the heart and produce a graphic tracing of the electrical impulses.

The heart's conduction system is made of specialized neuromuscular tissue. The movement of charged ions across the membranes of myocardial cells produces the wave forms on the EKG. EKG results determine abnormalities in heart rate, heart rhythms, and the strength and timing of the electrical signals as they pass through each part of the heart.

EKG Changes in Anorexia Nervosa

On an EKG, the QT interval reflects the time during which the left and right ventricles of the heart are triggered to contract and then build the potential to contract again. On an EKG reading, the QT interval usually lasts for one-third of a heartbeat cycle. This is known as depolarization and repolarization. As heart rate increases, the depolarization–repolarization must happen more quickly and the QTc, the corrected QT interval, adjusts for this.

It was once thought a ventricular arrhythmia caused by QT prolongation was responsible for sudden deaths in individuals with anorexia nervosa. Although studies have documented prolonged QT intervals in severely anorexic individuals, this has not been a consistent finding. According to *Eating Disorders: A Guide to Medical Care and Complications*, the prevalence and cause of prolonged QT interval is controversial. Currently, the assumption is that the QT interval is not inherently prolonged in anorexia nervosa, and it is not an independent cause of sudden death. A 2006 study published in the *International Journal of Cardiology* reported that in individuals with anorexia nervosa, the QT interval is usually normal, but individuals with severe hypokalemia (decreased serum potassium) are at risk for *torsade de pointe,* a life-threatening arrhythmia. If a person with anorexia nervosa has a prolonged QT interval, electrolyte imbalances should be considered.

In addition to a prolonged QT interval, other EKG changes result from electrolyte abnormalities. Severe hypokalemia can cause T-wave flattening, prominent U waves, and ST segment depression. Low magnesium and low calcium can also cause a prolonged QT interval and T-wave changes. QRS segment depression, ST segment alterations, and T-wave changes on an EKG can also be related to decreased thickness of the left ventricle wall and cardiac chamber size due to decreased muscle mass from starvation.

QT dispersion on an EKG is another marker for determining arrhythmia risk. The length of the QT interval is usually similar between each of the 12 leads. QT dispersion is the difference between the maximum QT interval and minimum QT interval occurring in any of the 12 leads. A 2005 study in the *International Journal of Eating Disorders* found when QT dispersion is increased, an individual may develop ventricular arrhythmias. The reason for an increased QT dispersion in individuals with anorexia nervosa is unknown, but it is hypothesized a decreased resting metabolic rate and decreased skeletal and cardiac muscles due to starvation increases QT dispersion.

EKG Changes in Bulimia Nervosa

Eating Disorders: A Guide to Medical Care and Complications reports that normal weight individuals suffering from bulimia nervosa have fewer cardiac complications than individuals with anorexia nervosa. EKG changes in individuals with bulimia nervosa are usually indicative of electrolyte abnormalities. Low blood levels of potassium and magnesium are a danger to the heart, especially in individuals who purge frequently by vomiting or using laxatives and diuretics.

EKG Changes and Refeeding

Most of the EKG changes can be reversed with the correction of electrolyte imbalances, hydration, and nutritional status; however, during refeeding, electrolytes must be carefully monitored because there may be alterations in phosphorus, magnesium, and potassium that can cause electrolyte abnormalities and EKG changes.

Shelly Guillory

See also: Medical and Health Consequences; Refeeding Syndrome

Bibliography

Facchini, M., L. Sala, G. Malfatt, R. Bragata, G. Redelli, and C. Invitti. "Low K+ Dependent QT Prolongation and Risk for Ventricular Arrhythmias in Anorexia Nervosa." *International Journal of Cardiology* 106, no. 2 (2006): 170–176. Accessed May 7, 2011. https://doi.org/10.1016/j.ijcrd.2005.01.041

Krantz, Mori J., William T. Donahoo, Edward L. Melanson, and Philip S. Mehler. "QT Interval Dispersion and Resting Metabolic Rate in Chronic Anorexia Nervosa." *International Journal of Eating Disorders* 37, no. 37 (2005): 166–170. Accessed May 6, 2011. https://doi.org/10.1002/eat.20082.

Lewis, Sharon M., Margaret Heitkemper, and Sharon Dirkson. "Fluid, Electrolyte and Acid-Base Balance." In *Medical-Surgical Nursing: Assessment and Management of Clinical Problems.* 5th ed., edited by Sally Shrefer, 324–326. St. Louis, MO: Mosby, 2000.

Mehler, Philip S., and Arnold E. Anderson. "Evaluation and Treatment of Electrolyte Abnormalities." In *Eating Disorders: A Guide to Medical Care and Complications*, 2nd ed., 96–107. Baltimore, MD: Johns Hopkins University Press, 2010.

Mitchell, James E., Claire Pomeroy, and David E. Adson. "Managing Medical Complications." *Handbook of Treatment for Eating Disorders*, 2nd ed., edited by David M. Garner and Paul E. Garfinkel, 383–393. New York: Guilford Press, 1997.

National Heart and Blood Institute. "Electrocardiogram." Last modified October 1, 2010. Accessed November 16, 2016. http://www.nhlbi.nih.gov/health/dci/Diseases/ekg/ekg _what.html.

Takimoto, Yoshiyuki, K. Yoshiuchi, H. Kumano, G. Yamanaka, T. Sasaki, H. Suematsu, Y. Nagakawa, and T. Kuboki. "QT Interval and QT Dispersion in Eating Disorders." *Psychotherapy and Psychosomatics* 73, no. 5 (2004): 324–328. https://doi.org /10.1159/000078850.

ELECTROLYTE IMBALANCE

Electrolytes are substances whose molecules dissipate or split into ions when placed in water. Ions are electrically charged particles. Positive ions, called *cations*, include sodium, potassium, calcium, and magnesium. Anions are negatively charged particles. Examples are phosphorus, chloride, and bicarbonate. Electrolytes are in blood, urine, and bodily fluids and help regulate nerve and muscle function.

Electrolytes help the body maintain the normal fluid levels in cells, the space around cells, and in the blood. The fluid in these three compartments should remain fairly stable; however, how much fluid a compartment contains depends on the concentration of electrolytes. To adjust fluid levels, the body actively moves electrolytes in and out of the cells. If the electrolyte concentration is high, fluid moves into a compartment. If electrolyte concentration is low, fluid moves out of a compartment.

Electrolyte Imbalances and Eating Disorders

Despite significantly low body weight, individuals with anorexia nervosa who do not engage in purging behaviors rarely present with severe electrolyte disturbances. Most electrolyte imbalances are seen in individuals with bulimia nervosa who purge through self-induced vomiting, laxative abuse, and diuretic misuse. According to one study, the most common abnormality seen in individuals with bulimia was elevated serum bicarbonate, but other abnormalities included hypokalemia (low potassium), hypochloremia (low chloride), hyponatremia (low sodium), hypomagnesemia (low magnesium), and decreased serum bicarbonate.

A separate study found hypokalemia and hyponatremia were the most frequently altered electrolytes. Hypomagnesemia and hypokalemia were most commonly found in individuals with bulimia who used diuretics to purge.

Metabolic Alkalosis and Metabolic Acidosis

A normal serum bicarbonate level is 22–28 mmol/L. In individuals with bulimia, metabolic alkalosis, which results in an increased serum bicarbonate level, is almost always the result of purging through self-induced emesis or diuretic abuse. An elevated bicarbonate level or other electrolyte imbalances inconsistent with an individual's self-reported history can alert doctors when a client denies purging.

Metabolic alkalosis develops from self-induced vomiting because of acid and sodium chloride (NaCl) lost in the vomitus. Lost NaCl causes a state of decreased intravascular volume from dehydration that stimulates the kidney's renin–angiotensin system. This causes the adrenal cortex to secrete high levels of aldosterone—a hormone that increases salt absorption and bicarbonate reabsorption in the kidney—to prevent low blood pressure and fainting. This sequence of events is the body's normal response to prevent dehydration despite ongoing purging behaviors.

Diuretics cause increased sodium and chloride excretion that decreases intravascular volume depletion and dehydration, activating the renin–angiotensin system. The metabolic alkalosis that occurs as a result of diuretic abuse, however, is often not as severe as in individuals who engage in self-induced vomiting. Most serum bicarbonate concentrations over 38 mEq/L are almost always the result of self-induced vomiting.

Self-induced vomiting and diuretic abuse cause metabolic alkalosis, but laxative abuse can cause either a metabolic alkalosis or a metabolic acidosis. Acute diarrhea can cause large amounts of bicarbonate to be lost in the stool, causing hyperchloremic (high serum chloride) metabolic acidosis. However, the more common acid–base balance caused by laxative abuse is a metabolic alkalosis with a low serum chloride and low serum potassium. The alkalosis is usually in the mild range of 30–34 mEq/L, but the hypokalemia can be severe.

Clinical Manifestations

Eating-disordered individuals with electrolyte imbalances may have complaints of weakness, fatigue, constipation, dizziness, or depression. The normal range for serum potassium concentration is 3.5–5.5 mmol/L. Clinical manifestations of hypokalemia (less than 3.6 mmol/L) include generalized muscle weakness, fatigue, constipation, and heart palpitations. In severe cases of hypokalemia (less than 2.5 mmol/L), an individual is at high risk for cardiac complications and sudden death. Cardiac complications can be seen on a client's EKG and include T-wave changes, ST segment depression, prominent U waves, and QT prolongation. Although it is rare to see cardiac complications in a client with a potassium level greater than 3 mmol/L, complications are increased in clients with co-occurring heart disease who have a potassium level of less than 3.9 mmol/L. A low serum magnesium level can complicate hypokalemia symptoms and further contribute to arrhythmias and sudden death. Hypomagnesemia and hypocalcemia can also cause a prolonged QT interval and T-wave changes.

Electrolyte Abnormalities during Refeeding and Rehydration

The metabolic alkalosis from dehydration must be reversed before normalizing potassium levels. Aldosterone production must be stopped to halt renal potassium excretion. Intravenous sodium chloride is used to treat severe metabolic alkalosis; mild cases can be treated orally with fluids that contain sodium. Treatment of an individual with severe hyponatremia is done slowly; rapidly correcting serum sodium can cause a neurological complication called central pontine myelinolysis. Magnesium deficiency can also cause potassium loss. Magnesium deficiency should also be evaluated in individuals who purge using diuretics, as all diuretics cause some loss of magnesium.

Electrolytes should also be monitored frequently during refeeding, especially for clients at risk for refeeding syndrome—a syndrome of metabolic disturbances that can occur when malnourished individuals begin to eat. Refeeding syndrome can be fatal if not recognized or treated properly. Hypokalemia, hypomagnesemia, and high blood sugar can occur, but hypophosphatemia (low serum phosphorus) is the main electrolyte disturbance during refeeding syndrome and it causes significant morbidity and mortality. A dangerous drop in phosphorus can occur in three days of initiating nutrition therapy. According to an article in *Nutrition Reviews,* complications from hypophosphatemia include cardiac failure, muscle weakness, immune dysfunction, and death.

Shelly Guillory

See also: Bulimia Nervosa; Dehydration; Diuretics; Medical and Health Consequences; Purging; Refeeding Syndrome

Bibliography

"Fluid and Electrolyte Balance." MedlinePlus.com. Last modified June 6, 2016. Accessed November 21, 2017. http://www.nlm.nih.gov/medlineplus/fluidandelectrolytebalance .html.

Johnson, Larry E. "Disorders of Nutrition and Metabolism: Minerals and Electrolytes." Merckmanuals.com. Accessed November 16, 2016. http://www.merckmanuals.com /home/disorders-of-nutrition/minerals/overview-of-minerals.

Lewis, Sharon M., Margaret Heitkemper, and Sharon Dirkson. "Fluid, Electrolyte and Acid-Base Balance." In *Medical-Surgical Nursing: Assessment and Management of Clinical Problems,* 5th ed., edited by Sally Shrefer, 324–326. St. Louis, MO: Mosby, 2000.

Marinella, Mark A. "The Refeeding Syndrome and Hypophophatemia." *Nutrition Reviews* 61, no. 9 (2003): 320–323. https://doi.org/10.1301/nr.2003.sept.320-323.

Mehler, Philip S. "Diagnosis and Care of Patients with Anorexia Nervosa in Primary Care Settings." *Annals of Internal Medicine* 134, no. 11. (2001): 1048–1059. https://doi .org/10.7326/0003-4819-134-11-200106050-00011.

Mehler, Philip S., and Arnold E. Anderson. "Evaluation and Treatment of Electrolyte Abnormalities." In *Eating Disorders: A Guide to Medical Care and Complications*, 2nd ed., 96–107. Baltimore, MD: Johns Hopkins University Press, 2010.

Miller, Karen K., Steven K. Grinspoon, Julia Ciampa, Joan Hier, David Herzog, and Ajnne Klibanski. "Medical Findings of Outpatients with Eating Disorders." *Archives of Internal Medicine* 135, no. 5. (2005): 561–566. https://doi.org/10.1001/archinte.165.5.561.

Wolfe, Barbara E., Eran D. Metzger, Jeffery M. Levine, and David C. Jimerson. "Laboratory Screening for Electrolyte Abnormalities and Anemia in Bulimia Nervosa: A Controlled Study." *International Journal of Eating Disorders* 30, no. 3 (2001): 388–393. https://doi.org/10.1002/eat.1086.

Wolfe, Barbara E., Mark E. Rosenberg, James E. Mitchell, and Paul Thuras. "Urine Electrolytes as Markers of Bulimia Nervosa." *International Journal of Eating Disorders* 30, no. 3 (2001): 288–293. https://doi.org/10.1002/eat.1085.

EMOTIONAL EATING

Emotional eating is the tendency to eat in response to negative or positive emotions. Rather than listening to biological cues of hunger and fullness, emotional eaters tend to consume more food when they experience anxiety, anger, depression, or elation, or when they are upset. By contrast, individuals who are not emotional eaters may actually lose their appetite or forget to eat when they experience similar emotions. Emotional eating has been associated with excessive eating and a greater tendency to indulge in one's trigger foods that are often high in sugar, salt, or fat (e.g., ice cream, chips, or cookies).

Emotional Eating and Eating Disorders

Therefore, being overweight and obesity may be the natural outcome of a pattern of overeating behavior. Additionally, emotional eating may be associated with dieting and yo-yo weight cycling, which contributes to obesity and eating disorders, such as binge eating disorder and bulimia nervosa. In a study of 129 Finnish college students, emotional dieters reported higher body dissatisfaction, perfectionism, drive for thinness, and maturity fears than nondieters, indicating a higher risk for eating disorders. Emotional dieters also had more depression, feelings of inadequacy, poorer body image, and lower self-esteem globally than nondieters. Emotional eaters had some overlap with restrained eaters, showing that emotional eaters tend to fluctuate between excessive food intake and food restriction. Therefore, individuals who have been diagnosed with binge eating disorder or bulimia nervosa often admit to struggling with emotional eating and have often lost a sense of when they are truly hungry (or full). In a treatment setting, emotional eating should be addressed so individuals develop a more biologically based approach to evaluating hunger or fullness. Individuals may benefit from intuitive eating, so they can listen to their bodies and move away from emotional eating patterns.

Emotional eating in response to strong feelings can occur in individuals of any weight or size. Although related to bulimia nervosa and binge eating disorder, emotional eating is strongly related to dieting and weight fluctuations. If emotional eating continues, overweight and obesity may result, or disordered eating may become more extreme. Therefore, it is important emotional eating be addressed as part of treatment and an individual adopt an intuitive eating approach.

Justine J. Reel

See also: Disordered Eating; Intuitive Eating; Nutrition Treatment Approaches; Obesity

Bibliography

Eldredge, Kathleen L., and W. Stewart Agras. "Weight and Shape Overconcern and Emotional Eating in Binge Eating Disorder." *International Journal of Eating Disorders* 19 (1996): 73–82. https://doi.org/10.1002/(SICI)1098-108X(199601)19:1<73::AID-EAT9>3.0.CO;2-T.

Lindeman, Marjaana, and Katarina Stark. "Emotional Eating and Eating Disorder Psychopathology." *Eating Disorders* 9 (2001): 251–259. http://dx.doi.org/10.1080/10640260127552.

Lowe, Michael R., and Edwin B. Fisher Jr. "Emotional Reactivity, Emotional Eating and Obesity: A Naturalistic Study." *Journal of Behavioral Medicine* 6 (1983): 135–149. https://doi.org/10.1007/BF00845377.

Van Strien, Tatjana, Gerard M. Schippers, and W. Miles Cox. "On the Relationship between Emotional and External Eating Behavior." *Addictive Behaviors* 20 (1995): 585–594. https://doi.org/10.1016/0306-4603(95)00018-8.

Waller, Glenn, and Miki Matoba. "Emotional Eating and Eating Psychopathology in Non-clinical Groups: A Cross-cultural Comparison of Women in Japan and the United Kingdom." *International Journal of Eating Disorders* 26 (1999): 333–340. https://doi.org/10.1002/(SICI)1098-108X(199911)26:3<333::AID-EAT11>3.0.CO;2-D.

Waller, Glenn, and Selen Osman. "Emotional Eating and Eating Psychopathology among Non-Eating Disordered Women." *International Journal of Eating Disorders* 23 (1998): 419–424. https://doi.org/10.1002/(SICI)1098-108X(199805)23:4<419::AID-EAT9>3.0.CO;2-L.

ENDURANCE SPORTS

Endurance sports are defined by the physiological and competitive requirements they share. Specifically, endurance sports are classified as sports that primarily depend on aerobic energy systems (i.e., with oxygen) and require lower intensity training of long duration. Endurance sports include cross-country and track, cross-country skiing, cycling, swimming, water polo, rowing, and speed skating. Perhaps the most studied endurance sport athlete in the eating disorder area is the endurance runner.

Energy Deficits

Some endurance athletes, especially marathon runners, have difficulty consuming enough calories to sustain their performance and other metabolic processes necessary for optimal bodily function. These athletes are thought to run on an energy deficit, with little dietary energy available for metabolic processes after exercise. But why does this happen? Scholars contend that some endurance athletes may lack a significant biological drive to consume enough calories and counterbalance the energy expended each day. In this case, energy deficits are unintentional.

However, others may purposefully restrict calorie consumption to manage weight or alter body composition for performance purposes. After all, many endurance athletes often strive for a leaner and lighter build simply to facilitate faster race times. Of most concern is that some endurance athletes may compulsively engage in pathological weight control behaviors, including severe calorie restriction to lose weight or body fat to improve appearance and performance.

Weight Pressures

Pressures to lose or maintain weight are evident in endurance sports. In a study of 62 female collegiate swimmers, the most frequently cited weight pressures were revealing swimming attire (45.2 percent), the belief that being lighter improves swimming performance (42 percent), the perception teammates notice weight (16.1 percent), and that spectators scrutinize their body (12.9 percent). In addition to swimming, some researchers postulated rowers may also experience weight pressures because their sport requires them to make a particular weight class. Female lightweight rowers may be especially at risk for disordered eating because of thin ideal standards for women in general and having to maintain a suitable weight for the lightweight category of their sport. Runners and cyclists may also face a unique set of weight pressures, including the belief that thinness means faster times. Although many athletes and coaches believe this to be true, evidence suggests that endurance athletes with the lowest body fat or body mass index (BMI) do not always have the fastest times. For example, in a study of 70 female distance runners, one of the best running performances was from an athlete with the highest percentage of body fat in the sample at 35.8 percent.

Body Image Concerns and Disordered Eating

Unsurprisingly, elite female endurance and aesthetic athletes tend to be leaner and at greater risk for disordered eating; they also have higher training volumes compared to other sport types, such as technical (e.g., golf) and ball game sports (e.g., soccer). The prevalence of eating disorders has been reported at 24 percent in elite female endurance athletes and 9 percent in elite male endurance athletes. At the high school level, the prevalence of eating disorders has been reported at 8 percent and 20 percent for male and female endurance athletes, respectively.

Disordered eating has been most extensively studied in swimmers, rowers, and runners as compared to other endurance sports. Unfortunately, the research has not been entirely optimistic. For example, in a study of 487 female and 468 male swimmers in the age group of 9–18 years, 15.4 percent of the girls and 3.6 percent of the boys reported engaging in at least one unhealthy weight control behavior, including fasting, self-induced vomiting, or the consumption of diet pills, laxatives, and diuretics. Binge eating, fasting, and vomiting may be a particular concern in rowers. Among 162 collegiate rowers (89 males and 73 females), 12.3 percent of the males and 20 percent of the females reported binge eating at least twice a week, 57 percent of males and 25.4 percent of females reported fasting, and 2.5 percent of males and 13.2 percent of females reported vomiting as a means of cutting weight. In a study of 412 high school, university, and track and field athletes, 11.8 percent of middle- and long-distance athletes, and 4.7 percent of sprint athletes reported symptoms indicative of an eating disorder. Together, research on these athletes suggests that although most do not engage in disordered eating behaviors, some do engage in extremely harmful weight control behaviors.

Regardless of the method or intentions for such behaviors, inadequate caloric intake can lead to a deficiency in important micronutrients (i.e., dietary minerals like iron and potassium) and macronutrients (i.e., major energy sources including fats, proteins, and carbohydrates) critical for optimal athletic performance and everyday functioning. Prolonged energy deficits in the body can place athletes at risk for developing components of the female athlete triad, including low bone mineral density and menstrual dysfunction. Low bone mineral density is a special concern in endurance athletes in sports like swimming, rowing, and cycling, where there is little impact loading on the bones to strengthen them and offset the effects of low energy availability and poor calcium intake. For endurance sports with high-impact loading, like running, low bone mineral density can lead to stress fractures, especially when combined with overtraining and inadequate nutrition.

Coaches of endurance athletes could play a major role in preventing disordered eating, the female athlete triad, and the associated consequences including stress fractures. Researchers agree education on proper training and nutrition is imperative. Unfortunately, preliminary evidence suggests some coaches are limited in an understanding of specific methods of recovery, sports nutrition, and eating disorders. Although resources are available at the more elite levels of sport (e.g., through the U.S. Olympic Committee and the National Collegiate Athletic Association), such educational tools are scarce in the youth and high school athletics.

Benefits

Although appropriate prevention measures should be taken in light of the risk for inadequate energy intake, unhealthy weight control practices, and components of the female athlete triad, it is critical to remember endurance sports can also be quite healthy when proper training and nutritional practices are employed. Aerobic exercise training in general is associated with a number of benefits, including reduced risk for cardiovascular disease and diabetes. In fact, healthy elite endurance-trained athletes to live longer than the general population, probably due to the reduced risk for disease. Other preliminary research suggests aerobic exercise training is associated with improvements in visuospatial memory and positive emotion in young adults. Education on nutrition and appropriate training for an endurance sport athlete is one important way to minimize the detriments and maximize the benefits of this type of sport participation.

Dana K. Voelker

See also: Coaches; Distance Running; Rowing; Sports; Swimming and Synchronized Swimming; Weight Pressures in Sport

Bibliography

Hausenblas, Heather A., and Kimberly D. McNally. "Eating Disorder Prevalence and Symptoms of Track and Field Athletes and Nonathletes." *Journal of Applied Sport Psychology* 16 (2010): 274–286. http://dx.doi.org/10.1080/10413200490485630.

Kellmann, M. "Preventing Overtraining in Athletes in High-Intensity Sports and Stress /Recovery Monitoring." *Scandinavian Journal of Medicine and Science in Sports* 20 (2010): 95–102. https://doi.org/10.1111/j.1600-0838.2010.01192.x.

Loucks, Anne B. "Low Energy Availability in the Marathon and Other Endurance Sports." *Sports Medicine* 37 (2007): 348–352. https://doi.org/10.2165/00007256-200737040 -00019.

Reel, Justine J., and Diane L. Gill. "Slim Enough to Swim? Weight Pressures for Competitive Swimmers and Coaching Implications." *The Sport Journal* 4 (2001): 1–3.

Rosendahl, J., B. Bormann, K. Aschenbrenner, F. Aschenbrenner, and B. Strauss. "Dieting and Disordered Eating in German High School Athletes and Non-Athletes." *Scandinavian Journal of Medicine and Science in Sports* 19 (2009): 731–739. https://doi .org/10.1111/j.1600-0838.2008.00821.x.

Sundgot-Borgen, Jorunn, and Monica Klungland Torstveit. "Prevalence of Eating Disorders in Elite Athletes Is Higher Than in the General Population." *Clinical Journal of Sports Medicine* 14 (2004): 25–32.

Thompson, Ron A., and Roberta Trattner Sherman. *Helping Athletes with Eating Disorders.* Champaign, IL: Human Kinetics, 1993.

ENERGY AVAILABILITY

Energy availability is energy available after exercise. In other words, energy availability equals dietary energy intake minus energy expenditure. Energy availability can fall along a spectrum ranging from optimal available energy to low energy availability. Low energy availability occurs when a female consumes insufficient food to support her level of physical activity as well as normal growth and development. Having too few calories (i.e., low energy availability) may reflect the presence of disordered eating associated with restrictive behavior and a desire to lose weight. Athletes may be at a particular risk for decreased energy availability that is harmful over time. For example, low energy availability may also occur when an athlete engages in strenuous training that expends too many calories. If this energy output associated with practice or competitions is accompanied by inadequate energy intake, energy availability can be affected. Inadequate intake to meet caloric demands may be due to low knowledge on an athlete's part about how many calories are required. However, low energy availability, like disordered eating, can have health consequences and may result in reproductive system disruption to conserve energy resulting in inadequate estrogen production.

In the 2007 female athlete triad position stand, the American College of Sports Medicine (ACSM) replaced disordered eating with energy availability for a component of the female athlete triad. Researchers have suggested low energy availability is predictive of exercise-induced menstrual dysfunction rather than low body weight or low body fat. Although the prevalence of low energy availability is unknown, one study found 15 percent of college female athletes and 26 percent of college male athletes consumed insufficient energy in the form of carbohydrates and proteins to meet nutritional needs.

Justine J. Reel

See also: Disordered Eating; Female Athlete Triad; Medical and Health Consequences; Nutrition Treatment Approaches

Bibliography

American College of Sports Medicine (ACSM). "Position Stand: The Female Athlete Triad." *Medicine & Science in Sports & Exercise* 39 (2007): 1867–1882. https://doi.org/10.1249/mss.0b013e318149f111.

Hinton, Pamela S., Tiffany C. Sanford, M. Meghan Davidson, Oksana F. Yakushko, and Niels C. Beck. "Nutrient Intakes and Dietary Behaviors of Male and Female Collegiate Female Athletes." *International Journal of Sport Nutrition and Metabolism* 14 (2004): 389–405. http://dx.doi.org/10.1123/ijsnem.14.4.389.

Loucks, Anne B., Bente Kiens, and Hattie H. Wright. "Energy Availability in Athletes." *Journal of Sports Sciences* 29, S1 (2011): S7–S15. https://doi.org/10.1080/02640414.2011.588958.

Loucks, Anne B., Nina S. Stachenfield, and Loretta DiPietro. "The Female Athlete Triad: Do Female Athletes Need to Take Special Care to Avoid Low Energy Availability?" *Medicine & Science in Sports & Exercise* 38, no. 10 (2006): 1694–1700. https://doi.org/10.1249/01.mss.0000239397.01203.83.

Thompson, Ron A., and Roberta Trattner Sherman. *Eating Disorders in Sport.* New York: Routledge, 2010.

EQUINE THERAPY

Equine therapy is horse-assisted therapy used in the treatment of psychological conditions. Animals have been used for mental health treatment since before 1792. In fact, ancient Greeks recognized the therapeutic effects of horses and would offer rides to individuals believed to have incurable or untreatable illnesses to improve their mood and outlook. Pet therapy is considered an evidence-based treatment for addressing a variety of mental disorders including eating disorders.

Equine therapy, also referred to as equine-assisted experiential therapy (EAET) or equine-facilitated psychotherapy (EFP), allows individuals to work on communication, trust, and living in the present and develop coping skills necessary for healthy recovery from eating disorders. Equine activities include performing daily chores such as caring for horses; grooming can occur as part of a client's daily schedule at a residential facility. Additionally, therapeutic exercises include role-plays to work on psychological issues during individual or group therapy. Equine therapy can provide an effective supplement or an alternative to traditional eating disorder treatment (i.e., talk therapy).

Benefits of Equine Therapy for Eating Disorder Treatment

Stigma remains a barrier for individuals in traditional mental health services who are hesitant to be open and to achieve sufficient treatment progress. However, a horse seems to act as a normalizing effect allowing many clients to relax and experience a safe environment for expressing emotions spontaneously and taking risks in a therapeutic environment. Additionally, treatment providers (e.g., psychologists) observe clients outside an office setting, which can provide valuable information about their ability to communicate and set boundaries. Importantly, equine therapy provides the opportunity to explore relevant metaphors regarding the role an eating disorder is playing for a client as well as the recovery process.

An example of the use of equine therapy in an eating disorder setting is described by Jo Christian's case study. Five buckets of feed labeled by a client as the five most important aspects of her life (education, ballet, family, friends, and health) are placed along the inside rail of the round arena. Meanwhile, the horses are labeled shame, control, and perfection using sidewalk chalk. The client is able to practice assertiveness by directing the horses to move to the particular buckets. She must use appropriate verbal and nonverbal communication to guide the horses in the right direction. During an equine-assisted exercise, a client's treatment team can observe and provide support and encouragement. After the exercise, a client can process emotions that arose during the real-life enactment of her life.

Justine J. Reel

See also: Art Therapy; Assertiveness Training; Integrative Approaches; Treatment

Bibliography

Bizub, Anne L., Ann Joy, and Larry Davidson. "It's Like Being in Another World: Demonstrating the Benefits of Therapeutic Horseback Riding for Individuals with Psychiatric Disability." *Psychiatric Rehabilitation Journal* 26, no. 4 (2003): 377–384. http://dx.doi.org/10.2975/26.2003.377.384.

Christian, Jo Ellen. "All Creatures Great and Small: Utilizing Equine-Assisted Therapy to Treat Eating Disorders." *Journal of Psychology and Christianity* 24, no. 1 (2005): 65–67.

Karol, Jane. "Applying a Traditional Individual Psychotherapy Model to Equine-Facilitated Psychotherapy (EFP): Theory and Method." *Clinical Child Psychology and Psychiatry* 12 (2007): 77–90. https://doi.org/10.1177/1359104507071057.

Klontz, Bradley T., Alex Bivens, Deb Leinart, and Ted Klontz. "The Effectiveness of Equine-Assisted Experiential Therapy: Results of an Open Clinical Trial." *Society and Animals* 15 (2007): 257–267. https://doi.org/10.1163/156853007X217195.

Rothe, Eugenio Quiroz, Beatriz Jimenez Vega, Rafael Mazo Torres, Silvia Maria Campos Soler, and Rosa Maria Molina Pazos. "From Kids and Horses: Equine Facilitated Psychotherapy for Children." *International Journal of Clinical and Health Psychology* 5, no. 2 (2005): 373–383.

Vidrine, Maureen, Patti Owen-Smith, and Priscilla Faulkner. "Equine-Facilitated Group Psychotherapy: Applications for Therapeutic Vaulting." *Issues in Mental Health Nursing* 23 (2002): 587–603. https://doi.org/10.1080/01612840290052730.

EXERCISE

The relationship between exercise and eating disorders is both positive and negative. On the one hand, if exercise behaviors are taken to the extreme and exercise is used as a purging method as part of an eating disorder, having a dysfunctional relationship with physical movement can be detrimental to treatment and recovery. Dysfunctional exercise has been referred to as activity anorexia, overexercise, exercise addiction, excessive exercise, exercise dependence, exercise abuse, and obligatory exercise. These are labels for pathological exercise that continue beyond injury and illness and result in an individual missing social, family, and work obligations for exercise sessions.

Conversely, exercise can be a positive coping mechanism for stress and anxiety and has been linked to improved mood, decreased depression, and increased self-confidence. Exercise therapy can be integrated into a comprehensive treatment program for mental health populations such as persons with mood disorders, substance abuse, and eating disorders.

History of Exercise and Eating Disorder Treatment

Historically, exercise has been severely limited during eating disorder treatment due to the presence of dysfunctional exercise by many clients and the concern movement would undermine necessary weight restoration goals. The excessive hyperactivity was observed in some of the earliest documented cases of eating disorders. However, in the 1970s, researchers discovered 25 out of 33 anorexia nervosa clients hospitalized for eating disorder treatment over a 10-year period showed symptoms of excessive exercise behaviors. Another research study discovered that 75 percent of anorexia nervosa clients exhibited excessive exercise (referred to as *intense athleticism* in that study).

Until the 1990s, clients with anorexia nervosa who entered treatment were placed on bed rest with all movement restricted. Any form of exercise as part of eating disorder treatment was considered controversial despite that 97 percent of clinicians and researchers admitted physical activity and eating-disordered behaviors were related and realized the benefits of exercise extended beyond health.

Beumont and his colleagues introduced the first structured exercise program into eating disorder treatment in 1994 to include anaerobic exercise (e.g., resistance training). The rationale for the exercise was that distorted beliefs surrounding exercise should be addressed and challenged in treatment. The need for exercise education (e.g., how to engage in healthy exercise and expand motivations to exercise) was important, and they realized the total elimination of movement had been ineffective and unrealistic for eating disorder clients.

Benefits of Exercise

In addition to numerous health benefits of physical activity (e.g., disease prevention, increased strength, improved cardiovascular functioning, and bone health), exercise has psychological benefits as well. In addition to well-researched mood benefits of exercise, including reduction of overall depression and anxiety, eating disorder clinicians and researchers know exercise can reduce anxiety around meals and improve program compliance. Exercise can also increase weight gain and body composition and prevent relapse. Ideally, exercise education can be used with actual movement to challenge distorted thoughts and emotions about exercise and help clients move from dysfunctional exercise behaviors and toward a more mindful approach to exercise.

Physical Activity Recommendations for Eating Disorder Treatment

Any movement during eating disorder treatment should be prescribed, supervised, and individualized to a client's needs and preferences whenever possible. Exercise education and a debriefing period to follow movement is optimal as part of the treatment process.

Prescribed

If a client is medically compromised, has a body mass index below 14, or is restricted to bed rest, he or she should wait to participate in exercise and movement sessions until cleared by a physician. Exercise provided in an inpatient or residential setting should be deliberate with specific functions. For example, stretching can be helpful for clients who have spent much time sitting and experience back pain. Light lifting or resistance training can be useful to provide impact to improve bone health. Other types of exercise associated with playfulness and enjoyment (e.g., Nia, Zumba, and yoga) and activities less likely to be abused by clients are ideal. Generally, running should be avoided during initial stages of treatment due to high caloric demands and potential for injury and stress fractures. Also, running often involves moving despite pain, which is the opposite of mindful exercise (i.e., listening to one's body and adapting exercise to what feels good). As a general rule, it is recommended a treatment program expose clients to a wide variety of movement patterns and types of exercise to deliver the message that there are many forms of activities as exercise.

In an outpatient setting it is recommended a treatment team include an exercise specialist knowledgeable of the specific needs and challenges associated with an eating disorder population. This specialist should work with a physician on a treatment team to prescribe an exercise routine that emphasizes quality over quantity. S client should be encouraged to begin exercise gradually and introduce a variety of movements. Generally, yoga, resistance training, and other forms of stretching are recommended over running and intense activities during initial treatment.

Supervised

Supervising physical activity is more manageable in a residential or inpatient setting. Nonetheless, all activity should be monitored throughout the day. Some treatment programs provide specific classes, such as yoga, but also have casual walks throughout the day between treatment groups. It is recommended all exercise and movement be structured (planned) and supervised by staff with exercise qualifications to gauge intensity of exercise. During exercise classes, an instructor can observe facial expressions to determine whether clients are abusing exercise or being overly intense during a session. An exercise instructor should be trained to change cues to support an eating-disordered population. The focus should be on enjoyment or health benefits, rather than burning fat and calories, or looking good. Some yoga postures may need to be modified to avoid competition in a group. Generally, mirrors are discouraged in a treatment setting, but if used should only be a guide for technique, not a way for clients to monitor weight changes and appearance.

In outpatient settings supervision becomes more difficult. Family members and others can support an exercise plan so clients do not engage in additional activities that lead to too much energy expenditure. Family members and friends may need to receive education on how prescribed exercise is actually helpful to treatment. Some personal trainers can monitor exercise routines for outpatient clients; however, few receive training in the needs of an eating-disorder population. A client may be encouraged to exercise with a friend who can set a moderate, less intense pace. It is recommended a treatment team consider whether a client is able to continue organized sports and other activities that may have contributed to exercise abuse prior to admission for treatment.

Individualized

The amount of exercise and types of movement should ideally be individualized like any type of prescription medication. For example, individuals with bulimia nervosa and binge eating disorder may be able to engage in aerobic exercise sooner than individuals with anorexia nervosa who are still working on weight restoration. Additionally, client preferences may allow for certain modifications in the types of activities performed. Some clients may be triggered (i.e., experience negative body image) by participation in yoga and may choose Nia or Zumba instead. Although individualizing exercise plans can be costly in a residential setting, each client should be provided with an exercise plan as she or he transitions to an outpatient setting.

For clients are in the outpatient setting, individualizing treatment is more manageable and is only limited by the types of exercise available in a client's community. An exercise therapist may not be able to screen every exercise class and may have to work with clients to cope with triggers in an exercise environment as they arise.

Exercise Education

Exercise education should accompany actual movement or exercise sessions so eating disorder clients learn about healthy forms of exercise and work to change dysfunctional mind-sets about exercise. An important topic to include is motivation to exercise. Although clients may enter treatment with a sole motive for exercise being to burn calories or lose weight, it is important to identify the many reasons why people choose to move their bodies. Clients can work on topics such as improving self-confidence and assertiveness in exercise classes (e.g., martial arts and self-defense).

Debriefing Feelings Following Exercise

Following exercise, clients should have an opportunity to process emotions that arose during the session. It is common for individuals to experience a full range of emotions—such as frustration that their body can actually feel less intense and shorter bouts of movement, and anxiety about not doing enough exercise to burn the calories consumed. It is especially powerful for individuals to process thoughts that occurred during movement such as being compulsive or detached from one's body or sensing joy associated with movement.

Types of Exercise

When clients are admitted for treatment they should be screened for dysfunctional exercise; the activities they abused prior to treatment should also be determined. Clients should initially be prescribed new activities that are less aerobic in nature. Throughout treatment clients will have the opportunity to practice many types of exercise; however, some of the more common forms of exercise at eating disorder treatment centers are yoga, Nia, horseback riding, and stretching. Exercise options are expanding and, depending on geographic location, clients may be able to engage in water aerobics, hiking, or ice skating. Zumba, which has recently gained popularity across the United States, shows promise for eating disorder clients. Similar to dance, Zumba encourages participants to embrace the music and learn steps and routines while moving in a low-impact fashion.

Justine J. Reel

See also: Exercise Dependence; Intuitive Exercise; Nia; Obligatory Exercise; Sports; Therapeutic Recreation; Yoga

Bibliography

Beumont, Peter J. V., Brenden Arthur, Janice D. Russell, and Stephen W. Touyz. "Excessive Physical Activity in Dieting Disorder Patients: Proposals for a Supervised Exercise Program." *International Journal of Eating Disorders* 15, no. 1 (1994): 21–36. https://doi.org/10.1002/1098-108X(199401)15:1<21::AID-EAT2260150104>3.0.CO;2-K.

Calogero, Rachel M., and Kelly N. Pedrotty. "The Practice and Process of Healthy Exercise: An Investigation of the Treatment of Exercise Abuse in Women with Eating Disorders." *Eating Disorders* 12 (2004): 273–291. http://dx.doi.org/10.1080/10640260490521352.

Calogero, Rachel M., and Kelly N. Pedrotty-Stump. "Incorporating Exercise into Eating Disorder Treatment and Recovery." In *Treatment of Eating Disorders: Bridging the Research to Practice Gap,* edited by Margo Maine, Beth Hartman McGilley, and Doug Bunnell, 425–443. London: Elsevier, 2010.

Hechler, Tanja, Peter Beumont, P. Marks, and Stephen Touyz. "How Do Clinical Specialists Understand the Role of Physical Activity in Eating Disorders?" *European Eating Disorders Review* 13 (2005): 125–132. https://doi.org/10.1002/erv.630.

Thien, Vincent, Alison Thomas, Donna Markin, and Carl Laird Birmingham. "Pilot Study of a Graded Exercise Program for the Treatment of Anorexia Nervosa." *International Journal of Eating Disorders* 28 (2000): 101–106. https://doi.org/10.1002/(SICI)1098-108X(200007)28:1<101::AID-EAT12>3.0.CO;2-V.

Tokumura, Mitsuaki, Shigeki Yoshiba, Tetsuya Tanaka, Selichiro Nanri, and Hisako Watanabe. "Prescribed Exercise Training Improves Exercise Capacity of Convalescent Children and Adolescents with Anorexia Nervosa." *European Journal of Pediatrics* 162 (2003): 430–431. https://doi.org/10.1007/s00431-003-1203-1.

Touyz, Stephen W., Wolfgang Lennerts, Brenden Arthur, and Peter J. V. Beumont. "Anaerobic Exercise as an Adjunct to Refeeding Patients with Anorexia Nervosa: Does It Compromise Weight Gain?" *European Eating Disorders Review* 1, no. 3 (1993): 177–182. https://doi.org/10.1002/erv.2400010306.

EXERCISE DEPENDENCE

The "exercise as medicine" movement largely touts the benefits of exercise, includ ing reduced stress and improved cardiovascular function, makes it difficult to view physical activity as a negative habit. However, *exercise dependence* is excessive physical activity with a dysfunctional psychological mind-set. Exercise dependence (referred to as exercise addiction or excessive exercise) can be identified by the presence of at least three of the following characteristics: tolerance (i.e., a need to increase exercise to avoid guilt), withdrawal effects (i.e., symptoms such as anxiety and fatigue when unable to exercise), intention effects (i.e., exercise is often in larger amounts or over a longer period than planned), lack of control (i.e., a persistent desire or unsuccessful effort to decrease or control exercise), time (i.e., longer time spent exercising), reductions in other activities (i.e., exercise is prioritized over social, occupational, or recreational activities), and continuance (i.e., exercising despite injury and illness). Furthermore, individuals who exhibit exercise dependence refuse to incorporate rest days into workout schedules and tend to engage in a rigid routine that does not include a variety of movement activities.

History of Exercise Dependence

The term exercise dependence was originally coined by de Coverley Veale in 1987 and has been described as a negative mood state experienced in the absence of a drug, object, or activity. In other words, exercise is a stimulant for the physiological arousal of the brain and the avoidance of negative emotions. For some individuals, exercise alters the mood in the short term and can occasionally stimulate a state of euphoria popularly referred to as the *runners' high* by competitive and recreational runners beginning in the 1970s. Veale used exercise dependence not runner's high to allow for a broader application across sports and recreational activities and capture the negative and compulsive nature of this condition. In recent years, the importance of identifying both an individual's psychological mind-set and reasons for exercise have become key to detectexercise dependence.

Symptoms of Exercise Dependence

The symptoms of exercise dependence include depressed mood, irritability, fatigue, anxiety, impaired concentration, and sleep disturbances. The negative effect on mood and evidence of depression has been observed in runners identified as having exercise dependence following just one day without exercise. Physical complications associated with exercise dependence include repeated soft tissue injuries and stress fractures, pressure sores (i.e., damaged skin caused by staying in one position for too long), gastrointestinal blood loss and anemia, myocardial infarction, and death. These harmful effects have been documented most comprehensively in long-distance runners since the late 1970s.

Primary versus Secondary Exercise Dependence

The classifications of exercise dependence are primary and secondary exercise dependence. In primary exercise dependence, exercise is an end in itself, but secondary exercise dependence goes beyond exercise addiction. Specifically, individuals with secondary exercise dependence engage in excessive exercise as a purging method as part of an eating disorder.

Primary exercise dependence is characterized by several symptoms. The most common is preoccupation with exercise and withdrawal symptoms, such as mood swings and irritability, are seen in the absence of exercise. Additionally, an individual with primary exercise dependence experiences distress or impairment in his or her physical, social, occupational, or other important areas of functioning. Also, to be primary exercise dependent, an individual's preoccupation with exercise is not aimed at another mental disorder (e.g., a means of losing weight or controlling calorie intake as in an eating disorder).

By contrast, individuals with secondary exercise dependence intentionally use exercise as a purging method to control weight as part of an eating disorder. As a typical pattern of secondary exercise dependence, an individual often selects cardiovascular fitness and exercises for a few hours once or more daily. Furthermore, the exercise intensity level and amount become excessively increased with subjective awareness of a compulsion to exercise over the years. An individual with secondary exercise dependency also relies on exercise to cope with the stress or fear of gaining weight and experiences withdrawal symptoms on cessation of an exercise schedule. Therefore, the individual with secondary exercise dependence prioritizes exercise over other activities to maintain an exercise schedule.

Secondary Exercise Dependence: Warning Signs

Secondary exercise dependence is commonly identified in eating disorders. Studies have reported secondary exercise dependence as identified in approximately 80 percent of anorexia nervosa and 55 percent of bulimia nervosa clients. The following warning signs are identified in secondary exercise dependence:

1. Exercising a couple of times a day, two to five hours total.
2. Counting calories to figure out what exercise is needed to burn them.
3. Rearranging one's day to fit in exercise.
4. When one's daily routine or cycle is disrupted by a constant need to exercise above all else; the individual will stop whatever it is he or she is doing, no matter how important, to exercise.
5. Food is viewed as the enemy.
6. Exercise becomes the sole activity and only social outlet.

The causes of exercise dependence are not entirely clear, but the motivation to lose weight or to keep weight low is a significant factor for both disordered eating and excessive exercise behaviors. Psychological characteristics of exercise dependence such as perfectionism, low self-esteem, and negative self-acceptance/self-image overlap with psychological characteristics associated with eating disorders.

Recently, researchers have found a potential link between brain activity and exercise dependence suggesting exercise dependence may have addictive qualities similar to substance abuse (e.g., cocaine, morphine).

Maya Miyairi

See also: Exercise; Intuitive Exercise; Obligatory Exercise

Bibliography

Adams, Jeremy, and Robert J. Kirkby. "Excessive Exercise as an Addiction: A Review." *Addiction Research and Theory* 10, no. 5 (2002): 415–437.

American Psychiatric Association. *Diagnostic and Statistical Manual of Mental Disorders*, 5th ed. (*DSM-5*). Washington, DC: American Psychiatric Association Publishing, 2013.

American Psychiatric Association. *Diagnostic and Statistical Manual of Mental Disorders*, 4th ed. Washington, DC: American Psychiatric Association Publishing, 2000.

Bamber, Diane, Ian M. Cockerill, Sue Rodgers, and Doug Caroll. "Diagnostic Criteria for Exercise Dependence in Women." *British Journal of Sports Medicine* 37 (2003): 393–400. https://doi.org/10.1136/bjsm.37.5.393.

Blaydon, Michelle J., Koenraad J. Linder, and John H. Kerr. "Metamotivational Characteristics of Exercise Dependence and Eating Disorders in Highly Active Amateur Sport Participants." *Personality and Individual Differences* 36 (2004): 1419–1432. http://dx.doi.org/10.1016/S0191-8869(03)00238-1.

Bratland-Sanda, Solfrid, Jorunn Sundgot-Borgen, Øyvind RØ, Jan H. Rosenvinge, Asle Hoffart, and Egil W. Martinsen. "Physical Activity and Exercise Dependence during Inpatient Treatment of Longstanding Eating Disorders: An Exploratory Study of Excessive and Non-Excessive Exercisers." *International Journal of Eating Disorders* 43, no. 3 (2010): 266–273. https://doi.org/10.1002/eat.20769.

Ferreira, Anthony, Fernando Perez-Diaz, and Charles Cohen-Salmon. "The Relationship between Physical Activity and Cocaine Intake in Mice." *Journal of Clinical Sports Psychology* 3 (2009): 232–243.

Ferreira, Anthony, Fabien Cornilleau, and Fernando Perez-Diaz. "Exercise Dependence and Morphine Addiction: Evidence from Animal Models." *Journal of Clinical Sports Psychology* 2 (2008): 17–24.

Gapin, Jennifer, Jennifer L. Etnier, and Denise Tucker. "The Relationship between Frontal Brain Asymmetry and Exercise Addiction." *Journal of Psychophysiology* 23, no. 3 (2009): 135–142. https://doi.org/10.1027/0269-8803.23.3.135.

Glasser, William. *Positive Addiction*. New York: Harper and Row, 1976.

Hagan, Amy L., and Heather Hausenblas. "The Relationship between Exercise Dependence Symptoms and Perfectionism." *American Journal of Health Studies* 18, no. 213 (2003): 133–137.

Hall, Howard K., Andrew P. Hill, Paul R. Appleton, and Stephen A. Kozub. "The Mediating Influence of Unconditional Self-Acceptance and Labile Self-Esteem on the Relationship between Multidimensional Perfectionism and Exercise Dependence." *Psychology of Sport and Exercise* 10 (2009): 35–44. http://dx.doi.org/10.1016/j.psychsport.2008.05.003.

Harmon, Kevin Bernard. "Are You an Exercise Addict?" *American Fitness* (2009): 52–53.

Hausenblas, Heather A., and Danielle Downs Symons. "Exercise Dependence: A Systematic Review." *Psychology of Sport and Exercise* 3 (2002): 89–123. http://dx.doi.org/10.1016/S1469-0292(00)00015-7.

Peñas-Lledó, Eva, Francisco J. Vaz Leal, and Glenn Waller. "Excessive Exercise in Anorexia Nervosa and Bulimia Nervosa: Relation to Eating Characteristics and General Psychopathology." *International Journal of Eating Disorders* 31 (2002): 370–375. https://doi.org/10.1002/eat.10042.

Reel, Justine J., and Katherine A. Beals, eds. *The Hidden Faces of Eating Disorders and Body Image.* Reston, VA: AAHPERD/NAGWS, 2009.

Russell, Michael. "What Is Dependence?" In *Drugs and Drug Dependence,* edited by Griffith Edwards. Lexington, MA: Lexington Books, 1976.

Shroff, Hemal, Lauren Reba, Laura M. Thornton, Federica Tozzi, Kelly L. Klump, Wade H. Berrettini . . . Cynthia M. Bulik. "Features Associated with Excessive Exercise in Women with Eating Disorders." *International Journal of Eating Disorder* 39 (2006): 454–461. https://doi.org/10.1002/eat.20247.

Veale, de Coverley. "Exercise Dependence." *British Journal of Addiction* 82 (1987): 735–740. https://doi.org/10.1111/j.1360-0443.1987.tb01539.x.

EXPOSURE THERAPY

Eating disorders have a widely accepted and long-standing association with anxiety disorders and symptoms, both in anecdotal evidence and in scientific studies. This association between eating disorders and anxiety has prompted investigation into the efficacy of exposure therapy to treat eating disorders. Exposure therapy is commonly used to treat anxiety disorders. Exposure therapy involves an incremental and controlled regimen of exposures to something that causes an individual anxiety. For example, someone with a crippling fear of dogs may start by simply imagining they are sitting in a park and can see a dog with its owner a distance away. Once a person is comfortable with this situation, the exposure moves up (i.e., the dog gets closer). The goal of exposure therapy is to desensitize a person to a fear-provoking stimulus.

Theoretical Basis of Exposure Therapy

Exposure therapy is widely used for the treatment of anxiety disorders, including specific phobias, post-traumatic stress disorder (PTSD), obsessive-compulsive disorder (OCD), and social phobia. The underlying theoretical basis for exposure therapy lies in Pavlovian theories of learning. Ivan Pavlov gained fame in the field of psychology for his experiments with dogs who learned to salivate at the sound of a bell. By repeatedly feeding the dogs concurrently with a bell chime, Pavlov was able to train the dogs to associate the bell tone with food, thus prompting a salivation response. In psychology, Pavlovian learning refers to the process of *conditioned learning*, or the pairing of a previously neutral stimulus (the bell tone) with something that produces a predictable behavioral response (food that causes salivation). Over time, repeated and predictable pairing of the neutral stimulus with the meaningful stimulus creates a strong cognitive association between the two, and eventually the behavioral response previously only associated with the meaningful stimulus occurs in response to the neutral stimulus.

Conditioned learning is thought to be central to the development of phobias, PTSD, and OCD. Danger is an extremely powerful physiological and psychological state for human beings, such that neutral stimuli can become associated with danger in a very short time. This association between danger and a neutral stimulus is known as *fear conditioning*, and it is involved in almost all anxiety spectrum disorders. For example, someone may have a particularly negative experience while giving a class presentation and come to associate public speaking with danger, giving rise to a form of social phobia. Fear conditioning is a largely unconscious, automatic process, and, in healthy individuals, it serves to keep us safe by learning to predict danger from environmental cues.

In anxiety disorders, it is not the process of fear conditioning that is thought to be dysfunctional. Instead, it is the complimentary process of *fear extinction* that seems to go awry in people who suffer from phobias, PTSD, etc. Fear extinction is the gradual breakdown of the learned association formed between neutral stimuli and behavioral responses. Returning to the example of Pavlov's dogs, if the dogs were trained to expect food after the bell tone (fear conditioning) and then were repeatedly exposed to the bell tone *without* any subsequent food, the association between bell tone and food would weaken. This is called fear extinction, and it is the degradation of unconscious associations learned through fear conditioning. For example, many children fall down several times learning to ride bikes. Although the association between biking and falling may produce some fear and anxiety in children for a short time, as children master bike riding and have more instances riding a bicycle without falling, that association slowly dissipates. In individuals with anxiety disorders, fear extinction does not occur as easily (or at all), meaning that the fear response to different environmental cues does not lessen over time. Exposure therapy seeks to force people to actively engage in fear extinction by gradually exposing them to their fear(s) in a safe, controlled environment and guiding them through a process of unlearning the association between environmental cue and the fear response.

Exposure Therapy in Eating Disorders

Exposure therapy has received significant attention for its potential to treat anorexia nervosa (AN). Treatment for AN routinely involves a focus on the feared outcome of weight gain, which offers an opportunity to incorporate exposure therapy. Many individuals who suffer from AN learn to avoid the sensations of fear and anxiety associated with possible weight gain through extreme dietary restriction or other forms of weight control. These behaviors are motivated by avoidance of the fear of gaining weight. In fact, research has shown periods of elevated anxiety correlate with more disordered eating behaviors in anorexia nervosa, further supporting the association between anxiety and eating disorders.

Although the underlying theory of anorexia nervosa seems to lend itself to exposure therapy, many studies that tested exposure therapy for eating disorders focused on bulimia and binge eating more so than anorexia nervosa. The high mortality rate associated with anorexia nervosa makes it very difficult to test experimental forms of treatment. However, there have been a handful of studies that investigated exposure therapy for the treatment of AN. These studies use graded food exposure to try and alleviate feelings of anxiety associated with food intake. Although the studies have produced generally encouraging results, researchers have raised concerns about whether these studies were natural enough for the results to be extrapolated to daily life.

Exposure therapy has been tested in the treatment of bulimia nervosa and binge eating disorder much more rigorously than for anorexia nervosa. In one study, women suffering from bulimia nervosa were exposed to either high-calorie foods or low-calorie foods for 20 minutes on subsequent days. Only the high-calorie foods prompted urges to binge, and the stress associated with the presentation of calorie-rich foods was significantly reduced on the second day compared to the first exposure. Another study used a specific type of exposure therapy known as exposure with response-prevention (ERP). ERP is the exposure of an individual to a fearful stimulus and removing the ability to participate in compensatory behaviors, such as vomiting in bulimia or compulsive hand washing in OCD. This study exposed women with bulimia nervosa and the binge–purge subtype of anorexia nervosa to their self-reported favorite foods. Participants were not able to taste or touch the foods, and they were prevented from purging in response to seeing the foods. While exposed to the foods, subjects were asked to complete a variety of self-report questionnaires; this procedure was repeated nine times over the course of three weeks. Overall, the participants reported lower levels of tension, guilt, and stress and a lessened desire to binge and/or purge as the study progressed.

Exposure therapy has also been used for stimuli other than. One study tested the effects of exposing women diagnosed with binge eating disorder to their physical appearance using a mirror over the course of two days. Compared to healthy individuals, the women with binge eating disorder reported lower body satisfaction and worse mood during the first exposure. During the second exposure, however, the binge eating sample reported higher self-esteem, body satisfaction, and elevated mood.

Virtual reality has also been explored as an option for exposure therapy in eating disorders. Several case studies have shown support for the efficacy of virtual reality simulations to treat eating disorders. Overall, studies using virtual reality for exposure therapy have shown encouraging results, with many participants reporting decreases in body dissatisfaction, fewer urges to participate in unhealthy eating or exercising behaviors, a lower drive for thinness, and general improvements in mood and health. A majority of these studies also incorporated other forms of treatment (e.g., physical training, cognitive behavioral therapy) with virtual reality exposure, so many researchers agree exposure therapy (and virtual reality–based exposures specifically) should be treated as one component in a comprehensive treatment plan.

Hannah J. Hopkins

See also: Treatment; Virtual Reality

Bibliography

Ferrer-Garcia, Marta, José Gutiérrez-Maldonado, and Giuseppe Riva. "Virtual Reality Based Treatments in Eating Disorders and Obesity: A Review." *Journal of Contemporary Psychotherapy* 43, no. 4 (2013): 207–221. http://dx.doi.org/10.1007/s10879-013-9240-1.

Hilbert, Anja, Brunna Tuschen-Caffier, and Claus Vögele. "Effects of Prolonged and Repeated Body Image Exposure in Binge-Eating Disorder." *Journal of Psychosomatic Research* 52, no. 3 (2002): 137–144. https://doi.org/10.1016/S0022-3999(01)00314-2.

Kennedy, Sidney H., Randy Katz, Christina S. Neitzert, Elizabeth Ralevski, and Sandra Mendlowitz. "Exposure with Response Prevention Treatment of Anorexia Nervosa-Bulimic Subtype and Bulimia Nervosa." *Behaviour Research and Therapy* 33, no. 6 (1995): 685–689. https://doi.org/10.1016/0005-7967(95)00011-L.

Koskina, Antonia, Iain C. Campbell, and Ulrike Schmidt. "Exposure Therapy in Eating Disorders Revisited." *Neuroscience & Biobehavioral Reviews* 37, no. 2 (2013): 193–208. https://doi.org/10.1016/j.neubiorev.2012.11.010.

Murray, Stuart B., Michael Treanor, Betty Liao, Katharine L. Loeb, Scott Griffiths, and Daniel Le Grange. "Extinction Theory & Anorexia Nervosa: Deepening Therapeutic Mechanisms." *Behaviour Research and Therapy* 87 (2016): 1–10. https://doi.org/10.1016/j.brat.2016.08.017.

VanElzakker, Michael B., M. Kathryn Dahlgren, F. Caroline Davis, Stacey Dubois, and Lisa M. Shin. "From Pavlov to PTSD: The Extinction of Conditioned Fear in Rodents, Humans, and Anxiety Disorders." *Neurobiology of Learning and Memory* 113 (2014): 3–18. https://doi.org/10.1016/j.nlm.2013.11.014.

EYE MOVEMENT DESENSITIZATION AND REPROCESSING

Eye movement desensitization and reprocessing (EMDR) is a therapy developed by Dr. Francine Shapiro to help people work through unresolved traumas. After successful cancer treatment, she was told her cancer would likely return. Shapiro decided to educate herself in psychoimmunology and the mind–body connection and developed a nonprofit organization, Metadevelopment and Research Institute, to synthesize different areas of learning. In 1987, EMDR was born when Shapiro noticed her life stress reactions were alleviated when she swept her eyes spontaneously back and forth during her daily walk through the park. She began to experiment and discovered that the process was effective for other people as well.

Overview of EMDR

EMDR entails having an individual recall a stressful past event while thinking about a positive self-chosen belief. Rapid eye movements during this dual thought process serve to actually reprogram the memory and soften the impact the traumatic or stressful memory has on an individual's ability to thrive. The key element to reprogramming memory lies in dual stimulation where a client thinks or talks about triggers, painful emotions, and memories while focusing on the therapist's moving finger. Other forms of bilateral stimulation can be used with similar benefit. Some people respond better to alternating hand taps or listening to a chime that sounds back and forth from ear to ear.

At the time a stressful or traumatic event occurs, strong emotions can interfere with one's ability to process the experience, and an event can then become frozen in time. Recalling the incident may seem as though one is reliving the trauma because the smells, sounds, images, and emotions are there in a frozen state and can be triggered in the present. When activated, the memories can cause a negative effect on one's daily functioning and interfere with self-concept and how one relates to others. EMDR therapy seems to directly affect the brain by unfreezing traumatic memories. The individual then has an opportunity to process the memories, find resolution, and move on.

EMDR and Eating Disorder Treatment

Eating-disordered individuals have a tendency to be shaped by traumatic events and fail to establish healthy and secure bonds with others. Although originally applied to the treatment of post-traumatic stress disorder (PTSD) and other anxiety disorders, EMDR has been found to be quite useful treating of eating disorders because perceived traumatic events and body image disturbance are often the root of eating disorders. A 2008 study found eating-disorder clients in a residential treatment facility who received EMDR therapy reported less distress about negative body image memories and lower body dissatisfaction at post-treatment, 3-month, and 12-month follow-up, compared to clients who did not receive EMDR.

EMDR therapy for eating-disorder treatment typically includes eight phases. Phase 1 includes history and treatment planning. A therapist typically does not discuss traumatic events in detail but learns a general timeline of significant events in a client's life. Phase 2, preparation, involves teaching a client self-care techniques (e.g., relaxation) to manage strong emotions that may occur between sessions. Phase 3, assessment, establishes a groundwork for the actual EMDR therapy sessions. A client is asked to identify (1) a specific scene or picture, (2) a negative belief, and (3) a positive belief. Beliefs are then rated on a scale of one to seven based on how strongly they are believed to be true. Locations in the body are identified where physical sensations are experienced related to the traumatic event. Phase 3 is a poignant intervention to help eating-disordered clients make a mind–body connection. In Phase 4, desensitization, a client concentrates on all the negative beliefs, disturbing emotions, and bodily sensations that surface as he or she focuses on the target image while following the therapist's finger back and forth. A client takes note of all the reactions to the processing and checks in with the therapist to assess the level of disturbance regarding the target image. Eating-disorder clients learn to identify how perceived traumas contribute to disordered-eating behaviors by understanding how their reactions support the eating disorder. In Phase 5, installation, a client is asked to focus on the identified positive belief to replace the old negative belief about the trauma while simultaneously tracking the therapist's finger with the eyes. The eating-disorder client learns to sense the physical body in a new way. Phase 6, body scan, includes checking for lingering tension or uncomfortable physical sensations that are targeted with bilateral stimulation until resolved. EMDR is often used in conjunction with other eating-disorder therapies (e.g., cognitive behavioral therapy) so integration occurs between resolution of lingering tension and cessation of disordered behaviors. Phases 7 and 8 focus on creating closure and evaluating a client's progress.

Juliann Cook Jeppsen

See also: Comorbidity; Trauma; Treatment

Bibliography

Bloomgarden, Andrea, and Rachel Calogero. "A Randomized Experimental Test of the Efficacy of EMDR Treatment on Negative Body Image in Eating Disorder Inpatients." *Eating Disorders* 16, no. 5 (2008): 418–427. http://dx.doi.org/10.1080/10640260802370598.

Dziegielewski, Sophia. "Eye Movement Desensitization and Reprocessing (EMDR) as a Time Limited Treatment Intervention for Body Image Disturbance and Self Esteem: A Single Subject Case Design." *Journal of Psychotherapy in Independent Practice* 1 (2000): 1–16. http://dx.doi.org/10.1300/J288v01n03_01.

Shapiro, Francine. *Eye Movement Desensitization and Reprocessing: Basic Principles, Protocols and Procedures.* New York: Guilford Press, 1995.

Shapiro, Francine. "Eye Movement Desensitization and Reprocessing (EMDR): Evaluation of Controlled PTSD Research." *Journal of Behavior Therapy and Experimental Psychiatry* 27 (1996): 313–317. https://doi.org/10.1016/S0005-7916(96)00029-8.

Shapiro, Francine. *EMDR as an Integrative Psychotherapy Approach: Experts of Diverse Orientations Explore the Paradigm Prism.* Washington, DC: American Psychological Association, 2002.

von Ranson, Kristen, and Kathleen Robinson. "Who Is Providing What Type of Psychotherapy to Eating Disorder Clients? A Survey." *International Journal of Eating Disorders* 39 (2006): 27–34. https://doi.org/10.1002/eat.20201.

F

FAD DIETS

A fad diet refers to eating that is a fashionable or popular way to lose weight. The hundreds of diets that have become popularized throughout the years have changed, but all fad diets involve restricting certain foods or entire food groups. The danger of fad diets is that they recommend a magic bullet or quick fix (e.g., rapid weight loss) without the evidence to back up claims. In other words, fad diets the scientific evidence associated with objective study. Another problem with fad diets is they can result in inadequate consumption of nutrients for a healthy diet. For example, by eliminating an entire food group, a person may risk not getting enough vitamins, which can create health-related problems.

From a psychological approach, fad diets also tend to identify foods as "good" or "bad," rather than promote a healthy lifestyle or a moderation approach. This dieting mentality is associated with contributing to negative body image and, in some cases, to disordered eating. Another concern is fad diets do not address a person's relationship with food, which means dysfunctional thought patterns, such as eating for emotional reasons remain. Dieting behavior has been shown to trigger disordered-eating thoughts and behaviors as it promotes a restrictive mind-set around food.

Unfortunately, most people gain the weight back that they lose while dieting. Given that disordered eating and eating disorders have been shown to be an outgrowth of dieting behavior, a healthy lifestyle approach is generally preferable to fad diets.

Types of Fad Diets

One of the earliest documented fad diets was a low-carbohydrate diet in 1825. The creator of Graham crackers purportedly pushed a high-fiber diet in 1830, and Englishman William Banting promoted a diet low in carbohydrates as a weight loss strategy in 1863. Fad diets have also included eating behavior strategies tied to weight loss such as chewing each bite of food 32 times, that the trend in 1903. Other diets over the years have included, but are not been limited to, the cigarette diet, banana-and-skim-milk diet, cabbage soup diet, and grapefruit diet.

Other popular diets have included the vegetarian diet (i.e., the elimination of meats) and the South Beach diet that focused on increasing protein while eliminating "white stuff" in one's diet (e.g., flour, sugar, pasta). The controversial Atkins diet was backed by a cardiologist and similarly limited sugar and carbohydrate intake. However, the Atkins diet allowed people to consume meat (even bacon) without worrying about fat intake. Finally, people were able to have their steak and eat it, too.

The Paleo diet, otherwise known as the caveman diet, discussed in a separate entry, purports to get back to the original way early humans ate. This meal plan excludes processed foods as well as dairy products. Once again, this fad diet made health-related claims and was backed by a doctor to gain credibility. The Paleo diet also underscored foods to eat and not eat, with an emphasis on meats, fish, fresh fruits, vegetables, and seeds.

The problem with diets with a narrow range of allowable foods is they become monotonous. Being overly rigid with food choices or amounts can be difficult to maintain. Unfortunately, most people gain back any weight lost while on a diet because weight maintenance is extremely challenging. Therefore, a sustainable approach to eating should be selected over an overly restrictive diet.

Justine J. Reel

See also: Detox Diets and Cleanses; Diet Pills; Paleo Diet; Vegetarianism

Bibliography

Eaton, Stanley B., and Stanley B. Eaton III. "Paleolithic vs. Modern Diets—Selected Pathophysiological Implications." *European Journal of Nutrition* 39, no. 2 (2000): 67–70.

"Fad Diets." Clevelandclinic.org. Last modified June 12, 2012. Accessed November 21, 2017. http://my.clevelandclinic.org/health/healthy_living/getting_fit/hic_Fad_Diets.

"Fad Diets." Eatright.org. Accessed September 27, 2016. http://www.eatright.org/resources/health/weight-loss/fad-diets.

Golden, Robert N., Fred L. Peterson, Gerri F. Kramer, William Kane, and Mark J. Kittleson. *The Truth about Eating Disorders*, 2nd ed. New York: Facts on File, 2009.

Lindeberg, Staffan, Tommy Jonsson, Yvonne Granfeldt, E. Borgstrand, J. Soffman, Karin Sjöström, and Bo Ahrén. "A Palaeolithic Diet Improves Glucose Tolerance More Than a Mediterranean-Like Diet in Individuals with Ischaemic Heart Disease." *Diabetologia* 50, no. 9 (2007): 1795–1807. https://doi.org/10.1007/s00125-007-0716-y.

Lynch, Rene. "A Brief Timeline Shows How We're Gluttons for Diet Fads." latimes.com. Last modified February 28, 2015. Accessed November 21, 2017. http://www.latimes.com/health/la-he-diet-timeline-20150228-story.html.

FAMILY INFLUENCES

In the 1980s, family members and particularly parental styles (i.e., overbearing mother and distant father figure) were solely blamed for causing eating disorders. However, researchers and clinicians have realized that, although families contribute to eating disorders, they also provide the necessary support to foster healthy treatment and recovery from eating disorders. Additionally, families provide a source of self-esteem and self-worth that serves as a protective factor against body dissatisfaction and body image disturbances. By contrast, a family's overemphasis on appearance or praise for slenderness can contribute to an environment that values beauty over other qualities (e.g., athletic ability, academic prowess). Furthermore, dieting and restricting certain foods in the home can heighten a mind-set of good and bad foods that may perpetuate disordered thoughts and an unhealthy relationship with food.

Family Dynamics

Family dynamics have been identified as key factors in the development and perpetuation of eating disorders. Dated studies and case reports of families that had a member with an eating disorder indicated the families tended to be intrusive, enmeshed, and hostile. In the past few years, several studies have suggested people who suffer from eating disorders seem to have insecure attachments to family members.

Eating-disorder clients have at times described a critical family environment with coercive parental control. Adolescents who report poor family communication and low parental expectations, as well as those who report sexual or physical abuse, seem to be at increased risk for developing eating disorders. Additionally, children raised by separated, divorced, or widowed parents are at higher risk and tend to engage in solitary eating more often, which has been found to be a contributing factor in the development of eating disorders. Single-parent families may be more likely to lack the ability to educate children regarding food habits and eating patterns, precisely due to the absence of one of two parents during meals. This parental input is believed to exert a very important influence to prevent eating disorders. Clients with bulimia nervosa also report parents who are intrusive, jealous, and competitive and that privacy is not respected. In contrast, perceived parental encouragement of autonomy is associated with less dieting behavior, which serves as a protective function against eating disorders.

Maternal Influence

Mothers provide a role model for eating and body image scrutiny for their daughters and sons. Mothers who make disparaging comments about their bodies may socialize their children to be critical of their body parts and perceived flaws. In some cases, mothers of daughters with eating disorders exhibited eating disorder behaviors themselves, which may have had an influence on their daughters' development of eating disorder pathology. According to one study, mothers with eating disorder symptoms fed their children at irregular times, used food for rewards and punishments, expressed concern about their children's weight as early as age two, and were more dissatisfied with the general functioning of the family system. By age five, these children exhibited greater signs of depression and anxiety than did offspring of mothers without eating disorders. One study conducted by Lilenfeld et al. suggested that 50 percent of children of mothers with eating disorders display symptoms of depression, anxiety, obsessive-compulsive disorder, and eating disorders. Furthermore, a mother's direct comments to her children seem to be more influential than her behavior regarding weight and body image concerns, although even modeling does appear to affect children's weight- and shape-related attitudes and behaviors. Several studies suggest a mother's critical comments increase the probability of eating disorder behaviors in daughter.

Paternal Influence

Fathers appear to play a significant role in their children's development of eating disorders. A noteworthy study by Canetti et al. found fathers of daughters with anorexia nervosa tended to be less caring and more controlling. According to the findings, controlling fathers did not predict the *severity* of their daughter's symptoms but did contribute to the *onset* and *maintenance* of the eating disorder symptoms. Furthermore, when the daughters viewed the fathers as displaying *affectionless control,* the daughters reported increased eating disorder symptoms. In addition, the researchers examined the roles of grandparents in a client's eating disorder development. Fathers who perceived their mothers (paternal grandmother to client) as less caring had daughters who reported increased eating disorder behaviors. Also, a father's controlling behavior and uncaring attitude toward his children was associated with the controlling behavior of his own father. The father–daughter relationship seemed to have a direct influence on the development of and maintenance of an eating disorder. These findings were consistent with other studies regarding the influence of parent–child relationships on children's eating disorders. Furthermore, the authors suggested when considering parent–child relationships, it is often difficult to determine if existing problems contributed to the development of the eating disorder or if the eating disorder contributed to the development of the existing relationship problems. For example, does the eating disorder change parents' behavior so parents become less caring, or does a real lack of care contribute to the development of an eating disorder? Similarly, does a defiant adolescent have a distorted perception that parents are controlling, or have the parents adopted a new parental attitude as a result of an effort to cope with the child's self-harming illness?

Sibling Influence

Currently, a paucity of research exists regarding the influence of sibling relationships on body image and disordered eating. In one study, researchers suggested the relationship with one's sister may be the most potent modeling agent of weight concerns in the family environment. Other studies noted that sisters were perceived to communicate equivalent pressures to be thin as both parents combined. As sisters may recognize more modeling cues from each other than either parent, they also engage in high levels of social comparison. The comparison may be more negative if one sister is perceived by societal others as more attractive. One study found sisters reported similar levels of internalization of the thin ideal and body image disturbance, especially within a familial subculture of thinness. Another study found sisters of clients with eating disorders did not demonstrate a significant disturbance in their perception of their body image. The authors also found a tendency toward overestimation of body fat in brothers compared to male controls. This finding, together with a higher muscularity overestimation, points toward a potential for more negative body perception in brothers of clients.

Ethnicity

Research has also examined the role of family ethnicity in the development of eating disorders. Caucasian subjects have frequently been found to report greater body dissatisfaction and eating concerns than either Asian or African American subjects. Conversely, one study demonstrated British Asian individuals showed higher dietary restraint scores than Caucasian contemporaries and a higher prevalence of eating disorders in Asian than Caucasian girls. Furthermore, a series of studies with New Zealand families from a range of cultural backgrounds showed vast differences in attitudes about eating. For instance, Maori and Pacific Islands women showed no concerns about their eating and body image/shape. However, Pacific Islander women who were raised in families that identified with Pakeha ways had a high incidence of anorexia and bulimia. Also, one study found the introduction of television into the lives of Fijian families resulted in a negative effect upon adolescent daughters' disordered eating attitudes and behaviors. Many studies have shown that a greater prevalence of eating disorders exists in families from industrialized societies than in families from developing societies.

Juliann Cook Jeppsen

See also: Causes; Family Therapy; Parents; Teasing

Bibliography

Becker, Anne, Rebecca Burwell, David Herzog, Paul Hamburg, and Stephen Gilman. "Eating Behaviors and Attitudes Following Prolonged Exposure to Television among Ethnic Fijian Adolescent Girls." *The British Journal of Psychiatry* 180 (2002): 509–514. https://doi.org/10.1192/bjp.180.6.509.

Benninghoven, Dieter, Nina Tetsch, and Gunter Jantschek. "Patients with Eating Disorders and Their Siblings: An Investigation of Body Image Perceptions." *European Child and Adolescent Psychiatry* 17 (2008): 118–126. https://doi.org/10.1007/s00787-007-0645-9.

Bulik, Cynthia M., Patrick F. Sullivan, and Kenneth S. Kendler. "Genetic and Environmental Contributions to Obesity and Binge-Eating." *International Journal of Eating Disorders* 33, no. 3 (2003): 293–298. https://doi.org/10.1002/eat.10140.

Canetti, Laura, Kyra Kanyas, Bernard Lerer, Yael Latzer, and Eytan Bachar. "Anorexia Nervosa and Parental Bonding: The Contribution of Parent–Grandparent Relationships to Eating Disorder Psychopathology." *Journal of Clinical Psychology* 64 (2008): 703–716. https://doi.org/10.1002/jclp.20482.

Coomber, Kerri, and Ross M. King. "The Role of Sisters in Body Image Dissatisfaction and Disordered Eating." *Sex Roles* 59 (2008): 81–93. https://doi.org/10.1007/s11199-008-9413-7.

Hodes, Marquis, Saw Timimi, and Patrick Robinson. "Children of Mothers with Eating Disorders: A Preliminary Study." *European Eating Disorders Review* 5 (1997): 11–24.

Lilenfeld, Lisa R., Walter H. Kaye, Catherine G. Greeno, Kathleen R. Merikangas, Katherine Plotnicov, Christine Pollice, Radhika Rao, Michael Strober, Cynthia Bulik, and Linda Nagy. "A Controlled Family Study of Anorexia Nervosa and Bulimia Nervosa: Psychiatric Disorders in First-Degree Relatives and Effects of Proband Comorbidity." *Archives of General Psychiatry* 55 (1998): 603–610. https://doi.org/10.1001/archpsyc.55.7.603.

Strober, Michael, Cloughton Lambert, William Morrell, James Burroughs, and Charles Jacobs. "A Controlled Family Study of Anorexia Nervosa: Evidence of Familial Aggregation and Lack of Shared Transmission with Affective Disorders." *International Journal of Eating Disorders* 9 (1990): 239–253. https://doi.org/10.1002/1098-108X(199005)9:3<239::AID-EAT2260090302>3.0.CO;2-7.

FAMILY THERAPY

Family therapy encompasses specific techniques beyond basic psychotherapy to assist families and couples overcome relationship difficulties. A family therapist typically works with a couple or family at the same time, instead of using individual sessions. Change is viewed in terms of the interactions between a couple or among family members. Family therapy is an important component of effective treatment for individuals who suffer from eating disorders. For adolescents who continue to cope with family dynamics at home, it is a critical piece for relapse prevention as part of a comprehensive eating disorder treatment plan. Family therapy for adult eating-disordered clients may be optional and depends on a continued relationship with family members (e.g., parents, siblings) and a need to address unhealthy bonds that trigger disordered eating.

History of Family Therapy

Family therapy as a unique professional practice originated in the 19th century with the marriage counseling and child guidance movements. The formal development of family therapy dates to the 1940s and early 1950s with the formation of the American Association of Marriage Counselors in 1942. Initial influence came from psychoanalysis and social psychiatry, and later from learning theory and behavior therapy. In the early 1950s, Dr. Bateson and his colleagues began to study the communication patterns that schizophrenic clients had with their families. He believed the thought processes of clients emerged out of bizarre communication patterns in the family. The team also observed that if a client improved, the family became destabilized and resisted or blocked a client's improvement. Essentially, for the family system to operate, a client needed to remain sick. Dr. Bateson's team described the family as a system with homeostatic tendencies, hierarchies, boundaries, coalitions, and conflicts between specific members. By the mid-1960s, a number of other distinct schools of family therapy (e.g., Adlerian, Cognitive Behavioral, Experiential, Family Systems, Feminist, Strategic, Structural) emerged, many of which have become integral parts in the treatment of eating disorders.

Adlerian Family Therapy

Founded by Alfred Adler in the 1920s, this approach examines a client in a family system. Treatment focuses on healing the underlying causes of the eating disorder and the purposes the eating disorder serves for an individual and his or her family. Adler asserted people are constantly striving to meet a real or fictional goal in life. With an eating disorder, perceptions are often distorted and can lead to destructive behaviors due to especially high sensitivity levels of eating-disorder clients and their misinterpretations of events. Adlerian techniques are used to assist a family to understand each member's role in the development and maintenance of an eating disorder and in reframing interpretations of events and family interactions.

Being the Sibling of a Person with an Eating Disorder: An Interview with "Molly"

"Molly" (pseudonym used to preserve anonymity) is a 27-year-old woman who resides in the United States and is graduating from college this year. She is studying to become an elementary teacher because she loves kids. She learned that her sister had an eating disorder when she was only 14 years old and that knowledge had a significant impact on her life. She remains proud of her sister's recovery and learned a lot as a result of the journey.

How old is your sister now and what age was she when you realized she had a problem? How old were you and what did you know about eating disorders before the problem emerged? What were the telltale signs that indicated she had an eating disorder?

My sister is currently 24 years old. She was always really big into sports. She played basketball all throughout junior high and high school. I started to notice a change in her when she was in 10th grade. She was becoming more involved with basketball and "eating healthy." She stopped eating meat and then eventually became a vegan. I didn't think anything of it at first, I just thought she was trying to stay healthy, but after a while it became more than that. It became an obsession. She obsessed over every little thing that she ate. It wasn't until her senior year when she was 17 and I was 14 years old that I realized she had a serious problem. I didn't connect it to an eating disorder at the time. I never thought that my sister would have an eating disorder because she was the skinniest of the three siblings. Once I found out that she had an eating disorder, I didn't know how to process the news. I didn't know a lot about eating disorders. We grew up with a father that was very critical of us so I definitely knew what it was like to hate yourself and your body, but I couldn't wrap my head around the fact that my skinny sister felt that she needed to starve herself and throw up.

How was the problem handled within your family? Did anyone confront your sibling about her eating disorder? How did the eating disorder affect your family dynamic (in other words, what changed within your family system as a result of your sibling's problem)?

I don't think my sister's eating disorder was handled in the best way. When we realized she had a problem our family was in the middle of a very messy divorce that involved my father being fired from his job due to inappropriate relationships with students. It also involved a lot of stalking and manipulation and late night calls to the police. Although I don't think her eating disorder was handled the best way, at the time we were just trying to survive and we were all doing the best we could to keep our heads above water. With my dad out of the picture, the only one that really confronted my sister at first was my mom. My mom put her in therapy and took her to see a nutritionist. My brother kept his distance as he coped with what was going on with our dad and I didn't exactly know what to say to my sister at that point. At the time it was just easier for me to ignore the problem. Her eating disorder changed our family dynamics greatly. Our relationship wasn't nearly as strong as it used to be. She became antisocial and would always stay in her room and she would have mood swings so it was hard to be around her. I felt like I had to filter everything I said around her because she was so easily offended and would snap at me over unimportant things. It put a lot of stress on my mom, which made my relationship with my mom difficult. I felt like I could never complain or have a bad day because she already had so much to worry about with my sister, in my mind she didn't need two daughters with issues. I had a hard time focusing on my life because I was so worried about my sister. Every time my phone rang my heart would race and I would get a sinking feeling in my stomach because I was worried I was going to answer it and have someone tell me that my sister was dead. I think it put a lot of stress on us individually and as a family I think for a while it tore us apart.

What do you believe were some of the contributing factors that played a role in the development of your sibling's eating disorder?
We grew up with a mentally, emotionally, and sexually abusive dad. I know for a fact that is what triggered her eating disorder. He played mind games with us all. She had all of the pressure on her to be the "skinny and athletic" daughter because I was the "heavier" daughter. He would hide food from us and reward her with food if she would go for runs and workout. He had to hide it so that me and my brother wouldn't eat it and gain more weight. All throughout our childhood we were pressured and forced to look like the perfect happy family. I grew up being taught "don't have a personality, it makes it easier for people to judge you." We were never good enough. I know my sister grew up feeling like she would never be good enough. I know this abuse was the cause of her disorder and the way she feels about herself.

How did the eating disorder change your relationship with your sibling? What does your relationship look like now that your sibling is recovered?
I feel like my sister lost herself to her eating disorder. She was hardly a person. We used to be really close but her eating disorder took over completely. She wasn't my sister. She was mean. She would say hurtful things. She was manipulative. She wasn't the fun sister that I grew up with. She was always locked in her room and would only talk to us when it was necessary. Here we are seven years later, yes our relationship has gotten better but it is not even close to what it used to be like. I feel like we grew apart. She was so caught up in her eating disorder she really wasn't a part of my life for years. Right now I think she is still trying to figure out who she is now that she is recovering. I think part of me will always be mad at her. I know the eating disorder wasn't her fault and was completely out of her control but it took away a lot of my life. She was my big sister. She was supposed to look after me and protect me, but it was the complete opposite. I was always looking after her. Making sure she wasn't hurting herself and going to the hospital when she did hurt herself. My life revolved around her eating disorder. My mind and thoughts revolved around her. Is she okay? Is she throwing up? Is she cutting herself? Will today be the day she kills herself? It was frustrating for me. For the most part I was patient and understanding but I got to a point where I was tired of trying to help her. You can't help someone that doesn't want it. I had to find space and detach because it was too painful to see my sister slowly kill herself and nothing I did or said would change that. We will never have the same relationship anymore. I love my sister more than anything but it is toxic being too close to someone with this disorder.

What did treatment entail for your sister? Do you participate in family therapy for your sibling's eating disorder treatment? What did that look like? What advice did you receive as to how to best support your sister?

My sister went to several different therapists and nutritionists. I feel like she was constantly at appointments. She ended up going to a rehab center, but she made it about three days before she decided she wanted to check herself out and go home so that wasn't successful. I have only ever been to one of her appointments. She was very private when it came to her appointments and never wanted anyone to go with her. The one appointment I sat in on she was very closed off. I could tell she wasn't comfortable with me there which is why I didn't go to any other ones with her. I don't necessarily think you need to sit in on appointments to be supportive. My sister knew I loved her unconditionally and always supported her. She knew I would do anything for her. In her case, therapy was easier for her to do alone. She is more open to discussing her feelings and struggles now than she was in the past, which is a huge improvement.

What would you tell other individuals who have just learned that their sister/brother has an eating disorder? Any advice you can offer about how to best cope with the stress placed on the family system?

The advice that I have for people in the same position as me is simple. Your sibling is not their eating disorder. You have to try and separate the two. They are sick. They need your unconditional love and support. Sometimes they need tough love and sometimes they just need a shoulder to cry on. It's not easy to be around and it is a long journey, but they need your help.

What support do you believe is necessary for family members of individuals who have an eating disorder?

I don't think people realize how hard it is on the family. I personally think support groups for those who have a family member with an eating disorder would be helpful. It would create a place where families can get together and share their struggles and get ideas of how to help their loved ones.

What else would you like to add from the perspective of a sibling who has a sister/brother with an eating disorder?

I don't think people are taking eating disorders as serious as they should. I watched my sister slowly disappear and become someone else. I watched her hate herself. I watched her punish herself. I watched her hurt herself. This isn't something that a person chooses to do. It needs to be taken seriously. I could have completely lost my sister because of this illness, but I was one of the lucky ones. I don't believe that you can ever completely recover from this disorder. I watched my sister slowly stop starving herself and making herself throw up, but it caused other issues like cutting. I think that you can somewhat recover but I think there will always be a part of them that struggles with the disorder. I have watched my sister over the years, she has come a long way and I am so proud of her but I know there are many things she still struggles with. She is not recovered. She is healing and is overcoming so much but I will always worry about her going back to her old habits and relapsing like she has in the past.

Cognitive Behavioral Therapy for the Family

John Gottman and Albert Ellis originally viewed family problems to be the result of operant conditioning. Operant conditioning in the context of family therapy refers to negative behaviors reinforced by a family's interpersonal exchanges that promote incentives for unhealthy behaviors. Eating disorder symptoms are viewed as unhealthy behaviors in response to a client's interpersonal family relationships. The goals of cognitive behavioral therapy for a family are to help (1) a family understand how members' eating disorder behaviors originate with maladaptive thoughts, then feelings; (2) a family identify negative consequences (i.e., a client's eating disorder symptoms) of their behaviors; and (3) family members change their thoughts, that change feelings, and then behaviors. Although family members are not to blame for a client's eating disorder, they can play a crucial role in recovery.

Experiential Family Therapy

This approach proposes growth and healing occur through a real-life encounter with a therapist who is intentionally authentic with clients without pretense, often in a playful way, as a means to foster flexibility in the family and promote individuation. Experiential therapy includes, but is not limited to, activities such as family sculpture, role-play, yoga, hiking, and art therapy to help family members explore their relationships and connections with one another. The therapist assists a family with enacting past and present emotional climates, giving family members a chance to view their relationships from a different perspective. For instance, a therapist uses family sculpture by having each family member take a position in a therapy room that symbolically represents the nature of their relationships with other family members. Also, a therapist may have family members role-play certain scenarios that happen in the family and may suggest changes that could improve relationships. The goal of experiential therapy in eating disorder treatment is to free a family from the unresolved emotions around their relationships, so that they are able to live in the present. Ultimately, self-discovery through resolving family emotional conflicts is a vital element for a patient in treatment because his or her self-identity is entangled in the development and maintenance of the illness.

Family Systems Therapy

Based on the work of Murray Bowen, this approach refers to conceptualizing family members as driven to achieve internal and external balance and often causing anxiety and emotional isolation. Family members become emotionally distanced from each other (internal) and the family unit becomes isolated from society (external). Societal isolation often stems from a lack of communication within a family that extends to outside relationships. Also, a family may be ashamed of its internal struggles that lead to external isolation. Eating disorder symptoms serve a function by absorbing the anxiety in a family system. A major focus of family systems therapy is to activate each individual in a family to develop initiative and to accept responsibility for his or her actions. At the same time, a therapist must address the forces in a family that may thwart individual motivation. Unresolved emotional issues are addressed, which bring awareness to the anxiety and other emotional processes in a family. Awareness of unfulfilled emotional needs creates room for options that may help a client manage eating disorder behaviors as other family members adapt to the change in relationships that occur as the client becomes well.

Feminist Family Therapy

This approach is based on the feminist perspective that eating disorders develop in social or familial contexts that view women as nurturers and places emphasis on their conforming to cultural norms of physical attraction. Social expectations are identified as the root of the problems, rather than a family system itself. Therapists following feminist family therapy work to model an egalitarian perspective of healthy family relationships (each family member holds equal status within the family) and use a less directive approach than other therapists to explore the way cultural values are expressed by the family. A therapist tends to ask questions and listen rather than give specific instructions to family members, so the family is empowered to take an active role in treatment and recovery. Feminist family therapy embraces a therapeutic attitude of equality, an opposition to the use of male power against women, and a special respect for the emerging individuality and femininity of a female eating-disorder client. Feminist family therapy is particularly powerful in addressing cultural pressures pertaining to an eating-disorder patient's body image distortion. A therapist may ask probing questions about media and other societal pressures to be thin, thus encouraging a client and family to explore and challenge their maladaptive beliefs.

Strategic Family Therapy

This approach is influenced by the work of Jay Haley (late 1960s) and views an eating disorder as a set of symptoms that purposefully maintain balance in a family hierarchy. A therapist's goal is to discover and disconnect the eating disorder symptoms from the roles the symptoms play in family interactions. A therapist will prescribe specific healthy behaviors for family members and guide family members as they practice healthy roles. As family members begin to change behaviors (e.g., having family meals), the eating disorder symptoms fade from a central role, a family organization shifts, and a client and family members develop adaptive ways of functioning.

Structural Family Therapy

The structural family therapy approach is based on Salvador Minuchin's early 1960s conceptualization of the psychosomatic family, which had major impact on the treatment of eating disorders. In this model, family problems are viewed as arising from maladaptive boundaries and subsystems, indirect communication, and avoidance of conflict that are created in the overall family system of rules and rituals that govern interactions. The focus of structural family therapy is to change a family's interactional patterns, thereby strengthening some bonds (i.e., between the parents), weakening other bonds (i.e., between the mother and the daughter/eating-disorder client), and promoting the eating-disorder client's autonomy. Essentially, a therapist challenges whatever it is in the family structure is contributing to curtailing a client's autonomy and growth. A therapist encourages all family members to speak for themselves and avoid saying how another person thinks or feels. This allows each person in a family system to claim his or her space that promotes self-discovery and individuation, which are vital components of eating disorder recovery.

Maudsley Approach or Family-Based Treatment

This approach was conceived by a team of child and adolescent psychiatrists and psychologists at the Maudsley Hospital in London during the early 1990s. The Maudsley Approach is covered in a separate section.

Juliann Cook Jeppsen

See also: Cognitive Behavioral Therapy; Family Influences; Maudsley Family Therapy; Parents; Treatment

Bibliography

Bateson, Gregory, Don D. Jackson, Jay Haley, and John Weakland. "Toward a Theory of Schizophrenia." *Behavioral Science* 1, no. 4 (1956): 251–254.

Becvar, Dorothy S., and Raphael J. Becvar. *Family Therapy: A Systemic Approach.* Boston: Allyn and Bacon, 2008.

Bowen, Murray. *Family Therapy in Clinical Practice.* Lanham, MD: Rowman & Littefield Publishers, 2004.

Eisler, Ivan, Christopher Dare, Marquis Hodes, Gerald Russell, Elizabeth Dodge, and Dominique LeGrange. "Family Therapy for Anorexia Nervosa: The Results of a Controlled Comparison of Two Family Interventions." *Journal of Child Psychology and Psychiatry* 41 (2000): 727–736.

Haley, Jay. *Leaving Home: The Therapy of Disturbed Young People*, 2nd ed. London: Routledge, 1997.

Hare-Mustin, Rachel T. "A Feminist Approach to Family Therapy." *Family Process* 17 (1978): 181–194. https://doi.org/10.1111/j.1545-5300.1978.00181.x.

Mayer, Robert D. *Family Therapy in the Treatment of Eating Disorders in General Practice* (Doctoral dissertation). London: University of London, 1994.

Minuchin, Salvador, Bernice L. Rosman, and Lester Baker. *Psychosomatic Families: Anorexia Nervosa in Context.* Cambridge, MA: Harvard University Press, 1978.

Nichols, Michael P., and Richard C. Schwartz. "Recent Developments in Family Therapy: Integrative Models." *Family Therapy: Concepts and Methods.* Boston: Pearson/Allyn and Bacon, 2006.

Rumney, Avis. *Dying to Please: Anorexia, Treatment and Recovery.* Jefferson, NC: McFarland & Company Publishers, 2009.

FAT BIAS/FAT DISCRIMINATION

Fat bias refers to negative judgments of individuals who appear overweight or obese. Fat discrimination is often a consequence of fat bias and refers to prejudicial action directed toward overweight and obese individuals. Overweight and obese individuals are often targets of bias and discrimination. Although large, rotund bodies were thought to be socially ideal in the past (e.g., prior to the 1920s) as they represented wealth and success, today, in Western society, lean, toned, and athletic bodies are idealized. These lean body ideals stand in stark contrast to reality as the World Health Organization estimates that 1.5 billion adults are overweight. Yet, a lean and thin body has come to be viewed as the physical display of self-discipline, motivation, and achievement, whereas a large, fat body is viewed as the ultimate failure publicly displayed for all to see and judge. Although there has been little research examining fat bias and discrimination in relationship to eating disorders, the evidence that exists suggests experiences of bias and discrimination are associated with a number of unhealthy eating behaviors and a negative body image.

Social Influences on Idealized Bodies

Social consciousness and awareness of the body in Western society are shaped and fueled by the booming diet industry, estimated to bring in $40–$50 billion each year. The mass media publicize an ultrathin physique as ideal, resulting in increased social value placed on a lean body. The combination of the current food environment (where food—especially high-calorie, low-nutrition food—is plentiful, accessible, and affordable) and the physical environment (where physical activity has been engineered out of the environment) creates a scenario that is extremely challenging for most people to navigate. The diet industry, playing off the socially-constructed body ideal, promotes and advertises that weight loss is easily attainable with enough effort, willpower, and motivation.

Television shows, such as NBC's *Biggest Loser* and Bravo TV's *Thintervention*, emphasize the need for discipline to achieve weight loss while disregarding biological, social, and environmental factors that influence eating and physical activity behaviors associated with weight. Moreover, research has documented that large individuals are rarely shown on television or in the movies, and when they are included, they are often stereotyped as unattractive and unappealing, are the target of jokes, or shown overeating.

Fat Bias and Discrimination as Acceptable

The assumed inherent value of thinness, where thin = good and fat = bad, contributes to the pervasive nature of fat bias and discrimination. Researchers from the UConn Rudd Center for Food Policy and Obesity suggest overweight and obese people constitute one of the last socially acceptable targets of bias and discrimination. While other forms of bias and discrimination, such as sex and race bias and discrimination, have become socially unacceptable and grounds for job dismissal, fat bias and discrimination are still prevalent. Research indicates that about

12 percent of adults experience fat discrimination and that fat discrimination is the fourth most prevalent form of discrimination.

Why is fat bias so pervasive? It is likely that because the body and weight are assumed to be controllable and malleable (as communicated by the diet industry and reinforced via mass media), there is an *ideology of blame*, a phrase coined by Crandall in 1994, when it comes to overweight and obesity. Attributions (or perceived causes) for weight are generally internal and controllable; in other words, people believe an individual's weight is the result of personal eating and activity habits, and those who are overweight or obese must lack willpower, be lazy, and overindulgent. Because the causes of obesity are believed to be within a person's control, individuals who are overweight or obese are thought to be deserving of any and all psychological, social, or physical consequences of their weight—they have only themselves to blame. Experiences of weight loss, though often unsustainable, seem only to strengthen such beliefs.

Experiences of Fat Bias and Discrimination

Overweight and obese individuals report experiencing fat bias and discrimination in a variety of ways, including others' negative assumptions about their abilities, critical comments about their weight and size from children, physical barriers and obstacles in public places, and disparaging comments from doctors and family members. Bias and discrimination are experienced in different settings, including home, work, school, and health environments. In a home environment, family members are the primary source of stigma, with mothers, spouses, fathers, and siblings rated the most common sources of negative and critical comments. In a work setting, overweight employees and prospective employees are often perceived as less conscientious, less agreeable, less emotionally stable, and less extroverted than thin employees. Interestingly, although these stereotypes are common, research contradicts these perceptions. Overweight employees do not differ from thin employees when it comes to personal characteristics. Unfortunately, overweight and obese individuals do face discriminatory hiring practices and tend to be paid lower wages, receive fewer promotions, and are terminated more frequently than thin employees.

Overweight and obese individuals report health care providers are the second most common source of fat bias and discrimination. Research has documented fat bias in obesity specialists, physicians and medical students, nurses, dieticians, fitness professionals, and physical education teachers. Physicians tend to report that they are not confident in their ability to treat weight problems. In fact, some physicians indicate the treatment of overweight and obesity is useless. Similarly, dieticians have negative perceptions of overweight clients, with common perceptions being that overweight clients lack commitment and motivation, have poor compliance with instruction, and have unrealistic expectations.

Interestingly, fitness preprofessionals and professionals also believe overweight and obese clients are likely to be lazy, lack willpower, and be unattractive. However, fitness professionals, unlike physicians, report being competent to prescribe exercise for weight loss and enjoy helping clients work toward and achieve weight-related goals. Physical educators also report negative attitudes toward overweight students and have lower expectations of them, yet report being motivated to help students develop physical skills and enjoyment of movement.

For young people, school is the prime setting in which they experience fat bias and discrimination. Peer teasing is common, and research has found children and adolescents believe thin people have many friends and are smart, healthy, and happy, whereas fat people have few friends, are lazy, and unhealthy. Moreover, young people are less willing to engage in activities with overweight and obese peers in comparison to average weight peers and in comparison to peers in a wheelchair, missing a limb, on crutches, or disfigured. In addition to facing teasing and social rejection from their peers, overweight and obese children and adults also face bias and discrimination from teachers.

Correlates and Consequences of Fat Bias and Discrimination

Negative attitudes directed toward overweight and obese individuals and stereotypes can result in negative interpersonal interactions, social rejection and bullying, and discrimination, all of which can have serious effects on physical and psychological health. Experiences of fat bias and discrimination are associated with poor psychological well-being as well as behaviors that can negatively influence physical health.

Psychological Well-Being

To date, few studies have examined the relationship between fat bias and psychological well-being; however, what research has been completed indicates depression, poor body image, low self-esteem, and low quality of life are associated with experiences of fat bias and discrimination in adults and children. The serious effects of poor psychological well-being have been well documented: depression is associated with risk of suicidal ideology and actions; low self-esteem is associated with depression; and poor body image is associated with disturbed eating. Thus, although additional research is needed to better understand the mechanisms underlying the relationships between fat bias and discrimination and psychological well-being, there is certainly enough evidence to suggest the effects are serious and harmful.

Health Behaviors

Unhealthy behaviors associated with experiences of fat bias and discrimination may include the delay and avoidance of health care due to weight-related concerns, physical inactivity, and overeating and binge eating. For example, overweight and obese individuals report fear of being weighed, concerns about not fitting into dressing gowns, and worries about negative weight-related comments associated with delaying health care. Overweight and obese women are less likely than average-weight women to seek gynecological health care. Delaying or avoiding health care can negatively affect the physical health of overweight and obese individuals.

Avoiding physical activity is another problematic behavior associated with fat bias and discrimination. Individuals who are overweight or obese may experience embarrassment or shame in physical activity or exercise settings, feel incompetent, and be self-conscious about body and appearance. Although it has been suggested some level of dissatisfaction with one's body may be motivation to lose weight, the reality seems to be just the opposite—when individuals are made to feel bad about or guilty about their bodies and their weight, rather than increasing activity, they actually become inactive to avoid the discomfort and negative attention.

Similarly, research has indicated individuals who experience fat bias and discrimination are more likely to binge eat. Indeed, one study documented eating was one of the most prevalent coping mechanisms for dealing with stigmatizing experiences. Thus, in response to negative attitudes, weight-related teasing, and experiences of bias, overweight and obese individuals may turn to overeating and binge eating to comfort themselves and stuff down negative emotions.

Approaches for Reducing Fat Bias and Discrimination

Increasing Awareness

Fat bias may be both conscious and unconscious. Research indicates moderate to low levels of conscious (e.g., implicit) bias but higher levels of unconscious (e.g., explicit) bias. It is likely social desirability influences responses to conscious measures of bias. Increasing the awareness of unconscious bias is particularly important as individuals are probably unaware of the degree to which they have internalized and automatized stereotypes of overweight and obese individuals. An online version of the Weight Implicit Associations Test (IAT) allows individuals to assess their unconscious associations by completing a pairing task where fat and thin faces are presented in conjunction with words representing personal attributes or characteristics such as motivated/lazy and good/bad. Individuals are typically faster and more accurate when thin faces are paired with good or positive personal attributes and slower and less accurate when fat faces are paired with good or positive attributes. The Weight IAT allows individuals to be more aware of their bias, which is a first step toward reducing the prevalence of fat bias and discrimination.

Challenging Perceived Social Consensus

Perceived social consensus refers to individuals' beliefs about the degree to which others endorse particular beliefs, such as fat people are unattractive and unhealthy. Research indicates when perceived social consensus is challenged, fat bias is reduced—that is, as individuals come to see that not everyone has negative attitudes toward or negative beliefs about overweight and obese people, they are more likely to challenge their beliefs and lessen biased attitudes.

Promoting Empathy

Promoting empathy for and understanding of overweight and obese individuals is another important step to reduce fat bias and discrimination. Although research demonstrating the efficacy of inducing empathy is limited, it is reasonable to expect that a sense of understanding of the challenges that overweight and obese individuals face would be beneficial. One way to promote empathy is providing people, especially professionals who work with overweight and obese individuals, opportunities to gain experience and perspective in simulated situations. The obesity empathy suit (http://www.empathysuit.com/) is a device that may be useful. The obesity empathy suit simulates the actual weight and bulk of being overweight—while wearing the suit, individuals can experience the challenges of daily living, such as carrying groceries upstairs, picking up items off a floor, and getting into and out of a car.

Revising Educational Training and Development Models

Educational training and professional development models should be revised to address fat bias and discrimination in health professionals and educators. Physicians, nurses, and dieticians need better training to work with overweight and obese clients, effective strategies for intervention, and to be comfortable and confident in their ability to work with clients. The Exercise Is Medicine initiative by the American College of Sports Medicine (ACSM) provides resources for health professionals who wish to talk with clients about weight. Moreover, educators need training specifically for dealing with weight-related teasing in bullying.

Resources on Fat Bias and Discrimination

The UConn Rudd Center for Food Policy and Obesity is the worldwide leader in research, education, and advocacy related to fat bias and discrimination. The center's website offers many resources for researchers, health professionals, teachers, parents, employers, youth, and policy makers. The Rudd Center has also produced several videos to highlight the myths and facts of fat bias, and experiences of fat bias and discrimination at home, school, and in health care settings. Additionally, resources for overweight and obese individuals interested in physical activity are available at *Active at Any Size* (http://win.niddk.nih.gov/Publications/active.htm).

Christy Greenleaf

See also: Binge Eating Disorder; Health at Every Size Approach; Obesity; Teasing; Weight Stigma

Bibliography

Ashmore, Jamile A., Kelli E. Friedman, Simona K. Reichmann, and Gerard J. Musante. "Weight-Based Stigmatization, Psychological Distress, and Binge Eating Behavior among Obese Treatment-Seeking Adults." *Eating Behaviors* 9 (2008): 203–209. http://dx.doi.org/10.1016/j.eatbeh.2007.09.006.

Blaine, Bruce E., Deanne M. DiBlasi, and Jane M. Connor. "The Effect of Weight Loss on Perceptions of Weight Controllability: Implications for Prejudice against Overweight People." *Journal of Applied Biobehavioral Research* 7 (2002): 44–56. https://doi.org/10.1111/j.1751-9861.2002.tb00075.x.

Crandall, Chris S. "Prejudice against Fat People: Ideology and Self-Interest." *Journal of Personality and Social Psychology* 66 (1994): 882–894. http://dx.doi.org/10.1037/0022-3514.66.5.882.

Drury, Christine Aramburu Alegria, and Margaret Louis. "Exploring the Association between Body Weight, Stigma of Obesity, and Health Care Avoidance." *Journal of the American Academy of Nurse Practitioners* 14 (2002): 554–561. https://doi.org/10.1111/j.1745-7599.2002.tb00089.x.

Faith, Myles S., Mary Ann Leone, Tim S. Ayers, Moonseong Heo, and Angelo Pietrobelli. "Weight Criticism during Physical Activity, Coping Skills, and Reported Physical Activity in Children." *Pediatrics* 110 (2002): e23.

Greenleaf, Christy, Heather Chambliss, Deborah J. Rhea, Scott B. Martin, and James R. Morrow Jr. "Weight Stereotypes and Behavioral Intentions toward Thin and Fat Peers among White and Hispanic Adolescents." *Journal of Adolescent Health* 39 (2006): 546–552. http://dx.doi.org/10.1016/j.jadohealth.2006.01.013.

Greenleaf, Christy, and Karen Weiller. "Perceptions of Youth Obesity among Physical Educators." *Social Psychology of Education* 8 (2005): 407–423. https://doi.org/10.1007/s11218-005-0662-9.

Latner, Janet D., and Albert J. Stunkard. "Getting Worse: The Stigmatization of Obese Children." *Obesity Research* 11 (2003): 452–456. https://doi.org/10.1038/oby.2003.61.

National Institute of Diabetes and Digestive and Kidney Diseases of the National Institutes of Health. "Active at Any Size." Accessed November 20, 2016. http://win.niddk.nih.gov/Pub lications/active.htm.

"Obesity Empathy Suit." Empathysuit.com. Accessed November 20, 2016. http://www.empathysuit.com/

O'Brien, Kerry S., Jackie A. Hunter, and M. Banks. "Implicit Anti-Fat Bias in Physical Educators: Physical Attributes, Ideology and Socialization." *International Journal of Obesity* 31 (2007): 308–314. https://doi.org/10.1038/sj.ijo.0803398.

Project Implicit. "Project Implicit." Accessed November 20, 2016. https://implicit.harvard.edu/implicit/demo/selectatest.html.

Puhl, Rebecca M., T. Andreyeva, and Kelly D. Brownell. "Perceptions of Weight Discrimination: Prevalence and Comparison to Race and Gender Discrimination in America." *International Journal of Obesity* 32 (2008): 992–1000. https://doi.org/10.1038/ijo.2008.22.

Puhl, Rebecca M., and Kelly D. Brownell. "Confronting and Coping with Weight Stigma: An Investigation of Overweight and Obese Adults." *Obesity* 14 (2006): 1802–1815. https://doi.org/10.1038/oby.2006.208.

Puhl, Rebecca M., and Kelly D. Brownell. "Psychosocial Origins of Obesity Stigma: Toward Changing a Powerful and Pervasive Bias." *Obesity Reviews* 4 (2003): 213–227. https://doi.org/10.1046/j.1467-789X.2003.00122.x.

Puhl, Rebecca M., and Chelsea A. Heuer. "The Stigma of Obesity: A Review and Update." *Obesity* 17 (2009): 940–964. https://doi.org/10.1038/oby.2008.636.

Puhl, Rebecca M., and Janet D. Latner. "Stigma, Obesity, and the Health of the Nation's Children." *Psychological Bulletin* 133 (2007): 557–580. http://dx.doi.org/10.1037/0033-2909.133.4.557.

Puhl, Rebecca M., Corinne A. Moss-Racusin, and Marlene B. Schwartz. "Internalization of Weight Bias: Implications for Binge Eating and Emotional Well-Being." *Obesity* 15 (2007): 19–23. https://doi.org/10.1038/oby.2007.521.

Puhl, Rebecca M., Marlene B. Schwartz, and Kelly D. Brownell. "Impact of Perceived Consensus on Stereotypes about Obese People: A New Approach for Reducing Bias." *Health Psychology* 24 (2005): 517–525. http://dx.doi.org/10.1037/0278-6133.24.5.517.

UConn Rudd Center for Food Policy and Obesity. "UConn Rudd Center for Food Policy and Obesity." Accessed November 20, 2016. http://www.uconnruddcenter.org/.

UConn Rudd Center for Food Policy and Obesity. "Videos Exposing Weight Bias." Accessed November 20, 2016. http://www.uconnruddcenter.org/weight-bias-stigma-videos-exposing-weight-bias.

Vartanian, Lenny R., and Jacqueline G. Shaprow. "Effect of Weight Stigma on Exercise Motivation and Behavior: A Preliminary Investigation among College-Aged Females." *Journal of Health Psychology* 13 (2008): 131–138. https://doi.org/10.1177/1359105307084318.

World Health Organization. "Obesity and Overweight." Last modified June 2016. Accessed November 21, 2017. http://www.who.int/mediacentre/factsheets/fs311/en/.

FEMALE ATHLETE TRIAD

In 1992, a group of esteemed scholars held a consensus conference called by the Task Force on Women's Issues of the American College of Sports Medicine (ACSM) to discuss the incidence of three interconnected disorders observed in female athletes with increasing frequency—disordered eating, amenorrhea, and osteoporosis. Although it was likely these conditions had been in female athlete populations for decades, increasing attention in the research literature sparked the initiation of a conference to address these medical conditions. In 1997, ACSM published a position statement identifying the term *female athlete triad* to describe the interrelationship between energy availability, menstrual status, and bone health

Since then, a growing body of research has informed a more recent ACSM position statement published in 2007 and has improved understanding of this complex phenomenon. More specifically, the components of the female athlete triad have been redefined as the interrelationship between energy availability, menstrual status, and bone health, where each component represents a continuum from a healthy to unhealthy. This important change is depicted in the following excerpt from ACSM's 2007 position stand:

> Low energy availability (with or without eating disorders), amenorrhea, and osteoporosis, alone or in combination, pose significant health risks to physically active girls and women. The potentially irreversible consequences of these clinical conditions emphasize the critical need for prevention, early diagnosis, and treatment. Each clinical condition is now understood to comprise the pathological end of a spectrum of interrelated subclinical conditions between health and disease.

The development of the female athlete triad follows a progressive pattern that typically begins with low energy availability and can result in serious disordered eating issues and menstrual and/or bone health concerns. Often, each component is linked directly or indirectly to another. In the most severe case, an athlete may develop a clinical eating disorder, extreme menstrual irregularities like amenorrhea, and a serious bone disease such as osteoporosis.

Energy Availability

Dietary energy (i.e., energy from food) is necessary to fuel the metabolic processes that sustain life. Energy availability is defined as the amount of energy left for these important metabolic processes after expending energy during exercise. This term is often better explained in the form of a simple equation: Energy Availability (EA; available energy left to use) = Dietary Energy Intake (EI; what you eat) – Exercise Energy Expenditure (EE; what you burn during exercise). When sufficient energy is available, the body can support healthy reproductive function and facilitate bone formation. However, when energy availability is low, reproductive functioning suffers and bones weaken.

Athletes have low energy availability when their energy expenditure during exercise exceeds their dietary intake. In other words, the amount of energy consumed does not match the energy expended. While some athletes may reach a point of low energy availability inadvertently, other athletes purposefully engage in disordered eating behaviors such as diet restriction to lose weight, alter body shape, or change their appearance in an attempt to achieve athletic success. This is especially true for athletes in aesthetic sports (e.g., gymnastics, figure skating) and endurance sports (e.g., running, cycling) that favor lighter and leaner athletes. In addition to conforming to sport-specific pressures, female athletes may also intentionally diet to achieve societal standards of appearance for women. In Western cultures, a long and lean figure or thin ideal is emphasized.

Menstrual Status

Low energy availability can lead to menstrual dysfunction in female athletes. More specifically, low energy availability is believed to deprive the brain of important carbohydrates necessary for proper hormonal secretion and release (e.g., gonadotropin-releasing hormone from the hypothalamus located in the brain and follicle-stimulating and luteinizing hormones from the pituitary gland). As a result, the functioning of the ovaries and subsequent production of estrogen and progesterone are disrupted.

Due to improper hormonal release and production, a variety of menstrual dysfunctions can ensue. For example, primary amenorrhea occurs in females who either have not developed secondary sex characteristics (e.g., breast development and body hair growth) and have not had their first menstrual cycle by the age of 14, or have experienced normal growth and development of secondary sex characteristics but have not had a first menstrual cycle by age 16. In contrast, secondary amenorrhea occurs in females who have had their first menstrual cycle but have not menstruated for three months or longer. Other menstrual dysfunctions can include luteal suppression (i.e., a shortened luteal phase of the menstrual cycle), anovulation (i.e., absence of ovulation), and oligomenorrhea (i.e., prolonged length of time between cycles). Because of the critical role hormones play in the menstrual cycle, serious menstrual disturbances may also be a sign an athlete's bone health is at risk.

Bone Health

Poor bone health can include a number of disorders ranging from osteopenia (i.e., a condition characterized by lower-than-expected bone thickness or low bone mineral density) to osteoporosis (i.e., a severe disease characterized by skeletal degeneration and loss of bone strength). Poor bone health can occur as a result of low energy availability and inadequate nutrition, as well as menstrual dysfunction.

As discussed, when athletes engage in disordered eating behaviors such as restrictive dieting, they consume far less than the recommended number of calories necessary to compensate for the energy expended in a sport. The little energy available is believed to be devoted to survival functions and sport training, as opposed to proper growth and maturational processes. Some researchers contend longitudinal growth (or height) in particular can be permanently or temporarily stunted by inadequate caloric intake.

In addition to the consequences of low energy availability in general, poor calcium intake is of special concern because of its crucial role in bone health, growth, and mass. Peak bone mass is not achieved until approximately 30 years of age and steadily decreases thereafter. Female athletes with poor nutritional habits, low energy availability, and inadequate calcium intake do not accumulate sufficient bone mass early in life and are therefore at risk for poor bone health across their lifespan.

Poor bone health also occurs as a direct result of the absence or disruption of the menstrual cycle. Estrogen is a principal hormone for the suppression of cells responsible for breaking down bone (i.e., bone resorption). In other words, estrogen prevents certain cells from eating the bone away. Irregular hormonal release and low estrogen levels due to menstrual dysfunction can lead to an increase in bone resorption and, therefore, a decline in bone quality. Research demonstrates missed menstrual cycles are associated with significant and potentially permanent losses in bone mineral density.

Athletes with poor bone health are at increased risk for stress fractures. Stress fractures are partial or complete breaks in a bone, often resulting from repetitive weight-bearing impact. The most common areas for stress fractures are the tibia (i.e., the shin), the ankle, and the foot. Weight-bearing exercises can work to strengthen bone. However, individuals with poor nutritional habits, low energy availability, menstrual dysfunction, or a combination of these factors tend to weaken the body's ability to repair injured bones over time. As a result, the wear and tear of everyday activities as well as sport training frequently lead to stress fractures, particularly in runners.

A Fourth Component to the Triad

Some scholars contend there may be a fourth component to the triad, endothelial dysfunction, because of the link between this condition, amenorrhea, and low estrogen levels. The endothelium is the inner lining of the blood vessels. Dysfunction of endothelial cells can impair functioning of the heart, reduce exercise capacity and blood flow to important muscles during exercise, and hasten development of cardiovascular disease and events (e.g., heart attacks). Oral contraceptives and folic acid supplements have been proposed as possible treatments for endothelial dysfunction. Although more research is needed to make strong conclusions about the presence of endothelial dysfunction in female athletes and its link to other components of the triad, these health concerns should certainly be taken seriously.

Prevalence of the Female Athlete Triad

The prevalence of all three components of the triad is relatively small. That is, few female athletes show low energy availability, menstrual dysfunction, *and* poor bone health. However, from a physical and performance perspective, signs of even just one component of the triad are cause for concern. Researchers provide prevalence estimates for each triad component suggesting that between 1 percent and 62 percent of female athletes engage in disordered eating, between 6 percent and 79 percent of female athletes experience menstrual dysfunction, and between 22 percent and 50 percent of female athletes have osteopenia. The variability of these percentages is due to differences in how each component of the triad was measured and defined as well as differences in the sample of individuals included in a study. Although determining precise prevalence estimates is difficult, what is certain is that some female athletes may have low energy availability, menstrual dysfunction, and poor bone health.

Prevention and Treatment of the Female Athlete Triad

The cyclical nature of the female athlete triad and the associated health risks warrant attention and concern. Many scholars have argued for the need to educate audiences about the female athlete triad and methods of prevention. The Female Athlete Triad Coalition is one such resource that works to prevent the triad. The National Collegiate Athletic Association (NCAA) has published materials to inform coaches to identify, manage, and prevent the female athlete triad. Coaches are believed to play an integral role in these processes because of the significant interaction they have with athletes as well as their influence as mentors and supportive adults. In addition to coaches, athletes and parents should be educated on the proper nutrition for adolescent and young adult athletes, characteristics of normal versus dysfunctional menstrual cycles, and the importance of accruing bone mass through regular weight-bearing exercise. Because the female athlete triad typically begins with disordered eating, ACSM specifically contends policies and procedures should be in place to safeguard against unhealthy and detrimental weight loss practices in female sports.

In addition to educational materials, other scholars contend a physical screening is necessary prior to sport participation. More specifically, school nurses and medical doctors are in an optimal position to detect and prevent the triad through preparticipation physical exams. Screening for disordered eating as well as menstrual dysfunction in adolescent and college-aged athletes is believed to be an important first step to prevent the development and progression of the triad. For example, if detected, menstrual dysfunction can be reversed with increases in energy availability. Unfortunately, research shows most high school athletic programs do not adequately screen for these signs and symptoms.

Relative to treatment, scholars and practitioners have long supported a multidisciplinary team approach of coaches, athletic trainers, team physicians, registered sport dietitians, sport psychologists, and sport administrators. Parents and teammates can also play supportive roles in the treatment process. ACSM contends increasing energy consumption or reducing energy expenditure is the first important step in treatment and may require nutritional counseling, psychotherapy, and/or restriction from training and competition. Pharmacological treatment may include antidepressants, oral contraceptive pills, or hormone replacement therapy. In all cases, social support for the at-risk or affected athlete is essential.

Dana K. Voelker

See also: Anorexia Athletica; Athletic Trainers; Coaches; Sports; Weight Pressures in Sport

Bibliography

Beals, Katherine A., and Amanda K. Hill. "The Prevalence of Disordered Eating, Menstrual Dysfunction, and Low Bone Mineral Density among US Collegiate Athletes." *International Journal of Sport Nutrition and Exercise Metabolism* 16 (2006): 1–23.

Beals, Katherine A., and Nanna L. Meyer. "Female Athlete Triad Update." *Clinics in Sports Medicine* 26 (2007): 69–89. https://doi.org/10.1016/j.csm.2006.11.002.

Ireland, Mary Lloyd, and Aurelia Nattiv. *The Female Athlete.* Philadelphia, PA: Saunders, 2002.

Lanser, Erica M., Karie N. Zach, and Anne Z. Hoch. "The Female Athlete Triad and Endothelial Dysfunction." *Physical Medicine and Rehabilitation* 3, no. 5 (2011): 458–465. https://doi.org/10.1016/j.pmrj.2010.12.024.

Manore, Melinda M., Lynn Ciadella Kam, and Anne B. Loucks. "The Female Athlete Triad: Components, Nutrition Issues, and Health Consequences." *Journal of Sports Sciences* 25 (2007): S61–S71. https://doi.org/10.1080/02640410701607320.

Nattiv, Aurelia, Anne B. Loucks, Melinda M. Manore, Charlotte F. Sanborn, Jorunn Sundgot-Borgen, and Michelle P. Warran. "The Female Athlete Triad Position Stand." *Medicine and Science in Sports and Exercise* 39 (2007): 1867–1882. https://doi.org/10.1249/mss.0b013e3181 49f111.

Otis, Carol K., Barbara Drinkwater, Mimi Johnson, Anne Loucks, and Jack Wilmore. "ACSM Position Stand: The Female Athlete Triad." *Medicine and Science in Sports and Exercise* 29 (1997): i–ix.

Thompson, Ron, and Roberta Trattner Sherman. *NCAA Coaches Handbook: Managing the Female Athlete Triad.* Indianapolis, IN: The National Collegiate Athletic Association, 2010.

Yeager, Kimberly K., Rosemary Agostini, Aurelia Nattiv, and Barbara Drinkwater. "The Female Athlete Triad: Disordered Eating, Amenorrhea, Osteoporosis." *Medicine and Science in Sports and Exercise* 25 (1993): 775–777. http://dx.doi.org/10.1249/00005768-199307000-00003.

Zach, Karie N., Ariane L. Smith Machin, and Anne Z. Hoch. "Advances in Management of the Female Athlete Triad and Eating Disorders." *Clinical Journal of Sports Medicine* 30 (2011): 551–573. http://dx.doi.org/10.1016/j.csm.2011.03.005.

FEMININITY IDEALS

Femininity is a socially constructed phenomenon that includes the roles, behaviors, and attributes that are believed to characterize women and girls. To be considered feminine in Western cultures, women and girls are often expected to fulfill traditional sex roles like housekeeping and childbearing, display passivity, submissiveness, modesty, and nurturance, and improve their physical appearance. Although feminine ideals have drastically changed over the past century, women and girls still face many pressures to conform to culturally defined standards, especially in relation to appearance and beauty.

History of the Ideal Female Body

The definition of beauty and physical perfection for women has dramatically evolved over time. During the Victorian era in the 20th century, fair-skinned women with a rotund or well-rounded figure were considered ideal and desirable by men and women alike. Drawings by the famous illustrator Charles Dana Gibson became popular icons of femininity throughout the early 1900s. His *Gibson Girl* drawings featured women with neatly placed thick hair and an hourglass figure with unimaginably tiny waists. Remaining popular until the end of World War I, the *Gibson Girl* image was considered the first pin-up girl, so named because of the posters placed in male locker rooms, auto shops, and other venues across the country. With increased freedom of expression, independence, and the right to vote in the 1920s, many women dressed as *flappers*—a style characterized by short skirts, long legs, and more skin. Also popular was the bob hairstyle, often cut to the ears and curled. Such short hair on women was considered androgynous because it challenged traditional feminine hairstyles and had both masculine and feminine features. With the rise of the film industry in the 1930s, female movie stars such as Carole Lombard and Judy Garland accentuated the long and lean figure desired by most men and women of this time. During the World War II era, curves became more popular, and Bettie Page became the staple of female beauty. Named Best Pin-Up Girl in the World in 1955, Bettie often posed partially nude and with props to engage audiences. She eventually became known as the girl with the perfect figure with curvy lines and long legs.

In the 1950s, actress Marilyn Monroe further popularized the voluptuous figure and, by today's standards, is estimated to have been a size 12. With her fame and good looks, Marilyn was considered the sex symbol of the century. However, while her curvy figure and proportions were applauded and revered in the acting world, models were becoming much thinner. Twiggy, a supermodel of the 1960s, signified a stick-thin, boyish, and even underdeveloped figure and has often been blamed for promoting an unhealthy body image for women and girls. Figures like that of model Kate Moss and contestants on the popular reality television show, *America's Next Top Model*, demonstrate the ultrathin ideal of today. Recent research has shown most fashion models are thinner than 98 percent of women in the United States.

Ultrathin Ideal, Body Image Concerns, and Disordered Eating

Both research and the popular press suggest the ideal image of the female body has continued to become thinner over time. Individuals in Western cultures tend to idolize thin female bodies, putting unrealistic pressures on women and girls in relation to weight, shape, and body size. Exposure to the ultrathin ideal could have major physical and psychological health implications for women and girls attempting to achieve this figure. Interestingly, some experts suggest the sociocultural demands to achieve and maintain an increasingly thinner female physique are at odds with what is physiologically possible. In other words, most females cannot become as thin as what their culture dictates.

Unfortunately, evidence suggests both males and females idolize this unrealistic ideal from childhood through adulthood. Primary school children as young as four years of age perceived thinner female bodies as more attractive than those perceived to be the norm. Moreover, female children between the ages of five and eight tended to show lower body esteem and greater desire for thinness following exposure to Barbie, the doll that has played a major role in defining the ideal female physique. These perceptions appear to persist well into the adult years and may affect women across race and ethnicity in the United States. For some people, early exposure and pressure to achieve the thin ideal can lead to long-term body dissatisfaction, the adoption of unhealthy weight management techniques, or serious clinical eating disorders.

Through an extensive examination of bulimia nervosa, researchers have proposed that families, peers, and the media are the three major sociocultural influences affecting women and girls today and contend that females become driven to achieve the thin ideal either through social reinforcement and a perceived pressure to be thin (e.g., by receiving disparaging comments from important others, being exposed to thin models in magazines) or modeling behavior (e.g., by observing and copying the weight management techniques of others). Women and girls exposed to these pressures are particularly vulnerable to internalization, the acceptance and application of societal values of thinness to one's personal image. Internalization of the thin ideal strongly predicts body image disturbances and disordered eating behaviors.

Femininity Ideals and Athletes

Recent studies have examined femininity ideals in the context of female athletics. Because the world of sports is predominantly masculine, female athletes have often been pressured to demonstrate their femininity to meet the sociocultural standards deemed appropriate for their sex. This is one reason media portrayals of female athletes tend to promote sex appeal and family-based ideals rather than athletic prowess. For example, famous tennis player Anna Kournikova is often portrayed in the media as a sex symbol posing in lingerie and swimsuits rather than as an elite athlete. Despite never winning a Women's Tennis Association singles tournament, she is one of the most well-known players because of the attention given to her looks off the court.

Some scholars argue female athletes are continually receiving mixed messages not only about how they should behave but also about how they are expected to look. For example, although many female athletes are proud of their athleticism and the muscles that allow them to succeed in their sport, muscles that are too big are often perceived as a negative attribute and a detriment to their femininity. Body image disturbances and disordered eating may be a concern for some female athletes attempting to meet the demands of their sport while striving to achieve societal expectations for their weight, shape, and body size.

Dana K. Voelker

See also: Body Image; Masculinity Ideals; Media; Models and Eating Disorders; Sports

Bibliography

Blowers, Lucy C., Natalie J. Loxton, Megan Grady-Flesser, Stefano Occhipinti, and Sharon Dawe. "The Relationship between Sociocultural Pressure to Be Thin and Body Dissatisfaction in Preadolescent Girls." *Eating Behaviors* 4 (2003): 229–244. https://doi.org/10.1016/S1471-0153(03)00018-7.

Brown, Felicity L., and Virginia Slaughter. "Normal Body, Beautiful Body: Discrepant Perceptions Reveal a Pervasive 'Thin Ideal' from Childhood to Adulthood." *Body Image* 8 (2011): 119–125. https://doi.org/10.1016/j.bodyim.2011.02.002.

Brownell, Kelly D. "Dieting and the Search for the Perfect Body: Where Physiology and Culture Collide." *Behavior Therapy* 22 (1991): 1–12. https://doi.org/10.1016/S0005-7894(05)80239-4.

Dittmar, Helga, Suzanne Ive, and Emma Halliwell. "Does Barbie Make Girls Want to Be Thin? The Effect of Experimental Exposure to Images of Dolls on the Body Image of 5- to 8-Year Old Girls." *Developmental Psychology* 42 (2006): 283–292. https://doi.org/10.1037/00121649.42.2.283.

Grabe, Shelly, Janet Shibley Hyde, and L. Monique Ward. "The Role of the Media in Body Image Concerns among Women: A Meta-Analysis of Experimental and Correlational Studies." *Psychological Bulletin* 134 (2008): 460–476. https://doi.org/10.1037/0033-2909.134.3.460.

Krane, Vikki. "We Can Be Athletic and Feminine, but Do We Want To? Challenging Hegemonic Femininity in Women's Sport." *Quest* 53 (2001): 115–133. http://dx.doi.org/10.1080/00336297.2001.10491733.

Krane, Vikki, Precilla Y. L. Choi, Shannon M. Baird, Christine M. Aimar, and Kerrie J. Kauer. "Living the Paradox: Female Athletes Negotiate Femininity and Muscularity." *Sex Roles* 50 (2004): 315–329. https://doi.org/10.1023/B:SERS.0000018888.48437.4f.

Murnen, Sarah K., and Linda Smolak. "Femininity, Masculinity, and Disordered Eating: A Meta-Analytic Review." *International Journal of Eating Disorders* 22 (1997): 231–242. https://doi.org/10.1002/(SICI)1098-108X(199711)22:3<231::AID-EAT2>3.0.CO;2-O.

Stice, Eric, Chris Ziemba, Joy Margolis, and Penny Flick. "The Dual Pathway Model Differentiates Bulimics, Subclinical Bulimics, and Controls: Testing the Continuity Hypothesis." *Behavior Therapy* 27 (1996): 531–549. http://dx.doi.org/10.1016/S0005-7894(96)80042-6.

Thompson, Kevin J., and Eric Stice. "Thin ideal Internalization: Mounting Evidence for a New Risk Factor for Body-Image Disturbance and Eating Pathology." *Current Directions in Psychological Science* 10 (2001): 181–183. https://doi.org/10.1111/1467-8721.00144.

FIGURAL RATING SCALES

Body image assessment has commonly included questionnaires that focus on satisfaction with one's overall shape and body parts and figural rating scales that measure body size satisfaction and discrepancies. The most widely used figural rating scale, the Figure Rating Scale (FRS), was developed by Dr. Stunkard in 1983 to examine obesity rates in 3,651 Danish adults ages 34–57. The FRS and other figural rating scales have been used extensively to measure body image with a variety of international populations and have been widely accepted as a way to assess body-size satisfaction.

Advantages of Figural Rating Scales

Figural rating scales, such as the FRS, include figures ranging from extremely thin or emaciated to extremely overweight or obese. The FRS provides nine figures for males and females represent current figure, ideal figure, and figure most attractive to the opposite sex. The participant is asked to select the actual silhouette that matches perceptions about size. Interestingly, figural rating scales vary in the number of figures from 2 to 13 silhouettes. Most commonly used scales present seven to nine figures in order from thinnest to heaviest in size.

One advantage of the figural rating scale is that because it is a visual instrument, individuals who have minimal education or reading ability can easily and quickly complete the assessment. In fact, the FRS has been used to measure body image with individuals who have an intellectual disability. The silhouette scales show size discrepancies clearly and participants can indicate whether they want to be smaller or larger, which is a representation of a desire to change one's size. Figural rating scales can be used to measure perceptual distortions as well, with an objective researcher assessing current size for comparison with a participant's response.

Disadvantages of Figural Rating Scales

Although figure rating scales provide the benefit of being easy to understand and efficient assessment tools for body image, there have been a criticisms of these instruments. For example, some researchers have argued the change from one figure to the next does not reflect proportional changes and lacks consistent size graduations. Another drawback of the figural rating scales is that research participants and clients do not always think the silhouettes resemble their actual dimensions and sizes.

Because height is not represented in the figures, the standardized silhouettes may represent different proportions (e.g., larger top than bottom). A respondent may indicate that some of her (or his) body parts are reflected by a few of the figures. Figures may not always capture cultural differences and may appear to have a Caucasian bias. In recent years, various researchers have attempted to develop silhouette scales to reflect different body types to include a muscularity scale (i.e., muscularity rating scale).

Justine J. Reel

See also: Assessment; Body Image; Body Image Globally; Intellectual Disabilities and Body Image

Bibliography

Ambrosi-Randic, Neala, Alessandra Pokrajac-Bulian, and Vladimir Taksic. "Nine, Seven, Five or Three: How Many Figures Do We Need for Assessing Body Image?" *Perceptual and Motor Skills* 100 (2005): 488–492. https://doi.org/10.2466/pms.100.2.488-492.

Furnham, Adrian, Penny Titman, and Eleanor Sleeman. "Perception of Female Body Shapes as a Form of Exercise." *Journal of Social Behavior and Personality* 9 (1994): 335–352.

Reel, Justine J., Sonya SooHoo, Julia Franklin Summerhays, and Diane L. Gill. "Age before Beauty: An Exploration of Body Image in African American and Caucasian Adult Women." *Journal of Gender Studies* 17, no. 4 (2008): 321–330. http://dx.doi.org/10.1080/09589230802419963.

Stunkard, Albert J., T. Sorenson, and F. Schulsinger. "Use of Danish Adoption Register for the Study of Obesity and Thinness." In *The Genetics of Neurological and Psychiatric Disorder,* edited by S. Kety, 115–120. New York: Raven, 1983.

Swami, Viren, Rosanne Taylor, and Christine Carvalho. "Body Dissatisfaction Assessed by the Photographic Figure Rating Scale Is Associated with Sociocultural, Personality and Media Influences." *Scandinavian Journal of Psychology* 52 (2011): 57–63. https://doi.org/10.1111/j.1467-9450.2010.00836x.

Thompson, J. Kevin, Leslie J. Heinberg, Madeline Altabe, and Stacey Tantleff-Dunn. *Exacting Beauty: Theory, Assessment, and Treatment of Body Image Disturbance.* Washington, DC: American Psychological Association, 1999.

FIGURE SKATING

Ice skating was a convenient means of transportation on the frozen canals of Nordic countries in the 1400s, was popular with the social elite in England in the 1600s, and became a competitive sport in Europe and the United States in the mid-1800s. The first World Figure Skating Championship was in 1896 and was open only to male skaters; women were allowed to compete in 1906. The first United States national competition was held in 1914. Today, U.S. Figure Skating, the official governing body of figure skating in the United States, reports having more than 176,000 members.

In the early- to mid-1800s, figure skating took place outdoors and involved creating and tracing intricate figures or patterns on the ice. Thus, the typical attire was geared toward warmth. As figure skating became more athletic, skating attire became more form-fitting and body-revealing. Sonja Henie, 10-time world champion and 3-time Olympic champion in the late 1920s and early 1930s, is credited with making short, leg-revealing skirts popular among female skaters. Moreover, as the technical and athletic aspects of figure skating became more demanding, skaters faced pressure to attain and maintain a very thin, lean body shape.

Figure Skating and Eating Disorders

A number of high-level skaters including Nancy Kerrigan, 1992 Olympic bronze medalist and 1994 Olympic silver medalist, and Jamie Silverstein, 2006 Olympic ice dancer, have reported experiencing disordered eating and weight-related pressures. Former figure skater, Jenny Kirk, world junior champion and world senior competitor, retired from figure skating in 2005 because of an eating disorder. Prior to the 2010 Winter Olympics, Kirk spoke about her experiences battling an eating disorder and discussed what she saw as pervasive eating and weight pressures in the world of figure skating.

Eating disorders and pathogenic eating behaviors and attitudes among figure skaters are problematic. Although specific clinical prevalence rates among skaters are unknown, previous research has documented elevated levels of psychological factors associated with eating disorders including drive for thinness and body and weight dissatisfaction. In a study of adolescent female figure skaters, Monsma and Malina found that 38 percent had elevated drive for thinness, 54 percent had elevated body dissatisfaction, and 8 percent of skaters had elevated scores on both risk factors. In a separate study, 30 percent of elite female figure skaters desired a thinner physique. Similarly, Ziegler and colleagues found 72 percent of female and 39 percent of male competitive skaters wanted to lose weight and 65 percent of female and 26 percent of male skaters had purposefully dieted to lose weight.

A number of factors contribute to an environment in which unhealthy eating behaviors and attitudes are present, including the physical demands of skating, the evaluative nature of figure skating, and weight-related pressures of figure skating.

Physical Demands of Figure Skating

Like athletes in many sports, figure skaters are motivated to perform at a high level, to be competitive, and to be successful in their sport. Having a thin, lean body is considered to offer a performance edge for skaters. Across the four primary disciplines in figure skating (i.e., singles, pairs, ice dance, and synchronized skating), skaters' bodies are required to perform a variety of complex physical stunts such as multiple rotation jumps, fast spins, and intricate footwork sequences with fast changes of direction. Moreover, in pairs skating, there is even greater pressure for female skaters who are lifted and thrown by male partners. In a study of female pairs and ice dance skaters, 92.7 percent reported pressure to maintain a low body weight. Synchronized skaters may face unique weight-related pressures as they are expected to present a uniform appearance with their teammates, which may heighten social comparison. In a study of collegiate synchronized skaters, 48.8 percent indicated they sensed pressure to maintain a low body weight.

Because skaters with thin, lean bodies are considered to have a performance advantage, some figure skaters engage in unhealthy behaviors such as caloric restriction, purging, and excessive exercise to attain or maintain a body they believe will allow them to perform at a higher level. For example, in a study of elite skaters, researchers estimated males consumed only 75 percent and females only 59.1 percent of the calories needed given their level of training. Another study found 9 percent of male and 26 percent of female skaters used excessive exercise to manage their weight. It is important to note that although there may be an initial performance improvement for figure skaters who have lost weight or maintain a lean, thin physique, there are serious health risks associated with low body weight and inadequate nutritional intake, such as fatigue, amenor-rhea, and increased risk of stress fractures.

Figure Skating as a Judged, Aesthetic Sport

In addition to the physical demands of figure skating that contribute to unhealthy eating attitudes and behaviors, the evaluative nature of the sport may also be associated with eating disorders. Figure skating is a judged, aesthetic sport. That is, performance is evaluated by a panel of expert judges who rate a skater's actual technical performance and physical appearance. Skaters are socialized to understand that appearance will be evaluated and they will be rewarded for having an attractive physical appearance, long lines (e.g., lean bodies), and graceful movements. In fact, in the International Judging System (IJS) used in competition, judges evaluate posture, style, and even personality. Thus, it is not surprising that in a sport like figure skating, with subjective evaluation, the skaters would be concerned about, and possibly engage in, pathogenic behaviors to maintain a low body weight to have an ideal figure skating physique. One study found 44 percent of male and 77 percent of female skaters were terrified of weight gain.

Sources of Weight Pressures in Figure Skating

Skaters may experience weight-related pressures from a number of sources, including significant others and form-fitting costumes. Skaters have reported that comments from judges, coaches, parents, and peers negatively influence how they think about their bodies. Some coaches have weigh-ins and require skaters to turn in food diaries; skaters struggling with body weight and bodies may respond by taking unhealthy actions to achieve a desired weight to gain approval from their coach. Parents may unknowingly reinforce pathogenic weight control behaviors by rewarding and praising improved performance associated with weight loss. Skaters, like other athletes, are likely to engage in social comparison, evaluating their bodies in relationship to other skaters, which may lead to body dissatisfaction. Form-fitting costumes typically worn in figure skating are another potential source of pressure for skaters. Wearing physique-revealing costumes may increase skaters' awareness of and concerns about their bodies and physical appearance and lead to body dissatisfaction. Because body dissatisfaction is a known precursor to disordered eating, it is important to recognize factors that contribute to skaters being unhappy with their bodies.

Christy Greenleaf

See also: Aesthetic Sports; Coaches; Sports; Weight Pressures in Sport

Bibliography

Coker, Lesleyann. "Jenny Kirk on Figure Skating's Eating Disorder Epidemic (Part I)." Huffingtonpost.com. Last modified May 25, 2011. Accessed November 21, 2017. http://www.huffingtonpost.com/lesleyann-coker/jenny-kirk-on-figure-skat_b_430032.html.

Coker, Lesleyann. "Jenny Kirk on Figure Skating's Eating Disorder Epidemic (Part II)." Huffingtonpost.com. Last modified May 25, 2011. Accessed November 21, 2017. http://www.huffingtonpost.com/lesleyann-coker/jenny-kirk-on-figure-skat_b_431698.html.

Greenleaf, Christy. "Weight Pressures and Social Physique Anxiety among Collegiate Synchronized Skaters." *Journal of Sport Behavior* 27 (2004): 260–276.

Jonnalagadda, Jatya S., Paula J. Ziegler, and Judy A. Nelson. "Food Preferences, Dieting Behaviors, and Body Image Perceptions of Elite Figure Skaters." *International Journal of Sport Nutrition and Exercise Metabolism* 14 (2004): 594–606.

Monsma, Eva V., and Robert M. Malina. "Anthropometry and Somatotype of Competitive Female Figure Skaters 11–22 Years: Variation by Competitive Level and Discipline." *Journal of Sports Medicine and Physical Fitness* 45 (2005): 491–500.

Monsma, Eva V., and Robert M. Malina. "Correlates of Eating Disorder Risk among Female Figure Skaters: A Profile of Adolescent Competitors." *Psychology of Sport & Exercise* 5 (2004): 447–460. http://dx.doi.org/10.1016/S1469-0292(03)00038-4.

Taylor, Gail M., and Diane M. Ste-Marie. "Eating Disorder Symptoms in Canadian Female Pair and Dance Figure Skaters." *International Journal of Sport Psychology* 32 (2001): 21–28.

U.S. Figure Skating. "Nutrition." Accessed November 20, 2016. http://www.usfigureskating.org/.

Ziegler, Paula J., Srimathi Kannan, Satya S. Jonnalagadda, Ambika Krishnakumar, Sara E. Taksali, and Judith A. Nelson. "Dietary Intake, Body Image Perceptions, and Weight Concerns of Female U.S. International Synchronized Figure Skating." *International Journal of Sport Nutrition and Exercise Metabolism* 15 (2005): 550–566.

Ziegler, Paula J., Chor San Khoo, Bonnie Sherr, Judith A. Nelson, Wendy M. Larson, and Adam Drewnowski. "Body Image and Dieting Behaviors among Elite Figure Skaters." *International Journal of Eating Disorders* 24 (1998): 421–427.

FIJI STUDY

The well-known Fiji study refers to an ethnographic study conducted over a decade (1988–1998) by Anne Becker, an anthropologist, of the Nahigatoka Village. Becker sought to better understand the interrelationships between cultural identity, body shape, the influence of media, and eating disorders within Fijian society. Becker's study is significant and frequently cited because it was one of the few opportunities to study a culture before and after Western media were introduced, while looking at a variety of factors. It is noteworthy that societal members who were largely unaware of body shape and expressed neutral thought about body image seemed to develop negative attitudes toward their bodies and the desire to lose weight after the introduction of Western media, which has been associated with ultrathin models and a strong emphasis on appearance. Furthermore, in a society devoid of eating disorders, dieting behavior has become increasingly more common with the influence of television and evidence of binge eating disorder is present in Fijian women.

Body Image and Fiji

Fiji provided an ideal study site to investigate body image because television was not introduced there until 1995, and, moreover, in Fijian culture, robust and larger body types were considered aesthetically pleasing. Traditional Fiji culture has been associated with feasts, and food was symbolic of social connectivity. The consumption of calorically dense foods with the encouragement to eat heartily has been evident (e.g., *"kana, mo urouro"* meaning eat, so you will become fat) at meals.

Fiji being a media-naive culture, Fijian females of all ages reported little desire to change their body shape. However, between 1995 and 1998, Dr. Becker found 83 percent of Fijian school girls thought television had influenced attitudes toward body shape and weight. These young females reported wanting to look like television characters and 40 percent thought that they would improve career prospects or become more useful at home if they lost weight or ate less. In addition, 30 percent of interviewees indicated television characters were powerful role models concerning work or career. The Fijian teenage females indicated that an intergeneration gap about body ideals was developing with the introduction of television. For example, 31 percent of teenagers responded that their parents encouraged higher food consumption than they thought was necessary.

Even among adult participants, body image–related responses varied between 1989 and 1998. Fijian adults in 1998 reported that body shape can be changed. They also showed decreased body satisfaction and demonstrated higher social comparison with others and the desire to trade one's body for another. This body dissatisfaction or motivation to change one's body shape is often predictive of dieting, disordered eating, and eating disorders.

Eating Disorders and Fiji

There was no illness category in Fiji that corresponded to the eating disorders in the *DSM* for mental health diagnoses. In fact, prior to the 1990s, anorexia nervosa and bulimia nervosa were thought to be nonexistent in ethnic Fijians. Conversely, Fijians have been more worried about *macake* (i.e., a cultural syndrome associated with appetite loss) and being too thin. Therefore, Westernized values of dieting and exercising for weight loss were not adopted by Fijian culture until the 1990s. When studying Fijian teenagers and adults in 1998, it was apparent that dieting behaviors had emerged since the introduction of television.

Binge Eating Disorder

When examining the presence of eating disorder symptoms, 10 percent of female participants reported symptoms consistent with binge eating and all these individuals reported that binge episodes caused distress. Only 4 percent of the sample met the full criteria for binge eating disorder (e.g., frequency requirements for binge episodes), which is consistent for a variety of Western populations. None of the participants reported purging behaviors associated with bulimia nervosa. One of the participants admitted to fasting behavior where she neglected to eat anything for 24 hours. However, bulimia and anorexia rates for Fijian women overall appeared lower than for the other samples.

Obesity and Fiji

Although a more robust figure has been traditionally viewed as most aesthetically pleasing, obesity rates have been on the rise. In 1989, 60 percent of Fijian subjects were overweight or obese (i.e., body mass index greater than or equal to 25) compared to 84 percent in 1998. In addition, the percentage of Fijian individuals with a body mass index higher than 30 increased from 30 percent in 1989 to 44 percent in 1998.

The Fiji study is an example of a culture affected by the media and the values associated with Western television. In a society that did not have a definition for eating disorders or body image, Fijian participants in 1998 showed significant increases in body dissatisfaction, desire to lose weight and change one's shape, dieting, and disordered eating behaviors. Likewise, overweight and obesity rates have risen between 1989 and 1998. When considering the powerful effect of the media, it is important to examine the health implications associated with these attitudes and behavioral shifts in Fiji.

Justine J. Reel

See also: Body Image; Body Image Globally; Media; Obesity

Bibliography

Becker, Anne E. *Body, Self, and Society.* Philadelphia: University of Pennsylvania, 1995.

Becker, Anne E. "Television, Disordered Eating, and Young Women in Fiji: Negotiating Body Image and Identity during Rapid Social Change." *Culture, Medicine and Psychiatry* 28 (2004): 2533–2559. https://doi.org/10.1007/s11013-004-1067-5.

Becker, Anne E., Rebecca A. Burwell, David B. Herzog, Paul Hamburg, and Stephanie E. Gilman. "Eating Behaviors and Attitudes Following Prolonged Exposure to Television among Ethnic Fijian Adolescent Girls." *The British Journal of Psychiatry* 180 (2002): 509–514. https://doi.org/10.1192/bjp.180.6.509.

Becker, Anne E., Rebecca A. Burwell, Kesaia Navara, and Stephen E. Gilman. "Binge Eating and Binge Eating Disorder in a Small-Scale, Indigenous Society: The View from Fiji." *International Journal of Eating Disorders* 34 (2003): 423–431. https://doi.org/10.1002/eat.10225.

Becker, Anne E., Stephen E. Gilman, and Rebecca A. Burwell. "Changes in Prevalence of Overweight and in Body Image among Fijian Women between 1989 and 1998." *Obesity Research* 13, no. 1 (2005): 110–117. https://doi.org/10.1038/oby.2005.14.

Becker, Anne E., and Paul Hamburg. "Culture, the Media, and Eating Disorders." *Harvard Review of Psychiatry* 4, no. 3 (1996): 163–167.

FLIGHT ATTENDANTS

The original flight attendants, cabin boys, or stewards in the 1920s were all men. Ellen Church, the first female flight attendant, was a 25-year-old nurse hired by United Airlines in 1930. Female flight attendants were called stewardesses or air hostesses and the job represented one of the few positions in the industry available to women in the 1930s. In 1935, 2,000 women applied to the Transcontinental and Western Airlines for roughly 35 spots. This represented the competitiveness for a flight attendant's job. In 1936, flight attendant requirements were described as petite, low weight (between 100 to 118 pounds), single, and 20–26 years old. Flight attendants were subjected to firing if they got married, exceeded formal weight requirements during weight-checks set by the airlines, or turned 32 or

35 years old (depending on the airline). This age restriction was eliminated in the 1970s and flight attendants were allowed to be married in the 1980s; however, the weight restrictions have persisted for flight attendants (but not pilots). In fact, in 1993, United Airlines reinstated weight requirements rationalizing that the measure would reduce costs for the company.

Body Image and Flight Attendants

Once airlines began hiring females for flight attendant positions, women's bodies became scrutinized for recruitment and retention of the cabin crew. Females hired by the airline industry were required to complete beauty and etiquette training and were expected to smile at all times and retain composure under pressure. Flight attendants have been a metaphor for femininity and their bodies have been monitored formally and informally since their employment in the 1930s. Although there has been documented evidence of weight limits, weigh-ins, and firing based on weight, it appears that flight attendants also engage in self-monitoring to further the tendency for body dissatisfaction, body checking, and attempts to change undesirable aspects of one's body or appearance. Female flight attendants have acknowledged that their bodies are under constant surveillance and scrutinized by the airlines, other crew members, and passengers. Female flight attendants have described the maintenance required to meet the aesthetic demands of the job including working out, expensive hair and nail treatments, makeup, and teeth straightening and whitening.

Beauty demands have historically been part of the recruitment and hiring process for female flight attendants. Applicants have been rejected for being too old, having blemished skin, short hair, messy hair, short or bitten nails, or poor posture; they have even been rejected for being out-of-proportion or otherwise unattractive with regard to a bodily feature. Interviews with flight attendants have revealed that female uniforms would be labeled a size larger to motivate flight attendants to be conscious of their weight and to create body concerns. Although many of the formal weight requirements disappeared in the 1990s for U.S. airlines, sociologists agree flight attendants continue to engage in aesthetic competitions where they compare themselves to one another and reap rewards for being the most slender, feminine, or beautiful.

Disordered Eating and Flight Attendants

It has been widely rumored for several decades that flight attendants have engaged in disordered eating, including restricting before weight-checks and flights, binge eating after flights, and purging behaviors. Their disordered eating behavior has been associated with airline weight requirements. A 1980s study of 466 flight attendants found that 26 percent weighed five or more pounds over the airline's limit for height and age. Forty-eight percent of these flight attendants reported purging by using self-induced vomiting and other methods. Over half of these individuals (62 percent) admitted that they began purging after they started working for an airline.

Current Events

In June 2010, 6,000 male and female flight attendants of Thai Airways International were subjected to body mass index (BMI) and waist circumference standards. Female flight attendants were expected to have a BMI of no more than 25 and a maximum waist measurement of 32 inches. Meanwhile, male flight attendants were restricted to a BMI of 27.5 or lower and a maximum 35-inch waist. The flight attendants were notified of the policy and given six months to comply with the standards. The flight attendants who did not meet the standards were told they could only fly on domestic flights, same day service. They were also expected to become ground crew within a year if they failed to meet the weight and waist requirements.

Justine J. Reel

See also: Body Checking; Body Image; Body Mass Index; Disordered Eating

Bibliography

Dar, Reuven, Nurit Rosen-Korakin, Oren Shapira, Yair Gottlieb, and Hanan Frenk. "The Craving to Smoke in Flight Attendants: Relations with Smoking Deprivation, Anticipation of Smoking and Actual Smoking." *Journal of Abnormal Psychology* 119, no. 1 (2010): 248–253. http://dx.doi.org/10.1037/a0017778.

Delaney, Justin. "Flight Attendant Weight Restriction Causes Uproar." *Gadling.* Last modified March 2, 2011. Accessed November 21, 2017. http://gadling.com/2011/03/02/flight-attendant-weight-restriction-causes-uproar/.

Graham, Frederick. "Winged Hostess: The Girl on the Plane May Also Be a Heroine." *New York Times*, January 7, 1940.

Hochschild, Arlie R. *The Managed Heart, 20th Anniversary Edition.* London: University of California Press, 2003.

Litvin, Michelle. "Flight Attendants' Weight Limit Brings on Turbulence." *Chicago Tribune.* Last modified May 2, 1993. Accessed November 21, 2017. http://articles.chicagotribune.com/1993-05-02/features/9305020252_1_flight-attendants-delta-air-lines-flight-united-flight.

Porter, Nicole B. "Sex Plus Age Discrimination: Protecting Older Women Workers." *Denver University Law Review* 81, no. 1 (2003): 79–112.

Tyler, Melissa, and Pamela Abbott. "Chocs Away: Weight Watching in the Contemporary Airline Industry." *Sociology* 32 (1998): 433–450.

FOOD ADDICTION

Eating disorders have been referred to as an addiction similar to substance use. In this case, the object of desire or euphoria is food or a particular type of food. Some people blamed being overweight or obese on an addiction to food or sugar. The cravings associated with food mirror those found for drug addiction. Consider the definition of "food craving" as an intense desire for a specific type of food that occurs without warning and needs to be satiated. These strong cravings can be tied to one's emotions or certain environmental triggers. For example, certain family dynamics may contribute to the presence of emotions around food and cravings.

When these patterns present themselves, the triggers reactivate the cravings. Interestingly, there seems to be a sex difference in the prevalence of food cravings with females having more food cravings than males.

Whether food addiction is backed by scientific evidence is controversial. Many people argue these addictions to food are real and are correlated with a tendency for overeating behaviors. But is the origin of a craving psychological or biological? Being depressed or experiencing strong emotions like sadness or madness can trigger a desire for certain kinds of food that tend to be sweet, salty, or fattening such as potato chips, cookies, or candy. Typically, food cravings are triggered by changes in mood and are thought to be psychological in nature. However, there are some valid biological explanations for sugar cravings linked to carbohydrate consumption.

Looking at this psychological versus biological debate for sugar addiction parallels the study of drug abuse as an addiction. A powerful example is chocolate, the most popularly reported food craving in Western society. The extreme popularity of chocolate is logical given its rich texture, a result of being dense in carbohydrates. People report having an almost euphoric feeling or high associated with eating chocolate. The argument for addictive qualities can be explained by the cocoa content of chocolate, which has been linked to mood-enhancing neurotransmitters within the brain.

Food Addiction and Eating Disorders

Food addiction is not currently included in the latest version of the *Diagnostic and Statistical Manual of Mental Disorders*. Although the idea of food addiction or classifying eating disorders as another addiction has been controversial in the scientific community and among practitioners, there are several advantages to this perspective. First, by providing some sense of legitimacy, more treatment and prevention options can be developed and implemented. Second, there may be some utility for evidence-based practices to address other addictions to people with eating disorders. If the underlying feelings of compulsion are seen as a common denominator, having strategies to address cravings in the immediate moment are critical as part of treatment. Food as an addiction presents a special challenge as the desire for the object cannot be extinguished as eating is a requirement of life. Finally, if treatment providers recognize eating disorders and food addiction as a real phenomenon, clients who express cravings will be validated during therapy sessions. To date, many clinicians will spend valuable time in session arguing that sugar and food addictions are a myth, which can be counterproductive.

Eating disorder and obesity prevention efforts should focus on decreasing the power of food and coping with cravings. Some support groups exist to provide some comfort to individuals who believe they are addicted to food or sugar. Food Addicts Anonymous offers face-to-face and virtual support groups that involve working the twelve steps. This organization supports people who struggle with what is believed to be a biochemical addiction to food.

Justine J. Reel

See also: Binge Eating Disorder; Obesity

Bibliography

Foddy, Bennett. "Addicted to Food, Hungry for Drugs." *Neuroethics* 4 (2011): 79–89 https://doi.org/10.1007/s12152-010-9069-1.

"Food Addicts Anonymous." FAA. Accessed November 20, 2016. http://www.foodaddicts anonymous.org/What-Is-FAA.

Gearhardt, Ashley N., Marney A. White, Robin M. Masheb, and Carolos M. Grilo. "An Examination of Food Addiction in a Racially Diverse Sample of Obese Patients with Binge Eating Disorder in Primary Care Settings." *Comprehensive Psychiatry* 54 (2013): 500–505. https://doi.org/10.1016/j.comppsych.2012.12.009.

Mason, Susan M., Alan J. Flint, Alison E. Field, S. Bryn Austin, and Janet W. Rich-Edwards. "Abuse Victimization in Childhood or Adolescence and Risk of Food Addiction in Adult Women." *Obesity* 21 (2013): E775–E781. https://doi.org/10.1002/oby.20500.

Steenhuis, Ingrid. "Guilty or Not? Feelings of Guilt about Food among College Women." *Appetite* 52 (2009): 531–534. https://doi.org/10.1016/j.appet.2008.12.004.

Tryon, Matthew S., Cameron S. Carter, Rashel R. DeCant, and Kevin D. Laugero. "Chronic Stress Exposure May Affect the Brain's Response to High Calorie Food Cues and Predispose to Obesogenic Eating Habits." *Physiology and Behavior* 120 (2013): 233–242. https://doi.org/10.1016/j.physbeh.2013.08.010.

Vilija, Maulinauskiene, and Malinauskas Romualdas. "Unhealthy Food in Relation to Post-traumatic Stress Symptoms among Adolescents." *Appetite* 74 (2014): 86–91. https://doi.org/10.1016/j.appet.2013.12.002.

Wagner, Heather S., Britt Ahlstrom, Joseph P. Redden, Zata Vickers, and Traci Mann. "The Myth of Comfort Food." *Health Psychology* 33, no. 12 (2014): 1552–1557. https://doi.org/10.1037/hea0000068.

Wallis, D. J., and M. M. Hetherington. "Emotions and Eating. Self-Reported and Experimentally Induced Changes in Food Intake under Stress." *Appetite* 52 (2009): 355–362. https://doi.org/10.1016/j.appet.2008.11.007.

FOOD ALLERGIES

Approximately 3 million children were identified as having food allergies in the United States in 2007. Food allergies are a negative response to a particular food that involves the body's immune system. In contrast to food intolerance, such as lactose intolerance, to be considered an allergy, the immune system needs to be part of the reaction. Examples of foods that may produce an allergic reaction include, but are not limited to, mango and other fruits, peanuts and other types of nuts, chocolate, and seafood. Interestingly, eight foods represent the lion's share (90 percent) of all food allergy cases. These foods are peanuts, soy, milk, eggs, fish, shellfish, wheat, and nuts that grow on trees (e.g., walnuts).

In general, food allergies are relatively rare and need to involve the immune system to receive a diagnosis. The trend has been toward increased awareness and diagnoses of food allergies in children. Responses to particular foods can be mild or deadly. Unfortunately, the best approach is to eliminate the noxious food from one's diet. A point of confusion is that food intolerance and food poisoning are often mistaken for food allergies because they may have similar symptoms. It is important for individuals with eating disorders to have medical documentation associated with self-identified food allergies so food avoidance problems are not reinforced.

Identification of Food Allergies

Common responses to consuming a particular food include sneezing, difficulty breathing, breaking out in hives, or feeling nauseous. Generally, only 4–8 percent of children are afflicted with true food allergies. The Centers for Disease Control and Prevention indicated a spike to 18 percent in children with food allergies from 1997 to 2007. There is evidence the diagnosis of a food allergy has become more common over the past 10 years for children in the United States. Many of these children, fortunately, can outgrow allergies and eat identified foods later in life. For adults, about one-third believe they have a food allergy.

Food allergies are often confused with food intolerance or food poisoning that result in an aversion to certain foods. Identifying a food allergy begins after symptoms have appeared and there is a need for a diagnosis. Questions will likely include how much of a food has been consumed, the duration of time before a reaction takes place, and how frequently the negative responses occur. A patient will likely be expected to maintain a food diary to record symptoms. Doctors may also impose an elimination diet of suspected foods to determine whether an allergy exists.

Unfortunately, drugs are not available for food allergies to lessen the response. Therefore, people with food allergies must eliminate the allergen from their diets. Moreover, people will need to read food labels carefully to ensure the food is not on an ingredient list. Food allergies can be inconvenient, but for some individuals who possess a severe allergy, consuming a particular food can produce a deadly reaction called anaphylaxis that involves difficulty breathing. To protect against this danger, a patient with severe allergies may wear a medical alert bracelet and likely carry a syringe filled with epinephrine (epi-pen) in the event of a severe allergic reaction and.

Eating Disorders and Food Allergies

As mentioned, food allergies are linked to the immune system. It is common for individuals with eating disorders to claim they have a food allergy to avoid the consumption of certain foods. However, eating disorder treatment centers require medical documentation of a suspicious food before removing it from a client's meal plan. It is important that people being treated for eating disorders address fear foods and that perceived food allergies be explored in more depth by medical professionals.

Justine J. Reel and Robert A. Bucciere

See also: Food Phobia; Orthorexia Nervosa; Picky Eating

Bibliography

American Psychiatric Association. *Diagnostic and Statistical Manual of Mental Disorders*, 5th ed. (*DSM-5*). Washington, DC: American Psychiatric Association Publishing, 2013.

Centers for Disease Control and Prevention. "Food Allergy among U.S. Children: Trends in Prevalence and Hospitalizations." CDC.gov. Accessed September 9, 2016. http://www.cdc.gov/nchs/products/databriefs/db10.htm.

Golden, Robert N., Fred L. Peterson, Gerri F. Kramer, William Kane, and Mark J. Kittleson. *The Truth about Eating Disorders*, 2nd ed. New York: Facts on File, 2009.

FOOD DESERT

Recent research has highlighted the importance of a person's immediate environment as it relates to food access for determining health outcomes. The term *food desert* is used to describe a neighborhood where availability of food—both in terms of quantity and quality—is limited. The U.S. Department of Agriculture defines a food desert as a census tract where 20 percent or more of residents live in poverty, the median household income is 80 percent or below that of surrounding areas, and at least one-third of residents in the tract live over a mile from the nearest supermarket. Recent estimates from the USDA report that over 23 million Americans live in these types of neighborhoods. Understanding food deserts is complicated due to the potential for a number of confounding factors, including disability status of residents, access and affordability of public transit, and alternative grocer programs such as Meals on Wheels.

Impact on Health Outcomes

Food deserts have been associated with negative health outcomes. Many researchers have noted that the a majority of food outlets in these neighborhoods are fast-food chains and convenience stores. Common food items found in these outlets tend to be high in fat, sugar, and sodium. Unsurprisingly, individuals who reside in these neighborhoods are more at risk for diseases and health complications associated with a poor diet, including diabetes, heart disease, and obesity.

Food deserts have also been shown to effect social functioning. A growing body of research supports the claim that substandard nutritional quality in early life is correlated with stunted cognitive development and poorer social skills in adulthood. One study found that low family income, lack of access to healthy foods, and lack of access to a vehicle (variables that characterize food deserts) all significantly predicted academic achievement in fourth graders. In other words, higher percentages of children living in food deserts predicted lower academic achievement scores, even after controlling for other predictive factors.

Research has also found that the food items available to persons living in food deserts may be less safe for consumption than food items in affluent areas. A recent study found that ready-to-eat produce, milk, and sandwiches served in supermarkets and food stores serving poorer neighborhoods had higher microbial counts than identical items in wealthier communities. Higher microbial counts indicate poorer sanitation of the food and may be a result of the supplier using unapproved transportation and storage methods. All these factors put consumers at elevated risk for foodborne illnesses such as *Yersinia*, *Listeria*, *E. coli*, and *Salmonella*.

What Causes Food Deserts?

Understanding the factors behind food deserts may by useful to identify at-risk areas, designing policies to counteract this phenomenon and guide subsequent urban planning to prevent the these types of neighborhoods from developing. Theories regarding what specifically causes a food desert to occur range in scope and discipline, with fields such as public health, marketing, and psychology all contributing explanations for this phenomenon.

Some credible theories have been conceptualized by anthropologists and sociologists. These theories focus on historical movements regarding inner-city demographics and economic factors. One theory cites competition from large chain supermarkets that are common on the outskirts of major metropolitan areas as the primary cause for smaller, independent, mom-and-pop grocers going out of business. The closure of these neighborhood grocers, which primarily served inner city communities in the earlier half of the 20th century, left large areas without access to affordable, varied food unless public or private transportation were available. Another theory claims when affluent households moved out of metropolitan areas into suburbs during the 1970s and 1980s, the economic disparity between inner-city and suburban areas increased. This shift caused a decline in the median income of inner cities, and thus resulted in the closure of almost half of all supermarkets in some of the most populous U.S. cities.

In addition to historical factors, food deserts are reinforced by a variety of economic and social factors. First, it is much easier and cheaper to purchase large tracts of land to accommodate bigger stores and parking lots in suburban areas than it is in inner-city neighborhoods. Additionally, zoning laws are typically less complicated and more business-friendly in these outskirt neighborhoods. Crime is also an important factor. In 2008, inner-city neighborhoods of the 100 largest U.S. cities reported an average of 2,129 incidents of violent crime and 4,477 incidents of property crime per 10,000 residents. Suburban neighborhoods in the same cities reported significantly lower crime rates of 1,062 and 2,616 incidents of violent and property crime, respectively. Developers for supermarket and grocery chains prefer to build in areas of lower crime to attract customers and save in costs associated with shoplifting and vandalism.

Problems with Studying Food Deserts

Studying food deserts is difficult for a number of reasons. Generally, researchers have struggled with controlling for a number of factors that complicate availability, which is central to the food desert definition. These factors include disability status of residents, access and affordability of public transportation, safety of the area for walking and/or bicycling, and the presence of nontraditional grocers and programs in the area. Clearly, each of these variables would vastly change the habits of residents regarding shopping and could either help or hinder accessibility to fresh and varied food options.

Food deserts also look different in urban versus rural communities. For example, inner-city neighborhoods tend to have food options, just typically not healthy ones that boast a selection of fresh produce or low-fat foods. Inner-city food deserts usually have fast-food restaurants and convenience stores. Rural food deserts, on the other hand, often have drastically fewer options altogether and have received far less attention in the research literature. To differentiate between rural and urban areas where healthy food availability is constrained, the term *food swamp* has been proposed to define inner-city neighborhoods where the quality of available food is lacking (as opposed to rural food deserts, where the quantity of available food is the limiting factor). Accounting for other differences in these two settings is also important. For example, an individual living in an urban neighborhood with a 45-minute commute to the nearest grocery store may end up paying significantly more in tolls, public transportation costs, and parking than someone in a rural area with a 45-minute commute. Further, individuals living in rural areas may have access to more locally sourced food options, such as homegrown produce and farm stands that are not captured in research on food deserts.

Another problem studying food deserts lies in understanding the complicated relationship between accessibility to quality resources and racial/ethnic demographics in a community. Research on food deserts has shown that ethnic minorities are more likely to live in these urban food desert neighborhoods. Along with this pattern comes a myriad of other factors that have negative effects on community health and may skew the outcomes associated with living in food deserts. For example, poor education regarding health behaviors and limited availability of affordable, quality health care have been associated with minority status in the United States. These factors may co-occurr with food desert factors and exacerbate the difficulties observed.

Hannah J. Hopkins

See also: Food Security

Bibliography

Adams, Anthony T., Monika J. Ulrich, and Amanda Coleman. "Food Deserts." *Journal of Applied Social Science* 4, no. 2 (2010): 58–62. https://doi.org/10.1177/19367 2441000400206.

Cerovečki, Irena Guszak, and Marko Grünhagen. "'Food Deserts' in Urban Districts Evidence from a Transitional Market and Implications for Macromarketing." *Journal of Macromarketing* 36, no. 3 (2016): 337–353. https://doi.org/10.1177/0276146 715612550.

Dubowitz, Tamara, Shannon N. Zenk, Bonnie Ghosh-Dastidar, Deborah A. Cohen, Robin Beckman, Gerald Hunter, Elizabeth D. Steiner, and Rebecca L. Collins. "Healthy Food Access for Urban Food Desert Residents: Examination of the Food Environment, Food Purchasing Practices, Diet and BMI." *Public Health Nutrition* 18, no. 12 (2015): 2220–2230. http://dx.doi.org/10.1017/S1368980014002742.

Frndak, Seth E. "An Ecological Study of Food Desert Prevalence and 4th Grade Academic Achievement in New York State School Districts." *Journal of Public Health Research* 3, no. 3 (2014): 319. https://doi.org/10.4081/jphr.2014.319.

Giang, Tracey, Allison Karpyn, Hannah Burton Laurison, Amy Hillier, and R. Duane Perry. "Closing the Grocery Gap in Underserved Communities: The Creation of the Pennsylvania Fresh Food Financing Initiative." *Journal of Public Health Management Practice* 14, no. 3 (2008): 272–279. https://doi.org/10.1097/01.PHH.0000316486.57512.bf.

Kneebone, Elizabeth, and Steven Raphael. "City and Suburban Crime Trends in Metropolitan America." Brookings. Last modified May 26, 2011. Accessed November 21, 2017. https://www.brookings.edu/research/city-and-suburban-crime-trends-in-metropolitan-america/.

Quinlan, Jennifer J. "Foodborne Illness Incidence Rates and Food Safety Risks for Populations of Low Socioeconomic Status and Minority Race/Ethnicity: A Review of the Literature." *International Journal of Environmental Research and Public Health* 10, no. 8 (2013): 3634–3652. https://doi.org/10.3390/ijerph10083634.

Reel, Justine J., and Brittany K. Badger. "From Food Deserts to Food Swamps: Health Education Strategies to Improve Food Environments in Urban Areas." *Journal of Obesity & Weight Loss Therapy* s4, no. 002 (2014): 1–2. https://doi.org/10.4172/2165-7904 .S4-002.

Walker, Renee E., Christopher R. Keane, and Jessica G. Burke. "Disparities and Access to Healthy Food in the United States: A Review of Food Deserts Literature." *Health & Place* 16, no. 5 (2010): 876–884. https://doi.org/10.1016/j.healthplace.2010.04.013.

FOOD PHOBIA

A person may have a food phobia when there are direct fears about eating food or certain textures of food. Although sometimes mistaken for picky eating or an eating disorder, like anorexia nervosa, the technical term for food phobia, *functional dysphagia*, is defined as a fear of swallowing foods. It is important to note that a phobia or aversion to food must be distinguished from an eating disorder like anorexia nervosa or bulimia nervosa. The avoidance of certain foods in this case does not relate to keeping caloric content low or fearing one will gain weight if an item is consumed. In fact, there is no presence of body image concerns or dissatisfaction for functional dysphagia. The food phobia should not be linked to any other medical condition that could explain low food intake or aversion to eating. Interestingly, this condition affects both males and females. Food phobia is common in younger children, but can also occur in adults. Individuals who exhibit severe and prolonged aversion to foods can be diagnosed with avoidant/restrictive food intake disorder (ARFID) as outlined in the *Diagnostic and Statistical Manual of Mental Disorders*, fifth edition.

For functional dysphagia, particularly, foods that are solid and lumpy in texture may be perceived as choking hazards. Typically, functional dysphagia results from a trauma that directly triggers a change in eating behavior. For example, someone who suffers from a food phobia may have witnessed someone choke on a particular food item such as a piece of meat, crab shell, or bone. Alternatively, a person may develop a food phobia if he or she has difficulty swallowing a particular food object. The belief that one can choke or die leads to an exaggerated phobia around eating regular meals. This complete refusal to eat (or even drink) can be related to another mental health disorder such as obsessive-compulsive disorder (OCD).

The resulting behavior related to having functional dysphagia is extreme anxiety around meals and a severely reduced diet. To avoid having to swallow foods, a person with functional dysphagia may choose to only eat blended foods like mashed potatoes and smoothies. Additionally, fruits, meats, and vegetables that require chewing might be avoided entirely. Problems associated with this highly restricted diet are not getting adequate nutritional content and caloric intake that may result in unhealthy weight loss. For children, they may be severely underweight for their age and height. Moreover, children may be teased for not eating like their peers. Meals can become a traumatic event for fear of choking or being bullied. It is important both children and adults seek treatment for their food phobia.

Treatment for Food Phobia

Treatment for food phobia needs to occur on a number of levels. Seeing a mental health professional will help an individual work through the traumatic events that contributed to a phobia around food and swallowing. An individual will also need to learn anxiety reduction techniques practiced around meals. There will be a need to gradually introduce a wider range of foods and expose the client to "scary" foods through a therapeutic approach called "cognitive desensitization therapy," to gradually reduce one's phobia of specific foods. The treatment team and family will need to provide support and reinforcement to achieve small goals that lead to a more well-rounded diet. Patience will be needed as a client is expected to be highly resistant to treatment and trying feared foods.

Justine J. Reel

See also: Avoidant/Restrictive Food Intake Disorder; Dietary Restraint; Exposure Therapy; Obsessive-Compulsive Disorder; Picky Eating; Selective Eating Disorder

Bibliography

American Psychiatric Association. *Diagnostic and Statistical Manual of Mental Disorders*, 5th ed. (*DSM-5*). Washington, DC: American Psychiatric Association Publishing, 2013.

Cardona Cano, Sebastian, Henning Tiemeier, Daphne Van Hoeken, Anne Tharner, Vincent W. V. Jaddoe, Albert Hofman, Frank C. Verhulst, and Hans W. Hoek. 2015. "Trajectories of Picky Eating during Childhood: A General Population Study." *International Journal of Eating Disorders* 48 (6): 570–579. https://doi.org/10.1002/eat.22384.

"Food Phobia Signs & Symptoms." Kartiniclinic.com. Accessed November 21, 2016. https://www.kartiniclinic.com/eating-disorder-treatment/food-phobia/signs-symptoms2/.

Kurz, Susanne, Zoé van Dyck, Daniela Dremmel, Simone Munsch, and Anja Hilbert. 2016. "Variants of Early-Onset Restrictive Eating Disturbances in Middle Childhood." *International Journal of Eating Disorders* 49 (1): 102–106. https://doi.org/10.1002/eat.22461.

Murphy, Jillian, and Kimberly R. Zlomke. 2016. "A Behavioral Parent-Training Intervention for a Child with Avoidant/Restrictive Food Intake Disorder." *Clinical Practice in Pediatric Psychology* 4 (1): 23–34. https://doi.org/10.1037/cpp0000128.

FOOD SECURITY

Eating disorder prevention programs are been implemented with individuals who face an overabundance of food, experience a dieting culture, and report pressure to be thin. For lower-income populations the assumption is that food insecurity would make eating disorders irrelevant. After all, food insecurity is a limited or unpredictable and uncertain availability of nutritionally adequate and safe foods.

Parent of a Son with an Eating Disorder: An Interview with "Tricia"

"Tricia" (pseudonym used to protect anonymity) is the mother of a 12-year-old son. She works full-time as a health educator in the community. She completed an undergraduate and master's degree in Health Promotion and Education as a nontraditional student. Tricia is athletic and has participated in sports throughout her life. She actively organizes local races and encourages others to be healthy and active.

How old is your son now and what age was your son when you realized he had a problem? What were the telltale signs that indicated he had an eating disorder?

My son is 12. I think he was 9 when we realized that there was a problem. I had gone up to his room and it smelled terrible. His room is always a mess, but I needed to figure out why it stunk, so I started cleaning it. There was tons and tons of food hidden all over his room. Breakfasts, lunches, dinners from weeks ago were all in there. It was really gross. I was concerned about this and so I had a little chat with him. After a lot of digging, he finally told me that the food was food that he had been given that he didn't want to eat because he didn't want to get fat. What? This kid is tiny! After this discussion, we noticed a few other things, like him throwing his meals away as soon as we left the room. We stopped leaving the room while he ate. We found out that he was throwing away his lunches at school. I started making his favorite foods to take in his lunch so he wouldn't throw them away. Sometimes that worked.

Later he started worrying about what was in food and not wanting to eat it because it had fat or sugar in it. I have never seen a 10-year-old who could read a nutrition label as well as he does. He started limiting his breakfast to one mandarin orange, so the whole family got the rule that all meals needed to be at least three food groups. This is still a bit of an argument as I don't think a boiled egg, a mandarin orange and a cup of milk is enough to sustain a 12-year-old until lunch. It is better, though.

Then came the clothing issues. He absolutely refused to wear a warm coat because it made him look fat. He likes to wear black because he thinks it makes him look skinnier. He also started worrying about folds of skin on his scrawny little arms and worrying about how his stomach went out when he breathes.

When he was in fifth grade, he had a teacher who was morbidly obese to the point where she had to use a wheel chair. That was a hard year for him. He has very little respect for fat people. She kept making comments about her weight to the class and he would develop ideas about what made a person fat from those comments. She said her problem was that she snacked too much, so Nathan stopped snacking. It was a rough year. I had to continuously educate about what did and didn't make a person fat. I had to educate about nutrients and what they were good for in the body. I had to show him that fat and sugars were needed in the diet. We had to calculate how many calories a 10-year-old boy needed just to stay alive and compare that to what he was getting, an average of 500 calories per day. It was a constant battle.

Did he get diagnosed right away or was there any resistance from the medical community based on gender? How has he been treated by health care providers? In other words have you sensed any gender bias toward your son?

I spoke to his pediatrician and he recommended getting him in to see a therapist. The one he referred me to was difficult to get in touch with. When I finally got an appointment, the lady cancelled as she quit working for the U. By that time, things seemed okay with him. We were handling things and I thought he might just grow out of it. Then he was getting ready to go to seventh grade and all heck broke loose. I think his anxiety about starting middle school triggered all kinds of issues. I got a referral from a friend who used to be a child therapist and we got in to see her. While she was hesitant to diagnose him with an eating disorder at first, it didn't take more than two sessions before she completely agreed with us. I never experienced any gender bias with him, except maybe for providers being more likely to believe that he really did have a problem. He was young and a boy, which is rare, so there must really be a problem. The issues that I identified were easily corroborated by Nathan, so if they ever had any thoughts that there wasn't really an issue, those were quickly put to rest.

What do you believe were some of the contributing factors that played a role in the development of his eating disorder?

We adopted Nathan from an orphanage in China where he didn't receive a lot of food, but it was more food than what he got with his biological parents. He was severely malnourished when he was taken into the orphanage at two years old. In therapy, it came out that when he didn't do what he was supposed to, the men wouldn't give him food. We adopted him when he was three. While most kids from these circumstances, end up hoarding food, Nathan went a different direction. He seems to be very worried that if he eats, he won't be able to survive a famine and he is training his body to not need food. I really think that the pain that he endured from losing parents that he was bonded to and being put into a situation where he didn't have enough food has led him to never want to feel that pain again. He wasn't able to control if he got food or not there, but in his mind, he is able to control whether or not the lack of food causes him pain. If he is adapted to it, they can't hurt him. He has other non–eating disorder behaviors and anxieties that would go along with this idea as well.

Do you believe that the eating disorder has looked different for him from the male perspective? Why or why not?

I really don't know on this one. I have never really seen it from either perspective. I only see it from Nathan's. I know that there is a lot of research in this area and that Nathan is pretty atypical. I would imagine that girls usually have a lot of peer pressure, which he doesn't have. He is well liked at school and quite the comedian. No one really knows that he has a problem. He isn't exposed to a lot of media images about his body, so I don't think that has a ton of influence on him where it does tend to with girls. I really think that this comes mostly from his own head and his struggles to cope with understanding why his parents didn't want him and why they would allow him to be in such a terrible place, if they loved him.

What are your biggest fears associated with your son's eating disorder?
I worry that he will struggle with this as an adult and won't always have people around him to help him. I worry that he will revert to this behavior when he is stressed. For now, I can hover in the kitchen while he eats. We all sit at the table at dinner and talk until everyone, including him, has finished. That's not a bad habit anyway. I can make sure that he always has plenty of his favorite foods available. What happens when he grows up and leaves home?

Has your son been willing to receive treatment for his eating disorder? What type of treatment is available for boys in your area?
He wasn't very excited to talk to the therapist. There were some major tantrums about it leading up to working with her. It has been the absolutely best thing for our family, though. She has helped him remember and address some of the issues from his abandonment and adoption. This has opened up some discussions between him and I that have been so very helpful. I think he has come to enjoy talking to her. She is fun and he is happier than he has been in a while. I really appreciate that she takes time to talk to my husband and me about what is going on and ways that we can help Nathan with his anxieties, his low self-worth and his feelings that his life is completely out of his control and that the world is a terrifying place with people who are bad and want to hurt him.

Other than therapy, I don't really know any other treatments. His therapist has said that he could take some medication, but we have decided that it needs to be Nathan's choice. He is really, really antimedication. So far, he is responding well to the therapy and his therapist is happy. She did say, however, that if he starts going through puberty and combines anxiety and depression with this, the medication may be necessary. We will take it as it comes. For now, Nathan having a choice, is more important.

We are working hard to help Nathan feel empowered in his own life. I will answer any and all of his questions completely honestly and help him do his own research on the things that scare him in his life. He has recently had a lot of anxiety about the elections. Research has helped him a lot with that. Watching the debates calmed a lot of his anxieties. Weird, it didn't have that effect on me! We work to help him identify things that he can choose to do to affect his life and then let him make the decision whether to adopt that behavior or not. We have enrolled him, one of my daughters and my husband in a karate class. This may seem strange, but it has been good for him. I hope he never, ever has to use his fists in real life, but him feeling like he could defend himself has been important for him to feel a little less powerless. His big brother said that if he gets his black belt, he will have to register his hands and feet as weapons. He LOVES that idea!

What should a parent do if he or she thinks their daughter or son has a problem?
Get help early. It was difficult for me to believe that my son might have a problem that I couldn't heal with more love and attention. I wonder if he would have gotten this bad if I had pushed and gotten him into therapy when he was 9 rather than waiting until he was 12. Thought patterns and behaviors are so much harder

to change when they have had time to solidify. He is doing well, but this is going to be a long haul with him.

What else would you like to add from the perspective of a parent who has a son with an eating disorder?
Don't let fear that you may have contributed to their eating disorder prevent you from getting them help. Nobody is perfect. We are all learning. Let go of any guilt. It is counterproductive to the healing process.

Therefore, providing healthy and safe food sources to low-income Americans, and impoverished communities globally, has been the focus of health promotion initiatives. Although rates of anorexia nervosa and bulimia nervosa are suspected to be low to nonexistent in these food insecure individuals, food insecurity has been linked to increased overweight, obesity, and binge eating behaviors.

Food Insecurity and Obesity

Food insecurity can exist with or without feelings of hunger (i.e., the physiological sensation of being without food). Food insecurity has been associated with both overnutrition (overeating) and undernutrition (undereating). Limited food availability and the access to cheaper, less nutritious, and higher caloric foods can contribute to a link between food insecurity and obesity.

A pilot study conducted in Uganda determined that 31.2 percent of men and 66.3 percent of women with food insecurity were overweight or obese. Food insecure females were less physically active and more likely to be overweight than females in the food secure group.

A separate study that examined food security in the United States found food insecurity was related to a significant decrease in the frequency of fruit and vegetable consumption with 74.4 percent of food insecure individuals consuming two or fewer fruits and vegetables per day compared with 51.6 percent of individuals in the food secure group. Disordered eating patterns (e.g., binge eating behaviors) were also observed for food insecure participants who consumed less potassium, fiber, and vitamins than food secure respondents. Similar findings have been revealed about food insecurity and poor nutritional habits across impoverished regions of the world.

Justine J. Reel

See also: Body Image Globally; Disordered Eating; Food Desert; Obesity; Prevention

Bibliography

Adams, Elizabeth J., Laurence Grummer-Strawn, and Gilberto Chavez. "Food Insecurity Is Associated with Increased Risk of Obesity in California Women." *The Journal of Nutrition* 133 (2003): 1070–1074.

Carter, Kristie N., Kerri Kruse, Tony Blakely, and Sunny Collings. "The Association of Food Security with Psychological Distress in New Zealand and Any Gender Differences." *Social Sciences and Medicine* 72 (2011): 1463–1471. https://doi.org/10.1016/j.socscimed.2011.03.009.

Chaput, Jean-Philippe, Jo Anne Gilbert, and Angelo Tremblay. "Relationship between Food Insecurity and Body Composition in Ugandans Living in Urban Kampala." *Journal of the American Dietetic Association* 107 (2007): 1978–1982. https://doi.org/10.1016/j.jada.2007.08.005.

Kendall, Anne, Christine M. Olson, and Edward A. Frongillo. "Relationship of Hunger and Food Insecurity to Food Availability and Consumption." *Journal of the American Dietetic Association* 96 (1996): 1019–1024. http://dx.doi.org/10.1016/S0002-8223(96)00271-4.

Murshed-e-Jahan, Khondker, Mahfuzuddin Ahmed, and Ben Belton. "The Impacts of Aquaculture Development on Food Security: Lessons from Bangladesh." *Aquaculture Research* 41 (2010): 481–495. https://doi.org/10.1111/j.1365-2109.2009.02337.x.

FULL OF OURSELVES

Full of Ourselves (FOO) is an educational program for female adolescents that promotes mental, physical, and social health to reduce the likelihood of body preoccupation and eating disorders. FOO is a primary prevention program that targets the general population rather than eating-disordered females. Although FOO was developed by Catherine Steiner-Adair and Lisa Sjostrom as a school-based program, FOO has been implemented in after-school programs, churches, and community settings (e.g., Boys and Girls Clubs) over the past decade.

Description of FOO Program

The program's title, *Full of Ourselves*, underscores the program's focus on building strength and confidence in females. Although FOO is an eating disorder prevention program, the program is framed in a positive light with an emphasis placed power, health, and leadership. In fact, eating disorders are not mentioned as part of the lessons. Power is addressed by teaching female participants body acceptance and assertiveness. Using an interactive format, girls practice conflict resolution and standing up to teasing or bullying from peers. To promote health, girls receive nutrition education and learn how to reject the popular diet mentality. To this end, FOO participants learn to replace the commonly held assumption of good versus bad foods with the idea of more or less powerful foods. Participants also practice mindful eating with raisins and candy, for example, to fully use the senses. Finally, girls have an opportunity to develop leadership skills.Each lesson ends with a Call to Action that serves as a homework assignment geared toward practicing skills at home with family and friends.

The program is organized into two phases directed at sixth, seventh, and eighth graders in the first phase (11- to 14-year-olds) and fourth and fifth graders (8- to 10-year-olds) in the second phase. The adolescent girls participate in eight FOO sessions in a group setting once or twice weekly for 45–60 minutes. Group leaders are two women who may be school teachers, nurses, counselors, or after-school personnel. The second phase allows girls who participated in the first phase to become group leaders for younger girls.

Evaluation of FOO Program

The FOO program was tested with 500 seventh-grade girls and determined to be feasible and safe for participants. In addition, participants showed changes in knowledge about health, appearance, weightism, and media literacy (understanding media messages that contribute to body dissatisfaction). Participants also reported improvements in body esteem after the program. In another study using a community sample, participants reported program satisfaction, increased awareness about intuitive eating, more positive body image, and confidence.

Justine J. Reel

See also: Body Esteem; Fat Bias/Fat Discrimination; Intuitive Eating; Media; Prevention

Bibliography

Reel, Justine J., Carlie Ashcraft, Rachel Lacy, Robert A. Bucciere, Sonya SooHoo, Donna Richards, and Nicole Mihalopoulos. "Full of Ourselves PLUS: Lessons Learned from an Obesity and Eating Disorder Intervention." *Journal of Sport Psychology in Action* 3, no. 1 (2011): 109–117. http://dx.doi.org/10.1080/21520704.2010.534545.

Sjostrom, Lisa A., and Catherine Steiner-Adair. "Full of Ourselves: A Wellness Program to Advance Girl Power, Health and Leadership: An Eating Disorders Prevention Program That Works." *Journal of Nutrition Education and Behavior* 37, no. 2 (2005): S141–S144.

Steiner-Adair, Catherine, and Lisa Sjostrom. *Full of Ourselves: A Wellness Program to Advance Girl Power, Health and Leadership.* New York: Teachers College Press, 2005.

Steiner-Adair, Catherine, Lisa Sjostrom, Debra L. Franko, Seeta Pai, Rochelle Tucker, Anne E. Becker, and David B. Herzog. "Primary Prevention of Risk Factors for Eating Disorders in Adolescent Girls: Learning from Practice." *International Journal of Eating Disorders* 32 (2002): 401–411. https://doi.org/10.1002/eat.100089.

GASTROINTESTINAL COMPLICATIONS ASSOCIATED WITH EATING DISORDERS

Gastrointestinal (GI) problems are common complications associated with eating disorders. Complications may occur any place along the GI tract from the mouth to the rectum. These complications may hinder progress in the treatment of eating disorders due to increased physical discomfort associated with eating. The most common GI problems associated with anorexia nervosa are constipation, gastroparesis, abnormal liver function tests, and acute gastric dilation. The GI complications associated with bulimia nervosa tend to have greater effect on the gastrointestinal tract. These complications include dental erosion and caries, parotid gland swelling, esophageal abnormalities, gastric dilation, and impaired colon function related to the use of laxatives and diuretics.

GI Complications Associated with Anorexia Nervosa

Constipation

Constipation is the most common GI complaint reported with anorexia nervosa. It is usually associated with a rapid decrease in food consumption and a decline in colon transit time. Although constipation rarely leads to severe medical complications, it may hinder treatment due to feelings of fullness and abdominal distention. Many individuals may rely on laxatives to treat constipation. However, this may lead to electrolyte imbalances, pancreatic damage, and further delay in intestinal motility. Weight restoration, frequent feedings, gradual increase in fiber-rich foods, and adequate hydration may decrease symptoms associated with constipation.

Gastroparesis

Gastric emptying is the time it takes for the stomach to eliminate its contents into the duodenum. *Gastroparesis* is delayed gastric emptying. Gastroparesis has been associated with anorexia nervosa. Although the exact mechanism remains uncertain, several mechanisms have been proposed. These include protein malnutrition leading to a decrease in the smooth muscle in the GI tract, adaptation to the stomach due to starvation and decreased food consumption, gastric dysrhythmias, and gastric adaptations associated with constipation. Weight restoration may improve gastric emptying, but it remains unknown if it is associated with nutrition rehabilitation, presence of food in the stomach, improved metabolic function, or actual weight gain. An increased dietary intake is necessary to promote weight gain but is often difficult due to increased feelings of early satiety, bloating, spontaneous vomiting, and abdominal discomfort with gastroparesis.

Abnormal Liver Enzymes

Liver function may be compromised by anorexia nervosa. Elevated liver enzymes (e.g., aspartate aminotransferase [AST], alanine aminotransferase [ALT], alkaline phosphatase [alk phos], and total bilirubin) may be identified in this population due to increased workload on the liver. Altered liver function abnormalities occur both in periods of weight loss and restricted food intake and during the early stages of refeeding. The levels generally normalize with slow increases in caloric intake.

Acute Gastric Dilation

Acute gastric dilation occurs when one consumes an amount of food greater than the stomach can hold. In anorexia nervosa, starvation causes the stomach to undergo muscular atrophy, and sudden consumption of food leads to gastric dilation. Although gastric dilation is rare, it is a potential complication that could occur during refeeding in a starved state. It is characterized by a rapid onset of abdominal pain, vomiting, and distended abdomen. Gastric fluids need to be removed from the stomach to prevent rupturing of the stomach.

GI Complications Associated with Bulimia Nervosa

Dental Erosion

Dental erosion is a result of repetitive exposure to gastric acid caused by self-induced vomiting. The degree of damage varies on the length of time of the disorder, the degree and frequency of behaviors, and oral hygiene habits. The hydrochloric acid breaks down the enamel and dentin of the teeth. Eroded teeth appear worn, chipped, and discolored. Although the elimination of vomiting will prevent further damage, dental erosion may require extensive dental treatments.

Dental caries, or cavities, are associated with both anorexia nervosa and bulimia nervosa. Diets high in carbohydrates have been associated with the development of dental caries. Sugar- and starch-containing foods are easily broken down by amylase and bacteria in the mouth, creating an environment to produce acids. This acid demineralizes the tooth structure leading to dental caries.

Parotid Gland Swelling

The parotid glands are the largest of the salivary glands. These glands are responsible for the secretion of saliva into the oral cavity. Saliva then facilitates mastication (chewing) and begins the process of starch digestion. Enlargement of the parotid glands are a result of frequent bingeing and purging. This gives the appearance of chipmunk-like cheeks. Parotid swelling tends to be soft to the touch and painless. It does not appear to alter salivary flow and is not infected. The onset of enlargement appears in three to six days following a binge–purge cycle. The severity of the enlargement is associated with the frequency and duration of purging. Swelling generally decreases as the binge–purge episodes cease. However, in some cases, enlargement may be permanent, causing an individual to seek cosmetic treatment.

Esophageal Complications

Complications associated with the esophagus range from mild esophagitis to esophageal rupture. The esophageal mucosa is damaged from the acidic contents regurgitated from the stomach. This leads to esophagitis, esophageal erosions, ulcers, and bleeding.

Heartburn and acid-reflux symptoms are a common complaint from individuals with bulimia nervosa. Chronic emesis causes relaxation of the esophageal sphincter, resulting in increased reflux symptoms. Barrett's esophagus, an alteration in the lining of the esophagus potentially leading to precancerous cells, may result from recurrent vomiting. Mallory-Weiss tears occur due to the trauma associated with purging and may lead to gastrointestinal bleeding.

Acute Gastric Dilation

Gastric dilation can also occur in bulimia nervosa. Unlike with anorexia nervosa, gastric dilation occurs as a result of binge eating. As with anorexia nervosa, if excessive gastric fluid is not removed, stomach rupture can occur, leading to death. Although gastric dilation is rare, it is a potential gastrointestinal complication seen as a result of binge eating.

Impaired Colon Function

Laxatives and diuretics are commonly used as a means to eliminate calories from the body. However, this is ineffective because a majority of nutrient absorption takes place in the small intestine, while the laxatives act in the large intestine and colon. There are five classes of laxatives grouped according to the mechanism of action: bulk laxatives, osmotic laxatives, surfactants, emollients, and stimulants. Stimulant laxatives are the primary class abused by individuals with bulimia nervosa. These laxatives have a mechanism of action that stimulates colon activity resulting in large amounts of watery diarrhea.

Cathartic colon occurs because of the decreased functioning of the colon nerves resulting from long-term stimulant-laxative abuse. Laxative stimulation prevents the colon from working properly, causing impairment in normal colon function. Cathartic colon is characterized by bloating, abdominal pain, feelings of fullness, and inability to fully eliminate feces. Eliminating the use of laxatives may help but full function of the colon may not return.

Hypovolemia and Electrolyte Disturbances

Vomiting, laxative, and diuretic abuse negatively impact electrolyte (potassium, chloride, and bicarbonate) balance due to increased fluid elimination from the body. Electrolyte imbalance, particularly potassium, affects smooth and skeletal muscles, including the heart. The loss of electrolytes can lead to muscle weakness, acute renal failure, cardiac arrhythmias, convulsions, and death.

GI Complications Associated with Binge Eating Disorder

Binge eating disorder may lead to similar complications as those resulting from the bingeing behavior in bulimia nervosa. These include heartburn, dental caries, and gastric dilation.

Amelia McBride

See also: Dental Complications; Medical and Health Consequences; Visceral Sensitivity

Bibliography

Gurenlian, JoAnn R. "Eating Disorders." *The Journal of Dental Hygiene* 76 (2002): 219–234.

Hadley, Sallie J., and B. Timothy Walsh. "Gastrointestinal Disturbances in Anorexia Nervosa." *Current Drug Targets-CNS and Neurological Disorders* 2, no. 1 (2003): 1–9. https://doi.org/10.2174/1568007033338715.

Mehler, Philip S. "Medical Complications of Bulimia Nervosa and Their Treatments." *International Journal of Eating Disorders* 44 (2011): 95–104. https://doi.org/10.1002/eat.20825.

Walsh, Judith M. E., Mary E. Wheat, and Karen Freund. "Detection, Evaluation, and Treatment of Eating Disorders—The Role of the Primary Care Physician." *Journal of General Internal Medicine* 15 (2000): 577–590. https://doi.org/10.1046/j.1525-1497.2000.02439.x.

Woolsey, Monika M. *Eating Disorder: A Clinical Guide to Counseling and Treatment.* Chicago: American Dietetic Association, 2002.

GENDER AND SEX

Historically, body image concerns and eating disorders have been viewed as women's diseases. Studies comparing the body dissatisfaction of males and females have consistently shown that, as a group, girls and women report more negative body image and higher eating disorder rates than their males. However, the way eating disorders have been identified, assessed, and diagnosed has been biased toward females. Therefore, it is important to continue to refine assessment, treatment, and prevention to develop an accurate picture of males who struggle with body image disturbances and eating disorders.

Prevalence Rates by Sex

For several decades, males have reportedly represented 10 percent, or 1 out of 10, of all eating disorder cases. Researchers and clinicians suspected that males might be suffering at higher rates but are more likely to go underdiagnosed and less likely to present for eating disorder treatment. Additionally, assessment tools are less likely to detect male body image disturbances or eating disorders. When disregarding amenorrhea as part of the diagnostic criteria for anorexia nervosa, women were 3 to 12 times more likely to have anorexia, 3 to 18 times more likely to have bulimia, and 1.5 times more likely to have binge eating disorder (BED). Males were more likely to struggle with BED or subclinical forms of disordered eating than anorexia or bulimia. Prevalence rates for males range from 0 to 2.5 percent for anorexia, 0.13–6.8 percent for bulimia, and 5.0–40.8 percent for the previous *Diagnostic and Statistical Manual of Mental Disorders* category of "eating disorder not otherwise specified" (that includes BED and other disorders that did not fit into anorexia or bulimia).

Sex Differences in Eating Disorders and Body Image Disturbances

A meaningful finding from a 2011 study was that females perceived eating disorders to be a more serious condition than males. Males were less likely to present for treatment until symptoms had become severe and required medical attention. Males may receive less support from family members and friends who may view eating disorders as primarily female disorders.

Males were more likely to report desiring a muscular and lean physique (i.e., reduction of body fat), whereas females often cited wanting to be thinner or slimmer. Males have reported wanting to increase the size of certain body parts (e.g., thighs, biceps) while maintaining low body fat. Therefore, some of the traditional body image assessment questionnaires with items like, "I wish my thighs were smaller" may be inadequate for measuring male body image. Items regarding menstrual disturbances should be removed for male respondents. Notably, males are more likely to struggle with muscle dysmorphia (i.e., body distortion resulting in feeling too small) which is discussed in a separate entry. Certain males may be more at risk for developing disordered eating or clinical eating disorders including wrestlers, bodybuilders, and those engaged in sports that emphasize weight (e.g., rowers, jockeys).

Justine J. Reel

See also: Assessment; Femininity Ideals; Masculinity Ideals

Bibliography

Culbert, Kristen M., Sarah E. Racine, and Kelly L. Klump. "The Influence of Gender and Puberty on the Heritability of Disordered Eating Symptoms." *Behavioral Neurobiology of Eating Disorders* 6 (2010): 177–185. https://doi.org/10.1007/7854_2010_80.

Dissing, Agnete Skovlund, Nanna Hasle Bak, Laura Ern Toftegaard Pedersen, and Birgit H. Petersson. "Female Medical Students Are Estimated to Have a Higher Risk for Developing Eating Disorders Than Male Medical Students." *Danish Medical Bulletin* 58, no. 1 (2011): 1–5.

Koskina, Nefeli, and Theodoros Giovazolias. "The Effect of Attachment Insecurity in the Development of Eating Disturbances across Gender: The Role of Body Dissatisfaction." *The Journal of Psychology* 144, no. 5 (2010): 449–471.

Mond, Jonathan M., and Anais Arrighi. "Gender Differences in Perceptions of the Severity and Prevalence of Eating Disorders." *Early Intervention in Psychiatry* 5 (2011): 41–49. https://doi.org/10.1111/j.1751.7893.2010.00257.x.

Sanftner, Jennifer L. "Quality of Life in Relation to Psychosocial Risk Variables for Eating Disorders in Women and Men." *Eating Behaviors* 12 (2011): 136–142. https://doi.org/10.1016/j.eatbeh.2011.01.003.

Stoving, Rene Klinkby, Alin Andries, Kim Brixen, Niels Bilenberg, and Kirsten Horder. "Gender Differences in Outcome of Eating Disorders: A Retrospective Cohort Study." *Psychiatry Research* 186 (2011): 362–366. https://doi.org/10/1016/j.psychres.2010.08.005.

GYMNASTICS

Gymnastics is a graceful and artistic sport requiring balance, coordination, strength, and agility. The sport of gymnastics has been around for over 2,000 years and dates to ancient Greece. Gymnastics was used by the early Greeks and Romans to prepare for war and was a mandatory part of ancient Greek education. Although gymnastics was part of the ancient Olympic Games, modern gymnastics reemerged in the late 18th and early 19th centuries as physical education for boys and young men. Friedrich Jahn, considered the father of gymnastics, developed the parallel bars, side horse with pommels, balance beam, ladder, and vaulting horse to create exercises.

Men's gymnastics became popular as a competitive sport and appeared in the first modern Olympics in 1896. Women began to compete in gymnastics in the 1920s, with the first female Olympic competitors in the 1928 games and the first U.S. women's gymnastics team in 1936. By 1954, gymnastics was standardized to a format including both individual and team competitions and a point system from 1 to 10.

Female gymnasts are associated with feminine grace of movement, beauty, and perfection. Nadia Comaneci became a societal sensation as a 14-year-old girl when she scored the first perfect 10, in the 1976 Summer Olympic Games in Montreal. Comaneci later admitted she suffered from an eating disorder. Additionally, U.S. gymnasts Cathy Rigby (a 1968 and 1972 Olympian) and Kathy Johnson (a 1984 Olympic silver medalist) publicly discussed battles with eating disorders. Rigby, who helped popularize gymnastics in the United States, admitted she struggled with bulimia nervosa for 12 years. She revealed she engaged in binge episodes and vomiting and was hospitalized twice due to electrolyte imbalance. Christy Henrich, an aspiring competitive gymnast, died from anorexia nervosa in 1994 at age 22. She was purportedly informed by a judge at an international event in 1989 that she needed to lose weight to be competitive and was told by her coach that she looked like the Pillsbury dough boy. This tragedy and the eating disorders reported by other competitive gymnasts underscore the risk of disordered eating and eating disorders in the sport.

Gymnastics and Eating Disorders

The prevalence of eating disorders and disordered eating has varied by the study. Most researchers found that gymnasts were actively dieting and using a variety of pathological methods to lose weight, such as restricting foods, self-induced vomiting, laxative abuse, fluid restriction, and diuretics. One study reported up to 62 percent of gymnasts were engaging in pathogenic weight control methods. Another study using more sensitive assessment measures found that 22 percent of college gymnasts met criteria for a clinical eating disorder. Gymnastics is considered an aesthetic sport and has been associated with a sport environment that has inherent risks for eating disorders and disordered eating.

Gymnastics as a Judged, Aesthetic Sport

Sports that are aesthetic in nature have been associated with higher drives for thinness and increased risk for eating disorders. Similar to figure skating and diving, gymnastics is based on a particular look judged using a subjective scoring system. Gymnastic stunts are scored higher when lines are more pronounced, often accomplished by a thinner, leaner physique and reduced feminine curves. Gymnasts may feel pressure to delay puberty and body-related changes due to the perception that they are more competitive at a smaller size.

Sources of Weight Pressures

Like other athletes from other aesthetic sports, gymnasts face sport-related weight pressures including form-fitting uniforms, coaching comments, comparison with peers, and judges. Gymnasts, like divers, have revealing team uniforms that show any perceived body imperfections and may increase body self-consciousness. The sport of gymnastics and its Olympic coaches have been exposed in books such as *Little Girls in Pretty Boxes* that have described daily weigh-ins and grueling physical training with restrictive food intake. Gymnasts have reported that coaches may comment about a gymnast's size, shape, or weight and that the thinnest gymnasts may be a coach's favorite. Gymnasts compete with other gymnasts in competitions and for spots in the competition and may use weight or size as a controllable factor. Finally, judges score in part based on aesthetic, with gymnasts who perform with the longest, thinnest lines given the highest scores.

Rhythmic Gymnastics

Rhythmic gymnastics was first recognized as a sport in 1962 by the International Gymnastics Federation. Participants in this form of gymnastics are expected to be feminine and graceful. A study conducted in Norway revealed that 8 of 12 rhythmic gymnasts had elevated drive for thinness and body dissatisfaction scores showing a risk for eating disorders, and that 33 percent of the gymnasts met the criteria for eating disorders. These researchers suggest disordered eating may be normative in rhythmic gymnasts due to the perception that extreme thinness is a requirement for success. Even extremely thin rhythmic gymnasts reported dieting to fight their natural body weight. This sport should be explored further as rhythmic gymnastics includes similar weight pressures as the more familiar form of artistic gymnastics—such as pressure from coaches, judges, and parents.

Justine J. Reel

See also: Aesthetic Sports; Celebrities and Eating Disorders; Coaches; Figure Skating; Sports; Weight Pressures in Sport

Bibliography

Beals, Katherine A. *Disordered Eating among Athletes: A Comprehensive Guide for Health Professionals.* Champaign, IL: Human Kinetics, 2004.

Harris, Mary B., and Debbie Greco. "Weight Control and Weight Concern in Competitive Female Gymnasts." *Journal of Sport & Exercise Psychology* 12 (1990): 427–433.

Klinkowski, Nora, Alexander Korte, Ernst Pfeiffer, Ulrike Lehmkuhl, and Harriet Salbach-Andrae. "Psychopathology in Elite Rhythmic Gymnasts and Anorexia Nervosa Patients." *European Child and Adolescent Psychiatry* 17, no. 2 (2008): 108–113. https://doi.org/10.1007/s00787-007-0643-y.

O'Connor, Patrick, Richard D. Lewis, Elisabeth M. Kirchener, and Dane B. Cook. "Eating Disorder Symptoms in Former Female College Gymnasts: Relations with Body Composition." *American Journal of Clinical Nutrition* 64 (1996): 840–843.

Petrie, Trent A. "Disordered Eating in Female Collegiate Gymnasts: Prevalence and Personality/Attitudinal Correlates." *Journal of Sport and Exercise Psychology* 15 (1993): 424–436.

Sundgot-Borgen, Jorunn. "Eating Disorders, Energy Intake, Training Volume and Menstrual Function in High-Level Modern Rhythmic Gymnasts." *International Journal of Sport Nutrition* 6 (1996): 100–109.

Thompson, Ron A., and Roberta Trattner Sherman. *Eating Disorders in Sport.* New York: Routledge, 2010.

HATTOU SHIN IDEAL

The Hattou Shin Ideal is a socially-constructed appearance ideal specific to Japanese culture and related to the head size and leg length of females. Japanese attractiveness ideals more closely resemble Western appearance ideals than any stereotypical images. In fact, Asian women report a Westernized body ideal that includes being tall, blonde, buxom, and thin with European facial features. In 1989, 48 percent of male models and 42 percent of female models in Japanese magazines were Caucasian. In recent publications, 74 percent of the ads featured Western models.

Body Image and the Hattou Shin Ideal

A unique aspect of Japanese body image has been the development and reinforcement of the Hattou Shin Ideal (i.e., length of one's head should equal one-eighth of one's height) since World War II. This ideal translated into the glorification of females with smaller heads and longer legs. Beginning in the early 1950s, Japanese magazine articles and advertisements actively promoted the Hattou Shin Ideal by including models with unusually long legs that were digitally enhanced to meet this Japanese cultural ideal. This body ideal of long and thin legs has been tied to weight management techniques such as skipping meals, obsessive exercise, vomiting, and using laxatives or diuretics to slim down and strive toward the Japanese ideal. Additionally, Japanese females will dress in a way that accentuates thinness by wearing high heels to make their legs appear longer.

Hailey E. Nielson

See also: Body Image Globally; Media

Bibliography

Chisuwa, Naomi, and Jennifer A. O'Dea. "Body Image and Eating Disorders amongst Japanese Adolescents. A Review of the Literature." *Appetite* 54 (2010): 5–15. https://doi.org/10.1016/j.appet.2009.11.008.

Iwao, Shunichiro. "Nihon-jin no Tai-gaikoki-jin Taido (Attitudes of Japanese toward Foreigners)." *Financial Review* 12 (1989): 1–10.

Mormoto, Mariko, and Susan Chang. "Western and Asian Models in Japanese Fashion Magazine Ads: The Relationship with Brand Origins and International versus Domestic Magazines." *Journal of International Consumer Marketing* 21 (2009): 173–187. https://doi.org/10.1080/08961530802202701.

Mukai, Takayo, Akiko Kambara, and Yuji Sasaki. "Body Dissatisfaction, Need for Social Approval and Eating Disturbances among Japanese and American College Women." *Sex Roles* 39 (1998): 751–763. doi: 0021-9630/94.

Nishizono-Maher, Aya, Yuko Miyake, and Akira Nakane. "The Prevalence of Eating Pathology and Its Relationship to Knowledge of Eating Disorders among High School Girls in Japan." *European Eating Disorders Review* 12 (2004): 122–128. https://doi.org/10.1002/erv.558.

Swami, Viren, Carolina Caprario, Martin J. Tovee, and Adrian Frunham. "Female Physical Attractiveness in Britain and Japan: A Cross-Cultural Study." *European Journal of Personality* 20, no. 1 (2006): 69–81. https://doi.org/10.1002/per.568.

HEALTH AT EVERY SIZE APPROACH

To combat the overweight and obesity problem, many researchers and practitioners focus on a weight loss approach that promotes dieting and, in some cases, can contribute to disordered eating and fear of fatness. Fat bias and weight discrimination (discussed in a separate entry, Fat Bias/Fat Discrimination) are a barrier for individuals who are overweight and obese, preventing them from receiving nonjudgmental and helpful treatment from the medical community. Like other *isms* (e.g., racism, sexism), being larger has been associated with stereotypes of being lazy, sloppy, or unmotivated by medical and health professionals. Therefore, a more long-term, health promotion approach that fosters self-acceptance as well as healthy eating and physical activity behaviors is needed.

Overview of the Health at Every Size Approach

The Health at Every Size (HAES) approach, conceived by Linda Bacon in 2005, strives to counteract the negative effects of dieting and traditional weight management approaches that emphasize weight loss. When programs focus on losing body weight, many individuals may be triggered by the emotional baggage associated with the number on the scale, rather than encouraged to develop lifestyle changes that favor a moderation approach. Therefore, the HAES paradigm views dieting and obsession with weight as unhealthy, celebrates diversity in body size, and promotes overall health. Rather than encourage dietary restraint, the HAES approach advocates eating in accordance with hunger and fullness cues (i.e., intuitive eating). It promotes physical activity for enjoyment rather than exercise solely for weight loss. Importantly, the HAES philosophy optimizes psychological and physical health at any weight. The Association for Size Diversity and Health (ASDAH) is an international professional organization committed to HAES principles. Its stated mission is to education, research and services to improve well-being without assumptions and discrimination.

Health at Every Size and Body Image

The HAES approach was developed after the realization that traditional weight management approaches were associated with dieting behaviors that were associated with overeating, depression, low self-esteem, poor body image, weight cycling, and eating disorders. The HAES approach promotes a balanced approach to eating and exercise while not compromising body image or creating an overemphasis on losing weight. HAES researchers believed overweight and obesity had been overemphasized. This view, supported by recent research suggesting health is not only about pounds, takes an unnecessary emphasis off of one's size, shape, or appearance.

Evaluation of the HAES Approach

A program evaluation using the HAES approach with 22 female participants showed significant improvement at 24 months for weight, exercise frequency, diastolic blood pressure, and systolic blood pressure. Interestingly, participants continued to lose weight after the program had finished, as they maintained their health lifestyle skills using a nondieting approach. In a separate study with 78 obese women, using the nondiet HAES approach yielded reductions in binge eating behaviors, depression, body dissatisfaction, and disordered eating. Initial findings for HAES studies show improvements in psychological and physical health; however, but studies with larger sample sizes are needed.

Justine J. Reel

See also: Emotional Eating; Fat Bias/Fat Discrimination; Intuitive Eating; Intuitive Exercise; Obesity; Plus-Size Models and Clothing; Weight Stigma

Bibliography

"Association for Size Diversity and Health." Sizediversityandhealth.org. Accessed August 22, 2011. http://www.sizediversityandhealth.org/index.asp.

Bacon, Linda, and Lucy Aphramor. "Weight Science: Evaluating the Evidence for a Paradigm Shift." *Nutrition Journal* 10, no. 9 (2011): 1–13. https://doi.org/10.1186/1475-2891-10-9.

Bradshaw, Alison J., Caroline C. Horwath, Lisa Katzer, and Andrew Gray. "Non-dieting Group Interventions for Overweight and Obese Women: What Predicts Non-Completion and Does Completion Improve Outcomes?" *Public Health Nutrition* 13, no. 10 (2009): 1622–1628. https://doi.org/10.1017/S1368980009992977.

Gagnon-Girouard, Marie-Pierre, Catherine Begin, Veronique Provencher, Angelo Tremblay, Lyne Mongeau, Sonia Boivin, and Simone Lemieux. "Psychological Impact of a 'Health at Every Size' Intervention on Weight Preoccupied Overweight/Obese Women." *Journal of Obesity* (2010): 1–12. https://doi.org/10.1155/2010/928097.

Hawley, Greer, Caroline Horwath, Andrew Gray, Alison Bradshaw, Lisa Katzer, Janine Joyce, and Sue O'Brien. "Sustainability of Health and Lifestyle Improvements Following a Non-Dieting Randomised Trial in Overweight Women." *Preventive Medicine* 47 (2008): 593–599. https://doi.org/10.1016/j.ypmed2008.08.008.

King, Carrie. "Health at Every Size Approach to Health Management: The Evidence Is Weighed." *Top Clinical Nutrition* 22, no. 3 (2007): 272–285. https://doi.org/10.1097/01.TIN.0000285381.24089.84.

Provencher, Veronique, Catherine Begin, Angelo Tremblay, Lyne Mongeau, Sonia Boivin, and Simone Lemieux. "Short-Term Effects of a 'Health at Every Size' Approach on Eating Behaviors and Appetite Ratings." *Obesity* 15, no. 4 (2007): 957–966. https://doi.org/10.1038/oby.2007.638.

Provencher, Veronique, Catherine Begin, Angelo Tremblay, Lyne Mongeau, Louise Cor-
neau, Sylvie Dodin, Sonia Boivin, and Simone Lemieux. "Health at Every Size and
Eating Behaviors: 1-Year Follow-Up Results of a Size Acceptance Intervention." *Journal of American Dietetic Association* 109 (2009): 1854–1861. https://doi.org/10.1016/j
.jada.2009.08.017.

Reel, Justine J., and Allison R. Stuart. "Is the 'Health at Every Size' Approach Useful for
Addressing Obesity Prevention?" *Journal of Community Medicine & Health Education* 2,
no. 4 (2012): 1–2. https://doi.org/10.4172/jcmhe.1000e105.

"Why Health Is Not Measured in Pounds." Princeton Bariatrics. Last modified November
24, 2014. Accessed November 21, 2017. http://princetonbariatrics.com/news/health
-is-not-measured-in-pounds/.

HEALTH CARE COSTS OF EATING DISORDERS

In addition to being the deadliest class of psychiatric disorders, eating disorders
are a significant financial burden to an afflicted individual, family, and health care
systems in general. Understanding the cost of an eating disorder on an individual
level requires an appreciation for treatment and medical expenses, as well as secondary effects (e.g., loss of employment) that can be associated with a disorder. If a
broader approach is taken and the goal is to quantify the economic burden of eating disorders on a societal level, carefully controlled research studies are necessary.

Eating disorders are costly, on both an individual and a societal level. Studying
the magnitude of costs is difficult as there is great variability. Inpatient treatment
(hospitalization and residential treatment facilities) ranges from $500–$2,000 per
day. Outpatient treatment is too varied and broad to accurately quantify, and the
duration of either in- or outpatient treatment has an important effect on estimating
costs. Insurance companies vary in the level of coverage offered and the treatments
qualified for coverage. Secondary costs, such as lower educational achievement
due to time taken off for treatment or inability to maintain employment, are even
more vague and difficult to study. On a societal level, eating disorders are comparable in treatment costs with other serious psychiatric disorders, such as depression
and schizophrenia.

Treatment Costs and Related Medical Expenses

Perhaps the most straightforward and intuitive manner to measure costs related
to eating disorders is to examine expenses related to treatment for an individual.
In this category, however, there is extraordinary variability based on an individual's level of insurance coverage, type of disorder, severity, treatment needs, location, and service(s) received. For inpatient treatment options, the general range
for all-inclusive care is estimated to be between $500 and $2,000 per day. Inpatient treatment usually takes one of two forms: hospitalization (usually only long
enough to achieve medical stability) or a residential treatment facility. Hospitalization is typically less expensive and is more commonly covered by insurance
plans; however, there is still great variability in the cost. For example, a study
conducted in 2004 compared the average treatment cost between usual care (14

days of inpatient hospitalization) and adequate care (45 days of hospitalization). The usual care model costs approximately $14,000, compared to an adequate care model that costs about $90,000.

Compared to hospitalization, residential treatment facilities offer more specialized and individual regimens of care, including medication management, counseling services, and nutrition classes. A recent study that evaluated 18 residential treatment facilities in the United States found that the average cost was $956 per day. The average length of stay at these treatment facilities was about 80 days, bringing the total cost for an entire stay to $79,348. Although this figure does not estimate out-of-pocket expense for someone after insurance coverage is calculated; few insurance companies provide coverage for a full-length stay at inpatient facilities. It is also common for insurers to deny coverage for inpatient treatment, citing that the research on treating eating disorders is scant or inconclusive and does not definitively identify a course of effective treatment.

Outpatient care is significantly more difficult to quantify based on the extreme variability in this form of treatment. In general, outpatient care has been found to be more cost-effective than inpatient treatment options. Outpatient care may include psychological counseling, medication management, group counseling, nutrition classes, and medical monitoring. Depending on the individual's needs, these various components can be combined in different ways to create a personalized treatment package. A recent study conducted in the United States found one outpatient family counseling session averaged $180 and average cost of each appointment with a doctor/primary care health provider was $150. Individual counseling appointments range from $75 to $150 per hour. The out-of-pocket cost for medication(s) ranges from $0 (if insurance covers the medications completely) to upward of several hundred dollars per refill. Outpatient care also varies significantly in length. Some individuals need only a few months of outpatient care, others participate in some form of outpatient treatment for decades.

Secondary Individual Costs

In addition to expenses associated with inpatient and outpatient treatment, eating disorders can have an immense financial burden on an individual's life. Individuals may be forced to leave jobs as a result of an eating disorder, and insurance companies may refuse to provide coverage for individuals with a history of a psychiatric diagnosis. Additionally, more intangible costs such as impaired social functioning and limits on educational attainment can also have tremendous effects. Very few attempts at studying these secondary financial effects of eating disorders have been made. Only one study, conducted in Germany in 2002, has produced an estimate of indirect costs. The only secondary cost examined was the impact of lost productivity due to an inability to work; average cost was 6,900 Euros per person (approximately $7,600 per person). In context, this figure is a rough estimate of the money each person receiving inpatient treatment following an eating disorder diagnosis lost as a result of being unable to work. No other secondary costs were studied.

Economic Burden of Eating Disorders on a Societal Level

Eating disorders are costly for affected individuals and their families and are also a financial burden at regional and national levels. Studies investigating costs and economic burden on a societal level are greater in number. Data from insurance companies, health care/treatment providers and governments often provide researchers with adequate information to draw conclusions about the societal cost of treatment. Expenses from these studies are often reported in terms of money spent per patient per year (a.k.a. per patient per annum, or PPP). The most comprehensive study conducted in the United States on this topic to date compared treatment costs (PPP) for males and females with anorexia, bulimia, and the diagnosis of eating disorder not otherwise specified (EDNOS) included in the fourth edition of the *Diagnostic and Statistical Manual of Mental Disorders*. The researchers found per patient costs were highest for women with anorexia nervosa ($6,045) and lowest for males with EDNOS ($2,165). When compared with the annual per patient costs for schizophrenia, anorexia and bulimia did not differ significantly. However, when compared with annual per patient costs for obsessive-compulsive disorder (OCD), both anorexia and bulimia were found to be significantly higher, reflecting the associated medical complications of these disorders. The annual costs for EDNOS treatment were lower than both schizophrenia and OCD.

Another study investigating annual costs per patient expended in the United States for eating disorders compared health care costs before and after an official eating disorder diagnosis was made. These figures were also compared to health care costs among a healthy sample and a psychiatric sample without an eating disorder. Costs for institutional care (e.g., hospitalization, residential treatment facilities), professional treatment (individual/group counseling), and medication expenses were compared. Researchers found health care costs rose dramatically following an eating disorder diagnosis, which suggests patients who receive a diagnosis are effectively educated about treatment options and are taking advantage of treatment options. Not surprisingly, health care costs per year were significantly higher for individuals who eventually received an eating disorder diagnosis than for healthy controls. Additionally, although the per year costs were similar in magnitude for eating disorders and the psychiatric non–eating disorder group, the latter experienced much more stable costs from year to year.

Hannah J. Hopkins

See also: Legislation on Eating Disorders; Levels of Care; Medical and Health Consequences; Treatment

Bibliography

Alderman, Lesley. "Treating Eating Disorders and Paying for It." *New York Times.* Last modified December 3, 2010. Accessed November 21, 2017. http://www.nytimes.com/2010/12/04/health/04patient.html.

"Early Diagnosis of Eating Disorders Cuts Costs." *Mental Health Practice* 18, no. 6 (2015): 6. http://dx.doi.org/10.7748/mhp.18.6.6.s4.

"Evaluating Residential Treatment Programs." *Eating Disorders Review* 17, no. 3 (2006). Accessed February 3, 2017. http://eatingdisordersreview.com/nl/nl_edr_17_3_7.html.

Harries, Chloe. "The Real Cost of Eating Disorders." *Community Practitioner* 85, no. 10 (2012): 14–16.

Lock, James, Jennifer Couturier, and W. Stewart Agras. "Costs of Remission and Recovery Using Family Therapy for Adolescent Anorexia Nervosa: A Descriptive Report." *Eating Disorders* 16, no. 4 (2008): 322–330. https://doi.org/10.1080/10640260802115969.

Mitchell, James E., Tricia Myers, Ross Crosby, George O'Neill, Jodi Carlisle, and Shamayne Gerlach. "Health Care Utilization in Patients with Eating Disorders." *International Journal of Eating Disorders* 42, no. 6 (2009): 571–574. https://doi.org/10.1002/eat.20651.

Simon, Judit, Ulrike Schmidt, and Stephen Pilling. "The Health Service Use and Cost of Eating Disorders." *Psychological Medicine* 35, no. 11 (2005): 1543–1551. https://doi.org/10.1017/S0033291705004708.

Striegel-Moore, Ruth H., Douglas Leslie, Stephen A. Petrill, Vicki Garvin, and Robert A. Rosenheck. "One-Year Use and Cost of Inpatient and Outpatient Services among Female and Male Patients with an Eating Disorder: Evidence from a National Database of Health Insurance Claims." *The International Journal of Eating Disorders* 27, no. 4 (2000): 381–389. https://doi.org/10.1002/(SICI)1098-108X(200005)27:4<381::AID-EAT2>3.0.CO;2-U.

Stuhldreher, Nina, Alexander Konnopka, Beate Wild, Wolfgang Herzog, Stephan Zipfel, Bernd Löwe, and Hans-Helmut König. "Cost-of-Illness Studies and Cost-Effectiveness Analyses in Eating Disorders: A Systematic Review." *International Journal of Eating Disorders* 45, no. 4 (2012): 476–491. https://doi.org/10.1002/eat.20977.

HISTORY OF EATING DISORDERS

Eating disorders were rarely discussed prior to the 1970s. Hilde Bruch published a groundbreaking book in 1973 entitled *Eating Disorders: Obesity, Anorexia Nervosa, and the Person Within*. Bruch detailed 70 case studies and argued eating disorders were more widespread than thought.

Prior to the 20th century, there was historical evidence of anorexia nervosa and other disordered eating behaviors. For example, in 700 BCE, binge and purge episodes were reported among the Romans during the time of Caesar. These wealthy Romans would gorge themselves on extravagant banquets until they were overfull. Then, they would purge by vomiting to continue feasting. Disordered eating behavior was revealed in ancient Egyptian hieroglyphics depicting monthly purges to prevent illness. There are additional examples of African tribes that engaged in fasting and restricting behaviors to the point of risking fatality, even after famines ended.

Religious fasting and showing hatred for one's body was also evident in women in the Christian era. In the 12th and 13th centuries there were examples of eating disorders tied to religious figures such as Saint Catherine of Siena, who was thought to have refused food to demonstrate her devout religious commitment and a denial of self. Early cases of eating disorders in the 17th century were referred to as the *wasting disease* to highlight the fasting behavior and marked weight loss of people. One such case was described in England during the 1680s: a 20-year-old woman died from the wasting disease, characterized as having a skeleton-like appearance that resembles the modern description of anorexia nervosa.

Sir William Gull was a physician who brought attention to the complexity of anorexia nervosa Gull realized anorexia, as a disease, represented more than a religious or biological eating practice. In addition to recommending force feeding female anorexic patients, Gull recognized the contribution of mental state and discussed the need for a change of scenery. He referred to the disease as *Anorexia Hysterica* to underscore the mental health component of the disorder anorexia nervosa, which literally means nervous absence of appetite. A French psychiatrist, Charles Lasegue, discussed the contribution of a family environment around meals creating stress and anorexia nervosa in children who refused food as a rebellion. He also argued women who were suffocated and stressed in a relationship may refuse food. Bulimia nervosa was less discussed in the medical community than anorexia nervosa. A case of a female patient struggling from bulimia was first identified in a medical context in 1903 by Pierre Janet. The patient was reported to secretly engage in binge episodes.

Interestingly, by the early 20th century anorexia nervosa was attributed to an endocrine problem. Thus, clients with eating disorders in the early 1900s were treated with pituitary hormones. There was also speculation by physicians that anorexia nervosa was a form of tuberculosis. In the 1930s, an emotional connection was identified with the disease to shift thinking in the medical community. Cases described underscored the obsessive nature around food and a drive for thinness by patients, leading to eating disorders and suicide. Discovering the multifaceted nature of this disorder was an important step in understanding an illness that remained very much a mystery.

A physiological and psychological connection to the disease was emphasized when anorexia nervosa was included in the first *Diagnostic and Statistical Manual of Mental Disorders* (*DSM*) in 1952, In the second edition (*DSM-II*) anorexia was listed under special symptoms in the feeding disturbances section; bulimia nervosa and binge eating disorder were absent from the manual. It was not until 1980 that bulimia nervosa was included as a mental health disorder in the newly designated eating disorder section in *DSM-III*. Although the clinical criteria for binge eating disorder were included in the appendix of *DSM-IV*, it was not until the recent edition of the *DSM-5* (2013) that binge eating disorder was included as a separate category in the eating disorders section.

Dieting became mainstream in the 1960s, 1970s, and 1980s. By the 1970s and 1980s, both anorexia nervosa and bulimia nervosa were widely documented in the medical community, but less understood by the general public. Early cases were thought to primarily afflict upper class females. Well-known musician and singer, Karen Carpenter, brought widespread attention to the severity of eating disorders when she died in 1983 from heart failure associated with her long-term anorexia nervosa. In the 1980s, eating disorders were thought to be primarily a disease that afflicted young affluent girls and young women. The first freestanding eating disorder treatment center in the United States, Renfrew Center, opened in 1984 in Philadelphia. Many more treatment centers opened throughout North America to provide residential level of care to eating disorder patients. In 1987, the first National Eating Disorders Awareness Week was launched to raise awareness about this disease. The National Eating Disorder Association (NEDA), formed in 2001 from two previous organizations, has taken the torch and currently has a nationwide NEDA week every February.

In the 1990s, eating disorders had a stronger presence in school health curricula and there was recognition of the dangers in the media. When Christy Henrich, an Olympic gymnast died in 1992 from complications associated with her eating disorder, the pressures associated with certain sports to lose weight were revealed. Research on eating disorders in athletics and the general population grew exponentially in the 1990s to better understand causes, treatment, and prevention. Heidi Gunther, a professional dancer, died in 1997 after being told she would lose her principal role if she gained weight. This death sent shock waves through the dance community and illuminated the need for improved awareness.

The late 1990s also saw widespread adoption of the Internet. With it came chat rooms and eventually social media sites. Alarmingly, pro-ana (websites that *promote* anorexia nervosa) and pro-mia (websites that *promote* bulimia nervosa) have been part of the Internet revolution. There is the realization the media's contribution to the development of eating disorders must necessarily include the Internet and social media platforms.

In the 21st century, there has been more attention paid to eating disorders in non-traditional populations. Now there is greater awareness of male sufferers of eating disorders as well as individuals from different ethnic groups experiencing negative body images and disordered eating. For example, in 2010 there was publicity around the death of male model Jeremy Gillitzer, who at the age of 38 weighed only 66 pounds after a long-standing battle with anorexia nervosa. Further, an official report published in 2009 by the Agency for Healthcare Research and Quality showed that hospitalizations for boys under 12 years old admitted for eating disorders increased 119 percent from 1999 to 2006. Treatment centers provide beds and specialized programming to male patients in recognition of this largely overlooked population. The Canopy Cove program in Tallahassee, Florida, reports it admitted the first male client in the 1990s.

Another trend in the 21st century has been a focus on the role of genes in the development of eating disorders. The developmental model proposed by Jeanine Spelt and her colleagues in 1995 acknowledged the role of genes and the environment in to the vulnerability to and development of eating disorders; however, genetics research has taken center stage in this century. By understanding the brain connection to eating disorders, there is hope we can determine effective treatment and prevention approaches in the future.

Selective eating disorder has been defined as having a narrow range of food choices. Originally viewed as *picky eating*, this form of disordered eating has received recent attention. For the first time, selective eating disorder was included in the fifth edition of the *Diagnostic and Statistical Manual of Mental Disorders* (2013). Other feeding disorders, such as orthorexia nervosa (i.e., an obsession with eating healthy and organic foods), are expected to be formally recognized in the future.

Justine J. Reel

See also: Anorexia Nervosa; Binge Eating Disorder; Bulimia Nervosa; *Diagnostic and Statistical Manual of Mental Disorders*; Selective Eating Disorder

Bibliography

American Psychiatric Association. *Diagnostic and Statistical Manual of Mental Disorders*, 5th ed. (*DSM-5*). Washington, DC: American Psychiatric Association Publishing, 2013.

Annus, Agnus M., Gregory T. Smith, Sarah Fischer, Megan Hendricks, and Suzannah F. Williams. "Associations among Family-of-Origin Food-Related Experiences, Expectancies, and Disordered Eating." *International Journal of Eating Disorders* 40, no. 2 (2007): 179–186. https://doi.org/10.1002/eat.20346.

Branca, Patricia. "Reviewed Work: Food and Drink in History." Edited by Robert Forster and Orest Ranum. *Journal of Social History* 14, no. 2 (1980): 315–316. Baltimore, MD: Johns Hopkins University Press.

Brown, Harriet. *Body of Truth: How Science, History, and Culture Drive Our Obsession with Weight and What We Can Do about It.* Boston, MA: Life Long, 2015.

Bruch, Hilde. *Eating Disorders: Obesity, Anorexia Nervosa, and the Person Within*, Revised Edition. New York: Basic Books, 1979.

Espejo, Roman, ed. *Eating Disorders: Opposing Viewpoints.* Detroit, MI: Greenhaven Press, 2012.

Hull, Holly R., Duncan Radley, Mary K. Dinger, and David A. Fields. "The Effect of the Thanksgiving Holiday on Weight Gain." *Nutrition Journal* 5, no. 29 (2006): 1–6. https://doi.org/10.1186/1475-2891-5-29.

McCarthy, Nicola. "A Lean Holiday Season." *Nature Reviews: Cancer* 7, no. 12 (2007): 892. https://doi.org/10.1038/nrc2286.

Procida, Mary A. "No Longer Half-Baked: Food Studies and Women's History." *Journal of Women's History* 16, no. 3 (2004): 197–205. https://doi.org/10.1353/jowh.2004.0070.

Spelt, Jeanine R., and Joanne M. Meyer. "Genetics and Eating Disorders." In *Behavior Genetic Approaches in Behavioral Medicine*, edited by J. Rick Turner, Lori R. Cardon, and John K. Hewitt. New York: Plenum Press, 1995.

IMPULSIVITY

Impulsivity is acting without thinking, having an inability to delay gratification, or acting without considering the risks of behavior. Impulsive behaviors are thought to be performed without conscious decision making or judgment and tend to be spontaneous action that involve insufficient planning. Impulsivity has been linked to eating disorders and other pathological behaviors, such as substance abuse, compulsive shopping, sexual promiscuity, and shoplifting. In fact, 37 percent of compulsive shoppers have eating-disordered symptoms. Two factors, reward-sensitivity and rash spontaneous impulsivity, have also been associated with impulsivity. Reward-sensitivity is the inability to delay reward and the tendency to choose small rewards over delayed ones; rash spontaneous impulsivity refers to a person rapidly responding without assessing the consequences of an action.

Eating Disorders and Impulsivity

One study found 17 percent of individuals with a history of eating disorders suffered from impulse control problems. Typically, impulsivity has been associated with increased binge episodes for eating-disordered individuals. For example, an individual who engages in uncontrollable eating patterns eats beyond the point of fullness despite the potential for weight gain, guilt, and negative health consequences. Most studies have found a higher prevalence of impulsivity in binge eaters diagnosed with binge eating disorder or bulimia nervosa than individuals with anorexia nervosa or nonclinical controls (i.e., people who do not have eating disorders). Therefore, impulsivity characteristics are thought to exist on a spectrum with binge eaters on one end and restrictive eaters (who are less likely to engage in risk taking) on the other end. Higher impulsivity in individuals with eating disorders has also been associated with increased severity of eating disorder symptoms, higher incidence of personality disorders, decreased psychological functioning, and an inability to cope.

Multi-Impulsivity versus Uni-Impulsivity

Researchers have distinguished between eating-disordered individuals who exhibit *multi-impulsivity* (i.e., several impulsive behaviors) and individuals who have one impulsive behavior). Individuals in the subgroup of multi-impulsivity engage in at least three distinct behaviors (e.g., alcohol or drug abuse, suicide attempts, self-mutilation, sexual promiscuity, and stealing) in addition to disordered eating behaviors. The multi-impulsive group has shown a stronger tendency to display comorbidity with other psychological disorders (e.g., substance abuse) and a higher dropout rate for treatment than the uni-impulsivity group. Therefore, it is important to consider the role of impulsivity in treatment and recovery for eating-disordered individuals.

Impulsivity has been widely linked to eating disorders. Although there is confusion over whether impulsivity is a risk factor for the development of disordered eating and eating disorders, it is evident impulsivity is more likely to be related to binge behavior. Impulsivity has also been related to increased eating disorder severity and decreased psychological functioning. Compared to individuals with binge eating disorder and bulimia nervosa, individuals who restrict food are less likely to engage in impulsive behaviors.

Justine J. Reel

See also: Binge Eating Disorder; Disordered Eating; Personality Characteristics; Recovery; Relapse; Substance Abuse; Suicide; Treatment

Bibliography

Boisseau, Christina L., Heather Thompson-Brenner, Kamryn T. Eddy, and Dana A. Satir. "Impulsivity and Personality Variables in Adolescents with Eating Disorders." *The Journal of Nervous and Mental Disease* 197, no. 4 (2009): 251–259. https://doi.org/10.1097/NMD.0b013e31819d96c0.

Claes, Laurence, Patricia Bijttebier, James E. Mitchell, Martina de Zwaan, and Astrid Mueller. "The Relationship between Compulsive Buying, Eating Disorder Symptoms, and Temperament in a Sample of Female Students." *Comprehensive Psychiatry* 52 (2011): 50–55. https://doi.org/10.1016/j.comppsych.2010.05.003.

Culbert, Kristen M., and Kelly L. Klump. "Impulsivity as an Underlying Factor in the Relationship between Disordered Eating and Sexual Behavior." *International Journal of Eating Disorders* 38, no. 4 (2005): 361–366. https://doi.org/10.1002/eat.20188.

Fernandez-Aranda, Fernando, Susana Jimenez-Murcia, Eva M. Alvarez-Moya, Roser Granero, Julio Vallejo, and Cynthia M. Bulik. "Impulse Control Disorders in Eating Disorders: Clinical and Therapeutic Implications." *Comprehensive Psychiatry* 47 (2006): 482–488. https://doi.org/10.106/j.comppsych.2006.03.002.

Fernandez-Aranda, Fernando, Andrea Poyastro Pinheiro, Laura M. Thornton, Wade H. Berrettini, Scott Crow, Manfred M. Fichter, Katherine A. Halmi, Allan S. Kaplan, Pamela Keel, James Mitchell, Alessandro Rotondo, Michael Strober, D. Blake Woodside, Walter H. Kaye, and Cynthia M. Bulik. "Impulse Control Disorders in Women with Eating Disorders." *Psychiatry Research* 157 (2008): 147–157. https://doi.org/10.106/j/psychres.2007.02.011.

Rosval, Lindsay, Howard Steiger, Kenneth Bruce, Mimi Israel, Jodie Richardson, and Melanie Aubut. "Impulsivity in Women with Eating Disorders: Problem of Response, Inhibition, Planning or Attention?" *International Journal of Eating Disorders* 39, no. 7 (2006): 590–593. https://doi.org/10.1002/eat.20296.

Waxman, Samantha E. "A Systematic Review of Impulsivity in Eating Disorders." *European Eating Disorders Review* 17 (2009): 408–425. https://doi.org/10.1002/erv.952.

INFERTILITY

There are numerous medical and health-related consequences that result from eating disorders such as anorexia nervosa, bulimia nervosa, and binge eating disorder. Infertility is defined as the inability to bear children despite refraining from contraceptive use for at least a year. Infertility affects 10–15 percent of married couples in the United States and has been linked to various psychological disorders including depression, obsessive-compulsive disorder, anxiety disorders, substance abuse, and eating disorders. Individuals with anorexia nervosa, bulimia nervosa, and binge eating disorder are more likely to experience infertility than the general female population due to extended menstrual cycle disturbances, hormonal imbalances, malnutrition, and vitamin deficiencies.

The pattern of higher proportion of eating-disordered individuals suffering from infertility was noted by Canadian researchers. Specifically, investigators who examined patients at infertility clinics discovered 1.5 percent of them had anorexia nervosa, 6 percent had bulimia nervosa, and another 9 percent had some other type of eating disorder or disordered eating, a higher proportion than would be expected in a community. The infertility was attributed to lack of ovulation. In addition to infertility, eating-disordered individuals may face problems with pregnancy and birth defects. Women with eating disorders may face greater risk for polycystic ovarian syndrome, characterized by changes to the ovaries such that multiple follicles accumulate in the ovaries without ovulation. The risk of infertility as a health consequence from an eating disorder may serve as the sole motivation for some women to seek treatment or desire to restore menstruation.

Justine J. Reel

See also: Medical and Health Consequences; Pregnancy

Bibliography

Abraham, Suzanne, and Derek Llewellyn-Jones. *Eating Disorders: The Facts.* New York: Oxford University Press, 1995.

Costin, Carolyn. *A Comprehensive Guide to the Causes, Treatments and Prevention of Eating Disorders,* 3rd ed. New York: McGraw-Hill, 2007.

Costin, Carolyn. *100 Questions & Answers about Eating Disorders.* Sudbury, MA: Jones and Bartlett, 2007.

Hall, Lindsey, and Leigh Cohn. *Bulimia: A Guide to Recovery.* Carlsbad, CA: Gurze, 2011.

Loucks, Anne B. "Energy Availability and Infertility." *Current Opinion in Endocrinology, Diabetes, and Obesity* 14, no. 6 (2007): 470–474. https://doi.org/10.1097/MED.0b013e3282f1cb6a.

Mehler, Philip S. "Bulimia Nervosa." *The New England Journal of Medicine* 349, no. 9 (2003): 875–882.

Mehler, Philip S., and Mori Krantz. "Anorexia Nervosa Medical Issues." *Journal of Women's Health* 12, no. 4 (2003): 331–340. https://doi.org/10.1089/154099903765448844.

Practice Committee of the American Society for Reproductive Medicine. "Current Evaluation of Amenorrhea." *Fertility and Sterility* 82 (2004): 266–272.

Sharagli, Chiara, Giuseppe Morgante, Arianna Goracci, Tara Hofkens, Vincenzo De Leo, and Paolo Castrogiovanni. "Infertility and Psychiatric Morbidity." *Fertility and Sterility* 90, no. 6 (2008): 2107–2111. http://dx.doi.org/10.1016/j.fertnstert.2007.10.045.

INTEGRATIVE APPROACHES

Many Americans have never heard of integrative health, but the holistic movement has left its imprint on many of the nation's hospitals, universities, and medical schools. The goal is to treat the mind, body, and spirit, all at the same time.

Groundbreaking research supports a strong interaction between brain and immune system, emotion, and disease.

An integrative approach to eating disorders traditionally includes treatment by an interdisciplinary team of professionals, including to primary care doctors, cardiologists, dentists, dietitians, psychotherapists, recreational therapists, and art therapists. More recently, additional modalities of mind–body–spirit intervention have been used to promote whole person healing.

Meditation

Mindfulness meditation includes an abundance of techniques to bring awareness to every aspect of daily life. For example, the popular *raisin meditation* is an experience of looking at, and then eating, a single raisin as mindfully as possible, as if a raisin has never been eaten before. This meditation takes only a few minutes, and many people report that it has a meaningful effect on their subsequent experiences with eating. Research based on sensory deprivation indicates compulsive eaters and chronic dieters are often disconnected from internal self-regulatory methods of control over their eating and are unduly influenced by external prompts, emotional signals, or belief systems. As such, the raisin meditation can be an appropriate introduction to increased self-awareness through meditation.

Other elements can also be used to increase mindfulness. Basic meditation techniques, such as *transcendental meditation,* involve a sitting or slightly reclined 20-minute meditation with repetition of a personal mantra. Focused breathing and simple yoga movements can also relax and reengage the body. Often, people with eating disorders simultaneously sense being disconnected from, yet completely defined by, their bodies. So, *meditative breathing* can be both a relaxation component and a powerful focusing technique. It works by balancing the autonomic nervous system and drawing attention to physiological processes that can be directly experienced without being threatening. Additionally, *guided meditations* can be used in a safe place to help people address their fears and experiences with hunger and fullness. Also, *forgiveness meditation* can address anger and hurt directed toward the self and others and can encourage nonjudgmental acceptance of feelings. A *spiritual wisdom* exercise can help people connect to values, strengths, and a higher life purpose through inner awareness and peace.

Therapeutic Massage/Touch

Therapeutic massage or therapeutic touch (TT) is an almost forgotten art of medicine, as many areas of the human body cannot be touched even by a physician without a specific reason for examination or biochemical treatment. Also, individuals who suffer from eating disorders often have a history of physical or sexual abuse that indicates a need for caution when employing of this powerful technique. Manual medicine includes sensitive touch, and can be a much more powerful tool than many modern physicians assume. Pains and discomforts can be eased by just touching the sick area and assisting the person to be in better contact with the distressed area of the body. People who suffer from eating disorders often disengage from their bodies, and this disengagement can be reversed by sensitive healing touch. When touch is combined with emotional therapeutic work, holistic healing is enhanced, and difficulties can be resolved in an effective way, often without the use of medication.

Acupuncture

In Eastern medicine, all illness is believed to be a result of mind–body–spirit energy imbalance. Acupuncture intends to restore health by readjusting and balancing energy. It is especially helpful for people with food allergies, digestive problems, and food cravings, conditions found in people with eating disorders. A recent study indicated that acupuncture may provide benefits to eating-disorder clients by improving their overall quality of life. The researchers found evidence of a lower anxiety and perfectionism, which may help people with eating disorders succeed in learning healthy eating behaviors.

Energy Psychology

Energy psychology is based on the premise that painful emotional, spiritual, and physical symptoms are the consequence of disruption in the energy system. Correcting the disruption reestablishes the body's natural ability to heal itself. Energy psychology is practiced in many forms beyond acupuncture, including meridian-tapping techniques, Thought Field Therapy, acupressure, Emotional Freedom Technique, and touch therapy. Traditional psychotherapy uses the influence of speech to transform or regulate emotions. By talking about emotions, one may come to a understanding of the self and new ways to respond to old issues. For individuals with addictions, anxiety, phobias, PTSD, and eating disorders, energy psychology techniques can complement traditional psychotherapy to release emotional blocks and promote healing. Specifically, meridian tapping involves repeating a neutral affirmation while rubbing a spot on the upper right or left chest, or tapping a karate chop point on the outside of either hand. Also, specific points on the face and body can be rubbed or tapped, depending on the symptoms. An affirmation could be, "Even though I have this eating disorder, I deeply and completely accept myself." If an individual has significant trauma, a therapist may walk her or him through each traumatic event one step at a time, while tapping to relieve troubling emotions.

Juliann Cook Jeppsen

See also: Eye Movement Desensitization and Reprocessing; Mindfulness; Treatment; Yoga

Bibliography

Bono, Joseph. "Psychological Assessment of Transcendental Meditation." In *Meditation: Classic and Contemporary Perspectives,* edited by Deane Shapiro and Roger Walsh, 209–217. New York: Aldine, 1984.

"Holistic Treatment Disordered Treatment." Mirasol. Accessed November 17, 2016. http://www.mirasol.net/integrative-treatment.php.

Marlatt, G., Alan L. Kristeller, and Jean L. Kristeller. "Mindfulness and Meditation." In *Integrating Spirituality in Treatment,* edited by William R. Miller. Washington, DC: American Psychological Association, 2000.

O'Connell, Daniel F., and Charles N. Alexander. *Self-Recovery: Treating Addictions Using Transcendental Meditation and Maharishi Ayur-Veda.* Binghamton, NY: Haworth Press, 1994.

Roucsh, Robert A. *Complementary and Alternative Medicine: Clinic Design.* New York: Haworth Integrative Healing Press, 2003.

Ventegodt, Soren, Niels Anderson, and Joav Merrick. "Holistic Medicine III: The Holistic Process of Healing." *The Scientific World Journal* 3 (2003): 1138–1146. http://dx.doi.org/10.1100/tsw.2003.100.

INTELLECTUAL DISABILITIES AND BODY IMAGE

People with intellectual disabilities (IDs) have received little attention in body image and eating disorder research, despite that this population may face additional pressures related to body shape, size, and culturally-constructed body ideals. This group has been the target of many stereotypes and faces stigma daily when interacting with others. Additionally, the terminology of individuals with ID versus persons with mental retardation has been controversial over the past several years. According to the *Diagnostic Manual-Intellectual Disability: A Clinical Guide for Diagnosis of Mental Disorders in Persons with Intellectual Disability,* there has been a shift since 2003 to using *intellectual disability.*

Definition of Intellectual Disability

An intellectual disability, often referred to as a "developmental delay," is determined by three criteria: (1) below average intellectual functioning (IQ < 70 or IQ-equivalent), (2) deficits in adaptive daily functioning, and (3) disability before age 18. Measurement of eating disorders and other mental disorders in this population can present some challenges as individuals with ID are a widely misunderstood and heterogeneous group. Persons with ID require just enough structure and cues to express their feelings in a spontaneous and unbiased fashion. Researchers have modified some surveys (e.g., Rosenberg's Self-Esteem Scale) developed for the general population to assess self-esteem and other psychological characteristics among individuals with ID.

Eating Disorders and Intellectual Disabilities

An individual who has an intellectual disability and has been diagnosed with an eating disorder may present with common stressors and indicators of an adult without an intellectual disability. For example, the individual with an intellectual disability may experience dysfunctional family dynamics, unhealthy eating habits, grief/loss issues, relationship issues, and other concerns that might complicate the eating disorder treatment. Poindexter and Loschen outlined the *DSM-IV* criteria for anorexia and bulimia nervosa and adapted it for people with severe to profound intellectual disabilities. Part of the criteria for anorexia nervosa is the refusal to gain weight and maintain age appropriate body weight. For example, a person with a severe/profound intellectual disability may exhibit a fear of gaining weight by avoiding food and restricting it during meals.

Approximately 6–42 percent of adults with intellectual disabilities in a hospital setting met the criteria for a clinical eating disorder including anorexia nervosa, bulimia nervosa, and the previous *DSM* diagnosis of "eating disorder not otherwise specified" (e.g., binge eating disorder). Another 19 percent in a community setting had a diagnosable eating disorder. However, these reported prevalence rates included individuals diagnosed with pica, severe/profound intellectual disabilities, autism, and other developmental diagnoses/genetic syndromes who would be unlikely to meet the full criteria for a clinical eating disorder (e.g., negative body image). Individuals who fit several of these diagnoses/syndromes tended to exhibit eating disorder–like characteristics. However, the similar presentation of psychopathology in individuals with intellectual disabilities and eating disorders make it challenging to distinguish an intellectual disability from an eating disorder. Additionally, the intellectual disability and eating disorder may coexist; therefore, it is important to differentiate a person with a dual diagnosis from one with only an intellectual disability.

Body Image and Intellectual Disabilities

Few studies have examined body image among individuals with intellectual disabilities. However, some recent attention has been given to a higher proportionate obesity rate for this population. A rare study explored body image in 100 adult males and females with ID and found trends similar to the general population. For example, males with ID chose a larger body size for their ideal body than female with ID, and men were more satisfied with their bodies than women. Both males and females expressed a desire to have a thinner physique; however, males also reported wanting to increase muscle size. To allow for more in-depth body image responses, participants were asked this question: if they had a magic wand, what, if anything, would they change. The two most common themes were the desire to be thinner or to have more muscles. Approximately 24 participants (23.3 percent) responded for open-ended items that they would like to lose weight or be skinnier. Although more females ($N = 15$) expressed an interest in losing weight, nine males reported wanting to be thinner. One male athlete (age 23) with a body mass index (BMI) of 27.5 stated, "I want to lose some weight—that is why I do basketball." Another male (age 61) with a BMI of 41.1 indicated he would like to "lose a bunch of weight here" as he pointed to his midsection. However, many male athletes expressed a desire to build muscles for the open-ended item as shown by the following comment from a 21-year-old male with a BMI of 25.7, "I want to have a six pack. No, an eight pack. Big muscles like Hollywood Hulk Hogan. I need to go to the gym."

Study results of females with ID resembled findings from previous body image studies about females without intellectual disabilities. Female participants desired to be thinner or to lose weight. One female (age 38) with a BMI of 42.9 expressed her intense body dissatisfaction. "I am too fat, too ugly, and not pretty. I am not cute." Another female participant stated she would change "my body, from my neck down to my toes" and yet another female indicated she wanted to "lose weight and date boys." Interestingly, only two participants identified their disability as something they would want to change. One female with ID (age 55) who was a quadriplegic with cerebral palsy shared, "I wish I could walk. I wouldn't want to be in this chair." A male with ID (age 54) echoed her sentiment, "I don't want to be in this chair." However, the characteristics associated with ID (e.g., larger head) were never discussed.

Justine J. Reel and Robert A. Bucciere

See also: Body Image; Media; Pica; Treatment

Bibliography

Bucciere, Robert A., and Justine J. Reel. "'Not So Different Than You': Body Image and Eating Disorders among Individuals with Disabilities." In *The Hidden Faces of Eating Disorders and Body Image,* edited by Justine J. Reel and Katherine A. Beals, 145–158. Reston, VA: AAHPERD, 2009.

Crabtree, Jason W., S. Alexander Haslam, Tom Postmes, and Catherine Haslam. "Mental Health Support Groups, Stigma, and Self-Esteem: Positive and Negative Implications of Group Identification." *Journal of Social Issues* 66, no. 3 (2010): 553–569. https://doi .org/10.1111/j.1540-4560.2010.01662.x.

Davis, Clare, Steven Kellett, Nigel Beail, and Jeremy Turk. "Utility of the Rosenberg Self-Esteem Scale." *American Journal on Intellectual and Developmental Disabilities* 114, no. 3 (2009): 172–178.

Dykens, E., K. Schwenk, M. Maxwell, and B. Myatt. "The Sentence Completion and Three Wishes Tasks: Windows into the Inner Lives of People with Intellectual Disabilities." *Journal of Intellectual Disability Research* 51, no. 8 (2007): 588–597. https://doi .org/10.1111/j.1365-2788.2006.00937.x.

Fletcher, Robert J., Earl Loschen, Chrissoula Stavrakaki, and Michael First. *Diagnostic Manual-Intellectual Disability: A Clinical Guide for Diagnosis of Mental Disorders in Persons with Intellectual Disability.* Kingston, NY: The NADD Press, 2007.

Gal, Eynat, Reem Hardal-Nasser, and Batya Engel-Yeger. "The Relationship between the Severity of Eating Problems and Intellectual Developmental Deficit Level." *Research in Developmental Disabilities* 32 (2011): 1464–1469. http://dx.doi.org/10.1016/j .ridd.2010.12.003.

Gravestock, Shaun. "Diagnosis and Classification of Eating Disorders in Adults with Intellectual Disability: the Diagnostic Criteria for Psychiatric Disorders for Use with Adults with Learning Disabilities/Mental Retardation (DC-LD) Approach." *Journal of Intellectual Disability Research* 47 (2003): 72–83. https://doi.org/10.1046/j.1365-2788.47 .s1.41.x.

Gravestock, Shaun. "Eating Disorders in Adults with Intellectual Disability." *Journal of Intellectual Disability Research* 44, no. 6 (2000): 625–637. https://doi.org/10.1111 /j.1365-2788.2000.00308.x.

Howes, Hannah, Stephen Edwards, and David Benton. "Female Body Image Following Acquired Brain Injury." *Brain Injury* 19, no. 6 (2005): 403–415. http://dx.doi.org/10.1080/02699050400025158.

Howes, Hannah, Stephen Edwards, and David Benton. "Male Body Image Following Acquired Brain Injury." *Brain Injury* 19, no. 2 (2005): 135–147. http://dx.doi.org/10.1080/02699050410001720077.

Keung Yuen, Hon, and Carolyn Hanson. "Body Image and Exercise in People with and without Acquired Mobility Disability." *Disability and Rehabilitation* 24, no. 6 (2002): 289–296. http://dx.doi.org/10.1080/09638280110086477.

Levi, Aurelia. "Orthopedic Disability as a Factor in Human-Figure Perception." *Journal of Consulting Psychology* 25, no. 3 (1961): 253–256. http://dx.doi.org/10.1037/h0038836.

MacMahon, Pamela, and Andrew Jahoda. "Social Comparison and Depression: People with Mild and Moderate Intellectual Disabilities." *American Journal on Mental Retardation* 113, no. 4 (2008): 307–318.

Murray, C. D., and J. Fox. "Body Image and Prosthesis Satisfaction in the Lower Limb Amputee." *Disability and Rehabilitation* 24, no. 17 (2002): 925–931. http://dx.doi.org/10.1080/09638280210150014.

Poindexter, Ann R., and Earl Loschen. "Eating Disorders." In *Diagnostic Manual-Intellectual Disability: A Clinical Guide for Diagnosis of Mental Disorders in Persons with Intellectual Disability,* edited by Robert J. Fletcher, Earl Loschen, Chrissoula Stavrakaki, and Michael First, 277–279. Kingston, NY: The NADD Press, 2007.

Potgieter, C., and G. Khan. "Sexual Self-Esteem and Body Image of South African Spinal Cord Injured Adolescents." *Sexuality and Disability* 23, no. 1 (2005): 1–20. https://doi.org/10.1007/s11195-004-2076-6.

Reel, Justine J. "Tailoring Eating Disorder Treatment for Diverse Clients: How to Avoid a 'Cookie Cutter' Approach." In *The Hidden Faces of Eating Disorders and Body Image,* edited by Justine J. Reel and Katherine A. Beals, 193–207. Reston, VA: AAHPERD, 2009.

Reel, Justine J., and Robert A. Bucciere. "Ableism and Body Image: Conceptualizing How Individuals with Disabilities Are Marginalized." *Women in Sport & Physical Activity Journal: Moving toward Justice* 19, no. 1 (2010): 91–97.

Shapiro, Deborah R., and Jeffery J. Martin. "Athletic Identity, Affect, and Peer Relations in Youth Athletes with Physical Disabilities." *Disability and Health Journal* 3, no. 2 (2010): 79–85. http://dx.doi.org/10.1016/j.dhjo.2009.08.004.

Stunkard, Albert J., Thorkild I. A. Sorenson, and F. Schulsinger. "Use of Danish Adoption Register for the Study of Obesity and Thinness." In *The Genetics of Neurological and Psychiatric Disorders,* edited by S. Kety, 115–120. New York: Raven, 1983.

Taub, Diane E., P. L. Fanflik, and Penelope A. McLorg. "Body Image among Women with Physical Disabilities: Internalization of Norms and Reactions to Nonconformity." *Sociological Focus* 36 (2003): 159–176. http://dx.doi.org/10.1080/00380237.2003.10570722.

INTERNATIONAL ASSOCIATION OF EATING DISORDER PROFESSIONALS

The International Association of Eating Disorder Professionals (IAEDP) is an organization formed in 1985 to provide quality training for eating disorder treatment providers from across the globe. Multidisciplinary professionals include physicians, psychiatrists, nurses, dietitians, psychologists, social workers, and other licensed health care providers who work with eating disorder clients in a variety of treatment settings. IAEDP has organized state and regional chapters to expand training opportunities at the local level in Arizona, California, Florida, New York, Utah, and Washington.

IAEDP offers the only recognized eating disorder treatment certification to professionals in the field with the goal of promoting high standards of care and continuing training and education. Professionals who treat eating disorders must meet requirements by taking educational classes and an examination. Mental health professionals (e.g., Licensed Professional Counselors [LPC], Psychologists, Licensed Clinical Social Workers [LCSW]) apply for certification to be a Certified Eating Disorder Specialist (CEDS) while registered dietitians are eligible to become a Certified Eating Disorders Registered Dietitian (CEDRD) if they meet the necessary requirements.

Justine J. Reel

See also: Academy for Eating Disorders; Advocacy Groups; Treatment

Bibliography

"International Association of Eating Disorder Professionals." IAEDP. Accessed November 17, 2016. www.iaedp.com.

INTERNET AND EATING DISORDERS

The Internet has become a double-edged sword when it comes to helping or harming one's mental health and tendency toward eating disorders. Although there are therapeutic approaches offered online, potential dangers have also come to light. For example, for individuals who are at risk for developing or who are currently struggling with an eating disorder, the Internet poses endless opportunities to find triggering images, exchange tips and tricks with others engaging in similarly unhealthy behavior, and reinforce their disorder. The recent emergence of pro-anorexia (a.k.a. pro-ana) and pro-bulimia (pro-mia) online communities is a perfect example of the dangers made possible. On the other hand, being online also poses a unique opportunity for anonymous, accessible, and low-cost therapeutic intervention. Research has been dedicated to developing, testing, and evaluating web-based treatment and prevention programs specifically targeted at eating disorders and body image. The benefits offered by these programs coupled with unique factors specific to Internet offer exciting potential for widespread treatment options.

The Dangers of the Internet

Although many researchers are optimistic about the possibilities offered by the Internet, recent research has also highlighted the dangers for people with eating disorders. Chief among the harms posed are online communities that promote eating disorders. These websites are often dubbed "pro-ana" for pro-anorexia and "pro-mia" for pro bulimia. There are also *fitspiration, thinspiration,* and *thintention* websites, which include blogs where users can document their weight loss, pictures designed to inspire users to remain adherent to dieting and weight-control behaviors, and a community board where users can interact with one another. Eating disorders are usually referred to in the first person and are given personalities, such as Ana and Mia. Many users refer to Ana/Mia as their best friend. A majority of individuals who create and visit these sites are young women, ages 18 to 25. Studies have found viewing these websites causes an increase in dieting behavior and body dissatisfaction. Viewing a pro-anorexia website just once caused individuals to experience a worsened mood and lower self-esteem, and viewers stated they were much more likely to compare themselves to the images of the women on pro-anorexia websites than to images of women on other websites (e.g., a fashion website). Clearly, pro-anorexia/pro-bulimia websites pose a threat to the well-being of individuals who may be at risk for, or currently combating, an eating disorder.

Another risk posed by Internet is the potential for exposure to misinformation. This is particularly critical for younger generations, who rely on Internet as a chief source of information and educational material. Many popular search engines, like Google, and video-content websites, such as YouTube, do not return search results based on the veracity of the information contained in the results. It is far more common for searches on any widely used website to return search results based on popularity; in some cases, certain companies pay search engines more to be higher in the results queue. These factors do not protect users from exposure to misinformation, particularly when it pertains to health. One study found almost 30 percent of the results retrieved in a YouTube search for anorexia were pro-anorexia material, meaning these results *promoted* anorexia rather than provided education around the health consequences of this disorder. Another study concluded there was very little quality information available on some of the most popular websites devoted to mental illness education; much of the information contained on these sites was outdated, unclear, contradictory, and blatantly incorrect. In a review of 79 articles testing the quality of general health information available on Internet, authors found 70 percent of the studies concluded that Internet provided poor-quality health information. Clearly, the availability of poor quality, inaccurate information related to health, mental illness, and eating disorders on the Internet is a major point of concern for researchers, health care providers, and the public.

Treatment Possibilities Using the Internet

Despite the dangers posed by Internet, many researchers and clinicians agree that being online represents an unparalleled opportunity for novel types of interventions. The new fields of e-mental health and e-therapy are rapidly growing in Western societies. E-therapy is particularly popular because, unlike traditional treatment options, using Internet as the medium for intervention allows individuals to stay anonymous, seek treatment from anywhere in the world (with Internet connection), and access these treatments at a fraction of the cost as traditional therapies. These opportunities are particularly compelling for eating disorders;

research has shown that fewer than 25 percent of individuals with an eating disorder actually seek treatment, and an even smaller percentage receive treatment due to barriers such as cost/insurance coverage and geographic location. The over 75 percent of individuals with an eating disorder who do not seek treatment often report fear of social stigma, shame/guilt, and lack of financial resources as reasons they did not seek treatment. Being online offers people an opportunity to remain anonymous during treatment, keep treatment private from others, and access it for little to no cost, e-therapies for eating disorders may be instrumental to reach a larger proportion of individuals who need treatment.

To date, research on the effectiveness of Internet-based treatment and prevention programs for eating disorders is mixed. Some studies have reported positive results with very low treatment dropout; others, however, have reported significant numbers of individuals who do not complete the online treatment protocol as well as limited benefits from the treatment. In a review of prevention, treatment, and relapse-prevention Internet-based programs, researchers from the UK concluded that the prevention-focused programs—specifically "Student Bodies," a cognitive behavioral treatment–based prevention program delivered via CD-ROM—were the most beneficial. Successful completion of the Student Bodies program resulted in a moderate reduction in overall disordered eating symptomology as well as a moderate reduction in the severity of bulimia nervosa. In general, Internet-based treatment programs seemed to have the largest effect on binge eating behaviors and cognitions associated with disordered eating (e.g., fear of gaining weight). Individuals with anorexia and bulimia had generally less positive reactions to Internet-based programs.

Researchers agree the available literature on the efficacy of Internet-based e-therapies is scant; therefore, it is important for researchers to continue to study and refine treatment programs being developed for Internet. Additionally, with widespread use of smartphones, researchers should investigate the utility of application-based interventions and how these programs can inform Internet-based programs. Last, the dangers posed by Internet need to be kept in mind when considering future directions for web-based programs. Research needs to be done to identify the specific dangers of Internet for individuals with eating disorders. Once these dangers have been identified, research on how to circumvent, combat, or minimize these risks is necessary.

Hannah J. Hopkins

See also: Media; Pro-Ana; Social Media and Eating Disorders

Bibliography

Aardoom, Jiska J., Alexandra E. Dingemans, Philip Spinhoven, and Eric F. Van Furth. "Treating Eating Disorders over the Internet: A Systematic Review and Future Research Directions." *International Journal of Eating Disorders* 46, no. 6 (2013): 539–552. https://doi.org/10.1002/eat.22135.

Bardone-Cone, Anna M., and Kamila M. Cass. "What Does Viewing a Pro-Anorexia Website Do? An Experimental Examination of Website Exposure and Moderating Effects." *International Journal of Eating Disorders* 40, no. 6 (2007): 537–548. https://doi.org/10.1002/eat.20396.

Homewood, Judi, and Maral Melkonian. "What Factors Account for Internalisation of the Content of Pro-Ana Websites?" *Journal of Neurology Neurosurgery & Psychiatry* 86, no. 9 (2015): e3. https://doi.org/10.1136/jnnp-2015-311750.37.

Levine, Michael P., and Sarah K. Murnen. "'Everybody Knows That Mass Media Are/Are Not [Pick One] a Cause of Eating Disorders': A Critical Review of Evidence for a Causal Link between Media, Negative Body Image and Disordered Eating in Females." *Journal of Social and Clinical Psychology* 28, no. 1 (2009): 9–42. http://dx.doi.org/10.1521/jscp.2009.28.1.9.

Loucas, Christina E., Christopher G. Fairburn, Craig Whittington, Mary E. Pennant, Sarah Stockton, and Tim Kendall. "E-Therapy in the Treatment and Prevention of Eating Disorders: A Systematic Review and Meta-Analysis." *Behaviour Research and Therapy* 63 (2014): 122–131. https://doi.org/10.1016/j.brat.2014.09.011.

Reavley, Nicola J., and Anthony F. Jorm. "The Quality of Mental Disorder Information Websites: A Review." *Patient Education and Counseling* 85, no. 2 (2011): e16–e25. https://doi.org/10.1016/j.pec.2010.10.015.

Syed-Abdul, Shabbir, Luis Fernandez-Luque, Wen-Shan Jian, Yu-Chuan Li, Steven Crain, Min-Huei Hsu, Yao-Chin Wang, Dojsuren Khandregzen, Enkhzaya Chuluunbaatar, Phung Anh Nguyen, and Der-Ming Loiu. "Misleading Health-Related Information Promoted through Video-Based Social Media: Anorexia on YouTube." *Journal of Medical Internet Research* 15, no. 2 (2013): e30. https://doi.org/10.2196/jmir.2237.

INTUITIVE EATING

Intuitive eating refers to decisions about eating based on biological cues of hunger and fullness rather than eating for emotional reasons. This popular approach has been defined as a nondiet, hunger-based approach to food and weight management. The overall goal of intuitive eating is to help individuals develop a healthy relationship with weight, self, and food and to reduce dysfunctional obsessive thought patterns related to food.

The basic premise of intuitive eating is individuals are born with an innate ability to decipher the amount and kinds of food ideal for their development. Most children are naturally intuitive eaters and do not eat past the point of fullness even when their favorite foods are offered. However, many adults have become emotional eaters, and rarely respond exclusively to biologically-based hunger cues. Learning intuitive eating gives an individual the ability to become reacquainted with the cues of hunger and satiety and encourages a response to these signals. Intuitive eating is part of the larger antidiet movement with similar programs including normal eating, wisdom eating, conscious eating, and mindful eating. Intuitive eating is also a component of the Health at Every Size movement.

History of Intuitive Eating

The term *intuitive eating* was first coined by Evelyn Tribole and Elyse Resch in their book *Intuitive Eating,* published in 1995. Tribole and Resch, registered dietitians working in California, began to recognize the ineffectiveness of traditional dieting and weight management approaches with clients. Their clients would follow elaborate meal plans to lose weight, only to regain the weight after leaving the program. The failure would cause clients to blame themselves and assume tremendous guilt. Tribole and Resch concluded traditional diet meal plans were ineffective and looked to existing antidieting movement for solutions. They thought the antidieting approach did not effectively address basic nutrition and created intuitive eating to bridge that gap. Since the book's publication, the intuitive eating approach has been a popular method for teaching healthy nutritional habits to individuals with eating disorders, disordered eating, chronic dieting, or obesity. By honoring hunger and relinquishing the power of foods, many individuals find they can maintain a healthy weight rather than a continual yo-yo weight fluctuation. Although eating-disordered individuals may take several months or more to use intuitive eating, they begin by learning about the philosophy and 10 principles of intuitive eating.

Ten Principles of Intuitive Eating

Tribole and Resch outlined 10 principles of intuitive eating to describe the overriding philosophy of intuitive eating:

1. **Reject the diet mentality.** To be an intuitive eater, you must first reject the idea that diets work. Many people spend endless time and money on diets that promise to make them effortlessly thin. The commercial diet industry has a failure rate of 95 percent; however, for most dieters, when they fail they blame themselves and not the process of dieting. To fully embrace intuitive eating, you must get rid of the diet books and magazine articles that promote dieting.
2. **Honor your hunger.** Deprivation leads to overeating as the body tries to physically compensate for the lost nutrition. Many people have learned to silence hunger cues and often go long periods without eating, followed by uncontrolled overcompensation. Honoring your hunger involves learning to identify your body's unique hunger cues. When you feel slight hunger, you respond by eating. Intuitive eaters are encouraged to eat whenever they are hungry, even if it is at nonmeal times, as the body's hunger signals a physical need for nourishment.
3. **Make peace with food.** The dieting mentality promotes the idea that food is the enemy. In this step, work is done to undo that damage and relate to food in a healthy way. Part of making peace with food includes giving oneself unconditional permission to eat. Dieting and deprivation lead to bingeing and guilt. By giving yourself permission to eat, you end the sense of deprivation and guilt that cause overeating.
4. **Challenge the food police.** Chronic dieters have trained themselves for years to decipher between good and bad foods. Often these dieters can recite calories, fat grams, points, or other numerical values when discussing food. Every food becomes good or bad in their minds, with the good foods low-calorie, healthy options and the bad foods anything calorie-laden or sweet. This leads people to have an internal voice that dictates whether they are good or bad, based on food choices they made that day. Intuitive eaters challenge these voices, realizing these voices are sabotaging a healthy relationship with food and weight.
5. **Respect your fullness.** Even though eating beyond fullness is uncomfortable, it is a common behavior. In this step, you pay attention to your fullness signals and stop when satisfied, rather than stuffed. This is most effectively done when you slow

down and enjoy your food. Intuitive eaters are encouraged to put their fork down throughout a meal and evaluate their fullness before continuing. They then stop when they are satisfied but give themselves permission to eat more if they become hungry again later.

6. **Discover the satisfaction factor.** In many cultures, the eating process is slow and social. Interestingly, these cultures often have lower rates of obesity. There is wisdom in the advice to slow down and savor your food. If you eat slowly, in a comfortable environment, you are more likely to taste each bite of food and feel more satisfied after the meal.

7. **Honor your feelings without using food.** In this step, you identify the emotional triggers that cause you to turn to food for support. It is important to understand food will not fix these problems. Once you identify emotional triggers, you work to find different distracters and alternative ways of coping that do not involve food.

8. **Respect your body.** Understanding and appreciating body diversity, including your own, is critical in self-acceptance. Showing respect for your body includes doing nice things for yourself and not delaying enjoyable experiences such as swimming or vacations because you are ashamed of how you look.

9. **Exercise—feel the difference.** Most dieters are either militant slaves of exercise or have completely given up on exercise. This step encourages you to find a physical activity you enjoy, such as walking, mountain biking, rollerblading, or rock climbing. The point of the activity is to make your body healthier and feel good about yourself. Forget about calculating calories burned or trying to lose weight, just get active to feel better.

10. **Honor your health—gentle nutrition.** In this last step, nutrition is finally addressed. The key is to make food choices that honor your health, but are also appetizing to you. You want to eat what you love, but be mindful of health where you can. It is important to address your feelings of deprivation. If you skip out on the chocolate chip cookies, will you feel deprived? If so, eat one when you are hungry. If not, choose something with more nutritional value.

Assessment of Intuitive Eating

The Hawks Intuitive Eating Scale (IES), a 30-item questionnaire, assesses one's relationship with exercise and eating using responses ranging from *strongly agree* to *strongly disagree*. For example, for relationship with food, one IES item states, "I seldom eat unless I notice I'm physically hungry." To address having a healthy relationship with exercise, another IES item is "One of my main reasons for exercising is to control my weight." This questionnaire has been used successfully with college students and is valid and reliable.

In 2006, another intuitive eating researcher, Dr. Tylka, developed a 21-item scale to measure the following components of intuitive eating: unconditional permission to eat, eating for physical reasons rather than emotional ones, and reliance on hunger and satiety cues. Sample items of this intuitive eating questionnaire include, "If I am craving a particular food, I let myself have it" and "I stop myself when I feel full (not overstuffed)." Item responses range from *strongly agree* to *strongly disagree* and the scale has been used with college students and women in midlife successfully.

Overall, intuitive eating has been shown to be a promising approach to disordered eating prevention, as it can transition participants away from a dieting mentality. High levels of intuitive eating are correlated with lower body mass index, lower triglyceride levels, high levels of high-density lipoproteins, and improved cardiovascular risk. In addition, intuitive eaters have increased enjoyment and pleasure with food and fewer dieting behaviors and food anxieties.

Men have higher total intuitive eating levels, meaning they have more traits of an intuitive eater, compared to women. Coercive feeding strategies from caregivers, association with individuals who are food/weight obsessed, and maladaptive personality characteristics negatively influence intuitive eating. Among obese women, intuitive eating was positively associated with self-esteem and negatively associated with uncontrolled emotional eating. Persons higher in intuitive eating are less likely to report binge eating, and there is a marginal association between intuitive eating and reduced depression, anxiety, and stress.

Intuitive Eating and Health at Every Size Approach

Researcher Linda Bacon conducted a 6-month randomized clinical trial with a two-year follow-up with white, female, obese chronic dieters in either a Health at Every Size (HAES) intervention or a diet intervention. The HAES program included intuitive eating as a dietary approach. Bacon found more people dropped out of the diet group compared to the HAES group. The members of HAES group maintained weight, improved on physical and psychological variables, and sustained improvements. The diet group participants lost weight and showed improvement in many variables at the one-year mark, but the weight was regained, and the variable improvement was not sustained after two years. From this study, she concluded the HAES approach, including intuitive eating, enabled participants to make long-term behavior change and resulted in improved health risks for obese women.

In the 2003 edition *Intuitive Eating,* Tribole and Resch added a chapter entitled, "Intuitive Eating: The Ultimate Path toward Healing from Eating Disorders." In this chapter, they discuss the practical use of intuitive eating as a nutritional recovery plan for individuals suffering from various eating disorders. However, intuitive eating cannot be embraced in the beginning of a serious eating disorder recovery. It is important that biological restoration and balance be achieved before a client learns about intuitive eating. Because most eating disorders begin with a diet, the intuitive eating approach is ideal for eating disorder recovery as it encourages a healthy relationship with food and does not dictate specific amounts of foods that must be eaten. Many eating disorder facilities around the country exclusively use intuitive eating as a dietary approach with clients.

TeriSue Smith-Jackson

See also: Emotional Eating; Health at Every Size Approach; Intuitive Exercise; Nutrition Treatment Approaches; Visceral Sensitivity

Bibliography

Augustus-Horvath, Casey L., and Tracy L. Tylka. "The Acceptance Model of Intuitive Eating: A Comparison of Women in Emerging Adulthood, Middle Adulthood, and Late Adulthood." *Journal of Counseling Psychology* 58, no. 1 (2011): 110–125. http://dx.doi .org/10.1037/a0022129.

Bacon, Linda. "Size Acceptance and Intuitive Eating Improve Health in Obese Female Chronic Dieters." *Journal of the American Dietetic Association* 105 (2005): 929–936. http://dx.doi.org/10.1016/j.jada.2005.03.011.

Cole, Renee E., and Tanya Horacek. "Effectiveness of the 'My Body Knows When' Intuitive-Eating Pilot Program." *American Journal of Health Behavior* (2010): 286–297. https://doi.org/10.5993/AJHB.34.3.4.

Hawks, Steven R., Hala Madanat, Jaylyn Hawks, and Ashley Harris. "Relationship between Intuitive Eating and Health Indicators among College Women." *American Journal of Health Education* 36, no. 6 (2005): 331–336. http://dx.doi.org/10.1080/19325037.2 005.10608206.

Hawks, Steven R., Ray M. Merrill, and Hala N. Madanat. "The Intuitive Eating Validation Scale: Preliminary Validation." *American Journal of Health Education* 35 (2004): 26–35.

Kroon Van Diest, Ashley, and Tracy Tylka. "Gender Differences in Intuitive Eating and Factors that Negatively Influence Intuitive Eating." Senior Honors Thesis, Ohio State University, 2008.

Smith, TeriSue, and Steven R. Hawks. "Intuitive Eating, Diet Composition, and the Meaning of Food in Healthy Weight Promotion." *American Journal of Health Education* 37, no. 3 (2006): 130–136. http://dx.doi.org/10.1080/19325037.2006.10598892.

Tribole, Evelyn, and Elyse Resch. *Intuitive Eating: A Revolutionary Program That Works.* New York: St. Martin's Griffin, 2003.

Tylka, Tracy L. "Development and Psychometric Evaluation of a Measure of Intuitive Eating." *Journal of Counseling Psychology* 53, no. 2 (2006): 226–240. http://dx.doi .org/10.1037/0022-0167.53.2.226.

INTUITIVE EXERCISE

Intuitive exercise is an approach to physical activity that encourages a positive and healthy relationship with movement. The term comes from a parallel philosophy called intuitive eating. Intuitive eating as a way of eating that relies on listening to bodily cues of hunger and fullness. This approach to eating moves away from emotional eating toward one that relies on biology. For individuals with eating disorders, these biological cues have been ignored and need to be relearned. It is also important that clients with eating disorders examine and improve their relationship with exercise.

Exercise provides numerous physical and psychological health benefits to people of all ages. In fact, exercise is viewed as medicine for mental health improvements like decreasing anxiety and depression. Likewise, exercise is a strong contributor to reduced risk of diseases, such as cardiovascular problems and cancers. Paradoxically, for clients with eating disorders, exercise might be taken to the extreme, where physical activity actually becomes detrimental to one's health. For individuals who exercise excessively and are compelled to exercise to compensate for eating behaviors, striking a healthy and balanced approach to exercise can be challenging.

Exercise and Eating Disorders: An Interview with Dr. Maya Miyairi

Dr. Maya Miyairi is an assistant professor in the department of Kinesiology and Health Science at Utah State University at Brigham City campus. She currently teaches courses for health education/health science programs through broadcast and online. She received her master's degree in Exercise and Sport Science and her doctoral degree in Health Promotion and Education at the University of Utah. She previously developed and implemented exercise education programs at eating disorders residential facilities in Utah. Her current research interests include weight bias, intuitive exercise, cross-cultural comparisons of disordered eating behaviors, and weight-related teasing as a form of bullying behaviors.

> **How do you know if a client has a problem with exercising too much or using exercise as a compensatory behavior (part of their eating disorder)? What are warning signs and flags parents, family members, and friends should look for?**
>
> Before making any assumptions, it is important to spend enough time to interview a client about her or his exercise behavior and build a trustful relationship first. This is for clients to feel safe to share their full stories with me, and this approach has helped me understand how each client engages in exercise and a relationship between her, exercise, and her eating disorder. There are a few questions that I always ask in order to evaluate client's exercise mind-set and behavior after asking general questions:
>
> - What types of exercise have you engaged in in the past year? And, how about your relationship with exercise in the past few months?
> - How often do you engage in exercise per week? And, how long does a typical length of exercise time last per day?
> - During your exercise time, what motivates you to continue exercise?
> - Can you describe specific thoughts and feelings you go through during exercise?
> - Where and with whom do you usually engage in exercise?

Although it is important to know frequency and amount of exercise, motives, and mind-set toward exercise are more critical evaluation points to determine if exercise is part of a client's eating disorder. For example, it really does not matter if she or he runs for 20 minutes or one hour as long as her or his motivations or intentions to run is to lose weight because dysfunctional motivations and intentions (i.e., burning calories, weight loss) can easily lead into more severe behaviors. The following behaviors are some examples of warning signs:

- Exercising alone multiple times per day,
- Choosing a particular cardiovascular exercise only (e.g., running),
- Obsessively counting calorie expenditure during exercise,
- Prioritizing exercise over social or family events,
- Engaging in a daily exercise schedule even on vacation or while being injured,
- Constantly increasing intensity levels, frequencies, and distance, and/or
- Refusing to participate in mind–body exercises (e.g., mindful walk, yoga)

What role should exercise play as part of an overall treatment strategy for addressing eating disorders?

Just think how exercise plays a part of healthy individuals' lives. Of course, we need to modify types of exercise and amount of activity time for clients with eating disorders. However, it is critical for a treatment team to promote a variety of ways to enjoy exercise so that clients can practice how to reengage in exercise in a healthy manner according to recovery levels. Ideally, an exercise specialist or exercise physiologist specialized in eating disorders needs to be involved as a treatment team member and provide a treatment plan to address a particular exercise behavior along with other areas of treatment plans. In addition, the treatment plan for exercise behavior should be accompanied with body image and nutrition challenges so that clients can overcome particular triggers caused by unhealthy exercise behaviors while they are in treatment.

What is "intuitive exercise"? How can you best teach this exercise approach to clients with eating disorders?

Intuitive exercise has been identified as a way to promote a healthy exercise manner in eating disorders treatment settings. Intuitive exercisers spontaneously choose a variety of types of exercise by listening to body cues and feelings in each moment and engage in exercise without being excessively conscious about dysfunctional motivations such as burning calories, weight loss, or getting rid of "fat." The concept of intuitive exercise can provide guidance to clients with eating disorders to reconnect with their own body and mind rather than relying on external cues such as counting numbers to control weight or follow rigid routines. Although mastering intuitive exercise is an ultimate goal, it is recommended to teach mindful exercise as a first step for clients with eating disorders. This is simply due to complexity of the intuitive exercise concept. Once clients understand a concept of being connected with their body and mind by responding to inner cues (e.g., thoughts, feelings), physical cues (e.g., muscle tightness, sweats), and being mindful of surroundings (i.e., leaf color, smell in the air) as part of mindful exercise, they will spontaneously recognize cues to engage in intuitive exercise.

Why is it so important for clients to address their negative thoughts and behaviors about exercise while they are in treatment?

Although it has been reported that 33–100 percent of clients with eating disorders misuse exercise as part of eating disorder behaviors, this trend is not limited to the population with eating disorders. Unfortunately, using exercise as a compensatory behavior to control their anxious feelings such as being "fat" or gaining weight has become a social norm in our society. Many family members and friends of clients with eating disorders may also engage in dysfunctional exercise even though they are not diagnosed with eating disorders. Due to this toxic social environment, clients with eating disorders must be able to protect themselves by identifying triggering situations and/or behaviors and choosing a healthy exercise behavior after their treatment. This will also prevent being relapsed from eating disorders. Therefore, it is critical for clients with eating disorders to address negative or triggering thoughts and behaviors about exercise, identify how to cope with the thoughts and behaviors, and practice mindful and intuitive exercise with an exercise specialist or exercise physiologist while they are in treatment.

What do you suggest to parents as far as ways to create a positive environment that encourages a healthy relationship with exercise?
I would suggest parents discuss how to create a positive environment for exercise with their child's treatment team. When I worked as an exercise specialist in a treatment setting, I provided a detailed discharge plan for exercise behavior to each client. I also communicated with parents before and after clients got discharged. Furthermore, it is important for both clients and parents to be on the same page so that parents should engage in prescribed exercise given by an exercise specialist or exercise physiologist with their child. This would help parents learn about the mindful and intuitive exercise concept and have better understanding of a healthy relationship with exercise for themselves as well.

Rather than engaging in moderate exercise, clients with eating disorders often display a dysfunctional mind-set surrounding exercise that mirrors other addictions. To underscore the addictive nature of exercise for individuals with eating disorders who experience euphoria, withdrawal, or guilt associated with physical activity, it is important to understand exercise presents a negative barrier to treatment and recovery. This negative relationship with exercise has been referred to as exercise addiction, compulsory exercise, or dysfunctional exercise.

Dysfunctional exercise is estimated to be present in more than 3 percent of the general population, 25–65 percent of athletes across competitive levels of sports, and 33–100 percent of eating disorder clients. Having a dysfunctional relationship with exercise is particularly poignant for eating-disordered clients given that having overexercise thoughts and behaviors at the time of discharge is one of the strongest predictors of relapse. Education for developing a healthy mind-set about exercise needs to happen during treatment programs. Many residential programs have now included healthy and moderate exercise classes and education around engaging in what is called intuitive exercise. Intuitive exercise is defined as listening to the body for cues about exercise, when to stop, and being a mindful exerciser. For example, if one is injured or sick, an intuitive exerciser will discontinue movement or lessen the intensity. Being a mindful exerciser means being present and attentive to the senses during exercise. Becoming an intuitive exerciser should be addressed in both prevention and treatment programs.

Intuitive exercise has been used in residential treatment settings but has been rarely described in the scientific literature. An operational definition for intuitive exercise is listening to the body for cues about when to start and stop exercise. Intuitive exercise also involves being a mindful exerciser rather than using distraction techniques (e.g., watching television, reading, or counting down). Incorporating senses while exercising may allow for the experience of feeling one's muscles more strongly to allow for pain to be felt and acknowledged. Furthermore, connecting with one's environment in a meaningful way can lead to noticing nature and surroundings. For example, using a meditative walk activity in a prevention program can encourage participants to notice the color and texture of leaves while listening to the noise of birds chirping. Incorporating diverse types of movement to maximize enjoyment is central to practicing intuitive exercise.

Assessment of Intuitive Exercise

Assessment tools that include exercise questions typically have focused on the quantity of exercise or one's dysfunctional relationship with movement. For example, the exercise dependence scale was developed to identify people compelled to exercise in a pathological manner. Recently, a tool was developed to measure one's relationship with exercise and ability to engage in intuitive exercise. The intuitive exercise scale includes 14 items that focus on an individual's ability to be a mindful exerciser and employ diverse types of activities. Having this assessment tool will allow for evaluation of exercise programming in treatment settings. Further, prevention programs should also teach intuitive exercise to promote a healthy relationship with exercise.

Justine J. Reel

See also: Exercise; Exercise Dependence; Intuitive Eating

Bibliography

American Psychiatric Association. *Diagnostic and Statistical Manual of Mental Disorders*, 5th ed. (*DSM-5*). Washington, DC: American Psychiatric Association Publishing, 2013.

Austin, S. Bryn. "The Blind Spot in the Drive for Childhood Obesity Prevention: Bringing Eating Disorder Prevention into Focus as a Public Health Policy." *American Journal of Public Health* 101, no. 6 (2011): e1–e4. https://doi.org/10.2105/AJPH.2011.300182.

Avalos, Laura C., and Tracy L. Tylka. "Exploring a Model of Intuitive Eating with College Women." *Journal of Counseling Psychology* 53, no. 4 (2006): 486–497. https://doi.org/10.1037/0022-0167.53.4.486.

Bacon, Linda, and Lucy Aphramor. "Weight Science: Evaluating the Evidence for a Paradigm Shift." *Nutrition Journal* 10, no. 69 (2011): 9–25. https://doi.org/10.1186/1475-2891-10-9.

Baer, Ruth A., Gregory T. Smith, Emily Lykins, Daniel Button, Jennifer Krietemeyer, Shannon Sauer, Erin Walsh, Danielle Duggan, and J. Mark G. Williams. "Construct Validity of the Five Facet Mindfulness Questionnaire in Meditating and Nonmeditating Samples." *Assessment* 15, no. 3 (2008): 329–342. https://doi.org/10.1177/1073191107313003.

Bombak, Andrea. "Obesity, Health at Every Size, and Public Health Policy." *American Journal of Public Health* 104, no. 2 (2014): e60–e67. https://doi.org/10.2105/AJPH.2013.301486.

Calogero, Rachel M., and Kelly N. Pedrotty-Stump. "Incorporating Exercise into Eating Disorder Treatment and Recovery." In *Treatment of Eating Disorders: Bridging the Research to Practice Gap*, edited by Margo Maine, Beth Hartman McGilley, and Douglas Bunnell, 425–443. London: Elsevier, 2010.

Carter, Jacqueline C., Emma Blackmore, Kalam Sutander-Pinnock, and D. Blake Woodside. "Relapse in Anorexia Nervosa. A Survival Analysis." *Psychological Medicine* 34, no. 4 (2004): 671–679. https://doi.org/10.1017/S0033291703001168.

Emery, Rebecca L., Kevin M. King, Sarah F. Fischer, and Kendra R. Davis. "The Moderating Role of Negative Urgency on the Prospective Association between Dietary Restraint and Binge Eating." *Appetite* 71 (2013): 113–119. https://doi.org/10.1016/j.appet.2013.08.001.

Irving, Lori M., and Dianne Neumark-Sztainer. "Integrating the Prevention of Eating Disorders and Obesity: Feasible or Futile?" *Preventive Medicine* 34, no. 3 (2002): 299–309. https://doi.org/10.1006/pmed.2001.0997.

Kabat-Zinn, Jon. *Wherever You Go, There You Are: Mindfulness Meditation in Everyday Life.* New York: Hyperion, 1994.

Muazzam, Amina, and Ruhi Khalid. "Development and Validation of Disorder Eating Behavior Scale: Identification, Prevalence, and Difference with Clinical Diagnosed Eating Disorders." *Pakistan Journal of Psychological Research* 26, no. 2 (2011): 127–148.

Neumark-Sztainer, Diane. "Integrating Messages from the Eating Disorders Field into Obesity Prevention." *Adolescent Medicine State of the Art Reviews* 23, no. 3 (2012): 529–543.

Oh, Katharine Hahn, Marcie C. Wiseman, Jill Hendrickson, Julia C. Phillips, and Eric W. Hayden. "Testing the Acceptance Model of Intuitive Eating with College Women Athletes." *Psychology Women Quarterly* 36, no, 1 (2012): 88–98. https://doi.org/10.1177/0361684311433282.

Penney, Tarra L., and Sara F. L. Kirk. "The Health at Every Size Paradigm and Obesity: Missing Empirical Evidence May Help Push the Reframing Obesity Debate Forward." *American Journal of Public Health* 105, no. 5 (2015): e38–e42. https://doi.org/10.2105/AJPH.2015.302552.

Reel, Justine J. "The Relationship between Exercise and Eating Disorders: A Double-Edged Sword." In *Doing Exercise Psychology*, edited by Mark B. Andersen and Stephanie J. Hanrahan. 259–273. Champaign, IL: Human Kinetics, 2015.

Reel, Justine J., Carlie Ashcraft, Rachel Lacy, Robert A. Bucciere, Sonya SooHoo, Donna Richards, and Nicole Mihalopoulos. "'Full of Ourselves PLUS': Lessons Learned When Implementing an Eating Disorder and Obesity Prevention Program." *Journal of Sport Psychology in Action* 1, no. 3 (2010): 109–117. https://doi.org/10.1080/21520704.2010.534545.

Reel, Justine J., Nick Galli, Maya Miyairi, Dana Voelker, and Christy Greenleaf. "Development and Validation of an Intuitive Exercise Scale." *Eating Behaviors* 22 (2016): 129–132. http://dx.doi.org/10.1016/j.eatbeh.2016.06.013.

Reel, Justine J., Kimber Harding, Brenna Sacra, Donna Richards, Glenn Richardson, and Nick Galli. "Implementing an Obesity and Eating Disorder Prevention Program among Mothers and Daughters in Utah." *Utah's Health: An Annual Review* 17 (2012): 54–60.

Reel, Justine J., Jacqueline J. Lee, and Abby Bellows. "Integrating Exercise and Mindfulness for an Emerging Conceptual Framework: The Intuitive Approach to Prevention and Health Promotion (IAPHP)." *Eating Disorders: The Journal of Treatment & Prevention* 24, no. 1 (2016): 90–97. http://dx.doi.org/10.1080.10640266.2015.1118951.

Reel, Justine J., and Maya Miyairi. "The Right 'Dose' of Activity: Health Educators Should Promote Mindful and Intuitive Exercise." *Community Medicine & Health Education* 2, no. 9 (2012): 1–2. https://doi.org/10.4172/2161-0711.1000e111.

Reel, Justine J., and Dana Voelker. "Exercise to the Extreme? Identifying and Addressing Unhealthy Exercise Behaviors." In *Athletic Insight's Writings of 2012*, edited by Robert Schinke, 301–314, New York: Nova Science Publishers, 2013.

Steiner-Adair, Catherine, and Lisa Sjostrom. *Full of Ourselves: A Wellness Program to Advance Girl Power, Health, and Leadership.* New York: Teachers College Press, 2006.

Stice, Eric, Heather Shaw, and C. Nathan Marti. "A Meta-Analytic Review of Eating Disorder Prevention Programs: Encouraging Findings." *Annual Review of Clinical Psychology* 3 (2007): 207–231. https://doi.org/10.1146/annurev.clinpsy.3.022806.091447.

Taranis, Lorin, and Caroline Meyer. "Associations between Specific Components of Compulsive Exercise and Eating-Disordered Cognitions and Behaviors among Young Women." *International Journal of Eating Disorders* 44, no. 5 (2011): 452–456. https://doi.org/10.1002/eat.20838.

Tribole, Evelyn, and Elyse Resch. *Intuitive Eating: A Revolutionary Program That Works*, 2nd ed. New York: St. Martin's Griffin, 2003.

J

JOCKEYS

A jockey is an athlete who competes in horseracing, a sport that dates back to the ancient Greek Olympics around 648 BCE. The first American racetrack was constructed in Long Island in 1665. This paved the way for organized horseracing, which accelerated in the late 1800s, due to increased gambling interest. The sport has been associated with high injury rates and unhealthy weight control methods. Weight restrictions, rationalized by safety concerns for the horse, have been in place for professional horseracing since its inception. However, since 1979, the average weight of jockeys has increased by 37 percent. Therefore, jockeys have needed to engage in numerous weight reduction strategies and disordered eating. In 2005, Emanuel Jose Sanchez, a 22-year-old jockey, died from a suspected eating disorder.

Eating Disorders and Jockeys

Depending on the event or the type of horseracing, weight requirements may range from 110 pounds to 140 pounds. Weighing in occurs before and after the race and requires athletes to make weight in their clothing, shoes, helmet, and horse tack (i.e., saddle, saddle pad, and crop). Generally, this results in at least three additional pounds before meeting an already restrictive weight. To meet the weight requirements, many jockeys engage in similar weight loss methods as wrestlers. Jockeys may engage in fasting, deliberate dehydration, and flipping or heaving, that refers to self-induced vomiting that often happens into "heave bowls." The most frequently reported weight loss method among jockeys at Delaware Park was the "Hot Box." Many jockeys admitted to sweating off pounds in rubber suits, steam rooms, and saunas. Every racecourse in the United Kingdom provides a sauna facility, which is used heavily by jockeys to make riding weight.

In a separate study, 75 percent of jockeys regardless of sex reported skipping meals as a weight management strategy, and at least a third of them missed a meal per day. Over half of jockeys (60 percent) needed to lose weight in preparation for race day. Twenty interviews with jockeys revealed 50 percent consumed nothing but coffee or an energy drink (e.g., RedBull, Monster) before they rode in the morning. This is a noteworthy finding because jockeys exercise horses for long hours each day, representing strenuous physical activity and energy expenditure. Additionally, jockeys have identified smoking as an appetite suppressant and reported using diet pills, diuretics, and laxatives to lose weight. Jockeys who engaged in wasting behaviors to meet a minimum weight tended to display more eating disorder symptoms, and 20 percent were considered to have eating disorders in one study. However, it is important to consider that like wrestlers, these unhealthy weight-related behaviors are normative for the jockey culture. Therefore, jockeys view flipping and hot boxes as part of the sport.

Equestrian Athletes

Horse-riding competitions are traditionally focused on show, beauty, and ceremony. Equestrian competitions, especially for dressage events, emphasize the physical appearance of the rider. Specifically, equestrian athletes must control their horse while appearing aesthetically pleasing, similar to a gymnast or figure skater. Generally, equestrian athletes with a lean physique are rewarded in the judging since scores are directly related to athletes' appearance. In a study of 138 female college equestrian athletes, 42 percent had eating disorders, 25 percent engaged in binge eating, 12 percent vomited to control weight or shape, and 15 percent abused diuretics, laxatives, or diet pills.

Justine J. Reel

See also: Diet Pills; Sports; Weight Pressures in Sport

Bibliography

Caulfield, Michael J., and Costas I. Karageorghis. "Psychological Effects of Rapid Weight Loss and Attitudes towards Eating among Professional Jockeys." *Journal of Sports Sciences* 26, no. 9 (2008): 877–883. https://doi.org/10.1080/02640410701837349.

Cotugna, Nancy, O. Sue Snider, and Jennifer Windish. "Nutrition Assessment of Horse-Racing Athletes." *Journal of Community Health* 36 (2011): 261–264. https://doi.org/10.1007/s10900-010-9306-x.

Hughes, Mark. "Jockeys Run Risk of Eating Disorders in Bid to Stay Slim." *The Independent.* Last modified March 10, 2008. Accessed November 21, 2017. http://www.independent.co.uk/sport/racing/jockeys-run-risk-of-eating-disorders-in-bid-to-stay-slim-793964.html.

"Jockeys Still Battle Weight Issues but Progress Being Made." ESPN. Last modified April 26, 2008. Accessed November 21, 2017. http://sports.espn.go.com/espn/wire?section=horse&id=3367868.

Labadarios, Demetre, Juan Kotze, D. Momberg, and Theunis J. Kotze. "Jockeys and Their Practices in South Africa." *World Review of Nutrition and Dietetics* 71 (1993): 97–114. https://doi.org/10.1159/000422352.

Moore, Jan M., Anna F. Timperio, David A. Crawford, Cate M. Burns, and David Cameron-Smith. "Weight Management and Weight Loss Strategies of Professional Jockeys." *International Journal of Sport Nutrition and Exercise Metabolism* 12 (2002): 1–13. https://doi.org/10.1123/ijsnem.12.1.1.

Torres-McGehee, Toni M., Eva V. Monsma, Jennifer L. Gay, Dawn M. Minton, and Ashley N. Mady-Foster. "Prevalence of Eating Disorder Risk and Body Image Distortion among National Collegiate Athletic Association Division I Varsity Equestrian Athletes." *Journal of Athletic Training* 46, no. 4 (2011): 431–437.

JOURNALING

Journaling is a self-reflection activity to elicit emotions through writing. Therapeutic writing and journaling exercises have been used as helpful interventions for a broad range of mental health conditions and are recommended as a useful treatment strategy for eating disorders in inpatient and outpatient settings.

Uses of Journaling in Eating Disorder Treatment

Because many eating-disordered individuals have difficulty identifying and expressing emotions, alternative therapies to talk therapy have been useful to reveal emotions. Journaling has been used with eating-disordered clients as a way to freely express themselves without fear of judgment or negative consequences. Clients may use a traditional diary format to write down events and emotions surrounding situations encountered that can later be discussed in therapy. Journaling can also be structured and involve having a client self-report positive or negative behaviors. For example, a therapist may assign journaling to track purging symptoms. A client and therapist can analyze the patterns in events precipitating purging as well as the specific times of the day when a client is more susceptible to disordered eating thoughts and behaviors.

Recently, some therapists have requested clients email their journal entries between sessions, text thoughts, or enter behaviors into a confidential website. By having a sense of the frequency of symptoms, triggers, or a client's response to situations, a therapist can gather information that can be used in treatment. In some cases, a clinician may be able to schedule an additional appointment to see a client sooner, if a client reports a marked increase in symptoms or reveals he or she is struggling. Some clinicians use computer programs or apps to tally behaviors and create bar graphs to show frequency of behaviors and change over time.

Barriers to Journaling in Eating Disorder Treatment

Although journaling can be an effective therapeutic tool for many clients, some individuals do not respond well to journal-type assignments. Clients may resist keeping a journal if they dislike writing or think there is a risk of a written diary being read by family members. To protect privacy, clients can be encouraged to keep journal assignments on a password-protected computer rather than in a diary. Clients who have difficulty with writing may be encouraged to use a different forum for expressing themselves (e.g., drawing, pastels), or told to write more informal blog-style entries or tweets.

When clients are asked to self-report disordered eating behaviors, they realize there is increased accountability for their actions. Therefore, clients less motivated to change or who are less ready for recovery may show resistance to documenting their symptoms. This resistance should be discussed in therapy.

Justine J. Reel

See also: Art Therapy; Integrative Approaches; Treatment

Bibliography

Wasson, Diane H., and Mary Jackson. "An Analysis of the Role of Overeaters Anonymous in Women's Recovery from Bulimia Nervosa." *Eating Disorders* 12 (2004): 337–356. https://doi.org/10.1080/10640260490521442.

Wolf, Markus, Jan Sedway, Cynthia M. Bulik, and Hans Kordy. "Linguistic Analyses of Natural Written Language: Unobtrusive Assessment of Cognitive Style in Eating Disorders." *International Journal of Eating Disorders* 40, no. 8 (2007): 711–717. https://doi.org/10.1002/eat.20445.

K

KETOACIDOSIS

Ketoacidosis is a metabolic state marked by extreme and uncontrolled elevated ketone levels in the body and is found commonly in individuals who have type 1 diabetes. According to *Medical-Surgical Nursing: Assessment and Management of Clinical Problems,* when insulin supply is insufficient, glucose cannot be used for energy. This condition causes the body to break down stored fats and proteins for energy. The liver metabolizes free fatty acids from stored triglycerides that are released, causing formation of large quantities of ketones. Ketones alter the pH of the body and cause acidosis. Loss of water occurs to balance the pH, as ketones are excreted in the urine and blood glucose rises to dangerous levels.

Ketoacidosis in Eating-Disordered Clients with Type 1 Diabetes

Binge eating disorder and bulimia nervosa are the most common types of eating disorders in individuals with type 1 diabetes. To control weight gain, an individual with an eating disorder may skip doses of insulin, which can lead to diabetic ketoacidosis.

Diabetic ketoacidosis can cause rapid weight loss, which is appealing to individuals with eating disorders. However, ketoacidosis is a life-threatening condition that can lead to coma and death. Some individuals with eating disorders may take just enough insulin to prevent ketoacidosis and avoid hospitalization.

Clinical Manifestation and Complications

Warning signs of ketoacidosis are deep, rapid breathing, dry skin and mouth, flushed face, nausea, vomiting, stomach pain, fatigue, frequent urination, and increased thirst. Acetone causes a fruity odor that can be smelled on the client's breath. Ketoacidosis can lead to serious diabetic complications, including eye disease, kidney failure, numbness and pain in the arms and legs, and vascular complications.

Treatment

According to an article in *Dimensions of Critical Care Nursing,* an individual with ketoacidosis should be stabilized medically, replacing fluid and electrolyte losses and initiating insulin therapy. Determining the degree of severity is done by assessing blood pH level, serum bicarbonate, and ketones present in the urine. During treatment an individual must also be monitored for hypokalemia (low serum potassium), high blood sugar, low blood sugar, overhydration, and cerebral edema. Frequent blood sugar assessment and supplemental doses of insulin may be needed to regaincontrol of an individual's levels. Bicarbonate is frequently administered to patients in severe ketoacidosis with a pH of less than 7.1 and bicarbonate less than 8 mEq/L. In addition, the eating-disordered individual and his or her family members should receive education about nutrition and exercise; psychotherapy is also recommended.

Ketoacidosis from Starvation

Chronic malnutrition, fasting, and starving can also induce ketoacidosis. Treatment includes correcting nutritional deficiencies and dehydration. According to an article in *Hospital Physician,* metabolic acidosis from starvation is mild and does not require treatment with bicarbonate.

Shelly Guillory

See also: Diabetes; Edema; Medical and Health Consequences

Bibliography

Charles, Joseph C., and Raymond L. Heilman. "Metabolic Acidosis." *Hospital Physician* 41, no. 3 (2005): 37–42.

Lewis, Sharon M., Margaret Heitkemper, and Sharon Dirkson. "Patients with Diabetes Mellitus." In *Medical-Surgical Nursing: Assessment and Management of Clinical Problems,* 5th ed., edited by Sally Shrefer, 1393–1397. St. Louis, MO: Mosby, 2000.

Rodin, Gary, Marion P. Olmsted, Anne C. Rydall, Sherry I. Maharaj, Patricia A. Colton, Jennifer M. Jones, Lisa A. Biancucci, and Dennis Daneman. "Eating Disorder in Young Women with Type 1 Diabetes Mellitus." *Journal of Psychosomatic Research* 53 (2002): 943–949. PII: S0022-3999(02)00305-7.

Ruth-Sahd, Lisa A., Melissa Shneider, and Briggitte Haagen. "Diabulimia: What It Is and How to Recognize It in Critical Care." *Dimensions of Critical Care Nursing* 28, no. 4 (2009): 147–153. https://doi.org/10.11097/01.CCN.0000384062.54832.89.

LANUGO

Lanugo is fine, downy soft hair that appears on the back, face, and abdomen of individuals who have eating disorders. This is a result of inadequate protein intake. Lanugo hair is normal for infants, but for adults, lanugo is a red flag that an individual is struggling with an eating disorder and is in a severe state of malnutrition. Lanugo is usually a pale and light color; however, it may be darker in individuals with darker complexions.

Lanugo and Eating Disorders

Lanugo is s response to loss of body fat, resulting from severe restriction that mimics starvation. To keep the body warm and prevent hypothermia, lanugo grows to prevent heat loss Lanugo is generally not present with bulimia nervosa and binge eating disorder. Lanugo, along with other clinical signs and a detailed health history, can help aid a physician in the diagnosis of anorexia nervosa. Lanugo hair begins to disappear naturally once an individual with anorexia nervosa restores weight and body fat and consumes adequate calories. Although lanugo hair is not dangerous, is no treatment for it, the appearance of lanugo usually signals an individual is not consuming enough protein and calories to maintain appropriate body weight. Once an individual begins eating disorder treatment and increases food intake, lanugo begins to disappear from the body.

Shelly Guillory

See also: Assessment; Medical and Health Consequences

Bibliography

Birmingham, C. Laird, and Janet Treasure. "Complications by System." In *Medical Management of Eating Disorders*, 2nd ed., edited by Larid C. Birmingham and Janet Treasure. New York: Cambridge University Press, 2010.

"Health Consequences of Eating Disorders." National Eating Disorders Association. Accessed November 17, 2016. http://www.nationaleatingdisorders.org/health-consequences-eating-disorders.

Nicholls, Dasha, and Russell Viner. "ABC of Adolescence. Eating Disorders and Weight Problems." *British Medical Journal* 330 (2005): 950–953.

Pritts, Sarah D., and Jeffrey Susman. "Diagnosis of Eating Disorders in Primary Care." *American Family Physician* 67, no. 2 (2003): 297–304.

Walsh, Judith M., Mary E. Wheat, and Karen Freund. "Detection, Evaluation, and Treatment of Eating Disorders." *Journal of General Internal Medicine* 15, no. 8 (2000): 577–590. https://doi.org/10.1046/j.1525-1497.2000.02439.x.

LATE LIFE AND LATE-ONSET EATING DISORDERS

It is clear women develop and suffer from eating disorders later in life. One study examined body image and eating behaviors in women ages 55–65 years old (middle-aged) and women 66 years and older (elderly); not surprisingly, the authors found all women regardless of age desired a smaller ideal figure. More recently, Mangweth-Matzek and colleagues (2006) found that 56 percent of the women (60–70 years) stated they restrict their food consumption to prevent weight gain and 86 percent of the women engaged in unhealthy weight loss methods such as fasting, vomiting, taking laxatives and diuretics, and spitting out food. Alarmingly, 18 women (3.8 percent) met the criteria for an eating disorder with a majority of them having eating disorder not otherwise specified (EDNOS) based on the Structured Clinical Interview for the previous edition of the *Diagnostic and Statistical Manual of Mental Disorders* (i.e., *DSM-IV-TR*) and 21 women (4.4 percent) reported single symptoms of eating disorders. A Canadian sample of women revealed symptoms of disordered eating were present in 1.8 percent of women aged 65 and older and 2.6 percent of women in the age group 50–64 years. A rare study with males found 11–19 percent of elderly males had abnormal eating attitudes and negative body image. Deaths due to anorexia nervosa in the elderly were 10 percent in the 55–64 years age group, 12 percent in the 65–74 years age group, and 28 percent in the 85 and older group.

Late-Onset Eating Disorders

Eating disorders in an elderly population can be classified as early onset or late onset. While early onset eating disorders represent eating disorders that began in the younger years and may persist into late life, it is also possible for a disorder to recur after an individual has been free from symptoms. By contrast, late-onset eating disorders, sometimes referred to as *tardive anorexia,* develop for the first time after an individual reaches age 50. A contributing factor for late-onset eating disorders is a history of trauma, including flashbacks to emotional connections to mealtimes earlier in life. Having a sexual abuse history is more common in women with late-onset eating disorders than the general population. Another factor associated with late-onset eating disorders is depression, which has been linked to eating disorders as a comorbid condition. Interestingly, substance abuse was less common in late-onset eating-disordered clients than in young adults.

Justine J. Reel

See also: Aging and Body Image; Body Image; Disordered Eating; Menopause; Mortality Rates

Bibliography

American Psychiatric Association. *Diagnostic and Statistical Manual of Mental Disorders*, 4th ed., text rev. Washington, DC: American Psychiatric Association Publishing, 2000.

American Psychiatric Association. *Diagnostic and Statistical Manual of Mental Disorders*, 5th ed. (*DSM-5*). Washington, DC: American Psychiatric Association Publishing, 2013.

Brandsma, Lynn. "Eating Disorders across the Life Span." *Journal of Women & Aging* 19 (2007): 155–172. https://doi.org/10.1300/J074v19n01_10.

Cumella, Edward J., and Zina Kally. "Profile of 50 Women with Midlife-Onset Eating Disorders." *Eating Disorders* 16 (2008): 193–203. https://doi.org/10.1080/10640260802016670.

Lapid, Maria I., Maria C. Prom, M. Caroline Burton, Donald E. McAlpine, Bruce Sutor, and Teresa A. Rummans. "Eating Disorders in the Elderly." *International Psychogeriatrics* 22, no. 4 (2010): 523–536. https://doi.org/10.1017/S1041610210000104.

Lewis, Diane M., and Fary M. Cachelin. "Body Image, Body Dissatisfaction, and Eating Attitudes in Midlife and Elderly Women." *Eating Disorders* 9 (2001): 29–39. http://dx.doi.org/10.1080/106402601300187713.

Mangweth-Matzek, Barbara, Claudia I. Rupp, Armand Hausmann, Karin Assmayr, Edith Mariacher, Georg Kemmler, Alexandra B. Whitworth, and Wilfried Biebl. "Never Too Late for Eating Disorders or Body Dissatisfaction: A Community Study of Elderly Women." *International Journal of Eating Disorders* 39 (2006): 583–586. https://doi.org/10.1002/eat.20327.

Midlarsky, Elizabeth, and George Nitzburg. "Eating Disorders in Middle-Aged Women." *The Journal of General Psychology* 135, no. 4 (2008): 393–407. http://dx.doi.org/10.3200/GENP.135.4.393-408.

Patrick, Julie H., and Sarah T. Stahl. "Understanding Disordered Eating at Midlife and Late Life." *The Journal of General Psychology* 136, no. 1 (2008): 5–20. http://dx.doi.org/10.3200/GENP.136.1.5-20.

Peat, Christine M., Naomi L. Peyerl, and Jennifer J. Muehlenkamp. "Body Image and Eating Disorders in Older Adults: A Review." *The Journal of General Psychology* 135, no. 4 (2008): 343–358. http://dx.doi.org/10.3200/GENP.135.4.343-358.

Scholtz, Samantha, Laura S. Hill, and Hubert Lacy. "Eating Disorders in Older Women: Does Late-Onset Anorexia Nervosa Exist?" *International Journal of Eating Disorders* 43, no. 5 (2010): 393–397. https://doi.org/10.1002/eat.20704.

Zerbe, Kathryn J. "Eating Disorders in Middle and Late Life: A Neglected Problem." *Primary Psychiatry* 10 (2003): 80–82.

LAXATIVE ABUSE

Common purging methods for individuals with bulimia nervosa are self-induced vomiting and laxative abuse. Laxatives can be purchased over the counter and should only be used in the short term for the treatment of constipation; however, individuals with anorexia nervosa or bulimia nervosa may take laxatives in large quantities to control their weight. According to a study in the *International Journal of Eating Disorders*, inducing diarrhea is a purging method used when an individual feels desperate, and many individuals report that emptying themselves is associated with gratifying weight loss and a sense of purification. The study further states it is questionable whether the weight lost from purging through laxatives is an effective form of weight control, because most of the weight loss is fluid. Nevertheless, individuals with eating disorders feel rewarded seeing a lower number on the scale and this is likely to cause them to continue using laxatives.

Types of Laxatives

According to the Mayo Clinic, there are five types of laxatives. The Mayo Clinic explains oral bulk formers such as Metamucil and Citrucel increase the bulk of stool by absorbing water, causing normal contraction of the intestinal muscles.

Oral osmotics, such as Milk of Magnesia, magnesium citrate, sodium phosphate, and Miralax, pull water into the colon from the body's tissues to allow for easier passage of stool. Oral and rectal stimulant laxatives, including senna, Ex-Lax, and suppositories, cause the colon to contract and stool is eliminated. Stool softeners such as Colace, and lubricants including mineral oil, help an individual strain less during the elimination of stool by providing moisture.

Medical Complications

In addition to diarrhea, laxatives taken in large quantities can cause cramping, nausea, and vomiting. When individuals with an eating disorder take more than the recommended doses, they can place themselves at risk for life-threatening medical complications, including gastrointestinal bleeding, which can cause anemia, dehydration, and electrolyte imbalances. Symptoms of dehydration include tachycardia (increased heart rate), fainting, and dizziness upon standing. Long-term use of laxatives can cause tolerance, especially to stimulant laxatives. Higher doses of laxatives are needed to produce a bowel movement.

Electrolyte loss can be severe in individuals who abuse laxatives. Loss of potassium (hypokalemia) can cause cardiac arrhythmias and renal damage. Large quantities of sodium may be lost, but because of water loss, hyponatremia (low sodium) is rare. Hypocalcemia (low calcium) and hypomagnesemia (low magnesium) can also occur.

In addition to these health consequences, individuals with eating disorders who abuse laxatives for years may develop impairment in colon function. In these clients, X-ray examination shows changes in the lining of the colon and the colon may appear shortened. These changes are often permanent.

Treatment Considerations for Laxative Abuse

Treatment of an individual with an eating disorder should include a detailed health history. If laxative abuse is suspected after an initial assessment, physical and laboratory tests will be necessary to rule out medical complications. Because withdrawal from laxatives can cause constipation and fluid retention, some individuals may feel heavier from the bloating and constipation that results. This may make it hard for some individuals to cease using laxatives.

Individuals withdrawing from laxatives should consume a high-fiber diet and drink plenty of water. Some individuals with eating disorders restrict the amount of water they consume to minimize fluid retention, but fluid restriction can cause dehydration and increase the risk of further constipation. In some cases, doctors prescribe psyllium-containing laxatives or osmotic-type laxatives for short-term use in individuals with severe constipation at risk for a bowel obstruction.

Electrolyte imbalances should be corrected, and vitamins and minerals lost through laxative purging should be replaced. It is important to explain to an individual undergoing treatment for laxative abuse that with continued treatment, constipation and bloating should resolve.

Shelly Guillory

See also: Dehydration; Diuretics; Electrolyte Imbalance; Medical and Health Consequences; Purging

Bibliography

Baker, E. H., and G. I. Sandle. "Complications of Laxative Abuse." *Annual Review of Medicine* 47, no. 1 (1996): 127–133. https://doi.org/10.1146/annurev.med.47.1.127.

Kovacs, Dora, and Robert L. Palmer. "The Associations between Laxative Abuse and Other Symptoms among Adults with Anorexia Nervosa." *International Journal of Eating Disorders* 36, no. 2 (2004): 224–228. https://doi.org/10.1002/eat.20024.

Mitchell, James E., and Lana Boutacoff. "Laxative Abuse Complicating Bulimia: Medical and Treatment Complications." *International Journal of Eating Disorders* 5, no. 2 (1986): 325–334. https://doi.org/10.1002/1098-108X(198602)5:2 325::AID-EAT2260050211 3.0.CO;2-Z.

Mitchell, James E., Dorothy Hatsukami, Richard Pyle, Elke D. Eckert, and Lana L. Boutacoff. "Metabolic Acidosis as a Marker for Laxative Abuse in Patients with Bulimia." *International Journal of Eating Disorders* 6, no. 4 (1987): 557–560. https://doi.org/10.1002/1098-108X(198707)6:4<557::AID-EAT2260060413>3.0.CO;2-Z.

"Over-the-Counter Laxatives for Constipation: Use with Caution." MayoClinic.com. Last modified June 6, 2014. Accessed November 22, 2017. http://www.mayoclinic.com/health/laxatives/HQ00088.

Pryor, Tamara, Michael W. Wiederman, and Beth McGilley. "Laxative Abuse among Women with Eating Disorders: An Indication of Psychopathology?" *International Journal of Eating Disorders* 20, no. 1 (1996): 13–18.

Roering, James L., Kristine J. Steffan, James E. Mitchell, and Christi Zunker. "Laxative Abuse: Epidemiology, Diagnosis and Management." *Drugs* 70, no. 12 (2010): 1487–1503. https://doi.org/10.2165/10898640-000000000-00000.

LEGISLATION ON EATING DISORDERS

Understanding the laws for eating disorders helps us understand the governmental views around treatment for this dangerous disease.

Laws Pertaining to Eating Disorders

Although less than 5 percent of all proposed legislation ever gets passed into law on the national level, many lobbyists and health professionals have voiced discontent over the lack of effective national legislative action pertaining to eating disorders. This discontent with government action was one of the principal motivations behind the formation of the Eating Disorders Coalition (EDC) in 2000, a special interest group dedicated specifically to eating disorders. Although the EDC has been successful in advocating for more legislative action within Congress, thus far the EDC has not seen a bill passed into law while it has existed.

The picture becomes less bleak when state legislation is taken into consideration. Several states have become pioneers in the field of eating disorder legislation. Political pundits, mental health professionals, and researchers alike have agreed that these states serve as the example upon which national policy makers should base their legislative actions regarding eating disorders. A bill signed into law in Missouri by Gov. Jay Nixon received particular praise as being the single strongest piece of legislation that exists to date for eating disorders. Missouri Senate Bill No. 145 of the 98th General Assembly became law in August 2016 and requires insurance companies to cover all aspects of treatment for eating disorders, including diagnosis, inpatient hospitalization, and follow-up care. Insurance companies were mandated to update policies to comply with this regulation. Many advocacy groups have heralded this bill as the gold standard they hope to replicate in other states as well as at the national level.

New York has also been lauded as a leader in enacting legislation related to eating disorders. In September 2014, Gov. Andrew Cuomo signed S2530/A5294 into law, amending public health law to establish the Eating Disorders Awareness and Prevention Program in the state's health department. This program is geared primarily at educating the public on early warning signs of eating disorders and improving access to services and resources for individuals struggling with an eating disorder. New York is home to the National Eating Disorders Association (NEDA), a national nonprofit dedicated to eating disorder awareness and prevention, and thus it has been considered a national leader in the field of eating disorder legislation for some time.

President Barack Obama's Patient Protection and Affordable Care Act (ACA) of 2010 mandates all US citizens to have health insurance and prohibits insurance companies from denying coverage on the basis of a pre-existing condition, which has particular implications for eating disorders. Individuals who suffer from eating disorders usually begin to show signs when they are teenagers. Therefore, when these individuals apply for health insurance, an eating disorder would qualify as a pre-existing condition and (before the Affordable Care Act) be grounds for denial. Additionally, the Affordable Care Act enables children and young adults to remain on their parents' insurance policy until they are 26 years old. Given that older teens and young adults are disproportionately affected by eating disorders, the Affordable Care Act provides a continuity of care that is essential to a well-managed and smooth treatment plan. Under the Affordable Care Act, 10 states now require coverage for eating disorders on the same basis as other mental disorders. Another 18 states offer equal coverage for eating disorders on certain providers (e.g., state employee and group health plans).

Legislation on Eating Disorders Currently under Consideration

The majority of national legislation that exists pertaining to eating disorders is in subcommittees or at the Senate/House level. The FREED (Federal Response to Eliminate Eating Disorders) Act, originally proposed in 2009, is the first comprehensive piece of legislature on eating disorders in the history of Congress. The FREED Act calls for the collection and analysis of epidemiological data on eating disorders, the establishment of various regulatory bodies designed to coordinate research efforts nationally on eating disorders, as well as the development of education materials for individuals in a variety of professions (e.g., educators, athletic trainers/coaches, psychiatrists, social workers) on identifying and treating eating disorders. The FREED Act was not passed in the 111th Congress (2009–2010), where it was originally introduced, or in either the 112th (2011–2012) or 113th (2013–2014) Congresses, where it has been reintroduced. In each case, the bill was referred to subcommittees for further review and was not brought back to the House or Senate prior to the end of the congressional season.

Many other bills have faced a similar fate. The Eating Disorders Awareness, Prevention and Education Act of 2000 is one such example. In each session of Congress since the bill's original introduction in 2000, this act has been put forth and has been unable to advance past subcommittee review. The Eating Disorders Awareness, Prevention, and Education Act focuses on raising awareness of eating disorders among parents, students (particularly in elementary and secondary schools), and educators. The Truth in Advertising Act of 2014 failed to progress past subcommittee review in 2014. This bill, if enacted into law, would require the Federal Trade Commission to provide Congress with a report detailing the extent to which images in advertising were manipulated using Photoshop and other post-production techniques.

Legislation That Has Impacted Eating Disorders Indirectly

Although the majority of eating disorders legislation on the national level has not yet been passed into law, a number of bills pertaining to mental health have become law and have had tremendous effects on the field of eating disorders. Chief among these is the Paul Wellstone and Pete Domenici Mental Health Parity and Addiction Equity Act (MHPAE) of 2008. This bill was originally introduced as its own piece of legislation but was later included under the Emergency Economic Stabilization Act of 2008 and become Public Law no. 110-343 on October 3, 2008. The MHPAE requires insurance companies to provide equal benefits for mental health disorders as for medical/surgical conditions. Prior to the MHPAE, insurance companies would frequently place limits on treatment for mental disorders. This was particularly dangerous for eating disorders, which have the highest mortality rate of all mental illnesses. Insurance companies would regularly impose limits on the number of doctor visits, prescription medications, length of stay in hospitals/inpatient facilities, and financial coverage. These restrictions often drove families and affected individuals to rack up crippling debt, declare bankruptcy, or suffer through years of inadequate health care. With the enactment of the MHPAE Act of 2008, insurance companies are now legally bound to provide coverage that is on par with the coverage offered for medical disorders, like diabetes.

While an important step in the right direction, the MHPAE Act of 2008 drew criticism from eating disorder advocates because it did not specify that eating disorder treatment falls under the umbrella of "mental health" treatment. As such, many insurance providers used this loophole to avoid offering full coverage for expensive residential treatment stays and other costly treatments. In December of 2016, the 21st Century Cures Act was signed into law, which corrected this oversight from the MPHAE Act by specifying that eating disorder treatment needs to be offered equal coverage along with other mental health and medical diagnoses.

Conclusion

Several states such as Missouri and New York have passed legislation that serves as a template for the rest of the country as well as the federal government. Missouri's Senate Bill No. 145 is the first law mandating complete coverage for all stages of care involved in eating disorder treatment. Several bills have been proposed at the national level—such as the FREED Act—but have been unable to progress past committee review. However, several major landmark laws have had impacts on the broader field of mental health and particularly in the case of eating disorders. The Mental Health Parity and Addictions Equity Act, the 21st Century Cures Act, and the Affordable Care Act have made important improvements in how insurance companies are required to treat coverage that impacts eating disorders.

Hannah J. Hopkins

See also: Advocacy Groups; Health Care Costs of Eating Disorders; National Eating Disorders Association

Bibliography

Canady, Valerie A. "Combating Eating Disorders Gains Ample Bipartisan Support." *Mental Health Weekly* 25, no. 33 (2015): 4–5. https://doi.org/10.1002/mhw.30311.

Canady, Valerie A. "Missouri Eating Disorders Law Could Become National Standard." *Mental Health Weekly* 25, no. 27 (2015): 3–4. https://doi.org/10.1002/mhw.30256.

Cogan, Jeanine C., Debra L. Franko, and David B. Herzog. "Federal Advocacy for Anorexia Nervosa: An American Model." *International Journal of Eating Disorders* 37, no. S1 (2005): S101–S102. https://doi.org/10.1002/eat.20127.

Dolan, Kerry. "Legislative Victory in New York!" National Eating Disorders Association. Last modified June 17, 2014. Accessed November 21, 2017. https://www.nationaleatingdisorders.org/blog/legislative-victory-new-york.

Dolan, Kerry. "Victory for Eating Disorders Awareness & Prevention in New York!" National Eating Disorders Association. Last modified September 25, 2014. Accessed November 21, 2017. https://www.nationaleatingdisorders.org/blog/victory-eating-disorders-awareness-prevention-new-york.

"Eating Disorders Coalition: Previous Policy Initiatives." Eating Disorders Coalition. Accessed February 3, 2017. http://www.eatingdisorderscoalition.org/inner_template/our_work/previous-policy-initiatives.html.

Goldberg, Hayley. "Congress Just Passed the First Ever Eating Disorder Legislation." *Self.* Accessed December 9, 2016. https://www.self.com/story/congress-just-passed-the-first-ever-eating-disorder-legislation.

"H.B. 3891-85th Texas Legislature: Relating to Coverage for Eating Disorders Under Certain Health Benefit Plans." Trackbill.com. Accessed November 28, 2017. https://trackbill.com/bill/tx-hb3891-relating-to-coverage-for-eating-disorders-under-certain-health-benefit-plans/1427627/.

Hewitt, Sarah. "A Time to Heal: Eliminating Barriers to Coverage for Patients with Eating Disorders under the Affordable Care Act." *Law & Inequality* 31, no. 2 (2013): 411–436.

"H.R. 1193-111th Congress: Federal Response to Eliminate Eating Disorders Act of 2009." Govtrack.us. Assessed February 3, 2017. https://www.govtrack.us/congress/bills/111/hr1193.

"H.R. 1424—110th Congress: A Bill to Provide Authority for the Federal Government to Purchase and Insure Certain Types of Troubled Assets for the Purposes of Providing Stability to and Preventing Disruption in the Economy and Financial System and Protecting Taxpayers, to Amend the Internal Revenue Code of 1986 to Provide Incentives for Energy Production and Conservation, to Extend Certain Expiring Provisions, to Provide Individual Income Tax Relief, and for Other Purposes." Congress.gov. Accessed February 3, 2017. https://www.congress.gov/bill/110th-congress/house-bill/1424.

Larson, Heather. "Eating Disorder Treatment and Obamcare—What Has Changed?" NetQuote. Accessed December 12, 2017. https://www.netquote.com/health-insurance/news/eating-disorder-treatment-and-obamacare.

Puhl, Rebecca M., Dianne Neumark-Sztainer, S. Bryn Austin, Joerg Luedicke, and Kelly M. King. "Setting Policy Priorities to Address Eating Disorders and Weight Stigma: Views from the Field of Eating Disorders and the US General Public." BMC Public Health 14 (2014): 524. https://doi.org/10.1186/1471-2458-14-524.

Puhl, Rebecca M., Dianne Neumark-Sztainer, S. Bryn Austin, Young Suh, and Dorothy B. Wakefield. "Policy Actions to Address Weight-Based Bullying and Eating Disorders in Schools: Views of Teachers and School Administrators." Journal of School Health 86, no. 7 (2016): 507–515. https://doi.org/10.1111/josh.12401.

"S. 1865—114th Congress: A Bill to Amend the Public Health Service Act with Respect to Eating Disorders, and for Other Purposes." Congress.gov. Accessed February 3, 2017. https://www.congress.gov/bill/114th-congress/senate-bill/1865.

"S.B. 769—97th General Assembly Missouri Senate: Requires Health Benefit Plans Cover Diagnosis and Treatment of Eating Disorders." Trackbill.com. Accessed November 28, 2017. https://trackbill.com/bill/mo-sb769-requires-health-benefit-plans-cover-diagnosis-and-treatment-of-eating-disorders/641981/.

LEPTIN

Leptin is a protein hormone found primarily in white adipose tissues. It is also produced in stomach tissue, skeletal muscle, hypothalamus, pituitary gland, bone marrow, and mammary gland. Leptin functions as part of the endocrine system and regulates appetite, energy expenditure, and body weight.

The hypothalamus is involved in appetite regulation by detecting leptin levels in the blood. Leptin indicates satiety and regulate metabolism. As weight is gained the body releases additional leptin, which binds to receptors in the hypothalamus, resulting in a suppression of appetite and an increase in metabolic rate. In theory, this would lead an individual to consume less food to return to a set weight point. With weight loss, the reverse occurs as well. The body reduces the amount of leptin released into the blood, resulting in an increase in appetite and reduction in metabolism to conserve energy, thus increasing body weight.

Leptin and Eating Disorders

Leptin and Anorexia Nervosa

Serum concentration levels of leptin have been found to be low in individuals with anorexia nervosa. The decreases in leptin levels appear to be an endocrine adaptation to prevent further weight loss. The body decreases its release of leptin from the adipose cells to increase appetite and decrease metabolic rate. Weight restoration appears to increase serum leptin levels; however, there is evidence that leptin levels may reach elevated levels when one is recovering from malnourishment. This may increase the difficulty with weight restoration due to an increase in the metabolic rate of an individual. Decreased serum leptin levels have been linked to exercise-induced amenorrhea as well as hypothalamic amenorrhea, suggesting low levels of leptin may be involved in amenorrhea in anorexia nervosa. Without increasing leptin levels through weight restoration, further complications associated with amenorrhea (i.e., bone loss and impaired fertility) may occur.

Leptin and Bulimia Nervosa

Serum leptin levels have been reported to be decreased, normal, or elevated in bulimia nervosa. Low serum leptin levels have been seen in normal weight individuals with bulimia nervosa, indicating leptin is not solely influenced by weight but is also affected by eating patterns. A longer duration of illness and frequency of binge–purge episodes appear to lead to decreased levels of leptin. Decreased leptin levels may result in menstrual irregularities in individuals with bulimia nervosa.

Leptin and Binge Eating Disorder

Research is limited on the effects of leptin levels in binge eating disorder. It appears leptin levels are increased in individuals with binge eating disorder, but it remains unknown if increased levels are related to the binge episodes, obesity, and/or weight fluctuations. Chronic elevations in leptin have been associated with obesity and may lead to the development of diseases, such as hypertension, metabolic syndrome, or cardiovascular disease.

Amelia McBride

See also: Gastrointestinal Complications Associated with Eating Disorders; Intuitive Eating; Medical and Health Consequences; Obesity; Visceral Sensitivity

Bibliography

Bluher, Susann, and Christos S. Mantzoros. "The Role of Leptin in Regulating Neuroendocrine Function in Humans." *The Journal of Nutrition* 134 (2004): 2469S–2474S.

Chan, Jean L., and Chritos S. Montzoros. "Role of Leptin in Energy-Deprivation States: Normal Human Physiology and Clinical Implications for Hypothalamic Amenorrhea and Anorexia Nervosa." *Lancet* 366 (2005): 74–85. http://dx.doi.org/10.1016/S0140-6736(05)66830-4.

Eckert, Elake D., Claire Pomeroy, Nancy Raymond, Peter F. Kohler, Paul Thuras, and Cyril Y. Bowers. "Leptin in Anorexia Nervosa." *Journal of Clinical Endocrinology Metabolism* 83 (1998): 791–795. http://dx.doi.org/10.1210/jcem.83.3.4661.

Haas, Verena, Simone Onur, Thomas Paul, Detlev O. Nutzinger, Anja Bosy-Westphal, Maren Hauer, Georg Brabant, Harald Klein, and Manfred J. Muller. "Leptin and Body Weight Regulation in Patients with Anorexia Before and During Weight Recovery." *American Journal of Clinical Nutrition* 81 (2005): 889–896.

Mitchell, James E., and Scott Crow. "Medical Complications of Anorexia Nervosa and Bulimia Nervosa." *Current Opinions of Psychiatry* 19 (2006): 438–443. https://doi.org/10.1097/01.yco.0000228768.79097.3e.

Monteleone, Pamiero, Antonio DiLieto, Eloisa Castaldo, and Mario Maj. "Leptin Function-ing in Eating Disorders." *CNS Spectrums* 9 (2004): 523–529. https://doi.org/10.1017/S1092852900009615.

Monteleone, Pamiero, Vassilis Martiadis, Barbara Colurgio, and Mario Maj. "Leptin Secre-tion is Related to Chronicity and Severity of the Illness in Bulimia Nervosa." *Psychoso-matic Medicine* 64 (2002): 874–879.

LET'S MOVE!

"Let's Move! America's Move to Raise a Healthier Generation of Kids" refers to an initiative designed to fight the childhood obesity problem in the United States. The campaign was introduced by then first lady Michelle Obama on February 9, 2010. The program was touted as a comprehensive, collaborative, and community-based effort to address contributing factors of obesity and to promote healthy lifestyles among children and their families.

Five Pillars of the Let's Move! Initiative

Coinciding with the launch of the Let's Move! campaign, President Barack Obama signed a Presidential Memorandum charging a new Task Force on Childhood Obe-sity with the project of reviewing current nutrition and physical activity programs and identifying relevant goals and objectives. As an outgrowth of their efforts, the task force recommended the following five pillars: (1) create a healthy start for chil-dren; (2) empower parents and caregivers; (3) provide healthy foods in schools; (4) improve access to healthy, affordable foods; and (5) increase physical activity. These pillars have been addressed by efforts to increase physical education, eliminate food deserts (i.e., areas in the industrialized world that have barriers to providing healthful and affordable foods), and provide healthier school lunches with the support of chefs.

Taking Action

The Let's Move! campaign has used technology (e.g., website, YouTube videos) to promote messages and provide resources on topics including healthy eating and movement. Additionally, "taking 5 steps to success" targets kids and parents as well as schools, community leaders, chefs, elected officials, and health care providers. Finally, Let's Move! offers citizens an opportunity to take a pledge for health. At the time of this publication, 312 cities across the United States had organized and posted Let's Move! face-to-face meetings to address childhood obesity at a com-munity level. To personalize the obesity issue, Michelle Obama created a video to address the need to make behavioral changes and launch this initiative.

Justine J. Reel

See also: Exercise; Obesity; Prevention

Bibliography

"Let's Move!" https://letsmove.obamawhitehouse.archives.gov/. Accessed November 22, 2017.

LEVELS OF CARE

.The five main levels of treatment are inpatient hospitalization, residential, partial hospitalization (PHP), intensive outpatient (IOP), and outpatient. A number of factors considered when an individual is assessed to determine the appropriate level of care, such as the medical status of the client, level of motivation to recover, amount of family support for treatment, and how much weight needs to be restored. Generally, treatment facilities (e.g., Center for Change, an eating disorder treatment center in Orem, Utah) provide a complimentary in-depth clinical interview/assessment prior to admission to fully understand a client's needs.

Types of Treatment

The most intensive level of care, inpatient hospitalization, is recommended when an individual requires medical stabilization, 24-hour supervision and support, or medical refeeding and meal supervision. This setting resembles a hospital and a client who has often shown severe restricting prior to intake is typically placed on bed rest or prescribed minimal movement beyond stretching. Medications are monitored carefully, and a client may be monitored for risk of suicide or self-harm behaviors.

Residential treatment is a step down from inpatient hospitalization and is similar to a dorm setting. Clients live at a treatment facility and actively participate in comprehensive treatment including therapeutic meals, and group and individual therapy. Some eating disorder treatment facilities also provide yoga, Nia, or other exercise classes to address exercise dependence issues. Although a client in residential treatment requires structure and is provided support round-the-clock, he or she is not medically compromised or actively suicidal.

Partial hospitalization (PHP) is often a step down or a transition from the residential level of care. Clients may live in a home environment or housing associated with a treatment center that involves less structure and supervision than a residential facility. Generally, PHP clients have one to two meals while in treatment and will participate in groups and individual treatment. Clients will be responsible for monitoring their outside meals and bathroom policies for PHP level of care.

Intensive outpatient (IOP) and outpatient levels of care represent the least restrictive levels of care. Although IOP programs may include some of the group and individual approaches found in PHP, less support is provided throughout the week or on the weekends. Outpatient is the least intensive level of care and can include weekly visits to one's therapist as well as regular checkups with a physician and dietitian who serve on a client's multidisciplinary treatment team.

Justine J. Reel

See also: Family Therapy; Health Care Costs of Eating Disorders; Residential Treatment; Treatment

Bibliography

American Psychiatric Association. *Practice Guideline for the Treatment of Patients with Eating Disorders*, 3rd ed. Arlington, VA: American Psychiatric Association Publishing, 2006.

Committee on Adolescence. "Identifying and Treating Eating Disorders." *Pediatrics* 111, no. 1 (2003): 204–211. https://doi.org/10.1542/peds.111.1.204.

Stewart, Tiffany M., and Donald A. Williamson. "Multidisciplinary Treatment of Eating Disorders-Part 1: Structure and Costs of Treatment." *Behavior Modification* 28, no. 6 (2004): 812–830. https://doi.org/10.1177/0145445503259855.

Turner, Hannah, Rachel Bryant-Waugh, and Robert Peveler. "A New Approach to Clustering Eating Disorder Patients: Assessing External Validity and Comparisons with DSM-IV Diagnoses." *Eating Behaviors* 11 (2010): 99–106. https://doi.org/10.1016/j.eatbeh.2009.10.005.

Wilson, G. Terence, Kelly M. Vitousek, and Katharine L. Loeb. "Stepped Care Treatment for Eating Disorders." *Journal of Consulting and Clinical Psychology* 68, no. 4 (2000): 564–572. https://doi.org/10.1037//0022-006X.68.4.564.

MASCULINITY IDEALS

There has been a growing focus on body image over the past several decades. The male physique, in particular, has become a means of differentiating gender and emphasizing masculinity. Western society has transformed the way gender roles and gender identity are portrayed and interpreted. Typically research in gender roles has focused on the female and the body image concerns associated with a thin ideal. Similarly, men can have body dissatisfaction concerns. This increase in dissatisfaction in both males and females is evidenced by the billions spent annually by Americans on gym memberships, exercise equipment, and cosmetic surgery.

Traditional Role Changes

The role of men in society, or the definition of manhood, is created by culture. The perfect man in the 18th century was expected to be a father, a gentleman, a model of virtue, refined, and classy. His identity was represented by strictly male occupations such as the work of frontiersmen, policemen, doctors, businessmen, or soldiers. By 2011, masculinity based on one's occupation has largely evaporated. Consequently, many men may struggle to find their identity and to understand what qualities distinguish them from women.

This gender transformation, which should be distinguished from the biological term *sex,* is a change defined by culture. It has required males to seek identities separate from earlier norms. One identity that has been embraced by the male gender is sexually-based—muscularity. Current societal expectations encourage a male to develop a lean, muscular, mesomorphic body type.

The word *muscle* originates from the French word *mus,* meaning mouse. Its original meaning implied that a woman during that period was to swoon when seeing either muscle or mouse. The symbolism of muscle and its interpretation as a highly male characteristic lingers, and the size of muscles has traditionally symbolized the difference between the sexes.

Gender Differentiation

This distinct difference between men and women has meant that the male physique has been portrayed as more powerful and has underscored feminine weaknesses. Gerzon cites five traditional archetypes that depict masculinity: frontiersman, soldier, expert, breadwinner, and lord. Today, the archetypes of frontiersman and lord no longer exist whereas the breadwinner and expert are shared by both males and females. Indeed, while a soldier may also be a female, the role remains as a viable male archetype expressing an image of a strong, muscle-bound body.

Women may also possess a muscular body, which men may view as a threat to how they perceive their masculinity After all, masculinity is driven by a fear of being feminine or less than what a man should be, and a female intruding in a male domain threatens to abolish the physical distinction between the sexes. A muscular woman can threaten a male's perceived dominance in the areas of sexuality, sex, gender, the workplace, and social power. Thus, men are searching for a feature that distinguishes them from the opposite sex. Muscles provide a visual reminder of the sex differences in society that exist even as gender roles continue to evolve.

Klein's insight is supported through the increasing muscularity of men over the past 50 years. For males, having a more muscular physique and lower body fat has been referred to as a drive for muscularity. Men's bodies are judged by the size of their muscles. A muscular physique can depict traits that include power, dominance, strength, sexual virility, and self-esteem.

Implications for Body Image

Although it is generally understood the ideal human form is a representative consensus of what is dictated by society, these ideals change over time and vary across cultures. Therefore, if a perceived self-image does not equal the ideal as defined by a culture, a distorted view of one's body may develop. With men, there is a risk of developing dangerous attitudes and behaviors (e.g., obsession about size) associated with physique. Specifically, there is an increased risk of taking unhealthy measures (e.g., extreme dieting, overtraining) to be muscular and lean. Unfortunately, an individual with an intense drive for muscularity who attempts to rapidly reduce his or her body fat and becomes pathologically body conscious may be at risk for developing muscle dysmorphia. Muscle dysmorphia is discussed in a separate entry.

Timothy M. Baghurst

See also: Body Image in Males; Dolls; Drive for Muscularity; Femininity Ideals; Gender; Muscle Dysmorphia

Bibliography

Alexander, Susan M. "Stylish Hard Bodies: Branded Masculinity in *Men's Health* Magazine." *Sociological Perspectives* 46 (2003): 535–554. https://doi.org/10.1525/sop.2003.46.4.535.

Baghurst, Timothy M., David Carlston, Julie Wood, and Frank Wyatt. "Preadolescent Male Perceptions of Action Figure Physiques." *Journal of Adolescent Health* 41 (2007): 613–615. http://dx.doi.org/10.1016/j.jadohealth.2007.07.013.

Gerzon, Mark. *A Choice of Heroes: The Changing Faces of American Manhood.* Boston, MA: Houghton Mifflin, 1982.

Goldberg, Jonathan. "Recalling Totalities: The Mirrored Stages of Arnold Schwarzenegger." In *Building Bodies,* edited by Pamela L. Moore, 217–249. London: Rutgers University Press, 1997.

Klein, Alan M. "Of Muscles and Men." *The Sciences* 33, no. 6 (1993): 32–37. https://doi.org/10.1002/j.2326-1951.1993.tb03135.x.

Peoples, James G. "The Cultural Construction of Gender and Manhood." In *Men and Masculinity*, edited by Theodore Cohen, 9–19. Stamford, CT: Thomson Learning, 2001.

Pope, Harrison G., Jr., Katharine A. Phillips, and Roberto Olivardia. *The Adonis Complex: The Secret Crisis of Male Body Obsession.* New York: The Free Press, 2000.

Wesely, Jennifer K. "Negotiating Gender: Bodybuilding and the Natural/Unnatural Continuum." *Sociology of Sport Journal* 18 (2001): 162–180.

MAUDSLEY FAMILY THERAPY

Maudsley Family Therapy (Family-Based Treatment [FBT]) is a family therapy introduced by Christopher Dare and his team in 1985 at Maudsley Hospital in London. This approach was originally to treat adolescents with anorexia nervosa, in a home environment with therapeutic oversight by a trained professional. The Maudsley Approach was later adapted for use in the treatment of bulimia nervosa. A study that compared individual therapy and family therapy found family therapy was the most useful approach for patients under 18 years of age and if undertaken in three years of illness onset, as determined by a decrease in eating disorder symptoms. In this study, individual therapy was found to be more effective for clients over 18. However, the Maudsley Approach has since been adapted for use with adults and with other eating disorders, including behaviors that lead to obesity.

Phases of Treatment

The Maudsley Approach involves three phases that together span more than a year, typically, and it includes 15–20 sessions in the home. The three phases are weight restoration, returning control of eating to the child, and helping an adolescent establish an identity separate from the eating disorder.

Phase I: Weight Restoration

In the first phase, a therapist addresses the dangers of malnutrition associated with anorexia nervosa. Dangers include hypothermia, growth hormone changes, cardiac dysfunction, and cognitive/emotional changes. A family's routine eating habits and interaction patterns are assessed and a therapist assists parents in refeeding their daughter or son. Every effort is made by the treatment team to help parents in a joint attempt to restore an adolescent's weight. At the same time, a therapist will attempt to align a client with his or her siblings to provide positive peer support. A family meal is used to assess the family's interaction patterns around eating and to educate parents about how to support the adolescent. During this phase, a therapist models for an uncritical stance toward the child. The Maudsley Approach maintains the philosophy that the a child is not at fault for distorted attitudes and behaviors, but rather, the symptoms are usually outside of a child's control. The therapist confronts any criticism or hostility from parents.

Phase II: Returning Control to the Child over Eating

The adolescent's acceptance of parents' demands for increasing the intake of food, along with a steady weight gain and a change in the family's mood are all signals of Phase II. Phase II helps parents empower a child to assume increasing control over his or her eating. A therapist continues to keep a family focused on weight gain with minimal tension. Other familial relationship difficulties that were postponed can now be addressed in the counseling sessions. A child's symptoms also remain central in the discussions between therapist and family.

Phase III: Establishing Healthy Adolescent Identity

Phase III starts when an adolescent can independently maintain weight above 95 percent of ideal weight, and no longer engages in self-starvation. The focus shifts to the effect anorexia nervosa has had on the individual's ability to establish a healthy adolescent identity. Key issues of adolescence are addressed along with an increase in support of autonomy for the adolescent. In addition, parents are encouraged to develop healthy boundaries, and a strong couple's relationship.

Juliann Cook Jeppsen

See also: Children and Adolescents; Family Influences; Family Therapy; Treatment

Bibliography

Alexander, June, and Daniel Le Grange. "My Kid Is Back." *Empowering Parents to Beat Anorexia Nervosa*. Australia: Melbourne University Press, 2009.

Eisler, Ivan, Christopher Dare, Matthew Hodges, Gerald Russell, Elizabeth Dodge, and Daniel Le Grange. "Family Therapy for Adolescent Anorexia Nervosa: The Results of a Controlled Comparison of Two Family Interventions." *Journal of Child Psychology and Psychiatry* 41, no. 6 (2000): 727–736.

Lock, James, and Daniel Le Grange. *Help Your Teenager Beat an Eating Disorder*. New York: Guilford Press, 2005.

Lock, James, Daniel Le Grange, W. Stewart Agras, and Christopher Dare. *Treatment Manual for Anorexia Nervosa: A Family-Based Approach*. New York: Guilford Publications, 2001.

"Maudsley Parents." Accessed November 18, 2016. http://www.maudsleyparents.org.

Russell, Gerald, George Szmukler, Christopher Dare, and Ivan Eisler. "Family Therapy versus Individual Therapy for Adolescent Females with Anorexia Nervosa and Bulimia Nervosa." *Archives of General Psychiatry* 44 (1987): 1047–1056.

"Training Institute for Child and Adolescent Eating Disorders." Accessed November 18, 2016. http://www.train2treat4ed.com.

MEDIA

Television, radio, print (e.g., magazines) and the Internet serve as vehicles for promoting advertisements, conveying information and news, providing entertainment, and exposing individuals to visual images. Due to the constant exposure to pictures that emphasize perfect skin, flawless appearance, and bodies sculpted to optimal fitness, the media have often been blamed for being a primary cause of body image disturbances and eating disorders. Although cultural ideals have changed over time, what has remained constant is the tendency to promote a particular *type* or *look* that represents beauty and serves as a marker for others (especially women) to try to emulate. Women in the 1950s favored a curvaceous, feminine body ideal represented by the likes of Marilyn Monroe. By contrast, women in the 1960s were inundated by ultrathin models such as Twiggy who were on display exposing gaunt body frames with sharp lines. The media goes a step further by showing solutions to beauty problems and flaws by educating society about products that can change body and appearance imperfections.

Body Dissatisfaction and the Media

Margaret Carlisle Duncan, a sociologist who studies sport, has used the metaphor that the media serves as a prison guard tower that provides a constant gaze over societal members and monitors bodily flaws. Individuals in society internalize their appearance imperfections thus reinforcing body dissatisfaction and the tendency to engage in dieting and other behaviors geared toward making one's appearance closer to the unattainable ideal. Many studies have supported the contention that the media contribute to negative body image. For example, studies have found females who read a fashion magazine or watched a commercial were more likely to report body dissatisfaction, decreased self-esteem, and negative mood following the media exposure. In a separate study, researchers confirmed that trying to look like same-sex persons in the media was a stronger risk factor for females than males. However, for both males and females, the media promotes highly unrealistic and unattainable images that represent either highly masculine or feminine qualities. The models in advertisements possess unusual genetic attributes, such as being above average height, being well-proportioned, and having a naturally thin waist; these attributes are accentuated in media images. It is unlikely that these genetically gifted models need or could benefit from the products (e.g., cellulite cream, antiwrinkle eye cream, fat burning supplements) they are promoting. However, it is not uncommon for even these genetic masterpieces to be airbrushed or digitally altered in the photographs. For example, waists are decreased, and moles and skin blemishes are eliminated.

Television and Body Image

Considering that in Western societies television is viewed daily for seven hours on average, with an average exposure of 35,000 television commercials per year, it is noteworthy that television commercials that promote women as young, thin, and attractive have been shown to have a stronger effect on negative body image than static images in fashion magazines. Alarmingly, similar negative impacts on body image have been observed among females in Fiji with the introduction of the Western media. Television advertisements display stimuli associated with eating and certain foods including trigger foods or binge foods (e.g., desserts); they also include dieting messages in many ads (e.g., yogurt brands). Several years ago, a shoe commercial promoted shape-up and tone-up properties targeted toward seven- and eight-year-old girls. In addition to commercials, television actors in weekly shows are most likely to fit the socially constructed body ideal and are less likely to be older, overweight, or unattractive.

Internet and Body Image

Although magazines and television have been powerful forces influencing body image, the Internet is tidal wave of messages and images. Ads serve as banners for websites and flash in the margins of social networking sites (e.g., Facebook). In addition, a number of Pro-Ana websites have popped up that encourage, promote, and reinforce dieting and pathological weight control methods and overtly champion eating disorders. Photos are posted to promote ultrathin images (e.g., protruding collar bones and rib cages) to encourage thinness and discipline. *Thinspirations* including poems and messages about staying on course with one's eating disorders are to motivate visitors to engage in disordered eating; there are also forums for individuals to post their struggles restricting and maintaining discipline for anorexia nervosa.

Justine J. Reel

See also: Books about Eating Disorders; Celebrities and Eating Disorders; Internet and Eating Disorders; Models and Eating Disorders; Movies and Eating Disorders; Pro-Ana; Social Contagion Theory; Social Media and Eating Disorders; Television Shows and Eating Disorders

Bibliography

Becker, Anne E., Kristen E. Fay, Jessica Agnew-Blais, A. Nisha Khan, Ruth H. Striegel-Moore, and Stephen E. Gilman. "Social Network Media Exposure and Adolescent Eating Pathology in Fiji." *British Journal of Psychiatry* 198, no. 1 (2011): 43–50. https://doi.org/10.1192/bjp.198.1.50.

Carper, Teresa L. Marino, Charles Negy, and Stacey Tantleff-Dunn. "Relations among Media Influence, Body Image, Eating Concerns, and Sexual Orientation in Men: A Preliminary Investigation." *Body Image* 7 (2010): 301–309. https://doi.org/10.1016/j.bodyim.2010.07.002.

"Do 7-Year-Olds Really Need 'Shape-Ups?'" *Today Show.* Accessed November 18, 2016. https://www.facebook.com/today/posts/10150256811306350.

Field, Alison E., Kristin M. Javaras, Parul Aneja, Nicole Kitos, Carlos A. Camargo, C. Barr Taylor, and Nan M. Laird. "Family, Peer and Media Predictors of Becoming Eating Disordered." *Archives of Pediatric Medicine* 162, no. 6 (2008): 574–579. https://doi.org/10.1001/archpedi.162.6.574.

Legenbauer, Tanja, Ilka Ruhl, and Silja Vocks. "Influence of Appearance-Related TV Commercials on Body Image State." *Behavior Modification* 32 (2008): 352–371. https://doi.org/10.1177/0145445507309027.

Mazzeo, Suzanne E., Sara E. Trace, Karen S. Mitchell, and Rachel Walker Gow. "Effects of a Reality TV Cosmetic Surgery Makeover Program on Eating Disordered Attitudes and Behaviors." *Eating Behaviors* 8 (2007): 390–397. https://doi.org/10.1016/j.eatbeh.2006.11.016.

Mousa, Tamara Y., Rima H. Mashal, Hayder A. Al-Domi, and Musa A. Jibril. "Body Dissatisfaction among Adolescent Schoolgirls in Jordan." *Body Image* 7 (2010): 46–50. https://doi.org/10.1016/j.bodyim.2009.10.002.

"The Photoshop Effect." YouTube.com. Accessed November 18, 2016. https://www.youtube.com/watch?v=YP31r70_QNM&feature=player_embedded.

Spettigue, Wendy, and Katherine A. Henderson. "Eating Disorders and the Role of the Media." *The Canadian Child and Adolescent Psychiatry Review* 13, no. 1 (2004): 16–19.

Van den Berg, Patricia, Susan J. Paxton, Helene Keery, Melanie Wall, Jia Guo, and Dianne Neumark-Sztainer. "Body Dissatisfaction and Body Comparison with Media Images in Males and Females." *Body Image* 4 (2007): 257–268. https://doi.org/10.1016/j.bodyim.2007.04.003.

"Yoplait Commercial." YouTube.com. Last modified June 2, 2016. Accessed November 18, 2016. https://www.youtube.com/watch?v=7TO208trnno.

MEDICAL AND HEALTH CONSEQUENCES

Eating disorders can lead to a wide array of medical complications affecting many body systems. These complications result from the stress exerted on the body due to the effects of malnutrition brought about by nutrient deficiencies and starvation; they can also be the result of binge episodes and purging behaviors. It is crucial that all body systems (e.g., cardiovascular system) be reviewed as part of the treatment of eating disorders to address any complications.

Cardiovascular Complications

Cardiovascular complications of eating disorders can be seen in either the short-term or the long-term duration of the illness. These complications generally result from electrolyte imbalances, dehydration associated with persistent purging, or a weakened heart due to muscular adaptations associated with malnutrition. The cardiac muscle adapts both structurally and functionally to preserve the body. Weight restoration and/or the elimination of compensatory (purging) behaviors allows for the reversal of these complications. However, extensive damage to the heart may lead to irreversible or life-threatening complications, such as heart failure. Common cardiovascular complications include electrocardiogram (EKG) abnormalities, bradycardia, mitral valve prolapse, hypotension, and congestive heart failure.

Electrocardiogram Abnormalities

Electrocardiogram abnormalities are commonly seen in both anorexia nervosa and bulimia nervosa patients. Anorexia nervosa and bulimia nervosa may result in prolonged QT intervals—the time it takes for the heart to contract and subsequently refill with blood in preparation for the next contraction—due to low levels of serum electrolytes (sodium, potassium, calcium, and bicarbonate), phosphorus and/or magnesium deficiencies, dehydration, and low body weight. Low serum potassium is commonly a cause of prolonged QT intervals in individuals with bulimia nervosa. The QT interval is generally normalized with the correction of the cause.

Mitral Valve Prolapse

The mitral valve is involved in the blood flow in the cardiac muscle. In normal physiology the mitral valve opens to allow blood to flow from the left atrium into the left ventricle. Anorexia nervosa may result in a change in the size of the

Medical Perspectives on Eating Disorders:
An Interview with Dr. Anne O'Melia

Anne Marie O'Melia, MS, MD, is medical director of Adult Services at Eating Recovery Center in Denver, Colorado. She is a triple board-trained physician, with board certifications in Pediatrics and General Psychiatry. She also holds subspecialty board certifications in Child and Adolescent Psychiatry and in Psychosomatic Medicine.

From a medical perspective, what are the biggest concerns (health consequences) for someone who has an eating disorder?

Unlike most other psychiatric illnesses, eating disorders are often associated with serious, sometimes life-threatening medical complications. Starvation and other eating disorder behaviors such as bingeing, frequent vomiting, laxative or diuretic abuse, and excessive exercise can cause significant damage to the human body. Further complicating matters, eating disorder patients are often secretive or ashamed of their behaviors, making medical assessment and treatment that much more difficult and increasing the medical risks and even the lethality of eating disorders.

For anorexia nervosa, health consequences associated with restricting food intake are related to the effects of severe and sustained malnutrition. Effects are seen in virtually every system as the body tries to adapt to starvation by budgeting its resources. The most serious problems resulting from inadequate energy intake are cardiac concerns, very slow heart rate and low blood pressure proceeds to heart failure. Most medical consequences of anorexia nervosa are reversible with sustained nutritional stabilization. The most concerning irreversible medical consequence is inadequate mineralization and bone density loss (osteoporosis).

Purging behaviors associated with bulimia nervosa can lead to serious concerns related to electrolyte imbalances, which affect the way muscles contract, especially the muscle of the heart. Imbalance of fluids, acidity of blood, and potassium, sodium, and chloride can lead to unsafe heart function and impact other organ systems. Also, the stress of bingeing and purging or laxative abuse can cause significant problems with the digestive tract including inflammation of the esophagus, peptic ulcers, gastroparesis, constipation, and pancreatitis. Permanent damage to the nerves of the colon can result from laxative abuse. Oral complications from frequent vomiting include loss of enamel and dentin on the teeth, cheilosis, and pharyngeal soreness. After an individual who frequently engages in vomiting stops the behavior, we often see sialadenosis (parotid gland swelling) which can last for weeks and is quite uncomfortable for patients. Patients with anorexia nervosa who also engage in purging behaviors are at the highest risk of severe medical consequences.

The health risks of binge eating disorder are the same as for obesity. These include hypertension, high cholesterol and triglycerides, heart disease, orthopedic problems, type 2 diabetes, gall bladder disease, and increased risk for cancer.

After a malnourished patient begins their journey to recovery, there are risks of refeeding problems. As metabolism switches from a system of catabolic metabolism to a metabolism that uses food as the main source of energy, the risks of refeeding syndrome must be well understood by care providers who must monitor eating disorder patients as they begin to stabilize their nutrition after significant nutritional deprivation. The greatest risk of these complications occurs during the first 2–3 weeks of refeeding. Problems are manifested by cardiovascular collapse after refeeding (oral, enteral, or parenteral). Phosphate levels, in particular, must be monitored as low phosphorus can result in cardiac arrest and/or delirium.

Although these complications are usually common and predictable consequences of eating disorder behaviors, most physicians are not trained to recognize or treat the medical concerns associated with eating disorders. As a result, patients and families are sometimes offered inappropriate reassurance or unhelpful and even dangerous care by well-intentioned health care providers who aren't experienced with eating disorder care.

I will give an example of a situation where a lack of understanding of the physiology of eating disorders can cause harm to our patients. Most medical professionals are largely unaware of the need to "detox" from eating disorder purging behaviors (including self-induced vomiting, laxative and/or diuretic abuse, etc.). When a patient develops the will to stop the purging behavior, they will often experience uncomfortable medical complaints (e.g., abdominal pain and constipation) after stopping their laxatives or significant edema resulting in weight gain. Edema results as a consequence of chronic severe fluid volume depletion, which has caused high levels of aldosterone production to compensate over time (pseudo-Bartter's syndrome). This syndrome is severely exacerbated when a patient who has recently stopped purging behaviors seeks care, is noted to have low blood pressure, dehydration, low potassium or acid–base imbalances, and is provided the standard medical response of a rapid infusion of IV saline fluids. Our chronically volume depleted patients will hold onto the fluids causing severe and sometimes dangerous edema and pulmonary or cardiac congestion. Further, our patients report such discomfort with the misunderstanding of their medical needs that they refuse any return visits and will often go back to purging behaviors to alleviate the uncomfortable symptoms that were not addressed in the community medical setting.

What are the medications used to treat eating disorders? How effective are they? Do you have concerns about the side effects that patients experience with these medications?

For many patients, especially those with bulimia nervosa (BN) and binge eating disorder (BED), medication can be a valuable addition to treatment, which would ideally include psychotherapy and nutritional counseling. There are presently only two medications with FDA indication for treatment of eating disorders. Fluoxetine (Prozac) at a dose of 60 mg per day is approved for the treatment of bulimia. Lisdexamfetamine (Vyvanse) was recently approved by the FDA for the treatment of moderate to severe BED. While the pharmacologic evidence for effectiveness of response for other medications is less compelling, many patients clearly benefit from the addition of other medications to manage eating disorder symptoms as well as to address common comorbid problems with anxiety, mood disorders, or ADHD.

Anorexia nervosa (AN): There is only minimal to moderate evidence that psychiatric medications are effective in treating patients with AN. Despite the prevalence of mood and anxiety symptoms in patients with AN, medications used to treat these conditions are not necessarily useful treatment adjuncts for reducing the symptoms of anorexia nervosa or even reducing symptoms of anxiety and depression, especially while a patient remains underweight. There may be more evidence for using antidepressants in the weight maintenance phase.

In addition to concerns regarding the efficacy of antidepressants in patients with anorexia nervosa, there is also considerable debate as to the efficacy of antipsychotics in treating the symptoms of anorexia nervosa. Low-dose antipsychotic medications may sometimes be useful in treating delusional beliefs regarding body image, intense ruminations about food, and the hyperarousal and as well as anxiety induced by having to face weight restoration. For patients with AN whose eating disorder symptoms have proven refractory to other evidence-based treatment interventions (psychotherapies, nutritional rehabilitation), the use of medication with the hope of offering relief of suffering from debilitating eating disorders, anxiety, or depressive symptoms is always worth considering.

Bulimia nervosa (BN): Effective treatment for BN should include medical stabilization, nutritional rehabilitation, psychotherapy, and, when indicated, psychiatric medication management. Patients benefit more from combined psychotherapy and pharmacotherapy than from either treatment alone.

Fluoxetine (Prozac), a selective serotonin reuptake inhibitor (SSRI), has been FDA-approved for treating symptoms of bulimia nervosa. Fluoxetine, which has been used to help regulate mood swings, also has been shown to reduce binge eating by creating a sense of satiety (i.e., fullness).

Other SSRI medications shown to be effective for the treatment of bulimia nervosa include citalopram (Celexa) and sertraline (Zoloft). Some concern for cardiac risk at higher doses of citalopram may limit its usefulness for treatment of eating disorders. Trazodone, an atypical antidepressant, studied at doses of 200–400 mg/day, has also been shown to be helpful for sustained control of BN in one small but well-controlled study.

Monoamine oxidase inhibitors (e.g., phenelzine) and tricyclic antidepressant medications (e.g., desipramine, imipramine, and nortriptyline) have also been shown to be effective in reducing symptoms of BN. However, because these medications have common and potentially dangerous adverse events associated with their use, they are generally reserved for refractory cases and for use by psychiatrists with considerable eating disorder expertise. Bupropion (Wellbutrin) has also been found helpful in controlling bulimia nervosa symptomology, but it has been associated with an increased risk for seizures and should not be used for the treatment of bulimia nervosa and other eating disorders.

Although many patients with bulimia benefit greatly from the use of antidepressants, it is important to recognize risks associated with use during pregnancy, possible risk of increased suicidality in adolescents and young adults, risk of manic symptoms in patients with bipolar disorder, and possible weight change as a side effect. Prior to initiating pharmacotherapy, patients should be counseled regarding these risks and carefully screened for additional risk factors and comorbidities.

The antiepileptic drug, topiramate (Topamax), has been found to be effective for bulimia nervosa treatment in two separate randomized, placebo-controlled studies. Average dosing of topiramate ranged from 100 mg/day to 250 mg/day. Topiramate was superior to placebo in reducing the frequency of binge and purge days and was also associated with reduced body weight. Although weight loss for bulimia nervosa patients who are obese or overweight may not be a medical problem, the potential destabilizing impact of weight loss for patients with BN must be considered before initiating this treatment and must be monitored closely over time. The FDA recently approved topiramate for migraine prevention in adolescents. Caution and screening for eating disorder risk factors is advised before using topiramate for headache prevention, as there are some reports of onset of eating disorder symptoms when it's used for this indication in adolescent patients.

Pharmacotherapy for BN may also be guided by the presence of co-occurring conditions. Antidepressants may be especially helpful for bulimia nervosa patients with a depressive or anxiety disorder. Patients with a seasonal pattern to depressive symptoms and bulimia may benefit from light therapy: 10,000 lux for 30 minutes each morning.

ADHD medicines, like atomoxetine (Strattera), or a psychostimulant like methylphenidate (e.g., Ritalin, Concerta) and lisdexamfetamine (Vyvanse), with careful monitoring, may be helpful in patients with BN and comorbid ADHD. These medications have also been shown to be helpful for control of eating disorder symptoms in patients with BED. The use of psychostimulents, in particular, may be limited by a high rate of discontinuation due to side effects (e.g., high blood pressure, anxiety, insomnia, fast heart rate) and by the risk of medication abuse and dependence inherent in the use of controlled substances.

Antiaddiction or anticraving drugs may prove helpful for some patients with co-occurring substance-use disorders. The opiate antagonist Naltrexone (Revia), at supratherapeutic doses (e.g., 200 mg/day), has been shown to be helpful in controlling bulimia nervosa symptoms. Although Naltrexone use carries the risk of liver damage, when used with consistent assessment for response and careful laboratory monitoring of liver function, the potential benefit of this medicine could outweigh the risk when used for select patients.

What role does the MD play on an eating disorder treatment team?
Physicians are important members of eating disorder multidisciplinary treatment teams. Primary care physicians play critical roles in eating disorder prevention and are on the front line in screening and helping patients initiate care with specialized care providers. Physicians who specialize in eating disorders are experts in assessing risks and determining the appropriate level of care. Psychiatrists assess for comorbid mental health concerns, prescribe and monitor psychiatric medications and oversee the medical and behavioral safety of the patient. They are in the best position to lead a multidisciplinary team and coordinate the care of complex patients. Internists, family practitioners, and pediatricians, along with specialists like gastroenterologists, neurologists, orthopedic specialists, gynecologists, endocrinologists, and cardiologists must understand and treat the varied and sometimes dangerous consequences of eating disorders.

What needs to happen for a patient with an eating disorder to begin to improve/ recover from an eating disorder?
Recovery generally happens in "phases" or "steps." The first priorities of care must be nutritional and medical stabilization and psychiatric safety. Adequate nutrition must be provided to the recovering brain while avoiding destabilizing medical problems that may threaten progress in treatment, and issues of suicidality or threat

of harm from others must be managed. Nobody has ever recovered from anorexia while they are underweight. Full weight restoration and normalization is a critical component of sustained recovery. As physical and nutritional health is regained, psychotherapy is aimed at understanding the functional role of the eating disorder, self-understanding, self-acceptance, and identification of individual noneating disorder goals and values. Eating disorder patients are usually temperamentally anxious, threat sensitive, and harm avoidant. In therapy, patients explore how they have used their eating disorder to manage their anxiety. Values-based anxiety management is implemented where we work with eating disorder patients to identify what they value in life and help them see how their values can trump their anxiety. We help them to understand that there's something they value more in life than escaping their anxiety and support them while they find the strength and the motivation to accept and experience their anxiety in the service of their real values.

What would you say to parents who are worried that their son or daughter may suffer from an eating disorder?
Keep asking questions until you are satisfied that a provider that understands eating disorders has evaluated your loved one and provided recommendations. Don't waste time and, if, you remain worried, don't accept reassurance from nonexpert providers. Early identification and intervention improves the chances of recovery. The longer your loved one engages in eating disorder behaviors and suffers from eating disorder urges, the harder their illness is to treat.

cardiac muscle, without changing the size of the supporting tissue. Consequently, the mitral valve bulges slightly upward into the left atrium, rather than closing smoothly. Mitral valve prolapse is characterized by a clicking sound after the contraction of the ventricle. Individuals with a mitral valve prolapse may experience chest palpitations or pain, dizziness, fainting, and fatigue. Mitral valve prolapse is generally not life threatening. Weight restoration will typically allow the heart to repair itself, thereby resolving mitral valve prolapse.

Bradycardia
Bradycardia (slowed heart rate) is a resting heart rate of less than 60 beats per minute. This condition is generally seen in individuals with anorexia nervosa and is a physiological adaptation associated with a hypometabolic state. Heart rates as low as 30 beats per minute may be seen in this population. Generally, there are no additional symptoms directly associated with bradycardia; however, it is often seen in conjunction with hypotension. As malnutrition is resolved and weight is restored bradycardia improves.

Hypotension
Hypotension is characterized by decreased blood pressure resulting from a decrease in cardiac output, arterial tone, and effective arterial blood volume. It is defined by a systolic blood pressure of less than 90 mm Hg and diastolic blood pressure of less than 50 mm Hg. Orthostatic hypotension results when blood pressure decreases by values greater than 20/10 mm Hg when going from a supine to

upright position. This is detected by measuring blood pressure in different positions (supine, sitting, and standing). Common symptoms associated with orthostatic hypotension include dizziness or fainting when changing positions (laying/sitting to standing). Malnutrition, dehydration (associated with inadequate fluid intake or excessive loss of fluids through vomiting and/or diarrhea), and cardiac problems are common causes of hypotension in eating disorders.

Congestive Heart Failure

Congestive heart failure results when the heart is unable to effectively pump blood into the body. It occurs as a result of fluid overload on a weakened heart or in the final stages of starvation. It is primarily a concern during refeeding due to rapid increase in intake either orally or enterally. Congestive heart failure has also been associated with severe hypokalemia or vitamin B deficiencies. Symptoms of congestive heart failure should be monitored in the early stages of refeeding.

Anorexia nervosa may result in various cardiac complications that can generally be reversed with weight restoration and nutrition rehabilitation. Cardiac complications of normal-weight individuals with bulimia nervosa are typically limited to electrolyte imbalances associated with frequent purging.

Gastrointestinal Complications

Gastrointestinal complaints are common in both anorexia nervosa and bulimia nervosa. These complications can occur at any point along the gastrointestinal tract. Many of the complications are linked to compensatory behaviors, such as self-induced vomiting, laxative abuse, and diuretic abuse. Prolonged use of compensatory behaviors may result in irreversible damage to the gastrointestinal tract.

Anorexia nervosa may lead to complications such as constipation, bloating, gastroparesis (increased gastric emptying time), and abnormal liver function tests. A decrease in food intake results in physiological adaptations of the gastrointestinal tract. Consequently, as increased amounts of food are reintroduced into the body, it leads to gastrointestinal discomfort including constipation, bloating, and gastroparesis. Although these symptoms may impact an individuals' ability to tolerate foods, symptoms generally improve as food intake normalizes and the gastrointestinal tract readapts to the presence of food.

Abnormal liver function tests may be seen as a result of weight loss and in the early stages of weight restoration. Frequent abnormalities include elevated levels of aspartate aminotransferase (AST), alanine aminotransferase (ALT), alkaline phosphatase, and total bilirubin. Levels generally normalize as increases in caloric intake stabilize and body weight improves.

Bulimia nervosa has greater impact on the gastrointestinal tract than anorexia nervosa. Complications include disruptions in the esophagus, stomach, small and large bowel, and rectum. Damages can be reversed if addressed, but long-term abuse of purging behaviors may result in irreversible consequences.

Chronic vomiting leads to repetitive exposure of the esophagus to the acid components of gastric content. The esophageal sphincter valve is weakened, leading to increased symptoms of heartburn and gastrointestinal reflux. Alterations along the esophagus may result in cellular changes leading to Barrett's esophagus. Mallory-Weiss tears may be seen in the esophagus due to the trauma of vomiting. These tears may lead to internal bleeding. Although rare, esophageal ruptures could occur in bulimia nervosa.

The chronic use of laxatives impairs the function of the colon. Laxatives disrupt the normal peristaltic function of the colon, decreasing mobility. Symptoms of constipation may increase as the body adapts to long-term use of laxatives. Normal bowel function can return if laxative intake is stopped, although it takes time for the body to readapt.

Gastrointestinal complaints are common in both anorexia nervosa and bulimia nervosa. Constipation, bloating, gastroparesis, and abnormal liver function tests are often seen in anorexia nervosa. These are a result of the reintroduction of foods into the gastrointestinal tract and will improve with continual intake. Bulimia nervosa may alter the lining of the esophagus and function of the colon depending on one's purging method.

Renal Complications

Kidneys eliminate of waste and urine from the body. Chronic dehydration and compensatory behaviors may lead to kidney and electrolyte imbalances. Electrolytes are involved in cell communication and muscle contraction, and alterations in serum electrolytes disrupt these processes. The electrolytes include sodium, potassium, chloride, and bicarbonate.

Vomiting causes the body to lose hydrochloric acid from the stomach leading to metabolic acidosis (elevated serum bicarbonate levels). Hypokalemia (low serum potassium levels) and hypochloremia (low chloride levels) are related to the frequency of purging behaviors. Metabolic alkalosis (low serum bicarbonate levels) results from the loss of alkaline fluids from the bowel due to laxative abuse. Hyponatremia (low serum sodium levels) may occur as a result of consuming large amounts of fluids. Hypernatremia (elevated serum sodium levels) is a result of inadequate fluid intake or excessive fluid loss via diarrhea and/or vomiting. Mixed compensatory behaviors may lead to multiple electrolyte imbalances. Electrolyte imbalances are seen less frequently in restricting behavior and are primarily associated with dehydration.

Endocrine Complications

The endocrine system is composed of glands that produce and secrete hormones. These hormones are involved in metabolism, growth, and development, and sexual development and function. Endocrine abnormalities in eating disorders primarily result from prolonged starvation.

Thyroid

The thyroid hormone is primarily responsible for regulation of metabolic processes and thermoregulation of body temperature. It is also involved in the cardiovascular system, central nervous system, and the reproductive system. The body adapts to starvation by lowering thyroid hormone production leading to decreased metabolic rate, increased cold intolerance, slowed heart rate, constipation, and fatigue. Weight restoration generally allows these symptoms to resolve.

Growth

Slowed growth has been associated with anorexia nervosa in children and adolescents. Inadequate energy intake leads to a reduction in the production of thyroxine and triiodothyronine, and sex hormones. Additionally, an elevation in cortisol levels and changes in growth hormones are commonly reported. These hormones are involved in growth, and alterations may affect linear growth during this critical time of growth and development. Anorexia nervosa in children and adolescents may prevent them from reaching their full height potential.

Amenorrhea

The presence of amenorrhea was previously a diagnostic criterion for anorexia nervosa. Amenorrhea, a warning sign for eating disorders, results from a physiological adaptation to starvation. Starvation leads the pituitary gland to decrease the production of follicle-stimulating hormone and luteinizing hormone resulting in a decrease in production of estrogen and progesterone. The decreased levels of these hormones result in the absence of menstruation. Although amenorrhea may impact fertility, it does not always cause anovulation; therefore, it cannot be seen as an assurance that pregnancy will not occur. Weight restoration appears to stimulate the production of estrogen and progesterone leading to restoration of menstruation.

Reduced Bone Density

A reduction in bone density is commonly associated with anorexia nervosa and may lead to osteopenia or osteoporosis. There are multiple factors believed to be related to low bone density including low estrogen levels, increased cortisol levels, poor nutrition, low calcium and vitamin D intake, and low body mass. Because amenorrhea reduces estrogen levels, there is a greater risk of lower bone density. Targeting the cause of reduced bone density is essential, but it should be noted complete bone density may never be fully restored. Bone mineral density does not seem to be impacted as greatly in bulimia nervosa.

Hypercholesterolemia

Hypercholesterolemia, or elevated cholesterol, is commonly identified in individuals with anorexia nervosa. High-density lipoprotein (HDL) concentrations are likely to be elevated because of high levels of exercise and weight loss. Elevations in low-density lipoprotein (LDL) concentrations have also been identified. Probable mechanisms are acceleration in cholesterol metabolism and abnormalities in estrogen, thyroid hormone, and glucocorticoids. Nutrition and weight restoration generally result in the normalization of cholesterol levels.

Cortisol

Elevated cortisol levels have been identified in persons with anorexia nervosa. Other symptoms such as hyperglycemia, hypotension, and skin atrophy associated with elevated cortisol levels are not present. This indicates that anorexia nervosa leads to a resistance of the tissues to glucocorticoids.

Endocrine abnormalities are associated with starvation. Individuals with anorexia nervosa may exhibit various endocrine complications. Early detection, monitoring, and evaluation of any endocrine irregularities may prevent long-term complications.

Neurological Complications

Eating disorders affect both the central and peripheral nervous systems. Complications associated with the central nervous system stem from structural and functional adaptations. The most common peripheral abnormality seen in eating disorders involves muscle weakness.

Images of the brain indicate eating disorders may impact its overall structure and function. Individuals with anorexia nervosa exhibit pseudoatrophy of the brain characterized by enlarged ventricles and external cerebrospinal fluid spaces. The mechanism behind this abnormality remains unknown, but it appears to reverse with weight restoration. Seizures, headaches, and syncope have been reported in eating disorders. These complications are thought to be associated with malnutrition and decrease as nutrition is improved.

Muscle weakness is common in anorexia nervosa and bulimia nervosa. Nutrient deficiencies, dehydration, and electrolyte imbalances appear to have the greatest impact on muscular weakness. As these conditions are addressed muscular weakness improves.

Hematological Complications

Hematological complications have been identified in anorexia nervosa. Bone marrow hypoplasia has been associated with states of malnutrition leading to an increased presence of anemia, leukoneutropenia, and thrombocytopenia. A low body mass has also been correlated with lower hemoglobin, leukocyte, red blood cell, and neutrophil counts. Anemia can also be related to factors including the state of starvation, increased blood loss through the gastrointestinal tract due to purging behaviors, and/or nutrient deficiencies (iron, vitamin B12, and folic acid). The improvement in dietary status will generally reverse the effects of anemia. Leukopenia (low white blood cell count) can be seen due to protein energy malnutrition. This does not appear to impact the immune system and improves as nutritional status recovers.

Dermatological Complications

Anorexia nervosa and bulimia nervosa both impact dermatological health. Dermatological symptoms may overlap between anorexia nervosa and bulimia nervosa. Common dermatological manifestations include acne, xerosis, lanugo, carotenoderma, hair and nail fragility, acrocyanosis, peripheral edema, and Russell's sign.

Dermatological complications are mainly aggravated by poor nutritional intake. Acne, both facial and back, is commonly seen during the weight restoration process. Weight loss results in the body reverting to a prepubescent state, including a decrease in hormone production. As weight is restored the body adapts to hormonal shifts resulting in acne.

Xerosis (dry skin) develops as a result of vitamin deficiencies. Lotions and creams may alleviate symptoms associated with dry skin; improved nutrition will resolve the condition.

Lanugo is fine, downy, pale hair that grows on the body in attempts to provide insulation for a malnourished individual. It is generally found on the face, chest, arms, legs, and back. The body will rid itself of the hair as improved thermoregulation is achieved.

Carotenoderma results in an abnormal yellow-orange hue on the skin, primarily on the ears, palms, and soles. It is a result of an accumulation of serum carotene. Carotenoderma is thought to be associated with a high intake of carotene-rich foods and/or an alteration in the hepatic breakdown of carotene. This will resolve with improved nutrition status allowing for the normalization of liver function.

Hair and nails may be brittle due to protein-energy malnutrition as well as a deficiency of vitamins and minerals. Increased hair loss may also occur. Restoration of nutrition leads to improved health of hair and nails.

Acrocyanosis results from a disruption in the circulatory system. This is often seen in anorexia nervosa as the body decreases blood circulation to the periphery as it conserves blood flow for vital organs. It is characterized by cold hands and feet resulting in a bluish-purple coloring of the fingernails and toenails. Weight restoration appears to improve circulation, thus reducing symptoms of acrocyanosis.

Peripheral edema is observed in individuals with anorexia nervosa and bulimia nervosa. Fluid retention occurs in the refeeding phase of anorexia nervosa, a result of the low basal metabolic rate and fluid shifts in the body. Binge episodes and purging (through self-induced vomiting, diuretics, and laxatives) interrupt the fluid balance in the body. Eliminating behaviors will cause the body to initially retain fluids, resulting in peripheral edema. Fluid retention is typically improved as the body adapts to increased intake and the cessation of purging behaviors.

Russell's sign is a distinguishing characteristic of using one's hand to force vomiting. It is identified by calluses or abrasions along the knuckles of the hands due to contact with the teeth. The abrasions may lead to permanent scarring.

Oral Complications

Oral complications are as a result of repetitive vomiting. Common oral complications include angular cheilosis, dental caries, dental erosion, and parotid gland swelling.

Angular cheilosis is characterized by dry, painful fissures along the corners of the mouth. It results from repetitive exposure of the mouth to the acidic content of the vomitus. It is not permanent, and like other wounds, will heal on its own, although it may leave scarring. Angular cheilosis is also associated with riboflavin deficiency. A correction of the deficiency may be necessary.

Dental caries is a potential result of both anorexia nervosa and bulimia nervosa. High intake of carbohydrate-rich foods provides a breeding ground for bacterial growth in the mouth. The increase in bacteria leads to a greater risk of developing dental caries.

Dental erosion is frequently associated with bulimia nervosa due to the long-term contact with gastric acid. This leads to the decay in dental and tooth enamel. This is likely to occur after two years of frequent excessive vomiting. Treatment includes eliminating vomiting behaviors and being diligent about dental hygiene.

Parotid gland swelling is characterized by chipmunk-like cheeks. It occurs as a result of recurrent bingeing and purging. It has been attributed to an increase in cholinergic nerve stimulation, repetitive stimulation of the gland due to bingeing behaviors, chronic elevated bicarbonate, and/or increased autonomic stimulation from the stimulation of lingual taste receptors. Parotid gland swelling generally occurs two to three days after a purging episode. Although it may be cosmetically unappealing, it is generally painless. A reduction in the frequency of purging behaviors leads to a reduction in the swelling of the glands.

Amelia McBride

See also: Amenorrhea; Dehydration; Dental Complications; Edema; Electrocardiogram; Gastrointestinal Complications Associated with Eating Disorders; Health Care Costs of Eating Disorders; Lanugo; Leptin; Mortality Rates; Nutritional Deficiencies; Visceral Sensitivity

Bibliography

Birmingham, C. Laird, and Janet Treasure. *Medical Management of Eating Disorders*, 2nd ed. Cambridge, UK: Cambridge University Press, 2010.

Katzman, Debra K. "Medical Complications in Adolescents with Anorexia Nervosa: A Review of the Literature." *International Journal of Eating Disorders* 37, no. 51 (2005): S52–S59. https://doi.org/10.1002/eat.20118.

Lamber, Michel, Catherine Hubert, Benevieve Depresseux, Bruno Vande Berg, Jean-Paul Thissen, Charles Nagant de Deuxchaisnes, and Jean-Pierre Devogelaer. "Hematological Changes in Anorexia Nervosa Are Correlated with Total Body Fat Mass Depletion." *International Journal of Eating Disorders* 21 (1997): 329–334. https://doi.org/10.1002/(SICI)1098-108X(1997)21:4<329::AID-EAT4>3.0.CO;2-Q.

Mehler, Philip S. "Medical Complications of Bulimia Nervosa and Their Treatments." *International Journal of Eating Disorders* 44 (2011): 95–104. https://doi.org/10.1002/eat.20825.

Mehler, Philip S., and Arnold E. Anderson. *Eating Disorders: A Guide to Medical Care and Complications*, 2nd ed. Baltimore, MD: Johns Hopkins University Press, 2009.

Mitchell, James E., and Scott Crow. "Medical Complications of Anorexia Nervosa and Bulimia Nervosa." *Current Opinions of Psychiatry* 19 (2006): 438–443. https://doi.org/10.1097/01.yco.0000228768.79097.3e.

Reiff, Dan W., and Kathleen Kim Lampson Reiff. *Eating Disorders Nutrition Therapy in the Recovery Process*, 2nd ed. Mercer Island, WA: Life Enterprises, 2007.

Rushing, Jona M., Laura E. Jones, and Caroline P. Carney. "Bulimia Nervosa: A Primary Care Review." *Primary Care Companion Journal of Clinical Psychiatry* 5 (2003): 217–224.

Walsh, Judith M., Mary E. Wheat, and Karen Freund. "Detection, Evaluation, and Treatment of Eating Disorders: The Role of the Primary Care Physician." *Journal of General Internal Medicine* 15 (2000): 577–590. https://doi.org/10.1046/j.1525-1497.2000.02439.x.

MEDICATIONS AND EATING DISORDERS

Similar to other mental health conditions, medications may be prescribed as part of a comprehensive treatment plan for eating disorders. The use of medications can be varied and may address underlying biological issues related to the disordered eating thoughts and behaviors that place an individual at risk for relapse. Psychopharmacology refers to the use of psychotropic medication to address the psyche associated with mental health concerns. For individuals with eating disorders psychotropic medications may be prescribed to treat comorbid conditions such as depression, anxiety, and obsessive-compulsive disorder that interfere with a person's ability to progress in their recovery. By clearing the fog with the use of antidepressants, clients may better focus on their treatment goals.

An important aspect of medication in treatment involves ensuring a client receives the right dose. Moreover, managing side effects, such as weight gain, constipation, and sleep disturbances, of the medication is also important because they can make taking the medication intolerable for a client. It is also necessary to supervise a client's course of treatment to determine the prescribed drug be taken for an adequate time to receive results. It is critical for a psychiatrist to manage medication therapy in the event dosage should be changed or if a medication should be changed due to adverse side effects.

Medications may also be used to assist with weight restoration for individuals who are severely underweight. Further, medications have been prescribed to alleviate and reduce purging behaviors and modulate mood. Hunger cues such as satiety may also be altered with the use of medication. Finally, medications may be used to reduce impulsivity or a tendency to respond in a self-destructive manner. Because of the frequent co-occurrence of other psychiatric conditions, it is common for an individual with an eating disorder to be prescribed a medication to treat depression or anxiety.

Types of Medications

Prozac, which has been used to treat depression, is frequently used as a treatment for bulimia nervosa. There has been some support to show the success of Prozac when coupled with cognitive behavioral therapy (CBT) in addressing bulimia nervosa. The benefit of this prescription drug has been fewer side effects than other psychotropic medications and purportedly longer lasting results. Antidepressants have also been found to have positive results in the reduction of binge episodes with clients who have binge eating disorder. Unfortunately, antidepressants have been less effective with anorexia nervosa and studies have shown mixed results. In general, psychotropic medications are ineffective to provide significant relief to clients with anorexia nervosa. This could be attributed to low body weight or the state of starvation present in individuals with anorexia nervosa.

Clomipramine has been prescribed for obsessive-compulsive disorder and may be used to decrease obsessive thoughts. However, this drug is known to cause weight gain that contribute to resistance on the part of eating disorder clients already worried about size and body weight. Having weight gain as a side effect, which is the case for many prescription medications, is problematic for treatment compliance in individuals with eating disorders. Another drug, Lithium, used for bipolar disorder to address mood swings, also contributes to weight gain.

Antianxiety medications, such as lorazepam, are frequently prescribed to reduce sensitivity to stress and general anxiety. Attention-deficit drugs are also been to individuals with eating disorders, but much more work is needed before a magic pill is identified to address this mental health disorder. Medication has been controversial among some treatment providers who believe prescribing psychotropic drugs feeds into a sick patient mentality. However, for some patients, medication can provide the much-needed relief and can address comorbid issues that prevent progress in treatment and recovery.

Justine J. Reel

See also: Anxiety Disorders; Health Care Costs of Eating Disorders; Treatment

Bibliography

American Psychiatric Association. *Diagnostic and Statistical Manual of Mental Disorders*, 5th ed. (*DSM-5*). Washington, DC: American Psychiatric Association Publishing, 2013.

Bryant-Waugh, Rachel and Bryan Lask. *Eating Disorders: A Parents' Guide*, 2nd ed. New York: Routledge, 2013.

Cogan, Jeanine C. 2000. "Question & Answer: Why Is Advocacy on Eating Disorders Needed?" Edited by Russell D. Marx. *Eating Disorders* 8 (4): 353–354. https://doi.org/10.1080/10640260008251242.

Costin, Carolyn. *A Comprehensive Guide to the Causes, Treatment, and Prevention of Eating Disorders: The Eating Disorder Sourcebook*, 3rd ed. New York: McGraw Hill, 2007.

"DSM-5 Diagnostic Criteria." The Alliance for Eating Disorders Awareness. Accessed November 22, 2016. http://www.allianceforeatingdisorders.com/portal/dsm-bed.

"Eating Disorder Treatment: Know Your Options." Mayo Clinic. Last modified July 29, 2014. Accessed November 22, 2017. http://www.mayoclinic.org/diseases-conditions/eating-disorders/in-depth/eating-disorder-treatment/art-20046234.

Gorla, Kiranmai, and Maju Mathews. "Pharmacological Treatment of Eating Disorders." *Psychiatry (Edgmont)* 2, no. 6 (2005): 43–48.

Smolak, Linda, and Michael P. Levine. *The Wiley Handbook of Eating Disorders: Volume 1 Basic Concepts and Foundational Research*. West Sussex, UK: John Wiley & Sons, 2015.

MENOPAUSE

Menopause refers to a developmental milestone that occurs as women age. A female in midlife stops having a period for at least 12 consecutive months and the lack of menses cannot be explained by other reasons (e.g., oral contraceptives).

Women usually experience menopause between ages 45 and 55 and can expect to encounter some biological changes that parallel pubertal changes in adolescence. These physical changes in the body (e.g., body weight and shape) for menopausal women include increased body mass index (BMI) and evidence of adipose (fat) tissue gathered around the abdominal region. Physiological changes such as decreased metabolic rate and changes in hormone levels also contribute to weight gain during menopause.

Women tend to gain weight as they grow older due to physiological reasons. Moreover, the percent of body fat also increases as menopause draws near. Although menopause is associated with changes in body weight and shape, the understanding of women's perceptions of body image during menopause is limited. As a result of decreased estrogen production, hot flashes, sweats, and sleep disturbances are common and symptoms may linger for five or more years. Generally, menopausal women report feeling less attractive, worry more about being fat, and diet more to lose weight than premenopausal women, supporting the contention that physiological symptoms, such as hot flashes, affect a woman's body image and make her feel like her body is out of control. Media often reinforces stereotypes about menopausal women being emotionally unstable, out of control, and crazy, leading many women to fear and fight this natural part of the aging process. Case studies of women in their 50s suggest eating-disordered behaviors may be triggered in midlife women in response to menopausal weight gain.

Justine J. Reel

See also: Aging and Body Image; Late Life and Late-Onset Eating Disorders

Bibliography

Cumella, Edward J., and Zina Kally. "Profile of 50 Women with Midlife-Onset Eating Disorders." *Eating Disorders* 16 (2008): 193–203. https://doi.org/10.1080/10640260802016670.

Deeks, Amanda A., and Marita P. McCabe. "Menopausal Stage and Age and Perceptions of Body Image." *Psychology and Health* 16 (2001): 367–379. http://dx.doi.org/10.1080/08870440108405513.

Kearney-Cooke, Ann, and Florence Isaacs. *Change Your Mind, Change Your Body: Feeling Good about Your Body and Self after 40.* New York: Atria, 2004.

Maine, Margo, and Joe Kelly. *The Body Myth: Adult Women and the Pressure to Be Perfect.* Hoboken, NJ: John Wiley & Sons, 2005.

North American Menopause Society (NAMS). "Basic Facts about Menopause." Accessed November 18, 2016. http://www.menopause.org/.

Peat, Christine M., Naomi L. Peyerl, and Jennifer J. Muehlenkamp. "Body Image and Eating Disorders in Older Adults: A Review." *The Journal of General Psychology* 135, no. 4 (2008): 343–358. http://dx.doi.org/10.3200/GENP.135.4.343-358.

SooHoo, Sonya, Justine J. Reel, and Judy Van Raalte. "Chasing the 'Fountain of Youth': Body Image and Eating Disorders among 'Older' Women." In *The Hidden Faces of Eating Disorders and Body Image,* edited by Justine J. Reel and Katherine A. Beals. Reston, VA: NAGWS/AAHPERD, 2009.

Zerbe, Kathryn J. "Eating Disorders in Middle and Late Life: A Neglected Problem." *Primary Psychiatry* 10 (2003): 80–82.

MILITARY

Eating disorders affect a variety of populations. Although there has been little research about eating disorders among members of the military, there is some evidence this group may be at risk for developing disordered eating tendencies. Recently, the importance of identifying and addressing mental health concerns in active duty members has been emphasized due to a recognition of workforce-related stressors on both an individual in the military and his or her family members.

As of 2014, there were roughly 1.4 million active duty military personnel and 20.7 million surviving veterans from the United States. Mental health care among the active duty and veteran populations has increased in popularity due to an increased awareness of disorders such as PTSD that play a particularly important role in health outcomes of this group. Members of the military are much more likely to have cardiovascular disease, poor mental health, diabetes, arthritis, and asthma (just to name a few) than the general population. Veterans are also among one of the top groups affected by suicide, with recent data suggesting approximately 20 combat veterans commit suicide per day. Research on the prevalence of eating disorders in the military has also received recent attention; the inclusion of women in the armed forces has contributed to this. Investigating eating disorders in the military is a complicated puzzle. Trauma, consistent stress, and unusual living circumstances that often accompany military life play contributing roles in the development of physical and mental disorders, including eating disorders. Additionally, the pressure to maintain certain rigorous physical standards both increases the occurrence of disordered eating habits and often discourages military members from reporting symptoms.

Although there is a substantial body of research pointing out the factors that predispose military personnel and veterans to the development of eating disorders, the research on this field is still expanding. Originally, the military was identified as a population of interest given the physical pressures imposed on its members and the parallels between this environment and competitive athletes. Military personnel and veterans face unique pressures that often prompt development of unhealthy eating behaviors.

History of Eating Disorder Research in the U.S. Military

Over the past 2 decades, the rise of female U.S. military members has prompted a focus on health topics stereotypically considered women's issues, of which eating disorders is common. Additionally, the exponential rise in veteran's health care costs and mental health awareness among this population has prompted an increased focus on eating disorders. One of the first studies to investigate this was in the late 1990s. This study compared the pressure to be active, physically fit, and maintain a specific physique/weight common in the military was comparable to the pressure found in organized sports. Female athletes—particularly those in aesthetic sports—were a widely studied population in the eating disorder literature, with the majority of research supporting higher rates of disordered eating among female athletes. Thus, the study predicted female military members would also demonstrate higher rates of eating disorders compared to the civilian population. This hypothesis was confirmed, with approximately 8 percent of military women (compared to 1–3 percent of civilian women) meeting criteria for an eating disorder, with an additional 26 percent considered at risk for developing an eating disorder.

This research study was among the first to draw attention to eating disorders in a military population. Subsequent studies have supported that military personnel are more likely to develop an eating disorder than civilians. Research has also extended this finding to male military members. Although research on this topic is growing, it remains understudied given the body of literature highlighting the number of risk factors for disordered eating and other mental health disorders for military members.

Risk Factors for Eating Disorders in the Military Population

A majority of research on this topic has identified aspects of the military lifestyle that may contribute to development of disordered eating, including: stressful combat situations (such as the possibility of seeing a companion get killed or having to kill another individual); rigorous physical standards and tests; changes in eating behaviors during service; weight restrictions and monitoring; and military sexual trauma. One study found a number of social variables, including the competition over opportunities for advancement and harassment from a supervisor over weight, were significantly associated with higher levels of disordered eating behaviors. The same study also reported purging behaviors caused 9.9 percent of women in the Navy, 7.4 percent of women in the Air Force, 10.2 percent of women in the Army, and 22.3 percent of women in the Marines to routinely skip menses, a common indicator of good health and nutrition.

In the veteran population, post-traumatic stress disorder (PTSD) has been heavily implicated in disordered eating. Historically, PTSD has been positively associated with obesity and weight gain in the veteran population. A recent study demonstrated the relationship between PTSD and weight gain/obesity was mediated by eating-disordered symptoms. In other words, the strength of the relationship between PTSD and obesity in veterans is explained by the presence of disordered eating symptoms. Additionally, veteran populations often struggle with substance abuse disorders, depression, and anxiety, all of which are strongly associated with eating disorders.

Hannah J. Hopkins

See also: Body Image in Males; Post-Traumatic Stress Disorder; Suicide

Bibliography

"Armed Forces Personnel, Total." Worldbank.org. Accessed February 3, 2017. http://data.worldbank.org/indicator/MS.MIL.TOTL.P1.

Bartlett, Brooke, and Karen Mitchell. "Eating Disorders in Military and Veteran Men and Women: A Systematic Review." *International Journal of Eating Disorders* 48, no. 8 (2015): 1057–1069. http://dx.doi.org/10.1002/eat.22454.

Beekley, Matthew, Robert Byrne, Trudy Yavorek, Kelli Kidd, Janet Wolff, and Michael John-son. "Incidence, Prevalence, and Risk of Eating Disorder Behaviors in Military Academy Cadets." *Military Medicine* 174, no. 6 (2009): 637–641. http://dx.doi.org/10.7205/MILMED-D-02-1008.

Larson, Robin J., and Gilbert Welch H. "Risk for Increased Utilization and Adverse Health Outcomes among Men Served by the Veterans Health Administration." *Military Medicine* 172, no. 7 (2007): 690–696. http://dx.doi.org/10.7205/MILMED.172.7.690.

Lauder, Tamara, Marc Williams, Carol Campbell, Gary Davis, and Richard Sherman. "Abnormal Eating Behaviors in Military Women." *Medicine & Science and Sports & Exercise* 31, no. 9 (1999): 1265–1271. https://doi.org/10.1097/00005768-199909000-00006.

McNulty, Peggy Anne Fisher. "Prevalence and Contributing Factors of Eating Disorder Behaviors in Active Duty Service Women in the Army, Navy, Air Force, and Marines." *Military Medicine* 166, no. 1 (2001): 53–58.

Mitchell, Karen, Barbara Porter, Edward J. Boyko, and Alison E. Field. "Longitudinal Associations among PTSD, Disordered Eating, and Weight Gain in Military Men and Women." *American Journal of Epidemiology* 84, no. 1 (2016): 33–47. https://doi.org/10.1093/aje/kwv291.

U.S. Census Bureau. "2010–2014 American Community Survey 5-Year Estimates, Table S2101—Veteran Status." Factfinder.census.gov. Accessed February 3, 2017. https://factfinder.census.gov/faces/tableservices/jsf/pages/productview.xhtml?pid=ACS_15_5YR_S2101&prodType=table.

Voelker, Rebecca. "Eating Disorders in the Military." *Journal of the American Medical Association Quick Uptakes* 282, no. 24 (1999): 2291. https://doi.org/10.1001/jama.282.24.2291-JQU90010-2-1.

MINDFULNESS

Mindfulness is the process of bringing increased attention and nonjudgmental awareness to the present moment experience. Mindfulness is linked with positive psychological health and is used as a skill to reduce depressed mood, anxiety, and other negative emotions. Mindfulness has gained recognition recently as a way to address and treat eating disorders including anorexia nervosa, bulimia nervosa, and binge eating disorder. Mindfulness (i.e., focus on the present) as emphasized through meditation and other modalities is also taught to the general population as a way to deal with stress, improve one's quality of life, and experience more personal life enjoyment.

Mindfulness and Eating

A mindfulness practice that the general population and individuals with eating disorders can benefit from is mindful eating. It is common in the United States to engage in distracted eating that involves eating while standing up, driving, or watching television. However, distracted eating negatively impacts one's dining experience; it results in the person not tasting the flavors of food and being disconnected with hunger and fullness cues. By not being mindful, individuals may eat more or less than the body needs and can trigger binge eating episodes. By contrast, mindful eating encourages the use of all senses to experience the food.

In addition to eating slowly and noticing the flavors of the food, an eater who is mindful does not eat in front of a television or at a desk at work. Mindful eating results in being in touch with one's hunger and being able to avoid overeating.

Mindfulness and Exercise

Eating-disordered individuals who engage in obligatory exercise are usually mindless exercisers. Similar to mindless eaters, mindless exercisers often engage in distracted exercise that is disconnected from the body. As a result, the mindless exerciser may exercise through pain, increasing risk for injuries or soreness. Mindless exercisers may use external cues (e.g., calorie counters on exercise machines) to determine duration of workout rather than how the body feels; therefore, they are likely to experience more boredom during exercise and less exercise enjoyment than mindful exercisers.

Exercise interventions that include mindfulness encourage participants to attend to the senses and the outside environment. A meditative walk or mindful walking may involve smelling, seeing, and listening to one's surroundings while moving at a more controlled pace. Mindful exercise also involves retraining oneself to listen to body cues to determine when to exercise and when to stop.

Mindfulness and Eating Disorders Treatment

Mindfulness has been shown to be a useful adjunct in eating disorder treatment for addressing distorted cognitions. For example, having a mindful outlook may help to cope with distressing cognitions (e.g., irrational thoughts or rigid thinking about a *bad food*) and feelings (e.g., desire to purge); it helps one view these cognitions and emotions as temporary events that will pass. Mindfulness has been directly incorporated into dialectical behavior therapy (DBT) to increase awareness and promote self-acceptance.

Similarly, mindfulness can be applied to experiences with body image. Mindfulness teaches a person to observe his or her body without judgment and emotional reaction to reduce the likelihood of impulsive and self-destructive reactions and behaviors. Furthermore, an individual is forced to become more mindful about the ways in negative body image thoughts occur in an automatic or mindless fashion. Body image disturbances represent a type of mindlessness (i.e., rigid, inflexible, and unwilling to adapt to an ever-changing bodily form) that should be viewed from multiple perspectives without judgment.

Justine J. Reel

See also: Coping Skills; Dialectical Behavior Therapy; Intuitive Eating; Intuitive Exercise; Self-Care; Treatment; Visceral Sensitivity

Bibliography

Boudette, Robin. "Integrating Mindfulness into the Therapy Hour." *Eating Disorders: The Journal of Treatment & Prevention* 19 (2011): 108–115. https://doi.org/10.1080/10640 266.2011.533610.

Hepworth, Natasha S. "A Mindful Eating Group as an Adjunct to Individual Treatment for Eating Disorders: A Pilot Study." *Eating Disorders: The Journal of Treatment & Prevention* 19 (2011): 6–16. https://doi.org/10.1080/10640266.2011.533610.

Lavender, Jason M., Bianca F. Jardin, and Drew A. Anderson. "Bulimic Symptoms in Undergraduate Men and Women: Contributions of Mindfulness and Thought Suppression." *Eating Behaviors* 10 (2009): 228–231. https://doi.org/10.1016/j.eatbeh.2009.07.002.

Masuda, Akihiko, and Johanna W. Wendell. "Mindfulness Mediates the Relation between Disordered Eating-Related Cognitions and Psychological Distress." *Eating Behaviors* 11 (2010): 293–296. https://doi.org/10.1016/j.eatbeh.2010.07.001.

Stewart, Tiffany M. "Light on Body Image Treatment: Acceptance through Mindfulness." *Behavior Modification* 28, no. 6 (2004): 783–811. https://doi.org/10.1177/0145445503259862.

Wanden-Berghe, Rocio Guardiola, Javier Sanz-Valero, and Carmina Wanden-Berghe. "The Application of Mindfulness to Eating Disorders Treatment: A Systematic Review." *Eating Disorders: The Journal of Treatment & Prevention* 19 (2011): 34–48. https://doi.org/10.1080/10640266.2011.533604.

MODELS AND EATING DISORDERS

Fashion models, like female athletes in aesthetic sports such as figure skating, have received significant attention in regard to eating disorders. The special attention given to this population is a result of several factors. First, professional models are expected to be thin to fit into designers' clothes. High-fashion designers typically only make clothing in the smallest sizes—zeros and twos primarily—for runway shows. Additionally, thinner models are preferred by designers because they show case clothing better. During an interview with Fox News, Emmy award–winning fashion designer Zyla said that women with fuller figures would upstage the designer's clothing. High-fashion models are often described as "hangers," referencing their role to display clothing without distracting a customer. Models who cannot fit into a designer's clothes, have too many curves, or who do not showcase clothing well enough are essentially failing to meet their workplace standards. Second, the tragic deaths of some prominent figures within the modeling industry (notably Luisel and Eliana Ramos, Ana Reston, and Hila Elmalich) from complications of anorexia nervosa has prompted an awareness of the dangers posed by the fashion industry's emphasis on thinness. And last, the negative impact of having an underweight body ideal reinforced by the modeling industry poses a public health threat and may increase the risk for development of disordered eating in the general population.

Many researchers have gone as far as to label the professional modeling industry as a toxic environment for triggering and exacerbating disordered eating symptoms. Although the pressure to maintain a low body weight is inherent in modeling, this emphasis on thinness is particularly relevant for models working at highly competitive, international agencies that cater to haute couture designers in Europe and the United States.

Understanding How Models Compare to the General Population

In the United States, the average woman is approximately five foot four and weighs 166 pounds. The average fashion model, in contrast, is five foot ten and weighs

107 pounds. This means the average model is thinner than 98 percent of American women. Not only are models typically thinner than the general population, but their average weight is low enough to be considered life threatening. According to the World Health Organization, having a body mass index (BMI), the common metric to assess weight status relative to height, lower than 16 is considered medically dangerous. The average international runway model has a BMI at or below that cutoff, putting her at risk for health complications, such as bone density loss, decreased immune functioning, cardiac failure, loss of menses, and infertility.

Despite an abundance of evidence that fashion models are thinner than the general population and an acknowledgment of the dangers that an environment valuing extremely thin bodies poses for those at risk for eating disorders, few research studies have investigated eating disorders in the modeling industry, and even fewer studies have done so on a large scale. One of the few studies to look at this topic reported that 1.2 percent of fashion models in the study met the full criteria for anorexia nervosa with an additional 12.7 percent exhibiting partial anorexia symptoms. These figures were significantly higher than in the control group, with 0.8 percent and 2.4 percent meeting full- and partial-criteria for anorexia, respectively.

Role of the Modeling Industry on Cultural Standards of Beauty

The prevalence of underweight models in the modeling industry has implications beyond the health of models themselves. The modeling industry is often considered the stage upon which cultural beauty standards are embodied, with the models acting as flesh-and-blood versions of a society's beauty ideals. The increased pressure on models to maintain a dangerously low body weight reflects a societal fixation on thin bodies. Central to the research on this topic is the distinction between *setting* and *symbolizing* cultural beauty standards; models themselves (and, to some extent, the industry at large) do not define beauty standards, they only represent standards by responding to consumer demand. However, that is not to imply that the industry is blameless. The reinforcement of beauty standards takes place when models who are dangerously underweight are displayed as symbols of haute couture, high fashion, and aesthetic beauty.

If the beauty ideals reinforce by the modeling industry actually encourage eating disorders is controversial and difficult to quantify. However, research indicates these beauty standards play at least *some* role in body dissatisfaction and the onset of disordered eating. A famous example of this is what is known as the Fiji Study that examined the impact of Western television programming had on adolescent female inhabitants of a remote area of Fiji. Traditional Fijian cultures report virtually no incidences of eating disorders, dieting or any number of common weight management techniques common in the West (e.g., use of laxatives, self-induced vomiting), or body dissatisfaction. In one previously media-naive region (no previous exposure to Western media), the percentage of adolescent girls who reported wanting to be thinner rose from 0 percent to 74 percent after three years of Western television programming. This study is one among several using similar research designs that demonstrate the generally negative impact the Western media has on body image, body dissatisfaction, and disordered eating. Given the modeling industry's front-and-center position in Western media, understanding how promoting the thin standard among models impacts the population generally is very important.

Recent Attempts to Regulate the Modeling Industry

Over the past few years, several countries have taken steps to hold the modeling industry more accountable for the health and well-being of employees, specifically fashion models. France recently passed a law, commonly referred to as France's anorexia rule, making it illegal for modeling agencies to employ a model whose BMI is below 18. Interestingly, a BMI of 18 is still considered underweight. Similar standards have been applied in Israel, Madrid, and Milan. However, despite the presence of these laws, enforcement has been tepid at best, with few infractions resulting in any sort of disciplinary action.

The U.S. fashion industry has been under pressure from public health advocacy groups and lobbies for several years to enact similar rules. Currently, the fashion industry in the United States, one of the most dominant and influential worldwide, has nothing in place to protect the health of fashion models. This fact is particularly surprising given the strict workplace health and safety standards that have been applied to other professions, such as mining, construction, and garment factories. Even though formal laws may not be in place to protect the health of models, several retail companies and fashion magazines have taken steps to promote a more inclusive and healthier body image through body-positive advertising campaigns, models with a variety of body types and weights, and not digitally enhancing or editing images.

Luisel and Eliana Ramos

Luisel and Eliana Ramos were sisters and famous Uruguayan fashion models. Daughters of Luis Ramos, a former soccer player for the Uruguayan squad Nacional, both girls were known across their native country and throughout Latin/South America for their modeling careers. Luisel was 22 years old when she collapsed following a catwalk in Montevideo, Uruguay, on August 2, 2006. Her cause of death was ruled as a heart attack due to malnutrition from anorexia nervosa. Rumors circulated throughout the modeling community that she had only been eating lettuce leaves for several months prior to her death.

Six months later, in February 2007, her younger sister Eliana, 18, was found collapsed in her family's home in the Uruguayan capital. Although many of Eliana's acquaintances and fellow models spoke out against the public speculation that she too had suffered from anorexia, an autopsy revealed she had died of a heart attack caused by malnutrition.

Ana Reston

Shortly following Luisel Ramos's death in 2006, Ana Carolina Reston, another South American model who had recently risen to international fame, died from complications of anorexia nervosa. Ana began her modeling career when she was just eight years old; she won the Queen of Jundiaí beauty contest in Jundiaí, a town about 40 miles north of São Paolo, Brazil. Following this first exposure to the world of modeling, Ana signed with Ford Models, one of the premiere modeling agencies in the world. Several years later she signed with Elite Modeling Management, marking her transition from teenaged beauty queen to serious supermodel.

Throughout her meteoric rise, Ana faced criticism for being too short and too overweight for the modeling industry. Friends and family report that Ana began struggling with anorexia during 2004, shortly after one of her first modeling trips internationally. A friend of Ana's said Ana only ever drank juice and was never able or willing to eat solid foods. It was around this time that Ana became financially responsible for supporting her mother, adding another source of pressure in her life. Throughout the next two years, agencies and companies working with Ana frequently mentioned her weight as a concern; a representative from Giorgio Armani reportedly called Ana's agent to say that she was too thin for a photoshoot. In late October 2006, Ana began complaining of pain in her sides. She was hospitalized two days later and spent the remaining three weeks of her life in the intensive care unit at Hospital Municipal dos Servidores Publicos in São Paolo. Ana Reston was 21 years old when she died on November 15, 2006, of multiple organ failure, septicemia, and urinary infection, all connected to her anorexia. She weighed just over 80 pounds.

Hila Elmalich

Hila Elmalich was an Israeli fashion model who died from complications of anorexia nervosa in late 2007, shortly before her 34th birthday. According to Israeli news reports, Hila was five foot six and weighed 49 pounds at her death. Hila struggled with an eating disorder for years and had been hospitalized several times prior to her death. Adi Barkan, an Israeli fashion photographer and personal friend of Hila, remembered how difficult it was to see Hila grow increasingly more thin and sick at the end of her life. When asked about a recent visit he had paid Hila at a hospital, he recalled holding her felt "like I took hold of something from the grave."

Israel was one of the first countries to enact rules and restrictions designed to protect models from being too thin. These rules were first enforced in 2006, but it was too late for Hila. Hila's death came just a few months after the deaths of Luisel Ramos and Ana Reston in 2006 and Luisel's younger sister, Eliana, a few months before Hila's death.

Isabelle Caro

One of the fashion industry's most well-known cases of anorexia-related deaths was the young French supermodel Isabelle Caro. Isabelle began struggling with anorexia when she was just 13 years old and continued to battle the disorder throughout her young adult life. Many of Isabelle's friends and family believe her modeling career accentuated her disorder. Isabelle, however, believed that a difficult childhood was the underlying factor for her disorder. In her memoir, *The Little Girl Who Didn't*

Want to Get Fat, Isabelle described her dysfunctional relationship with her mother, who suffered from depression and was overprotective of Isabelle from a young age. Isabelle wrote her mother often criticized her for being overweight, particularly when Isabelle started puberty. It was around this time Isabelle began dieting, sometimes eating no more than one square of chocolate and one cup of tea per day. This extremely restrictive dieting continued throughout puberty and into Isabelle's early 20s, when she repeatedly had to be hospitalized after falling unconscious or, in some instances, slipping into a temporary coma. At five foot four, Isabelle weighed approximately 55 pounds at her lowest weight. The severity of her illness caused her to lose several teeth, suffer sores and extreme dryness on her skin, and lose her hair.

After years of battling the disorder privately, Isabelle went public in a "no anorexia" photoshoot campaign in 2007. The photos, which depict Isabelle nude, highlight her skeletal frame, and were promoted to increase understanding and awareness of anorexia. Isabelle also discussed her personal story with anorexia in tabloids and news outlets all over the world, encouraging individuals with the disorder to seek help. The photo campaign, while designed to raise awareness, was heavily criticized for being too shocking and exploitative. In fact, the photos were eventually banned in Italy, with many claiming that the photos glamorized the disorder and could be potentially dangerous for people on the brink of the disorder. Although Isabelle made some progress in her health following the 2007 campaign, in the three years after the release of her photos, her weight hovered around 66 pounds, and she ultimately died November 17, 2010, at age 28.

Hannah J. Hopkins

See also: Celebrities and Eating Disorders; Media; Plus-Size Models and Clothing

Bibliography

Becker, Anne E., Rebecca A. Burwell, David B. Herzog, Paul Hamburg, and Stephen E. Gilman. "Eating Behaviours and Attitudes Following Prolonged Exposure to Television among Ethnic Fijian Adolescent Girls." *The British Journal of Psychiatry* 180, no. 6 (2002): 509–514. https://doi.org/10.1192/bjp.180.6.509.

Beckford, Martin. "Sister of Tragic 'Size Zero' Model Found Dead." *The Telegraph.* Last modified February 15, 2007. Accessed November 22, 2017. http://www.telegraph.co.uk/news/uknews/1542707/Sister-of-tragic-size-zero-model-found-dead.html.

Carollo, Kim. "French Model Isabelle Caro's Death Highlights Tough Personal Battles against Anorexia." ABCNews.com. Last modified December 30, 2010. Accessed November 22, 2017. http://abcnews.go.com/Health/MindMoodNews/anti-anorexic-model-isabelle-caro-dies/story?id=12509780.

Entwistle, Joanne, and Elizabeth Wissinger. "Keeping Up Appearances: Aesthetic Labour in the Fashion Modelling Industries of London and New York." *The Sociological Review* 54, no. 4 (2006): 774–794. https://doi.org/10.1111/j.1467-954X.2006.00671.x.

Garces, Raul. "2 Uruguayan Sisters, Both Models, Die." *Washington Post.* Last modified February 14, 2007. Accessed November 22, 2017. http://www.washingtonpost.com/wp-dyn/content/article/2007/02/14/AR2007021401624.html.

Grimes, William. "Isabelle Caro, Anorexic Model, Dies at 28." *New York Times.* Last modified December 30, 2010. Accessed November 22, 2017. http://www.nytimes.com/2010/12/31/world/europe/31caro.html.

Hareyan, Armen. "Ilanit Hila Elmalich, Israeli Model Dies of Complications." HULIQ. Last modified November 20, 2007. Accessed November 22, 2017. http://www.huliq .com/42452/ilanit-hila-elmalich-israeli-model-dies-complications.

Hildesheimer, Galya, and Hemda Gur-Arie. "Just Modeling? The Modeling Industry, Eating Disorders, and the Law." *International Journal of Feminist Approaches to Bioethics* 8, no. 2 (2015): 103–138. https://doi.org/10.3138/ijfab.8.2.103.

Phillips, Tom. "Dying for Fashion: How One Young Girl's Dream Turned into a Nightmare." *Daily Mail.* Last modified September 1, 2007. Accessed November 22, 2017. http:// www.dailymail.co.uk/femail/article-479286/Dying-fashion-How-young-girls-dream -turned-nightmare.html.

Phillips, Tom. "Everyone Knew She Was Ill. The Other Girls, the Model Agencies . . . Don't Believe It When They Say They Didn't." *The Guardian.* Last modified January 13, 2007. Accessed November 22, 2017. https://www.theguardian.com/lifeandstyle/2007 /jan/14/fashion.features4.

Pike, Kathleen M., and Patricia E. Dunne. "The Rise of Eating Disorders in Asia: A Review." *Journal of Eating Disorders* 3, no. 33 (2015): 1–14. https://doi.org/10.1186/s 40337-015-0070-2.

Preti, Antonio, Ambra Usai, Paola Miotto, Donatella Rita Petretto, and Carmelo Masala. "Eating Disorders among Professional Fashion Models." *Psychiatry Research* 159, no. 1–2 (2008): 86–94. https://doi.org/10.1016/j.psychres.2005.07.040.

McGregor-Wood, Simon, and Karen Mooney. "Did Model Die from Pressure to Be Thin?" ABCNews.com. Last modified November 19, 2007. Accessed November 22, 2017. http://abcnews.go.com/GMA/Health/story?id=3883944&page=1.

McKay, Hollie. "Pills, Injections and Plain Starvation: The Dangerous Extremes Models Go to for the Fashion Week Runways." *FOX News Entertainment.* Last modified September 5, 2012. Accessed November 22, 2017. http://www.foxnews.com /entertainment/2012/09/05/pills-injections-and-plastic-suits-dangerous-extremes -models-go-to-to-walk.html.

Record, Katherine L., and S. Bryn Austin. "'Paris Thin': A Call to Regulate Life-Threatening Starvation of Runway Models in the US Fashion Industry." *American Journal of Public Health* 106, no. 2 (2016): 205–206. http://dx.doi.org/10.2105/AJPH.2015.302950.

Santonastaso, Paolo, Silvia Mondini, and Angela Favaro. "Are Fashion Models a Group at Risk for Eating Disorders and Substance Abuse?" *Psychotherapy and Psychosomatics* 71, no. 3 (2002): 168–172.

Swami, Viren, and Emilia Szmigielska. "Body Image Concerns in Professional Fashion Models: Are They Really an At-Risk Group?" *Psychiatry Research* 207, no. 1–2 (2013): 113–117. https://doi.org/10.1016/j.psychres.2012.09.009.

Treasure, Janet L., Elizabeth R. Wack, and Marion E. Roberts. "Models as a High-Risk Group: The Health Implications of a Size Zero Culture." *The British Journal of Psychiatry* 192, no. 4 (2008): 243–244. https://doi.org/10.1192/bjp.bp.107.044164.

MORTALITY RATES

Mortality means fatality or death. Since Karen Carpenter's death in 1983, eating disorders have been increasingly recognized as severe illnesses with a mortality risk. Individuals with anorexia nervosa, bulimia nervosa, and binge eating disorder may be at increased risk for premature death due to medical complications (e.g., cardiovascular problems) as well as self-harm behaviors and suicide. Mortality rates vary across studies; however, it is known eating disorders represent the highest mortality rate among psychiatric disorders.

Anorexia Nervosa and Mortality

Mortality has most commonly been associated with anorexia nervosa with one study showing the mortality rate for this disorder as 0.56 percent per year or approximately 5.6 percent per decade. Another study reported a 4.0 percent mortality rate across anorexia nervosa cases. The combination of low body weight, potential use of purging behaviors, severe restriction, and mental health issues (e.g., self-harm and suicide) predicts a higher mortality rate in individuals with anorexia nervosa. Research has shown only 46 percent of individuals fully recover from anorexia nervosa, and 20 percent suffer from anorexia nervosa chronically leading to increased risk for death. These findings are a matter of great concern.

A 10-year mortality study conducted in France found mortality risk for anorexic inpatients was 10 times higher than the mortality risk for the general female French population. During the study, 40 deaths were recorded and half of these occurred in the three years following hospitalization. Interestingly, several characteristics were found to predict mortality among anorexia nervosa clients: older age, longer eating disorder duration, history of suicide attempt, and diuretic use. Additionally, French researchers found the lower the desired body mass index and the more severe the eating disorder symptoms, the higher the risk of death.

Other Eating Disorders and Mortality Risk

Although most attention has been given to mortality risk associated with anorexia nervosa, bulimia nervosa and other disordered eating cases like binge eating disorder also present serious concerns. In one study, crude mortality rates were 3.9 percent for bulimia nervosa and 5.2 percent for other types of disordered eating, compared with 4.0 percent for anorexia nervosa. It is well-recognized that the substantial medical complications (e.g., electrolyte disturbances) are associated with purging behaviors (e.g., vomiting, laxatives, diuretics) pose severe risk. Moreover, individuals with bulimia nervosa and other forms of disordered eating may exhibit impulsivity, which is associated with substance abuse and higher suicide risk.

Most studies conclude anorexia nervosa yields the highest mortality rate due to medical complications and increased suicide rates. However, it is important not to discount the severity of bulimia nervosa and other forms of disordered eating when considering risk for mortality. Predictors for mortality include longer duration of eating disorder, older age, purging behaviors, and suicide attempts.

Justine J. Reel

See also: Anorexia Nervosa; Binge Eating Disorder; Bulimia Nervosa; Carpenter, Karen; Medical and Health Consequences; Substance Abuse; Suicide

Bibliography

Arcelus, Jon, Alex J. Mitchell, Jackie Wales, and Soren Nielsen. "Mortality Rates in Patients with Anorexia Nervosa and Other Eating Disorders." *Archives of General Psychiatry* 68, no. 7 (2011): 724–731. https://doi.org/10.1001/archgenpsychiatry.2011.74.

Huas C., A. Caille, N. Godart, C. Foulon, A. Pham-Scottez, S. Divac, A. Deschartres, G. Lavoisy, J. D. Guelfi, F. Rouillon, and B. Falissard. "Factors Predictive of Ten-Year Mortality in Severe Anorexia Nervosa Patients." *Acta Psychiatrica Scandinavica* 123 (2011): 62–70. https://doi.org/10.111/j.1600-0447.2010.01627.x.

Kaye, Walter. "Eating Disorders: Hope despite Mortal Risk." *American Journal of Psychiatry* 166, no. 12 (2009): 1309–1311.

Preti, A., M. B. L. Rocchi, D. Sisti, M. V. Camboni, and P. Miotto. "A Comprehensive Meta-Analysis of the Risk of Suicide in Eating Disorders." *Acta Psychiatrica Scandinavica* 124 (2011): 6–17. https://doi.org/10.1111/j.1600-0447.2010.01641.x.

Rosling, Agneta, Par Sparen, Claes Norring, and Anne-Liis von Knorring. "Mortality of Eating Disorders: A Follow-Up Study of Treatment in a Specialist Unit 1974–2000." *International Journal of Eating Disorders* 44, no. 4 (2011): 304–310. https://doi.org/10.1002/eat.20827.

Suzuki, Kenji, Aya Takeda, and Aihide Yoshino. "Mortality 6 Years after Inpatient Treatment of Female Japanese Patients with Eating Disorders Associated with Alcoholism." *Psychiatry and Clinical Neurosciences* 65 (2011): 326–332. https://doi.org/10.1111/j.1440-1819.2011.02217.x.

MOTIVATIONAL INTERVIEWING

Motivational interviewing is a therapeutic approach used help people work through barriers, commit to change, and enhance intrinsic motivation. This client-centered approach assesses an individual's readiness for change as represented by his or her stage of change for an addictive disorder or health behavior.

Stages of Change Model

The Stages of Change model, also known as the Transtheoretical model, was first developed by Prochaska to promote smoking cessation. Clients were moved through the stages of change beginning with working with individuals who were highly resistant to treatment and moving toward actively maintaining a smoke-free lifestyle. The treatment is tailored to a client's particular stage of change that include precontemplation, contemplation, preparation, action, or maintenance. Precontemplation refers to a stage in which an individual is not consciously aware of a problem or concern. Contemplation, on the other hand, represents a stage when an individual begins to think about change, but has not acted. Preparation indicates a stage in which an individual begins taking steps to change behavior (e.g., purchases a gym membership). When the individual is exercising more consistently he or she is classified as in the action and maintenance stages.

The Stages of Change model has been used as the guiding framework for motivational interviewing techniques with a variety of target populations (e.g., those with exercise, gambling, substance abuse problems). Motivational interviewing combines a supportive and empathic counseling style with a directive method for decreasing client ambivalence and helping a client focus on a direction for change. Clients are encouraged to form an argument for change (i.e., change talk) to represent the desire, ability, and need to change. As a result, clients engaging in motivational interviewing show a greater commitment to the process of change.

Motivational Interviewing and Eating Disorder Treatment

Because eating-disordered individuals are notoriously resistant to change and difficult to treat, motivational interviewing has shown much promise as a treatment approach. Researchers and clinicians view motivational interviewing as a natural fit to help with addictive aspects of eating disorders while reinforcing and enhancing a client's motivation to change. Motivational interviewing has been used as a stand-alone intervention or in combination with other forms of treatment (e.g., cognitive behavioral therapy) for anorexia nervosa, bulimia nervosa, and binge eating disorder.

A noteworthy study of 108 women with binge eating disorder and were assigned to either the motivational interviewing treatment group or a control group found the women who received motivational interviewing were more confident in their ability to change binge eating patterns and tended to abstain from binge eating episodes at a higher rate compared than the control group (27.8 percent versus 11.1 percent).

Although more outcome studies are needed that use motivational interviewing to treat eating disorders, initial findings show that this approach can be helpful to treat clients resistant to change. Motivational interviewing has been used successfully with substance abuse and other addiction populations and can be used to assess an eating-disordered individual's stage of change so an intervention can be matched to the readiness for change.

Justine J. Reel

See also: Cognitive Behavioral Therapy; Treatment

Bibliography

Brennan, Leah, Jeff Walkley, Steve F. Fraser, Kate Greenway, and Ray Wilks. "Motivational Interviewing and Cognitive Behavior Therapy in the Treatment of Adolescent Overweight and Obesity: Study Design and Methodology." *Contemporary Clinical Trials* 29 (2008): 359–375. https://doi.org/10.1016/j.cct.2007.09.001.

Cassin, Stephanie E., Kristin M. von Ranson, Kenneth Heng, Joti Brar, and Amy E. Wojtowicz. "Adapted Motivational Interviewing for Women with Binge Eating Disorder: A Randomized Controlled Trial." *Psychology of Addictive Behaviors* 22, no. 3 (2008): 417–425. https://doi.org/10.1037/0893-164X.22.3.417.

Hettema, Jennifer, Julie Steele, and William R. Miller. "Motivational Interviewing." *Annual Review of Clinical Psychology* 1 (2005): 91–111. https://doi.org/10.1146/annurev.clinpsy.1.102803.143833.

Towell, Down Baker, Sally Woodford, Steven Reid, Barbara Rooney, and Anthony Towell. "Compliance and Outcome in Treatment-Resistant Anorexia and Bulimia: A

Retrospective Study." *British Journal of Clinical Psychology* 40 (2001): 189–195. https://doi.org/10.1348/014466501163634.

Wade, Tracey D., Anna Frayne, Sally-Anne Edwards, Therese Robertson, and Peter Gilchrist. "Motivational Change in an Inpatient Anorexia Nervosa Population and Implications for Treatment." *Australian and New Zealand Journal of Psychiatry* 43 (2009): 235–243.

Wilson, G. Terence, and Tanya R. Schlam. "The Transtheoretical Model and Motivational Interviewing in the Treatment of Eating and Weight Disorders." *Clinical Psychology Review* 24 (2004): 361–378. https://doi.org/10.1016/j.cpr.2004.03.003.

MOVIES AND EATING DISORDERS

Understanding how movies affect eating disorders requires an appreciation for the immensely important role movies play in modern society and in our daily lives. Most Americans watch an average of 13 hours of movies per month, the equivalent of about five full-length films. With the rise of online movie streaming websites like Netflix as well as easy rental options like RedBox, movies are becoming increasingly more accessible and affordable. The faces of the men and women in the movie industry are some of society's most well-known and loved celebrities, with megastars like Jennifer Lawrence and Leonardo DiCaprio being household names. However, the film industry—along with modern media generally—has come under scrutiny recently for its perpetuation of unattainable beauty standards.

What Makes Modern Media Different?

How do we make sense of the role that movies play in mental disorders? Answering this question requires understanding the complexity surrounding media, societal standards, and the psychological processes behind how we interpret visual media. One particularly crucial point to explore is how modern media differs from the media that permeated society in previous centuries. Modern media forms (such as filmography and editorial photography) differ in one very important way from historical forms of media, like portraiture and frescoes: these modern forms of art blur the line between reality and fantasy. Historically, paintings and other visual art forms depicted romanticized, otherworldly subjects, as is the case with Botticelli's *Venus*. Even portraiture follows this general rule, with the formality of the dress, setting, and style of the subject conveying a sense of fantasy.

Modern media have not preserved this sense of otherworldliness. Instead, modern art forms tend to market themselves as snapshots of reality but in truth employ a number of techniques to hide imperfections. These techniques involve applying makeup digitally; brightening eyes, skin and hair; digitally elongating limbs; airbrushing away skin imperfections (pores, a naturally occurring part of human skin fall into this category); minimizing certain parts of the body, such as the waist; and changing bone structure. Photoshop techniques are also used on males, with jaw elongation and enhancement of the abdominal muscles being among the most common alterations to male media images. Therefore, the movies and pictures a viewer sees, while often interpreted as reality, represent extensive editing and refinement.

The Cost of Keeping Up with the Joneses

In addition to digital manipulation, the actors and actresses in movies invest significant time and money into appearance, much more than the average American is either willing or able to spend. According to an article in the *Daily Mail*, Jennifer Aniston, one of America's wealthiest actresses, spent a reported $8,000 per month on beauty products and procedures. This totals $96,000 per year, which is more than the average American family earns per year. Celebrities have received attention for their extravagant beauty expenditures, including 24-karat gold weekly facials, six-week personal training programs, private home chefs, and personal stylists who choose their outfits. In addition to these routines, actors spend hours prior to shooting a scene in a movie or TV show having their hair, makeup, and outfits meticulously prepared.

Even though the manipulation techniques used in the media as well as the spending habits of the rich and famous have received attention nationally, a significant percentage of the American audience believes the images and movies they see depict reality. A recent poll conducted among women ages 18 to 65 that 15 percent of 18- to 24-year-olds thought magazine photographs, movies, and TV shows all depict actors/actresses as they truly look. A third of all women reported their standards for beauty were unattainable for them.

How We Respond to What We See

Viewing a movie is not as passive an activity as many may think. Being exposed to media has important psychological effects that relate to eating disorders. *Internalization* is the process through which an individual accepts a set of standards or norms through socialization. Much of the literature on media exposure and eating disorders references the "internalization of the thin ideal." In other words, through repeated exposure to images, films, and TV shows that glorify thin body types, we identify these thin bodies as the ideal body type. Internalizing the thin ideal has been linked to eating disorder symptomology, body dissatisfaction, dieting and overexercising, and higher rates of depression and anxiety. Over the past several decades, research has sought to explain how internalization of the thin ideal occurs and what factors make someone prone to internalizing the messages seen in the media. Several factors that have been isolated as risk factors for internalization of media beauty standards include: lower self-esteem; higher exposure to media at a younger age; exposure to specific types of media (including films that focus on attractive characters, soap operas, and music videos); and a tendency to compare oneself to others.

Eating Disorders and Acting Professionals

Movie viewers are not the only ones affected by the pressure to be thin; actors seen as the harbingers of the thin ideal are also victims. Actors are often instructed to lose or gain significant weight for roles, drastically change their physique (adding muscularity is a common requirement for male actors), or change their appearance in other significant ways. Cynthia Bulik, the director of the University of North

Carolina at Chapel Hill's eating disorder treatment program, has cautioned that celebrities experience the same detrimental physical and psychological side effects of this body preoccupation as the public. The bodies and weights of actors are routinely criticized and evaluated. The actress Keira Knightley successfully sued a British tabloid for publishing a story claiming that, despite Knightley's repeated denials, she suffered from anorexia. Actress Lilly James was also a source of public skepticism after her 2015 movie *Cinderella* was released, in which she had what many thought was a too-thin frame. Other big names in movies, including Rebel Wilson, Melissa McCarthy, and Val Kilmer, have publicly revealed they have been personally targeted by derogatory remarks about their weight.

Documentaries and Eating Disorders

Eating disorders have been a topic of particular attention in documentary filmography. A number of documentaries depicting the struggles of disordered eating and recovery have received high praise from critics, viewers, and eating disorder survivors. HBO's documentary *Thin* and NOVA's *Dying to Be Thin* are among two of the most watched and praised documentaries on eating disorders. It is important to acknowledge that, although documentaries may not be as popular as fictional films, they contribute to a stronger knowledge base and less stigma in the public. One research study found that individuals who watched a documentary about mental illness learned more and exhibited many more positive attitudes regarding mental disorders than those who watched a fictional film with identical information. So, although popular media plays a role reinforcing unhealthy beauty standards, other genres, such as documentaries combat, those standards and increase the knowledge of the public.

For the Love of Nancy

For the Love of Nancy was a made-for-television movie released in 1994 and based on a true story. It depicts Nancy Walsh, a young woman obsessed with her weight and shape during the first semester in college. Although her parents (played by Jill Clayburgh and Cameron Bancroft) do not notice the severity of her disorder, Nancy's neighbors and specifically her brother Tommy (Mark-Paul Gosselaar) become concerned over Nancy's extreme weight loss. Nancy's brother and neighbors convince her parents Nancy's health is at risk; her parents eventually confront her regarding her disorder and Nancy she is anorexic. Although Nancy's family attempts to hospitalize her and enroll her in different treatment options, Nancy can control her treatment regimen since she is over 18. After several failed attempts on her family's part to force Nancy into treatment, a doctor advises the family that, if Nancy is going to get better, she needs to have someone become her legal guardian who can control her medical care. Nancy's father goes to court against his daughter to win guardianship of Nancy; seeing her family suffering and taking such extreme measures resonates with Nancy and she cedes guardianship to her father. The movie concludes after showing Nancy's stay in a hospital, where she begins to gain weight and pursue a healthy lifestyle.

For the Love of Nancy was based on the true story of Nancy Walsh, a young woman who was diagnosed with anorexia shortly after starting college in 1991. Following almost a year of extremely unhealthy weight loss—she was five foot ten and was 83 pounds at her lowest—and battling medical care providers, friends, and family, Nancy settled the guardianship court with her father outside of court. This film was received positively by critics as well as by survivors of anorexia. Many praised its realistic portrayal of the disorder. Much of that praise was attributed to the performance of the main actress, Tracey Gold, who herself had recently recovered from anorexia at the time of filming.

The Best Little Girl in the World

The Best Little Girl in the World was a made-for-television movie released in May 1981. Jennifer Jason Leigh stars in this film, portraying a teenaged girl named Casey Powell who begins to starve herself in high school. Casey drops 25 pounds in the span of several months after pressure to stay thin for dance and cheering teams and discord between her parents at home. Ultimately, Casey's parents must resolve their differences and come together to help their daughter overcome her anorexia. *The Best Little Girl in the World* received some praise, including one prime-time Emmy nomination. The lead actress, Jennifer Jason Leigh, was also lauded for her performance, which included an intensive dieting regimen that began months before filming to capture her character's thinness.

Starving in Suburbia

A more recent release, *Starving in Suburbia* was a Lifetime movie released in 2014. It depicts the story of a young girl who, in the search of support for her weight loss, turns to the thinspiration online community. Although she is at first able to balance her wish to be thin with her health, Hannah (the main character, portrayed by Laura Wiggins) slowly becomes more and more obsessive until her anorexia reaches dangerous levels. Although *Starving in Suburbia* represented an attempt to speak to the dangers of online communities in the eating disorder world, many criticized the film for its heavy-handed theatrics and horror movie–esque aesthetic.

Justine J. Reel

See also: Books about Eating Disorders; Celebrities and Eating Disorders; Media; Television Shows and Eating Disorders

Bibliography

The Best Little Girl in the World. Directed by Sam O'Steen. 1981. Accessed February 3, 2017. https://www.youtube.com/watch?v=AoliDaTHgK4.

"CBS News Poll: Americans and the Movies." *CBS News.* Last modified February 22, 2015. Accessed November 22, 2017. http://www.cbsnews.com/news/cbs-news-poll -americans-and-the-movies/.

"Celebs Who Have Been Body-Shamed." CNN.com. Last modified September 30, 2016. Accessed November 22, 2017. http://www.cnn.com/2015/06/05/entertainment/gallery /body-shaming-celebs/index.html.

Feinberg, Scott. "'Awards Chatter' Podcast—Jennifer Jason Leigh ('The Hateful Eight')." *The Hollywood Reporter*. Last modified February 22, 2016. Accessed November 22, 2017. http://www.hollywoodreporter.com/race/awards-chatter-podcast-jennifer-jason-867679.

For the Love of Nancy: Based on a True Story. Directed by Paul Schneider. 1994. Accessed February 3, 2017. https://www.youtube.com/watch?v=wU2T7xf7AMk.

Gedeon, Kimberly. "Beyonce Spends HOW Much on Her Looks?! The Cost of Perfection . . . by the Numbers." MadameNoire. Last modified February 25, 2015. Accessed November 22, 2017. http://madamenoire.com/514126/beyonce-spends-much-looks-cost-perfection-numbers/.

Hanley, Robert. "Parents File Suit to Battle 19-Year-Old's Anorexia." *New York Times*. Last modified July 18, 1992. Accessed November 22, 2017. http://www.nytimes.com/1992/07/18/nyregion/parents-file-suit-to-battle-19-year-old-s-anorexia.html.

Harrison, Kristen. "The Body Electric: Thin-Ideal Media and Eating Disorders in Adolescents." *Journal of Communication* 50, no. 3 (2000): 119–143. https://doi.org/10.1111/j.1460-2466.2000.tb02856.x.

Kimmerle, Joachim, and Ulrike Cress. "The Effects of TV and Film Exposure on Knowledge about and Attitudes toward Mental Disorders." *Journal of Community Psychology* 41, no. 8 (2013): 931–943. https://doi.org/10.1002/jcop.21581.

Luhby, Tami. "Typical American Family Earned $53,657 Last Year." CNN Money. Last modified September 16, 2015. Accessed November 22, 2017. http://money.cnn.com/2015/09/16/news/economy/census-poverty-income/index.html.

O'Rourke, Jill. "To Say Lifetime Movie *Starving in Suburbia* Was Intense Would Be an Understatement." Crushable. Last modified April 27, 2014. Accessed November 22, 2017. http://www.crushable.com/2014/04/27/entertainment/lifetime-movie-starving-in-suburbia-review/.

Thompson, J. Kevin, and Eric Stice. "Thin-Ideal Internalization: Mounting Evidence for a New Risk Factor for Body-Image Disturbance and Eating Pathology." *Current Directions in Psychological Science* 10, no. 5 (2001): 181–183. https://doi.org/10.1111/1467-8721.00144.

Vagianos, Alanna. "Proof We Still Need to Talk about Photoshop." *The Huffington Post*. Last modified November 29, 2013. Accessed November 22, 2017. http://www.huffingtonpost.com/2013/11/27/photoshop-survey-women_n_4350263.html.

Van Camp, Jeffrey. "180 Million Americans Watch Movies and TV Online Each Month." Digital Trends. Last modified January 20, 2011. Accessed November 22, 2017. http://www.digitaltrends.com/computing/180-million-watch-movies-and-tv-online-each-month-in-the-u-s/.

"Weight, Size and Media Lies: The Numbers Don't Add Up." Beauty Redefined. Last modified July 18, 2013. Accessed November 22, 2017. http://www.beautyredefined.net/weight-size-media-lies/.

Wellman, Victoria. "$2,000 on the Face and $6,000 on the Body: Jennifer Aniston's Monthly Beauty Bill Broken Down." *Daily Mail*. Last modified March 14, 2012. Accessed November 22, 2017. http://www.dailymail.co.uk/femail/article-2114414/Jennifer-Anistons-monthly-beauty-broken-down.html.

MUSCLE DYSMORPHIA

Originally called reverse anorexia or bigorexia, muscle dysmorphia is a proposed psychiatric disorder characterized by an intense desire to gain muscle mass while simultaneously reducing one's body fat. Muscle dysmorphia is not exclusive to males; however, muscle dysmorphia in females is rare. Its prevalence is unknown, although it has been suggested up to 90,000 men may meet the criteria for this disorder. It is difficult to estimate an accurate number since men are unlikely to admit that they are struggling to avoid embarrassment or shame. The millions of gym memberships sold to males each year in the United States could be associated with the desire of males to change their bodies. Furthermore, there is evidence to suggest male adolescent use of steroids is to improve athletic performance, but many use steroids for the sole purpose of enhancing appearance.

Muscle Dysmorphia and Body Image

It should be noted that while many men may be unhappy with their lack of muscularity, it does not always mean they struggle with muscle dysmorphia. However, a problem may occur when a discrepancy exists between what someone perceives as an ideal physique and one's actual physique. This perception must be combined with the belief coming closer to this proposed ideal will generate some kind of reward.

Male body image satisfaction exists on a continuum with one extreme men who have no interest in or care little about their physiques. The middle of the continuum represents men who may be somewhat dissatisfied with their physiques but are not at a pathological level for concern. However, a male who falls on the opposite extreme of the continuum is highly preoccupied with his physique and is willing to take extreme actions to change his appearance and muscularity.

Classification of Muscle Dysmorphia

Muscle dysmorphia is not included in the *Diagnostic and Statistical Manual of Mental Disorders*, fifth edition (*DSM-5*). This is primarily because its classification has yet to be established. This condition includes traits that are characteristic of other disorders, such as anorexia nervosa. It remains unclear whether it is a spectrum disorder of obsessive-compulsive disorder or a somatoform disorder. Some researchers argue that muscle dysmorphia should fit under obsessive-compulsive disorder and, subsequently, a type of body dysmorphic disorder. Body dysmorphic disorder is defined as a preoccupation with an imagined or slight physical defect concerning a particular body part (e.g., nose). The individual believes this perceived flaw is unappealing or ugly, even though in reality the flaw is negligible or even nonexistent to others.

Some researchers believe muscle dysmorphia should be categorized as an eating disorder diagnosis because the condition has characteristics similar to those of anorexia nervosa. Previously, many individuals with muscle dysmorphia were diagnosed as having an eating disorder not otherwise specified (EDNOS) under the older *DSM-IV-TR* criteria. Thus, muscle dysmorphia is and remains a proposed psychiatric disorder. Research about muscle dysmorphia is in its infancy, and more research is needed before a clear understanding of its traits and characteristics can be obtained.

Etiology of Muscle Dysmorphia

What causes muscle dysmorphia or where it comes from is not entirely clear. In fact, attributing it to a single factor is shortsighted and it is likely to be caused by a combination of factors. Although most research would suggest that muscle dysmorphia begins in teenage or early adulthood, an understanding of physique may begin much earlier.

Various models have been proposed to explain the etiology of muscle dysmorphia and similar factors appear in them. Poor self-esteem, body dissatisfaction, and distortion play a significant role where poor self-perception leads to steps to alter physique. The media are also a frequently cited source. Seemingly perfect images of muscular, toned males portrayed in the media allow for comparison between images and the self. As a consequence, a negative or upward social comparison may occur where a comparison against a seemingly superior physique can lead to decreased self-esteem and negative affect.

Peer experiences and the effect of parents is another contributor to muscle dysmorphia. Parents appear to exert more influence than peers, particularly a father figure. Other influences during youth can include action figures and dolls, discussed in a separate entry.

Perhaps a key element to be considered in relation to muscle dysmorphia is the gender transformation that has occurred over the past several decades. Men have traditionally attained their masculinity from their work, and they have enjoyed dominance in certain vocations such as business and security forces. However, these vocations are no longer exclusive to males, thereby leaving males to seek identity through alternate means. Muscularity is a visible entity where differentiation clearly remains.

Consequences of Muscle Dysmorphia

For those with muscle dysmorphia, there are potentially serious physical, psychological, and environmental risks; these are in addition to other negative attitudes and behaviors associated with an extreme desire for muscle mass. Examples of physical consequences include heart failure, renal failure, dehydration, and sometimes death. In part, these effects can be caused by the abuse of illegal substances, such as anabolic steroids. They can also be caused by extreme dieting, overtraining, and exercise addiction.

An individual may also experience negative social, recreational, and occupational hazards including depression, social physique anxiety, low self-esteem, neuroticism, and perfectionism as a result of muscle dysmorphia. It is interesting that men with muscle dysmorphia are often highly muscular and lean, and yet they exhibit intense vulnerability with respect to their body image leading them to continually build their bodies in pursuit of an unattainable goal.

Perhaps some of the least discussed aspects of muscle dysmorphia are the social and recreational effects. Someone seeking an ideal body expects rewards, such as a fuller life, happiness, and successful romantic relationships. However, these rewards are seldom realized, as muscle dysmorphia creates a preoccupation that supersedes other responsibilities and desires. For example, sexual activity may be impaired due to fears that one's small physique will be exposed or because of the perception that sex wastes energy needed for working out. Because of the strict diets required to achieve muscularity with low body fat, eating out socially can be difficult. Exposing one's physique at a doctor's office or a beach may cause extreme discomfort. A sufferer may become so preoccupied with working out that he could give up his job or career to spend more time in the gym. Or he may build a gym in his home so he can work out continually without fear of physique comparisons that occur at a gym.

Measurement of Muscle Dysmorphia

Measurement tools for muscle dysmorphia are quite varied primarily because there has been little agreement regarding diagnostic criteria for the condition. Although each measure has limitations, there have been several attempts to measure muscle dysmorphia or the drive for muscularity. These include the Swansea Muscularity Attitudes Questionnaire, Muscle Appearance Satisfaction Scale, Bodybuilder Image Grid, Drive for Muscularity Scale, Somatomorphic Matrix, and Muscle Dysmorphia Inventory.

The Swansea Muscularity Attitudes Questionnaire assesses the perceived positive attributes of being muscular and the desire to be muscular, but it has not been well tested. The Muscle Appearance Satisfaction Scale (MASS) is a 19-item measure to assess symptoms of muscle dysmorphia. The self-report measure includes five factors: bodybuilding dependence, muscle checking, substance use, injury, and muscle satisfaction. The MASS includes injury-related statements to address tendencies to overuse body parts that increase injury risk, which are not part of the general characteristics of muscle dysmorphia. The Bodybuilder Image Grid (BIG) uses a series of two-dimensional pictures on a grid that vary in muscularity and body fat. Again, the BIG has been little used in empirical research.

One of the most commonly used assessment methods is the Drive for Muscularity Scale, a 15-question survey assessing drive for muscularity traits. Although initially designed and tested with adolescents, it has been widely used in subsequent research and has been well tested for reliability and validity.

The Somatomorphic Matrix includes 100 images, placed in a 10 x 10 matrix database computer program, that allow a user to increase or decrease the fat-free mass index or body fat percentage of the image being shown. Participants only see one image at a time. The advantage of the Somatomorphic Matrix is that both muscularity and body fat are assessed as determinants of body image. Although the scale has good construct validity, it is not adequately reliable and further testing is needed.

The Muscle Dysmorphia Inventory (MDI) identifies characteristics associated with muscle dysmorphia. It uses 27 questions on a Likert scale to assess characteristics associated with muscle dysmorphia that are then divided into subscales of size/symmetry, physique protection, exercise dependence, supplement use, dietary behavior, and pharmacological use. Subscales are measured separately, as each measures conceptually independent traits. Although the MDI appears to be a valid and reliable method for assessing traits associated with muscle dysmorphia, the inventory should not be employed as a diagnostic tool.

Future Directions

The challenge for researchers is to assess and treat muscle dysmorphia. The term is barely a decade old, and the field remains fertile for research. Perhaps the most important need is a clear understanding of where the condition fits in the spectrum of other mental disorders. Furthermore, there is no consistent method for identifying someone with muscle dysmorphia. Thus, one cannot be categorically identified with muscle dysmorphia, but one can exhibit characteristics associated with the proposed condition.

Although the general definition of muscle dysmorphia has been relatively consistent, what traits or characteristics the definition includes is still debatable. For example, while steroid use is a commonly assumed characteristic, there is research to suggest individuals may not necessarily use steroids, and yet they can still be excessively concerned about their physiques. Physique protection is also a characteristic that needs further research. For example, why do some individuals exhibit extreme preoccupation with displaying their physique while others appear to seek affirmation as much as possible through the praise of others or through mirror checking.

Timothy M. Baghurst

See also: Bigorexia; Body Image in Males; Bodybuilding; Dolls; Drive for Muscularity; Masculinity Ideals

Bibliography

Baghurst, Timothy M., and Dan B. Kissinger. "Perspectives on Muscle Dysmorphia." *International Journal of Men's Health* 8 (2009): 82–89. http://dx.doi.org.10.3149/jmh.0801.82.

Baghurst, Timothy M., and Cathy Lirgg. "Characteristics of Muscle Dysmorphia in Male Football, Weight Training, and Competitive Natural and Non-natural Bodybuilding Samples." *Body Image* 6 (2009): 221–227. http://dx.doi.org/10.1016/j.bodyim.2009.03.002.

Bahrke, Michael S., Charles E. Yesalis, Andrea N. Kopstein, and Jason A. Stephens. "Risk Factors Associated with Anabolic-Androgenic Steroid Use among Adolescents." *Sports Medicine* 29 (2000): 397–406. https://doi.org/10.2165/00007256-200029060-00003.

Davies, Rebecca, and Dave Smith. "Muscle Dysmorphia among Current and Former Steroid Users." *Journal of Clinical Sport Psychology* 5 (2011): 77–94.

Lantz, Christopher D., Deborah J. Rhea, and J. L. Mayhew. "The Drive for Size: A Psychobehavioral Model of Muscle Dysmorphia." *International Sports Journal* 5 (2001): 71–86.

Leit, Richard A., James J. Gray, and Harrison G. Pope Jr. "The Media's Representation of the Ideal Male Body: A Cause for Muscle Dysmorphia?" *International Journal of Eating Disorders* 31 (2002): 334–338. https://doi.org/10.1002/eat.10019.

Leone, James E., Edward J. Sedory, and Kimberly A. Gray. "Recognition and Treatment of Muscle Dysmorphia and Related Body Image Disorders." *Journal of Athletic Training* 40 (2005): 352–359.

McCreary, Donald R., and Doris K. Sasse. "An Exploration of the Drive for Muscularity in Adolescent Boys and Girls." *Journal of American College Health* 48 (2000): 297–304. http://dx.doi.org/10.1080/07448480009596271.

Morgan, John F. "From Charles Atlas to Adonis Complex: Fat Is More Than a Feminist Issue." *Lancet* 356 (2000): 1372–1374. https://doi.org/10.1016/S0140-6736(05)74051-4.

Murray, Stewart B., Elizabeth Rieger, Stephen W. Touyz, and Yolanda L. De La Garza Garcia. "Muscle Dysmorphia and the SDM-V Conundrum: Where Does It Belong? A Review Paper." *International Journal of Eating Disorders* 43 (2010): 483–491. https://doi.org/10.1002/eat.20828.

Olivardia, Roberto. "Body Image Obsession in Men." *Healthy Weight Journal* 16 (2002): 59–64.

Olivardia, Roberto. "Mirror, Mirror on the Wall, Who's the Largest of Them All? The Features and Phenomenology of Muscle Dysmorphia." *Harvard Rev Psychiatry* 9 (2001): 254–259.

Olivardia, Roberto, Harrison G. Pope Jr., John J. Borowiecki III, and Geoffrey H. Cohane. "Biceps and Body Image: The Relationship between Muscularity and Self-Esteem, Depression, and Eating Disorder Symptoms." *Psychology of Men and Masculinity* 5 (2004): 112–120. http://dx.doi.org/10.1037/1524-9220.5.2.112.

Pope Jr., Harrison G., A. J. Gruber, Precilla Choi, Roberto Olivardia, and Katharine A. Phillips. "Muscle Dysmorphia: An Unrecognized Form of Body Dysmorphic Disorder." *Psychosomatics* 38 (1997): 548–557. http://dx.doi.org/10.1016/S0033-3182(97)71400-2.

Pope, Jr. Harrison G., Katharine A. Phillips, and Roberto Olivardia. *The Adonis Complex: The Secret Crisis of Male Body Obsession.* New York: The Free Press, 2000.

Tucker, Readdy, Patti L. Watkins, and Bradley J. Cardinal. "Muscle Dysmorphia, Gender Role Stress, and Sociocultural Influences: An Exploratory Study." *Research Quarterly for Exercise and Sport* 82 (2011): 310–319. http://dx.doi.org/10.1080/02701367.2011.10599759.

MYTH OF THE "FRESHMAN 15"

The "Freshman 15" refers to the catchphrase related to gaining 15 pounds during a freshman year of college. This phenomenon has been popularized in the media and is frequently discussed by college students, but it appears to be more a myth than an evidence-based phenomenon. A few freshmen do gain weight, but studies have found only about half of students gain any weight during their freshman year, and the average weight gain is around five pounds.

The concept of the Freshman 15 first appeared in an academic journal article in 1985, but was not popularized until the late 1990s. Since that time, the Freshman 15 has been used as a marketing tool for gyms, grocery stores, and restaurants trying to appeal to customers who are interested in seeking a healthy lifestyle. As a result of media exposure and marketing, the Freshman 15 has become a topic of conversation among students. The vast majority of college students are able to accurately define the Freshman 15 and up to 60 percent are at least moderately concerned that they will gain weight. This concern can turn into a self-fulfilling prophecy when college students sabotage their health behaviors by eating unhealthy foods and not exercising because they think the Freshman 15 is inevitable. Even though the Freshman 15 concept has been exaggerated, the concern about weight gain appears to negatively affect some students by distorting the way they think about weight, leading to an increasingly negative body image.

Although gaining 15 pounds during a freshman year is often a gross overestimation of actual weight gain, many students do gain at least some weight the first year of college. In fact, studies have shown college students gain weight between 6 and 36 times faster than the general population. Although both genders are affected, women gain slightly more weight than men. Almost all college women have an ideal weight that is less than their current weight and roughly half are currently dieting. Ironically, dieting during a freshman year often contributes to weight gain rather than weight loss for most college students. This is due to a decrease in metabolism because of the diet, combined with a greater likelihood of overeating postdiet. There are a number of environmental and social reasons for weight gain during the freshman year of college, including changes in eating habits, physical activity, stress, and societal pressure.

Eating Habits

Dietary Freedom

For many students, going to college is the first time they have total freedom to make dietary choices. This freedom may result in students opting for their favorite-tasting foods that may be less nutritious, high-calorie options. Many students are initially attracted to the unhealthy foods because they can eat them without parental restraint. Parents are no longer there to encourage fruits and vegetables and discourage excessive fried foods and sweets. Students must learn to self-regulate their eating to match their calorie output.

Dining Halls

Many universities offer on-campus dormitory housing and some require the purchase of a meal plan that allows students to eat at cafeterias with buffet style, all-you-can-eat menus. These buffets can be problematic for both nutritional quality and portion control. At some universities, these meal plans can also be used to purchase items from snack carts, fast food kiosks, or vending machines. One study found students who ate in a dining hall felt thought ate more and left with a greater sense of fullness. This communal eating may encourage constant overeating.

As students adjust to a new living situation, they must also learn to balance obligations at school, work, and with families and friends. With the chaos of their lives, convenience may be the single most important factor in food choices. Students report eating fewer meals per day while in college than they did in high school. They may opt for quick, processed meals, fast food, or vending machine snacks. Many college campuses are surrounded by fast-food restaurants, making fast foods a quick and easy option for meals. These foods are high in fat and low in vitamins and minerals and serving sizes have gotten increasingly bigger each year. Research has found the larger the serving, the more an individual will eat. The accessibility of vending machines at schools as well as in some dormitory halls may contribute to weight gain, as individuals who snack more are likely to gain weight.

Late-night parties and pulling all-nighters to study for exams may also contribute to excessive snacking for college students. Most people do not appear to compensate for the food they eat while snacking by lowering their calorie content at meals.

Alcohol Consumption

Another common health problem tied to weight gain among college freshmen is the consumption of large quantities of calorically dense alcohol. The use of alcohol becomes more prevalent during the early college years, and college students are more likely to engage in binge drinking. Though not extensively studied, it is hypothesized that the additional calories consumed from alcohol use may contribute to weight gain for some people. Increased alcohol use during the freshman year has also been linked to disordered eating and alcohol abuse. The effects of smoking and illicit drug use on weight gain during the freshman year require further study.

Contradictory Evidence

Although most studies support the common causes of freshman weight gain, there are some contradictory findings. For example, a few studies have found living in residential halls where food is provided is not related to weight gain; the amount of fruits and vegetables and high-fat fast foods consumed does not change; and, the transition to college does not significantly change eating patterns. This contradictory evidence is likely to be due to the complex nature of weight gain and the varying experiences at individual universities.

Calorie Intake

Given dietary freedom, dining halls, hectic lifestyle, and alcohol consumption, it is assumed a college student's caloric intake would be considerably higher than in high school. However, research suggests the average calorie intake usually remains constant or decreases during the first year of college. The decrease in caloric intake and increase in body weight suggests that a change in physical activity may be primarily responsible for freshman weight gain.

Physical Activity

College students vary in their physical activity levels, and lack of activity can contribute to weight gain. Many students report that the busier schedule allows less time for recreational and organized sports. Fewer students have the opportunity to play collegiate sports than high school sports. In addition, having more hectic schedules makes it difficult to make exercise a priority. Individuals who were relatively inactive in high school may find their activity levels actually increase as they walk around campus and no longer rely on a car for transportation. One research study found all students dramatically decreased their exercise during the beginning of the school year, but many students returned to their previous level of exercise after the initial college transition. However, the participants in the study who gained weight during their freshman year had decreased physical activity levels when compared to high school. Another study found participation in exercise to be stable throughout the school year, although aerobic exercise was declining.

Stress

Many students encounter stress as they transition from home and to a university. This stress may be short-lived, lasting only till the student adjusts to college life, or it may be chronic as the academic pressures are continual. Students who fail to adjust may indulge in unhealthy behaviors and experience negative physical and psychological health. Universities typically are a competitive academic setting, so while a student may have performed well in high school, he or she may struggle at the university level. Some students reported an increased workload, more rigorous class schedules, and less lenient grading contributed to stress for new students. The severity and frequency of stress has been associated with weight gain or weight loss. Students who are stressed may turn to food to unwind and feel better, thus increasing their emotional eating. People who eat emotionally are more likely to have trouble managing their weight, as they may eat unneeded calories throughout the day. Stress is also more likely to affect an individual when he or she is sleep deprived. Research has found freshmen sleep far less on average than they did during their high school.

Societal Pressure

The societal pressure to be thin for women and to be muscular for men may contribute to weight dissatisfaction for this population. Freshmen are bombarded by media, peers, and family members outlining an ideal that is nearly impossible to achieve. Students think the university setting intensifies the comparison between peers and perpetuates weight dissatisfaction. The effect of weight dissatisfaction during the freshman year has been primarily researched in women, though it is postulated that men would have similar experiences. For freshman women, weight dissatisfaction intensifies as actual weight increases. Students with greater weight dissatisfaction are more likely to develop worsening symptoms and further eating pathology during college. Weight dissatisfaction is related to dieting, which is related to weight gain for freshman women.

Eating Disorders and Obesity

Research has found a higher weight was significantly positively correlated to concern about the Freshman 15. Students who weighed more upon entering college were more worried about gaining additional weight. The more overweight the individual, the less likely he or she is to have healthy eating habits and exercise. An overweight college freshman is more likely to eat more and be more dissatisfied with additional weight gain.

The overall prevalence of clinical eating disorders does not appear to increase during the freshman year; however, disordered eating and eating disorder symptoms do increase in persons without clinical eating disorders. This means more individuals have behaviors that could be symptoms of eating disorders, while not having a full diagnosable case. Researchers speculate for most women, eating disorders are established before college, but self-image, dieting behaviors, and eating disorder symptoms are common during college. In one study, about a fourth of the freshman class started a diet for the first time during their freshman year. Similarly, for females, about 15 percent began binge eating for the first time during their freshman year.

Prevention of the Freshman 15

Health professionals fear that the unhealthy habits that cause freshman weight gain may persist throughout adulthood, continually adding extra weight to these individuals, thus putting them at risk of obesity, heart disease, and diabetes. Given the threefold increase in the prevalence of overweight and obesity when comparing adolescent and adult age groups, the college years appear to be an appropriate time for prevention programs. Many universities work to prevent the Freshman 15 by helping freshmen to understand the facts, along with some of the possible causes of the Freshman 15, through presentations during courses or at orientation can address some of the underlying emotions that may perpetuate the problem. Universities can also offer healthier eating options in dining rooms and in vending machines. Access to equipment for exercise can also decrease the likelihood of gaining weight during the first year of college. In addition, universities offer nutrition and/or physical education courses helping students to make better food choices and increase physical activity.

TeriSue Smith-Jackson

See also: Media; Obesity; Sorority Women

Bibliography

Brown, Cecelia. "The Information Trail of the 'Freshman 15'—A Systematic Review of a Health Myth within the Research and Popular Literature." *Health Information and Libraries Journal* 25, no. 1 (2008): 1–12. https://doi.org/10.1111/j.1471-1842.2007.00762.x.

Butler, Scott M., David R. Black, Carolyn L. Blue, and Randall J. Gretebeck. "Changes in Diet, Physical Activity and Body Weight in Female College Freshman." *American Journal of Health Behavior* 28, no. 1 (2004): 24–32. https://doi.org/10.5993/AJHB.28.1.3.

Cooley, Eric, and Tamina Toray. "Body Image and Personality Predictors of Eating Disorder Symptoms during the College Years." *International Journal of Eating Disorders* 30, no. 1 (2001): 28–36. https://doi.org/10.1002/eat.1051.

Cooley, Eric, and Tamina Toray. "Disordered Eating in College Freshman Women: A Prospective Study." *Journal of American College Health* 49, no. 5 (2001): 229–235. http://dx.doi.org/10.1080/07448480109596308.

Delinsky, Sherrie S., and Terence G. Wilson. "Weight Gain, Dietary Restraint, and Disordered Eating in the Freshman Year of College." *Eating Behaviors* 9, no. 1 (2008): 82–90. http://dx.doi.org/10.1016/j.eatbeh.2007.06.001.

Graham, Melody A., and Amy L. Jones. "Freshman 15: Valid Theory or Harmful Myth?" *Journal of American College Health* 50, no. 4 (2002): 171–173. http://dx.doi.org/10.1080/07448480209596023.

Hajhosseini, Laleh, Tawni Holmes, Parinez Mohamadi, Vida Goudarzi, Lucy McProud, and Clarie B. Hollenbeck. "Changes in Body Weight, Body Composition and Resting Metabolic Rate (RMR) in Freshmen Students First-Year University." *Journal of the American*

College of Nutrition 25, no. 2 (2006): 123–127. http://dx.doi.org/10.1080/07315724
.2006.10719522.

Hoffman, Daniel J., Peggy Policastro, Virginia Quick, and Soo-Kyung Lee. "Changes in
Body Weight and Fat Mass of Men and Women in the First Year of College: A Study of
the 'Freshman 15.'" Journal of American College Health 55, no. 1 (2006): 41–45. http://
dx.doi.org/10.3200/JACH.55.1.41-46.

Holm-Denoma, Jill M., Thomas E. Joiner, Kathleen D. Vohs, and Todd F. Heatherton.
"The 'Freshman Fifteen' (the 'Freshman Five' Actually): Predictors and Possible
Explanations." Health Psychology 27, no. 1 (2008): S3–S9. http://dx.doi.org/10.1037
/0278-6133.27.1.S3.

Jung, Mary Elizabeth, Steven Russell Bray, and Kathleen Anne Martin Ginis. "Behavior
Change and the Freshman 15: Tracking Physical Activity and Dietary Patterns in
1st-year University Women." Journal of American College Health 56, no. 5 (2008): 523–
530. http://dx.doi.org/10.3200/JACH.56.5.523-530.

Lowe, Michael R., Rachel A. Annunziato, Jessica Tuttman Markowitz, Elizabeth Didie,
Dara L. Bellace, Lynn Riddell, Caralynn Maille, Shortie McKinney, and Eric Stice.
"Multiple Types of Dieting Prospectively Predict Weight Gain during the Freshman
Year of College." Appetite 47, no. 1 (2006): 83–90. http://dx.doi.org/10.1016/j.appet
.2006.03.160.

Mihalopoulos, Nicole L., Peggy Auinger, and Jonathon D. Klein. "The Freshman 15: Is It
Real?" Journal of American College Health 56, no. 5 (2008): 531–533.

Rozin, Paul, Jordana Riklis, and Lara Margolis. "Mutual Exposure or Close Peer Relationships Do Not Seem to Foster Increased Similarity in Food, Music or Television Program Preferences." Appetite 42, no. 1 (2004): 41–48. http://dx.doi.org/10.1016/S0195
-6663(03)00115-6.

Serlachius, Anna, Mark Hamer, and Jane Wardle. "Stress and Weight Change in University
Students in the United Kingdom." Physiology & Behavior 92, no. 4 (2007): 548–553.
http://dx.doi.org/10.1016/j.physbeh.2007.04.032.

Smith, TeriSue, Justine J. Reel, and Rosemary Thackeray. "Coping with 'Bad Body Image
Days': Strategies from Freshmen College Women." Body Image: An International Journal
of Research 8, no. 4 (2011): 335–342. https://doi.org/10.1016/j.bodyim.2011.05.002.

Vohs, Kathleen D., Todd F. Heatherton, and Marcia Herrin. "Disordered Eating and the
Transition to College: A Prospective Study." International Journal of Eating Disorders 29,
no. 3 (2001): 280–288. https://doi.org/10.1002/eat.1019.

Zielke, Judi. "Just for Teens. Mood Swings. Not the Freshman 15." Diabetes Forecast 56, no.
11 (2003): 47–48.